Advance Praise for *The Romans*, Second Edition

"This is the best textbook of Roman history I have read. It is very well conceived, thorough, and well written. . . . The maps are excellent and the captions for the well-chosen illustrations are really helpful to the reader."

Guy MacLean Rogers, Wellesley College

"This text is a very straightforward and organized full-length treatment of Roman history. It balances historical narrative with excellent explanations for terms and concepts that are unfamiliar to the students . . . it succeeds marvelously at reaching its audience."

Vanessa B. Gorman, University of Nebraska-Lincoln

"*The Romans* presents a unified narrative voice despite having been written by four authors. The narrative flows seamlessly throughout the text from beginning to end. In addition, the maps and their captions are both useful and informative."

Debra L. Nousek, University of Western Ontario

"*The Romans: From Village to Empire* is a very good introduction to ancient Roman history. It is clear and engaging, and the numerous pedagogical devices are well conceived and quite helpful for the beginner."

Carlos F. Noreña, University of California, Berkeley

"*The Romans*, in general, is of outstanding quality. It provides a coherent narrative of Roman history with a strong emphasis on the development of the Roman state . . . The writing style is extremely clear and lively, making for an engaging read."

Denise Demetriou, Michigan State University

"This is the best textbook for students coming to Roman history for the first time. Its main qualities are an attractive and varied presentation, balance in the material, and readability . . . the writing style is attractive and clear."

Brian McGing, Trinity College, Dublin

THE ROMANS

From Village to Empire

SECOND EDITION

Mary T. Boatwright

Daniel J. Gargola

Noel Lenski

Richard J. A. Talbert

NEW YORK   OXFORD
OXFORD UNIVERSITY PRESS

Oxford University Press, Inc., publishes works that further Oxford University's objective of excellence in research, scholarship, and education.

Oxford   New York
Auckland Cape Town Dar es Salaam Hong Kong Karachi
Kuala Lumpur Madrid Melbourne Mexico City Nairobi
New Delhi Shanghai Taipei Toronto

With offices in
Argentina Austria Brazil Chile Czech Republic France Greece
Guatemala Hungary Italy Japan Poland Portugal Singapore
South Korea Switzerland Thailand Turkey Ukraine Vietnam

For titles covered by Section 112 of the US Higher Education Opportunity Act, please visit www.oup.com/us/he for the latest information about pricing and alternate formats.

Published by Oxford University Press, Inc.
198 Madison Avenue, New York, New York 10016
http://www.oup.com

Oxford is a registered trademark of Oxford University Press

Library of Congress Cataloging-in-Publication Data
The Romans : from village to empire / Mary T. Boatwright ... [et al.]. — 2nd ed.
    p. cm.
Includes bibliographical references and index.
ISBN 978-0-19-973057-5 (acid-free paper) 1. Rome—History. I. Boatwright, Mary Taliaferro.
DG209.B58 2012
937—dc23   2011036879

Frontispiece: *Head from Italica.* This magnificent marble head (2 ft/60 cm in height) was found in a public area of Italica in southern Spain, one of the earliest Roman communities established outside Italy (see Chapter Three). Today the head is in Seville's Archeological Museum. The diadem and high tower signify that the figure is the city's goddess of Fortune, a vital protective deity. The style of the head—deeply carved hair and lips contrasting with smoothly finished cheeks and brow—is characteristic of sculpture dating to the first half of the second century A.D. This was when Italica, as the prosperous ancestral home of the emperors Trajan and Hadrian, proudly embarked upon an ambitious expansion program requiring large public buildings and much new statuary. Thus this serene female image symbolizes the city, and by extension Roman civilization, at the peak of its glory.

Cover: Kurşunlugerme aqueduct bridge. The vicinity of Constantinople, the New Rome, could not furnish such a large city with an adequate supply of water. It had to be brought from far to the west, necessitating even longer aqueducts than those built for Rome itself and other cities such as Nemausus in Gaul (see Figure 10.9). In the 360s/370s (when Valens was emperor) and again in the early fifth century A.D., aqueduct lines were built from various springs; the most distant of these are situated about 75 miles (120 km) from the city in a straight line, although the constant curves essential to maintain a steady gravity flow required the channels to run for over four times that distance. About sixty bridges in all carried the channels across valleys. The best preserved bridge is at Kurşunlugerme. Its three tiers rise as high as 130 ft (40 m); the middle tier, with six arches, carried a channel on either side, while the top one, with eleven arches, carried a single channel. With successive restorations, Constantinople's amazing Roman aqueducts continued in operation until the eleventh century.

Printing number: 9 8 7 6 5 4 3 2

Printed in the United States of America
on acid-free paper

We dedicate this second, expanded edition
to our teachers and to our students

CONTENTS

1 Archaic Italy and the Origins of Rome

2   Republican Rome and the Conquest of Italy

3   The Beginnings of a Mediterranean Empire

4 Italy and Empire

 5 Italy Threatened, Enfranchised, Divided

6   The Domination of Sulla and Its Legacy

9 The Early Principate (A.D. 14–69): The Julio-Claudians, the Civil War of 68–69, and Life in the Early Empire

14 The Final Years of the Western Empire and Rome's Revival in the East

MAPS

FIGURES

PLATES

PREFACE TO THE
SECOND EDITION

This second edition, which is appearing eight years after the first, has offered a welcome opportunity to rethink certain aspects of the book in the light of the three authors' own classroom experience and of the varied reactions offered by students and other readers, as well as by fellow instructors. The latter have voiced one concern time and again—namely that, despite the misgivings articulated in the original preface, the chronological scope should be extended. In response, the most striking new feature of the second edition is that its coverage continues for a further two centuries, to around A.D. 500. For this purpose, Noel Lenski kindly consented to rewrite the final chapter of the first edition and to add two fresh chapters. Meantime, the opening five chapters of the first edition have been reworked and trimmed to become four, so that there is now only one more chapter than before (fourteen instead of thirteen). Another distinctive feature of the second edition is the inclusion of sixteen pages of color plates grouped in two sections, a marvelous enrichment which it has been a delight to provide. In addition, social, cultural, and religious history now receive more attention. Considerable changes have been made to Boxes (now Sources), Suggested Readings, and the presentation of the maps; redesign of the Timeline renders it more concise and comprehensible.

New to this Edition
- Timeline of the book has been expanded by about 200 years, down at least to the fall of the western empire in the late fifth century
- Chapters 1 and 2 have been combined: Archaic Italy and the Origins of Rome

- Two new chapters:
  - Chapter 13: The Rise of Christianity and the Growth of the Barbarian Threat (324–395)
  - Chapter 14: The Final Years of the Western Empire and Rome's Revival in the East
- Now features two 8-page full color inserts

Mary T. Boatwright, Durham, North Carolina
Daniel J. Gargola, Lexington, Kentucky
Noel Lenski, Boulder, Colorado
Richard J. A. Talbert, Chapel Hill, North Carolina

PREFACE TO THE FIRST EDITION

The descendants of the first settlers on the hills overlooking a ford across the Tiber River eventually controlled most of Europe, the Near East, and North Africa for centuries. Still today, a millennium and a half later, the legacy of this extraordinary achievement by the Romans exerts a powerful influence in a rich variety of spheres worldwide—not least among them, architecture, art, language, literature, law, and religion. Although the writings and material remains that survive are inevitably no more than a tiny, random sample of what once existed, there is still quite enough to impress and engage us, and to permit a fair degree of insight into many dimensions of the nature and development of Roman civilization. Of course there are aspects—related to politics or strategy or social practices, to name only three areas—which we can never hope to understand fully. Even so, that does not deter a large body of interested inquirers from continuing to formulate questions and discuss answers as part of an ongoing dialogue. This activity has proved especially fruitful since the mid-nineteenth century: From then onwards, at an increasing pace, advances in scholarship, technology, and exploration have hugely improved the control and appreciation of the material at our disposal. These advances have also led to many exciting new discoveries, as well as stimulating ventures into fresh areas of inquiry over a broader range than ever. The expanding pursuit of inquiry, discovery, and (re)evaluation is sure to continue. Current knowledge, interests, and opinions are by no means fixed or exhausted; each generation chooses its own mix of elements in Roman history.

The distinctiveness of this book lies in its synthesis of the Roman state's changing character and expansion from earliest beginnings to the fourth century A.D. It is a book aimed primarily at average college-educated readers who lack prior engagement with ancient Rome, but who are eager to gain something more than a superficial introduction to its history. Our editor, Robert Miller, invited us to plan and write the book as a partner for Oxford's successful *Ancient Greece* by S. B. Pomeroy, S. M. Burstein, W. Donlan, and J. T. Roberts. What clinched our acceptance of his invitation was a shared awareness (as Roman history instructors) of the patent need for such a treatment; nothing for quite this central purpose has been published in recent decades.

Our scope, we determined, would be the evolving nature of the Roman community, its state institutions, and forms of rule, together with its expansion and some of the consequences. Next to no background knowledge would be expected, nor any acquaintance with languages (ancient or modern) other than English. For Rome's history to unfold most meaningfully for newcomers to it, we concluded that the presentation needed to be mainly, though by no means invariably, narrative. Yet since we are covering a truly vast canvas in terms of time, space, and human interaction, many topics and trends can only be touched on here, despite the fact that it would in principle be possible to discuss them at length in their own right. In these instances, our book consciously limits itself to providing no more than the foundation and context essential for proceeding further.

An important feature that distinguishes our treatment from others now available is that its focus on Rome's political and institutional history is coupled with an awareness of how such a narrative is inseparable from social, cultural, economic, art historical, and other types of history. We have sought to offer at least glimpses of many different aspects of Roman life, particularly through quotations from ancient writings, maps, line drawings, and illustrations with substantial captions. Although ours does not set out to be a book about "Roman civilization" as such, we hope that it will lay the foundation for a sound appreciation of Roman culture—in plenty of its manifestations—as well as of Roman history in a more strictly defined sense.

We returned time and again to the issue of where to close. Discussion and experiment convinced us that a book of this length could hardly find space for the major fourth-century developments following the emperor Constantine's attainment of sole control (A.D. 324) without seriously impairing the coverage up to that date. We acknowledge that this endpoint makes our book less appealing to readers whose interests postdate the Roman Republic and fix instead on the period when Rome was a world-class power ruled by emperors—say, from the time of Julius Caesar or Augustus into the fifth or sixth century. A focus on this later period, however, calls for a different book altogether from one beginning with early Italy a millennium before.

Our variation of the amount of narrative at each stage, and of its pace overall, is also deliberate. Often indeed, our choices are limited by immense variations in the quantity, quality, and range of surviving source material from period to period; repeatedly, the means to answer a key question or to probe some significant shift just does not exist. In the opening chapters, a complex array of Roman institutions and practices has to be introduced, and for the early centuries of the Republic only a sketchy impression at best can be offered of Rome's external affairs; so the narrative here covers long periods briefly, and proceeds thematically. From the mid-second century B.C., by contrast, our knowledge improves, and a succession of developments occurs, both at home and abroad, which have to be grasped in more depth not only for their individual importance but also for their cumulative impact. The ensuing end of the Republic, and the emergence from it of a stable regime that halted a ruinous cycle of civil wars, are such fundamental, well documented changes that they justify closer attention. Thereafter, once the Roman Empire is enlarged and stabilized from around the beginning of the Christian era, we have tried to balance narrating affairs of state with introducing more topics thematically, since both these approaches are invited by a relative abundance of literary, documentary, and archeological evidence. Throughout, we have had to make hard choices about which dates, events, ideas, names, topics to mention (and at what length), and which to omit. We have deliberately sought to reflect only opinions that—while often perforce remaining controversial—at least enjoy some measure of acceptance among current experts. We recognize that any introductory book, no matter how thorough or absorbing, can only open the way to learning more. We hope that our efforts will encourage teachers and students alike to supplement, question, and explore further all the material offered here.

With these aims in mind, at the start of each chapter we briefly survey the main sources that form the basis of knowledge for the period it covers, and at intervals we insert "boxes" that reproduce a variety of ancient writings to give a vivid sense of their character and historical value. Each chapter closes with a short listing of books recommended for further reading. In addition, at the end of the book, we offer a timeline, a glossary, and a listing of the principal ancient authors mentioned.

Our book's aims, and its presentation, are carefully matched, therefore. At the same time, we adhere to practical stipulations about length, format, illustrations, and the like, set by our publisher. As coauthors, we determined that, broadly speaking, each of us should take responsibility for three successive stages—Gargola far into the second century B.C., Talbert to the end of the Republic and establishment of the Principate, Boatwright thereafter. At every stage each partner would (and did) review drafts by the other two, as well as consider comments made correspondingly. Our goal was to ensure that the treatments should integrate into a coherent whole, although, naturally enough, three individual voices are still detectable. That seems fitting enough: It was the achievement of the Romans themselves, after all, to forge from many different peoples a distinctive and compelling history.

Mary T. Boatwright, Durham, North Carolina
Daniel J. Gargola, Lexington, Kentucky
Richard J.A. Talbert, Chapel Hill, North Carolina

ACKNOWLEDGMENTS

Our original editor has been succeeded by Charles Cavaliere, and we thank him warmly for steering this second, expanded edition to publication. We are also grateful to the many colleagues who offered recommendations for improvement: among them, James C. Anderson, University of Georgia; Ron Legon, University of Baltimore; Robert Morstein-Marx, University of California–Santa Barbara; C. Robert Phillips, Lehigh University; Walter Scheidel, Stanford University; Raymond Starr, Wellesley College. Faith Orlebeke's editorial assistance was invaluable to Noel Lenski in drafting the new chapters. Staff at the Ancient World Mapping Center most ably made, or remade, all the maps: Dr. Brian Turner (Acting Director), Ray Belanger, Steve Burges, Ashley Lee. The terrain depiction on all the maps (except city plans) is calculated from Environmental Systems Research Institute SRTM Shaded Relief, on ESRI Data & Maps 2006 [DVD-ROM], Redlands, CA.

NOTES TO THE READER

To assist further investigation of the themes introduced by this book, suggested readings are listed at the end of each chapter. In addition, two works to be referred to throughout are the revised third edition of the *Oxford Classical Dictionary (OCD)* edited by Simon Hornblower and Antony Spawforth (Oxford: Oxford University Press, 2003), and *Religions of Rome*, Vol. 1, *A History*; Vol. 2, *A Sourcebook*, by Mary Beard, John North, and Simon Price (Cambridge: Cambridge University Press, 1998). For the fourth century A.D. onwards, a further invaluable work of reference is Alexander P. Kazhdan et al. (eds.), *The Oxford Dictionary of Byzantium* (3 vols., Oxford: Oxford University Press, 1991). Rigorous coverage of Rome's entire history is offered by the second edition of the *Cambridge Ancient History* (Cambridge: Cambridge University Press), beginning at Volume VII Part 2 (1984); the presentation of this extensive work, however, is at a very advanced scholarly level.

A timeline, a glossary, and a listing of the principal ancient authors mentioned are to be found at the end, together with an index and a gazetteer for the maps.

The Ancient World Mapping Center at the University of North Carolina, Chapel Hill, offers free digital copies of each map that it produced for this book: visit http://www. unc.edu/awmc/mapsforstudents.html.

Some "Sources" translate Latin texts to be found in the periodical *L'Année Epigraphique* (*AE*) and in Hermann Dessau (ed.), *Inscriptiones Latinae Selectae* (Berlin: Weidmann, 1892–1916) (*ILS*). One quotation is a translation from Henrica Malcovati, *Oratorum Romanorum Fragmenta Liberae Rei Publicae* (ed. 4, Turin: Paravia, 1976) (*ORF*).

ABOUT THE AUTHORS

Mary T. Boatwright is Professor of Ancient History in the Department of Classical Studies, Duke University. Her books include *Hadrian and the City of Rome, Hadrian and the Cities of the Roman Empire,* and *Peoples of the Roman World.* She has also examined the roles, status, and images of Roman women in numerous articles.

Daniel J. Gargola is Associate Professor of History at the University of Kentucky, Lexington, and the author of *Lands, Laws, and Gods: Magistrates and Ceremony in the Regulation of Public Lands in Republican Rome* (1995).

Noel Lenski is Associate Professor of Classics at the University of Colorado at Boulder. He is the author of *Failure of Empire: Valens and the Roman State in the Fourth Century A.D.* (2002) and editor of *The Cambridge Companion to the Age of Constantine* (2006).

Richard J. A. Talbert is Kenan Professor of History and Classics at the University of North Carolina, Chapel Hill. Books authored or edited by him include *Barrington Atlas of the Greek and Roman World, Classical Courts and Courtiers, Rome's World: The Peutinger Map Reconsidered,* and *The Senate of Imperial Rome.*

ARCHAIC ITALY AND
THE ORIGINS OF ROME

For centuries before the formation of cities, Italy was a land of villages and the outside world impinged on life only fitfully. Urban life appeared here long after it had emerged in other parts of the Mediterranean basin. Over time, some settlements slowly became larger and more complex socially, economically, and politically, and the leaders of these more highly structured towns and villages gloried in their connections with the wider Mediterranean world. In the seventh and sixth centuries B.C., some communities achieved the status of cities, with elaborate social systems, monumental buildings and temples, and formal public spaces; others would follow in later centuries. These urban centers would long remain the chief centers of power in Italy.

ITALY AND THE MEDITERRANEAN WORLD

Italy (Italia in Latin) is a long peninsula, encompassing slightly less than 100,000 square miles (260,000 sq km), that juts out from the northern or European coast of the Mediterranean Sea (Latin, Internum Mare). In the far north, the Alps (Latin, Alpes) divide Italy from the rest of Europe. To their south, the valley of the Po (Latin, Padus)—Italy's largest river—contains land with great agricultural potential. Except for the plains along the eastern coast, the Apennine mountains separate the Po Valley from the rest of Italy. Peninsular Italy begins south of the Po Valley. The peninsula is about 650 miles in length (1,040 km), and it never is more than 125 miles wide (200 km); the sea is always fairly close. The Apennines dominate the peninsula. From their northwestern end, where they meet the western Alps and the sea, these mountains run almost due east in a narrow and virtually unbroken line that nearly reaches the Adriatic Sea; this portion of the chain separates the Po Valley from Etruria, an early center of urban life. As they approach the eastern coast, the mountains turn sharply to the south, running in a series of parallel ridges that in places reach almost 10,000 feet in height (3,000 m). In its northern half, the main chain lies much nearer to the Adriatic than it does to the Tyrrhenian Sea on the western side of the peninsula. South of Rome, however, the mountain chain gradually leaves the eastern coast and approaches the western, ending in the southwestern promontory of Bruttium. The mountains on the island of Sicily (Latin, Sicilia), separated from the mainland only by a narrow strait, are a continuation of this chain, which ultimately reappears in the mountains of Tunisia, Algeria, and Morocco in North Africa.

The first great centers of population and civilization arose in the coastal regions. The Adriatic coast, with few harbors and little space for large-scale settlement, was for a long time backward. For much of their length, the Apennines leave no more than a narrow coastal plain. Only in the south, where the mountains approach the Tyrrhenian coast more closely than they do the Adriatic, are there broad plains. Much of the plateau of Apulia, however, is semi-arid; only a few river valleys here were sufficiently fertile and well-watered to support substantial populations. The peninsula's southern (Ionian) shore also has narrow plains or semi-arid ones. The mountains of Bruttium closely confined some coastal communities. Even so, in some more favored areas, sufficient land and water could be found for large settlements. Towns appeared early here, and some became wealthy and important.

The west coast was the most favored. Here, well-watered and fertile lands proved capable of supporting large populations, many harbors gave access to the sea, and four rivers—the Arnus (modern, Arno), Tiberis (modern English, Tiber), Liris, and Volturnus—all navigable in small boats, barges, and rafts for some distance, gave easy passage to the interior. Three of the regions facing the Tyrrhenian Sea had especially prominent places in the history of ancient Italy. Etruria, the land of the ancient Etruscans, is the northernmost; this region of fertile hills, forests, and lakes, roughly bounded by the Arno and Tiber rivers, saw some of the earliest centers of urban life. Next, two regions each with an important plain occupy the coast to the south of Etruria. First comes Latium. East to west, the Latin plain ran from the sea to the foothills of the Apennines. North to south, it covered the stretch of coast between the lower Tiber River and the northern limits of Campania. Rome itself (Latin, Roma) would rise here on the banks of the Tiber, just across the river from the southernmost Etruscan centers. Centering on the Bay of Naples and its hinterland, the Campanian plain is the southernmost of the three regions.

The surrounding mountains and seas did not isolate the peninsula. Although the Alps seem quite formidable from the Italian side, large-scale movement across them has always been possible, and the inhabitants of the Po Valley have often had closer cultural links and firmer and friendlier relations with groups across the northern

Map 1.1 *Archaic Italy*

mountains than they did with peoples to their south. From an early period, ships have traveled from Italy across the Mediterranean, moving goods, people, ideas, and institutions. Much of this traffic was only local, but at times long-distance commerce developed and flourished. Before Rome succeeded in dominating the peninsula, seaborne connections flourished only fitfully along the Adriatic, although the mouth of the Po River on occasion received much trade. The peninsula's southern and western shores were more open. Good harbors could be found along the coasts of the Ionian and Tyrrhenian seas, and the richer and more extensive plains provided valuable hinterlands.

Italy occupies a strategic point in the Mediterranean world. The island of Sicily, off the southwest tip of the peninsula, divides the Mediterranean Sea in two, and maritime traffic between east and west necessarily passes by the island. Ships seeking to enter the Tyrrhenian Sea from the Ionian and Sicilian seas had to pass through the narrow Straits of Messina before they could proceed north along the Italian coast or west along the north shore of Sicily. This passage could be dangerous: Greek writers would place there the whirlpool Charybdis and the monster Scylla, who fed on ships' crews. Other important routes passed to the south of the island, eventually funneling through the passage between western Sicily and Cape Bon in modern Tunisia, about 100 miles away (160 km). The island could also serve as a virtual bridge between Italy and North Africa, facilitating north-south traffic across the central Mediterranean. In later periods maritime powers often fought for control of the island, and the state that ultimately would dominate it could expand east and west with some ease.

THE EVIDENCE

Archeological investigations provide the evidence for the history of Italy before the appearance of cities and organized states, because writing develops only as urban life was emerging. The material remains of ancient cultures can provide insights into important aspects of societies: how people organized and arranged their houses and their settlements; the ways they earned their living; the objects they made and how they used them; the commercial and cultural contacts they established with neighbors and with more distant peoples. At first glance, moreover, the recovery of the physical traces of the lives of earlier inhabitants seems to avoid many of the problems associated with the interpretation of often biased and value-laden texts (see further below).

But archeological evidence also has its own limitations. Only a few activities leave clear physical traces, and the remains are often very difficult to date and to interpret. Archeologists, moreover, often restrict their investigations to a limited range of sites. Thus, tombs and monumental public buildings for long received more attention than ordinary houses or settlements. Archeologists now often focus more on settlements and houses, and they regularly employ surface surveys—involving the systematic examination of traces on the surface left by centuries of human use—to learn more about settlement patterns. At the same time, in order to shed light on the environment and the economy, excavators have sought to recover plant and animal remains and to subject them to increasingly sophisticated analysis. Yet there are limits to these approaches. Much of life remains inaccessible. Excavations and surveys usually reveal more about a society's technology, settlement patterns, and economy than they do about the events that shaped the inhabitants of a community, about the political and social institutions and practices that organized their lives, and about the system of beliefs that guided relationships with neighbors, family members, rulers, and ruled.

This necessary emphasis on the material, technical, and economic aspects of communities has a further, and important, consequence. Archeologists often identify "cultures" on the basis of a number of shared traits, practices, and forms in funerary rites, in technology, in material goods, and in economic life; but these archeological cultures should not be confused with cultures defined through other means. After all, groups that differ in many ways can construct similar buildings, they can make virtually identical tools and ornaments, and they can earn their livings in many of the same ways. Artifacts and techniques, in other words, can cross ethnic, linguistic, and political borders. Archeological cultures, then, are collections of traits in material goods, in technology, in funerary practices, in settlement forms, and in economic life. They are not political or linguistic units, nor need they have a single ethnic identity, either in their own eyes or in the opinions of their neighbors.

In addition, the broader significance of finds is not always apparent, and major problems in interpretation can arise. Many of the most significant of the recovered objects have been found in tombs. The burial rites of many ancient communities required that grave goods be interred with the deceased, but the extent to which tombs and grave goods reflect the organization of society is controversial. Some burials, for example, are richer than others in the same cemetery, and the usual inference is that the deceased, in life, stood out in wealth and in status. In other cemeteries, burials may have been very similar in layout and in their contents. Here, scholars often suggest that the associated settlements had a more egalitarian social structure. Neither of these inferences is certain: burials are the remains of a burial rite, and fashion or belief may well have had more influence on deposits than other factors. At the same time, it is far from certain that all members of settlements received formal burials of the kind that have left detectable and datable traces in the archeological record. What survives, then, may be evidence for the practices of only a portion of the inhabitants of the towns and villages associated with a particular cemetery. Votive deposits, another important category of evidence, provide similar problems in interpretation. In Italy and in much of the Mediterranean world, worshippers deposited objects in sacred places to fulfill a vow or to thank the presiding deity for favors. When these sanctuaries, shrines, caves, or groves became crowded with gifts, those in charge would make room by burying the offerings. Again, the finds primarily illuminate the range of objects deemed suitable as a gift to a god, although they may also reveal something about the kinds of objects available in the community and the techniques involved in their manufacture.

ITALY BEFORE THE CITY

The basic pattern of social and economic life in peninsular Italy was established early. For centuries after the first appearance of agriculture around 4000 B.C., Italy was a land of villages with simple forms of economic and social organization. Settlements were very small, usually with no more than a few huts and outbuildings and less than one hundred inhabitants. Villagers planted barley and several types of wheat, and they raised sheep, goats, cattle, and pigs. Their technology was simple, and signs of occupational specialization are few. For millennia, Italian communities produced pottery in a range of styles and forms. At other times and places, the production of pottery could be a highly skilled craft, and devices were in use which require great expertise, such as the potter's wheel, which allows for more regular shapes, and high-temperature kilns, which provide harder and finer surfaces. In Italy, neither of these devices was used before the appearance of cities. In earlier centuries, too, specialized potters were almost certainly not involved in the craft; the manufacture of ceramics, in other words, was primarily a household activity. Tools necessary in everyday life were generally made of wood, bone, or stone.

The use of metals provides the only clear example of more sophisticated techniques and some craft specialization. Around 2000, copper tools and ornaments appear in the material remains. In the succeeding Early (c. 1800–1600) and Middle (c. 1600–1300) Bronze Ages, a limited range of tools, weapons, and ornaments were made of bronze, an alloy of copper and tin. Metalworking was a task for specialists, since it requires both expertise and organization: materials must be acquired, often from great distances, and the processes of refining the ore and casting the metal require knowledge and skill. In the Middle Bronze Age, throughout peninsular Italy artifacts of copper and bronze exhibit much standardization in form and techniques of manufacture; this may indicate that experts moved from village to village in search of markets for their skills.

Beginning in the ninth century, there occurred a series of developments in Italy leading, by the seventh century, to the appearance of the cities that would turn out to dominate Italian history. Archeologists refer to the years between the start of the ninth century and the last third of the eighth as the Iron Age. The extraction of metal from the ore and the working of the iron require complex and sophisticated techniques, and the making of steel is an even more elaborate process. Iron has important advantages over bronze. Iron ore is relatively common, so that the acquisition of this metal is a much simpler and cheaper process; when used in the form of steel, tools and weapons can be made harder and better able to retain an edge. Eventually, the use of iron would lead to cheaper products, which can be employed for a wider range of functions and by a larger portion of the population. For centuries after the introduction of iron, however, a wide range of objects, utilitarian and otherwise, continued to be made of bronze, wood, bone, and stone.

In the ninth and eighth centuries, Etruria, Latium, and Campania saw the rise of an inter-related group of cultures that would eventually develop into major centers of power and wealth. In Etruria, the Iron Age culture of these centuries is known as "Villanovan" from the estate near modern Bologna where archeologists first found traces of its material culture. Beyond Etruria, Villanovan settlements also appear in some areas just across the Apennines—such as around modern Bologna especially—and in Campania, where Capua and other centers show close connections with southern Etruria by sea or by the land route up the valleys of the Liris, Anio, and Tiber rivers. One of Villanovan culture's most significant traits was the greatly increased size of its settlements. Beginning around 900, certain ones began to grow larger, sometimes through the abandonment of earlier villages and the concentration of population at a few centers. For the most part, these central places were on easily defended plateaus, where the natural features of the site, occasionally reinforced by ditches and banks, formed the primary defense. In southern Etruria, which has been more fully researched, settlements at the future sites of Caere, Tarquinii, and Veii may each have had over one thousand inhabitants. To judge by the distance between them, the chief centers may have controlled territories as large as 350–750 square miles (900–1,940 sq km). At first, land away from the core may have only been sparsely inhabited, but by the eighth century some large settlements seem to have established smaller secondary ones near the limits of their territory, perhaps as a way of securing control over their borders, or because the main center was now too densely inhabited to accommodate further population growth.

In their internal organization, these new and larger settlements still remained relatively simple, consisting of clusters of huts separated by small open spaces. Each of the smaller clusters that together made up the whole may have represented a kinship group or the inhabitants of an earlier, now abandoned village. Settlements often had several cemeteries, each used by a single cluster of huts or by a few neighboring groups, a sign that they perceived some common identity. Farming and the raising of pigs, cattle, sheep, and goats remained the primary economic activities. Since these settlements show no sign of elaborate social systems or clearly identifiable distinctions in wealth, let alone of formal layouts and public buildings (all marks of the cities that would emerge in the eighth and seventh centuries), they are best characterized as "proto-urban," rather than as "urban."

Placed between Villanovan Etruria and Campania, Latium developed its own regional culture around 1000. This "Latial culture" was once seen as a variant of Villanovan, and it shares many of its features. For the most part, Latin settlements were located on hills or on spurs that projected from the Apennines into the plain. Iron Age settlements in Latium generally were smaller than their counterparts in

Etruria. In all likelihood, no village in Latium ever had more than one hundred inhabitants at any point during the ninth century. After about 800, however, a number of settlements there, like their Villanovan neighbors, began to expand because of internal growth and the abandonment of outlying villages.

For the ninth and early eighth centuries, the burials at the site of the future city of Gabii provide some evidence for the social order of a Latin settlement. Graves in its two cemeteries were arranged by rite and by the age and gender of the occupant. Adult men lie at the center; here cremation was the exclusive rite in one cemetery and the dominant practice in the other. Around the center were situated the graves of women and of young men; here, inhumation was the dominant practice. Young women interred on the periphery were often buried with bronze objects and ornaments of glass paste and of amber. These cemeteries seem to have been family burial grounds, and the different practices show that certain status distinctions were determined by age and by gender. Yet there are signs that some men possessed a distinctive position in the community. In the male cremation burials miniaturized weapons, such as swords and spears, are common—they are not found in male inhumation graves—and the occupants may have claimed some special status related to warfare. Toward the end of the ninth century, these cremation burials end, but the status groups associated with them may well have persisted, expressing their social position in new ways (see next section).

Greeks and Phoenicians in the Central Mediterranean

Outside contacts markedly affected both the pace and the nature of change in the centers of the Villanovan and Latial cultures. In the late ninth century, as well as in the eighth, maritime contact with the eastern Mediterranean became a prominent factor in the development of central Italian societies. The Phoenicians led the way. The coastal regions of the modern states of Syria and Lebanon on the eastern shore of the Mediterranean were their homeland, and the first traces of their civilization appear there around the beginning of the second millenium B.C. The Phoenicians' world centered on a number of cities, each with its own king, priests, palace, and temples, and each ruling the surrounding countryside. Long-distance trade by land and by sea was important in the social and political order of a Phoenician city-state; kings and temple priesthoods participated, as did associations of rich and powerful merchants. Around 1000, these cities, especially Tyre and Sidon, began to send out settlers and trading expeditions, first to the nearby coast of Cyprus, but soon as far away as Spain. Eventually, Phoenician settlers would establish a series of new cities along the coasts of western Sicily, Sardinia, northern Africa, and southern Spain. Carthage (Latin, Carthago), probably founded around 800 in the territory of modern Tunisia, would become the most powerful of these new settlements—and Rome's great rival.

Greeks followed shortly afterward. By 775, some Greeks established a settlement on the island of Pithecusa in the Bay of Naples, and a few Phoenicians may also have settled there. In this new community, and in others that would be founded later, trade and access to metals played an important role—Pithecusa shows signs of ironworking on a large scale—but the search for farmland was vital, too, and before long would become the most important factor. Greek settlements on the mainland soon sprang up. Cumae, founded around 750, was the first, and others would follow in the seventh, sixth, fifth, and fourth centuries. Eventually the eastern, southeastern, and northern coasts of Sicily would be dotted with Greek city-states, as would the south and west coasts of Italy as far north as Campania. Later, Romans would call these mainland areas of Greek settlement "Great Greece" (Latin, *Magna Graecia*). In the seventh and sixth centuries, the Greek colonies here, like communities in Greece itself, would develop more or less similar institutions that led to the formation of city-states.

THE RISE OF CITIES

Beginning in the middle of the eighth century and continuing over the next three centuries, Etruria, Latium, and Campania witnessed a series of political, social, and cultural innovations that would result in the formation of the first central Italian city-states. The appearance of this new form of social and political life was a broad phenomenon that characterized many Mediterranean regions and ethnic groups. In Italy, city-states became the dominant form of organization in Etruria, Latium, Campania, and the Greek regions of Sicily and southern Italy. Broad similarities in form, however, should not mask the great diversity in detail and the many local variations that could be found in important aspects of urban life. Cities, in other words, could share many of the ways they organized government, war, and religion without really being very much alike.

A city-state was both a kind of settlement and a form of political, military, and social organization. Fully developed city-states usually possessed a clearly defined urban core, with special areas designated for elite and for communal activities, and cemeteries encircling it. Beyond, its surrounding territory contained scattered shrines, hamlets, and farmsteads, along with a few settlements, smaller than the central city and without a fully developed communal life. The scale of these city-states varied greatly. In the contemporary Greek world, a "typical" one may have had approximately one thousand inhabitants and perhaps a territory of around forty square miles (100 sq km); its army would have numbered no more than a few hundred men. In central Italy, many of the emerging city-states would have been somewhat larger; by the end of the sixth century, some had populations of several tens of thousands.

Some formal political organization was essential. In a typical city-state, elite residences, political life, and communal religious activity were all concentrated in and about the center. Here, members of elite families displayed their status, competed with their peers, and exercised leadership over their own followers, even,

on occasion, over the city as a whole. At first, aristocratic families and their retainers dominated most emerging city-states. In the seventh and sixth centuries, kings
reigned in some. By the early fifth century certain cities possessed formal offices
and priesthoods, filled by a process of election, and held for terms of one year.
Arrangements such as these would eventually become standard in communities
with a city-state form of organization.

City-states emerged through a number of interrelated processes. First, an
aristocracy, with its own distinctive way of life, developed. This process almost
certainly began before it becomes visible in the archeological remains. Over time,
aristocratic families concentrated in the larger settlements, making them centers of
wealth and power. The leaders here began to construct larger and more elaborate
buildings, and to set aside formal spaces where the population would gather for
occasions deemed important to the city. Eventually, institutions regulating the
community as a whole appeared and began to overshadow individual families
and their leaders.

In central Italy, scholars divide the formative age of the city-state into two broad
phases: the Orientalizing Period (c. 725–580) and the Archaic Period (c. 580–480).
This division has much to do with artistic styles and with clear, direct foreign influ-
ences. The Orientalizing Period is so named because of the appearance in tombs
and votive deposits of luxury goods imported from the "Orient"—Greece, Syria,
and Egypt—or of locally made imitations of these imports. These two periods also
mark, if only roughly, other developmental stages. In the earlier period, monumental architecture commissioned by the elite becomes conspicuous, as does literacy. From around 600, the basic communal institutions of the city-state come into
view, the governing elite broadens in some ways, and large-scale warfare between
cities begins. The course of these developments probably varied considerably from
city to city, and the evidence rarely allows a full picture of the process to be reconstructed for any one place. The history of Rome in this period, however, is the best
documented of all (see further below).

Beginning of Writing

During the eighth century, writing came to Italy, and written texts now supplement the archeological evidence. Around 740, someone in the Greek settlement of
Pithecusa scratched into the surface of a jug a short text in Aramaic, a script and
language of Syria. At about the same time, mourners placed in a grave a cup
inscribed in Greek, one of the earliest examples of the Greek alphabet found anywhere in the Mediterranean world. The Greek language and script were to have
a long life in Italy and would exert great influence there. By 700, texts in one or
another of the languages of Italy itself appear, written in scripts derived from the
Greek. The earliest known Etruscan documents date from the very beginning of
the seventh century; known texts of the seventh and sixth centuries now number
in the many hundreds. Early documents in Latin are less common. Only a very

few can be placed in the seventh century, and less than one hundred in the sixth and fifth centuries.

The surviving texts of the eighth through the fifth centuries are generally short, difficult to interpret, hard to date, and not very informative. Inscribed on stone, bronze, or pottery, the languages in which they are written are often not well understood today. These texts identify the occupants of tombs, or the owner or maker of an object, or the dedication of gifts placed in temples and shrines. A few texts are longer, but these are only preserved in fragments for the most part, and their contents are obscure. No evidence survives of a bureaucratic use for writing, such as occurs in some other Mediterranean societies. Even so, writing in Italy was closely associated with the elites of its cities, and the earliest written texts accompany their activities.

Appearance of an Elite

Toward the end of the eighth century, some families in the coastal regions of Etruria, Latium, and Campania began to demonstrate that they possessed wealth, status, and power on a scale far greater than others in their communities had attained. These emerging elite families, like many others in the Mediterranean world at the time, sought to distinguish themselves in their communities through a distinctive way of life with the appropriate personal ornaments, weapons, and other marks of status. Many of the objects, and the imagery of wealth and power associated with them, had their origins in Greece and the Near East, where they were used in a similar fashion.

Tombs provide the earliest signs of elite families and their pretensions. In the eighth century, rich deposits of grave goods become more common. At Gabii, some tombs of the mid-eighth century are markedly richer than others, and a few exceptionally rich ones contain chariots. By the end of the century, powerful families proclaimed their position in their town or village in the so-called "princely" burials. These emphasize families and their place in their communities. In many instances the builders constructed them so that they could receive multiple burials over the years, a sign that each was intended to be for a family or a lineage. Grave goods reveal a broad concern among the elite for conspicuous displays as well as the willingness to expend much wealth in pursuit of these ends. Tombs and burials, after all, are arranged by the survivors, and in them the kin of the deceased can make clear statements about the social position they think that the dead occupied in life—not to mention the position which the survivors themselves wish to be seen as maintaining. Families often placed their tombs along the main roads into the settlement, where they could be seen and admired.

Tombs in this new manner were much more elaborate and required a larger commitment of resources than was the case earlier. One at Etruscan Caere in the seventh century, known today as the Regolini-Galassi Tomb, has a corridor over 120 feet long (36 m) and six feet (1.8 m) wide and a burial chamber on either side of this aisle. Its builders cut the lowest part of the wall into the underlying rock, and built the upper portion with large stone blocks that formed a vault over the aisle. Finally, they covered the entire structure with a large earth mound or *tumulus* about 150 feet (45 m) in diameter, and set up a low stone wall surrounding its base.

The contents of the tombs in turn served to distinguish the new burials from their predecessors and from those of their less fortunate contemporaries. Elite tombs often contain large quantities of metal objects and fine pottery, imported or of local manufacture. At Castel di Decima in Latium, mourners in the late eighth century buried a young man with personal ornaments of silver and bronze, iron weapons, a chariot, bronze tripods, other bronze vessels, and a range of Greek and Phoenician pottery. In another, later burial in the same cemetery, a young woman was interred with over ninety bronzes and imported ceramics, while her body was covered with gold, silver, and amber jewelry. Most finds of Greek and Phoenician pottery, jewelry, and other metal work—and of locally produced imitations too—have been made in tombs of this kind.

The new aristocratic tombs were not a single artistic or social phenomenon, nor were they restricted to only one ethnic or linguistic group. Instead, they attest to the formation of a broad central Italian elite culture. Burials on this pattern can be found along the west coast of Italy from the north of Etruria to the south of Campania, and later they can be found well inland too. The practice certainly crossed linguistic divides. It is present in areas whose inhabitants spoke Etruscan, and in others where Latin was the dominant language. Under this broad diffusion, there could be much local variation in practices, as well as in the layout and construction of tombs. Some were even larger than the Regolini-Galassi, while many others were smaller. Some had many burial chambers, while others had only one. Funeral rites, whether cremation or inhumation, varied from place to place (and sometimes from tomb to tomb), as did the wooden or stone coffins or sarcophagi in which bodies were buried, and the funerary urns in which ashes were placed. What these burials have in common are the prestige objects deposited in graves and many of the decorative themes on walls and on sarcophagi. Over time, much of this original unity would break down, as local elites each followed their own course of development.

Associated with these ways of death was an aristocratic way of life. In the emerging cities members of the leading families also came to adopt and display a distinctive lifestyle, which marked them off from the mass of the population and often united them with the leading families in other communities. Again, evidence from tombs is central, since mourners deposited there objects that played a prominent role in an aristocratic self-image, especially ones used in the ceremonies that defined and proclaimed this image. Thus, horses, chariots, rich armor and weapons, personal ornaments, and the equipment for feasting and drinking were all particularly important in this connection (Fig. 1.1).

Much of this new lifestyle remains obscure, but a comparison with the Greek world, which influenced Italy greatly, may help to clarify some of its features.

Greek aristocrats proclaimed their position through elaborate displays of family, wealth, and leadership in war. Male members saw themselves as heroes, which explains in part the popularity of epics such as Homer's *Iliad*. Warlike display was certainly important among central Italian elites too. Their burials regularly contained arms and armor, and the frequent representations of combat may well reflect claims to fighting skills and leadership in war. The presence of weapons in women's tombs, too, could indicate that skill in war was seen as a family attribute rather than just an individual one. Certain finds, such as the large bronze shields often embossed with elaborate designs, are too light and fragile for use in battle, although they are highly suitable for display on ceremonial occasions.

Ceremonial drinking and feasting occupied a prominent place in the aristocratic lifestyle in many parts of the Mediterranean world. In Greece, male aristocrats held ceremonial drinking bouts or *symposia* (singular, *symposium*), in which poetry, song, displays of wit and invective, and conversation all had an important place. In these gatherings, elite males in a community and their guests from elsewhere created links among themselves and proclaimed their distinction from others. Essential implements in such gatherings—bowls for mixing wine, cups, and tripods—were often expensive, and they served as symbols of a special, and highly desirable, way of life. The bulk of the bronze vessels and tripods included in Italian elite graves, along with most of the imported ceramics and their local imitations, were designed and made specifically for these occasions, which suggests that formal feasting and drinking occupied a similar position in the self-definition of the Italian elite. In Greece, guests at symposia were virtually all male; in the Italian world, artistic representations show that wives participated too.

Extravagance was a prominent feature of elite burials of the eighth and seventh centuries, but their sixth- and fifth-century successors were on a much-reduced level. The "princely" burials of the eighth and seventh centuries are relatively rare; clearly, they held the remains of only a tiny portion of the population. The elite tombs of the following centuries exhibit a wider range of sizes,

Figure 1.1 *Chariots occupied a prominent place in public displays of status, and they were often highly decorated for that purpose. This bronze panel covered the front of a chariot-body interred in a grave high in the Apennines around 550. The two sides of the chariot were similarly decorated. The relief depicts what is probably an arming scene, where the woman on the left hands the man on the right his shield and helmet. The birds flying over their heads may represent good omens. The side panels, not shown here, depict two warriors fighting over the body of a third, and a warrior driving a chariot pulled by winged horses. The chariot was probably produced in an Etruscan workshop.*

Figure 1.2 *Banquet scenes were common in the art of archaic Italy. This drawing reproduces such a scene on a terra-cotta frieze from the palace at Murlo. The artist shows the guests reclining on couches (as was customary in the Greek world too), attended by four servants. A mixing bowl of the kind often found in aristocratic tombs rests on a stand between the two couches. One of the guests plays a lyre. Hunting dogs crouch beneath tables laden with food.*

and grave goods generally are fewer, less costly, and less exotic. Despite the reduced scale, these burials were still the prerogative of a select group, and their builders shared some values with their seventh-century predecessors. Burial chambers often replicated rooms in the houses that the deceased would have occupied when alive. The walls, moreover, were covered with elaborate frescoes, certainly a task calling for skilled artisans; scenes of feasting were common, illustrating some continuity with earlier ideals. More families may have interred their members in a relatively expensive manner than was the case earlier. At Etruscan Volsinii, for example, inscriptions deposited between 550 and 500 reveal the presence of at least ninety families rich enough to build tombs. Placing a tomb was no longer solely the choice of the family. At some major centers, formal cemeteries or *necropoleis* (singular, *necropolis*), located on the margins of the settlement, contained the burials, while grids of streets determined the placing of tombs. In later periods, communal institutions overshadowed any single elite family, and the broadening of the elite from the sixth century may well reveal an early stage in this process.

Cities and Monumental Architecture

In the ninth and eighth centuries, settlements in Etruria, Latium, and Campania consisted of collections of huts with no traces of planning, formal organization, or public buildings, let alone private dwellings on a significantly larger scale than their neighbors. From the beginning of the seventh century, however, members of elite families began to construct larger, more elaborate, and more expensive structures in the main centers of population. They also began to lay out and ornament the public spaces that would define communal life for centuries, all signs of their ability to muster resources and labor on an increasingly lavish scale.

Residences of the elite form the earliest among these new kinds of edifices that are visible in the archeological record. From the beginning of the seventh century, the wealthy and powerful started to construct larger houses made of brick or stone and roofed with terracotta tiles. Some possessed elaborate and colorful exterior ornamentation. These new structures, built with techniques that had reached Italy from the eastern Mediterranean, required more capital and more labor than did earlier dwellings; surrounded by lesser structures, they would have proclaimed their owners' status much more clearly. Later, intermediate groups in the towns, not quite as wealthy or powerful, would copy these structures on a smaller scale.

A few buildings display wealth and status more appropriate to rulers than to aristocrats, perhaps the residences of the kings that legends and histories later associated with this time. The large structure constructed around 575 at Murlo in the countryside near modern Siena provides the clearest example (Fig. 1.3). This so-called "palace" consisted of four blocks of rooms around a central courtyard. The courtyard itself was surrounded on three sides by a colonnade, while the fourth side probably held a shrine, and it may also have had a place for a throne. Builders covered the rooms with over 30,000 square feet (2,800 sq m) of terracotta rooftiles, which would have required a formidable outlay of resources in fuel, kilns, and labor. The palace at Murlo had an earlier, less well-known seventh-century predecessor, which was destroyed by fire. Acquarossa, near modern Viterbo, saw the construction of a similar house during the sixth century. At Rome, another palace, known as the Regia, was built according to the same general plan toward the end of the seventh century.

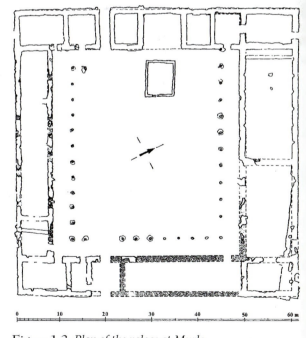

The elaborate decorations of the palace at Murlo reveal some of its functions and much of the same ethos already seen in tombs and in grave goods. Walls and rooflines were adorned with elaborate terracotta sculptures and friezes, some depicting human and divine figures and real or mythical animals, and others representing banquets, processions, horse races, and groups of warriors marching behind leaders in chariots—all prominent forms of elite behavior and display (Fig. 1.2).

Figure 1.3 *Plan of the palace at Murlo.*

Certain scenes show standing and seated human figures apparently engaged in some ceremony or public business, and one carries a special curved staff or *lituus* that would serve in Etruria and Latium as a symbol of office for nearly a thousand years.

The ways in which the palace at Murlo was used are not entirely clear. It may have served as a residence for a ruler or for the leading family in the town. Certainly, some of the ceremonial activities depicted in the friezes must have taken place within its courtyard. Fragments of fine pottery attest to banquets and symposia. The presence of a shrine indicates that religious rites were performed in the palace too; the Regia at Rome also possessed shrines to several gods. Possibly the ruler held court there in the presence of his followers and the leaders of other prominent lineages.

Slightly later, many ruling families began to establish larger and more elaborate meeting places for the residents of their cities. Structures like Murlo could have accommodated relatively few participants and observers. In later periods, the leaders of cities regularly gathered the citizens in public assemblies to announce political decisions and to mobilize popular support for them. Leaders also staged elaborate public and ceremonial displays. Religious rituals addressed to the gods of the city typically played a prominent part, for the performance of such rites also emphasized the dominant role of the elite families. Large-scale gatherings of the residents of a community, and the rituals that often accompanied them, served as a visual sign of the increasing unity of the city-state. Hence the governing elites of many emerging city-states established well-defined public spaces—together with temples and shrines surrounding them—to serve as the stage for their activities and the center of such limited government as these communities possessed.

As part of this development, the ruling elites of central Italy made the cult places of their communities grander and grander. From around 600, some cities and towns began to build large, elaborate temples to their gods. These edifices, which shared many features with the earlier palaces, especially in their decorations, were often located on the central square of a settlement or on a hill overlooking it, where they would dominate the city's physical appearance. Although there could be considerable variation in ornament and in details, temples in central Italy generally were built upon a high platform or *podium*, fronted by a porch with columns; crowning the structure were a peaked roof of terracotta tiles and such terracotta decorations as statues, friezes, and antefixes (Fig. 1.4). In later periods, these structures had an important place in communal identity, and they served functions beyond the strictly religious. In Rome, for example, officials performed many of their duties here, and speakers addressed their audience from a temple podium, where they would be highly visible.

These new cult places in some ways were an elaboration and a monumentalization of earlier practices. Organized cults did not begin with the seventh century. Excavations at the sites of some sixth- and fifth-century temples have unearthed votive deposits that contained objects much older than the temples. In the Latin

Figure 1.4 *This reconstruction of the so-called Portonaccio Temple at Veii (built c. 500) illustrates some of the typical features of a central Italian temple. It was built upon a high platform or* podium. *In front was a deep colonnaded porch, and behind was the chamber or* cella *where the cult statue of the god and some of the most precious offerings were stored. Along the ridge and edges of the roof, terracotta sculptures were placed (termed "acroterial" statues after the bases or* acroteria *on which they stood); see Fig. 1.7. The altar would have been somewhere in front of the temple; most ceremonies here would have been outside (not inside) and public.*

city of Satricum, the area later occupied by a temple had been the site of a simple hut of ninth-century date (with a hearth) that may have served as a cult place. Around the middle of the seventh century, this hut was replaced by a rectangular stone building with terracotta roof decorations; a votive model of this structure clearly shows it to have been a temple. Comparable development from hut to temple may also be seen at Velitrae, Lanuvium, and Gabii. At other places, sacred groves or open-air altars first occupied the sites of later temples.

Temples and open-air shrines formed the stage for many of a city's most important religious rites, as well as for elaborate displays of wealth and power by the governing elite. Votive offerings were prominent in central Italian cult places. These objects, offered to thank a god for answering a prayer or for giving some other sign of divine favor, could vary greatly in kind, in expense, and in quality. Individuals occupying a wide range of statuses made dedications, but those made by members of elite families would have stood out. Some of these more prestigious gifts bore inscriptions identifying the person who had made the dedication—one of the earliest uses of writing in Italy—and in the process, they would have marked this individual, in the eye of the viewer, as one favored by the god.

As wealth came to concentrate in cities and towns, many communities began to expend resources on their defense. For centuries, villages were often located on easily defensible hills or plateaus, which the inhabitants might strengthen with ditches, dikes, and palisades. From the eighth century, some communities began to construct more elaborate and expensive defensive systems. Many fortified themselves by first digging a deep, broad ditch (*fossa*), and then using the excavated earth to construct a thick, high mound (*agger*) inside it. In general, however, only the most vulnerable areas were strengthened in this manner. A few cities built still more elaborate fortifications. At the beginning of the sixth century, the Etruscan city of Rusellae built itself a wall of large mud bricks mounted on a stone base, and in the sixth and fifth centuries, the Etruscan centers of Caere, Tarquinii, Vulci, and Veii built walls with stone blocks. Again, these fortifications seldom extended completely around the settlement.

Warfare in the Orientalizing and Archaic Periods

The eighth, seventh, and sixth centuries saw major changes in the frequency of warfare, as well as in its scale and degree of organization. The new ways of making war affected not only relations between the emerging cities, but also the role and power of aristocracies, the political and social organization of the communities themselves, and their physical layouts. In the fourth century and later, when our evidence is much better, it is clear that some cities made war in a very formal and highly organized manner. They fielded large armies led by the political leaders of the city as a whole, and these armies fought formal battles in which soldiers were massed in large and regular formations. Before this date, however, simpler and less structured forms of warfare prevailed. There were few or no set battles; quick raids for cattle and other loot predominated; warriors served not as members of the community, but rather as followers of an aristocratic leader who had organized the enterprise. While the nature of the transition from one mode of warfare to another is clear enough, the stages and the timing of the shift are very obscure; it was probably a long process with much local and regional variation. From 600, however, the evidence shows traces of an ever-intensifying warfare between cities, while later literary sources even provide the names of prominent leaders in war.

Some aspects of the shift stand out more than others. The increasing scale and sophistication of the fortifications that came to surround many communities plainly illustrate both the greater intensity of warfare and higher levels of organization. By contrast, shifts in military formation and tactics, and changes in the political and social structures that may have accompanied them, are far more obscure. In the Greek world, which was the source of important innovations, the new way of war-making centered on hoplite infantry, who were protected by body armor or corselets (made either of metal or of leather reinforced with metal), bronze greaves (leg armor), and bronze helmets. These hoplites carried a large circular shield or *hoplon*, and were armed with both a spear and a sword or dagger. This new equipment was better suited to close combat than to fighting at a distance with weapons that were thrown. At the same time it made combatants less mobile in the field, so that hoplites fought in a dense formation, or phalanx, where men were protected and reinforced by those on either side. The new tactic emphasized formal battles over raid and counter-raid. It also favored the larger formation over the smaller, so that communities had a positive incentive to increase the number of men serving in their armies. The development of the hoplite phalanx was a long process. The new equipment appeared first (perhaps as early as the last decades of the eighth century), but the phalanx itself developed only slowly.

The cities of central Italy may have followed a broadly similar course of development. After around 700, weapons and body armor became more expensive, more complex, and perhaps more widely diffused over the adult male population. The presence of the equipment in graves, however, does not necessarily imply the existence of large armies fighting in regular formations. First, the range of forms for shields, helmets, weapons, and body armor seems too variable for the degree of standardization often associated with the hoplite phalanx. Moreover, grave goods, votive deposits, and new artistic representations provide very uncertain evidence for changes in tactics (Fig. 1.5). Objects deposited in graves or in sanctuaries are the relics of rites whose relationship to other aspects of communal life must remain somewhat problematic. Some shields, helmets, and corselets seem too ornate and too fragile ever to have been used in combat; objects such as these probably had more to do with ceremonial displays than with the actual conduct of war. Even the presence of serviceable equipment on the hoplite pattern need not imply that the original owner fought in a phalanx, because the prominent exhibition of foreign, and especially Greek, objects (or local copies) was a notable feature of aristocratic self-presentation. The significance of the dense groups of marching warriors seen on vases or friezes is also controversial (compare Fig. 1.6). Some experts view them as depictions of phalanxes marching into battle, while to others they are processions and armed ritual dances. Nevertheless, it is certain that some cities did slowly adopt more regular and larger-scale ways of making war.

Perhaps the most obscure aspects of these changes are leadership and recruitment. Early in the history of the Greek city-state, aristocratic families and factions dominated the life and the decision making of their communities. Fighting forces consisted of

Figure **1.5** *This Umbrian bronze votive figure of a warrior wears some of the equipment of a hoplite, including a helmet with a high, very prominent crest. It probably dates from the fifth century.*

Figure 1.6 *This mid-sixth-century terracotta frieze from the palace at Acquarossa depicts two warriors equipped as hoplites on the far left, following in procession behind a man with a bull and a chariot with two riders. The winged horses signify that the procession belongs in the realm of myth. The man with the bull may be identified as the Greek hero Heracles, the Latin Hercules.*

members of the elite and their retinues and dependents, while military leadership was largely a function of the ability to raise and lead a personal armed following. Among the developed Greek city-states of the fifth century, communal institutions such as citizen assemblies and election of officeholders had superseded the earlier aristocratic leadership in many areas of civic life, and communal norms and institutions had come to be central to warfare. For the most part, equipment was standardized across the army, and military service had become a function of citizenship and wealth rather than merely the result of birth or dependence on a leading family. In the larger cities, at least, adult males were ranked according to wealth in a way that determined eligibility for military service along with a range of other political rights and duties. They came to elect their own military leaders, and formally voted on matters of war and peace.

In central Italy, certain cities slowly made a similar transition, although some of them may never have taken it very far. In these emerging urban communities, the leading families dominated in war; just as in the Greek world, the ability to raise a personal military following was a prominent aspect of leadership and an important prop to aristocratic power. Really outstanding individuals, moreover, were able to attract followers from distant places—often younger members of aristocratic families elsewhere—who were looking for adventure, fame, and wealth. In some cities—Rome is the best-known—communal institutions would also come to overshadow individual families in making war. Yet it is possible for armed followings based on a powerful individual or a leading family to coexist for considerable periods of time with other modes of recruitment based on citizenship or residence. Indeed, it is possible that Rome's preeminence, and that of a few other towns, may have been due, to some degree, to its reorganizing while neighbors did not.

Social and Economic Organization

Elite families dominated the social and economic life of their cities just as they did their political, religious, and military organization. The wealth and power of the upper classes rested upon their control over their followers and other dependents as well as over land. Prominent individuals mobilized groups of men for war, led them in battle, and, if successful, distributed the fruits of victory: land, cattle, captives, and the movable goods of the defeated. In peacetime, leading families also assembled dependents to farm their land, guard their herds and flocks, and attend to household tasks. Agriculture was becoming more complex, more capital-intensive, and perhaps more profitable. Beginning in the eighth century, the cultivation of grape vines, so essential to a culture with ceremonial drinking, spread to central Italy, along with the planting of olive trees. Powerful families probably played an important role in this process and in the accumulation of wealth that would have accompanied it. In the late seventh and sixth centuries, potters in Etruscan coastal centers made pottery vessels, *amphorae,* for the storage of olive oil and wine; some of these wine amphorae have been found along the coasts of southern France and northeast Spain.

Long-term ties of dependency bound many of the inhabitants of the new cities to aristocratic leaders. Links between members of the elite and their followers could be defined in terms of "patrons" and "clients." Ideally, the patron granted protection to his clients, who followed this protector in war and in politics and served him in other ways when appropriate. In some cases, a powerful family may have controlled entire villages or clusters of dwellings in a larger settlement. The communities of central Italy possessed what has been called a "gentile" organization. Romans, for example, belonged to a clan or *gens* (plural, *gentes*). At first, a gens consisted of an aristocratic lineage or group of lineages and some of their lesser followers and dependents. A special system of nomenclature characterized groups formed in this fashion. Members were identified by a name or *nomen* (plural, *nomina*) that identified their gens, and they also had a first or personal name, the *praenomen.* Names in this style appear on inscriptions from the seventh century, although it is unclear whether that is a recent development or just the first appearance in writing of an already established practice. All of a city's residents need not have been either aristocrats or dependents of some aristocratic family. In some cities, independent elements of the population could certainly be found. Eventually, they too came to be organized into gentes, so that every member of a community would belong to a gens.

For many, dependence on the rich and powerful was unavoidable. So long as communal organizations were relatively weak, only powerful families, with their many armed retainers, could offer protection from war and other forms of violence. Debt formed another route to dependency. In many societies of the ancient Mediterranean world, debt established—and was intended to establish—a long-term relationship between borrower and lender. Farmers who possessed only a small plot of land were highly vulnerable to crop failure, and they had great difficulty in assembling a surplus that would see them through bad years. In the semiarid environment of much of the Mediterranean basin, crop failures or low yields because of drought were fairly frequent, a circumstance that regular warfare could only aggravate. Many men were forced to turn to their wealthier neighbors for assistance, borrowing to feed their families or to plant their next crop.

Debt incurred in this fashion, it should be noted, would probably never be repaid; debtors would never gain enough wealth to repay in full, and they would continue to need further assistance in lean years. Instead, debt created a permanent relationship in which debtors lost control of their land and their labor, while creditors gained followers and a permanent workforce. In many early city-states of Greece and Italy, debt formed one of the chief sources of social conflict.

The production of luxury goods, and trade in them too, probably focused on elite households. In the Mediterranean world of the time, the specialists who made the prestigious products desired by the rich and powerful were for the most part itinerant. They made their living, in other words, by moving from place to place, offering their services to the wealthy in each. While employed, they would be supported by their customers, who would maintain them in their households. In the seventh and sixth centuries, some producers of ceramics and metalwork certainly came to Italy from abroad, usually Greece, but on occasion from Phoenician areas too.

The leaders of some cities took a clear role in sponsoring and protecting long-distance trade, and the presence of foreign prestige items in sanctuaries and elite tombs confirms that local elites were eager to benefit from such trade. In the sixth century, Caere and Tarquinii set up secure locations in which foreign merchants could operate, and they also made treaties with other cities to protect shipping. The Greek city of Sybaris, moreover, founded dependent colonies at Laus, Scidrus, and Poseidonia on the west coast of the peninsula, so that merchants could travel from Sybaris to Campania and farther north by land, thus evading the tolls imposed by Rhegium on ships using the narrow straits between Sicily and Italy (Map 1.2).

One should not imagine, however, that the ruling elites of such cities participated personally in long-distance trade. A desire to own goods from distant places need not imply a personal interest in arranging their acquisition and transport. Indeed, the exchange of goods could be a very complex phenomenon. Members of the Greek upper classes, for example, professed contempt for trade and traders, but they still engaged in exchange with outsiders. Roman elites at a later date (see Chapter Four) also professed scorn for commerce and traders, and there are Etruscan inscriptions showing the existence of a Greek-style culture of gift giving. Leading individuals could benefit from trade without entering into a commercial relationship, and perhaps without even coming into much contact with traders. Italian aristocrats, in other words, were not merchants.

GREEKS AND ETRUSCANS

The seventh, sixth, and fifth centuries were the great age of the Etruscan and Greek cities of Italy and Sicily. In addition to the evidence provided by archeology and occasionally by inscriptions, the histories of these societies are illuminated by a few literary texts in Greek. Some of them are even contemporary with the last stages of the Archaic Period; they identify major figures and events, and shed light on social

Map 1.2 *Southern Italy and Sicily*

and political organization. All these texts, however, were composed at a considerable distance from the communities themselves. Unlike the Greeks, the Etruscans are largely silent. Some probably did write histories and chronicles of their own cities, but only a few, slight traces of these works remain. The cities of coastal Etruria sometimes appear in the writings of later Greek and Roman historians. In the Greek texts, the Etruscans appear as enemies, competitors, and pirates, cruel and faithless. The Roman writers were less hostile, but no less ethnocentric.

Greek Cities of Southern Italy and Sicily

By the end of the eighth century, some of the Greek colonies of Sicily and southern Italy began to take on the forms of city-states (Greek, *polis*). Several became notably powerful, dominating extensive hinterlands and large populations — only a fraction of whom, however, would have been citizens of the polis, because these Greek cities made sharp distinctions between citizens and noncitizens. Syracuse (Latin, Syracusae) came to dominate a large territory thus, as did Gela and Acragas (both on the south coast of Sicily), and also the south Italian cities of Taras (Latin, Tarentum), Sybaris, and Croton. The Greek cities of Sicily and Magna Graecia typically suffered from sharp internal divisions. Narrow oligarchies, composed of the descendants of the first settlers, for a long time controlled the best land and the public offices. Strife between oligarchs and the mass of citizens, as well as the sharper divide between Greek and non-Greek, made the internal stability of many cities precarious. Civil wars and coups were common, and could result in the establishment of a tyranny, the personal rule of a single individual backed by an armed following.

From the middle of the sixth century, these Greek city-states, already disturbed by internal problems, entered into a period of wider, more serious conflict. The more powerful cities, able to dominate the native populations in their hinterlands, began to press on the territories of others. During the sixth century Sybaris was the most powerful Greek city in Italy; in 510, however, after being weakened by civil strife, it was defeated and destroyed by its neighbor Croton. Then in the fifth century, Rhegium and Locri (both farther west) ended Croton's preeminence. During this century, Syracuse successfully dominated many of its smaller Greek neighbors.

Etruscans

Beginning in the late eighth century, a number of communities in southern Etruria—Caere, Tarquinii, Vulci, and Veii—began to develop rapidly into city-states (Map 1.3). By the end of the seventh century, others could be found in northern Etruria, at Populonia, Rusellae, and Volaterrae, as well as inland in the valleys of the Tiber and Arno rivers. These cities possessed a common language, and many features of their government, social organization, and religion were similar; they also had some sense of a shared identity. Yet Etruscan city-states were never united politically, and frequently they were rivals and even enemies.

Map 1.3 *Northern Italy*

The major centers of Etruria controlled substantial territories. Political power and public cult were concentrated at the core, reducing other settlements in the territory to a subordinate role, or forcing their abandonment when the inhabitants were moved to the city. The larger cities often spread over several hundred acres, although buildings did not occupy all of this space. Smaller dependent settlements, some as extensive as twenty-five acres (10 ha), could be found toward the fringes of a larger community's territory, too far away for the land there to be cultivated by people from the center. Villages occupying less than about ten acres (4 ha) surrounded the central city, as did hamlets or isolated farms that covered two to three acres (1 ha) at most. In certain instances some lesser settlements contained a religious structure or elite dwelling, and even fortifications. In addition, a few towns of intermediate size, seldom exceeding one hundred acres (40 ha), preserved a precarious independence in zones that were isolated from major settlements. Most such towns, however, eventually succumbed to their stronger neighbors: Murlo was destroyed twice, first c. 600 and finally c. 530; Acquarossa was eclipsed around 500.

Shrines in the territories of some cities promoted relations both between communities in Italy and with the outside world. In the Orientalizing Period, aristocratic households may have mediated much long-distance trade, but in the sixth century a broader institutional involvement developed in some places. At Graviscae and Pyrgi, the ports of Tarquinii and Caere respectively, elaborate temple complexes received dedications from local notables as well as from Greek, Phoenician, Latin, and Etruscan merchants. In some cases, local gods were identified with foreign ones. At Graviscae, the local Turan was equated with the Greek Aphrodite, while at Pyrgi the Caeretan deity Uni was linked with the Phoenician Astarte. Around 500, in a long inscription in Etruscan and Phoenician, the ruler of Caere recorded a dedication he had made; his choice of languages illustrates the importance of Phoenicians here (coming from Carthage perhaps, or from another western colony). Thus, as elsewhere in the Mediterranean, cult places such as these served as centers of interaction between peoples of different origin under the patronage of the host community.

Traces of Etruscans are not limited to Etruria. In some places, Etruscan settlements followed Villanovan predecessors, just as they did in Etruria itself: Capua and Nola in Campania, as well as Felsina (modern Bologna), across the Apennines, are good examples. New Etruscan centers appeared elsewhere in the Po Valley in the course of the sixth and fifth centuries. Small groups of Etruscans also inhabited places that remained essentially non-Etruscan, as we know from inscriptions in the Etruscan language found in many places in Latium (including Rome itself), Campania, and Umbria.

In the Archaic Period, Etruscan elites were among the most active in Italy. For example, in the sixth century, two brothers from Vulci, Caeles and Aulus Vibenna (Caile and Avle Vipinas in Etruscan), stand out because they left traces in the mythologies of several Etruscan cities and may even have ruled in Rome for a time. However, the nature of the interaction between prominent Etruscans and non-Etruscan communities is not always clear. It has been suggested that

Etruscan practices spread with the movement of elites and their followers, who would come to dominate a preexisting community. Some of the Etruscan centers in the north may have begun in just this way: Hatria, from which the Adriatic Sea received its name, and Spina, a major trading center from the closing decades of the sixth century, may originally have been Greek cities. Roman writers of a later date thought that two of Rome's last three kings were of Etruscan descent, and they believed that some of Rome's core institutions and practices were of Etruscan origin.

Even so, it is by no means clear how far the emergence of cities in regions such as Latium is to be credited to Etruscans. In the seventh and sixth centuries, the chief Etruscan communities were among Italy's richest and most powerful urban centers; as such, they would plainly have had marked influence, either imposed directly through the power they exerted over their neighbors, or indirectly through the models they provided for others. The similarity in material culture that many scholars regard as signifying the undoubted presence of an Etruscan elite may rather be due to the formation of an international elite style—one that crossed ethnic boundaries, and was shared by numerous local elites imitating each other to increase their own prestige. By the same token, the presence of Etruscan speakers may indicate only that the newly forming city-states in many regions were for a time open to outsiders. The Romans, it should be noted, thought that Lucius Tarquinius Priscus—the first Etruscan king of Rome, and father of the second—came to Rome from Tarquinii as an immigrant, not as a conqueror.

THE EMERGENCE OF ROME

Rome occupied a group of hills overlooking the Tiber River (Map 1.4). The location was a favorable one. Water was plentiful, and defense easy. Two of the most important routes in central Italy passed by the site, one from the salt pans at the mouth of the Tiber along the banks of the river into the interior, and the other the coastal road from Etruria to Campania, which crossed the Tiber by a ford here, the closest place to the sea where this was possible. A small stream running through a marshy valley separated three of the hills that proved especially important in early Rome: the Capitol, the Palatine, and the Velia. When drained in the seventh and sixth centuries, this valley would become the *Forum Romanum* (Roman Forum), the city's political and religious center (Map 1.5). Along the banks of the Tiber, where the stream that drained the Forum valley joined the river, a small plain gave access to the Tiber ford; this plain would become the *Forum Boarium*, the chief market and harbor of urban Rome.

The hills and valleys here were inhabited for centuries before Rome became a city. Finds show that several small clusters of huts occupied the hills, and perhaps also the valleys between them and the plain by the river. Some of these hamlets shared cemeteries, but it would seem that no sense of common identity linked

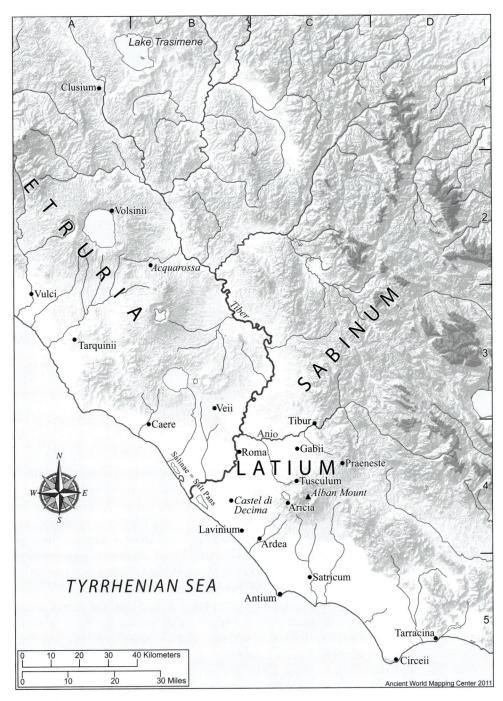

Map 1.4 *Rome and Environs*

all the hamlets on the hills. In this respect, early Rome was little different from other Latin centers, although it may have been more populous than most.

After c. 800, signs appear that a larger and more highly organized community was emerging. Burials begin to concentrate at a few large cemeteries on the margins of the settled area; meanwhile the scattered cemeteries, each shared by a few hamlets, begin to fall into disuse. The first graves in the Esquiline *necropolis*—in the seventh and sixth centuries Rome's chief cemetery—date to this period. At the same time, finds of Greek pottery on the site of the Forum Boarium may show not only that the inhabitants of Rome were in contact with distant places, but also that the plain along the Tiber River had already taken up its later role as market and port. Later too, this area would be the site of the *Ara Maxima*, an altar dedicated to the Greek hero Heracles (Latin, Hercules) and associated with commerce; his cult may have been established here as early as the eighth century.

Perhaps the most striking indications that a more highly organized community now occupied the site of Rome have emerged along the northeast slopes of the Palatine hill. Here, recent excavations have uncovered a mid-eighth-century wall, built of clay and timber on a stone foundation, running along the bottom of the hill. The wall's function is uncertain. Some scholars believe it to be a fortification, while others suggest that it marked some sacred boundary. Between 675 and 550, three successive stone walls followed the same line, but by around 530 the usefulness of all these walls had ended. Even though the construction of the first one naturally required much organization and effort, the identity of the workforce remains obscure. Residents of the villages on the Palatine may have been responsible, although it is possible that people from other hills also participated, making the wall an early sign of an increasingly united community.

From the middle of the seventh century, the Romans began to transform the valley separating the hills into the civic and religious center of the city, the Forum Romanum. Earlier, this valley—much of which was marshy and liable to flooding—held no more than a few clusters of huts and some cemeteries. The first phase of construction, which began around 650, turned part of the valley into a place where Romans could gather for communal events; for this purpose, the huts were cleared, the valley's lowest areas were drained and filled, and a rough surface of beaten earth was laid. A quarter of a century later, this pavement was refurbished and extended by filling in more wetlands. Henceforth the Forum would serve as the chief place for large public assemblies and ceremonies in the city.

As the political center of the city, the Forum also became Rome's most prominent building site. Near the end of the seventh century, the *Regia* (see below, Politics and Society Under the Kings) was erected along its edge. At the end of that century, builders laid out another public space, later known as the *Comitium*, and along its edges they constructed a large stone building that is probably to be identified with the later *Curia Hostilia*. The original uses of the Comitium and the Curia Hostilia are obscure. In later periods at least (and possibly from the outset too), they were crucial to the functioning of the Roman state. The Comitium was

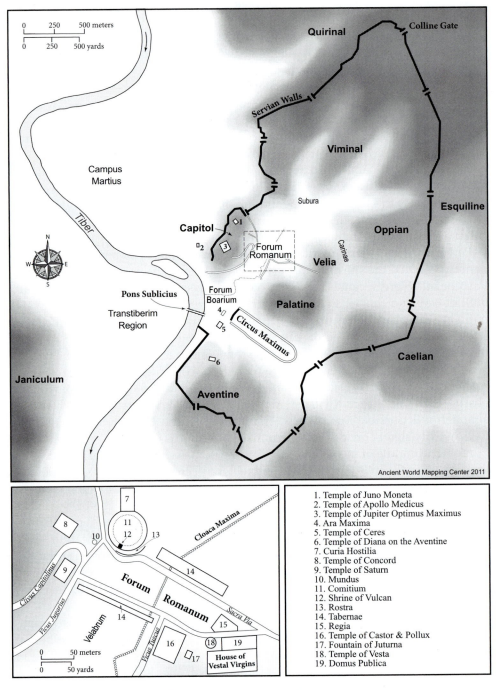

1. Temple of Juno Moneta
2. Temple of Apollo Medicus
3. Temple of Jupiter Optimus Maximus
4. Ara Maxima
5. Temple of Ceres
6. Temple of Diana on the Aventine
7. Curia Hostilia
8. Temple of Concord
9. Temple of Saturn
10. Mundus
11. Comitium
12. Shrine of Vulcan
13. Rostra
14. Tabernae
15. Regia
16. Temple of Castor & Pollux
17. Fountain of Juturna
18. Temple of Vesta
19. Domus Publica

Map 1.5 *Rome in the Early Republic (before 300 B.C.)*

a sacred space where officials would summon citizens to vote, to hear legal cases, and to make (or be informed about) important public decisions; the Curia Hostilia served as one of the meeting places for the council of elders known as the *senate*. Around the beginning of the fifth century, temples to Saturn and to Castor and Pollux were constructed on the south side of the Forum.

In addition to the Forum Romanum, two other major centers of Rome's civic and religious life, the Forum Boarium and the Capitol, began to be adorned with larger, more elaborate structures. At the end of the seventh century, builders cleared the huts from part of the plain along the banks of the Tiber and established a sacred space, which in all likelihood contained an altar. The first temple here, probably dedicated to Fortuna, was built in the second quarter of the sixth century; it was rebuilt a generation later, and decorated with terracotta friezes and statues of the Greek hero Heracles and the Greek goddess Athena. On the Capitoline hill, the Romans began to construct the temple of Jupiter Best and Greatest (Jupiter Optimus Maximus) around the beginning of the sixth century; when completed toward the end of the century, this structure was one of the largest temples in Italy. Last but not least (although the matter is controversial), the Romans of the sixth century may have protected parts of their city by excavating a *fossa* that was fifty-five feet (16.5 m) wide in places, and by constructing an *agger* to a height of forty feet (12 m).

A wealthy and powerful elite lived in the city. Goods deposited in seventh-century tombs reveal the presence of aristocratic families able to expend resources in large-scale displays of their status. Wealthy Romans also constructed buildings for their personal use. By 625, houses built of stone and roofed with tiles had replaced some of the huts on the Velia. More such houses would soon follow on the Palatine and other hills. Around 530, the walls that had marked the northeast corner of the Palatine were covered by a large earth platform. On it at least four substantial private dwellings were constructed, with large reception rooms or *atria* (singular, *atrium*) and other rooms grouped around enclosed gardens—features that would mark Roman aristocratic houses for centuries. By the end of the sixth century, dwellings spread over most of the hills, making Rome one of the largest cities in Italy.

THE ROMANS AND THEIR EARLY HISTORY

The evidence of archeology and the brief, fragmentary texts of archaic inscriptions are eventually supplemented for us by an active tradition of history-writing at Rome. These histories merged myths of Rome's origins with detailed accounts of the achievements of prominent individuals who may once have lived. According to the version that became standard, Rome was founded as a result of a conflict in the ruling family of the mythical city of Alba Longa. The king, Numitor, was deposed by his brother Amulius, who forced Numitor's daughter Rhea Silvia to become a virgin priestess of the goddess Vesta ('Vestal Virgin'). However, the god Mars—according

Figure 1.7 *This terracotta statue of the Greek god Apollo decorated the roof of the Portonaccio Temple at Etruscan Veii, which was probably dedicated to the goddess Minerva (see Fig. 1.4). Other acroterial statues attached to the temple represent Heracles and possibly Hermes. A sculptor from Veii named Vulca is said to have made the cult statue of Jupiter Best and Greatest on the Capitol, which was dedicated in 509— about the same time, in other words, as the Portonaccio shrine.*

to some versions—made her pregnant, and she gave birth to twin sons, Romulus and Remus. Amulius gave orders for them to be drowned in the Tiber, but the basket carrying them washed ashore at the foot of the Palatine hill. There, a she-wolf suckled them and, later, a shepherd rescued them. Once adult, they overthrew Amulius, restored Numitor to his throne, and decided to found a city where they had been saved. The brothers quarreled, however, and Remus was killed, so that Romulus would become Rome's sole founder.

This tale, or a close variant of it, is at least as old as the beginning of the third century. In 293, two officials erected a statue of the twins and the wolf on the Palatine; around thirty years later, the same image would feature on some of the earliest silver coins minted at Rome. For Rome's historians, Romulus was the first of seven kings and the one who established its most important political institutions (Table 1.1). His successor Numa Pompilius set the pattern for Rome's religious life. The kings that followed built temples, founded further institutions, and, like their predecessors, waged war on Rome's neighbors. Servius Tullius, the sixth king, was virtually a second founder of the city. Accounts of the reign of Tarquinius Superbus, Rome's last king, justify his fall and the end of the monarchy. The dates that Roman scholars gave to Romulus' foundation of the city vary widely, although most fall in the eighth century. Marcus Terentius Varro (116–27 B.C.), one of Rome's greatest scholars, thought that Romulus founded Rome in 753, a date that came to be generally adopted.

The reliability of these histories is far from certain. Their authors wrote centuries after the events they recounted; they filled their works with anachronisms and patriotic mythmaking; they regarded the city as unchanging in many important ways; they presented its history in a fashion that often ignored or minimized the influence of neighbors and allies. Romulus certainly is a figure of myth. His name merely means "the Roman," and he serves to explain both the existence of the city and its name. The remaining monarchs may actually have

TABLE 1.1 Dates of Rome's Kings According to Varro

Romulus, 753–715;

Numa Pompilius, 715–673;

Tullus Hostilius, 673–642;

Ancus Marcius, 642–617;

Lucius Tarquinius Priscus (Tarquin the Elder), 616–579;

Servius Tullius, 578–535;

Lucius Tarquinius Superbus (Tarquin the Proud), 534–510.

lived and ruled—their family names were all in use at some time in Rome—but the achievements attributed to them are full of myths, moralizing tales, fabrications, and the political propaganda of later ages.

The Greeks taught the Romans to write histories. Greek and Roman historians came to develop clear ideas about how one should write history and why. Historians, it was thought, should either compose accounts of a single, significant event, such as a war; or they should record a city's history from its foundation to the author's own day; or they should describe in general the history of the civilized world. The first two of these choices would prove popular among Roman authors. Moreover, proper histories should glorify one's city, as well as entertain and instruct one's readers. In order to entertain, historians offered quantities of vivid and dramatic stories adorned with colorful details. To instruct, they focused on leading individuals, the situations that these faced, and the effects of their actions on their city. Such accounts, it was hoped, would provide memorable examples of actions that good citizens should either imitate or avoid.

The first Greek histories were written in the fifth century, but the earliest Roman ones did not appear until over two centuries later. Quintus Fabius Pictor, the first Roman historian, offered an account—written in Greek, not Latin—of Rome's history from its foundation to his own day (c. 200). Others soon followed. Half a century later, Marcus Porcius Cato the Elder wrote the first prose history in Latin; its title, *Origins*, indicates one of its major themes. These early works do not survive, although their influence persisted. In fact both Greek and Roman historians composed their works in ways that nowadays we would more or less equate with plagiarism, since they often incorporated segments of the works of others into their own. Today, our knowledge of this historiographical tradition of early Rome derives from two Roman writers in particular—Marcus Tullius Cicero (106–43), and Livy (Titus Livius, 59 B.C. to A.D. 17)—as well as from such Greek authors as Diodorus Siculus (mid to late first century B.C.), Dionysius of Halicarnassus (late first century B.C.), Plutarch (before A.D. 50–after 120), and Cassius Dio (late second and early third centuries A.D.).

Roman historians only rarely undertook what a modern historian might recognize as research. Undoubtedly, Romans of a later age had access to information regarding earlier centuries that was, in modern terms, reliable. Some documents

did survive, although later Romans found them difficult to decipher and interpret. Monuments often carried very brief inscriptions identifying their builders
and perhaps the occasion for their construction. One group of priests, the pontiffs,
maintained a year-by-year account of significant events, the so-called pontifical
annals. These annals identified the chief elected officials who held office each
year, noted victories and perhaps defeats, recorded the foundation of temples,
and set out a wide range of unusual or dramatic events that were thought to
reveal the will of the gods in some way—including famine, earthquakes, freak
storms, and lightning strikes sustained by prominent buildings or monuments.

However, few Roman historians seem to have consulted the old texts directly.
Instead, they largely relied on interpretations of them (not always accurate)
encountered in the works of earlier writers. They also resorted to other sources
that modern historians might find less dependable. For example, popular or
priestly aetiologies—stories told to explain or justify a religious rite by setting out
an account of its first appearance—often found their way into histories. Historians
made use of family traditions too. In fourth-century Rome, as well as later (see
Chapter Two), a relatively small circle of prominent families held most of the high
offices and commanded most of the armies. These families asserted their greatness
by proclaiming the offices and deeds of their ancestors; in the process, it was often
suspected, they also exercised their powers of imagination.

SOURCE 1.1: *When recounting Rome's early history, both Roman and (later) Greek his-*
torians often imagined the city's first leaders as initiating and performing practices that later
would be typical of its officials. Here Plutarch presents Romulus as founding Rome with just
the same rites that the founders of Rome's own colonies used in the fourth century and later
(see Chapter Two).

Plutarch, *Romulus* 11: Romulus buried Remus in the Remonia, together with the servants who had reared him. He then began to build his city, after summoning experts
in sacred customs and writings from Etruria, who taught him everything as if in a religious rite. A trench was dug around what is now the *Comitium*, and in it were deposited first fruits of whatever was considered good by custom and necessary by nature.
And finally, each man brought a small portion of their native soil and threw it in,
where it mixed together. They call this trench the *mundus*, as they do the heavens.
Then, they marked out the city in a circle around this center. And the founder, after
placing a bronze ploughshare on the plough and yoking to it a bull and a cow,
ploughed a deep furrow around the boundary lines, while those who followed behind
turned the clods thrown up by the plough inwards toward the city, leaving none to
face outward. With this line, they mark out the course of the wall, and it is called by
contraction the *pomerium*, in other words 'behind the wall' (*post murum*). And where
they intended to place a gate, they lifted the plough and left an empty space. And this
is why they regard the entire wall as sacred except for the gates.

Moreover, Roman historians, like their Greek models, felt free to invent parts of their narratives. In principle, historians were bound by the facts. They should describe only wars that had actually taken place, and they should accurately identify the victors and the vanquished. But they could also embellish their narratives when they had little factual guidance. Thus they added minor actions, claims about motives, and even specific words and deeds when they thought their accounts required them. To be sure, there were a few agreed guidelines. Attributions should be plausible; they should be both true to character and illustrative of it; and they should not contradict known events. Inevitably, however, a common consequence of such additions was to project back into the past the attitudes and practices of the author's own day. Roman historians tended to think that their city, in its essentials, was unchanging from an early date. Thus, they had no difficulty in believing that Romans of earlier centuries had the same attitudes and values as did their descendants, and that in the distant past the city had functioned socially and politically in much the same way as it would later.

Separating fact from fancy is always a difficult task, and modern scholars have long disagreed over the degree to which Roman tradition can be considered reliable. In this regard, today's scholars are often better disposed to the Romans than their predecessors were. Roman histories do contain an uneasy mixture of fact, supposition, and outright invention. Much is doubtless true. From the sixth century on, the main outline of wars, conquests, and the dedication of new temples is in all likelihood substantially correct. The prominent individuals we read of may not only actually have lived, but they may also have done things that resemble, if only remotely, the accomplishments attributed to them. This said, there are also unquestionably elements that were shaped by their dramatic possibilities, or by their usefulness as a means of praising virtue and condemning vice. There is no shortage of lurid stories and moralizing tales in which heroic men and women do great deeds or suffer tragic fates, and no dearth of villains either, some of whom suffer for their misconduct.

As a result, the Roman historical tradition, when coupled with the evidence from archeological excavations and from inscriptions, does permit the broad outlines of the city's early history to be known with some confidence—for the sixth and fifth centuries especially. On some specific points, moreover, this picture of the city and its institutions in the Orientalizing and Archaic periods can be supplemented by using evidence from later practices. The earliest forms of these institutions may well have varied considerably from later and better-known versions, but in certain cases we can be sure that they were present in one form or other.

POLITICS AND SOCIETY UNDER THE KINGS

Kings certainly once ruled in Rome. *Rex*, the Latin word for king, appears in two fragmentary sixth-century texts, one an inscription from the shrine of Vulcan, and the other a potsherd found in the Regia. And kingship persisted in Rome in the form of a priestly office, the *rex sacrorum*, that continued the king's religious functions long after the political and military powers had been lost. Rome was not the only Italian city with a king, but it is far from clear how common monarchy was. Tyrants, who seized power forcefully and often ruled in the same way, governed many of the Greek cities of southern Italy and Sicily during the sixth and fifth centuries. Kings led a number of Etruscan cities too, from the seventh century into the opening years of the fourth. Roman historians did believe that their monarchy had not been hereditary, so that each king had to establish his right to rule. In the traditional list of seven kings, it should be noted, there is only one instance where a father and his son both held the throne, although even here the reign of another intervened.

Romans of a later date associated their kings with leadership in war, the construction of temples and other public buildings, the performance of religious rites, and the granting of judgments in legal disputes. These early rulers, we are told, defeated many of the surrounding towns and villages, forcing some of their inhabitants to move to Rome, while others were permitted to remain in what would become no more than small rural centers without much civic life. Archeologists have found the remains of towns near Rome, some of which were wealthy and powerful in the seventh century, but no more than fortified villages in the sixth. In later periods, the Romans regularly celebrated rites that marked the boundaries of their territory centuries earlier. Certain rituals preserved the memory of a time when Roman territory encompassed only about seventy-five square miles (190 sq km), and Rome's frontiers were no more than five miles (8 km) from the city in any direction. By the end of the sixth century, however, Rome had become a much larger place. Its territory probably covered almost 300 square miles (780 sq km), while the population may have been as high as 35,000.

The area around the Forum Romanum contained a number of places linked to rites and activities that Roman historians later associated with kingship. Around 625, the Regia was constructed along the same general pattern as the "palaces" at Murlo and Acquarossa, with small chambers surrounding a central courtyard. The building had a clear religious function. In it, shrines to Mars and Ops Consiva, the gods of war and of wealth, served as the focus of a range of sacred tasks performed by the kings and their priestly successors. In the sixth century, the Regia probably formed part of a larger complex that included the temple of Vesta, containing the sacred hearth of the city, and the *domus publica*, later the house of the leader of an important group of priests and quite possibly the sixth-century dwelling of the kings. Not too far away, in the area sacred to the god Vulcan, was found a long sixth-century law, today very fragmentary (the so-called *Lapis Niger*, "Black Stone"), which seems to record regulations of a ritual nature that in some way involved the king.

The aristocracy, too, had its own political, religious, and military roles in the city. Roman historians later held that the leaders of the city's aristocratic families met in a council of elders known as the senate, which chose the kings, helped them make policy, and on occasion resisted their initiatives as they saw fit. Aristocratic councils were common in the world of the city-state. Like kings, prominent members of the Roman elite also had their own religious roles. Later Romans believed that certain aristocratic families enjoyed especially close relations with the gods; in time, too, prominent families certainly did come to monopolize the most important priestly offices.

Like other cities of central Italy, Rome seems to have witnessed a certain mobility of elite families during the seventh, sixth, and early fifth centuries. Some aristocrats and their followers moved from city to city, taking up in the new place the position they had abandoned in the old. The Elder Tarquin was thought to have moved to Rome from the Etruscan city of Tarquinii. Around 500, the aristocratic family of the Claudii, which centuries later would provide emperors for Rome, first came to the city with a great body of clients, having left its native Sabine country to the northeast after suffering political setbacks there. A few leaders of private armies gained an especially prominent place in the history of central Italy during the sixth and early fifth centuries. Some dominated their own cities, while others sought wealth and power away from home. Romans of a later age liked to believe that their kings had ruled with the consent of the leading families and the people. In practice, however, the entry of powerful individuals and their followers into a new city may have been tantamount to conquest. As late as 460, Appius Herdonius, a Sabine, seized the Capitoline hill with armed clients and tried—without success—to dominate the city.

One of the chief characteristics of a fully formed city-state was a citizenry organized communally to fulfill its roles in politics, religion, and war. In Rome, the mass of adult male citizens was known as the *populus Romanus*. At some indeterminate point, this populus gained the right to give assent to officeholders and their policies, a practice that would eventually become formalized as a vote. The bulk of Rome's population was integrated into the city's institutions through intermediary groups known as *curiae* (singular, *curia*). These curiae, supposedly thirty in number, came together to form three tribes, the Tities, Ramnes, and Luceres.

Like other elements of Rome's social and political order, the curiae had important religious functions. In later, better-documented times, they met for communal meals during major festivals and for the performance of their own religious rites. Their only known officials, *curiones*, *libones*, and *flamines*, either were priests or at least possessed many priestly attributes. Rome's oldest aristocratic families dominated these positions, and they would maintain this control long after they had lost their monopoly of other priestly offices at the end of the fourth century (see Chapter Two).

The tribes had an essential role in Rome's political and military organization. When the city made war, its army—the followers of the king and of powerful members of the elite, along with some sort of general levy—was organized by tribes, with each one providing its own unit of cavalry and of infantry. Aristocratic families probably dominated their tribal contingents just as they did the curiae.

During the sixth century, a reform superseded this organization of tribes and curiae, but did not eliminate it. The sixth king, Servius Tullius, supposedly created new forms of classifying and organizing the population—the beginnings of the Roman *census*, in other words, which in later periods would be one of the central institutions of the city (see Chapter Two). The core of the new arrangement was the regular compilation of a list of adult male Romans, in which they were classified by wealth and by residence, rather than by kinship. In the world of the city-state, citizens provided their own arms and armor when serving in the army. Aristocrats clearly possessed the resources to equip themselves in this manner—they certainly could afford to deposit military equipment in their tombs—and they may have supplied weapons and armor to their followers too. Tullius' census divided Romans into those who could afford to equip themselves for service on foot (known as the *classis*, "those summoned"), and those who could not (*infra classem*, "below those summoned").

Citizens who belonged to the classis—probably along with those who could serve in the cavalry, and just possibly those who were judged to be infra classem also—were further subdivided into units known as centuries (*centuriae*; singular, *centuria*). In the strictest sense, the term centuria should denote a group of exactly one hundred men; however, in later periods at least, the size of a centuria could be quite different from this supposed norm.

Units likewise termed centuriae also occupied a primary position in the organization of Rome's armies in the field, and in fact the use of the term in this military context almost certainly preceded its adoption for the census. Roman commanders raised armies by summoning citizens to gatherings where they chose their soldiers from those eligible to serve. The force raised in this way was called a legion (*legio*; plural, *legiones*), which signified that it stemmed from a selection process—the verb *legere* meaning either "to collect" or "to pick." Under the kings, the legion selected each year was the army of the city. In later centuries, the term came to denote a unit of several thousand men serving under one of the commanders who held office for the year (see Chapter Two). From the earliest period for which we have information, a legion was always subdivided into sixty centuries. The centuries of the census, however, were not the same as the centuries of the legion. Later, for certain, the former came to comprise voting units in one type of citizen assembly (see Chapter Two), and this function may even have been original, so that from the outset this "assembly of centuries" represented the citizenry under arms.

Although it may not have been part of the original census, citizens soon came to be assigned to tribes that received their members from defined territories. Servius Tullius supposedly divided the city itself into four "urban" tribes for its residents, and this number was never increased. At the same time or shortly after, "rural" tribes were added for the inhabitants of the countryside, and their number was to grow as Roman territory expanded. These territorial tribes served as the mustering units of the Roman army. Residents of the city assembled for military service in their four tribes. Members of the rural tribes probably gathered in a tribal mustering center, which would have been a prominent, and no doubt fortified, place in its territory.

Tullius' creation of these tribes did not require the elimination of the three original ones, which continued to perform some of their old functions. Consequently,

Roman citizens now belonged to two tribes in two different tribal systems. Over time, however, the new tribes came to be considerably more important than the old, and membership in one became a mark of citizenship. By the first century B.C., there were even some Romans who did not know their own curia, but all would have been able to name their territorial tribe.

Accounts of Servius Tullius' life and reign are full of dramatic events, turns of fortune, and tales of divine intervention, and many of the incidents recorded about his life may be more a matter of myth than of history. Descriptions of his reforms, moreover, contain elements that only became standard at a later date. Nonetheless, the key features were probably in place by the early fifth century at the latest. The oldest territorial tribes, those closest to the city, bear the names of families who were prominent in the first decades of the Republic, but less prominent later. Later Roman historians thought that Tullius ruled without the consent of the senate, and that he was sometimes hostile to it. In some contemporary Greek cities, where institutions like the Roman census can also be found, the creation of a list of citizens and the reassignment of the population to new subunits certainly did have the effect of lessening aristocratic control; newly created means of organization acted to decrease the importance of older ones in which members of the elite had possessed hereditary rights of leadership. The reforms credited to Tullius may well have had similar goals—an early stage in the long process whereby political power based on a personal armed following would give way to power gained and exercised through more formal, communal, and regulated means. But it is possible that practical considerations also played a role. In the sixth century, Rome's territory now greatly exceeded its size in the seventh, so that smaller territorial tribes, and more of them, would make the mustering of the army a quicker, more convenient operation.

ROME AND THE LATINS

A shared identity linked the cities of Latium. Much later, Roman writers would maintain that the ancestor of all Latins was Aeneas, a noble Trojan who escaped from Troy as it fell to the besieging Greeks. After many adventures, Aeneas landed in Latium near the future city of Lavinium, where he formed a new people from his own followers and from the aboriginal inhabitants of the area. His son would found Alba Longa, the seat of kings who would rule Latium and found the other Latin cities. This tale certainly does not depict historical events. Latins were not Trojans, and Alba Longa probably never existed as a city and as the seat of a powerful dynasty of kings. But the myth does serve a distinct purpose. It expresses an unmistakable sense of a perceived relationship between the cities of Latium, and it also connects them to one of the most important "events" in Greek myth, celebrated in the epic poems, Homer's *Iliad* and *Odyssey*, that were so central to Greek culture. Moreover, the inhabitants of Latium did have much in common. They shared the name of Latin (*nomen Latinum*), and they used variants of the Latin language. From the beginnings of the "Latial culture" around 1000, they also possessed a common material culture.

The belief in an identity that transcended the separate communities of Latium received clear expression in religious ritual. At certain festivals, Latin settlements came together for the performance of communal rites. The Latin Festival, or *Latiar*, held in honor of Jupiter Latiaris (Jupiter of the great feast of the Latins), was the most prominent. Each spring, towns and villages possessing the right to take part—the Romans later knew of thirty—shared common sacrifices and banquets on the Alban Mount, the supposed site of Alba Longa. The Latin festival survived the end of the political independence of the Latin communities in the fourth century (see Chapter Two), because Roman officials continued to supervise its performance for centuries thereafter. The Latins also possessed common cults at other sites. At Lavinium, a group of Latin cities, probably thirteen in number, sacrificed at a shrine to the Penates, or household gods; centuries later, when Rome had taken over the shrine, Roman officials still performed rites there to the Penates of the Roman People. Another cluster of cities, towns, and villages shared worship in the grove of the goddess Diana at Aricia, and there may have been further groups that made common use of sacred groves near Tusculum and Ardea. The Roman king, Servius Tullius, allegedly established another shrine to Diana on the Aventine hill, just outside the limits of the city of Rome, for all the Latins to use.

These sanctuaries and the rites that took place in them are certainly old, although the date of their first appearance is unknown. At two of the sites, prominent cult structures appeared in the sixth century, at just the time when cities were also first building temples to their own gods. At Lavinium, archeologists have found the sanctuary of the Penates just outside the city's fortifications. In it, beginning in the sixth century, were built thirteen monumental altars, each of which probably belonged to one of the cities that sacrificed there (see Fig. 1.8a). Later representations of the cult statue of Diana on the Aventine, which would have been housed in her temple there, show it to have been of a sixth-century type. Temples built within cities during the sixth and fifth centuries often occupied the sites of open-air sanctuaries at which cult activity would date much further back. The same may well be true of the interurban sanctuaries at Rome, Lavinium, and other places.

Latins' sense of a shared identity also found expression in other ways. In the Greek world, the ideal city-state or *polis* was a closed community; few outsiders became citizens, intermarriage with noncitizens was sometimes discouraged, and the right to own land was restricted to citizens. Latin cities were less exclusive—at least with other Latins. Later, all Latins possessed the right of *conubium*, permitting them to make a lawful marriage with a resident of any other Latin city (children of the marriage gained the citizenship status of the father; children born outside marriage received their mother's status). Equally, the right of *commercium* allowed Latins to own land in any of the Latin cities and to make legally enforceable contracts with their citizens. In addition, all Latins had the right (*ius migrationis*) to

Figure 1.8a, b *In the 1960s an open-air sanctuary with a row of thirteen monumental stone altars [a] was discovered by Italian archeologists just outside the walls of Lavinium, a Latin city not far south of Rome. The altars—never all in use simultaneously—seem to have been built at various times between the sixth and fourth centuries, and the sanctuary remained in use to the end of the third century. The likelihood is that different Latin cities each commissioned an altar and sacrificed to the Penates here. Nearby, also just outside the city walls, a temple of the goddess Minerva was built around 500. In the third century, the temple was apparently cleaned and remodeled, and over one hundred terracotta statues were placed in a votive deposit. The statue shown [b] was found there, and represents Minerva in armor, probably the temple's original cult statue, an imposing 6.5 ft tall (2 m).*

take up citizenship in any other Latin city merely by establishing residence there. These rights achieved formal expression no later than the fourth century, although it is likely that they were, in some form, much older. Such shared rights—and the common religious rites too—may be relics of the time before the appearance of cities divided the people of Latium into clearly separated communities.

Despite all this sharing, the Latins were not politically unified. The proliferation of rites and cult centers, shared by cities in various combinations, plainly demonstrates the absence of any single overarching organization, religious or political, during the seventh and sixth centuries. Latin communities certainly waged war against one other, and the largest and most powerful of them competed among themselves for primacy, often at the expense of the weaker communities. In these circumstances, cities grew by war, and the political institutions that would later unite the Latin communities resulted from the domination of a few centers, and eventually from the leadership of just one, Rome.

Roman authors later thought that their city, under its kings, had led the other Latins. Although the extent of Rome's power remains uncertain, this claim is to some degree correct. Polybius (*Histories* 3.22), a Greek historian of the second century B.C., recorded a treaty between Rome and the North African city of Carthage that he claimed had been preserved in an inscription. In this treaty, probably concluded around 500, the Carthaginians pledged not to injure any Latin city subject to Rome, and not to attack any other Latin city. The treaty specifically named some of these subject cities, lying along the coast: Ardea, Antium, Lavinium, Circeii, and Tarracina—the last about sixty miles (96 km) south of Rome. This treaty, then, clearly illustrates Rome's claim to leadership of the Latins, and also shows that its rule was contested or resisted by some Latin cities. As Rome's fortunes waxed and waned, its ability to control these cities may have tightened or weakened accordingly.

SUGGESTED READINGS

Aubet, Maria Eugenia. 2001 (second edition). *The Phoenicians and the West: Politics, Colonies and Trade*. Cambridge: Cambridge University Press.

Banti, Luisa. 1973. *Etruscan Cities and Their Culture*. Berkeley, Los Angeles, London: University of California Press.

Cornell, Timothy J. 1995. *The Beginnings of Rome: Italy and Rome from the Bronze Age to the Punic Wars (c. 1000–264 B.C.)*. London and New York: Routledge. An intensive survey of Rome's early centuries based on archeological and literary evidence. Since the ancient historical writers who treated this period all wrote several centuries later, the value of their testimony continues to be hotly debated by modern scholars. Professor Cornell's view of the accuracy of Roman traditions is a more favorable one than that reflected in the first two chapters of the present book.

Gabba, Emilio. 1991. *Dionysius and the History of Archaic Rome*. Berkeley, Los Angeles, London: University of California Press. A study of how the Greek historian Dionysius of Halicarnassus put together his account of the history of early Rome.

Grandazzi, Alexandre. 1997. *The Foundations of Rome: Myth & History*. Ithaca and London: Cornell University Press.

Miles, Gary B. 1995. *Livy: Reconstructing Early Rome*. Ithaca and London: Cornell University Press.

Smith, Christopher J. 1996. *Early Rome and Latium: Economy and Society c. 1000-500 B.C.* Oxford: Oxford University Press.

Smith, Christopher J. 2006. *The Roman Clan: The* Gens *from Ancient Ideology to Modern Anthropology*. Cambridge: Cambridge University Press.

Spivey, Nigel. 1997. *Etruscan Art*. London: Thames and Hudson. This work is broader than its title indicates, covering art throughout central Italy and placing it in its social context.

REPUBLICAN ROME AND
THE CONQUEST OF ITALY

In the sixth century, Rome was one of the largest and wealthiest cities in Italy. At the end of the century, however, Rome and many of its neighbors entered into a period of great turbulence. In Rome itself, this coincides with an important shift in rule with the end of the monarchy and the beginning of the Roman Republic. Over the next two centuries, Roman political institutions took on their longstanding form and Rome succeeded in dominating peninsular Italy. The first century of the Republic is nearly as obscure as the history of regal Rome. Once again, our evidence for the city's history in this period rests on archeology, on a few inscriptions, and on the same literary sources introduced in the previous chapter. In the following century, the evidence becomes more detailed and more reliable; some events, moreover, can be confirmed in sources composed outside of Italy.

THE EARLY REPUBLIC

Rome's monarchy ended with the sixth century in the midst of decades of strife that seems to have shaken many of the cities of Italy. Rome's historians later described the expulsion of the last king, Tarquinius Superbus, in terms that justified his fall, presenting him in the conventional garb of a tyrant, and providing the details appropriate to such a figure and to his family. The central episode in his fall was an assault by his son, Sextus Tarquinius, on Lucretia, the wife of Lucius Tarquinius Collatinus, and her subsequent suicide. Because of this and other crimes, we are told, prominent members of the Roman elite, especially Lucius Junius Brutus, Collatinus, and Publius Valerius Publicola (or Poplicola), exploited the king's absence to take over the city and begin the Republic. Whatever the facts of the matter, it is certain that kings once ruled Rome and just as certain that, in the fifth century, they no longer did. Rome was not alone in this transition, for some Etruscan cities made a similar shift in the sixth and fifth centuries.

Romans of a later date believed that the end of the monarchy marked the beginnings of the major political institutions of the Republic, but the transition was definitely not so sharp and clear. Powerful leaders still possessed armed followings, and it may have seemed an open question to contemporaries whether or not a new king appeared. A fragmentary inscription in archaic Latin found in 1977 at the Latin city of Satricum, the so-called *Lapis Satricanus*, records a dedication made to the god Mars by a group identifying itself as the *soudales* of Poplios Valesios. Soudales are either the members of a cult association of equals, or the elite companions of a prominent individual; just conceivably, their leader could have been the Publius Valerius Publicola known from later Roman authors. In any case, the text shows that some kind of leader with a personal following was active in Latium around 500. In the fifth century, it should be noted, the nearby Etruscan city of Veii first expelled its king and then, after a substantial interval, installed another.

In the Roman Republic, magistrates took the king's place. Magistracies spread power more widely among the rich and powerful, which is perhaps why so many cities eventually discarded their kings. The frequent replacement of kings by elected officials, moreover, may well be a sign that the aristocratic families of many Italian cities had never become fully reconciled to the rule of one man; in later periods, at least, resistance to monarchy and tyranny would be a central element in their ideology. Rome would eventually possess a hierarchy of offices, each with its own tasks and powers. Each office was annual—its occupants served only for a year—and collegial; more than one individual shared the powers of the position at the same time, and each could check improper actions by a colleague. Later, limited terms and shared tenure in office would be seen as a chief prop of liberty, and this may well have been true from an early date. Other cities, too, came to rely on officials like those at Rome, although there were significant variations in the number of magistrates and in their powers.

For much of the fifth century, there was some instability and experimentation in Rome's offices and in the rules surrounding them. Roman historians later would identify the Republic with the two consuls who were elected yearly (see below). The predominance of the consulship, however, would not become fixed until the fourth century. During the second half of the fifth and early in the fourth centuries, the Romans chose military tribunes with consular powers (*tribuni militum consulari potestate*). At first these tribunes served in groups of three or four, but eventually six would be chosen in most years. Later Roman historians thought that the consular tribunate was inferior to the office of consul in its powers and its religious prerogatives; why the Romans resorted to it for a period remains obscure. Perhaps having a larger number of officeholders was occasionally more important than having fewer, but more powerful, magistrates.

In times of emergency, the Romans resorted to the dictatorship, an office with extraordinary powers. The practice during the fourth and third centuries was for magistrates to appoint one man to serve as dictator in emergencies, or in a major war when a unified command seemed desirable. Dictators were not elected. Instead, a consul designated a single man for the post in a ceremony that took place in the dead of night. The new dictator then appointed a "master of cavalry" (*magister equitum*) as second-in-command to assist him. Dictators were thought to possess the undivided authority of the old kings of the city, and they surrounded themselves with symbols of royal power; perhaps for this reason, they were bound by a series of ritual prohibitions limiting their conduct. A dictator remained in office for six months or for the duration of the emergency, whichever was shorter; meantime the consuls remained in office, but served under the dictator's command. The roots of this office certainly lie in the wars and civic disturbances of the fifth century.

Annual magistracies require a process of selection. Citizen assemblies certainly fulfilled this function during the fifth century, and they may even have done so under Rome's kings, but little is known of their powers and mode of operation then. In the first century B.C., an assembly of curiae (*comitia curiata*) met to ratify the choice of officials made by others, to witness the inauguration of priests, and to approve certain adoptions and wills. By that date, when this "curiate" assembly met, each of the thirty curiae was represented by a single citizen, who cast its vote. In early Rome, its meetings must have been better attended, but its functions may not have been different. Registering assent or witnessing the actions of leaders may have been all that ever was expected of it. Assemblies organized by tribes or by centuries also operated during the first century of the Republic's existence. In later periods, the "Centuriate" assembly chose the highest officials and rendered judgments in important cases. It is uncertain when it gained these functions, but the mid-fifth-century law code of the Twelve Tables does mention a "greatest assembly" that gave judicial rulings in the same kinds of cases later judged by the centuries. The adjective "greatest" itself demonstrates that this was not the only citizen assembly at the time.

Some fifth-century laws give a glimpse of contemporary Roman society. According to Rome's historians much later, popular agitation to limit the consuls' power and to make the laws public by writing them down for the first time led to the creation in 450 of a special commission of ten men or "decemvirs" (*decemviri*). They were to hold supreme power for one year, superseding the consuls, and by the end of this year they were to produce a body of laws to regulate the Republic. In some accounts, a second such commission was chosen for the following year to complete the task. The final result was the "Laws of the Twelve Tables," which served for centuries as the fundamental text in Roman law. Accounts of both commissions are filled with the kind of elaboration typical of our sources. The second group of decemvirs was painted in especially tyrannical colors. One of them, Appius Claudius, lusted after Verginia, whose father killed her in order to prevent her from being seized by the would-be tyrant. This tale bears obvious similarities to the story of Lucretia and, like it, serves to justify attacks on the holders of legitimate offices. Claudius' actions supposedly resulted in the fall of the decemvirs and in the moderation of some of their measures. The laws, however, did exist, and some of their provisions survive.

That said, these Laws of the Twelve Tables were not a code in the modern sense. They attempted no systematic treatment of all of the law. Instead, they were a collection of specific, detailed, and narrowly focused provisions. They best fit a society where the family and the household are the fundamental units of social life, and agriculture and animal rearing the primary economic activities. The authors of the laws addressed aspects of marriage and divorce, inheritance, and the rights of a father over members of his household. They attempted to regulate disputes over the ownership of land and its boundaries, farm buildings and fences, livestock, fruit-bearing trees, and slaves, as well as conflicts that arose over injuries to persons or property. Procedural matters loom large. Plaintiffs themselves were responsible for notifying the other parties, for ensuring their attendance in person for trial in the Forum or Comitium, and for collecting any judgments awarded. When defendants did not appear for trial, the Twelve Tables authorized plaintiffs, after summoning witnesses, to seize defendants by force and bring them to court.

Debt and its consequences were among the lawmakers' central concerns. At Rome, as in other cities of the ancient Mediterranean world, debt could force small-scale farmers into a state of permanent dependency (see Chapter One). The Twelve Tables prescribed that creditors must assure the debtor's appearance in court, and must carry out all judgments. Debtors had thirty days to pay a debt in default or to satisfy a judgment against them. In the event that a debtor did not pay in time, the creditor could seize and hold him, unless some other person pledged to pay the debt if the debtor ran away. The creditor next brought the debtor to the Forum on three successive market days; if the debt still remained unpaid, he could then sell him into slavery "abroad, across the Tiber." Etruria lies across the Tiber from Rome and the rest of Latium, so these words "abroad, across the Tiber" may indicate that Romans could not legally be held as slaves in Rome itself or in Latium. Although the Twelve Tables mention it only in passing, one other way that a debtor might satisfy a creditor was by entering into a relationship of debt-bondage, or *nexum*; such individuals (*nexi*) served their creditor as long as the debt remained unpaid.

Rome and Its Neighbors in the Fifth Century

The circumstances in which the Romans found themselves changed dramatically around 500. In consequence, the fifth century seems to have been a difficult time for the inhabitants of Latium, Campania, and the Greek cities of the south. The settled coastal plains of the west and south were disturbed by the movements of peoples and bands of warriors beyond their margins. The inhabitants of the valleys and plateaus of the central Italian highlands did not live in an urbanized social environment. Villages were the chief settlements here, and in their economies the herding of animals seems to have been more important than agriculture. Raiding may well have been ubiquitous; some villages shared fortified hilltop places of refuge where they and their herds could take shelter when attacked. By the beginning of the fifth century, ruling elites had begun to merge and form federations. Although these combinations did not result in cities and the more highly organized life associated with them, they were capable of collective action on a larger scale than before, especially when it came to raiding, warfare, and self-defense.

By the beginning of the fifth century, the highlanders had begun to press on the coastal plains. In 473, the Greek cities of Tarentum and Rhegium attempted to prevent the Messapii of Apulia from sending out new settlements, and in consequence they suffered a very severe defeat (Map 1.2). The cities of the west coast—Greeks, Latins, and the Etruscans of Campania—also came under attack. In Campania, a warband from the highlands of Samnium captured Etruscan Capua in 423 and Greek Cumae around 420 (Map 2.1). Farther south, Lucanians attacked Thurii (a newly founded city on the site of Sybaris) in 433, and captured Poseidonia in 410. By the end of the century, Velia and Neapolis (modern Naples) were the only Greek cities remaining on the Tyrrhenian coast. Along the southern (or Ionian) coast, the major Greek centers survived, although by now their prosperity and power were largely eclipsed.

Latium suffered too, and very severely in the case of some cities. Sabines, Volsci, and Aequi emerged from the hills that bordered Latium in an arc from northeast to southeast; archeologists have found some of their fortified hilltop refuges. Rome itself suffered from their depredations, and several Latin cities fell. Roman authors would later report battles quite close to the city, and they would claim that Rome led the other Latins in the common defense. It may well be the Romans took this kind of lead, but we still remain ignorant of how it compared to the role played by other important Latin centers such as Tibur and Praeneste. In any event, by the end of the century Rome and its Latin allies had the upper hand. Steadily, Volsci, Aequi, and Sabines were first repelled, and then pushed back. In the process, Latin cities that had fallen or been abandoned were reoccupied as colonies (*coloniae*, singular, *colonia*). Here the victors established new settlers to serve as garrisons, gave them land around the town that had been freed by the victory, and organized it as a city-state with officials of its own. Last but not least, the new foundation was assigned a recognized place as an ally of Rome and the other Latin cities.

Roman tradition associated model figures with these wars. Gnaeus Marcius Coriolanus, who earned his third name or *cognomen* from his leadership of the army that captured the Volscian town of Corioli (its exact location is no longer known), left Rome because of his unpopularity there and took refuge with the Volsci he had previously defeated. Coriolanus then led their armies against the Romans with great success, and (we are told) failed to capture Rome only because he heeded the pleas of his mother Veturia and his wife Volumnia, models of the

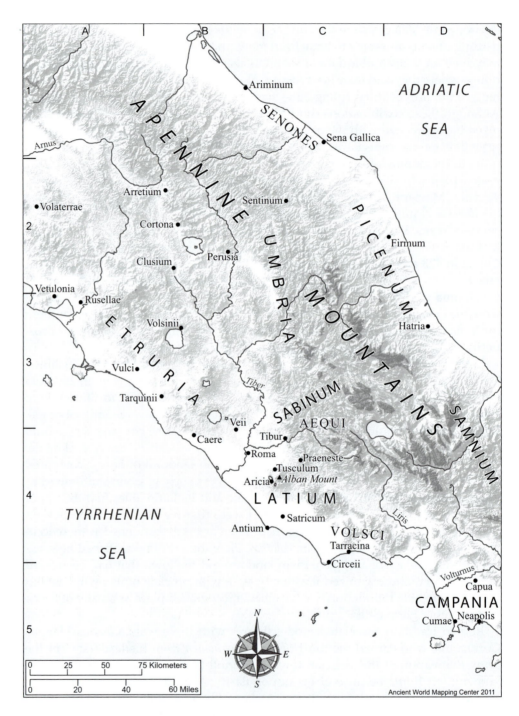

Map 2.1 *Latium and Southern Etruria*

virtuous Roman matron. Lucius Quinctius Cincinnatus provides a more positive example. In 458, Cincinnatus was summoned from his fields to serve as dictator after the Aequi had trapped a Roman army in the mountains. Within sixteen days, he had gathered an army, defeated the Aequi, rescued the beleaguered Roman army, resigned his dictatorship, and returned to his farm. There could be no better model of the modest and dutiful citizen. Although there is much embellishment in these stories, which undoubtedly grew in the telling, real people and situations may lie behind them.

Struggle of the Orders

In the fifth and early fourth centuries, Rome also faced severe internal conflicts that accompanied its foreign wars. Roman historians later recorded frequent reports of famine, and of strife over land and debt. Food shortages and quarrels over fields and their produce are common occurrences in small-scale agricultural societies, and the warfare of the fifth century, with its disruption of social arrangements and the devastation of fields, must have aggravated the situation. Competition between members of the Roman elite for leadership in the city may often have led to violence and disorder. This strife, however, was worsened by deeper conflicts, reflecting aspects of the basic organization of the Republic and of Roman society in general. Modern scholars call this conflict the "Struggle of the Orders."

Certain kinds of conflict were endemic in the archaic city-states of both Italy and the Greek world. One concerned access to magistracies because, after the expulsion of a king, leading families often tried to monopolize the new offices in their communities. A second area of conflict concerned the ability of officials to punish at will. A third and final one involved the roles of magistrates and citizen assemblies, in particular the ability of such assemblies to choose officeholders freely and to make laws requiring or forbidding certain actions by magistrates. Each of these sources of strife was present in Rome during the fifth and fourth centuries, although all need not have been matters of controversy simultaneously.

Roman historians of a later date believed that a long conflict between two opposing groups, *patricians* and *plebeians*, characterized the first centuries of the Republic. To be a patrician, a Roman had to belong to one of a very few families. The origins of the patriciate are unknown. From the eighth century, in Rome and elsewhere, wealthy, powerful families assumed leading roles in their communities, and some, or most, of those that made up the Roman patriciate may have had their origins here. At any rate, Roman patricians claimed privileges that ensured their leadership of the city. Later, Rome's historians thought that patricians enjoyed the exclusive right to hold high office under the Republic. This belief can only be accepted with modifications, however. In the lists of those who served as consuls or military tribunes with consular powers during the fifth and early fourth centuries, the overwhelming majority of names do indeed belong to gentes that were either patrician or are known to have included patricians. But some entries, most of them concentrated in the first half of the fifth century, bear names that were plebeian at a later date. In a few instances, an official with a seemingly plebeian name may have belonged to a patrician branch of his family that subsequently died out without leaving a trace, but as a general explanation, this probably will not do. So in all likelihood, with the foundation of the Republic, certain families were able to establish a monopoly over the new offices, although it was perhaps neither as secure nor as absolute as Roman authors later believed.

Patricians also claimed to have exclusive rights over the religious life of Rome, a central aspect of communal life. It is true that priestly offices long remained the prerogative of the patriciate, and claims to secular offices also rested on a religious foundation. Roman kings and the magistrates who succeeded them possessed as a mark of their office the right to take the auspices (*auspicium*), rites by which an officeholder sought the approval of the gods to take up his office for the first time and, while serving, divine consent for all of his official actions (see Plate 1a). Patricians regarded the auspices as their own possession. In later centuries, in the rare instances when both consuls died in office, the auspices were thought in some way to return to the patricians. A patrician senator was then chosen as *interrex* for five days, followed by others in turn until one was able to arrange the election of new consuls. Roman historians believed that the interrex was a regal institution, with *interreges* serving between the death of one king and the installation of his successor. The name itself—"between kings"—would seem to confirm this belief.

The plebeians are much more shadowy than the patricians. Plebeians certainly far outnumbered patricians, but they need not have encompassed all of the inhabitants of Rome outside the patrician group. It remains possible, for example, that the clients of the great families counted as neither patricians nor plebeians. The Roman plebs was not a very homogenous group, since it contained individuals with a range of statuses and roles in the city. Some were not even poor, although most probably were. In the fifth and early fourth centuries, plebeians were able to supply leaders from their own ranks, so that some plebeians clearly had standing in the community. As a result, the mass of plebeians may not have been very unified in its concerns. Matters of land distribution and of debt would probably have concerned the poor more than the well-to-do, while access to office may have interested the leaders of the plebeians more than the bulk of their followers. In these circumstances, the plebeian leadership may have been more capable of mustering followers at times when debt, high food prices, and poverty were proving especially burdensome. Roman historians later believed that the plebeians' main weapon was the "secession," a kind of strike in time of war, and that their major successes derived from this. In a secession, plebeian members of an army would withdraw to a hill outside of Rome, choose their own leaders, and refuse to cooperate with the magistrates of the city until their grievances had been addressed.

Successes by the plebeians created a dual organization in the city. Consuls and military tribunes were seen as leaders of the Roman people as a whole, the populus Romanus, and they were expected to provide political, military, and religious leadership in matters of general concern. Meantime, the plebeians created a parallel organization of officials and cults that addressed only matters specific to the plebs and, at least in theory, did not affect the rest of the populus Romanus. The plebeians' first major gain (in the 490s) was the right to choose their own leaders, the tribunes of the plebs (*tribuni plebis*); their title may have been intended to provide a clear contrast with the military tribunes (*tribuni militum*, literally "tribunes of the soldiers") who were, in many of these years, the Republic's chief officials. At the same time, plebeian tribunes, and the plebeian *aediles* who assisted them, established their own cult site at the temple of Ceres, the goddess of grain, on the Aventine hill; the close relationship between the chief officials of the city itself and the temple of Jupiter Optimus Maximus on the Capitol may have served as a model. In later periods, the Roman plebs met in tribes to elect tribunes, and this may well have been the case in the fifth century too.

Much of the early history of the tribunate is obscure. Roman historians later believed that the powers of the office all began with the elections of the first tribunes, but this almost certainly would not have been the case. By the second century, the tribunes of the plebs held a wide range of functions—protecting individuals, blocking official actions they considered improper, convening the senate, proposing legislation—but they did not acquire them all at once. At first, their responsibilities may have been limited to providing leadership, and to protecting individuals threatened with severe treatment by magistrates. Roman historians later agreed that a key complaint by plebeians concerned their vulnerability to arbitrary actions by magistrates. There are numerous tales of consuls executing or punishing individuals because of personal enmity, political differences, or the desire to seize their possessions. Many of the details may well be inventions, but the basic claim is probably accurate. *Auxilium*, the giving of aid, was central to the tribunes' office. They even had the right to intervene physically between an official and the targets of his wrath, freeing the victims or preventing the official and his attendants from seizing them. The authority of their physical presence was reinforced by their "sacrosanctity." Plebeians took an oath to regard anyone who laid hands on a tribune as an outlaw liable to be killed without penalty; the phrase used to indicate the nature of the penalty—"let him be accursed" (*sacer esto*)—shows that the culprit was in some way regarded as condemned to pay a penalty to the gods.

Fall of Veii and the Sack of Rome

Early in the fourth century, a Roman victory made the city preeminent in its region. Around 396, the Romans succeeded in capturing the Etruscan city of Veii after a siege. Veii, about ten miles (16 km) from Rome, was a wealthy and powerful city-state, which, like Rome, dominated some of its smaller neighbors. In the fifth century, Rome and Veii had fought over land and over the leadership of smaller cities, without either gaining a distinct advantage. Now the Romans marked their victory by eliminating Veii as an autonomous city-state. Veii's land became Roman territory, and some of its citizens became Roman citizens. Rome enslaved or expelled the remainder of the population, and settled some Roman citizens on parts of Veii's territory that were made vacant as a result. Although the site of the city itself remained inhabited, it no longer possessed a full range of civic institutions, and functioned instead as a center for Romans dwelling nearby.

Rome's victory was matched by a defeat. Around 387, a large army of Gauls that had been plundering in the upper Tiber Valley moved down the river toward Rome, defeated a Roman army, and entered the city. In the opening decades of the fourth century, Gauls dominated the valley of the Po River and the northern portion of the plains along the eastern coast of the Italian peninsula. Their origins lie across the Alps in central Europe, and their advance into northern Italy formed part of a larger movement that would carry Gallic tribes to the margins of the Greek world, and even (in the third century) into Asia Minor. By the end of the fifth century, the Etruscan cities north of the Apennines were hard-pressed by Gauls, and some may already have been wiped out.

The Gauls did not have an urban culture and the social and political organization that went with it. Instead, their political life centered on aristocratic families and their armed retainers. Prominent leaders could assemble large forces, and they faced relatively few communal restraints on their actions. Gallic warbands, some apparently fairly large, would often raid across the Apennines. Cities of northeast Etruria and the upper Tiber Valley were especially vulnerable to them, but their southern neighbors were not immune either. Such Gallic raids would persist, with decreasing frequency, well into the third century. Greeks and Romans would long continue to regard Gauls as uncivilized, warlike, predatory, and expansionistic. The Gallic sack of Rome did not have as long-lasting effects as the Roman capture of Veii, but the symbolic significance that came to be attached to it was immense: Romans remembered it as the only time their city had fallen to a foreign enemy. Reports of Gallic invasions could lead to panic in Rome for centuries thereafter (Fig. 2.1).

Roman historians would later make Marcus Furius Camillus the hero both of the final war against Veii and of the recovery after the sack of Rome. As dictator, he commanded the Roman army that captured Veii. After the Gauls had entered Rome, Camillus was supposedly once again made dictator, defeated the Gallic army, and recovered the treasure that the Gauls had taken from the city. As dictator yet again, he was reported to have had a central role in opening the highest offices to plebeians in 367, a crucial event in the Struggle of the Orders (see next section). In all, Rome's historians thought that he had been military tribune with consular powers six times and dictator five times. Camillus is perhaps as much a figure of myth as of history; details of his life seem to have been continually embellished

Figure 2.1 *This stretch of wall on Rome's Esquiline hill formed part of defense works built to encircle the city and attributed to King Servius Tullius in the sixth century. While Rome may well have had some defenses at that early date, the encircling wall, of which several stretches survive today, is more likely to have been constructed after the Gallic sack of the city around 387. The tufa blocks for the wall were cut from a quarry near Veii, Rome's nearby rival until its capture around 396. Even though the wall as it stands today is up to 13 ft thick (4 m), and can rise to over 30 ft high (10 m), it in fact formed just one component in a more complex construction which included a massive* agger *(rampart) of earth reinforcing the wall on its city side, and a deep* fossa *(ditch) beyond it.*

from the fourth century to the first century B.C. By the latter date, he had become, in history and in legend, virtually a second founder of the city. As a result, to tease out his actual accomplishments from the myth may well be impossible. Even so, the stories of a sole savior with extraordinary military and civil power underscore how fragile Rome's new republican institutions were likely to have been in this period when magistracies were opened to a wider group of citizens.

THE CITY AND ITS INSTITUTIONS IN THE FOURTH CENTURY

The political order that would govern Rome in later, better-documented centuries emerged in a series of reforms and reorganizations that began during the mid-fourth century and continued into the early third century. Roman government required the direct participation of citizens, although all did not have equal responsibilities. Officials, priests, senators, and citizens performed their roles in and around the temples, public squares, and processional routes of the city. Most official actions took place in the open, under the gaze of others. Because Rome lacked a bureaucracy, officials dealt directly with those that they were in the process of governing. Roman assumptions about government were markedly hierarchical, and, in all periods, a few leading families dominated public life. In the fourth century, magistracies and priesthoods formed the focus of conflicts and competition. These conflicts over offices, priesthoods, and the powers of citizen assemblies were part of the larger Struggle of the Orders. Plebeians sought eligibility for the highest offices, and many patricians resisted such demands.

Officials

A small number of officeholders occupied the center of public life. At the top, beginning in 366, military tribunes with consular powers were no longer elected, and instead two consuls were chosen each year. During their year in office, the consuls served primarily as generals in Rome's wars. When they were present in the city, they made sacrifices and performed other rites of the public cults, presided over meetings of the senate, addressed assemblies of citizens, listened to complaints, and rendered judgments.

Consuls could be identified at a glance. The Roman citizen's robe (*toga*) that they wore was a special one bordered in purple, the *toga praetexta*, and they sat on a distinctive chair inlaid with ivory, the *sella curulis* or "curule" chair. Generally, they were surrounded by attendants of various kinds: messengers, heralds to make public announcements, scribes to record their decisions, and, for each consul, twelve lictors, who maintained order in his presence and carried the *fasces*, double-headed axes bound in rods. The fasces were old marks of royal power in Rome and in Etruscan cities; they symbolized quite starkly the consuls' power to punish those who disobeyed them. In public, consuls took their places on platforms that elevated them over those who were to witness their actions, and their movements from place to place within the city often took on many of the attributes of processions.

Roman historians later would connect the replacement of military tribunes by consuls with an important episode in the Struggle of the Orders. After years of conflict, two tribunes of the plebs, Gaius Licinius Stolo and Lucius Sextius Lateranus, successfully had a series of laws passed known as the Licinian-Sextian Laws; according to some authors, Camillus, as dictator, helped secure patrician acceptance of these measures. Some provisions of the legislation allegedly addressed matters of land use and debt, but the most important ones (we are told) fixed the office of consul as the highest in the city and permitted plebeians to compete for it. Even though many of the stories surrounding the Licinian-Sextian reforms are improbable, it is quite clear that the Roman political order did shift around this time. Over two decades later, another tribune, Lucius Genucius, had a law passed requiring that at least one of the two consuls chosen each year be a plebeian. Surviving lists of the occupants of Rome's highest offices confirm that from the mid-fourth century pairs of consuls do invariably comprise one patrician and one plebeian each year—until 172, when, for the first time, both the consuls chosen were plebeian. The practical result of the reforms, it should be noted, was not the opening of offices to the entire citizen body, but rather the creation of a new political elite, composed of some patrician families and some plebeian ones (see Chapter Three).

The Licinian-Sextian reforms also created the new office of *praetor* (initially, one elected to hold office each year). Praetors were the leading officials in Rome when the consuls were absent on campaign. When necessary, a praetor could himself command an army. Because of their regular presence in the city, holders of this office often heard testimony and issued judgments against those thought to have injured the community. Praetors would come to exercise a great deal of influence over the ways in which private disputes between citizens were resolved; thereby, they would assume a major role in the development of Roman law. Plebeians would successfully gain access to this office, too; a plebeian was praetor for the first time in 337. Almost a century later, in 242, the Romans would add a second praetor, who divided responsibilities in the city with the first. In the decades thereafter, the number would be increased to meet the needs of Rome's developing empire outside of Italy (see Chapter Three). Like the consuls, praetors were surrounded by visible signs of their power: toga praetexta, curule chair, lictors with fasces, heralds, messengers, and scribes. Their power, however, was deemed inferior to that of the consuls, and in the presence of the higher official, they were expected to give way.

Both consuls and praetors possessed a wide range of powers and functions that were regarded as dependent upon their *imperium* and *auspicium*. Auspicium denoted their right to seek the approval of the gods for their tenure in office, and for their official actions, through the rituals of divination known as the auspices. Along with a dictator and his second-in-command, the *magister equitum*, every consul and praetor possessed a special right to command known as imperium, a term that is related to the verb *imperare* meaning "to order" or "to command." For Romans, imperium had strong religious associations, and its possession was what provided the essential basis for a higher magistrate's authority to lead armies and to punish offenders.

This said, a consul's or praetor's powers varied according to the place where he chose to exercise them. Whenever he headed an army, his right to command was virtually unlimited, and the special nature of his imperium at these times was indicated by addition of the noun *militiae* ("on campaign"). Within the *pomerium*, the sacred boundary of the city of Rome,* however, consuls and praetors possessed only a more limited kind of imperium, qualified by the term *domi* ("at home"); here, they had no authority to command troops, or to ignore or brush aside all lesser officials. More generally, imperium was associated with certain symbols thought to derive from the kings, such as lictors bearing fasces, the special toga (toga praetexta), and the curule chair. To symbolize their superiority, consuls had twelve lictors, while (in the third century at least) their inferiors the praetors had only two. On the other hand, dictators—greater than the consuls— had twenty-four lictors, supposedly the number possessed by the kings. Within the pomerium, the fasces were carried with the axes removed, so as to symbolize the officeholder's more limited right of punishment here.

In addition to consuls and praetors, the Romans also filled a number of lesser positions. From 366, they elected two *curule aediles* annually, an office created as the

---

*Its actual course is too poorly known to mark on a map.

counterpart to the two plebeian aediles. Between them, the four aediles maintained temples and the city's streets, and they also supervised its markets, where they judged disputes arising from business there. *Quaestors*—an office that apparently dated back to the mid-fifth century—took care of public money. In particular, this responsibility required them to supervise the treasury (later, at least, located in the temple of Saturn), as well as to oversee the funds that generals took on campaign.

The ten tribunes of the plebs were the most important of the lesser officeholders. Like consuls and praetors, they possessed the right to summon citizens to vote. However, many of their most important powers were essentially negative, because it was they who—through their ability to block public actions that they considered unlawful or inappropriate—guaranteed the rights of citizens against ill-treatment by other magistrates. Tribunes were very much officials of the city, and, in later periods at least, they were prohibited from spending much time outside of it. Beyond the first milestone outside the pomerium, tribunes no longer possessed the ability to prevent consuls and praetors from acting as they wished, so that they could not interfere with a general on campaign.

Later, in the third and second centuries, it was tribunes of the plebs who secured the passage of nearly all laws, but the early history of Roman legislation remains controversial. Roman laws or *leges* (singular, *lex*) were usually limited in scope, instructing or permitting officials to take certain actions, or setting up rules to regulate officeholders. A law was generally known by the name of the one or more officials who placed it before the citizens for a vote. Thus, a law proposed by Gaius Licinius and Lucius Sextius would be a *lex Licinia-Sextia*. During the last secession of the plebs, which took place sometime around 287, the dictator Quintus Hortensius sponsored a law, the *lex Hortensia*, that supposedly gave to citizen assemblies meeting under the presidency of a tribune of the plebs the right to enact laws binding on the entire community, rather than just on the plebs. However, later Roman historians thought that tribunes had begun to sponsor legislation right from the time when their office was first established in the early fifth century; thus many notices of such laws, and brief summaries of their contents, are preserved. At a very early date, patricians had possessed the right to approve all legislation before it was presented to the people, but the senate subsequently claimed this as its exclusive prerogative. Later, only tribunes and the Plebeian assembly were exempted from having to seek senatorial approval. It is possible that any legislation proposed by tribunes had once required the senate's consent if it was to be binding on all Roman citizens, and that what the lex Hortensia did was to free tribunes and the Plebeian assembly from this restriction hereafter.

The two *censors* held the only office that was not annual. From 443, these censors replaced the consuls as supervisors of the *census*; usually elections would be held every five years, and the successful candidates would hold office for around eighteen months. The census counted only Roman citizens. However, it was much more than a mere enumeration of them; rather, in time it developed into an elaborate operation that assigned them to their proper places in the city

Figure 2.2 *The Ficoroni Cista. In the late fourth century, Rome was the center of a wealthy elite who had assembled around them craftsmen capable of making highly desirable products. This large* cista, *a container for small objects of high value, was found at the Latin city of Praeneste. It carries an inscription announcing that it was made in Rome by Novios Plautios, a sign of the city's economic strength. As the engravings on the sides depict the Greek myth of Jason and the Argonauts, we may also glimpse the cultural sophistication and pretensions of the elite in Rome and Praeneste. The cista is bronze and has an overall height of 2 ft 6 in (0.75 m).*

(see further below). Censors were important figures, therefore, and this importance only increased after they began to choose the senate from the last decades of the fourth century. Their decisions could cause conflict. For example, critics of Appius Claudius Caecus, censor in 312, claimed that he passed over better qualified men for inclusion in the senate, and that he enrolled some residents of Rome itself (probably poorer citizens and freed slaves) in rural tribes rather than in the four urban tribes, which were considered to be less prestigious. Similar conflicts would recur in the following centuries.

Senate

This collection of officials did not form a government on the modern pattern; there need be little coordination among them, and there was no central direction of policies. Officials were expected to consult others before acting. In Rome itself, the senate filled this advisory role. Away from the city, officeholders sought advice from a smaller group, although it might include some senators who had accompanied an official from Rome. The senate met only when called together by a consul or a praetor, or later, by a tribune of the plebs, and it met in the presence of that official. By strict rule, it could meet only in a place dedicated to the gods, usually in a temple. Before citizens gathered to vote, senators met near the place of assembly—thus typically in the Curia Hostilia next to the Roman Forum, or in the temple of Jupiter on the Capitol, which was adjacent to an open space, the *area Capitolina*, sometimes used for voting. When conferring with a consul who had already taken up his military command, and was thus barred from entering the city itself, the senate would meet in a consecrated place on the *Campus Martius*, just beyond the pomerium.

The senate's role would change greatly over the course of the fourth and third centuries. In theory, it was merely advisory, and senators should discuss only the matters put to them by the official who called them together. However, the senate would gradually assume a much more active role. In particular, it came to make decisions in matters of religion, supervise public finances, receive embassies from both allies and enemies, and determine military assignments for consuls and praetors. This shift in the senate's place in the Roman order did not go uncontested, and it sometimes led to conflicts between the senate and individual officeholders.

In part, the shift may have been due to changes in how the senate's members were chosen. During the third and second centuries, every five years the censors compiled a ranked list of around 300 senators; the member placed at the head of the list gained the honorific title *princeps senatus*. Censors eventually included everyone who had held elected office, from quaestors to former praetors and consuls; exclusion of any former officeholder was a mark of disgrace. In these circumstances, therefore, membership in the senate effectively became lifelong, and officeholders would spend the bulk of their political careers there. As a result, senators had a strong sense of belonging to a well-defined and honored group in society, and, on occasion, they could be quite willing to assert the senate's power and prestige against magistrates and assemblies.

The senate's membership and its role under the kings, as well as during the first century of the Republic, are obscure. Without question, some kind of council, almost certainly aristocratic in character, did function then. According to the Roman antiquarian Festus (p. 290L), the tribune Ovinius (in office sometime between 339 and 318) had a law passed transferring to the censors the duty of compiling a list of senators, and requiring each censor to take an oath that he would choose "the best men of all orders"—a phrase which probably means that the senate was to be recruited from those who had never held any office as well as from former magistrates. Before Ovinius' law, Festus claims, the consuls and military tribunes with consular powers used to choose their advisors themselves "from among their closest friends among the patricians and then from among the plebeians." To be sure, it must have been some informal practice of this nature that was followed before the censorship was first established in the mid-fifth century. Later, if Festus is accurate, the impact of Ovinius' law would have been to transform the senate from a temporary collection of individuals, poorly placed to assert themselves as a group against magistrates, into a long-serving body independent of the annual magistrates and much better fitted to exert its collective weight in Roman public life.

At the same time, the Roman elite seems to have asserted itself against its more powerful and popular members. In the fourth century, a very small number of individuals dominated officeholding in Rome. Consequently, in the years between 366 and 291 fourteen men between them held fifty-four consulships, over one-third of the total, and eight of these fourteen held the office as many as thirty-eight times. These same men also held other offices, some more than once. The patrician Lucius Papirius Cursor was consul five times, served once as dictator, and once as magister equitum. Another patrician, Marcus Valerius Corvus, was consul six times and dictator twice; he is known to have held office twenty times. The plebeian Quintus Publilius Philo served as consul four times, and he also was chosen dictator, magister equitum, and censor. These repeated electoral victories are clear signs that such successful individuals possessed enduring prestige and popularity in the citizen assemblies, and it may well be that especially prominent officeholders would have faced few checks on their actions beyond the need to maintain popularity among the voters. By contrast, less fortunate members of the elite would have faced all the greater difficulty in reaching high office and in asserting themselves against their more powerful competitors.

Such concentration of power in a very few hands did meet resistance. In 342, Lucius Genucius, a tribune of the plebs, had a law passed that prohibited the holding of more than one office at the same time, or of the same office more than once in any ten-year period, a practice known as "iteration." For two decades or so, this law proved effective, with few men holding the consulship more once. In the 320s, however, when Rome was under pressure from war, some again held further consulships within ten years. The goal of restricting iteration would ultimately be attained, showing that opposition to the practice was strong, at least among the Roman elite. After 290, Romans who achieved success in their political careers were rarely consul more than once, only a few gained the office twice, and no more than a handful more than twice.

This limitation on multiple officeholding had important consequences. First, it spread the available offices over a slightly larger group, enabling some individuals to rise higher now than they had previously been able. Second, it meant that virtually every holder of an office was now inexperienced in it, and thus in need of advice. Finally, it lessened, although it did not eliminate, the importance of popularity; for anyone to court popularity in the hope of staying in office over an extended period was now pointless. As a result, in the course of their career politically active individuals were more likely to focus their attention on the senate; its importance rose as a result, and senators were more prone than ever to be very supportive of its claims to privilege.

Assemblies of Citizens

Underpinning offices and senate were assemblies of citizens who chose new officeholders and authorized important public actions. Roman assemblies, however, were not representative bodies of the kind found in modern states. Instead, adult male Roman citizens listened to debates personally, and voted directly not only to elect new leaders every year, but also to approve (or reject) proposed laws. Elections, the enactment of laws, decisions on war and peace, trials for public crimes, and discussions of other state business all took place in large, open-air meetings where citizens, by their votes, chose officeholders, accepted (or rejected) policies and laws, and issued verdicts in trials. These gatherings were open to any citizen who wished to come, so that attendance could vary markedly from one occasion to another, and the composition of no two assembly meetings would ever have been exactly the same. Seating was not provided. In any case, were an assembly to attract an exceptional crowd, all eligible citizens could hardly have been accommodated. In the Campus Martius—the place where elections of consuls, praetors, and censors were usually held—there was space for only about 70,000 people at most, in other words an increasingly small fraction of Rome's citizen body as it expanded over time.

In these public meetings, the officials of the city kept a firm control over the agenda. Only holders of certain offices—consuls, praetors, and tribunes of the plebs—possessed the power to summon citizens to meetings to elect new officeholders, to discuss matters of importance, and to decide on laws and policies. *Contiones* (singular, *contio*) were occasions just for discussion and debate. The official who had called the meeting addressed the crowd himself, and also brought forward others whose opinions he wished citizens to hear. *Comitia* and *concilia* were assemblies where they actually voted. These assemblies met only at

Rome—so that any citizen resident elsewhere who wished to vote had to come to the city to do so—and the voting had to be completed within a single day. Once again, the official who called the meeting controlled the agenda, and the assembled voters could do no more than accept or reject the candidates or the proposals put before them. When assemblies gathered for a discussion or a vote, the senate met at the same time in a nearby temple or other sacred building to provide advice. At any assembly, therefore, ordinary citizens had little freedom of speech or initiative. There was no opportunity for any of them to address the meeting; they could not put forward any proposal or any candidate for election; nor could they seek to amend a proposal presented by the presiding official. All they could do was to vote for or against. In practice, however, despite this official control of both the agenda and the speakers, citizens could still register dissatisfaction with the proceedings informally, through demonstrations, heckling, and occasionally even by destroying an official's insignia of office, such as his fasces or his official chair.

The fact that Roman citizens did not cast their votes in a mass made the census one of the city's vital political institutions. By the fourth century, the census had become highly complex, and had come to serve a larger range of functions than when it was first instituted in the sixth or early fifth century. Property, reputation, and place of residence remained fundamental to the operation of the developed census. Once new censors were chosen, all citizens made declarations to them, in which they identified themselves and their places of residence, and listed their property and their dependents. From these declarations, and on their assessment of each citizen's character, the censors assigned men to centuries and tribes and also made distinctions of age. Censors assigned the wealthiest to the centuries of the cavalry, while they placed those who were too poor to serve in the army in the single century of the *proletarii*. All those considered eligible for service in the infantry were placed in a further group of centuries, ones that were now arranged in a series of classes, each signifying minute gradations of wealth and status. Throughout this entire process, it should be remembered, censors maintained the right to examine any citizen's physical condition and way of life. They could express their disapproval of a citizen in various ways—by rebuking him publicly, by registering a cause for complaint in a "note" (*nota*) attached to his name in the roster of citizens, or by imposing penalties.

By the fourth century the census had shifted from being primarily an aspect of military organization. Membership in a century set voting rights as well as military duties, and it also determined liability for payments of *tributum*, assessments of money for emergencies that fell most heavily on the members of the wealthiest centuries. Centuries, moreover, no longer strictly corresponded to forms of military service. For example, the *equites*, the cavalry in wartime, were now not recruited exclusively from the so-called equestrian centuries, and some of the men placed in the leading centuries of the infantry must have served on horseback. At the same time, in all probability the complex hierarchy of the infantry centuries no longer corresponded closely to any distinctions in the military service that their members actually performed.

The categories established at regular intervals in the census were the basis of all assemblies. The Centuriate assembly (*comitia centuriata*), which only an official with imperium could summon, was organized like the army with the presiding official acting as a commander and the voters as soldiers. For this reason, it met outside the sacred limits or pomerium of the city, since commanders could not issue binding orders to their soldiers within Rome. Voting was oral, and each citizen, when summoned to vote, signified his acceptance or rejection of any candidate or proposal by word of mouth. This voting was organized and tallied by centuries, which voted in turn. Each century possessed one vote, which was itself determined by the votes of a majority of the century's members who were present. Victory in a straight majority of centuries determined the outcome. In general, the Centuriate assembly elected new consuls, praetors, and censors, and voted on matters of war and peace.

Procedures in this assembly favored any presiding official, and also the wealthiest citizens. In elections, the former was entitled to accept or reject the names of would-be candidates, although it is unclear how freely this right was exercised in practice. The votes of the rich carried far more weight than those of the poor, since the rich occupied a large number of small centuries. The eighteen

SOURCE 2.1: *When recounting the alleged activities of Servius Tullius, sixth king of Rome, the historian Livy (1.42.4–43.9) described in detail his creation of the census. Together with a similar passage in Dionysius of Halicarnassus' Roman Antiquities (4.16.1–18.3), this is the most complete surviving account of the classes that made up the census. There remain problems with both accounts—in particular, elements of speculative reconstruction are detectable—and the link between a census class and its members' military equipment was almost certainly not as rigid as portrayed here. In any event, Livy's census certainly fits third-century conditions better than those of the sixth, where both he and Dionysius place their descriptions. Note that juniores were male citizens between seventeen and forty-five years of age, while seniores were older. Later, during the second century, the distribution of centuriae may have been changed in a way that reduced the influence of the first class.*

Servius Tullius then began by far the greatest work of peace. Just as Numa was the author of religious laws, so Servius shone among posterity as the founder of all distinctions within the city and of the orders that mark out the grades of fortune and dignity. For he began the census, a most useful measure for so great a future empire, since it distributed the burdens of war and peace, not individually as before, but according to level of wealth. From the census, for use in war or peace, he then defined classes and centuries and the following gradations.

From those who had a census of 100,000 *asses* [a monetary unit] or more, he formed eighty centuriae, forty each of seniores and juniores; all were called the first class. The seniores were to be ready to guard the city, the juniores to wage war abroad. For armor, they were to provide helmet, round shield, greaves, and breastplate, all of bronze, as protection for their bodies; as weapons, they were to have a spear and a sword. Two centuriae of carpenters and smiths, who served without weapons, were added to these; they had the duty of making siege machines in war. The second class was instituted from those who had a census of between 75,000 and 100,000 asses; from these, both seniores and juniores, twenty centuriae were enrolled. They were to use a long rectangular shield instead of a round one; except for the breastplate, their remaining arms were the same as for the first class. Servius Tullius wished the census of the third class to be 50,000 asses. Here, he made the same number of centuriae as in the second class, with the same distinctions of age. There was no difference in their equipment, except that the greaves were omitted. In the fourth class, the census was 25,000 asses. The same number of centuriae were formed, but their equipment was different, because they had to provide only a spear and a javelin. The fifth class was larger, and thirty centuriae were formed for it; these men carried slings and stones for missiles. With them were hornblowers and trumpeters divided into two centuriae. The census of this fifth class was 11,000 asses. Those whose census was less than this, the remainder of the population, formed a single centuria and were exempt from military service.

When the equipment and distribution of the infantry had been arranged, he enrolled twelve centuriae of cavalry from the leading men of the city. He also formed a further six centuriae of cavalry—three had been instituted by Romulus—under the names by which they had been inaugurated.

equestrian centuries voted first, and, as each finished voting in turn, the results were publicly proclaimed to guide the vote of the remaining citizens. Next, the richest centuries of the infantry voted, followed in turn by those who were progressively poorer.* As the vote went down the scale, moreover, the number of centuries diminished, so that many more voters were crammed into fewer voting units. The *proletarii*, too poor to be eligible for military service, all occupied the single century which was slated to vote last. In any case, voting always ceased as soon as a sufficient number of centuries had voted to settle the outcome for or against. Frequently, therefore, the lower centuries, which contained the great mass of citizens, would never have been called upon to vote at all, in particular whenever the rich showed themselves to be in broad agreement.

Assemblies of tribes were neither as complex nor so blatantly weighted toward the rich as was the Centuriate assembly, although poorer citizens, especially if they lived far from the city, may have found it hard to attend these assemblies, too. As we have seen, every Roman citizen belonged to a tribe determined by place of residence. Those who lived in Rome itself filled four "urban" tribes, while those resident elsewhere belonged to one of the "rural" tribes whose number was slowly increased as Rome's power expanded; by 241 that number had reached thirty-one, where it remained. Potentially, therefore, the votes of members of "rural" tribes could carry more weight in these assemblies, if those members could afford to be present.

---

*Eventually, a slight modification was introduced whereby a single century chosen each time by random lot from among the wealthiest juniores centuries of the infantry voted before the cavalry.

Tribunes of the plebs summoned citizens by tribes to elect their successors as tribunes or to accept or reject proposed laws; whenever a tribune did this, the assembly was known as the Plebeian assembly or *concilium plebis*. On other occasions, consuls or praetors summoned the tribes to fill certain minor offices (they probably did not preside over assemblies to vote on legislation until much later). In the tribal assemblies, citizens cast their votes one tribe after another. The voting order was determined on every occasion by lot, with each tribe in turn accepting or rejecting the candidates or the proposals under consideration. The first candidates acceptable to a majority of the tribes filled the offices. A law, too, passed (or was rejected) as soon as the bare majority of tribes for or against was attained; voting ceased at that point. In these assemblies, therefore, many of the citizens present could not know until well into the day itself whether or not they would in fact be called upon to vote.

The City, Its Gods, and Its Priests

Religion formed an important part of Rome's organization, and the prominent remains of cult places show that this was true from the beginning of the city. Roman religion cannot be separated from the city and its public institutions or from the social groups and settlements that made up the Roman people; all these had their own divinities, which they worshipped in their own ways. Thus, Rome itself had its protecting divinities, and the city's officials and priests took the lead in cultivating them. Households contained shrines to the *lares*, ancestral spirits, and the *penates*, the protective divinities of the house, while old aristocratic families maintained their special relations with major gods. Away from Rome, the towns and villages inhabited by Roman citizens had their temples, shrines, and

TABLE 2.1 Roman Assemblies

	Centuriate assembly	Tribal assembly	Plebeian assembly
Composition	All citizens	All citizens	Only plebeians
Voting Units	193 centuries	35 tribes (after 241 B.C., 31 rural and 4 urban)	35 tribes
Presiding Officials	Consul or praetor	Consul or praetor	Tribune of the plebs
Elections	Elects consuls, praetors, and censors	Elects curule aediles, and quaestors	Elects tribunes of the plebs, and plebeian aediles
Legislative Powers	Normally votes only on issues of war and peace	Votes on proposals made by a consul or praetor	Votes on proposals made by a tribune of the plebs
Judicial Powers	Hears citizens' appeals on capital charges	Issues verdicts in trials	Issues verdicts in trials

cult activities. In the countryside, some forms of religious activity concentrated around crossroads.

Other practices centered on individuals and their concerns, and they were not as bounded by family, neighborhood, or even citizenship as were the cults of the Roman people. When confronted with difficult choices or stressful situations, many people made vows to favored deities, to be fulfilled if and when the desired outcome should be achieved. Those about to undertake journeys or projects could try to determine the attitude of the gods towards their plans through rites of divination. Some especially prominent shrines, even outside of Roman territory, drew such pilgrims from considerable distances. The temple of Fortuna Primigenia in the allied city of Praeneste, for example, drew many seeking good fortune in their activities (see Fig. 5.3). In the fourth century and later, healing shrines dotted much of rural central Italy; at many, archeologists have found terracotta feet, hands, limbs, eyes, and other anatomical models left by worshippers as tokens of their vows (Fig. 2.3).

From an early date, the city and the nearby countryside were full of cult places: temples, altars, sanctuaries, and sacred groves. In and around the city, processions, animal sacrifices (usually of cattle, sheep, or swine), contests, banquets at cult sites, prayers, and vows were a regular feature of life. On especially important occasions, magistrates and priests led processions which could include the male and female children of prominent families, young men about to reach adulthood, charioteers, musicians, singers, dancers, and attendants bearing the images of the gods or the treasures of city and temple. Great festivals or *feriae* formed prominent elements in the religious year. On certain days fixed in the religious calendar, public officials staged sacrifices, processions, and ritual contests or *ludi*. The Roman Games (*ludi Romani*) and the Plebeian Games (*ludi plebeii*), supposedly the earliest, may go back to the early Republic, although their forms certainly changed over time. From the late fourth century, some *ludi* began to include theatrical performances or *ludi scaenici*. The surviving plays for these performances—the comedies of Plautus and Terence—date to the early second century.

In general, the chief elected officials of Rome performed the major rites of the city. Consuls, praetors, censors, and other officials each had their

Figure 2.3 *In the case of some terracotta anatomical models left at Italian shrines, it is hard to be sure just which organ is meant, and even whether it is intended to be human or animal. No such doubt attaches, however, to human uteri, which are rendered oval, flat on one side, and with transverse ridges on the other. Even so, the additional pear-shaped feature sometimes found extending down from the mouth—either to the left, or to the right (as here, a votive recovered from the Tiber river)—remains a puzzle. There is no agreement on whether this feature represents some defect in need of healing, say, or a plea for a child of a particular sex. At least, any explanation which presupposes a confident grasp of gynecology should be treated with caution, because in all likelihood the human body was not well understood.*

own religious program of sacrifices, festivals, games, processions, and rites of divination. In these matters, magistrates were often assisted and advised by priests, who served for life and (until the last century of the Republic) were chosen by other priests. A few gods, such as Jupiter, Mars, and Quirinus, each had their own priest or *flamen*. The holders of priesthoods, it should be noted, came from many of the same families as the city's political leaders, and many priests also held elective offices.

"Colleges" or groups of priests sharing the same function had an important role in Roman public life. The pontiffs (*pontifices*, singular, *pontifex*), headed by the *pontifex maximus*, exercised a general supervision over a wide range of rites as well as over the calendar of the Republic itself. Individual pontiffs advised officials on how best to perform rites, and the college could give an opinion on whether a ritual had been properly performed (if it had not, they could recommend that it be performed again until satisfactory, a procedure known as *instauratio*). Their supervision of the calendar meant more than knowing the days on which certain rites were to be performed. The calendar also identified the days when it was permissible for magistrates to conduct public business or hold assemblies. Originally, the pontiffs numbered three, and only patricians could serve. By the end of the fourth century, the number had increased to nine and plebeians now made up about half the total; the number would be further increased to fifteen in the first century B.C. Pontiffs served for life. When a vacancy occurred, the surviving pontiffs chose the new priest, who was often a relative (although not necessarily a close relative) of the man he replaced. From the third century, seventeen of the tribes, chosen by lot, elected the pontifex maximus from among the serving pontiffs—a limited assertion of control by the citizen body.

The "augurs" were at least as important. Like the pontiffs, they possessed their own areas of expertise, central to the political organization of the city. The first of these were the auspices, essential to an official's power. Before taking office or before beginning any public action, an official was expected to consult Jupiter, the god of the auspices. This could be done by watching the flight of birds or by observing the feeding of chickens kept for the purpose (compare Plate 1a). Although magistrates performed the rite, it was the augurs who were thought to be the experts in its proper forms and in the interpretation of the results. Augurs also possessed knowledge of the rituals necessary to "inaugurate" certain places. Consequently, magistrates and pontiffs could dedicate sacred sites, such as temples and shrines, only after the augurs had prepared the location. Augural responsibilities for rendering sites sacred had political implications. Places where magistrates performed many of their essential functions had to be inaugurated, as did locations where the senate met and the people voted. At first, there were only three augurs, but by the end of the fourth century their number had been increased to nine; at this time, plebeians were permitted to serve, filling about half of the positions. Like the pontiffs, the augurs too were increased to fifteen in the first century B.C.

SOURCE 2.2: *Dionysius of Halicarnassus (Roman Antiquities 7.72.1–13) offers a long description of a procession that accompanied the performance of the Roman Games or ludi Romani, which he attributes to the first performances of the games early in the fifth century. He derives his description (slightly abbreviated here) from the work of Quintus Fabius Pictor, the first Roman historian (c. 200), and he claims to have seen a similar procession in his own day (end of the first century B.C.). These Roman Games certainly were in existence by the middle of the fourth century, and the procession described by Dionysius may well have been instituted around this time, since it shares features with other Roman ceremonies of the same date.*

Before beginning the games, the chief magistrates conducted a procession honoring the gods from the Capitol through the Forum to the Circus Maximus. Romans' sons nearing manhood and of the right age led the procession—on horseback if their fathers were qualified to be equites, on foot if they were to serve in the infantry. Those on horseback went in troops and squadrons, those on foot in divisions and companies as if they were going to training school. This was done so that outsiders might see the flower of the young men of the city and how numerous and fine they were. Charioteers followed, some driving four horses abreast, some two, and others riding unyoked horses. Next came the contestants in both the light and the heavy games, their bodies naked except for a waistband.

After the contestants came numerous bands of dancers, divided into three groups, one of men, the second of youths, and the third of boys. They were accompanied by flute players, using old-fashioned flutes that were small and short, as is done even today, and by lyre players, who plucked ivory lyres of seven strings and the instruments called *barbita*. Their use has ceased among the Greeks of my time, traditional though it used to be, but the Romans still use them in all their ancient sacrificial ceremonies. The dancers wore red tunics with bronze belts. Swords hung at their sides, and they carried spears of shorter than normal length. They also wore bronze helmets with prominent crests and plumes. One man led each group, and he gave the figures of the dance to the others, taking the lead in displaying quick, warlike steps, usually in a four-beat rhythm. After the armed dances, other dancers marched in procession as satyrs, performing the Greek dance called *sicinnis*. Those dressed as *silenoi* wore shaggy tunics, called by some *chortaioi*, and streams of all kinds of flowers; those portraying satyrs wore belts and goatskins and erect manes on their heads, along with other similar items. These men mocked and mimicked the serious dancing, turning it into a comic performance.

After the bands of dancers, many flute players and lyre players came in procession. And after them came men who carried censers in which perfume and frankincense were burned along the entire route of the procession, along with other men carrying vessels made of gold and silver, some that were sacred to the gods and others belonging to the Republic. Last of all came the images of the gods, carried on men's shoulders.

Figure 2.4 *In this fifth-century relief from Clusium, officials on the left observe contestants in* ludi. *The farthest left of the participants in these games is probably an armed dancer, while a female dancer and flute player are immediately to his right. The figures on the platform are clearly officials, since the one in the middle carries a curved staff or* lituus *(compare Plate 1a). The seated figure to his right is a scribe, writing the results of the games (or of the judges' decisions) on a tablet.*

The *decemviri sacris faciundis* ("ten men in charge of sacrifices") were concerned with signs of divine displeasure as revealed through prodigies, such as lightning striking prominent buildings, exceptionally severe storms and floods, earthquakes, and weird behavior by animals. These decemvirs were the custodians of the "Sibylline Books," the Books of Fate. When some highly unusual occurrence indicated that the *pax deorum*—the state of peace between Rome and its gods—had been ruptured, the senate would instruct the decemvirs to consult the Books and determine what rites might placate the gods' anger. Priests often linked prodigies to specific acts by Roman officials that supposedly had offended the gods, so that their expiation might constitute not just a public judgment on an officeholder's behavior but also a divine one. Initially there were only two men in charge of sacrifices (*duumviri*), but this number was raised to ten early in the fourth century, and eventually to fifteen (*quindecimviri*) in the first century.

Women possessed a more prominent place in the religious life of the city than they did in politics. The six Vestal virgins performed the rites of Vesta, the Roman goddess of the hearth, from her shrine near the Regia in the Forum Romanum. Among their tasks was to tend the sacred flame; its extinction would endanger the city itself. The wives of the pontifex maximus and of the *flamen* or priest of Jupiter (the *flamen Dialis*) shared in some of their husbands' ritual responsibilities. Women of elite families, moreover, were thought to have dedicated the temple of the Fortune of Women (*Fortuna Muliebris*) early in the Republic, and it long served as a center for their religious activities. Women and girls had defined places in processions and in other celebrations. Some of the larger conflicts of Roman society made themselves felt in this sphere too. In 295, patrician women prevented the participation of Verginia, a patrician woman who had married a plebeian, in rites at the temple of Patrician Chastity (*Pudicitia Patricia*); she then founded on her own a new shrine of Plebeian Chastity (*Pudicitia Plebeia*).

Broadly speaking, therefore, Roman cult may be seen as a system of communication between individuals or the community on the one hand, and the gods on the other. Both private citizens and public officials entreated the gods for benefits by offering sacrifices, vows, and prayers. In rites of divination, such as the auspices, magistrates sought permission to perform certain public acts. Through prodigies, a god might signal anger over some fault or omission; equally, an individual or official might avoid the consequences through rites of expiation. Much of this public cult, then, rests upon the conviction that the gods can be influenced, and even persuaded to change their minds. Indeed, rites were often repeated until a successful outcome was forthcoming. As Romans saw it, their scrupulous attention to the signs observed by the augurs, and their sensitive interpretation and expiation of prodigies played a primary role in securing success for the city in its wars and other public undertakings. Only in the first century B.C. did concern over the auspices and prodigies gradually decline, in part due to the growing influence of certain Greek conceptions of divinity which likened the gods to forces of nature that could not be deflected from their course, and in part because powerful political figures became less willing to submit to such restraints.

ROME AND CENTRAL ITALY

During the fourth century and the opening decades of the third, Rome became the dominant city in Italy. Wars, battles, victories, and defeats—all illustrated by acts of Roman heroism and the perfidy of Rome's enemies—fill Roman accounts of this century. Despite this wealth of detail, however, a clear narrative of the wars is not possible. There is the usual problem of exaggerated victory claims, not to mention a desire to blame Rome's enemies for all conflicts. Furthermore, the changing alliances of the period confused later authors, and Roman opportunism among these shifts may have embarrassed some. In addition, Roman families descended from the commanders in these wars occasionally made claims for their ancestors that were unjustified. Indeed, in some instances, Roman historians were unable to decide who had commanded in a battle or a campaign because several families claimed that their ancestors had been in charge.

No single continuous narrative is preserved for much of the early third century. The surviving books of Livy's monumental history break off in 290, and they only resume with a full account of the century's last two decades. The third-century portions of Dionysius of Halicarnassus' history, which originally reached to 264, survive only in fragments. From the biographer Plutarch we possess a life of Rome's enemy Pyrrhus. In other sources, records of the foundation of colonies are almost certainly near complete and their dates dependable; they serve as a good indicator of the spread of Roman power and the fates of nearby communities. By contrast, the details of wars and battles, accounts of diplomacy, and the assignment of credit for victory and blame for defeat, are all probably much less reliable.

Warfare and the Civic Order

War occupied a central place in the civic and religious structure of many city-states, but this was especially true of Rome. By the fourth century, Rome had evolved a pattern of warfare that centered on campaigns undertaken almost every year, a level of intensity and regularity that is unique among ancient city-states. In the process, warfare came to be deeply entrenched in Roman political and religious life, shaping the highest offices as well as the lives and careers both of the community's leaders and of its citizens. Military service was one of the central duties of the citizen body. The boundaries between citizen and soldier were neither firm nor long-lasting, and each year large numbers of adult males performed both roles. Soon after the new consuls had entered office, citizens eligible for military service came to Rome for the levy, or *dilectus*, in which some were chosen to be soldiers in the consuls' armies in the upcoming season. On occasion, an additional levy could be held later in the year if it proved to be necessary. After a season's campaigning, soldiers were discharged, returning to their places in civil life.

In Rome, as in other city-states, warfare followed a clear seasonal pattern. Direct attacks on cities or long sieges of fortified places were relatively rare. Instead, commanders of invading armies more often sought to interfere with the ability of the inhabitants of the targeted city to cultivate their lands and feed their families. Offensive operations usually began before the grain harvest, which in central Italy took place in late May or early June. After marching into an enemy's territory, soldiers of the invading force would live off the land, harvesting the nearly ripe crops in the field and attempting to prevent the defenders from doing the same. Defenders could seek to prevent the enemy from inflicting such damage by fighting a formal battle; alternatively, if they were weaker or did not wish to risk such an engagement, they could retreat within the fortifications of their city and wait until the invaders left. In these circumstances, campaigns were generally brief, and soldiers were often discharged after only a few weeks or months. In those few instances when soldiers had to be kept under arms throughout the year, the Romans imposed a payment known as *tributum*, which bore most heavily on the wealthiest citizens, in order to contribute to the soldiers' support.

Even successful wars could have few permanent results. Some wars were encompassed within a single summer's campaigning, while others consisted of a series of annual campaigns, each with a different commander and army. Sometimes, campaigns ended in truces that could run for several years; on other occasions, defeated cities might accept the dominance of the victor. When Roman commanders had secured a clear victory over an enemy city, they sometimes forced the defeated to perform a total surrender known as a *deditio in fidem*. Through this ceremony, the officials of the newly subjected city handed over all its components to the Roman people to do with as they wished (see Source 5.1).

Backed by the senate and the citizen assemblies, Roman commanders could then in theory exact any terms they wished, although they were supposedly limited by Roman good faith, or *fides*, which imposed a moral imperative not to prescribe excessively harsh conditions. Sometimes, it should be noted, communities would seek this relationship with Rome voluntarily in order to gain protection. It was the belief of Rome's leaders that such a formal surrender established a permanent relationship of subordination. However, certain defeated communities plainly did not share this view, and Roman armies sometimes had to force them into submission repeatedly. Altogether in ancient Italy, none but the strongest of cities was able to exert long-term dominance over a substantial number of others. During the fourth century, Rome became just such an exceptional city.

Rome in Latium and Campania

Rome's victory over Veii profoundly changed relations among the cities of central Italy. Rome, already a relatively large and populous city, came to overshadow its neighbors even more starkly. Strength in war was closely related to a city's population and to the numbers of its adult males who could afford to serve in its army. Rome's treatment of Veii enlarged its own citizen body, and in addition the land then distributed to poorer citizens gave still more Romans the necessary means to equip themselves as soldiers. These new circumstances affected Rome's relations with other cities in turn. The elimination of Veii, along with the extension of Roman frontiers and influence, meant that Rome now had new neighbors and new competitors in both Etruria and Umbria. Meantime in Latium itself, Rome's new power seems to have disturbed the leaders of many Latin communities, who worried about Roman domination.

The impact of the Gauls' sack of Rome was apparently no more than momentary. In Latium, some Latin communities did seek to escape Roman domination. Tibur and Praeneste, the most powerful Latin cities after Rome, attacked several times, sometimes in alliance with the Volsci and, on at least one occasion, with bands of Gauls. Roman armies retained the upper hand in these wars, however. This was a mark of their greatly increased strength, although they did not win all their battles nor were all their victories final. Even so, according to the antiquarian Festus (p. 498L), Titus Quinctius, dictator in 380, was able to dedicate a large gold crown to Jupiter in the temple on the Capitol with an inscription, still visible centuries later, recording that "in nine days, he had taken as many towns, and on the tenth, Praeneste."

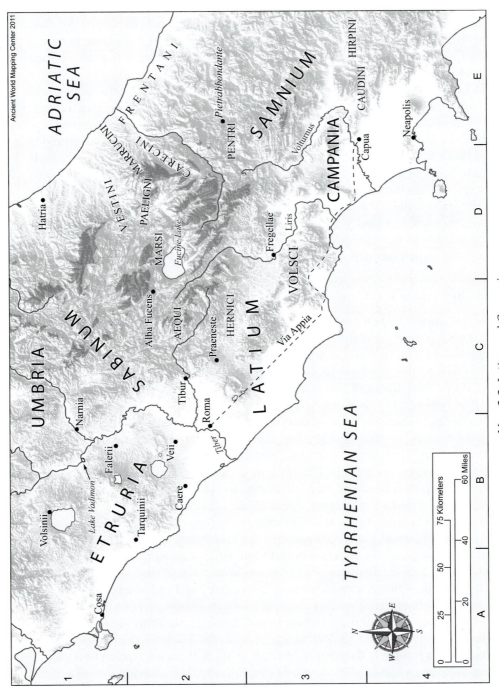

ADRIATIC SEA

F R E N T A N I

MARRUCINI

CARECINI

VESTINI

PAELIGNI

Hatria

UMBRIA

SABINUM

MARSI

Fucine Lake

Alba Fucens

AEQUI

Narnia

Tibur

Praeneste

HERNICI

Roma

Tiber

Veii

Faleri

Lake Vadimon

ETRURIA

Volsinii

Tarquinii

Caere

Cosa

PENTRI

Pietrabbondante

SAMNIUM

Volturnus

CAMPANIA

CAUDINI

HIRPINI

Capua

Neapolis

VOLSCI

LATIUM

Fregellae

Liris

Via Appia

TYRRHENIAN SEA

N E S W

0   25   50   75 Kilometers

0   20   40   60 Miles

A   B   C   D   E

1

2

3

4

Map 2.2 *Latium and Campania*

In the third quarter of the fourth century, Roman commanders proceeded to wage wars and make alliances with states that were more powerful than their nearest Latin or Etruscan neighbors; in the process, they succeeded in extending Roman power over all of Latium and northern Campania. In Campania, the invasions of the fifth century had not eliminated city life. Instead, victorious groups of warriors from the highlands had largely adopted the urban lifestyle of those they had defeated, creating in the process a culture with marked Greek, Etruscan, and Italic elements. In the fourth century, the cities of northern Campania had rallied around the leadership of the largest city, Capua. These *Campani* fought against the cities of southern Campania, against Neapolis (modern Naples) and other cities of the coast, and against the Samnites to their east.

During the fourth century, the Samnites were the strongest group in the central highlands. In the valleys of Samnium, archeological evidence reveals a dense pattern of rural settlement with the inhabitants living in scattered villages, where they raised crops, vines, and livestock. City-states had not taken root here, but a powerful military confederacy of tribes had emerged. The district, or *pagus*, governed by its own magistrate and assembly, was the basic political unit. Each pagus comprised a few neighboring villages, a shared fortified hilltop refuge that was often small and inaccessible, and rural sanctuaries that served as cult centers for the scattered population. Groups of *pagi* in turn formed larger units or tribes—Hirpini, Caudini, Carecini, Pentri—each with its own officials and assemblies. Together, the four tribes named made up a larger Samnite confederacy, with its own leaders and cult sites, such as the large rural sanctuary at modern Pietrabbondante (Plate 4). Both the tribes and the Samnite confederacy itself, it should be noted, really only functioned as groups in time of war. The Samnites were very aggressive, and they possessed a formidable military reputation.

In the late 340s and early 330s, Roman armies fought Latins, Volsci, Campanians, and possibly Samnites, while Campanians and Samnites also conducted wars of their own. The details of all these conflicts are obscure, marked by shifting alliances that would greatly confuse later Roman writers. Capua and its allies appealed to Rome for help against the Samnites, who were pressing against communities in the lower Volturnus River valley, one of the chief routes from the Samnite highlands to the coastal plains of southern Latium and Campania. The result was what later authors would call the First Samnite War (343–341), although it is far from clear how much fighting between Romans and Samnites actually took place.

At about the same time, the Latin War (341–338) marked the end of any autonomy for the Latin cities. Fearing Roman encroachment, some of these cities joined to oppose Rome, an event that Roman authors later would portray as a revolt. The Latins received some assistance from Volscian and Campanian communities; the Samnites, on the other hand, because they had ambitions in the valley of the Liris River, took Rome's side in this war. In 340, the Romans won a major victory in northern Campania. The actions of one of the consuls in command went into legend. Titus Manlius Torquatus, this consul's son, killed an enemy soldier in single combat, but was then put to death by his father for disobeying the explicit order given that no Roman should engage in single combat—an example of the virtuous official placing the welfare of the city and its laws above family. By 338, the war essentially had ended, although scattered communities did continue to resist for a few years afterwards.

The end of the Latin cities' independence was the clearest result of these wars. First, the victors ended all alliances and religious associations that had linked the inhabitants of various Latin cities; as a result, responsibility for maintaining many of the cults that had been shared by a number of Latin towns became the task for Roman officials (see Chapter One). Then, the Romans bound each town directly to Rome alone. Most Latin communities were incorporated into the Roman state, just as Veii had been over half a century earlier; their citizens became Roman citizens and their land Roman territory. Their urban centers continued to exist as units of no more than local government with restricted freedom of action. Such towns were styled *municipia* (singular, *municipium*). They retained much of their old civic organization, electing officials, maintaining the local equivalent of a senate, and performing their traditional religious rites. They could not make war or peace on their own, however, and their citizens, when drafted, served in the Roman army. They could vote in Roman assemblies if they were present in Rome.

A few Latin communities—in particular Tibur and Praeneste, the largest ones—did maintain a formal independence and were not absorbed directly into the Roman citizen body. Even so, they became Roman allies, were completely surrounded by Roman territory, and were no longer capable of any independent action. Some Latin colonies formed during the wars of the fifth century continued in a special status that would eventually be known as "allies of the Latin Name" (*socii nominis Latini*). They preserved the customary Latin rights of intermarriage, contract and the ownership of land, and of migration (see Chapter One), but they could now only exercise them with Rome and with Romans, since there was to be no further interaction between Latin communities except through Rome.

Certain cities, primarily the Volscian communities of southern Latium, which were separated from Rome by greater distances, suffered a different fate. The Romans declared them too to be municipia, a sign that they wished to incorporate them in some manner

Figure 2.5 *This bone plaque (8 × 2 in / 20 × 5 cm), originally attached to a wooden box as decoration, was found at the Latin city of Praeneste. It depicts a warrior in the panoply of a hoplite; his shield can be seen behind his left leg. The plaque was carved in the late fourth century, when Praeneste was firmly an ally of Rome.*

into the larger Roman political community; but citizens of these municipia could not vote in Roman elections. Later, these nonvoting municipalities (*municipia sine suffragio*) were seen as occupying an inferior position to those with the full rights of Roman citizenship. However, the original intention may have been different; the right to vote in Roman elections, after all, would have been much less valuable to those who lived far from Rome, and the ability to bind such citizens fully into the Roman civic order would have been weaker. Perhaps, therefore, the original purpose of creating nonvoting municipalities was no more than to link these communities firmly and permanently to Rome. Even so, they maintained separate identities as city-states in a way that was not open to communities nearer to Rome, although this identity no longer permitted an independent foreign or military policy. Capua, a large and powerful city, became a municipium sine suffragio at some stage during the late fourth century; a century later, the great majority of its citizens still thought of themselves as Campani rather than as Romans (see Chapter Three).

Incorporation of municipia into the larger Roman state did not necessarily involve a drastic rearrangement of these communities' internal social arrangements. Like Rome, their social orders were firmly hierarchical. Some leading families may not have survived their city's defeat or lost their social position in new circumstances, but many others did survive and continued to dominate their communities; so long as they remained loyal, Roman magistrates would preserve them against internal unrest. For certain of these municipal elites, their newly acquired Roman citizenship would have proven especially valuable. The leading families of many Latin communities, which for long had had close, if sometimes tense, relations with Rome, may have intermarried with prominent Roman families from a relatively early date; incorporation within the larger Roman community apparently accelerated this process. Wealthy families in some municipia sine suffragio, such as Capua, also formed marriage alliances with Roman families, although this may have been a slower development. Eventually, some municipal families would become part of the Roman political elite, holding offices and serving in the senate of Rome itself. Centuries later, the elites of many Italian communities, including Rome, would be linked by networks of family relationships.

This said, the Romans also treated some defeated communities in ways that did disrupt their social and political arrangements. Victorious Roman armies plundered the camps of armies they defeated in battle as well as the cities they took by storm, and Rome often imposed penalties on communities that had fought too hard or resisted too long, confiscating land and displacing or enslaving the inhabitants. Roman citizens, as individuals, could take up small allotments of some of this captured land in what are known as "viritane" assignments. Other substantial tracts of it went to groups of settlers in colonies.

Seeking to hold new territory or allies by founding colonies was an old Roman and Latin practice, but now the process became considerably more formalized and under Rome's exclusive control. Colonies were to be fully functioning city-states with their own fighting forces and capable of their own defense. In some colonies, the settlers remained Roman citizens and were enrolled in a tribe. Such citizen colonies were small—300 adult men—and they were generally situated along the coast, at harbors, or at the mouths of rivers. Most colonies were larger, however, with 2,500, 4,000, or 6,000 adult male settlers; colonists in these new communities lost Roman citizenship, but they received instead the privileges enjoyed by the citizens of towns with Latin status. From the late fourth to the early second century, the Romans established at least fifty-three colonies in Italy at locations open to enemy attack, in recently subjugated regions liable to revolt, at strategic river crossings and road junctions, and on vulnerable sections of coastline (see Plate 2). One Roman writer later would describe colonies like these as "small images of the Roman people" (Gellius, *Attic Nights* 16.13.9).

So, in these wars of conquest and the political accommodations that followed, Roman officials developed the military alliances and the institutions that would enable them to dominate Italy and, later, much of the Mediterranean world. Rome, like other city-states, did not possess a bureaucracy or an elaborate political and administrative establishment. It would be an impossibility for Roman officials to continue expanding their state indefinitely if they intended to govern new territories and their inhabitants directly, or if they wished to exploit subordinate communities to the full. Rather, in their efforts to bind communities, the Romans instead created a hierarchy of settlements defined by relationship to themselves. Thus some were deemed to be fully a part of the Roman political order; others shared partially in Roman rights; still others remained ostensibly independent. All, however, maintained some local self-government. As a result, the Romans could lead many communities without having to make the adjustments in their own government that any consistent attempt to manage others at the local level would have required.

The resulting system of alliances and incorporated communities was primarily military in nature. After the actual conquest, the Roman state did not seek any specific and direct financial benefit from the defeated, since it imposed no taxes or tribute. Instead, the Romans sought to exercise their leadership primarily in war. Colonies, municipia, and allies were expected to defer to Rome, to follow its leadership in war and peace, and to provide soldiers for its wars. Such an assemblage of communities could field formidable military forces, and it could be expanded indefinitely. Each new acquisition of land or people would lead to the creation of new colonies and new municipia, and would only increase Rome's military strength for the next round of wars.

Samnite Wars

Once again wars with the Samnites loomed large in Rome's history during the last quarter of the fourth century and the opening decade of the third. Both powers, after all, were expansionist, and they were now neighbors. Around their city,

Roman forces had united Latium, northern Campania, and the territory of Veii together with some of its subordinate cities. Only the Samnites possessed a nearly equivalent power, so that the Roman-Samnite wars really did determine which would be the leading power in Italy.

The Second Samnite War (326–304) was a long struggle for dominance. It began over the Roman foundation of a colony at Fregellae, on the eastern bank of the Liris River, in territory that the Samnites apparently considered to be their own. In the next year, Rome went to war with the Greek city of Neapolis, and the Samnites came to its assistance. This phase of the war ended at the Battle of the Caudine Forks (Latin, *Furculae Caudinae*) in 321, when Samnite forces succeeded in ambushing a Roman army in a mountain valley and forcing its surrender. In the resulting peace, the Romans gave up their colonies at Fregellae and Cales. Fighting resumed on a large scale in 316. For the next few years, Roman historians record Samnite invasions of Latium and Campania, but Rome's armies did recover and would then invade Samnium yearly until peace was made in 304. During this war, Rome founded several colonies in southern Campania, and one, Luceria, far away in Apulia, in an apparent attempt to create bases for further operations against Samnium.

As censor in 312, Appius Claudius Caecus began two large public works projects that illustrate the increased scale of the Roman state. The first was the construction of an aqueduct, *aqua Appia*, to bring water to the city from some distance away. This project can only suggest that population growth had by now rendered local sources of water no longer adequate; construction of another aqueduct in 272, *Anio Vetus*, by the censor Manius Curius Dentatus, confirms continued growth. The second project was a long road from Rome to Capua in Campania that would become known as *via Appia*. Primarily military in purpose, it was intended to give armies a faster, easier march from Rome, where they first were mustered, into the region around Capua. Its construction is a clear sign of how intense operations were in Rome's wars with the Samnites, and probably also an indication that Roman leaders expected these wars to be long-lasting. Later, other censors would arrange for the construction of further roads to speed armies into regions of intense campaigning.

From 312, the Romans also sent commanders and armies against other cities and confederations, a proof of the state's extensive resources. In 311, Roman armies advanced up the Tiber Valley against the Etruscan cities of Perusia, Cortona, and Arretium, and three years later, they would campaign against another Etruscan city, Volsinii. These wars generally ended in truces, either for a single year or sometimes for as long as fifty years. In 299, however, the Romans did found a Latin colony at Narnia, less than fifty miles (80 km) up the Tiber from the city. Between 306 and 304, Roman armies overcame the Hernici and the Aequi, in the hills to the southeast of Rome. These campaigns were said to have been especially harsh, with many of the hill towns of the Aequi destroyed and their populations massacred. Their neighbors—Marsi, Paeligni, Marrucini, Frentani, and Vestini—made peace with Rome, presumably on Roman terms, between 304 and 302. Again, the Romans founded several new colonies on confiscated lands.

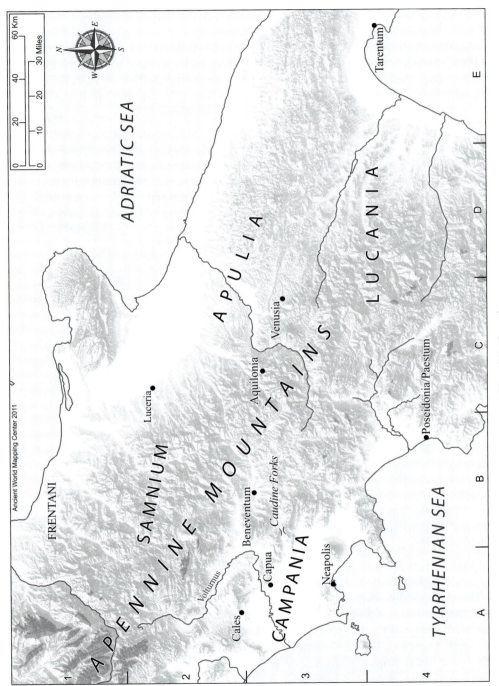

Map 2.3 *Samnium*

The Third Samnite War (298–290) secured Rome's leadership. Hostilities seem to have begun over Roman activities in Lucania. By the end of 297, a coalition of Samnites, Etruscans, Umbrians, and Gauls formed, although its actions were not well-coordinated. In 295, the two consuls of the year decisively defeated a force of Samnites, Umbrians, and Gauls in a great battle at Sentinum in Umbria. This victory was later to be closely associated with the consul P. Decius Mus, who lost his life in the same act of self-sacrifice that his father had made in a battle against the Latins in 340. Like his father, at a crucial point in the fighting the son "devoted" or pledged his life to the gods if they would claim the enemy too; he then rode alone into the enemy ranks, causing his own death, but also theirs so as to ensure their defeat. In 291, another Roman consul defeated the Samnites at Aquilonia; soon afterwards, the Romans would establish the colony of Venusia south of there. After this defeat, the Samnites again made peace.

EXPANSION OF ROMAN CONTROL OVER ITALY

In the century between the fall of Veii and the end of the Third Samnite War, therefore, the Romans had united Latium, parts of northern Campania, Veii and some of its smaller neighbors, and the former territories of the Aequi and Hernici as far as the Fucine Lake (Latin, Lacus Fucinus). In the wars of this period Rome had also emerged as the most powerful state in Italy. Away from its core, however, Roman power rested only on a few isolated colonies, dependent upon Rome for their safety, together with a number of often unwilling allies who were forced by circumstances to accept such a relationship for a time. Many of these communities were restive, some were hostile, and virtually all wished to pursue interests of their own. So here Roman ambitions and claims to leadership had to be continually reasserted; even so, the ample reserves of men of military age provided by the network of colonies and municipia gave Rome an advantage that would become more marked through the third century.

Wars in Central and Northern Italy

The pattern of annual campaigns in central and northern Italy that had characterized the last decade of the fourth century continued well into the third. In 290, just after the Roman victory in the Third Samnite War, the consul Manius Curius Dentatus ravaged the land of the Sabines, who lived in scattered villages, and then reached the Adriatic Sea. As a result of this campaign, the Romans established a Latin colony at Hatria, and made the Sabines Roman citizens without the right to vote. Roman armies also conducted regular campaigns into Etruria and Umbria, especially along the valley of the Tiber. These wars were complicated, with shifting alliances between states, and they often involved Gauls. In 284, the Gallic Senones defeated a Roman army at Arretium in northern Etruria. In the following year, by contrast, another Roman army defeated the Gallic Boii and some of their Etruscan allies at Lake Vadimon, about fifty miles (80 km) north of Rome. By 283, the Romans had expelled the Senones from a portion of their territory, which would become known as the *ager Gallicus*. There, the Romans would establish colonies at Sena Gallica (in 283) and Ariminum (in 268; modern Rimini).

In the 280s and 270s, Roman armies forced most of the cities of Etruria and Umbria into a dependent status. By 280, the Romans had made alliances with the Etruscan cities of Vulci, Volsinii, Rusellae, Vetulonia, Populonia, Volaterrae, and Tarquinii. Caere was treated more severely: upon its defeat in 273, it became a municipium (without the vote) and some of its land was confiscated. By the 260s, few, if any, communities in Etruria, Umbria, and Picenum possessed any real independence. Attempts to reassert it were severely punished. The Picentes revolted in 269. When defeated, they lost territory—a Roman colonial commission established the colony of Firmum there—and they were made citizens without the vote; some Picentes were also deported to the southern margins of Campania. In Etruria, the revolt of Falerii in 241 was the last. A Roman army captured and destroyed the city, and then forced its inhabitants to settle at a nearby location more open to attack. Falerii's chief deity, the goddess Minerva, was moved to Rome as *Minerva Capta* (Captured Minerva).

Sharp internal conflicts characterized many Etruscan cities. The majority of their populations had only a restricted role in community government, and this limitation may have contributed to the persistent Etruscan defeats. In 265, the wealthiest and most powerful families of Volsinii lost control of their city and sought Roman intervention. Marcus Fulvius Flaccus, consul in 264, captured and destroyed the city, although some of the survivors were then permitted to settle at a less defensible site nearby. When civic disturbances occurred in allied cities, Roman officials and the Roman senate usually supported the leading families, a policy which in many instances may well have encouraged them to submit to Roman leadership.

Conquest of the South

At the end of the Third Samnite War in 290, Rome's hold over the Samnites and Lucanians was precarious, and its power over more distant communities was virtually nonexistent. Nonetheless, during the first half of the third century the Romans also regularly involved themselves in hostilities in the southern regions of the Italian peninsula. Here they encountered a different kind of enemy, leading to changes in Roman methods of making war.

In 285, Thurii appealed to Rome for protection from the Lucanians and Bruttii. Gaius Fabricius Luscinus then forced the Lucanians to abandon their siege of Thurii, and he left a Roman garrison there for its protection. Shortly afterwards, other cities—Locri, Rhegium, and Croton—also successfully sought Roman protection. This growing Roman presence now alarmed the citizens of Tarentum, the largest Greek city in the region and often ambitious to lead the others. In 282, the Tarentines attacked and sank some Roman warships that had appeared outside their harbor, apparently in violation of an agreement between the two cities. The Tarentines then marched on Thurii, expelled its Roman garrison, and replaced the ruling oligarchy with a more democratic regime. Tarentum took these actions, it should be noted, while Rome was heavily involved in wars against Etruscans, Umbrians, and Gauls.

In the far south of Italy, the Romans were entering a region in turmoil. Tensions between oligarchic and democratic factions were common in the Greek cities there and in Sicily. Such strife could lead to violence, providing one of the chief reasons for other states to be called upon for help. Roman leaders already had a well-deserved reputation for favoring oligarchic groups over democratic. At the same time, the Greek cities along the south coast of Italy were often under fierce pressure from the Samnites, Lucanians, and Bruttii and would appeal to fellow Greeks for help. In the decades before Rome's intervention, the Tarentines and their neighbors had sought the aid of several military leaders who possessed more powerful armies than did most city-states. Agathocles was the most recent of them to respond. By the end of the fourth century, he had made himself ruler of the Sicilian city of Syracuse, and had begun to build up a military state—based on large numbers of mercenary soldiers—that encompassed much of the island and several cities in southern Italy. He died in 289 and his empire fell apart, but the Greek cities of southern Italy continued their appeals. So in 281, when a Roman consul and his army entered Tarentum's territory in reaction to its earlier attacks, the Tarentines sought assistance from Pyrrhus, king of the Molossians in Epirus across the Adriatic (Map 3.5). His intervention would differ from earlier ones in its scale and consequences.

Dramatic changes occurred in the political, social, and cultural life of the Greek world around 300. During the fifth century, monarchy had largely disappeared except on its barbarous margins, and city-states dominated. In the fourth century, however, monarchy re-emerged as a powerful political institution; at the same time, military operations grew larger in scale and more innovative. Mercenaries reinforced citizen levies, and increasingly elaborate techniques for fighting battles and besieging cities were developed. City-states lacked the resources to sustain warfare on this scale, but kings could muster them.

The rise of the kings of Macedon was central to these shifts. Philip II (reigned 359–336) gained control of Greece. His son and successor, Alexander III, "the Great," vastly extended his father's rule by conquering the mighty Persian empire in campaigns that were ended only by his death in 323 aged thirty-three. The phenomenal nature of these conquests—which extended through central Asia to the Indian sub-continent, and south to Egypt—made Alexander a towering figure, widely considered to be a god. For centuries afterwards, too, he remained a source of inspiration to many leaders (Romans among them), who sought to imitate him. After his death, his empire soon fragmented into several states whose rulers called themselves kings and vied for wealth and power; Greek city-states were largely eclipsed. A new culture—now known as "Hellenistic"—was created, and was to exercise marked influence even beyond the area ever ruled by Greeks or Macedonians. Hellenistic kingship was personal. These kings ruled because the

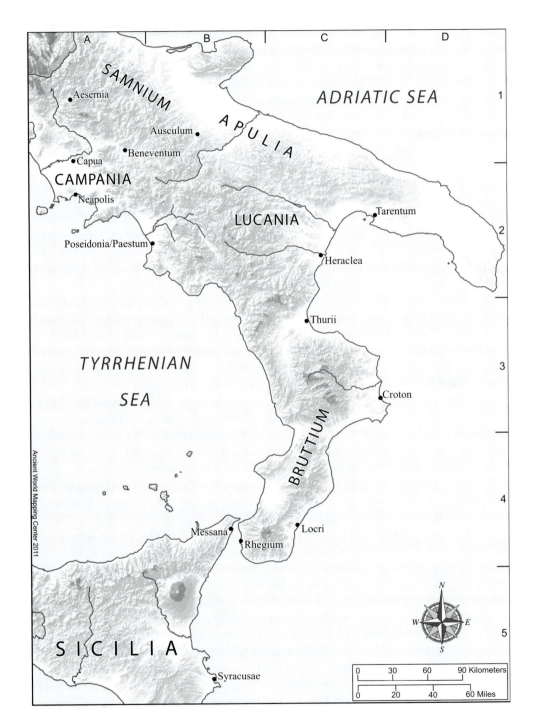

Map 2.4 *Southern Italy*

necessary resources and authority were theirs, not because they held a traditional position. Hence they stressed the material bases of their power: great wealth and large armies. They also advertised their personal qualities, exaggerating or inventing accomplishments and characteristics that showed favor by the gods or even identity as a god or godlike being. In the capitals and courts from which they ruled, these kings acted with pride as patrons of the arts and literature, and with grand ceremonies displayed their wealth, luxurious lifestyle, and military strength and prowess. Such elements of the public culture of the Hellenistic monarchies would find many imitators, not least among members of Rome's governing elite.

Pyrrhus matched this model. When he received the Tarentines' invitation, he resolved to seek opportunities in the West and assembled his forces at Tarentum itself in 280. Molossians and other Epirotes formed the core of his army, which included about twenty war elephants; to this core, Pyrrhus added large numbers of mercenaries. The Tarentines contributed their citizen army. Meantime the Romans, who also were fighting in Etruria and Umbria, had their own forces in the south. Lucius Aemilius Barbula, who as consul in 281 had commanded the Roman army ravaging Tarentum's territory, had remained nearby over the winter (one of the earliest known instances when a Roman army did not return home after a summer's campaigning). The armies of Pyrrhus and Barbula engaged at Heraclea, southwest of Tarentum. After a hard-fought battle, Pyrrhus won, but with immense loss of life, giving rise to the expression "Pyrrhic victory" for a battle won at such cost that it almost amounted to a defeat. A bronze plaque found at the sanctuary of Zeus at Dodona in Epirus records the dedication of some of the plunder following this victory: "King Pyrrhus and the Epirotes and the Tarentines to Zeus Naios from the Romans and their allies."

After the battle at Heraclea in 280, the war spread. Lucanians, Samnites, the Bruttii, and some of the Greek cities that had been allies of Rome, all decided to join Pyrrhus. With his army and allies he now invaded Campania, but without capturing any major community or inspiring any to desert Rome and join him. Next he turned toward Rome itself, approaching to within fifty miles (80 km) of the city. By this time, however, another Roman army which had been campaigning in Etruria returned to protect Rome, and Pyrrhus hesitated to press on. Instead, he returned to Tarentum, where he began offering peace terms. Our sources preserve different versions of his demands (conveyed through his envoy Cineas), which seem to have either confused Roman historians or offended their patriotic sensibilities. According to one account, Pyrrhus demanded that the defeated Romans give up all the land they had taken from the Samnites, Lucanians, and Bruttii and become his allies, in effect thereby ending both their empire and their independence. Nonetheless an elderly, blind senator, Appius Claudius Caecus, who had been censor in 312, is credited with having persuaded the senate to reject these inordinate demands; copies of his speech may have survived into the first century B.C.

The war resumed again in the following year (279). Pyrrhus brought over reinforcements from Epirus, hired more mercenaries, acquired new elephants, and raised additional funds from his allies. The financial contributions imposed on them may have undermined his popularity for a time. Certainly they were onerous. A number of inscribed bronze tablets, which record the finances of the temple of Zeus Olympius at Locri, probably date to this year. They record the payment of over 300 tons of silver from the temple treasury "to the king." Pyrrhus led his army through Apulia with the apparent intention of marching on through Samnium toward Rome. He met the Romans at Ausculum, and another lengthy, fearsome clash ensued. Once again, Pyrrhus proved victorious in battle, but at terrible cost.

At this point, therefore, he decided to direct his forces elsewhere. Certainly, his failure to win a decisive victory underlines the depth of Rome's resources. Unlike other city-states, Rome, with its colonies and municipia, was able to muster citizen troops on a scale that made it possible to compete with, and eventually overcome, the armies of Hellenistic rulers. In a report to Pyrrhus, Cineas compared Rome to a mythical Greek monster with many heads, the hydra; as soon as an attacker cut off one of its heads, it grew two more. The Greek cities of Sicily provided the occasion for Pyrrhus' departure. After Agathocles' death in 289, his kingdom of Syracuse became embroiled in civil war. Carthage, which controlled the western part of Sicily, took advantage of this disorder and attempted to establish its control over the entire island. In these circumstances, the Syracusans in 278 offered Pyrrhus the supreme command of their forces if he would bring his army to assist them. In the two years that Pyrrhus then spent in Sicily, he did succeed in driving the Carthaginians out of most of the island, but he was not able to expel them altogether nor could he defeat the stronger Carthaginian fleet. His allies in Italy suffered much in his absence. Lists of Roman commanders who achieved great victories—the so-called *fasti triumphales*—record defeats of Samnites, Lucanians, and Bruttii in 277 and 276.

In 275, Pyrrhus returned to Italy, prompted perhaps by renewed appeals from his Italian allies as well as increasing dissatisfaction with his leadership in Sicily. Later that year, he clashed with the Romans at Beneventum in Samnium, and this time the Roman army won. The victorious consul, Manius Curius Dentatus, would later build an aqueduct at Rome from his share of the plunder. By the end of the year, Pyrrhus had crossed the Adriatic and returned home. There he would achieve some success for a time, only to be killed during street fighting at Argos in southern Greece in 272.

Pyrrhus' failure proved disastrous for many of his allies, who in consequence would lose their independence to Rome and suffer harsh treatment. In 272, Tarentum became a Roman ally. Wars with the Samnites and the Lucanians continued into the 260s. The foundation of Latin colonies at Paestum in 273, Beneventum in 268, and Aesernia in 263 mark their defeat. By this time, the Romans had reduced to the status of allies, voluntarily or otherwise, around 150 once-independent communities. Another important consequence of Rome's war with Pyrrhus and the associated involvement in the affairs of the

Greek cities of the south was an altogether closer engagement with the Greek world and its culture. Although there would be no direct Roman participation in the wars of the Hellenistic states until the last decades of the third century, well before that Rome was no longer just an Italian power. Hellenistic monarchies and leagues of Greek cities now had to factor Rome into their plans, and their wars affected Rome.

WAR AND THE ROMAN STATE

In over a century of virtually continuous warfare, Roman officials and armies established their city as the most powerful in Italy, and they erected around it a network of alliances that made Rome a key participant in the larger politics of the Mediterranean world. This pattern of regular warfare merits explanation, although no single element or cause can serve as the key to all of Rome's wars.

Several features of Roman society and politics encouraged acceptance of frequent wars, and perhaps the active search for them. Possession of the military virtues was central to the self-image of the Roman elite, to the ways they competed among themselves for offices and honors, and to their claims to leadership in their city and over other communities (see Chapter Three). Regular warfare provided ambitious Romans with the opportunity to display their bravery and skill, and thus to spread their fame among the citizens—vital achievements for those who wished to reach high office. Indeed, the office of consul, the highest in Rome and the focus of elite competition, was itself substantially military in nature, and its occupants would have expected, and probably desired, to command armies in the field. Not least, they felt obliged to punish cities that challenged Rome or refused to remain subordinate, and equally to protect dependent communities or groups within them who proved loyal.

Decisions over war and peace were not just for the most prominent members of Rome's elite to take. The Roman practice of campaigning virtually every year required consensus among the populace and between the voters and the members of the ruling elite. Citizens voting in assemblies regularly chose the men who would lead them in war, and it was citizens again who fought the wars; mercenaries were not hired for the purpose. Successful warfare brought tangible benefits to many Roman citizens. For example, victorious armies plundered, and even common soldiers could expect to share in the loot (see Source 4.1). Land, too, was a prize. The captured land distributed in the colonies and viritane assignments of the period would have enabled many poorer Romans to receive a plot that was sufficient to support themselves and their families. Elsewhere, demands from the poor for land redistribution were often the cause of turmoil, but this pattern did not repeat itself at Rome; wealthy Romans had comparatively little cause to fear that their property was in danger. In the last decades of the fourth century, moreover, our sources preserve regular accounts of mass enslavements of defeated enemies. Some of the newly enslaved probably were sold outside of Italy. Others were put to work on the lands and in the households of Roman citizens, beginning a gradual shift away from the labor systems of archaic Rome, which had been based on dependent clients and debt-slaves. It may be no accident that a law passed near the end of the fourth century prohibited the old practice of *nexum*, which condemned Roman citizens to bondage if they failed to repay their debts.

Altogether, the acquisition of wealth through regular campaigns no doubt reduced the level of internal conflicts in the city. Accounts of the fifth and much of the fourth century record recurrent strife between the elite and segments of the populace over land, debt, and access to offices. Such conflicts seem to have lessened in the late fourth and early third centuries, and this shift—which included an end to the Struggle of the Orders—may itself have been a consequence of the wars. The demands of the poor for land and freedom from debt, and the desires of the rich for a dependent labor force for their estates, could all now be met at the expense of Rome's neighbors.

Internal factors are not the whole picture, however. Roman historians later regarded these wars as essentially defensive in nature, aimed at restraining aggression by others or at punishing disloyalty by cities which had supposedly accepted Roman leadership. From this perspective, therefore, Roman expansion was a successful response to the aggressive actions of others. Such a viewpoint may indeed plausibly explain some campaigns against some enemies, but it is unlikely to apply universally. Even so, it is important to recognize that other states, whether friend or foe of Rome, had their own agendas, ambitions, and military traditions. Some of these communities were themselves aggressive and expansionist, and they may, on occasion, have forced the Romans to respond to their initiatives. Unfortunately, the surviving evidence, which focuses so strongly on Rome itself, does not permit the full recovery of these other, less successful histories.

SUGGESTED READINGS

Cornell, Timothy J. 1995. *The Beginnings of Rome: Italy and Rome from the Bronze Age to the Punic Wars (c. 1000–264 B.C.)*. London and New York: Routledge.

Eckstein, Arthur M. 2006. *Mediterranean Anarchy, Interstate War, and the Rise of Rome*. Berkeley, Los Angeles, London: University of California Press.

Hanson, Victor Davis. 1998. *Warfare and Agriculture in Classical Greece*. Berkeley, Los Angeles, London: University of California Press. Although Greek cities of the fifth and fourth centuries form the focus, the book's conclusions are equally applicable to war between the city-states of Italy.

Harris, William V. 1979. *War and Imperialism in Republican Rome, 327–70 B.C.* Oxford: Oxford University Press. A controversial examination of Roman attitudes toward war and the ways that they shaped Roman actions.

Rüpke, Jörg. 2007. *Religion of the Romans*. London: Polity Press.

Salmon, E. Togo. 1967. *Samnium and the Samnites*. Cambridge: Cambridge University Press.

Scheid, John. 2003. *An Introduction to Roman Religion*. Edinburgh: Edinburgh University Press.

THE BEGINNINGS OF A
MEDITERRANEAN EMPIRE

In the 130 years following the end of the war with Pyrrhus, the Roman Republic became the dominant state in the Mediterranean. In the city itself, moreover, a new elite group, the nobility, emerged to take the lead in Rome's political structure; at the same time its foremost members became some of the wealthiest and most powerful individuals in the Mediterranean world. Participation in wars over a far wider geographical span, together with the consequent expansion of Roman power beyond the Italian peninsula, would now put major strains on the Republic's traditional structure and on its customary ways of making war and forging alliances.

SOURCES

No single continuous narrative survives for the entire period, but from the last two decades of the third century through the first third of the second century, the evidence is reasonably full and some of it is contemporary. The surviving books of Livy's history of Rome break off in 290 and resume with a full account only in 218; from this point, they run without interruption until 167, when the surviving text comes to an end. The biographer Plutarch wrote lives of five Roman commanders of the period: Quintus Fabius Maximus, Marcus Claudius Marcellus, Titus Quinctius Flamininus, Marcus Porcius Cato the Elder, and Lucius Aemilius Paullus. Earlier, the Greek author Polybius (c. 200–after 118) wrote a "universal history," in which the theme of Rome's expansion from the middle of the third century to his own day was central; extensive portions of this work survive. As a young man, Polybius was active in Greek political and military matters, but after

167 he lived mostly in Rome, where he became closely acquainted with important members of the Roman elite. At the same time, inscriptions (Greek as well as Latin) offer us insights and information about a range of Roman practices both in Italy and elsewhere in the Mediterranean.

THE NOBILITY AND THE CITY OF ROME

The opening of offices and priesthoods to plebeians that occurred during the fourth and third centuries resulted in the formation of a new governing elite in Rome with a distinctive way of life. Collectively known as the "nobles" or *nobiles*, it would govern Rome and its empire throughout the period of expansion in the third, second, and first centuries. Archaic Rome had been governed by relatively few individuals from a small group of families. However, the city's new leadership, although still a group of limited size, would differ from the old in significant ways. The patriciate was always an aristocracy of birth; in addition, certain leaders of the archaic period possessed personal followings that made them important whether or not they held an office. Although some patrician families would achieve prominence in the new elite too, it was not an aristocracy of birth, nor did its leading members possess significant military forces of their own. Instead, individuals and families had to establish and maintain their place in the city within a framework of elective offices, priesthoods, and formal religious and political institutions.

Officeholding was central. The new nobility rested on its members' ability to win offices and gain priesthoods. In this context, it was above all the magistracies that a man held which marked out his own position in the city as well as that of his family. Indeed, the Latin word *nobilis*, in its most restricted sense, designates an individual with an ancestor who had been chosen consul. By its very nature, this new order was a highly competitive one. More contestants, patricians as well as plebeians, now sought a limited number of positions. In Rome, as in other city-states, offices were in practice open only to the rich, and, more particularly, only to those rich who maintained a respectable way of life—whose wealth, in other words, derived primarily from landholding, and not from trade or from the practice of a "sordid" profession, such as auctioneer or scribe or buying and selling in the market. The position of the new elite families, however, was less secure than that of the patriciate of the past. In each generation, they had to provide new and successful seekers of offices; families that failed to do so could otherwise drop out of the governing elite. Meanwhile, a few men from families that had never held office did succeed in gaining at least lower magistracies; these individuals were termed "new men" (*novi homines*). If their descendants maintained and improved upon this success, they could become new members of the nobility.

The rise of the nobility accompanied, and reinforced, other developments in Roman public life. The emphasis on offices—and especially the office of consul—would result in the gradual creation of a hierarchy of positions, each of which conferred on its holders a successively higher status. In its developed form, these offices, from lowest to highest, would be quaestor, tribune of the plebs, aedile, praetor, and consul. The prohibition against holding the consulship more than once or twice became firmly established in the third century, and enabled two men to hold this office each year who had never done so before. The other offices tended to be held earlier, and since there was a greater number of openings for them, more families were able to compete successfully at this level. Some families in fact gained the lower offices for generations without ever achieving a consulship. The tribunate of the plebs now came to serve not only as an office of value in its own right, but also as a desirable early stage in the career of members of prominent plebeian families. As a result, the tribunate lost much of its radical nature—although it retained the powers for this to return later—and tribunes became part of the established order, as did the Plebeian assembly over which they presided.

It was during the third and second centuries that the senate took on its leading role in the city, and these centuries in many ways marked its high point. This was the period when its "influence" or *auctoritas* peaked, in other words when its direction of affairs won highest respect. The censors began to enroll primarily former officeholders, who in practice would serve for life. At some point in these centuries, tribunes of the plebs gained the right to summon meetings of the senate; they also came to be enrolled in it after holding office. These two developments (which cannot be dated precisely) mark the integration of plebeian officials into the official order of the city. As a gathering of former officeholders, the senate came to be organized internally in the same hierarchical fashion as were the magistracies. Former consuls tended to lead in the senate because they had held the highest office, and those individual senators who were considered to have the most prestige dominated the meetings. Thus, the senate came to be seen as a store of virtues, prestige, and experience.

In this competitive and hierarchical environment, prominent individuals could be very protective and assertive of their claims to status. Members of Rome's elite liked to think that the pursuit of praise or fame (*laus*) and glory (*gloria*) was integral to their way of life. The Roman public virtues were primarily military— indeed, the primary meaning of the Latin noun *virtus* is manly courage—and they were closely linked to the holding of offices. It was above all military success that led to laus and gloria. In the first century B.C. the historian Sallust would even claim (*Catilinarian War* 7.3–6) that competition for gloria was one of the key factors in Roman expansion. The primary source of fame was officeholding, and the higher offices earned a man greater esteem or *dignitas* than the lower. In the late second and first centuries, other forms of elite activity, such as skill in public speaking or in the law, also came to be seen as praiseworthy, but never to the same extent as holding magistracies. Officeholders wished their term of office to stand out in some way. Leading Romans missed no opportunity to proclaim their merits and accomplishments, and often asserted their superiority over the achievements of their competitors. Failure to recognize someone's accomplishments to the degree he expected—to be disrespectful to his dignitas, therefore—could provide a cause for lasting enmity.

Two examples may serve to illustrate the drive. First, in 221 Quintus Caecilius Metellus, who would be consul in 206, gave the funeral oration (*laudatio*) for his father; a summary of it is recorded by Pliny the Elder in the first century A.D. (*Natural History* 7.139–40):

> Quintus Metellus—in the oration in which he gave the highest praise to his father Lucius Metellus, who was *pontifex*, twice consul, dictator, *magister equitum*, member of a board of fifteen men to distribute land, and the one who first led elephants in a triumph during the First Punic War—wrote that his father had accomplished the ten greatest and best feats which wise men seek in their lifetime. He had wished to be the top warrior, the best orator, the bravest commander, to have personally directed the greatest affairs, to have the highest honor, to be the most wise, to be esteemed the most distinguished senator, to acquire immense wealth in a good way, to leave many children, and to be the most celebrated figure in the city. It fell to him to achieve all this, and no one else since Rome's foundation had been his match.

Second, the earliest of the epitaphs in the third-century tomb of the Scipios records that: "this man Lucius Scipio [consul in 259], as most agree, was quite the best of all good men at Rome." Both this epitaph and Metellus' funeral laudatio stress that the deceased had accomplishments that were greatest and best; perhaps even more significantly, both insist that the two men were widely seen as having had them.

The great pressure to assert a man's claims changed not just public life, but also Rome's physical appearance. The third and second centuries saw increasing elaboration of the city's ceremonial and religious life in ways that emphasized the power and glory of the official who staged the rites. Displays of wealth, luxury, and military power were at first limited to officeholders, but other members of wealthy and powerful families would eventually mount them too so as to add to the collective glory of their family (Chapter Five).

Since war was the chief arena in which members of the elite could exhibit their virtue and gain fame and glory, leading citizens craved public recognition of their military accomplishments. The chief celebration of victory was the triumph, a formal procession of a victorious general and his army through the city. The triumph was in fact an old ceremony in Rome. At first, the triumphal procession, which may have originated among the Etruscans, was primarily a rite intended to purify an army returning from battle or to thank the gods for a victory. In the late fourth and third centuries, however, under the influence of the elaborate ceremonies of the Hellenistic kingdoms to the east, the Roman triumph became less a celebration by the community and the army than a glorification of the virtues and achievements of the officeholder who had commanded the army in its victory. In the triumph, the victorious general or *triumphator*, accompanied by senators and other elected officials, led his army through the city together with prisoners, displays of captured property, and tableaux and paintings depicting key episodes in his victory.

The figure of the triumphator stood out clearly, because he wore the gold and purple costume of the old kings, he painted his face to resemble the cult statue of Jupiter Best and Greatest in the temple on the Capitoline Hill, and he rode in a four-horse chariot, just as did representations of the god.

The triumph was the single most important ceremony that any Roman in public life could hope to perform. Eventually a list of triumph-winners, the *fasti triumphales*, would be put on prominent display in the city to mark out their accomplishments for all time. The decision over whether or not a victory warranted a triumph was too important to be left to the commander alone. At some point, the senate asserted its control. In consequence, victorious commanders and their armies waited outside the *pomerium* while the senate debated their accomplishments. Because a triumph was so prestigious, conflicts were common. When the senate denied one to Gaius Papirius Maso, consul in 231, for his efforts on the island of Corsica, he proceeded to stage his own at the Alban Mount, the old cult center of the Latins, without senatorial approval. Other disappointed commanders,

---

SOURCE 3.1: *The triumph of Scipio Africanus at the end of the third century as described by the historian Appian* (Punic Wars 66). *Note that mocking rituals formed a part of the triumph, just as they did of the processions that marked the Roman Games (see Source 2.2).*

Everyone in the procession wore crowns. Trumpeters led the advance, and wagons laden with spoils. Towers were borne along representing the captured cities, and pictures illustrating the campaigns; then gold and silver coin and bullion, and similar captured materials; then came the crowns presented to the general as a reward for his bravery by cities, by allies, or by the army itself. White oxen came next, and after them elephants and the captive Carthaginian and Numidian leaders. Lictors wearing purple tunics preceded the general; also a chorus of harpists and pipers—in imitation of an Etruscan procession—wearing belts and golden crowns, and marching in regular order, keeping step with song and dance. One member of the chorus, in the middle of the procession, wearing a body-length purple cloak as well as gold bracelets and necklace, caused laughter by making various gesticulations, as though he were dancing in triumph over the enemy. Next came a number of incense-bearers, and after them the general himself in a richly decorated chariot.

He wore a crown of gold and precious stones, and was dressed, in traditional fashion, in a purple toga woven with golden stars. He carried a scepter of ivory, and a laurel branch, which is invariably the Roman symbol of victory. Riding in the same chariot with him were boys and girls, and—on the trace-horses either side of him—young men, his own relatives. Then followed the men who had served him on campaign as secretaries, aides, and armor-bearers. After these came the army itself marshalled in squadrons and cohorts, all of them crowned and carrying laurel branches, the bravest of them bearing their military prizes. The men praised some of their officers, and ridiculed or criticized others; during a triumph there are no restrictions, and everybody can say whatever they like. When Scipio arrived at the Capitol the procession came to an end, and he hosted the traditional banquet for his friends in the temple.

too, would come to celebrate triumphs here on their own authority, and although these ones offered less prestige than those which ended at the Capitol in Rome, they likewise were recorded and remembered.

Lesser magistrates also had opportunities for public display. From an early date, the great religious festivals of the Roman state had included games or *ludi*. At first, these comprised a procession, followed by chariot-racing in one of the open spaces, the Circus Maximus or the Circus Flaminius, just outside the pomerium. In the mid-fourth century, occasions for dramatic performances (*ludi scaenici*) were added to these circus games. During the third, second, and first centuries, such festivals would become more and more spectacular, as an increasing number of contests and plays in the Greek style were added to the traditional events. By the second century, if not earlier, the senate budgeted funds to finance the spectacle, but the presiding official was expected to add more of his own so as to increase the display and his own fame. Indeed, the opportunities for self-advertisement were so attractive that more festivals and festival days were steadily added to the public calendar. In addition, prominent Romans could stage games of their own on days not designated for any in the city's official religious calendar. Dedicators of temples, for example, did this to mark their dedications, and from the end of the third century generals also began to do so in order to thank the gods for bringing them victory.

A public figure was particularly concerned to preserve the memory of his accomplishments. By their very nature, victories were ephemeral. Memories of rites would fade, too, and new victors and new victories would always be occurring to obscure the old. Hence, from the last decades of the fourth century, leading Romans sought to enshrine the memory of their accomplishments in prominent monuments; the Latin word *monumenta* (singular, *monumentum*) is actually related to the verb meaning "to remind" or "to instruct." Often, initiatives of this type involved the official religion of the city, which in turn was so closely connected to its political life and to its leading families. When beginning a campaign or preparing for battle, for example, Roman commanders made vows in which they promised new temples, adornments for existing shrines, and elaborate rites to favored deities should they prove successful. As a result, generals would come to build dozens of temples in prominent places both inside the city and immediately outside its walls (see Plate 1b). In addition to statues of the gods and altars for their worship, temples often housed statues of the victor and prominent inscriptions recording his name and the names of the peoples he had defeated. Perhaps to highlight their prowess further, some commanders even introduced new gods especially associated with victory: Bellona Victrix in 296, Jupiter Victor in 295, and Victoria in 294. These novel deities reflect not only Roman preoccupations, but also the similar cult of Victory developing in the Greek world at the same period, especially around Hellenistic kings. By the end of the third century, monuments to past leaders surrounded the places where magistrates performed their tasks, where the senate held its meetings, and where assemblies of citizens gathered to hear debates and to vote.

Advancement of a family's claims to status came to involve remembering and celebrating the specific offices held by its members in earlier generations and their notable achievements in those capacities. Certain types of display were designed simply to encourage family members to imitate or outclass their ancestors. Other types were more public, because the successes of famous ancestors helped advance the claims to office made by their descendants, who supposedly had inherited their virtues. This desire to proclaim the glory of one's ancestors led some aristocrats to stress an additional name, the *cognomen*, which, when added to their *praenomen* and *nomen*, announced their descent from a particular member of their *gens*; thus, the Cornelii Scipiones used the cognomen Scipio to identify themselves as lineal descendants of a common ancestor within the larger gens Cornelia. It seems that some families were not entirely honest in their claims. Livy (8.40.4–5) would later complain that families claimed magistracies and victories for themselves falsely, and, in the process, compounded the historian's difficulties.

Portrait masks of wax, or *imagines* (singular, *imago*), offered another means of proclaiming the greatness of a family's ancestors (Fig. 3.1). Prominent Romans kept masks of those ancestors who had held high offices or performed famous exploits in the *atria* or reception halls of their houses, where they would be visible to visitors and passersby. Funerals provided an especially important occasion for such families to display the imagines of officeholders in their past, and to proclaim their versions of the family history. The more public stages of the funeral began at the house of the deceased, where the body had lain in state. From the house—decked with signs of mourning—a funeral procession with relatives, friends, musicians, dancers, and professional mourners, made its way to the Forum. There, a prominent male member of the family, a son if one was available, delivered a funeral speech or *laudatio* to the assembled citizens, describing the offices that the dead noble had held and the memorable feats he

Figure 3.1 *Because wax is a far from robust material, no imagines of a prominent Roman family's ancestors survive. All the same, the impact made by such commemorative objects is vividly recalled by this marble statue (5.5 ft/1.7 m tall)—the so-called "Togato Barberini"—where a dignified male figure wearing a toga stands proudly holding a bust of one man in his left hand, while resting his right hand on the bust of another man placed atop a column. The two busts seem realistic renderings of individuals rather than idealized ones, and the men portrayed may be family members, possibly of different generations. The statue is difficult to date, but stylistic criteria point to the late first century B.C.; the head seen here of the standing figure is evidently not the original one.*

had accomplished. According to Polybius (6.53.1–54.5), who witnessed these funerals in the middle of the second century, actors riding in chariots actually wore the family's imagines in the procession, with each carrying the symbols of the offices held by the man whose imago he wore. In the Forum, the actors sat on the ivory chairs of officeholders placed around the speaker's platform. Then, after the speaker had finished praising the deceased, he would proceed to list the offices and praise the accomplishments of each of the men whose imagines were displayed around him.

Like other public ceremonies, these funerals became more elaborate over time. From the middle of the third century, combats between pairs of gladiators also formed part of the proceedings. The first known gladiatorial games were staged during the funeral of Decimus Junius Brutus in 264; by the end of the third century, the sons of Marcus Aemilius Lepidus would put on combats with twenty-two pairs of gladiators. In addition, leading families sought to expand the number of public funerals they could stage. At first, these were restricted to office-holders, but families eventually began to stage them for male members who had held no office and for women of the family; both would provide occasions for the display of ancestral virtues. It also became the practice for wives to bring the imagines of *their* ancestors to their husbands' houses, adding to the display.

WARS WITH CARTHAGE

Wars with Carthage—called Punic from the Latin adjective *punicus* or Phoenician—dominate Roman history in the middle and late third century. Carthage was the most powerful of the cities that had emerged from the Phoenician colonization of the ninth through sixth centuries (see Chapter One). Carthage came to control, directly or indirectly, a considerable territory. In North Africa, the Carthaginians and other Punic cities nearby held the richest parts of modern Tunisia. By one means or another, the city of Carthage and members of its elite also exploited subordinate communities of their territory's original population. By the end of the fourth century, the Carthaginians controlled an area almost equivalent to Latium and Campania combined, although they restricted their citizenship much more than did the Romans. Still farther away, Carthage exercised some leadership, if only intermittently, over rulers of various tribes and confederacies; the Numidians, in modern Algeria, were the most important.

Carthage also expanded its power and influence by sea. From the end of the seventh century, the Phoenician settlements of western Sicily, Sardinia, and the Balearic Islands were subordinate to Carthage in some way. By the end of the sixth century, the Carthaginians controlled the coasts of Sardinia, where they established colonies of their own and controlled mines in the interior. In the sixth, fifth, and fourth centuries, Carthaginian armies fought, with varying degrees of success, against the Greek cities of Sicily. Carthage also had contacts, if sometimes distant and indirect, with cities in Italy. As part of their struggles with the Sicilian Greeks and to protect their trade, the Carthaginians concluded treaties with some central Italian communities, including Rome. The first of these Roman-Carthaginian agreements was probably made as early as c. 500, and others followed, although the precise number made thereafter is uncertain.

First Punic War (264–241)

War broke out between the Romans and the Carthaginians as a result of a three-way struggle between Carthage, Rome, and Syracuse over the strategic city of Messana (modern Messina), which controlled the straits between Italy and Sicily. Initially, Carthage and Syracuse vied to gain influence here, while Rome hesitated to intervene. The senate was divided on the issue, but one of the consuls of 264 (in all likelihood Appius Claudius Caudex) successfully proposed to a citizen assembly that Messana be given Roman protection. Claudius was certainly the consul who then set off to Sicily with his army. Hostilities escalated in 263, when Rome sent out both consuls, with a large force of Romans and allies. When it advanced into Syracusan territory, the self-made king of Syracuse, Hiero, negotiated peace terms and became Rome's ally. The consuls of the next year advanced further west into Sicily and besieged the Greek city of Agrigentum (modern Agrigento). Here, despite heavy losses, they drove off a large Carthaginian force, captured the city, plundered it, and sold thousands of the citizens into slavery. Meanwhile the Carthaginians replaced their unsuccessful commander with Hamilcar Barca, who would continue to command the Carthaginian forces on the island for the remainder of this long war.

After the sack of Agrigentum in 262, a period of stalemate ensued. Some cities that had previously defected to the Romans now resumed their alliance with Carthage, while others joined Rome for the first time. Both sides faced extraordinary difficulties. Carthage possessed one of the most powerful war fleets in the Mediterranean, but it depended upon mercenaries to fill out its armies. Because of this strength at sea, Carthaginian forces were able to hold towns on the coast, where reinforcements could easily be landed. Rome, on the other hand, had a large army, though only a small fleet, with its Greek allies providing many of the ships and crews. Roman commanders were able to bring armies across the narrow straits between Sicily and Italy, but the strength of the Carthaginian fleet made it impossible for them to expel Carthaginian forces from Sicily.

The Romans responded by building warships to challenge Carthage at sea. This was not an easy task. Shipbuilding was complex and expensive. Commanding ships and fleets, moreover, was a skilled operation that differed greatly from the leadership of an army, and warships by definition required large numbers of skilled oarsmen to propel them and maneuver them in battle. Here, the Carthaginians, with their long naval tradition and large fleet, had a great advantage, but the Romans were able to adapt remarkably quickly. Copying Carthaginian methods of construction, the Romans began by building about one hundred large warships, and over the course of the war, they would build many more. For sailors and oarsmen, they turned to their allies and also recruited

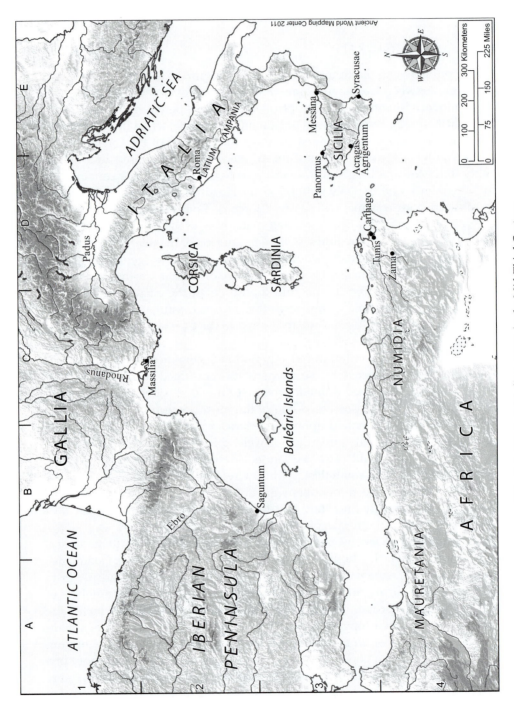

Map 3.1 *Western Mediterranean in the Mid-Third Century*

Roman citizens too poor to serve in the army. Roman fleets soon began to win battles at sea, although they also lost many ships, failures which they often attributed to inclement weather. In a bid to transfer their talent for land warfare to the sea, they invented a boarding device called the "crow" (*corvus*). A Roman ship fitted with it drew alongside an enemy vessel, and a gangplank was let down with a metal spike projecting underneath; with this embedded in the enemy's deck, Roman soldiers then swarmed across to engage them in close combat. Practical limitations discouraged the Romans from persevering with use of the corvus, but its invention reflects their determination and ingenuity, and it certainly succeeded in shocking the Carthaginians. Gaius Duilius, consul in 260 and commander in one of the earliest of Rome's naval victories, celebrated the first triumph gained at sea; as a striking monument to his victory, he set up a column in the Forum decorated with the bronze rams of captured ships.

For a time, Rome and Carthage both won victories and suffered defeats, but neither side could gain a decisive advantage. In 256, both consuls took the further initiative of crossing to North Africa with an army and a fleet, so as to attack Carthage itself in the hope of bringing the war to a quick conclusion. One of these consuls, Marcus Atilius Regulus, duly defeated the Carthaginians in battle, captured the city of Tunis (near Carthage), and provoked a rebellion among some of Carthage's Numidian allies. Early in 255, however, Xanthippus, a Greek mercenary commander in Carthaginian service, defeated and captured Regulus.

Roman writers would later turn this humiliation, so offensive to Roman sensibilities, into a patriotic myth that contrasted the supposed virtues of the consul and the vices of his captors. According to this tale, the Carthaginians allowed Regulus to return to Rome in order to negotiate either a peace or an exchange of prisoners, making him promise to return if his efforts were to prove unsuccessful. When the senate refused to negotiate, Regulus returned to Carthage where he died, exhibiting in the process the good faith (*fides*) that members of Rome's elite thought to be a defining characteristic of their class and their city. Some versions, moreover, would maintain that the Carthaginians tortured Regulus to death—Roman authors thought cruelty to be one of the chief traits of Carthaginians—but this may well have been an attempt to counter reports that Regulus' wife tortured Carthaginian prisoners.

After the failed invasion of North Africa, warfare continued on land and sea for fifteen years. In Sicily, Roman commanders slowly gained the advantage, since the Carthaginians lacked sufficient resources to fight simultaneously against the Romans and against their former Numidian allies in North Africa. In the process, much of Sicily was devastated. In 254, for example, the Romans captured Panormus (modern Palermo), the most important city on the north coast of Sicily; many of its citizens paid a ransom, but those who could not afford the payment set by Rome were enslaved. In 241, the Carthaginians gave Hamilcar, their commander in Sicily, authority to negotiate a peace. The result was that they agreed to leave Sicily and pay Rome a large indemnity.

Hostilities did not end here, however. At the end of the war, the Carthaginians had insufficient funds to pay their mercenaries, who were owed for many years of service. So the large mercenary army assembled in North Africa mounted a revolt, which soon spread to some of Carthage's Libyan and Numidian allies. The whole conflict here led to atrocities by both sides, until 237, when the Carthaginian army finally succeeded in gaining the upper hand. Meantime elsewhere, mercenaries serving Carthage in Sardinia joined the revolt and killed their general. When Carthage dispatched more mercenaries to the island, these too revolted. Eventually, after achieving victory in North Africa, the Carthaginians planned to send another army to Sardinia, but before they could, the mercenary commanders there begged Rome for assistance. Disregarding earlier agreements with Carthage, Roman officials now chose to intervene, threatening war and insisting that Carthage abandon the island and pay a further substantial indemnity. The Carthaginians, exhausted by interminable warfare, agreed.

Although Roman magistrates and senators may not have realized it at this point, it was in fact victory in the First Punic War that led to the creation of Rome's first permanent commitments outside Italy. In the decade following the assertion of Roman claims to Sardinia, nine consuls and at least one praetor campaigned against the inhabitants of the island, as well as against those of the neighboring island, Corsica. Campaigns in the interior of both islands would continue intermittently for a further century. While fighting Carthaginian forces in Sicily, Roman commanders had already granted protection to communities there, and had probably even made arrangements of a more permanent nature with some. Previously, when the Romans had forged alliances and granted protection to communities in Italy, they had made few commitments that required the permanent presence of Roman officials and Roman forces. Now, the senate may at first have intended that friendly cities in Sicily should enjoy the same sort of undemanding relationship. By 227, however, the decision had been made to station a commander and troops permanently in Sicily, Sardinia, and Corsica. In that year, the Centuriate assembly elected four praetors for the first time, with the intention that one of them should regularly be sent to Sicily and another to Sardinia-Corsica. Thus these islands became the first of Rome's "provinces" outside the Italian peninsula (see A Mediterranean Empire below).

The First Punic War, and to a lesser degree the war with Pyrrhus that preceded it, also marked an important new stage in how Rome waged war. The traditional pattern was for consuls and praetors to raise armies each spring and discharge them in the fall after the end of the campaigning season. Consequently, Roman soldiers could be self-supporting, since they always returned home in time to plant their crops and provide for themselves and their families in the following year. In some of the wars of the third century, however, this long-established practice no longer met Roman needs. Although they did still raise armies and fleets for less than a year's service, they also kept armies in the field over the winter and maintained garrisons in distant towns and forts. In part, this modification to traditional

Figure 3.2 *In addition to silver coins—which at first appear to have circulated primarily in southern Italy, where the use of money was long established—the Romans began to cast bronze in the form of ingots or coins; there is little doubt that these circulated more locally, and may have been intended for distribution to soldiers. This bronze ingot, dating between 275 and 242, bears an elephant on one side and a sow on the other; the elephant is probably a reference to the war with Pyrrhus.*

practice may have been a response to the greater distances that Roman armies now had to travel in order to reach their enemies. But Rome had also begun to compete with cities and kings who raised their forces in a different way. In particular, the mercenary armies of Pyrrhus and the Carthaginians typically remained in the area of operations over the winter, and were quite capable of seizing towns and forts during the Romans' absence.

In response to the new forms of warfare, Roman practices underwent some adjustment. Fleets required money for the construction and supply of ships; their crews could not live off the land as an invading army could. Soldiers kept through the winter in garrisons or camps distant from their farms also needed some means of support. Traditionally, Roman commanders had for the most part sought to supply their armies either by living off the land, or by demanding the necessary funds and provisions from allies and subjects in the vicinity. Rome's administrative organization, like that of most city-states, was rudimentary, and its ability to direct a range of activities correspondingly limited; it possessed little in the way of a permanent apparatus. To be sure, from time to time the state needed supplies and labor for religious rituals, for public building projects, and for the army. In these circumstances, however, officials would typically turn to private contractors or *publicani* (singular, *publicanus*) to fulfill needs that a more bureaucratized society would accomplish with state officials. Some publicani were undoubtedly involved in equipping and supplying Roman fleets and armies.

By the middle of the third century, there are clear signs that the Romans were expending public funds on a larger scale than they had in the past. Roman citizens were not subject to regular taxation, but when some exceptional, urgent need arose, a citizen assembly could authorize magistrates to collect a special payment or *tributum*, assessed on the basis of the *census*. It was when ancient communities faced the necessity of making regular payments on a large scale—either for war or for other public projects—that they usually began to mint coins in silver. When the

Romans first made use of such high-value coins, late in the fourth century, they relied on ones produced at irregular intervals by Campanian mints. During the Pyrrhic War, however, they began to mint their own, using Greek weights and designs. Eventually, in the last two decades of the third century, they introduced a complete range of denominations with Roman weights and designs. Rome's traditional style of warfare had not called for substantial sums of money. Now, however, Roman officials and the senate would face a steady need for cash, especially in the largest wars.

Second Punic War (218–201)

The Second Punic War broke out over Spain. Leadership of the Phoenician cities of the Iberian peninsula, together with influence in the interior there, had long been a major prop of Carthaginian power. The Carthaginians used Iberian mercenaries to fight in their wars; Iberian gold, silver, and other metals to pay and equip their soldiers and sailors; and Iberian timber to build their ships. After the end of the First Punic War, they attempted to extend their power in the peninsula and increase their access to its rich resources. In 237, Hamilcar Barca, previously Carthage's general in Sicily, landed in Spain; from then on, he regularly conducted military operations and extended Carthaginian power there until his death in 229. At that point he was succeeded by Hasdrubal, his son-in-law, who governed and campaigned until he too died in 221. After Hasdrubal's death, Hannibal Barca, Hamilcar's own son born in 247, became the chief Carthaginian commander in Spain.

This increase in Carthage's power provided the occasion for a new war with Rome. The diplomatic activity lying behind its outbreak is very obscure, mainly because our sources are pro-Roman and anti-Carthaginian and seek to put Hasdrubal, and especially Hannibal, in the wrong. In 226, the Roman senate—for reasons unclear to us—dispatched an embassy to Hasdrubal, and pressed him to agree to limit Carthaginian power in Spain. The result was a treaty in which the Carthaginians undertook not to send any military force across the Ebro River. A few years later, however, Hannibal attacked the city of Saguntum, south of the Ebro, and the Saguntines appealed to Rome. The senate apparently claimed that Saguntum—despite its location—was in some way dependent upon Rome or had a right to Roman protection; but again there is no knowing when or how this supposed relationship with Rome had developed. In any event, Rome sent no relief force, and Saguntum fell to Hannibal in 219. In the following year, and apparently after some debate, the senate sent an ultimatum to the Carthaginians, demanding that they hand over Hannibal. The Carthaginians refused, and the Roman envoys then declared war.

The senate evidently expected to be able to predict where the war would be fought. It instructed one of the consuls of 218, Publius Cornelius Scipio, to lead his army and fleet to Spain, while the other, Tiberius Sempronius Longus, was to go first to Sicily in order to prepare an invasion of North Africa from there. Hannibal, however, did not wait in Spain for the arrival of Roman forces. Instead, in the spring of 218, he left his headquarters in Spain and surprised Rome by daring to attempt the long march to Italy. Scipio failed in an attempt to stop Hannibal's army from crossing the Rhone River (Latin, Rhodanus) in what is now southern France. After this failure, Scipio sent most of his own men on to Spain under the command of his brother, Gnaeus Cornelius Scipio, while he himself returned to Italy. Later in the year, despite difficulties and much loss of life, Hannibal successfully crossed the Alps into Italy. Here, at the Trebia River, he defeated Tiberius Sempronius Longus (who had rushed north), and virtually destroyed his army in December 218.

Despite these remarkable achievements by Hannibal, however, the Romans still possessed most of the advantages. Rome's fleet far outclassed that of Carthage. For this reason, Rome's leaders had apparently expected to be able to fight the war in Africa and Spain, both of which they could reach by sea. At the same time, Rome's control of the sea meant that Hannibal could only receive limited reinforcements by ship while in Italy. Here, the Romans possessed great reserves of manpower, although they could not mobilize all their potential soldiers at one time. According to Polybius (2.23), several years before the war, the Romans had ordered their allies to compile lists of men eligible for military service. The lists showed that 250,000 Romans and Campanians could be summoned to serve in the infantry and 23,000 in the cavalry, along with 80,000 Latins who could serve on foot and 5,000 potential cavalrymen. Altogether, Samnites and Lucanians, along with Messapians and Iapygians from Apulia, could provide up to 150,000 infantry and 26,000 cavalry, while several small groups in the mountains of central Italy could muster another 20,000 infantry and 4,000 cavalry.

The record as transmitted by Polybius is plainly incomplete—there are no Etruscans, Umbrians, Bruttii, or Greeks here, for example—and it is unclear whether those actually serving in Rome's armies at the time were included in the totals given. Even so, there can be no question that Hannibal had far fewer soldiers. Polybius (3.56) saw a bronze tablet that Hannibal later erected in the south of Italy; his claim here was that he had 12,000 African and 8,000 Iberian infantry, and no more than 6,000 cavalry, when he entered Italy. He may have hoped to win victories that would be sufficiently impressive to encourage the Romans to make peace, or Rome's allies to revolt. If so, he would be only partially successful in achieving such aims.

When Hannibal crossed the Alps, he entered a region disturbed by warfare between Romans and Gauls. In 232, a tribune of the plebs, Gaius Flaminius had proposed and carried a law instructing officials to assign land taken from the Gauls here in small parcels to citizens. One consequence was that the two largest tribes, the Boii and Insubres, became more openly hostile. In 225, they crossed the Apennines into Etruria with a large force of infantry, cavalry, and chariots, and defeated a Roman force. Later in the same year, the two consuls—one of them hurriedly recalled with his army from Sardinia—trapped the Gauls between their

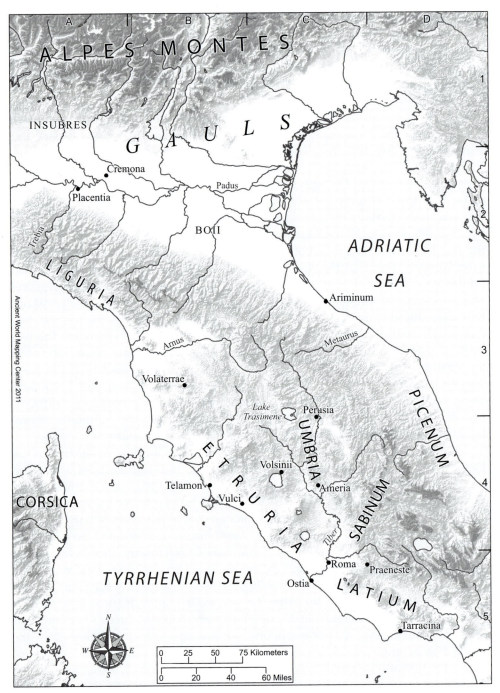

Map 3.2 *Northern Italy*

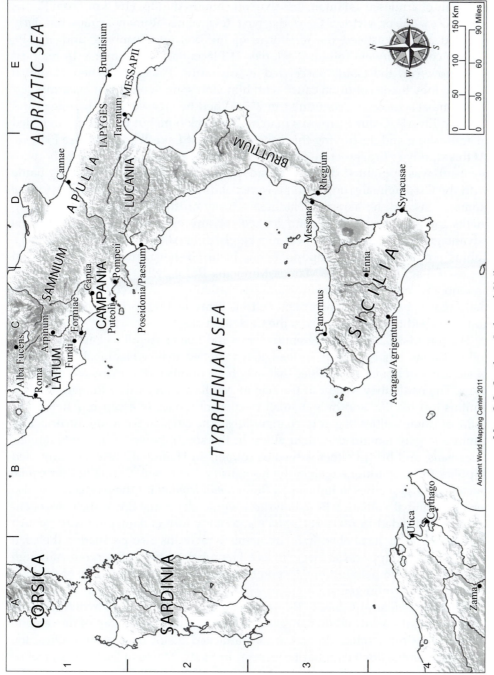

Map 3.3 *Southern Italy and Sicily*

Ancient World Mapping Center 2011

own pair of armies at Telamon, less than one hundred miles (160 km) from Rome, and won a major victory. Over the next few years, Roman armies regularly invaded and devastated the territories of the Boii and Insubres, and, in 219, Roman commissioners founded colonies at Placentia and Cremona. In the next year, however, the Gauls succeeded in capturing Placentia. When Hannibal arrived, they made common cause with him, and some would join his army.

Hannibal's successes continued in 217. When he crossed the Apennines and invaded Etruria, Gaius Flaminius marched to block him, but Hannibal succeeded in ambushing and destroying this consul's army at Lake Trasimene (see Plate 3). At this starkly critical juncture for Rome, Quintus Fabius Maximus, already twice a consul, was appointed dictator. He adopted a firm strategy of avoiding battle with the Carthaginians unless there were conditions especially favorable for the Romans. Instead, he harassed Hannibal's army on the march, attacked detachments foraging for supplies, and looked for any opportunity to exploit some advantage. For this reason, he was mockingly dubbed "the Delayer" (*Cunctator*). Fabius' strategy was most unpopular, and incurred sharp criticism not least from his own magister equitum, Marcus Minucius Rufus, who persuaded a citizen assembly to make him co-dictator, an unprecedented post. According to accounts that favor Fabius, Rufus then deployed his army rashly, and his more cautious colleague had to rescue him from the Carthaginians.

The consuls of 216, Gaius Terentius Varro and Lucius Aemilius Paullus, did not follow Fabius' strategy either. Instead, they marched against Hannibal with a combined army of Romans and allies that may have numbered as many as 80,000 soldiers. The battle they fought at Cannae in Apulia was a further Roman disaster: Paullus lost his life, and only a small fraction of the army escaped. Afterwards, some of Rome's allies began to change sides. The cities in Sabinum, Etruria, and Umbria largely remained Roman allies. In the south, however, many Samnites, Lucanians, and Bruttii either served as soldiers in Hannibal's army, or provided supplies for it, or fought against the Romans on their own. Capua in Campania, one of the largest cities in Italy and a Roman *municipium* for the past century, also joined Hannibal's alliance; Roman writers would claim that it was the mass of citizens who decided to reassert Capua's autonomy in this damaging way, against the wishes of the local elite. In Sicily, some Syracusans also persuaded their fellow citizens to support Carthage. In 212, Hannibal captured Tarentum, although a Roman garrison held out in a fort on the harbor, preventing the use of the only major port he would gain.

After the defeat at Cannae, Roman commanders reverted to avoiding battle with Hannibal's army, while harassing it and limiting its freedom of movement. At the same time, other Roman armies attacked disloyal cities and allies, too many in number for Hannibal to protect. In Sicily, Marcus Claudius Marcellus captured Syracuse in 213. Two years later, Capua fell, and the Roman commander then ordered the executions of the city's leading citizens and sold much of the population into slavery. In 209, the Romans recaptured Tarentum too, sacked it, and enslaved its inhabitants. After this date, Hannibal and his depleted army were more or less confined to Bruttium in the extreme south of Italy.

In the midst of the war in Italy, the magistrates and senate searched for signs of divine disfavor and for ways to bring better fortune to Rome. They took great care to perform the traditional rites flawlessly, while increasing their scale and grandeur. Should this approach fail to appease the gods, they also made elaborate vows which promised unprecedented sacrifices in the event of Roman victory. In 217, for example, the people voted, on the recommendation of the senate and the

SOURCE 3.2: *After offering his readers an extended description and evaluation of the institutions of the Roman Republic, Polybius concludes Book Six of his* History *with an account of this one episode, which he considers a perfect illustration of Rome's extraordinary strength:*

After winning the battle of Cannae [in 216], Hannibal gained control of the 8,000 Romans guarding the camp. He made them all prisoners, and agreed to a deputation being sent home to discuss their ransom and release. Ten very distinguished men were chosen, whom he dispatched after making them swear that they would return to him. One of those chosen said—just after leaving the camp—that he had forgotten something, went back and retrieved it, and then departed again, thinking that by returning in this way he had kept faith and was now released from his oath. On reaching Rome, the delegation begged and pleaded with the senate not to deny the prisoners their release, but to permit each man to be returned to his family on payment of three minas [Greek unit of currency]. Hannibal agreed to this, the delegates claimed, adding that the men for their part deserved release because they had not proven cowards in battle nor done anything that discredited Rome; instead, they had been left behind to guard the camp and, when all the rest perished in the battle, they became the victims of circumstance and fell into the enemy's hands. However, despite the major setbacks which the Romans had suffered on the battlefield, as well as the prospect that they were now losing in effect all their allies, together with the likelihood that Rome itself was in imminent peril, they did not react to what the delegation said by losing their dignity in the face of calamity, nor did they omit to consider all the appropriate concerns. They grasped that Hannibal's object was the desire to gain funds in this way and at the same time to reduce his opponents' ardor for battle by demonstrating that the defeated still had a hope of release. They were so opposed to acting upon any of the delegation's requests that they even discounted sympathy for the men's relatives as well as their potential value to the Roman cause. Rather, they overturned both Hannibal's calculations and the hopes he based on them. They rejected ransom for the captives, and laid down the rule that in battle Rome's soldiers must either win or die, with no other hope of rescue if defeated. So, in the light of this decision, they dismissed the nine of the delegates ready to return willingly in accordance with their oath; the one, however, who had contrived to release himself from it they returned to the enemy in chains. Consequently, Hannibal's satisfaction at having defeated the Romans in battle was surpassed by his dismay at the steady resolve these men displayed in their discussions. (6.58.2–13)

pontiffs, to sacrifice to Jupiter all the pigs, sheep, goats, and cattle born in the following spring, "if the Roman Republic and its people are preserved for the next five years in these wars…." Livy's history of this time is filled with reports of freak storms and uncanny events in which the gods revealed their displeasure. Expiation of these prodigies could change the ritual life of the community. In 212, after a dramatic series of prophecies, the senate and the *decemviri sacris faciundis* decided that games to the god Apollo, *ludi Apollinares,* should be performed; later, these would be repeated annually. In 205, in the wake of consistently distressing prodigies, the senate consulted Roman priests and the Greek oracle at Delphi. Both recommended bringing the Great Mother (Greek, *Megale Meter;* Latin, *Magna Mater*) from her sanctuary in Asia Minor to Rome. So, when the ship conveying her cult image—a black meteorite—and some of her priests arrived the next year, a delegation went down the Tiber from Rome to meet it at Ostia. The day on which the image reached the city itself was later marked by games in honor of the goddess, the *Megalesia.* However, the senate seems not to have realized what her worship entailed—self-castrated priests, ecstatic rites, and wild singing and dancing. In consequence, shocked Roman officials then saw to it that citizens were prevented by law from participating in the more disturbing forms of the cult, and were isolated from the priests. Even so, over time the cult became established, and a temple to Magna Mater was built on the Palatine hill at Rome.

The war in Spain proved decisive. Here, for the most part, the Carthaginians had never gained a firm grip. Their power rested on the Phoenician and Punic colonies along the coasts and in the valley of the Baetis River (modern Guadalquivir), a region of towns and villages where they and their Phoenician predecessors had long been active. In the years before the outbreak of the war, Carthaginian commanders had expanded their influence northward along the narrow plain between the coast and the eastern edge of the great central plateau that makes up much of Spain. This too was a region of towns and villages, but it also held a few coastal cities, Greek or Phoenician in origin, and some Spanish communities, which were in the process of becoming cities. Hasdrubal's foundation of New Carthage (Latin, Carthago Nova; modern Cartagena), where he built a strongly fortified city on a fine harbor, and Hannibal's capture of Saguntum mark two important stages in this advance. Within the region, Carthaginian power rested on some of the coastal cities, garrisons in important places, a large and well-trained field army, and a constantly shifting network of alliances. On the central plateau itself, Carthaginian power was even more limited. Here, communities generally were small, with economies based primarily on herding and only secondarily on the limited cultivation of crops. Settlements possessed no more than rudimentary forms of political organization, and unstable leadership. On this plateau the Carthaginians found mercenaries as well as allies, although typically not dependable ones; at the same time, other communities here were hostile.

In 218, Gnaeus Scipio landed at Emporiae (modern Empúries), a coastal settlement on the far northeast coast of Spain; his brother, Publius Scipio, joined him in

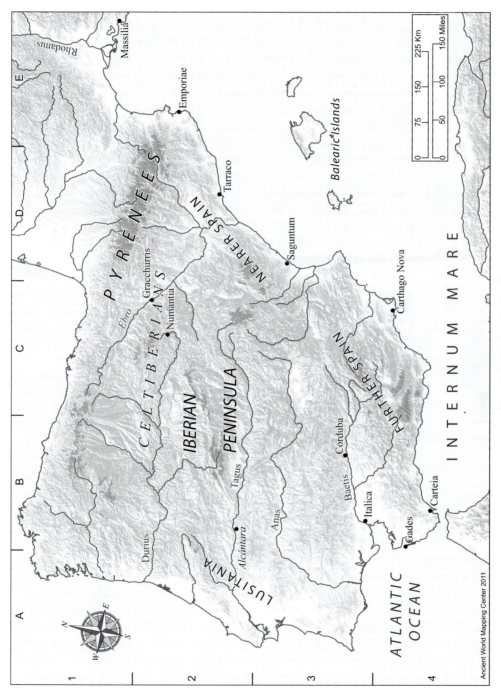

Map 3.4 *Iberian Peninsula*

Ancient World Mapping Center 2011

the following year. Before the beginning of the second war with Carthage, the Greek city of Massilia (modern Marseille, in France) established friendly diplomatic relations with Rome. The Massiliots had founded a series of colonies and trading posts along the coasts; Emporiae was one of the most successful. At the outset, then, Roman armies intervened as enemies of the Carthaginians, but also perhaps as allies and protectors of some small cities in the region. In the first years of the war, Rome's commanders duly secured the safety of Greek communities under their protection, expelled small Carthaginian garrisons from towns near the mouth of the Ebro River, and established control over the lower Ebro Valley and along the coast, perhaps as far south as Saguntum. Amid these campaigns, they made Tarraco (modern Tarragona) their main base of operations; it would become one of the chief centers of Roman power and influence in the peninsula.

The effort to support armies and fleets in Spain soon strained the capacity of the Roman state. In 215, the Scipios reported that they were unable to secure sufficient supplies from Spain itself, and they requested that food, clothing, and provisions for their navies be sent from Italy. Because of the many demands elsewhere, the senate concluded that it was incapable of meeting this request. Instead, it instructed a praetor to seek bids for contracts to supply the Roman commanders in Spain on condition, however, that the contractors would receive payment only when the necessary funds became available. Nineteen such contractors (*publicani*), organized into three companies, made successful bids, although they stipulated that they should be exempted from military service and that the state should insure their ships and cargoes on the way to Spain.

Figure 3.3 *From around 211, the Roman state began to mint silver coins known as denarii with its own original designs and with Latin inscriptions. The* denarius *would long remain the most common silver coin. This early example bears a helmeted image of the goddess Roma on the obverse, and the Dioscuri (Castor and Pollux, twin sons of Jupiter) on the reverse. These designs, too, would long remain standard.*

Gnaeus and Publius Scipio remained as commanders in Spain until their deaths in battle in 211. As early as the following year, Roman voters assigned the Spanish command to another Publius Cornelius Scipio, in fact the son of Publius and the nephew of Gnaeus. His post was atypical, one of the deviations from proper procedure that the pressure of the war permitted. He held no formal magistracy but was sent out instead as a private citizen with the right to command, a *privatus cum imperio*. In 209, he captured Carthago Nova, one of the chief centers of Carthaginian power. In the next year, he succeeded in crossing the mountains between the coast south of Saguntum and the headwaters of the Baetis River. In the latter area—a valley of vital importance to the Carthaginians—the remaining major battles of the war in Spain were fought. However, even though Hasdrubal, Hannibal's brother, was defeated by Scipio, he was then able to follow his brother's route into Italy and attempt to join their two armies. But in 207, at the Metaurus River along the Adriatic coast of Italy, Hasdrubal's army was stopped and beaten, and he lost his own life, thus extinguishing any hope that significant reinforcements might reach Hannibal. By the end of 206, the Romans had overcome virtually all Carthaginian forces in Spain.

As consul in 205, Scipio's task was to prepare for the invasion of North Africa. In the following year he and his army landed outside the city of Utica not far north of Carthage, and with the help of the Numidian ruler Masinissa defeated the Carthaginians in battle. The Carthaginian leaders then summoned Hannibal back to Africa, and he obeyed even though he had to leave his army behind in Italy. The decisive encounter between the Roman and Carthaginian forces occurred in 202 at Zama, where Scipio won another victory. He then returned to Rome for a lavish triumph (see Source 3.1), and added Africanus to his other names, immortalizing his victory for his descendants. Later, stories circulated claiming that Jupiter Optimus Maximus, chief god of the city, held him in special favor.

Peace was concluded in 201. The terms of the treaty severely restricted Carthaginian power and blocked any prospect of its revival. The Carthaginians surrendered their fleet, were burdened with crippling indemnity payments, lost all their territory outside of the core around Carthage and the other Punic cities in northern Tunisia, and were prohibited from waging war outside this territory without Roman permission. Meantime, Masinissa emerged as a staunch Roman ally with control of an enlarged Numidian kingdom.

Altogether, this seventeen-year war had imposed grave strains upon the Roman authorities, its citizens, and the citizens of allied states. Much of Italy was devastated by the continuous campaigning there. For the entire duration, the Romans had to maintain armies in Spain, Sardinia, and Sicily, as well as in Italy. The consequent need for numerous commands disrupted traditional political arrangements, while the many armies and the high casualty rates required an unusually large percentage of the male population to be drafted. Some of the allies proved incapable of providing more soldiers, and to fill the ranks Rome drafted even criminals and slaves. At Cannae, around eighty senators were said to have been killed, in addition to the many thousands of ordinary soldiers who lost their lives there; this depletion of the senate was so substantial that men who had never held office were chosen to make up its numbers. Nonetheless, despite all the setbacks, Rome remained undaunted throughout, and emerged from the war with a dominant position in the central and western Mediterranean that its leaders would exploit in the following decades.

A MEDITERRANEAN EMPIRE

After the Second Punic War, Roman power soon spread through much of the Mediterranean world. At the start of his work the Greek historian Polybius, who witnessed this development personally, described the fifty-three years following the end of the second war with Carthage as a period that was unique in history, since within this short span the Romans succeeded in subjecting "nearly the entire civilized world" to their rule. Once again, no single cause explains all of Rome's wars at this date. In region after region, the governing elite seems to have had no clear plan for expanding Rome's power or for establishing its authority. Instead, they just seem to have made arrangements piecemeal as they responded to the unfolding of events. Moreover, despite the Roman state's need for funds, there appears to have been no desire at first to promote the systematic exploitation of conquered communities' economic resources, although awareness of this type of potential would slowly gain ground.

Governors, Provinces, and Empire

During the Second Punic War and in the decades that followed, Roman armies were stationed in many places, often distant from Rome. Since Roman political and military leadership was closely tied to the tenure of a limited number of annual offices, these far-flung campaigns put great burdens on officeholders. First, the number of armies often exceeded the number of consuls and praetors, Rome's traditional military commanders. Then, some assigned areas of operations were so far from Rome that the time needed to travel there reduced the amount of actual campaigning which could be undertaken during a magistrate's year in office. Last but not least, generals operating in ever more distant theaters gained greater freedom of action, because they were far away from observation by other magistrates and by the senate.

Some of these difficulties were met by increasing the number of high officials. During the closing stages of the First Punic War, Roman assemblies elected not only two consuls but also two praetors annually. After the end of that war, the Romans expelled the Carthaginians from Sicily, Sardinia, and Corsica. Accordingly in 227, Roman voters began to choose two additional praetors to serve as commanders in Sicily and Sardinia respectively, an apparent recognition of the regular need for officials to watch over Roman interests there. After the Second Punic War, the number of praetors was again increased by two to provide leaders for Roman forces in Spain. Within a few years, this arrangement too was modified, and it became the practice to elect four praetors one year, then six the next, alternately. In fact this number of consuls and praetors still did not suffice to provide commanders for all Rome's armies, but nevertheless expansion of the number of officeholders ceased until the first century B.C. Tenure in these offices, after all, was the primary route to fame and glory, and to continue increasing the number of occupants meant diluting their prestige markedly.

To meet the increased demand for commanders, the Romans also resorted to extending the terms of some officials, a procedure known as "prorogation." In the late fourth century and during the First Punic War, a few officials with a limited task to complete had occasionally continued in office for a short time after their magistracies had expired. In their additional period of service, such officeholders were known as *proconsul* or *propraetor*, because each served in place of a consul or a praetor. During the Second Punic War, when the need for commanders was high, the practice became more common, and commands were sometimes extended for a year or more, as with the Scipio brothers' commands in Spain. After the war, prorogation became a regular practice. Prorogued officials had a different legal status from those actually in their year of office, and they had no authority in Rome itself, where they held no magisterial rank. Commands were extended in one of two ways. Sometimes, voting assemblies extended the commands of serving officials, or even assigned provinces to private citizens, where they were to serve as promagistrates; on other occasions, the senate did likewise on its own authority. During and after the Second Punic War, it was most common for the senate to act, although it was a citizen assembly that conferred proconsular *imperium* upon Publius Cornelius Scipio (Africanus) in 210.

More generally in the late third and second centuries, the senate took the lead in the conduct of wars and diplomacy. It received ambassadors from other states and gave them a hearing. From time to time, it chose some of its own members to serve as legates (*legati*; singular, *legatus*) to go on embassies outside of Italy, or to advise a governor who was winding up a major campaign. The senate also took the primary responsibility for assigning duties to officials. Each year, senators decided the tasks that would be divided among the new consuls and praetors. After the election, the new consuls cast lots to determine the consular assignment each would have, while the new praetors shared out their tasks in the same fashion. Alternatively, the new consuls had the right to determine assignments by mutual agreement before lots were cast, a process known as *comparatio*. Romans believed the casting of lots to reflect the will of the gods; this method also avoided contentious debates in the senate as rival magistrates sought to convince their fellow senators to give them the most attractive assignments.

Roman officials abroad often had considerable freedom of action to wage war, make alliances, and set the terms of peace—perhaps greater freedom than many senators found desirable. In practice, most sanctions took the form of judgments on a magistrate's actions after he had returned to Rome and left office. Even so, the senate sometimes refused to accept treaties that a commander had negotiated, leaving his successor to establish new arrangements. On several occasions, senatorial decrees sought to force officials to free defeated enemies who had been improperly enslaved, but efforts to remedy such injustices were seldom wholly successful. The most persistent problem, however, concerned charges of extortion and corruption. In the late third and second centuries, prosecutions for official misconduct, such as cowardice, incompetence, and corruption, served as the primary means of controlling an official's behavior in office (see Chapter Four). This said, such prosecutions could only take place after an official had returned to Rome and laid down his office.

Engagement beyond Italy grew steadily during the second century, but still this extension of Roman power and influence developed very unevenly and with much variation, as officials and senate responded to events. The creation of "provinces" was the main vehicle for Roman expansion. In modern English, a province usually denotes a subdivision of a larger state or country with well-defined borders and a capital of its own; today, a state's creation of a province often involves the formal subordination of the territory and its reorganization according to a definite plan. In time, the Latin term *provincia* would gain this meaning too, but for long it did not denote anything so fixed or definite. In the late third and early second centuries, and probably earlier, the term merely denoted the sphere of operations given to a Roman official, defined by task and location. In theory, colleagues in office all possessed the same powers and functions, but in practice they were usually expected to exercise them separately. Some served at the same place, but had different *provinciae*. Of the two praetors who usually remained in Rome, one, known as the "urban" praetor, was assigned the supervision of lawsuits between citizens, while the other, called the "peregrine" praetor, handled disputes involving noncitizens. Consuls and praetors who were assigned the command of armies as their provincia typically campaigned in different regions, although in large-scale conflicts more than one could be assigned the same region and they then had to share authority somehow.

Provinciae could be short-lived and ill-defined, although their number at any one time could never exceed the total of available consuls, praetors, and promagistrates. In some cases, officials were assigned provinciae that remained in existence only for a single project, campaign, or war. In others, provinciae remained in existence for some time, receiving new officials as soon as the previous ones left office. A consul's or praetor's provincia was primarily military in character. Equally, a governor's actions were largely shaped by his need to command his and his allies' army against Rome's enemies, to protect friendly cities from attack, and to obtain the money and supplies needed to support his forces. Gradually, in the longer-lasting provinces, governors took on other tasks, such as arbitrating disputes between cities, hearing legal cases, and supervising financial arrangements.

The Roman elite did not believe its leadership to be restricted to the regions—more or less well-defined—where Rome happened to be maintaining provinciae. Whenever a community surrendered or put itself under Rome's protection, magistrates and senate thought that it thereby became part of the *imperium* of the Roman people (*imperium populi Romani*). Although this word is the root of the English "empire," the Latin term does not denote a clearly delimited territory, nor does it imply any administrative responsibilities by the victors or prescribed duties by the defeated. As was the case with the imperium of magistrates, the Roman leadership considered that it had the right to command the defeated and to be respected by them, even though it did not necessarily make such demands very often.

At the beginning of the second century, the Roman state lacked the institutions or the administrative apparatus needed to exploit thoroughly the regions that were in some way its dependencies. Outside of Italy, the Romans slowly adopted different practices as they began to develop more financial sophistication in government. To gain necessary supplies and funds, governors would now impose payments of tribute on some communities and individuals, and require the contribution of supplies by others; any funds or items demanded had to be gathered together by the communities themselves. Meantime, certain especially favored cities and persons would be freed from all but the most extraordinary demands.

In addition, state contractors or *publicani* were active outside of Italy, although the extent of their operations is unclear. As we saw above, during the Second Punic War publicani in Rome contracted to supply the forces in Spain with food, clothing, and equipment; almost half a century later, others would contract to provide clothing and horses to Roman forces in Greece. Arrangements such as these may not have been the norm, however. On other occasions, the senate instructed governors of provinces such as Sicily to purchase grain locally and arrange for its shipment to the combat zone. Yet there were areas in which the use of publicani did expand, although it remains uncertain whether these individuals were Romans, citizens of other Italian communities, or residents of the provinces. From at least the 170s, Roman magistrates, acting on decrees of the senate, leased the exploitation of certain lands and resources. Toward the end of the second century, officials in Rome would also arrange contracts for the collection of taxes and rents from entire provinces and cities; this was to become the most prominent and controversial function of publicani in the first century.

Spain

To judge from its actions, the senate seems to have had no well-defined notion of how to proceed in Spain following the end of the Second Punic War. Some senators may have wished to disengage, but Rome had become too entangled in the affairs of the peninsula to leave easily. Other senators were evidently eager to punish communities that they thought had betrayed Rome or had proven to be especially bitter enemies; Roman commanders did in fact take such punitive action over several years. Roman officials also had allies and interests to protect, and these allies often attempted to persuade Rome to intervene in struggles with their neighbors. Toward the end of his time in Spain, Scipio Africanus had settled some of his wounded veterans at Italica—not far from modern Seville in the lower valley of the Baetis River—probably to protect his forces against any return by the Carthaginians. This town would become a major center of Roman power. From the start, it was a mixed settlement with firm local roots; the Roman and Italian veterans who formed the core of its population would have sought wives locally. The decision in 198 to choose two more praetors each year may well amount to an acknowledgment by the senate that Rome's involvement in the peninsula was to be long-lasting.

The nature of a command in Spain during the early second century can be appreciated from the campaigns of 195 and 194, one of the few instances at this date when Nearer Spain received a consul as governor. Accounts are especially detailed, and they probably derive in large part from the writings of the commander himself, Marcus Porcius Cato the Elder, who was lavish with self-praise. Once arrived in Spain, he first assisted the citizens of Greek Emporiae (Rome's main port of entry into the peninsula), who were so frightened of their Iberian neighbors that they forbade Iberians to come inside their city walls and refused to leave the town at night except in large groups. At the same time, Cato sought to supply his troops as well as train them by seizing crops and plundering the countryside, thereby in all likelihood only worsening much of the tension around Emporiae. Later in his term of office, Cato campaigned in the lower Ebro Valley and farther south along the coast. In the course of these wars, he plundered freely, ignored arrangements made by earlier commanders, and claimed to have firmly settled the affairs of his province. The amount of captured treasure he displayed in his subsequent triumph and the size of the "donatives"—a commander's distributions of money to his soldiers at the end of a campaign—together testify to his success in plundering, but later events confirm that Nearer Spain was far from settled; succeeding governors would continue campaigning in the same areas for several decades.

For almost forty years, Spain received praetors as commanders. The senate usually assigned two provinciae: Nearer Spain (*Hispania Citerior*), centered on Tarraco, the Massiliote colonies, and the lower Ebro Valley; and Further Spain (*Hispania Ulterior*), the valley of the Baetis River. Both governors conducted small-scale campaigns with relatively limited forces, at first near the centers of their power and later at some distance, fighting against groups and confederations on the peninsula's central plateau. Away from the coast and the Baetis Valley, Roman commanders found it difficult to establish control over the scattered population, or to form any lasting ties of alliance and subordination. Some attempted to establish settled communities, which might prove easier to control. Thus Tiberius Sempronius Gracchus, governor of Nearer Spain in 180 and 179, created a number of new towns, one of which he named Gracchurris after himself.

From the middle of the 150s, warfare became more serious and larger in scale, and the senate often assigned provinciae to consuls. These wars centered on two groups, the Lusitanians and the Celtiberians; later, the historian Florus (1.33) would claim that these two were so troublesome because they were the only ones with competent leaders. The Lusitanians inhabited the region to the northwest of the Baetis Valley and to the southwest of the central plateau crossed by the Tagus and Anas rivers (modern Tejo and Guadiana). According to Roman historians, Lusitanian raiders ravaged the fields of Rome's subjects, and in 155 they even defeated the armies of two praetors. In 150, Servius Sulpicius Galba, commanding in Further Spain, invaded Lusitania and persuaded some Lusitanians to surrender, but he then massacred thousands and sold the survivors as slaves. This Roman treachery helped Viriathus (who had escaped the massacre) to emerge as a powerful leader and to assemble a following among both his fellow Lusitanians and other disaffected groups in Spain. He waged war with marked success, defeating several Roman armies. Eventually in 139, Quintus Servilius Caepio, having failed to defeat him in battle, arranged for his assassination. The inspiring memory of Viriathus' heroic resistance to Rome remained strong among the Lusitanians. Now, however, Decimus Junius Brutus, consul in 138, was able to make peace, giving Viriathus' surviving followers land to cultivate. Brutus then began to campaign even further toward the northwest of the peninsula.

At about the same time, the Romans also entered into a lengthy series of wars with the Celtiberians. Their settlement at Numantia occupied a strong position on a high ridge in the upper reaches of the valley of the Durius River (modern Douro). In the 150s, 140s, and 130s, no less than five Roman consuls commanding in Nearer Spain made unsuccessful attacks on it, and two of them—Quintus Pompeius in 141 and Gaius Hostilius Mancinus in 137—had to negotiate peace terms, which the senate later rejected, in order to secure the safe withdrawal of their armies. Publius Cornelius Scipio Aemilianus, the victor over Carthage in the Third Punic War (see North Africa section) and chosen consul for the second time for 134, finally put an end to this war. After an eight-month siege, the Numantines—reported as numbering 4,000—surrendered to Scipio in 133. Traces still survive of the wall he constructed to surround the town, and of the seven camps he built for his soldiers; the remains of six other camps testify to earlier, failed attempts on the town (Fig. 3.4).

Through all these wars, Roman arrangements in Spain were becoming more settled and more profitable to the Roman state. Parts of Spain became the home of Romans and Italians, not to mention others who claimed Roman or Italian ancestry. In 171, the senate ordered a Roman commander to settle the children of Roman soldiers and Spanish women—under Roman law, the children of such marriages would not have been Roman citizens—at Carteia on the south coast, where they were to form a new community with the same rights that Latin colonies possessed in Italy. Either early in the 160s or in 152 (he served in Spain twice), Marcus Claudius Marcellus founded Corduba (modern Córdoba), another mixed settlement like Italica, further up the Baetis River. There can be no question that during the same period some Roman citizens and Italian allies migrated to Spain privately in search of opportunities and profit, although few traces of such individuals happen to survive in our sources.

In the decades immediately following the end of the Second Punic War, Roman financial arrangements in Spain were for the most part simple. Commanders raised money to pay their troops, and food to feed them, through plunder and forced contributions. Each commander, moreover, seems to have made his own arrangements, disregarding any pattern established by his predecessors whenever a change was felt to be convenient or necessary. However, the command of Tiberius Sempronius Gracchus in Nearer Spain in 180 and 179 marks a turning point. During his time in the province, he tried to specify more clearly the obligations of some of the allied communities under his authority, and to regularize their financial contributions. By

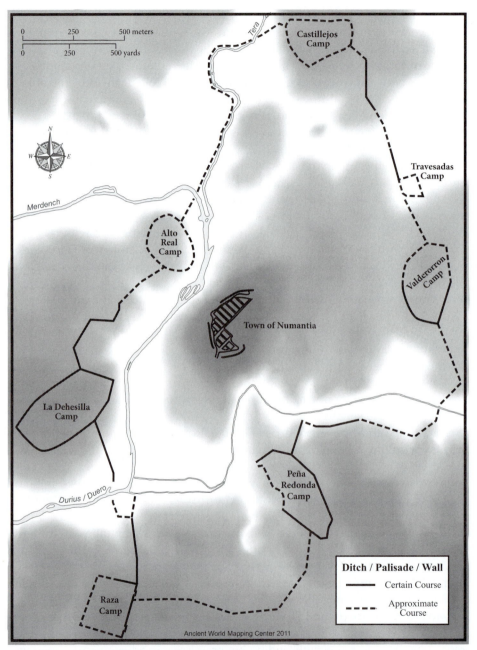

Figure 3.4 *According to the historian Appian (Iberian Wars 90-91), Scipio Aemilianus encircled Numantia with seven forts. He linked them by a ditch and a palisade more than forty-eight stades (6 miles/9.6 km) long; behind these works he constructed a stone wall with towers every 100 feet (30 m). Last but not least, he blocked the river with tree trunks. By these means, he closely surrounded the city and cut it off from its countryside. Substantial traces of the forts on their hilltops and of the wall are still visible. Scipio's own headquarters was probably at the northernmost fort, know as Castillejos.*

midcentury, some communities in both provinces provided 5 percent of their grain each year, while others paid a fixed sum of money. Even so, there was no single system that regulated all of Rome's Spanish subjects.

Over time, the Romans also began to exploit Spain's mineral resources more systematically. In 195, Cato the Elder in some way arranged for the operators of certain mines north of the Ebro River to make regular contributions of iron and silver. The deposits of ore here were limited in fact, and the collection of this tax in metals need not have been very complicated, let alone notably profitable. Later operations were on a larger scale, however. Mines on the fringes of the Baetis Valley and in the hills behind Carthago Nova certainly proved more lucrative. Polybius (34.9.8) described the latter mines as extending over an area of about one hundred square miles (260 sq km), where 40,000 miners working in the pits recovered enough silver each day to provide the Roman state with as much as 10,800 pounds (4,900 kg) of ore annually. Diodorus Siculus (5.36–38) claimed that Italians exploited these mines, using a vast workforce of slaves who toiled day and night under horrific conditions and frequently died from exhaustion.

Greece and Asia Minor

After the end of the Second Punic War, the Romans also began to intervene more regularly in the politics and diplomacy of the Balkans and Asia Minor. Polybius (1.3.6) maintained that, after their defeat of Carthage in 201, the Romans reached out to grab Greece and Asia. But the truth was undoubtedly far more complex than a simple scheme of Roman aggression.

The eastern Mediterranean was a bewildering mix of kingdoms, tribal states, city-states, and leagues of city-states, all with shifting alliances and enmities. Three kingdoms tended to dominate. First, the kings of Macedon had long sought to extend their power over the Greek cities of the south, the islands of the Aegean, and neighboring kingdoms in the Balkans. Second, the Seleucids of Syria had once ruled an extensive state that reached from the Mediterranean to the frontiers of India, but by now much of it had fallen away from their rule. Third, the Ptolemies of Egypt fought Syria for control over Palestine; with their powerful fleet, they also dominated and protected some of the islands in the Aegean, and they often intervened in the affairs of cities on the Greek mainland. Around these three great monarchies, there were many lesser states, sometimes allied with larger ones and commonly on the lookout to pursue their own advantage. Unlike in Spain, the Romans would employ elaborate diplomatic and administrative protocol to confront these well-established and powerful states to the east; consequently this gave Roman intervention here a very different character.

Roman forces first crossed the Adriatic Sea before the Second Punic War. In 229, both consuls campaigned against an Illyrian ruler whose ships had attacked vessels belonging to Italian merchants who were citizens of communities under Roman protection. In this brief war, the consuls helped the Greek cities of Corcyra,

Apollonia, and Epidamnus to expel their Illyrian garrisons, and they then placed these communities under Roman protection. Almost a decade later, the consuls of 219 received as their shared *provincia* a war against another Illyrian ruler seeking to expand his power southwards.

Roman actions in Illyria and Epirus came to involve another, more powerful ruler. The First Macedonian War (215–205) grew out of the Second Punic War. After Rome's defeat at Cannae in 216, Philip V, the Macedonian king, probably suspicious of Roman interventions across the Adriatic, began to negotiate with Hannibal. Discovery of their alliance led to war between Rome and Macedon. The senate sent a praetor with ships and soldiers, and, after several years of campaigning, he began to assemble a coalition of cities, leagues, and kings that felt threatened by Macedon. The two most important were the Aetolian League—communities in western Greece that elected leaders, made war as a group, and were feared as pillagers—and Pergamum in western Asia Minor, a long-time enemy and rival of Macedon, ruled by King Attalus I. This coalition of allies did not make war according to a common strategy, nor did the Romans, with so many commitments elsewhere, pursue the war vigorously. Attalus disengaged in 208, and the Aetolians made peace with Philip in 206. In the next year, Philip and the Romans made peace, the so-called Peace of Phoenice, in which both sides essentially kept what they held.

The Second Macedonian War (200–196) marked the beginning of the next stage of Roman intervention. Immediately after the end of the war with Carthage, Rome's former ally Attalus of Pergamum, together with some Greek cities, successfully urged intervention in Greece, a plea that must have gained strength from resentment among the Roman elite over Philip's earlier alliance with Hannibal. The first Roman commanders campaigned in the west, shielding allies and trying to force the passes over the mountains into Macedon itself. Titus Quinctius Flamininus, consul in 198 and proconsul for several years after, reached the plain of Thessaly, and—with the assistance of his Greek allies—was able to defeat Philip's army at Cynoscephalae in 197. In the peace that followed, Philip agreed to withdraw his garrisons from Greek cities, surrender most of his fleet, and pay Rome a large indemnity. Shortly afterwards, therefore, the senate ceased assigning *provinciae* in this area.

Rome's actions here stand in stark contrast to its behavior in Spain. To judge by actions alone, the Roman senate could be thought to have had no desire for a permanent military presence in the region. It would be mistaken, however, to infer that consequently Rome's leaders did not regard themselves as preeminent here. After his victory, Flamininus proclaimed the freedom of a number of Greek cities at the Isthmian Games, where thousands had gathered for the festival. Proclamations of freedom had a long and honored place in Hellenistic diplomacy, and Flamininus' decree shows how Romans adapted themselves to local practices while maintaining their own leadership. Kings typically issued proclamations of freedom to win over allies, and to weaken rivals by encouraging their subject-cities to defect. Such "freedom" usually meant no foreign garrisons, no

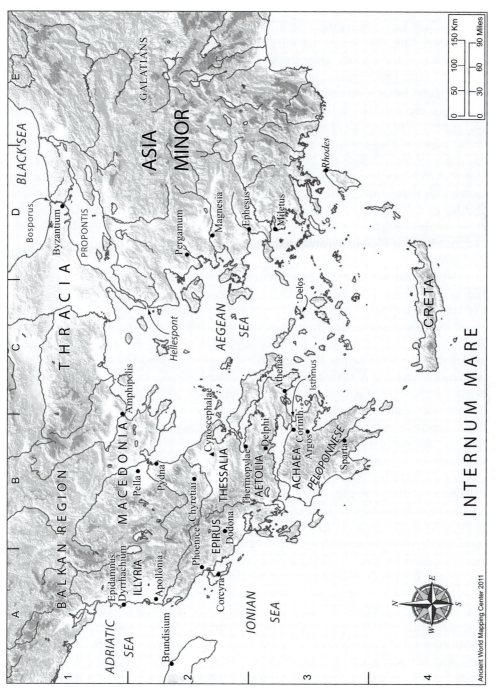

Map 3.5 *Greece, the Aegean, and Western Asia Minor*

Ancient World Mapping Center 2011

tribute, and no change to existing laws; however, it did not mean that the newly freed city could also omit to acknowledge the leadership of a larger and more powerful state.

Subsequent events would reveal how seriously the senate took its claims to leadership. The first major military intervention following the Second Macedonian War came shortly after the withdrawal of Roman armies. Antiochus III, king of Syria, had restored much of the grandeur and power of the Seleucid dynasty, and, after a seven-year campaign into eastern Iran, he was regarded by some as a second Alexander. While Rome was engaged with Philip V, Antiochus had extended his power in Asia Minor, largely surrounding the small kingdom of Pergamum; he had even recovered part of Thrace, which had once belonged to his predecessors. Before the beginning of the Syrian War (192–189), he had frequent exchanges of embassies with the Romans, as well as with a number of Greek cities and rulers; there were also such exchanges among the Greek cities and leagues themselves. In all this diplomacy, Antiochus achieved some success, most notably an alliance with the Aetolians, former allies of Rome, who felt they had not been sufficiently rewarded for their participation in the Second Macedonian War.

Hostilities began in 192, when Antiochus sent a small force across the Aegean Sea to Greece, where it joined with the armies of some allied states. Early in 191, the consul Manius Acilius Glabrio crossed with his army from Brundisium to Apollonia, marched across the mountains into Thessaly, and defeated Antiochus and his allies at Thermopylae. In the next year, the senate sent a commander with an army and a fleet across the Aegean, where they joined forces with Eumenes, who had succeeded Attalus as king of Pergamum. Finally in 189, Lucius Cornelius Scipio, the brother of Africanus, defeated Antiochus' army at Magnesia. Antiochus had to abandon all his claims to Asia Minor, refrain from making alliances in Greece and around the Aegean, surrender most of his ships and his war elephants, and pay an exceptionally large indemnity. In Asia Minor, Roman officials and legates then divided Antiochus' territory among Eumenes and other allies.

Gnaeus Manlius Vulso followed this victory with a campaign against the Galatians, Gallic migrants who had entered Asia Minor in the previous century and had for decades posed a threat to the kings of Pergamum as well as to settled communities throughout the region. Vulso's campaign was highly successful, devastating many of the communities of the Galatians and forcing them to accept peace on Roman terms. Within a few years, the senate again assigned no more provinciae in Greece, the Balkans, and Asia Minor for some time.

A primary goal in these wars was stability in Greece together with preservation of Rome's position in the Greek world. Roman forces returned to Greece because Antiochus III appeared to be challenging Rome's leadership there, and because some of Rome's allies seemed to be willing to join him. Such a desire to lead, but not necessarily to rule or to exploit systematically, evidently lay behind other Roman actions in the area. At first, it would seem, the senate attempted to assert Roman preeminence largely through diplomatic means. The Greek world possessed a complicated political and diplomatic culture. Here, rulers and cities both formed and broke alliances as needs and opportunities arose, the weaker sought protection from the stronger, and the parties to a dispute (be it domestic or foreign) sought arbitration by outside powers. For the powerful, alliances, calls for protection, and requests for arbitration were signs of their strength and their benevolence. For the less powerful, they were means to gain benefits that were otherwise unattainable, in exchange for giving public thanks and acknowledging dependent status.

Rome's elite adapted to these practices. The senate itself received foreign embassies and, when possible, granted their requests. Senatorial legates arbitrated boundary disputes, decided which cities should be free and self-governing and which should be subject to another, forced kings to give up garrisons, and sometimes merely observed. We have evidence of some Greek cities thanking prominent Romans for their benefactions in the proper way. Chyretiai, for example, honored Flamininus for returning property that the Romans had seized during the war against Philip V by erecting a monument on which his letter granting the city's requests was inscribed. In the letter, Flamininus used appropriate language for a benefactor, claiming that he wished the citizens to "learn of our nobility of character," and announcing that the Romans did not wish "to be avaricious, but instead thought good will and a good reputation to be of the highest importance." In their interventions, the senate and its legates tended to act most willingly and firmly against those who resisted giving due recognition to their leadership, or who seemed likely to disrupt it, or even to contemplate supplanting it.

The Third Macedonian War (171–168) ended the Macedonian monarchy. For years, prominent Romans had distrusted Philip's son and successor, Perseus, and were willing to listen to complaints against him. Perseus' marriage to a daughter of Seleucus IV, Antiochus' successor as king of Syria, no doubt increased their suspicions. In 172, Eumenes of Pergamum came to Rome with a long list of complaints against Perseus, and, with these as pretexts, the senate decided on war. The result was that in 168 Lucius Aemilius Paullus defeated Perseus at Pydna, where he had concentrated his army. The terms of the peace were severe. Perseus was transported to Rome, where he was paraded in Paullus' triumph; later, he was imprisoned in the Latin colony of Alba Fucens. Macedon was divided into four regions each with its own assembly and elected officials. The king's lands and mines became the property of the Roman state and, within a few years, contractors had doubtless begun to exploit them. Some Greek cities faced substantial penalties for real or imagined offenses. Hundreds of Aetolians were put to death for anti-Roman activities, and the Achaean League had to send 1,000 men from leading families to Rome as hostages; the historian Polybius was one.

While reorganizing Macedon and imposing terms on Greek communities, Paullus also marked his victory by a ceremonial demonstration of Roman power. At Amphipolis in 167 he put on a grandiose and expensive festival thanking

Rome's gods for his victory. Not to be outdone, Antiochus IV of Syria chose to stage a festival of his own in the very next year, 166. Just after the victory at Pydna in 168, a Roman embassy led by Gaius Popillius Laenas had forced Antiochus to end his invasion of Egypt under threat of war (Source 3.3). Following this rebuff and probably seeking to restore his prestige, Antiochus invited cities and kings to come to Antioch for a festival thanking Apollo for his victories; he thus rivaled Paullus, and some even judged the quality of his performances to be higher. Antiochus followed his festival with more military campaigns in regions far from the Romans.

Roman expansion created opportunities in many areas for Italian businessmen or *negotiatores* (singular, *negotiator*), individuals who were at once speculators, merchants, and financiers. In the second century, such negotiatores make their appearance in many regions of the Mediterranean, and especially in the east where the potential for profit was so high. The names of negotiatores—preserved

---

SOURCE 3.3 *A memorable act of diplomatic bravado in 168 by the Roman senate's envoy Gaius Popillius Laenas sufficed to forestall an invasion of Egypt (under the rule of King Ptolemy VI) launched by King Antiochus IV of Syria. Strictly speaking, Rome had no right to intervene here, but by this date the senate had become concerned with relations between the states of the entire eastern Mediterranean and the balance of power there. In the aftermath of Rome's shocking defeat of King Perseus of Macedon at Pydna earlier the same year, Antiochus could only acknowledge that it would be suicidal for him to persist with his invasion of Egypt against the senate's wishes. More generally, it is no wonder that Polybius came to be so awestruck by the rapid growth of Roman power in the fifty-three years following the end of the Second Punic War. Polybius narrates:*

Just as Antiochus was approaching Ptolemy in order to gain possession of Pelusium [entry-point to Egypt at the eastern end of the Nile delta], the Roman commander Popillius—being hailed with a greeting by the king, who held out his hand—had the document containing the senate's decree ready and so passed it to him, directing Antiochus to read it first. I imagine Popillius thought it inappropriate to make the usual gesture of friendship before establishing whether the recipient regarded him as friend or foe. The king, having read the decree, said that he would like to communicate the circumstances to his advisers. Popillius' reaction was to do something that seemed severe and utterly outrageous. Taking a stick of vine-wood that he had in his hand, he used it to draw a line around Antiochus and instructed him to give his reply to the document from within this circle. The king was amazed at such assertion of authority by this means, but after brief hesitation declared that he would comply with all the Romans' demands. With handshakes Popillius' entire entourage then greeted him warmly. The document ordered him to abandon his war against Ptolemy at once. So, within the period that he was permitted, he led his forces back to Syria, aggrieved and protesting, but for the time being submitting to the situation. (29.27.1–9)

on inscriptions they left in the cities of Greece and Asia Minor—show that they came from many regions of Italy, but that residents of Campania, where commerce had long been important, were especially numerous.

The small island of Delos became one of the great commercial centers of the Aegean, and the chief place of business for many Italian *negotiatores*. At the end of the Third Macedonian War, Roman officials punished the city of Rhodes by removing Delos—sacred to the god Apollo and the site of an important sanctuary—from its control and transferring it to Athens. Merchants and bankers began to concentrate on the island, and their number increased sharply after a Roman army destroyed the wealthy commercial city of Corinth in 146; the island's annual festival to Apollo became one of the chief occasions for merchants to meet in the Aegean world. On Delos, wealthy individuals financed the construction of temples, places of assembly, and luxurious private dwellings. The activities of Italians here were varied. Inscriptions record the presence of bankers, oil and wine merchants, and shipowners. Later in the century, the merchants of Delos took a pivotal role in the trans-shipment of slaves—captured by pirates, often with the connivance of kings—from the eastern Mediterranean to Italy.

Roman armies intervened again less than twenty years after the end of the Third Macedonian war. In 149, Andriscus, who claimed to be a son of Perseus, declared himself king of Macedon. In the next year, Quintus Caecilius Metellus (later known as Macedonicus) defeated the self-proclaimed monarch and ended his reign. From this time onwards, the senate regularly assigned Macedon as a *provincia*. Roman commanders there spent much of their time guarding against incursions made by Balkan peoples to the north; these were wars that Rome now inherited from Macedonian monarchs. By contrast, the Roman commanders in Macedon probably did not intervene much in the affairs of the Greek cities to their south and east. In 148, however, the Roman senate did assert itself against the Achaean League to the south, sending legates to order it to give independence to some cities under its control. When the Achaeans refused to comply, war began. In 146, Lucius Mummius defeated the League's army and captured Corinth, one of the richest and most famous cities in Greece. As a dire warning to other Greeks, he then plundered and destroyed it, and sold many of its citizens into slavery.

North Africa

To the west, Roman armies and fleets were waging war against Carthage at the same time. The Third Punic War (149–146) began as a result of longstanding quarrels between the Carthaginians and Masinissa, king of the Numidians (as noted earlier in the chapter). For years, Masinissa had been making provocative demands of the Carthaginians, and in the resulting arbitrations, Roman ambassadors had generally supported the Numidian king. For equally long, too, some leading Romans had not hesitated to voice the enmity and suspicion they felt towards Carthage. In particular, according to one tradition, for several years before Rome finally declared war, Cato the Elder ended every speech he made in the senate with the demand that Carthage must be destroyed. Eventually, the exasperated Carthaginians used force to resist Numidian claims, and the senate made this step the cause for war. When a Roman army and fleet arrived in 149, however, the Carthaginians immediately surrendered in the apparent hope that they would receive acceptable terms. At first, the Roman commander demanded hostages, and then, when the Carthaginians complied, the surrender of all Carthaginian arms. When these too were handed over, the Carthaginians were next told to abandon their city and live elsewhere. At this point, they finally acknowledged that there was no viable option but to resist.

For over two years, Roman forces besieged the city. It was not until early in 146 that, under the leadership of Scipio Aemilianus (grandson through adoption of Scipio Africanus), they were able to force their way inside. In days of street fighting, they killed thousands of Carthaginians, enslaved many thousands more, and completely destroyed the city. Afterwards, Scipio and his senatorial advisors imposed heavy penalties on the Punic cities that had remained loyal to Carthage, while rewarding those that had changed sides. From now onwards too, the senate regularly assigned Carthage's former territory here as a provincia called "Africa." This destruction of Corinth and Carthage during the same year marked the end of an era in Roman expansion; Roman historians later would believe that both events also signaled the beginning of Rome's moral decline.

SUGGESTED READINGS

Eckstein, Arthur M. 2006. *Mediterranean Anarchy, Interstate War, and the Rise of Rome.* Berkeley, Los Angeles, London: University of California Press.

Flower, Harriet. 1996. *Ancestor Masks and Aristocratic Power in Roman Culture.* Oxford: Oxford University Press.

Goldsworthy, Adrian K. 2000. *The Punic Wars.* London: Cassell.

Gruen, Erich S. 1984. *The Hellenistic World and the Coming of Rome.* Berkeley, Los Angeles, London: University of California Press.

Gruen, Erich S. 1992. *Culture and National Identity in Republican Rome.* Ithaca, New York: Cornell University Press.

Harris, William V. 1979. *War and Imperialism in Republican Rome, 327–70 B.C.* Oxford: Oxford University Press.

Hoyos, Dexter (ed.). 2011. *A Companion to the Punic Wars.* Malden, Mass.: Wiley-Blackwell.

Richardson, J. S. 1986. *Hispaniae: Spain and the Development of Roman Imperialism, 218–82 B.C.* Cambridge: Cambridge University Press.

ITALY AND EMPIRE

After the Second Punic War, Roman power spread throughout much of the Mediterranean world. This expansion was accompanied by major changes in the social, political, and cultural life of Rome and many other Italian communities as a result of the burdens of military service, the great wealth acquired through conquest, the consequent movements of people, and the deeper exposure to foreign ideas and practices. The first half of the second century marked the high point of the domination of the state by the senate and the nobility. Thereafter, in the third quarter of the century, a steady accumulation of political tensions and divisions would lead to the emergence of new forms of political activity that would undermine the senate's leadership.

SENATORS, OFFICIALS, AND CITIZEN ASSEMBLIES

During this heyday of power and prestige for the senate and nobility, it was the norm for members of a relatively few families to hold the offices of consul and censor. At the same time, the consensus of senators, expressed in the form of decrees, exercised a strong influence over policy making. In the second century, the 300 senators were chosen from former officeholders, and each senator, once chosen, served for life unless he was convicted in court, or unless a subsequent pair of censors dropped him from the senatorial roll for some moral failing. When an officeholder consulted the senate, senators registered their opinion in the form of an advisory decree or *senatus consultum*, rather than an order, since the formal role of the senate was to advise. Senatorial decrees were not determined by a strict majority vote. Instead, leading senators or *principes* (singular, *princeps*)—the members who generally had held the highest offices, belonged to the leading families, and had acquired the greatest fame and glory—sought to create a broad consensus for or against policies and individuals.

Since the late fourth century, the senate had taken for itself a wide range of rights and privileges that enabled its members to exercise considerable influence over public affairs. In the years following the Second Punic War, the senate determined the tasks that magistrates would perform, fixed the funds that governors would receive to finance their operations, selected the magistrates whose terms in office would be extended, and ruled on the acceptability of treaties that generals in the field had negotiated. On occasion, the senate chose some of its members to serve as "legates" (*legati*; singular *legatus*) to go on embassies or to assist a governor in his province. At some point, the senate also acquired the power to determine the validity of rulings issued by priestly colleges on matters of sacred law and ritual procedure. Altogether, the senate's place in the Roman political order rested on its great prestige and authority, and on the acquiescence of elected officials who themselves were senators. At the same time, however, the fact is that the senate lacked any specific power to command, to punish, to enact laws, or to implement policies.

In law and by custom, Rome's "government" corresponded to the officeholders who were elected to fill specific posts for limited periods of time. Only they could call meetings of the senate and of citizen assemblies, hear legal cases and issue judgments, command armies, and perform public rites and ceremonies. In the city, individual consuls and praetors could each block the actions of colleagues who held the same office and possessed identical powers; there was no requirement that they work in partnership. Equally, higher magistrates lacked the authority to command or instruct lesser ones, although in certain circumstances they could forbid them to take any action at all. In particular, the ten tribunes, who were empowered to block *any* magistrate's action, were under no obligation to coordinate. Accordingly, even a single tribune was entitled to proceed with a proposal or other step without regard for his colleagues' opinions. This said, it is important to appreciate that an act of obstruction by any magistrate always required his personal intervention. He himself had to confront directly the colleague whose action he sought to block. "Intercession" (*intercessio*), the technical term for this step, derives from a Latin verb meaning "to step between."

In the city, too, state religion forced many magistrates to adhere closely to established procedures; on occasion, religion could equally serve to check their activities. In particular, when consuls and praetors were in Rome, a wide range of mandatory rituals surrounded their public actions. Moreover, omissions or flaws in the performance of rites could have serious consequences. If colleges of priests found fault, and if the senate concurred, the official's act would be declared invalid. On other occasions, even a single augur could order the postponement of a public meeting, for example, if he announced that he had seen signs that the gods desired such a delay. This right of priests and senate to nullify magisterial actions in the city did not extend to the tribunes of the plebs, although some senators would advocate making them, too, subject to the same checks.

However, the tribunes of the plebs, who had once mobilized citizens against the governing elite during the Struggle of the Orders (see Chapter Two), had now become more a part of the established order. In the first decades of the second century, tribunes generally put forward proposals that had already met with senatorial approval, or blocked actions by magistrates in the city that were known to displease many senators. In consequence, with seldom any candidates outside the elite to support for election or tribunes to put forward proposals, the mass of Roman citizens could make their opinions known only through demonstrations and heckling.

Few officials defied a senatorial consensus for long. To be sure, the senate's decrees were only advisory and it could not formally compel obedience, yet still the great majority of officials largely followed its wishes. Officeholders had an interest in preserving the power and position of a body to which they themselves belonged. In addition, the senate collectively, and leading senators individually, could obstruct the political advancement of senators who had isolated themselves too much from the majority of members. Only the senate could grant triumphs, for example—essential distinctions to maintain a commander's fame and glory (see Chapter Three). Candidates for office, moreover, required allies in the senate at election time, and the more prestigious these allies were, the better. Last but not least, the senate's assumption of the power to assign tasks to each group of officials annually allowed it to exercise great influence.

Meantime it should not be forgotten that some of the governing elite were concerned to prevent prominent and popular senators from overshadowing their peers by too wide a margin. Senators after all, especially the most prominent among them, were participants in a constant competition for fame and glory, and certain very ambitious individuals within this circle may occasionally have desired to achieve an unduly preeminent place in the city. From the beginning of the senate's rise in the late fourth and early third centuries, officials made attempts therefore—probably with the support of most senators—to limit an individual's ability to stand out too far above his peers (see Chapter Three). Limits on the number of times that anyone could hold high office were clearly a key restriction in this respect. The great fame achieved by commanders both in the Second Punic War and in the numerous subsequent wars may well have induced many senators to favor restricting their most ambitious colleagues still further, although such legislation was not always successful.

However, during the decades following the Second Punic War a series of laws did now attempt to force senators' careers into a more regular, obligatory pattern. It became a formal requirement that anyone who stood for election as quaestor (the lowest senatorial office) had to have already completed ten years of military service. Moreover the offices were formed into a fixed hierarchy, within which individuals had to advance step by step from lesser offices to higher. In the fourth century and earlier, by contrast, it could happen that a more powerful office would sometimes be held before a lesser one; even in the early third century, some men were consul before they became praetor. However, a law enacted after the Second Macedonian War made it mandatory that from now onwards anyone seeking election as consul must have already served as praetor. In 180, a tribune Lucius Villius successfully proposed the first law fixing the minimum age at which the offices of praetor and consul could be held, and requiring that at least ten years should always elapse before a holder of either of these offices should be able to hold the same one again. Later, after this interval had not been observed when Marcus Claudius Marcellus gained the consulship for the third time in 152, further legislation prohibited holding the office of consul more than once.

Altogether, the eventual result was the development of a standard *cursus honorum* or hierarchy of senatorial offices within which contemporaries competed against one another to move up from quaestor to praetor to consul, and even censor. At each stage, of course, more competitors would fail to advance, because successively fewer positions were available. In addition, the offices of tribune of the plebs and aedile were optional—no patrician could even seek the tribunate unless he irrevocably renounced his status and became a plebeian—but most senators tried to gain one of these two offices in between serving as quaestor and seeking election as praetor.

Threats of prosecution were the sole check on the actions of officials when away from the city of Rome. In practice, only a limited number of perceived offenses against public order were investigated. In most such instances—especially when ordinary citizens were the suspects—Roman officeholders personally conducted investigations (*quaestiones*) commissioned by the senate or by a law passed in a citizen assembly. With the advice of assessors whom they chose themselves (usually fellow senators), presiding officials received accusations, sought out evidence against those suspected of crimes, listened to arguments in defense, proclaimed their verdicts and ordered punishments, and rewarded informants. The punishment usually followed soon after the verdict.

When senators or former magistrates were themselves the subject of the investigation, a different procedure was followed. In the late third and second centuries, prosecutions for official misconduct—charges such as cowardice, incompetence, and corruption—generally took place before assemblies of citizens, who would vote on the fate of the defendants. From the second century onwards, prosecutions of former officials in fact became a common feature of the Roman political order. Trial hearings offered a natural opportunity for a prominent citizen's rivals to try and damage his prestige, and many leading senators faced multiple prosecutions in the course of their careers. Even Scipio Africanus eventually withdrew from public life to avoid further such harassment.

From 149, a series of laws began to create permanent courts—so-called *quaestiones perpetuae*—to try certain specific offenses by magistrates and senators. In that year, a tribune Lucius Calpurnius Piso carried a law establishing such a court to hear charges of extortion in the provinces (see Chapter Five). According to this Calpurnian law, accusers presented their cases to juries chosen from members of the senate, who would then issue verdicts that could not be appealed. Later, similar permanent courts for other offenses would be established, in some of which it was permissible to prosecute non-senators too. In time, as we shall see below, the question of who should comprise the juries of all the permanent courts would become a contentious political issue.

ITALY AND THE CONSEQUENCES OF EMPIRE

Italy had long been a land with marked regional differences in language, in economic and social organization, and in political and religious life. By the end of the Second Punic War, communities with Roman citizenship were concentrated in Latium, Campania, southernmost Etruria, Sabinum, and a few adjacent areas along the Adriatic coast; those cities possessing full citizenship were mostly nearer to Rome than those with only partial citizen rights. Both levels of citizen community still also maintained much of their original culture, although they did adapt themselves to some Roman forms and procedures. The citizen communities aside, substantial regions of Italy—for example, most of Etruria, Umbria, Lucania, Samnium, Bruttium, and the Greek cities of the south—all remained as allies with their own customs and practices, and no Roman citizen rights.

During the second century, however, much of Italy experienced profound changes that disrupted long-established political and social practices. Some of the changes stemmed from wartime devastation and from the harsh peace that Rome forced on disloyal allies. Others derived from the movements of people within the peninsula made possible by the greater integration of Italian communities. Still others were consequences of the vast influx of wealth derived from Rome's wars outside of Italy. At the same time, as the result of warfare, diplomacy, and business dealings, members of the elite throughout Italy gained a closer familiarity with Greece and Asia Minor; the societies they encountered here were older, wealthier, and more complex, and offered attractive models to emulate in many respects.

Changing Relations Between Rome, Its *Municipia*, and Allies

The Second Punic War and its aftermath imposed severe strain on Rome's network of alliances and cities with shared citizenship. Some remained loyal, but at great cost in lives and resources lost to the war effort, devastated farms and fields, and increased internal political tensions. Others abandoned their relationship with Rome, and sought greater freedom of action in an alliance with Hannibal and Carthage. When Rome recaptured the cities of former allies, its commanders unflinchingly ordered the executions of leading citizens and the enslavement of many others. In the course of the arrangements made after the end of the war, moreover, many communities in southern Italy suffered massive confiscations of land, which badly hurt their citizens and their economies. In the second century, too, Roman officials came to involve themselves more deeply in the internal affairs of cities, and to distinguish more sharply between Roman citizens and their Italian allies. By the end of the century, relations between Rome and some of its allies had worsened considerably.

In the Po Valley and in peninsular Italy, Roman officials conducted large-scale settlement projects. In 200, immediately after the Second Punic War, commissioners settled veterans of campaigns in Spain, Sicily, and North Africa on some of the land confiscated from rebellious allies. Over the next two decades, the senate and assemblies ordered the establishment of a dozen new colonies, and the reinforcement of five existing ones in the territories of allies they presumably considered to be untrustworthy. During the 180s and 170s, Roman officials established eight more colonies in connection with campaigns in northern Italy, and in 173 they distributed small plots of land taken from the Gauls to Romans and Latins in more scattered settlements, without the formation of any new urban center to serve as the focus of self-government. Altogether, these various projects may have settled as many as 50,000 men and their families in colonies, together with an unknown number of other recipients in the veteran assignments of 200 and in the land distributions of 173. In 180, moreover, Roman officials moved up to perhaps 50,000 Ligures from their homes in northern Italy, and settled them on confiscated land in the south.

During the war with Hannibal and for two decades after its end, the senate had regularly instructed magistrates and promagistrates to search out signs of disloyalty in some allied cities and to punish those suspected of it. This task was by definition intrusive, and, on occasion, such magistrates' actions may well have been harsh. Attempts to search out perceived threats to good order wherever they might be found were not limited to charges of assisting Rome's enemies. Three times between 184 and 179, the senate assigned to praetors the task of investigating the many poisonings said to be taking place. For the Romans, the crime of poisoning (*veneficium*) included not only doing harm through drugs or potions, but also causing injuries through magic and the casting of spells; it was, thus, a category of offense readily open to rumor and panic.

Another series of investigations may have been even more intrusive and extensive. In 186, Roman officials and senators became disturbed by the practices and wide diffusion of the cult of the god Bacchus, the Greek Dionysus. This Bacchic cult was deeply entrenched in the cities of Campania and the south, but its devotees could also be found in Rome and other cities. In Etruscan Volsinii, for instance, a grotto was dedicated to Bacchus in a public space in the city during the third century. His worship often involved groups with no official sanction, outside of a city's normal religious and political framework. Moreover, in these rites there could be shouting, frenzied dancing, the use of cymbals and drums, drinking, and some sexual license. In Rome itself, the cult may have become more active in recent years, mixing men and women, some from prominent families, and performing nocturnal rites in secret.

According to the historian Livy (39.8–19), Spurius Postumius Albinus, one of the consuls of 186, began the investigation after receiving reports that worshippers included ritual murders and poisonings in their nocturnal rites. The senate then issued a decree ordering a search for Bacchic priests in both Rome and the rest of Italy, forbidding initiates to gather for rites, and instructing investigators to seek out criminals and performers of immoral acts. Lesser officials were to guard against nocturnal meetings and fire, always a danger in a crowded city such as Rome. Other provisions of this senatorial decree—which is known from an inscription found in Bruttium—ordered the dismantling of shrines, prohibited the mixing of men and women on ritual occasions, forbade men to be priests, and banned

Figure 4.1 *Late in the second century, a number of objects associated with the worship of Dionysus were placed in a votive deposit just outside the north gate of the Etruscan city of Vulci. Among them were a terracotta statue of a seated Dionysus and a small terracotta model of a temple. The two reclining figures in the pediment of the temple represent Dionysus and Ariadne (Etruscan, Fufluns and Ariatha) in a sacred union.*

secret rites and the swearing of oaths. The deliberate destruction of the Bacchic grotto at Volsinii early in the second century may have been prompted by the decree. The consul Postumius in fact spent his entire year implementing it, and Livy believed that his investigations resulted in many executions. Two years later in 184, the senate assigned Apulia to a praetor as his province and ordered him to look into the cult, end its troublemaking there, and prevent the worship from spreading. In the next year, another praetor received the same assignment.

An expansion of full Roman citizenship and a hardening of the distinctions between Romans and non-Romans accompanied greater Roman surveillance over local affairs in Italy. Among Romans, the chief division had been between residents of municipia with the right to vote in Roman elections, and residents of communities without this right. Over much of the third and second centuries, the full citizenship with voting rights was gradually extended to more cities that had not previously possessed it. The Sabines received this privilege in 268, while Arpinum, Formiae, and Fundi became municipia with it in 188. Because of the patchiness of our surviving evidence, the stages and rapidity of the process remain unclear. By the end of the second century, however, in all probability only a few citizen communities would not have gained the right to vote. All these extensions of the right to vote, it should be remembered, required assigning each community concerned to a Roman tribe; this was now done, not by creating new tribes, but by assigning new communities to existing ones.

At the same time, the distinctions between Romans and Latins became more pronounced. In the first decades of the second century, the right of Latins to take up Roman citizenship by moving to Rome was progressively restricted. Acting on the complaints of Latin communities that feared losing their citizens, the senate first agreed to require all Latins who wished to move to Rome (and thereby acquire Roman citizenship) to leave behind in their community a son who could fill their place. In the 180s and 170s, the senate also assigned magistrates the task of expelling Latins from Rome, and removing from the rolls of Roman citizens those who had improperly acquired the status.

One incident can illustrate changed perceptions of the relationship between Rome and its Italian allies. In 173, the consul Lucius Postumius Albinus, while traveling to Campania on official business, sent a message ahead to Praeneste (an allied city in Latium) instructing its officials to come out to meet him (a mark of special honor), to prepare to accommodate and entertain him at their own expense, and to provide pack animals for his baggage. The historian Livy (42.1.7–12), who reports the incident, claims that it was unprecedented. The senate customarily supplied Roman officials with mules and tents so that they might not be a burden to the allies. Prominent Romans, when journeying away from the city, normally stayed with other wealthy individuals with whom they shared hospitality, housing their hosts when they came to Rome. Only ambassadors, forced to make a sudden journey from Rome, could require more, and they were limited by law to one pack animal from each city through which they passed. Postumius' demands proved successful, however, and Livy reports that such behavior became more common. Outside of Italy, it is true, for some time past Roman officials had provided for their own maintenance in this arrogant fashion; now, some were treating Italian allies—who had borne many of the burdens of Rome's wars—just as they did Roman subjects elsewhere.

At the same time, the Romans seem to have gradually shifted more of the burdens and fewer of the benefits of waging war to the Latins and other Italian allies. Here, the evidence is too uncertain to do more than outline a general trend. At any rate, during the second century the numbers of Roman citizens probably increased more rapidly than did the populations of Latin and allied cities. Many of the latter, after all, had suffered badly in the Second Punic War, and some had lost land that would later be distributed to Roman citizens. No doubt the Romans had always apportioned the burdens and benefits of warfare unequally, but there are signs now that allied communities were carrying more of the burdens for a smaller share of the profits. During the second century, the ratio of Roman citizens to Latins and other allies in Rome's armies varied between rough equality to two allies for each Roman. By the end of the century, however, allied contingents seem to have regularly outnumbered Roman ones. In addition, in 167 the senate suspended the collection of *tributum* from citizens, since the treasury was full with the profits of expansion (the Third Macedonian War had proved especially lucrative: see Chapter Three). By contrast, Latin and allied cities in all likelihood still had to tax themselves to maintain their own soldiers.

This movement toward increased differentiation between Rome and its Italian allies was accompanied by a greater imitation of Roman institutions and practices. Latin colonies, founded by Roman officials, had long been organized in a Roman manner. Now, some allied communities began to imitate Rome more closely. Especially in the south of Italy, more communities began to use Latin in official inscriptions, and there are signs of an increased use of Roman law, even in communities that were not formally bound by it. Moreover, some allied communities began to give to their officials Latin titles, such as aedile or quaestor, or to call their own advisory council a senate.

Roman and Italian Elites

The political and social orders of Rome and its municipia and allies each rested on small groups of wealthy, prominent families, who held magistracies and priesthoods, and who filled out the ranks of the senate or its equivalent in the many smaller cities of Italy. In the second century, these ruling elites of Rome and of many other Italian cities grew richer through the profits of empire. They began to beautify their cities, and to proclaim their position in them through public building projects on an ever-larger scale. They also came to adopt an increasingly similar way of life, strongly influenced by Hellenistic Greece.

The social orders of Italian towns and cities were complicated and hierarchical. All forms of wealth were not considered equally honorable or desirable. The holders of magistracies based their wealth on land, on government, and on the profits of war; by contrast, direct participation in trade, even on a fairly large scale, could threaten their status. In Rome itself moreover, senators were specifically debarred from participating in trade and from holding public contracts as *publicani*. Even so, ways could be found around the limits imposed by law and custom. Finance, for example, was honorable if undertaken on a sufficiently large scale, and if the lending of money was divorced from any direct participation in the activities funded.

Status certainly affected the ways in which individuals could profit from Roman expansion. Roman magistrates and senators had the greatest opportunities and the greatest benefits. In Italy, transfers of wealth had long accompanied Roman warfare. The wars outside of Italy, in Greece and Asia Minor especially, resulted in seizures of property and enslavements on a scale that the Romans had never experienced before. Immense wealth certainly changed hands amidst combat and the disorder that followed. Prominent Romans also arranged for the transfer home of art treasures, furniture, and other valuables in addition to objects of gold, silver, and precious metals. Through plunder, the seizure of royal and sacred treasuries, and the imposition of tribute, commanders came to control large amounts of wealth. Some they probably apportioned to allies, but they brought the bulk of their gains back to Italy, where they displayed it in their triumphs. Afterwards, they distributed some formally to their soldiers according to rank, turned over another part to Rome's treasury, and retained a portion for their own use (Source 4.1).

Plunder was not the only reward of victory. Commanders who were assigned *provinciae*, together with their assistants, as well as legates either on embassies or on other missions, all had regular opportunities for personal gain. Members of the

---

SOURCE 4.1: *Plunder was a major source of wealth for commanders and soldiers alike, and the Romans developed highly formalized ways of acquiring it and distributing it. In the first passage, Polybius describes the manner in which the army of Scipio Africanus looted Carthago Nova in 209. Some of the wealth gained in this fashion was displayed in the commander's triumph, and, after he had left office, he often distributed a portion to his soldiers as a "donative," as Livy's account of the triumph of Gnaeus Manlius Vulso in 187 illustrates.*

Polybius (10.15.4–16.9): When Scipio thought that a sufficient number of soldiers had entered the city, he sent most of them—as is the Roman custom—in pursuit of the inhabitants, with orders to kill everyone they encountered, sparing nobody, and not to start pillaging until the order was given. They do this, I think, to inspire terror, so that when cities are taken by the Romans, one may see not only the bodies of human beings, but also dogs cut in half, and the dismembered limbs of other animals. On this occasion, these scenes were many, because of the number of people in the city. . . . After this, once the signal was given, the massacre stopped and they began to plunder. At nightfall, those Romans who had received orders to remain in the camp did so, while Scipio with his thousand men camped in the citadel. Through the military tribunes he ordered the rest of the troops to leave the houses, and then instructed them to collect their plunder in the forum, maniple by maniple, and to guard it by sleeping there. . . . On the next day, the plunder collected in the forum was divided among the legions in the usual way. After capturing a city, the Romans deal with this matter as follows. Depending on the city's size, on some occasions a certain part of each maniple and, on others, whole maniples are assigned to collect plunder, but never more than half of the army does this, the rest remaining under arms either inside the city or outside, ready for any trouble. . . . All the men who are ordered to plunder bring back what they have taken, each to his own legion, and, after this has been done, the military tribunes distribute the loot equally among everyone, including not only those in the protecting force, but also those guarding the camp, the sick, and anyone absent on a special assignment.

Livy (39.7.1–5): In his triumph, Gnaeus Manlius carried 212 gold crowns, 220,000 pounds of silver, 2,100 pounds of gold, 120,000 Attic *tetradrachmai* [a silver coin], 250,000 *cistophori* [another type of coin], and 16,320 gold *Philippei* [yet another coin]. There were also many Gallic arms and spoils carried in carts, and 250 enemy leaders were led before his chariot. To his soldiers, he gave forty-two *denarii* [the standard Roman silver coin], and to centurions twice this; in addition, he gave infantrymen double pay, and cavalrymen triple.

Roman elite in the provinces routinely demanded that the local inhabitants feed and house them, often at great expense, and provide them with transport. Some even demanded gifts as an inducement to reduce requisitions or to grant exemptions from them altogether. In addition, governors and their closest advisors received or extorted gifts from people who wished to ingratiate themselves or to receive favors. The acquisition of new wealth on a large scale was not limited to magistrates, senators, and members of their entourages. *Negotiatores* were certainly present in Greece in some number, and they could probably be found in Spain too (see Chapter Three). State contractors or publicani also profited from the desire of Roman commanders to erect monuments to their achievements. There were increased opportunities for publicani outside of Italy as well, although the extent of their operations is unclear initially.

The vast influx of wealth into Italy changed the appearance of many cities and the ways of life of their leading families. Wealthy Romans now built elaborate private houses and financed the construction of temples, public buildings, and monuments in prominent locales. Many members of the local elites that dominated the other cities (both citizen and allied) of the peninsula behaved in a similar manner, building houses—some of which rivaled royal palaces in size (Fig. 4.2)—and adorning their cities with temples, baths, theaters, and monuments to their own accomplishments. Cities in Latium and Campania— the core of Roman power, and home of the richest local elites—led the way. The wealthiest and most powerful of the Samnites followed,

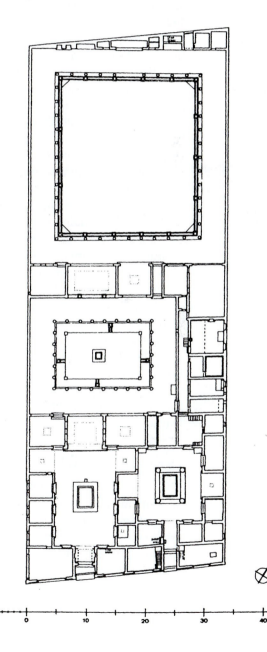

Figure 4.2 *The "House of Faun" at Pompeii in Campania is one of the most elaborate second-century houses known in Italy. Later extended, it covers 31,000 square feet (2,800 sq m). The only known residences of comparable size at this date are royal ones, such as at Pella in Macedon. The lower part of the plan shows the house's two reception halls or atria; above them are its two peristyle courtyards. In all, this house, which probably belonged to a member of the local elite, is more reminiscent of Greek palaces and public buildings than of the earlier dwellings of central Italian aristocrats.*

5   0   10   20   30   40M

turning their sanctuary sites into elaborate complexes. The Etruscans, farther away from the main commercial centers, also participated, but to a lesser degree (Fig. 4.3). For many of these projects, architects and builders imitated a Hellenistic style of building in both private houses and public structures.

Imitation of the Greek world was not limited to styles of building. In the third and early second centuries, magistrates staging festivals had come to favor playwrights—such as Livius Andronicus, Gnaeus Naevius (died in 201), Plautus (died c. 184), and Terence (died c. 159)—who imitated Greek styles. Later, participation in a Hellenizing literary and philosophical culture came to be a mark of elite status that linked individuals across communities. By the end of the Second Punic War, some members of Rome's elite were writing histories, at first in Greek and later in Latin too (see Chapter One). During the second century, members of the leading families in Rome and many other Italian cities, eager for political careers, sought training in Greek rhetoric, the highly formal art of public speaking. Some more restricted circles began to find the study of Greek philosophy stimulating. In the households of the rich, learned slaves served as secretaries and tutors, while especially prominent families invited rhetors and philosophers to live and teach in their houses. In these instances too, the regional elites of Italy did not all participate equally. It became the norm for a Roman of high rank to form ties of mutual hospitality with leading families in Italy, especially those who lived near Rome, or near his estates, or close to the routes that Roman officials often took to their assignments. These contacts served to reinforce the movement toward a common way of life within the Italian elites.

Greater wealth, more lavish lifestyles, and closer familiarity with Greek culture provoked a response among certain members of the Roman senate. Some—Cato the Elder was the most prominent—denounced luxury and, when in office, sought to limit it. Others were unsettled by Greek philosophy, which encouraged the questioning of fundamental truths, or by Greek rhetoric, since its techniques could be used to persuade without apparent regard for the moral value of a position. From time to time, therefore, magistrates and the senate ordered the expulsion of philosophers and teachers of rhetoric. Other prominent members of the Roman elite, however, clearly desired their presence, so that the expulsion of learned Greeks had little permanent effect.

Demographic and Economic Changes

The wars that established Roman leadership of the Italian peninsula had been accompanied by serious disruptions to the population levels and settlement patterns of the peoples involved. In the midst of these movements, Rome and a few other cities grew much larger. Firm statistics for Rome's population do not exist, and modern estimates have large margins for error, but it seems likely that, in the second century, several hundreds of thousands of people inhabited the city. They were highly diverse in class, in legal status, and in place of origin. Some came from the towns and villages of Italy, seeking opportunities in the city or fleeing changes

Figure 4.3 *This terracotta funerary urn from Perugia, dating to the second half of the second century, contained the ashes of Arnth Velimnas; the inscription is in the Etruscan alphabet. The artist has depicted the deceased as a banqueter, as was commonly done in Etruria at the time. The banqueting couch is heavily carved, an embellishment considered to signify conspicuous—indeed almost scandalous—luxury. A branch of the family successfully joined the Roman elite under the name Volumnii.*

in the countryside. Wealthier newcomers sometimes sought a place among Rome's elite. Many new residents came from outside the peninsula, some voluntarily, lured by its riches, while others were imported as slaves to work in the households of the wealthy. Much of Rome's population was ill-housed and led only a marginal existence. Tensions between rich and poor seem to have become more pronounced.

Changes in the countryside accompanied the growth of cities and fueled it. The constant wars outside the peninsula added to the mobility of the population of Italy. Some sought opportunities in Spain or the east, while many served in Rome's armies there. Wars in distant places made military service more burdensome for some Romans and allies. In the first half of the second century, the total free population of Italy probably numbered around three million. The Romans kept a substantial proportion of the adult males from citizen and allied communities under arms: perhaps 120,000 men in a typical year, and, on occasion, even more. Soldiers who served outside of Italy could be away for four to six years, with some men serving for over a decade. Military service on this scale and of this duration disrupted communal life and the organization of labor. Most soldiers were small-scale farmers, and prolonged absences must have weakened their ability to maintain themselves and their families on their lands. Indeed, the pressures of military service may well have encouraged some to abandon the land and move to the cities. Some Roman authors also believed that the demands of military service led wealthy landowners to shift away from hiring free laborers to employing slaves, who were not subject to conscription, to work their lands. There is certainly the distinct impression that throughout Italy more land than ever before was now controlled by wealthy families.

Warfare outside the peninsula also disrupted long established patterns of agriculture. The traditional economies of Italian city-states were based on farming and herding. In most districts, the arable land would be divided among the relatively few estates of the rich and a far larger number of smallholdings, cultivated by the owner and his family with perhaps the assistance of a few slaves. The ownership of land was closely tied to citizenship. The chief landowners of a city were its ruling elite, and its small-scale farmers formed the mass of its military levy. Under Roman law, only Romans and Latins could own land around Rome, in colonies, and in municipia. The Roman elite, although far wealthier than the elites of municipia and allied cities, probably concentrated the bulk of its holdings relatively close to the city. At the beginning of the second century, senators primarily owned lands in Latium, southern Etruria, Campania, and those portions of Sabinum that were closest to the city.

Land was the chief prop of the fortunes of the powerful, but landowning on any scale is always dependent on the availability of labor to farm it. During the fourth and early third centuries, Rome's elite increasingly turned to slaves, either born and raised in the household, or taken in large numbers in Roman wars, or purchased from abroad, the victims of piracy and other people's wars. In addition, from the beginning of the second century, if not earlier, Roman landowners employed tenant farmers, sharecroppers, and occasional free laborers. During the second century, slavery in Italy became larger in scale and importance as Roman armies forced larger numbers into slavery, and as more slaves became available as a result of warfare and piracy elsewhere in the Mediterranean world.

Slavery in Italy was a complex phenomenon. Some slaves worked in the fields, or guarded the herds and flocks of their owners. Others were servants in the households of the wealthy. Still others served as managers, accountants, and teachers. Masters typically employed skilled slave craftsmen to make products for domestic use and for sale in the market. For some, slavery was a temporary condition. Slaveowners in Italy often permitted slaves to acquire personal property, and some could purchase their freedom by this means. For other slaves, freedom could come as a reward for services. In either case, freedmen and freedwomen received the prized status of Roman citizens, if their former owners were citizens. However, they were still expected to continue to provide services and owe deference and loyalty to their former owners; freedmen frequently served as managers and business agents.

The influx of wealth and slaves from foreign wars, and the vulnerability to military service of tenant farmers, sharecroppers, and hired laborers, presented members of the landholding elites of Italy with a range of options. In the middle of the second century, Cato the Elder wrote a handbook *On Agriculture* (*De Agricultura*) that illustrates some ideal features of one type of holding. Cato's estate of around 100 acres or 40 hectares (one of several its imagined owner would possess) was operated by either a slave or a free man as manager; he supervised no more than a few dozen slaves—the most that could be kept fully employed throughout the year—and also hired seasonal free laborers to help with planting and the harvest. This holding specialized in a single crop, grapes for wine or olives for oil, which was to be sold for the owner's profit. Such intensive cultivation of a single crop depends on the proximity of a market sufficiently large to absorb its produce and the produce of other similar estates in the region. Perhaps for this reason, Cato placed his estate in southern Latium or northern Campania, near to Rome and the Campanian cities. Both Cato's handbook and others thought to have been written about the same time give the impression that specialized holdings of this type were a relatively recent phenomenon, perhaps a response to Rome's growth.

The raising of animals was another option for those with capital, land, and slaves. The second century witnessed an expansion in the practice of transhumance. Owners assembled large herds of cattle and flocks of sheep and goats, which they turned over to slaves to guard and to lead. These slave shepherds took their charges on long journeys each year while seeking out sufficient pasturage to feed them. During winter, the shepherds concentrated their animals in meadows in the warmer lowland, then during summer they led them to highland pastures. The migrations from highlands to lowlands and back again crossed many civic boundaries, and, if care was not taken, they could badly damage fields and crops. Transhumance requires a great deal of land (not necessarily of very high quality), and it was most common in the south of Italy where the population was less dense. Herding on this scale also requires the existence of a market in large cities where the owners or their agents can convert meat, leather, or wool into cash.

The use of slaves on a large scale presented dangers for the Roman political system. In 185, the praetor Lucius Postumius Tempsanus was assigned to suppress an uprising in Apulia, where groups of slave shepherds were robbing people in the countryside; he is said to have condemned around 7,000 men to death, although Livy (39.29.8–9) reports that many escaped execution. In the Roman world, pastoral slavery often was associated with brigandage. Slave shepherds, whose occupation made them difficult to supervise, were generally armed to protect their flocks from carnivorous animals and thieves, and sometimes it was only by resorting to force that they could assert their right to use pastures and springs.

The most alarming instance of the danger created by extensive use of slaves occurred in Sicily, in full view of the Roman elite. The island's economy, like that of Italy, was complicated and diverse. In some regions, estates produced grain on a large scale; in fact, the island was one of the primary sources for food for the city of Rome. In other regions, pastoral slavery was common. The First Slave War began around the city of Enna in the middle of the island. Eunus, its leader, a slave from Apamea-on-the-Orontes in Syria and a wonderworker who claimed the patronage of the Syrian goddess Atargatis, recruited a number of slave-shepherds. One night in 136, he gathered them outside the city, encouraged them to break into the slave barracks on the estates that surrounded it, and to free the field slaves housed there, who were usually kept shackled. With this force of several hundred, he then broke into Enna, and began a massacre in which some slaves resident in the city joined. The next day, he declared himself to be king. A month later, another rebellion began around the city of Agrigentum, where more massacres took place. Eventually, the rebellion spread to include about half of the island. Its suppression proved a long, hard task (see Fig. 4.4). At first, the Roman praetors who held Sicily as their provincia attempted without success to defeat the rebels, suffering several defeats in the process. In 134, the

a   *b*

Figure 4.4 *There have been many random finds of lead slingshots used in Roman wars. Typically, such shots measure about 1.3 in (3.5 cm) long, and weigh 1.5 to 2 oz (40–60 g). They often carry brief inscriptions in relief—a war-cry, for example, a leader's name, or some insult to the enemy; these were incised in the clay molds within which the shots were made. The two shots illustrated were found in Sicily, both of them likely to have been fired by slaves resisting Roman armies in the two Slave Wars of the late second century B.C. Their inscriptions are in Greek: the first [a] proclaims NIKH ('Victory'); the second [b] is the name of a slave leader in the second war, in the genitive, with a qualifying noun to be understood: "Athenion's [shot]." See Chapter Five for this second war.*

senate decided to make Sicily a consular province, an indication of its serious concern. The third of these consular commanders finally ended the war in 132.

ROMAN POLITICS FROM THE MID-SECOND CENTURY

In the third quarter of the second century a few members of Rome's governing elite began to base their position in the city more on their ability to court popularity and to mobilize crowds than on their standing with their fellow senators. Some of these men were charismatic military figures, eager to reach new offices and fresh heights of glory; others were more confrontational tribunes. In many ways, the shift they initiated represents a return to an older style of leadership, before the reforms of the late fourth and early third centuries began to elevate the senate above any individual officeholder. Both the growth of the city of Rome and the changes in the Italian countryside may have fueled the new development. The population of the city was now disturbed by starker contrasts between rich and poor, as well as by the presence of many people who had been forced through changes in the countryside to migrate to the city. As a result, crowds in Rome would have been larger, and their emotions more easily stirred. Crowds could also prove fickle, as seen in a cautionary tale about a member of the Scipio family expecting to be elected curule aedile. While out canvassing, he clasped rather tightly someone's hand that had been toughened by farm work, and by way of a joke asked him: "You're not in the habit of walking on your hands, are you?" The remark was picked up by bystanders and spread among the populace. As a result, Scipio failed to win election because all the rural tribes felt that he had criticized them for being poor, and they expressed their anger at his insulting city wit (Valerius Maximus 7.5.2).

In many ways, the institutional basis of the senate's position was weak. Because of the nature of the Roman political order, the senate's leadership depended on its high prestige and on the willingness of officeholders and candidates to abide by senatorial consensus in important matters. At the same time, by law officeholders possessed considerable powers of self-assertion, and, if they sought popular support, there was little to restrain them. Tribunes, in particular, possessed formidable powers to act, as well as to block the actions of others, should they wish to exercise this authority. From the late 150s, a few tribunes become notably more active. In 151, for example, following popular resistance to a consular levy of soldiers for Spain, tribunes imprisoned the consul when he ignored their vetoes. In 145, another tribune, Gaius Licinius Crassus, attempted unsuccessfully to enact a law removing the right to choose new priests from the priestly colleges and transferring it to citizen assemblies instead. In 139, the tribune Aulus Gabinius enacted the first law requiring secret ballots, rather than having citizens declare their votes in full view of the city's leaders. Two years later, another tribune's proposal instituted the use of secret ballot for trial verdicts.

During this period, figures such as Scipio Aemilianus and Tiberius and Gaius Gracchus would develop new styles of popular leadership, ones that would be much imitated in succeeding generations. There is no continuous narrative history of the years from 167 to 121 and beyond, however. The career of Scipio Aemilianus may be pieced together out of Appian's accounts of the Third Punic War and the Numantine War (written in the mid-second century A.D.), and from Plutarch's biography of Scipio's father, Lucius Aemilius Paullus. The tribunates of the two Gracchi are better documented. Plutarch wrote biographies of both brothers, while Appian opened his account of Rome's civil wars with their activities. Tiberius and Gaius Gracchus, moreover, were famous orators, and later authors preserved extracts or summaries of some of their speeches (see Source 4.2). Further, more occasional, references can be found in works by a range of authors. Yet problems remain. The brothers' actions and characters became the focus of much bitter controversy, and the propriety of their conduct and the responses of their opponents were vigorously disputed. As a result, the political positions of our sources have strongly influenced the representations of both brothers.

Scipio Aemilianus

Scipio Aemilianus was born in 185 or 184. His father was Lucius Aemilius Paullus, the victor over Perseus at Pydna in 168, and his grandfather was one of the consuls defeated at Cannae in 216. He was adopted by Publius Cornelius Scipio, the son of Scipio Africanus, who had defeated Hannibal. Scipio Aemilianus first served as consul in 147. In the previous year, he had initially sought election as aedile. However, popular discontent over the failure of Rome's generals to win a quick victory in the Third Punic War created an opportunity that he exploited, and he switched his candidacy to the consular election. His success here was extraordinary. He was considerably below the minimum age for consul, and he had yet to hold the office of praetor; he was, in other words, just the kind of candidate that the laws regulating the *cursus honorum* sought to bar.

With the backing of the senate, the consul who presided over the elections duly sought to bar Scipio's candidacy. According to Appian (*Punic Wars* 112), widespread protests were then voiced in the assembly, and some in the crowd asserted that the people possessed the right to elect whomever they wished. When one of the tribunes announced his intention to prevent any vote unless the consul permitted Scipio to stand, the senate gave way, instructing the tribunes to put forward a law permitting this, on the understanding that the regular requirements would once again be upheld the following year. After the election, Gaius Livius Drusus, who was chosen to fill the other consular position, requested that lots be cast to determine their *provinciae*, the normal procedure. Again, a tribune intervened, proposing that a citizen vote determine the assignment of provinces. Accordingly, in this exceptional way Scipio was assigned the war against Carthage.

Plate 1a Tomb of the Augurs *In this fresco of around 500 B.C. from the "Tomb of the Augurs" at Tarquinii, two men wrestle over three metal cauldrons which are probably the prizes of their contest. The cloaked figure to the left carries a curved staff or* lituus, *which was a sign of kingship and, at Rome, a mark of the priests known as augurs, who had charge of the "auspices." One of the chief ways to take the auspices was by defining a field of vision with a lituus, and then observing within it the behavior of birds. Here, the cloaked figure seems to be supervising the contest, while the lituus and the birds flying over the combatants may indicate that he was seeking to foretell the result.*

Plate 1b Marble temple, Rome *The innovative design and costly materials of this temple dating to the late second century/early first century B.C. reflect the growing fascination for Greek culture felt by many upper-class Romans at this period (see Chapter Four). Neither the Roman who commissioned the temple, nor the deity to whom it was dedicated, can be identified, although the latter is likely to be Hercules with his links to commerce among other attributes. The temple – about 48 ft (14.8 m) in diameter – is situated in the Forum Boarium area of Rome (see Chapter One), close to the Tiber, and is the city's oldest surviving building in marble. In this instance it was specially imported from Greece, and was used both for facing the entire exterior of the circular structure and for its twenty Corinthian columns, 35 ft (10.6 m) in height. The temple suffered damage in antiquity as well as later, but owes its survival to conversion into a church; the roof and many of the columns are not original.*

Plate 2 Roman land division in the Po valley   *From as early as the fourth century* B.C., *whenever Romans acquired new territory they normally commissioned surveyors* (agrimensores) *to mark out the cultivable land within it in square or rectangular parcels* (centuriae), *which could then be further subdivided. Roads and settlements (Roman colonies especially) were integrated into this distinctive pattern of land division. The resulting stamp of Roman control painstakingly imprinted upon a landscape even remains to this day in certain regions, as seen here from the air in Italy's Po valley near Modena, where a* centuria *is square with sides about 765 yards (700 m) in length.*

Plate 3 Site of Roman defeat at Lake Trasimene   *This view from Lake Trasimene in Umbria shows the area to the north where on the upper slopes Hannibal concealed many of his forces and brilliantly ambushed a large Roman army marching unawares below along the lakeshore. The rash Roman commander, the consul Gaius Flaminius, had omitted to reconnoiter the way ahead, and a low morning mist off the lake only served to blind his men further. When attacked, they were trapped and did not even have time to group in regular battle formation; as many as 15,000 were said to have been slaughtered, including Flaminius himself. This encounter in June 217 B.C. was the first of the catastrophic defeats which Hannibal inflicted upon Roman armies (see Chapter Three). For a no less devastating ambush by Germans in A.D. 9, see Chapter Eight and Figure 8.11.*

Plate 4 Samnite sanctuary, Pietrabbondante   *At modern Pietrabbondante – a superb site with panoramic outlook in Italy's Molise region – the Samnites established a sanctuary to a god of war as early as the fifth century* B.C. *Laid out along two mountainside terraces, it reached its most developed form during the second century, boasting two temples and the (restored) theater seen here. In all likelihood this sanctuary became a meeting-place of the entire Samnite confederacy (see Chapter Two). Following the Social War, however, and Sulla's massacre of Samnites (see Chapters Five and Six), the site came to be abandoned; since the mid-nineteenth century it has been unearthed and investigated by archeologists.*

Plate 5a Lucus Feroniae villa *This large villa of the Volusii family, situated on the outskirts of the town of Lucus Feroniae about 12.5 miles (20 km) north of Rome, was discovered during the construction of the Milan-Naples Autosole motorway in 1961. The luxurious nucleus of the villa (the part near the modern two-story house) dates from the middle of the first century B.C. It was greatly enlarged in the Augustan period by the expansive peristyle (to the left here) and other adjacent structures. The sparse decoration and functional character of the latter denote their use for housing slaves and other dependents, and for storing the villa's agricultural produce (especially grain) destined for the markets of Rome. The Volusii were prominent in public life at Rome for some 150 years, with members of the family attaining the consulship as late as A.D. 92. The excavated villa is striking proof of their success.*

Plate 5b Settefinestre villa garden wall *Miniature round turrets surmount the wall of the garden which is overlooked by the owner's quarters at the grand Settefinestre villa in Etruria: see its plan, Figure 6.4, at bottom right. This unusual architectural embellishment – which makes the garden wall resemble that of a fortified city – acts to reinforce the sense of wealth and authority projected by the entire villa. Below the garden, underground, is extensive vaulted basement space.*

Plate 6 Augustan victory monument, La Turbie   *This victory monument was built around 7 B.C. at modern La Turbie (France), high above modern Monaco where the mountains plunge down to the sea, a site brilliantly chosen for its visibility from all directions. The lost topmost part cannot be reconstructed with confidence, but it is clear that a tall square podium formed the base, upon which rose a round tower encircled by 24 columns; even in its surviving damaged condition the monument reaches a height of 118 ft (36 m). An inscription on the landward side of the podium (to the left in this view) records Augustus' subjugation of "all the Alpine peoples from the Upper Sea [Adriatic] to the Lower"; the names of forty-five peoples follow. This monument is to be compared to Augustus' commemoration of his victory at Actium (see Figure 8.5a,b), and it may well have been intended to match trophies erected by Pompey at the eastern end of the Pyrenees after his Spanish campaigns in the 70s (see Chapter Six).*

Plate 7 Prima Porta villa fresco *The frescoed decoration of a large subterranean room (approx. 132 by 66 ft/40 by 20 m) in Livia's villa at Prima Porta, 7.5 miles (12 km) north of Rome, is to be seen today in Rome's Palazzo Massimo alle Terme Museum. The four walls exhibit a continuous grove of trees, shrubs, and plants, including quince, pomegranate, palm, oleanders, myrtles, and pines, simultaneously flowering and bearing fruit with no regard for actual seasons. Against the misty background, realistically depicted birds flit about in the vegetation and nest there. This beautifully decorated room dates to perhaps around 30 B.C., and may have been used as a summer retreat. Its combination of Italic beauty and encyclopedic knowledge conveys the aspirations of the early Augustan period.*

Plate 8a Isis Giminiana (Ostia tomb painting) *This tomb painting from Ostia is now in the Vatican Museums. It shows the loading of grain ("res" here) onto a small, purpose-built river-boat that was hauled (probably by slaves) up the Tiber to Rome. Two longshoremen carrying sacks climb a gangplank onto the deck, where the grain is measured to check for theft during its transfer either from a larger seagoing vessel or from storage in one of the warehouses at the port (see Figure 11.2). "Master" Farnaces may be the ship's captain. Abascantus, who is depicted larger than the other figures, may be its owner (and the occupant of the tomb); the man to the left of him holds what seems to be a measuring device. "Isis Giminiana," perhaps the boat's name, acknowledges the importance of Egypt to Rome's food supplies by invoking Isis, one of Egypt's most important gods. The boat's prow rises above the water, and its stern even higher; the keel is very curved; sails and oars (except for steering) are absent; a tow-rope would be attached to the mast, set very far forward.*

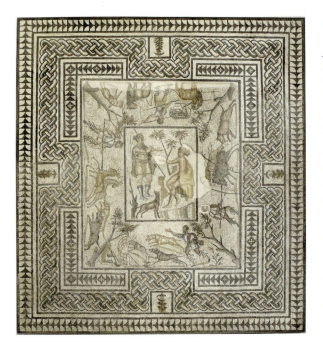

Plate 8b Mosaic with hunting scenes *This large Gallo-Roman mosaic (98.5 by 88.5 ft/30 by 27 m) of colored marble, limestone, and glass cubes (tesserae) is centered on an encounter between the goddess Diana and her companion the nymph Callisto; around them runs a continuous band of hunting scenes, enclosed within intricate figured borders. Produced in the third century A.D., the mosaic was found in a rustic but opulent villa near Villelaure in southern France; today it is in the Los Angeles County Museum. Its design reflects the literary interests of wealthy provincials of the period, intermingling Greco-Roman mythology with scenes of daily life, including the seated shepherd who wears a "Gallic" hooded cloak (lower left). Although hunting was a mark of status among rich landowners, wild animals' meat also represented a vital source of protein for rich and poor. Some animals were captured alive to be sold for wild beast hunts in the arena (venationes; see Figure 10.8).*

There, he would prove very successful, destroying the city in 146 and earning the cognomen of Africanus, as had his grandfather through adoption.

This election reveals some of the potential weaknesses of the senate's rule. Restrictions on eligibility for office—a vital means by which senators sought to protect themselves against their more popular peers—had force only so long as no one mobilized mass outrage against them, and no tribune asserted the citizens' right to vote as they wished; in that event, angry crowds and obstinate tribunes could force magistrates and senate to yield. Scipio's reputation for bravery and military skill, gained in Macedon, Spain, and North Africa, may have been the source of much of his popularity, but popular support, to be effective, must be organized and directed. Suspicion that a candidate had sought office improperly or too eagerly could lead to threats of prosecution. When a less prominent candidate defeated an opponent who was higher in the nobility, complaints that the winner was guilty of *ambitus*, the excessive pursuit of offices and popularity, were sometimes made. On at least two occasions in the first half of the second century, laws regulating ambitus were passed. In addition, other laws of this period limited large-scale, elaborate entertainments, which were often mounted by candidates to attract popular support. Clearly, Scipio and his chief supporters were somehow able to find the means of mobilizing the support required in 148.

Scipio showed the same willingness to rely on popular support later in his career. In 142, he sought election as censor, an office that was both prestigious and powerful, usually held by former consuls. His rival, Appius Claudius Pulcher, is said to have been backed by the majority of the senate, while Scipio had more support from the city populace. A central element in campaigning involved *ambitiones* (singular, *ambitio*), formal walks through the Forum, where the candidate, accompanied by prominent supporters, greeted citizens and requested their support. To have prominent supporters was thought to reflect well upon a candidate, and thus candidates for office liked to be surrounded by especially prominent men as they made their ambitiones. According to Plutarch (*Aemilius Paullus* 38), Scipio instead went to the Forum with men of low birth, some of them freedmen, who were able to gather a crowd and force issues by shouting and stirring up passions. He won the office of censor too.

In 135, Scipio again sought election as consul. When he first stood for this office, Roman armies had proven unsuccessful against Carthage. Now, a series of Roman commanders had failed against Numantia in Spain. Once again, his tremendous military prestige helped him gain office. As in his first campaign for the consulship, he also had to overcome a legal prohibition on his candidacy. After Marcus Claudius Marcellus had been consul for the third time in 152, a new law prohibited holding the office more than once. Scipio eventually found a way around the prohibition (although just how he did so remains unclear), and he was chosen consul for 134. The majority of senators then showed their dissatisfaction by refusing to vote him funds for the campaign in Spain, and by prohibiting him from drafting new soldiers. Scipio's spirited reaction was evidently to raise 4,000 men through voluntary contributions of troops by allied cities and by foreign kings who wished to gain or hold his favor; at the same time wealthy friends offered him funds. His campaign against Numantia was successful, increasing his prestige and glory still further.

In Scipio's day, a successful political career usually rested on the goodwill of one's fellow senators (gained largely through the exchange of favors), on some display of military prowess, and on popularity among the voters of the city. Individual senators were likely to possess such qualities in different proportions. Scipio proved to be one who often seemed indifferent to the wishes of a majority of his fellows. As a result, his career provoked sharp responses among his ostensible peers in the senate. Some were his close friends and allies. For example, Gaius Laelius, consul in 140, had served under his command at Carthage and remained a close associate for many years. Others, most notably Appius Claudius Pulcher and Metellus Macedonicus, were bitter enemies. In more turbulent times later, however, Scipio came to be seen as a more conventional figure than he may have appeared to his contemporaries. Cicero, a prominent orator and political figure of the following century, would present him as a paragon of the senatorial order in *On the Republic* (*De Republica*), his depiction of an ideal Roman constitution.

Tiberius Gracchus

Tiberius Sempronius Gracchus' tribunate in 133 marked a sharp break in Roman political development. Cicero would later claim that his death divided the Roman people into two camps. Tiberius Gracchus came from a wealthy and powerful family. The Sempronii Gracchi had served as consuls from the mid-third century, and the tribune's father, the elder Tiberius Sempronius Gracchus, held the office twice—a rare honor at this time—triumphed twice, and served as censor. His wife, the mother of the later tribune, was Cornelia, the daughter of Scipio Africanus, the victor over Hannibal in the Second Punic War. After her husband's death around 150, she never remarried, and raised her two sons and a daughter alone (the only three of her twelve children to survive to adulthood). Several Roman authors have preserved exemplary stories praising Cornelia's learning, her skill at speaking, and the care she took over her children's education. Some also accused her of instilling in her sons great ambition and a love of fame, but these were traits that were widely admired among Rome's elite.

Soon after he began his term as tribune, Tiberius Gracchus introduced a law regulating the use of the "public lands of the Roman people" (*ager publicus populi Romani*), in other words lands seized in Rome's various wars, but not yet distributed to settlers or leased to provide revenue. The core of the measure was an old law, long ignored, that limited to 500 *iugera* (about 300 acres or 120 hectares) the amount of "public" land which a single individual could exploit merely by occupying it. Use of such lands in this manner was legal, but occupiers never legally gained ownership, and Roman magistrates and assemblies had the right, rarely exercised, to reclaim it if the state had need of it. Tiberius proposed to enforce this limit and confiscate the excess, which would then be distributed in small allotments to landless Roman citizens. As compensation for lost holdings, the law made the remaining portions of occupiers' holdings their private property and thus immune from further seizures and distributions.

The law's most innovative feature was also its most controversial. In the past, when senate and assemblies decided to found colonies or make viritane assignments on captured land, they had chosen special magistrates—groups of three (triumviri) for colonies, and of ten (decemviri) for individual assignments—who were to travel to the scene, supervise personally the division of the land into small plots, and assign them directly to the beneficiaries. Under this arrangement, such commissioners had limited powers of discretion. The law that authorized their election specified where the assignments were to be, who was to benefit and in what numbers, and how long they themselves could remain in office. Tiberius' proposal likewise gave responsibility for enforcing its provisions to a group of three, but with wider powers. These triumvirs were to be able to assign land to as many recipients as they could, potentially making assignments to many thousands more than had their predecessors. At the same time, they possessed the power to determine themselves which lands were "public" and which private, and they were permitted to exercise it virtually anywhere in Italy.

The Gracchan agrarian law aimed at resolving serious problems that the reformer and his associates thought to threaten the state. Some later historians—in accounts that probably go back to Tiberius and his circle—hold that he considered the increase in the size and the number of slave-run estates to be both an injustice and a danger to the state. The flight of small-scale farmers from the land lowered the number of potential recruits for Rome's army and increased the burdens of conscription—and the desire to resist them too—among those who remained on the land. The large number of slaves there was itself a threat, as the difficulty of defeating the slave rebels in Sicily had clearly indicated. Tiberius' proposal addressed both of these problems by breaking up certain estates and by settling the poor on small plots of land. At the same time, it should be noted, his reform would also remove large numbers of poor people from Rome, lessening the burdens on urban institutions and removing a source of tension and instability. Other accounts, less friendly to the reformer, insist that he was motivated by a desire for fame and by rivalry with some of his contemporaries. The different versions are not incompatible.

Tiberius' reform had important supporters and opponents. Publius Mucius Scaevola, one of the consuls of 133, helped draft it, as did his brother, Publius Licinius Crassus Mucianus, who had already served as praetor and would serve as consul in 131. Other senators may also have thought that the problem was both real and serious. Scipio Aemilianus' friend, Gaius Laelius, had introduced an agrarian proposal of his own years before, but then abandoned it in face of strong opposition. Tiberius' proposal provoked intense opposition. Some Roman authors attributed this to a desire

SOURCE 4.2: *In composing* Lives, *Plutarch for the most part chose as his subjects Greeks and Romans he considered to be good men and inspiring role models for his readers. As the extract here makes abundantly clear, this is how he presents Tiberius Gracchus. An awareness on his part that Tiberius was in fact a polarizing figure—hated as well as idolized—also emerges clearly, but Plutarch was not concerned to be even-handed. His prime concern as a biographer was to probe moral character, not to duplicate the focus on political and military affairs adopted by historians. From the specimen of Tiberius' oratory that this extract preserves, we gain a vivid glimpse of his skill in appealing to the emotions of the crowd at a time of tremendous tension in Rome.*

[Tiberius] certainly did not draft the law just by himself, but consulted citizens of outstanding merit and reputation, including Crassus the *pontifex maximus*, the jurist (and consul at the time) Mucius Scaevola, and his own father-in-law Appius Claudius. Never, one might think, was a law aimed at such injustice and greed drafted more mildly and delicately. … But despite the tact with which matters were made right, and the readiness of the people to put the past behind them provided these wrongs would not recur, greed nonetheless led the men of wealth and property to detest the law and—in their rage and rivalry—its proposer. They attempted to change the minds of the people by arguing that Tiberius was introducing land redistribution to throw the state into turmoil and stir up revolution. Their efforts failed, however. The fact was that Tiberius—battling for a worthy, just cause with an eloquence capable of enhancing far less reputable ones—proved formidable enough to outclass any opponent whenever he took his position on the rostra and spoke about the poor, with the people thronging around him: "Every wild creature that lives in Italy has its own den and place to sleep and shelter. But the men who fight and die for Italy have a share in nothing more than its air and light. With their wives and children they roam homeless and unsettled. It's a lie when the commanders urge soldiers in battle to protect their graves and shrines from the enemy. Not one of them has a family altar, none of these Romans has an ancestral tomb. They go to war and die, rather, for the sake of others' wealth and luxury. 'Lords of the earth' they're hailed, but not one clod of it is theirs." (*Life of Tiberius Gracchus* 9)

on the part of many senators to preserve their own landholdings. Political considerations may also have had a role. Securing the passage of welcome reforms would have increased Tiberius' popularity and prestige, and, in the highly competitive atmosphere of Roman elite politics, this could only come at the expense of his rivals for office. It is perhaps no surprise that, unlike other tribunes, he omitted to seek senatorial approval for his measure before presenting it to the Plebeian assembly.

In the meetings that Tiberius Gracchus called to publicize his law and to mobilize support for it, another tribune, Marcus Octavius, emerged as his chief opponent. Octavius announced his intention to use his power as tribune to prevent a vote. In the past, tribunes had generally used their vetoes against consuls and praetors. A tribune's interference with the actions of another tribune was relatively rare, and the tribune who sought to veto a proposal of a colleague usually gave way if the colleague was able to muster popular or senatorial support against the obstruction. In dramatic confrontations in public meetings, Tiberius sought unsuccessfully to persuade or to pressure Octavius to withdraw his veto. He even attempted to increase the pressure on his opponent by blocking other public business himself and by locking the public treasury. Finally, he sought to remove his intransigent colleague from office—a step that was also unprecedented—seeking to justify the action by the assertion that a tribune who attempted to obstruct the people's ability to vote had failed in his duty to protect their rights. Here, he was successful, and the Plebeian assembly did remove Octavius from office, and then replaced him with another tribune. Soon after, the assembly enacted the agrarian law. In a later assembly, voters chose Tiberius himself, his brother Gaius, and his father-in-law, Appius Claudius Pulcher, to be agrarian commissioners.

Tiberius' efforts to enact his law and the attempts of his opponents to block it had escalated through a series of unprecedented actions, which must have increased tensions between the participants and among the citizen body as a whole. This escalation and the rancor that accompanied it did not end with the law's passage. The senate had long had the right to determine the amount of public funds that magistrates would receive to perform their duties. Now, senators voted the Gracchan triumvirs only a trivial sum. At this time, by coincidence, word reached Rome of the death of Attalus III, king of Pergamum, who had no heirs and had left his kingdom to the Romans in his will. In consequence, Tiberius acted in a way that undercut the senate's claims to manage Rome's foreign affairs and its finances. He successfully introduced to the Plebeian assembly a new proposal turning over Attalus' treasure to the triumvirs, so that they could finance their operations and give benefits to those poor for whom there was insufficient land.

Tiberius then announced that he would run for reelection as tribune, another act without apparent precedent. His motive, we are told, was fear that his enemies would seek to prosecute him when he left office, and that they would attempt in some way to nullify his agrarian law. In the electoral assembly, after the first two tribes had voted for Tiberius, his opponents began to assert that it was illegal for him to seek reelection, and, amid arguments, the assembly was adjourned. As the day for the new vote approached, crowds began to gather around the Capitol where the vote would be held, while the senate met in the nearby Temple of Fides. Here, Tiberius' opponents apparently argued that he was seeking to make himself tyrant, and they sought unsuccessfully to persuade the presiding consul Scaevola to authorize the use of force against him. Then, Scipio Nasica, the *pontifex maximus*, with a number of other senators and their retainers, left the meeting of the senate and attacked Tiberius and his supporters with wooden cudgels, according to one account killing two to three hundred. One of Tiberius' colleagues as tribune beat him to death with the leg of a stool. This may well have been the first political murder of a Roman officeholder for a very long time; the only possible precedents lie as far back as the fifth century. When Scipio

Aemilianus at Numantia heard of Tiberius Gracchus' death, he quoted a verse from Homer's *Odyssey*: "So may perish all others who venture on such wickedness." After his return to Rome, when he made clear his disapproval of Gracchus' law, Scipio lost the popularity he had held for so long.

In the following year, 132, the senate assigned both consuls the task of conducting a formal investigation into the conduct of Tiberius' supporters. Their investigation was harsh, and they are reported to have ordered executions, although no other senators seem to have suffered. Alarming portents convinced the senate and the members of the priestly college charged with their interpretation that the goddess Ceres, patron deity of the tribunate, was angered by the murder of the sacrosanct tribune, and expiatory sacrifices were made.

Tiberius Gracchus' murder did not result in the clear triumph of his opponents. The land commission, in particular, continued to operate. Crassus replaced Tiberius Gracchus on the triumvirate, and when he and Claudius died, Marcus Fulvius Flaccus and Gaius Papirius Carbo were chosen to replace them; Flaccus and Carbo would both reach the office of consul. A few inscribed boundary markers document the commission's impact in Campania, Picenum, Samnium, Lucania, and Apulia, areas where large tracts of land had been confiscated at the end of the Second Punic War. The Gracchan commissioners seem to have encountered much resistance, and some disorder may have accompanied their judgments and settlements. In 129, however, Scipio Aemilianus succeeded in blocking further action, by claiming (on grounds that are now obscure) that the commission was interfering with the rights of allied communities.

Gaius Gracchus

When Gaius Gracchus sought the tribunate for 123, his candidacy was much anticipated by opponents and supporters alike. In the years after his brother's death, lines of conflict had hardened; many hoped for a revival of reform, while others feared it. As quaestor in 126, Gaius had been assigned to accompany the consul Lucius Aurelius Orestes to Sardinia. The senate prorogued Orestes' governorship three times, perhaps to keep Gaius away from Rome. In 124, however, Gaius returned to Rome without waiting for an end to the consul's promagistracy. He apparently received a hero's welcome in the city, where many expected him to be the new advocate for the citizenry. Huge and enthusiastic crowds came to Rome for the election. Despite attempts to undermine his popularity, Gaius' candidacy was successful. In 123, he even gained reelection as tribune, an action that had led to his brother's death. His associate Marcus Fulvius Flaccus also sought and won election as tribune for 122, an unprecedented act for a former consul.

In our sources, Gaius Gracchus appears as a more complex and more confrontational figure than his brother. Tiberius' reform had limited goals at first; he became more controversial as opposition grew. Gaius introduced a large number of laws, covering a wide range of matters, which suggests that he had a clear legislative agenda. His laws are the only direct evidence for his plans, and their provisions and chronology are often unclear. Analysis of this legislation, moreover, can support different views of his goals. In an unfriendly account, Diodorus Siculus (34/35.25) claimed that Gaius Gracchus sought to bring down the senate, and for this reason tried to stir up others against it. More probably, Gaius merely wished to curb some of the excesses of the senate's rule, rather than eliminating it altogether.

As tribune, Gaius began a long, fast-moving series of actions that must have greatly encouraged his supporters, while arousing the fears of his opponents. He is reported to have been an electrifying speaker, perhaps the best of his day, capable of moving crowds with tremendous displays of enthusiasm and emotion. Our sources often depict him as surrounded by crowds of associates and well-wishers. The frequent meetings of the citizen body necessary to enact his many laws would have created a constant feeling of excitement among supporters and opponents alike. Like his brother, he probably did not bring any of his proposals to the senate for discussion. Even so, he too had supporters among his fellow senators, although they seem a more shadowy group and on the whole less senior than Tiberius' had been. Perhaps the most prominent was Marcus Fulvius Flaccus, a member of the agrarian commission alongside Gaius himself, and consul in 125. On occasion, others cooperated too, although the depth of their commitment is far from certain.

Among Gaius' earliest measures were laws aimed against the investigations that had led to the execution of so many of his brother's supporters. In the past, the senate had authorized most investigations, and, by extension, the punishments that had resulted from them. Laws passed by citizen assemblies authorized other prosecutions; the juries of senators that judged cases of extortion, for example, were authorized by a law proposed by a tribune in 149. One of Gaius' laws now prescribed a capital sentence for any magistrate who had imposed a capital sentence as a result of a *quaestio* or investigation that had not been authorized by the vote of a citizen assembly. After the passage of this law, Publius Popillius Laenas, who as consul in 132 had presided over the executions of Tiberius' supporters, went into exile, no doubt to avoid prosecution. Another law, probably connected in some way with the first, imposed the death penalty on anyone serving as a judge in some quaestio, who accepted a bribe to declare an innocent defendant guilty.

Gaius also introduced a range of laws that he probably expected to be popular among the bulk of the city's population. He renewed his brother's land law, but with some modifications. His commissioners no longer had the power to determine which lands were "public" and which were private, an apparent recognition of the controversy that these powers had caused and the resistance they had inspired. Later, he would secure the passage of laws authorizing the foundation of several colonies in Italy and one—to be named Junonia—in North Africa on the site of Carthage. Another early measure would also have contributed to his popularity in Rome. In all likelihood the city's poorer residents often faced difficulty in obtaining sufficient grain at a price they could afford. The aediles had long supervised the city's markets—where they sought to ensure, for example, that merchants used the proper weights and measures, that they did not mix any gravel with grain, and did not hoard grain in the hopes that prices would rise. More recently, some officials had sought to increase the amount of grain available in the city. Gaius Gracchus took this initiative one step farther. His law now guaranteed citizens the right to purchase in Rome a set amount of grain each month at a fixed price. Thus the state now had to arrange for a regular supply of grain, and to make up the difference whenever the fixed price for citizens turned out to be lower than the market price; it also had to construct granaries and improve harbor facilities.

Certain measures may have been crafted to define and limit some of the senate's most important prerogatives, although it is possible that they were merely aimed against prominent abuses. One law required that senators decide before elections the provinces that would be allocated between the new consuls. Gaius may have intended this law—which remained in effect after his death—to free the process of determining provinces from the intrigues of new consuls, their friends, and their opponents. Another law prescribed that taxes in the new province of Asia (formed out of the old kingdom of Pergamum) should be collected by Roman publicani bidding for contracts at Rome—the first known instance when these state contractors collected the revenues from an entire province. Some have seen this measure as sign that Gaius wished to mobilize the publicani against the senate, but it may have been aimed simply against official corruption in the province.

Perhaps the most important limitation of the senate's role concerned membership on the juries of the standing courts. In 149, a tribunician law had determined that juries made up of senators would judge cases involving corruption in the provinces. Here, accusers petitioned the urban praetor to put together a jury comprising selected senators. These jurors heard testimony and then rendered their verdict, which could not be appealed. Since only former officeholders and senators could be defendants in these cases—only they were in a position to extort money from provincials—the result of the measure was that in these matters senators would judge other senators. Gaius Gracchus' jury law now created a new list of jurors that evidently excluded senators altogether, perhaps a response to the way in which senatorial jurors had handled prominent trials. Instead, lists of potential jurors were in future to be chosen from the class of citizens called *equites*. Clauses that survive on a bronze tablet may be part of this law. If the identification is correct, Gaius plainly went to great lengths to exclude any senator or any juror closely related to one.

The equites formed an important part of the Roman elite, and, in the late second century, they seem to become more clearly distinguished from the membership of the senate. In Rome, an *eques* (plural, *equites*) literally meant a cavalryman. Originally, officials conducting the *census* had enrolled those eligible to serve in Rome's cavalry in the equestrian centuries. Later, probably during the fourth century, others who possessed sufficient wealth to supply their own horses were also expected to serve in the cavalry, although censors did not enroll them in the equestrian centuries; they too came to be called equites, even though they did not possess the voting privileges held by those who were actually enrolled in the designated centuries. Publicani who undertook major contracts would certainly have been included in their numbers. A few years before Gaius' tribunate, there appears to have been an attempt to bar senators from membership in these centuries, perhaps in an effort to create an equestrian order distinct from the senatorial, or merely an attempt to create more spaces for nonsenators. Much later, the historian Appian (*Civil Wars* 1.3.22) would claim, with some exaggeration, that Gaius had made the equites "rulers over the senate and the senators virtually their subjects."

Probably in Gaius's second term (122), he and Marcus Fulvius Flaccus proposed to extend Roman citizenship. During the second century, as we have already observed, Rome's allies came to bear more of the burdens of empire while receiving a declining share of the benefits, and Roman officials began to treat their Italian allies in many of the same harsh ways that they treated their subjects outside of Italy. Tiberius Gracchus' land reform may have aggravated the problem, since most of the activity of the commissioners seems to have taken place in the lands of allies. In 126, a tribune Marcus Junius Pennus carried a law ordering the expulsion of all non-Romans from Rome. Flaccus, when consul in 125, had proposed extending Roman citizenship more widely, and giving those who did not want citizenship the right of appeal against harsh actions by Roman magistrates; the matter had to drop, however, when he left for his province. Now in 122, Gaius Gracchus unsuccessfully proposed a law which would give Roman citizenship to all Latins, and the privileges of Latins to all the Italian allies. This measure, which is unlikely to have been popular among the citizens of Rome, may have begun the decline in Gaius' popularity that would result in his death.

Gaius' opponents did not confront him in the same manner that their predecessors had opposed his brother Tiberius. No tribune seems to have dared to block his laws, as Octavius had done a decade earlier. Instead, some of his enemies attempted to win away his followers through programs of their own and through shameless appeals to citizens' selfishness. Gaius Fannius (consul in 122) challenged a crowd: "You think, I imagine, that if you give citizenship to the Latins, you are going to have a place, as you do now, in the assembly (*contio*) in which you are standing, and to gain admittance to games and festivals? Don't you realize that they will fill up everything?" (*ORF* fr. 3). In 123, Quintus Fabius Maximus, a governor in Spain, shipped grain from his province to Rome in an apparent attempt to undermine Gaius' popularity among the beneficiaries of his grain law. Gaius' most successful opponent was Marcus Livius Drusus the Elder, tribune of the plebs in 122. Like Gaius, Drusus was an effective speaker, and was often surrounded by crowds of enthusiastic supporters. In an apparent effort to undermine the popularity that Gaius had gained by reenacting his brother's agrarian law and by his own colonial laws, Drusus proposed to found a series of colonies in which land would be given to more people. While Drusus campaigned for his measure, Gaius

Gracchus and Flaccus left Rome to direct the foundation of the colony at Carthage. When they returned, the political situation had changed drastically, and their popular following was not as large or as secure as it had once been. In ways that are obscure to us, Gaius also lost ground among the equites.

After his return, Gaius sought a third term as tribune for 121. This time, he was unsuccessful. The details of his defeat are unclear, but his supporters apparently alleged that the vote had been manipulated in some way. In 121, when Gaius was now out of office, the consul Lucius Opimius and several of the tribunes began to try to revoke some of his laws. Plutarch (*Gaius Gracchus* 13.1) claims that they also tried to provoke Gaius and Flaccus into some action that could be branded illegal. An attempt to repeal the law authorizing the foundation of the colony at Carthage began the final confrontation. Gaius and Flaccus, with a large following, attended the meeting where one of the tribunes was seeking to marshal support for the proposed repeal. At this assembly, in a confrontation between the supporters of both sides, a herald of the consul Opimius was killed. Opimius treated the death as a direct and deliberate attack against the state, and he summoned Gaius and Flaccus to the senate to defend themselves. When the two failed to appear, Opimius called on wealthy citizens to gather with their servants to defend the state. Gaius, Flaccus, and their supporters then withdrew to the Aventine hill, so long associated with the Roman plebs. Opimius offered no concessions, and even imprisoned a son of Flaccus, who had come to him as an envoy. Opimius then ordered an attack, in which some archers from the island of Crete whom he had stationed nearby joined—a possible indication that he had planned for just this outcome. Flaccus was killed in the fighting, and Gaius Gracchus committed suicide. Three thousand of their supporters are reported to have died in the fighting and in the prosecutions that followed.

Opimius based his actions on what came to be called the "Final Decree of the Senate" (*senatus consultum ultimum*), where senators instructed the consul "to take care that the state suffered no harm"—that is, to do what he considered necessary to preserve the political and social order without regard for the normal protections and rights due to citizens. These events leading up to Gaius' death were the first occasion on which the senate passed such a decree, and its legality would long be contested. In this "ultimate decree" (the SCU), senators asserted their ability to authorize investigations and punishments just as they had done after the death of Tiberius Gracchus, and in just the way that Gaius Gracchus had tried to prevent in his own laws.

The tribunates of Tiberius and Gaius Gracchus were to begin a tumultuous period in Rome's domestic politics, and their careers and their fates illustrate both the strengths and the weaknesses of this office. As long as a popular leader could muster a large following as they did, he could exercise considerable power in the city. This popularity had to be constantly reinforced, however. Some of the laws and issues of these years—land and grain distributions, control of the courts, and extensions of citizenship—would long remain prominent in the programs of ambitious tribunes. At the same time, opponents had little ability to block popular tribunes through normal means, so that resorting to violence would also remain an option.

In the following decades, a sharp division in political styles would develop among members of the Roman governing elite. Some would follow the traditional methods of competition within the senatorial order, making the traditional alliances and building coalitions of senators to back their plans and their ambitions. Those who furthered their careers in this manner came to be known as *optimates*, a label that marks their self-identification as the best people in the city. Others sought wider popularity among the citizen body as a way to advance careers and agendas, and the term *popularis* (plural, *populares*) identified them. In some cases, it should be noted, ambitious Romans could behave as optimates or as populares at different times in their careers.

SUGGESTED READINGS

Astin, Alan E. 1967. *Scipio Aemilianus*. Oxford: Oxford University Press. Despite Scipio's absence from Rome in 133, this book includes two admirably clear, full chapters on the tribunate of Tiberius Gracchus.

Bradley, Keith R. 1989. *Slavery and Rebellion in the Roman World, 140 B.C.–70 B.C.* Bloomington: Indiana University Press.

Erskine, Andrew. 2010. *Roman Imperialism*. Edinburgh: Edinburgh University Press. Concise analysis with marked attention to the second century B.C., followed by extracts from key sources in translation.

Morley, Neville. 1996. *Metropolis and Hinterland: The City of Rome and the Italian Economy, 200 B.C.–A.D. 200*. Cambridge: Cambridge University Press.

Rosenstein, Nathan. 2004. *Rome at War: Farms, Families, and Death in the Middle Republic*. Chapel Hill and London: University of North Carolina Press. This study reinterprets Italy's social and economic problems in the period prior to the tribunates of Tiberius and Gaius Gracchus, and thus challenges the standard perspective adopted in the present chapter.

Stockton, David. 1979. *The Gracchi*. Oxford: Oxford University Press.

ITALY THREATENED, ENFRANCHISED, DIVIDED

Any Romans who had hoped that the brutal elimination of Gaius Gracchus and his associates in 121 might mark an end to violence and turmoil were to be sadly disappointed by the outcome of events during the following twenty years or so. Unfortunately, the surviving ancient accounts of this period (and well beyond) are for the most part too sketchy for us to monitor the unfolding of events in depth, let alone offer satisfactory explanations for many of them. A senator of the mid-first century, Sallust (Gaius Sallustius Crispus), made the war with Jugurtha the subject of a moralizing, rhetorical monograph. For a broader perspective, however, we must rely above all on the biographer Plutarch, whose *Lives* of Marius and Sulla survive, and the narrative of Rome's civil wars composed by the historian Appian.

CHANGES IN ROMAN SOCIETY

The transformation of Roman society and politics that began in the second century and continued into the first also altered Roman private life and the roles and status of Roman women. Our grasp of these changes is by no means firm, and it is really only from the second century that we gain any knowledge of individual named Roman women; even then they are so few that it is hard to assess the representativeness of someone like Cornelia, the mother of the Gracchi brothers (Chapter Four). Nevertheless, by assembling and analyzing literary, documentary, visual, and legal evidence, we can gain important insights into Roman social history of the mid- to late Republic.

The basic unit of Roman society was the "house" or extended family, conceived of as a tightly knit unit obedient to the "father of the family" (*pater familias*) and under his authority. The conceptual family was the husband and wife, and all their children, slaves, freedmen and freedwomen, and other dependents such as young orphaned relatives who had been entrusted by a court of law to the pater familias. He controlled all property, and all transactions were to be authorized by him. Even grown sons—who advanced to manhood and liability for military duty when they assumed the *toga virilis* between the ages of fourteen and sixteen —were under their father's authority until he died or they were otherwise "freed" by him. If a woman passed into her husband's control at her wedding (in what is termed a *cum manu* marriage), she, too, could make no legally binding decisions without her husband, and owned no major property of her own. In an alternative form of Roman marriage (*sine manu*), however, the wife nominally remained under the power of her father, which meant that "her" property did not become her husband's.

Women, like men, were expected to marry, and to bear and raise children. Respectable opinion expected a first-time bride to be a virgin, and Roman law in fact allowed her to be as young as twelve (and her husband fourteen). Even so, in practice it would be more typical for a woman to marry during her late teens to a man in his late twenties, except at the top social level, where the ages of both bride and groom might well be a few years lower. Marriages are prominent in at least some of Rome's political alliances during the second century, linking together the Scipio and the Gracchus families, for example. But it is probably a mistake to see women simply as pawns here. Despite the traditional power of the pater familias, we know of no instances of a woman being forced into a marriage, and by the first century women such as Cicero's daughter Tullia definitely had a say in the choice of their husbands.

The ideal of the pater familias was not only reinforced by Roman law beginning with the Twelve Tables, but was also tied to the equally powerful Roman ideal of the farmer-citizen who remained on his property except for periodic skirmishing with hostile neighbors, voting in Rome, or otherwise fulfilling civic duties. Although women could also be classified as citizens and could play a role in Roman religion, only citizen men could participate in most activities that clearly defined a Roman: military service (from the lowest duties to commands), voting on legislation and candidates for office, and holding an elective position either locally or at Rome. Only men could be appointed to any magistracy or administrative or judicial office. As Rome expanded, however, the ideal of the farmer-citizen became increasingly hard to maintain. Numerous changes for Roman families and households were set in motion, not least by the overseas wars beginning in the third century; these kept many men away from home for years on end. Such prolonged absence of a pater familias must have been especially shocking to families in which the wife and other relatives were under the husband's control. Roman women were usually not educated in a way that might prepare them for involvement in property and business transactions or in legal and ethical deliberations. The level of education that they typically received was lower than that arranged for male siblings (in a society where no community provided any schooling, let alone made it compulsory). It was to sons alone that the handbooks written by Cato the Elder and other authors were addressed, and we have nothing at all written by a woman until the end of the Republic. Women were expected to help run the household, educate their children (as did Cornelia), and undertake many religious duties; they must have consulted with their husbands and other family members on these and other matters in the normal Roman way. Even so, there can be no question that long-term absence on the part of their spouses deprived Roman women of legal and other support, and added to their burdens.

Such strain may be one reason why very few Roman women were married *cum manu* by the first century. This change, which can be dated only generally, could have given a wife more agency during the times that her husband was away, because the property of a wife married *sine manu* was not subsumed to that of his, although legally she was still under the control of her father. In any case, the change is one among several that suggest the emergence of a little more individuality, independence, and respect for women, at least at the top of Rome's society.

Whether the prospects for poorer Roman women likewise improved at the same period is doubtful, however. It was households headed by men, not women, which stood to benefit from the new schemes that offered land and a fresh start in the countryside. Meantime poor rural families evidently migrated in large numbers to Rome and other cities; but no industries were to be found there, and very few occupations were open to women. If a woman were fortunate enough to possess the appropriate skills or education, she could work as a nurse or midwife, or at some craft or trade. Less training was needed to eke out a living as a musical entertainer, barmaid, or prostitute—all of them professions that the law grouped together. Freeborn women might also work as a wet-nurse, nanny, servant, or personal attendant, although in rich households slaves usually held these positions.

Richer, more politically active families used the growing cities as showcases, and women increasingly played a part in the exhibition of prestige. Rome's first sumptuary law, the *Lex Oppia*, was passed in 215 when the severe losses in the Second Punic War demanded extraordinary measures. This law debarred women from having more than a small amount of gold, wearing multi-colored clothes, or using vehicles drawn by an animal within a city or a one-mile radius beyond, except during public religious festivals. These measures demonstrate that wealthy women were by no means confined to their homes, that they customarily took part in their community's religious ceremonies, and that their style of dress could attract attention. Moreover, to judge by surviving representations from the period, there is no cause to think that women's clothing covered their faces or otherwise masked their appearance. By 195, six years after the successful conclusion of the Second Punic War, the Lex Oppia was repealed. Despite fierce objections from Cato the Elder, voters were persuaded by arguments that clothing, gold, and other refinements were marks of status for women, just as magistracies, priesthoods, triumphs, and war trophies were for men (Livy 34.8). During the second century the female relatives of the Scipios became well known for the opulence of their dress and carriages, their sacrificial utensils, and the crowds of their female and male attendants during Rome's religious festivals. A public funeral for a woman was held in the Forum—by a prominent senator for his mother Popilia—for the first time around 102. There can be no doubt that this greater visibility of wealthy women stems from the increasingly competitive politics of the period.

WAR WITH JUGURTHA (112–105)

Despite our uneven understanding, two developments in the years after Gaius Gracchus' death emerge clearly enough as special challenges for the state and the source of lasting change. Both were external, and both took Rome by surprise. At the center of the first was a Numidian named Jugurtha, who had been adopted by King Micipsa, the son and (since 148) successor to Rome's longstanding ally Masinissa; Jugurtha's own father was a brother of Micipsa who died prematurely. Micipsa, however, also had two sons of his own, both younger than Jugurtha. So on Micipsa's death, around 118, the kingdom was left jointly to all three. But any hopes of a working partnership were soon dashed, especially after Micipsa's sons had complained of how Jugurtha was placed above them. Consequently, Jugurtha had one (Hiempsal) murdered, and the other (Adherbal) driven out of Numidia altogether. Adherbal then begged help from Rome, so in 116 the senate dispatched a commission of inquiry headed by Lucius Opimius, the brutal consul of 121; it divided the kingdom, assigning the west to Jugurtha and the more developed east to Adherbal. Jugurtha's acceptance of this settlement is notable, as is the senate's willingness to intervene so deeply in what were, after all, the affairs of a foreign state. To be sure, Numidia was an old ally of Rome, it now had a long common border with the Roman province of Africa, and Rome naturally wanted a stable neighbor there. Perhaps the senate's hope was that this degree of intervention would suffice to ensure long-term stability.

If so, Jugurtha soon demonstrated otherwise by invading Adherbal's territory; by 112 he had him trapped in his capital Cirta (modern Qacentina/Constantine, in eastern Algeria). The senate's protests left Jugurtha unmoved. Eventually Adherbal surrendered, and Jugurtha executed him along with some Italian businessmen in Cirta who had been Adherbal's supporters. Romans' sharp reaction to these outrages now impelled the senate to send forces to discipline Jugurtha, though their campaigns had limited success at best. Diplomacy was tried again, too, but proved futile, especially in 111 when Jugurtha even came to Rome, only to

Map 5.1 *Rome's Foreign Wars, 113–82*

E   F   G

BLACK SEA

PONTUS

THRACIA

Danube

Byzantium

BITHYNIA

PAPHLAGONIA

CAPPADOCIA

MACEDONIA

Dardanus

Pergamum

ASIA

CILICIA

AEGEAN SEA

Orchomenus

Ephesus

Antioch

Orontes

SYRIA

Chaeronea

Athenae

Apamea

CRETA

INTERNUM MARE

Alexandria

Pelusium

Cyrene

AEGYPTUS

Nile

Ancient World Mapping Center 2011

be required by a tribune's veto not to speak there at all. In 110, the senate rejected a treaty made by a Roman commander in the field, and general dissatisfaction with its whole handling of the Numidian problem came to a head. Understandably, Jugurtha was suspected of having bought the silence or support of various senators; after all, he had had close personal links with upper-class Romans from an early age, after serving at Numantia under Scipio Aemilianus.

The effectiveness of the Roman forces in Numidia improved under Quintus Caecilius Metellus in 109–108, and likewise from 107 onwards under the commander who displaced him (in circumstances treated below), Gaius Marius. Only in 105, however, was the war at last brought to an end when Marius' quaestor, Lucius Cornelius Sulla (another figure we shall return to), successfully persuaded Jugurtha's ally King Bocchus of Mauretania to betray him to the Romans. Jugurtha was then executed after being paraded in Marius' triumph the following year. Meantime Bocchus was granted part of Numidia to add to his own kingdom, while a brother of Jugurtha was made ruler of the rest. Roman honor was thereby restored, and an unreliable neighbor to the province of Africa removed. Otherwise, however, it is striking how minimally the settlement of 105/4 differs from what Opimius' commission had determined just over a decade earlier. Rome exacted no direct permanent gain from this costly, prolonged series of embarrassments; there was no wish to annex Numidia. The fundamental shortcoming—just as on several occasions earlier in the second century—was the senate's lack of capacity for determining the extent and the timing of any Roman intervention in the affairs of a foreign state.

ITALY THREATENED FROM THE NORTH (113–101)

The second development that surprised and challenged the Roman state towards the end of the second century was a migration south by groups of German peoples, principally the Cimbri and Teutoni. Why they left their homeland in north Jutland is not certain; possibly they were suffering from a combination of population growth and the loss of low-lying land to encroachment by the sea. By 113 they had drifted as far as the eastern Alps, where they defeated a Roman consul and his army who had been sent to observe them. Next, by entering the Rhone river valley, they posed a threat to Rome's province of Transalpine Gaul (formed in 121), in particular after they had defeated another consul and his army in 109. Further Roman defeats followed in 107, and again most seriously of all at Arausio (modern Orange) in 105, where the catastrophic losses stemmed in part from the refusal of Quintus Servilius Caepio (a noble who had been consul in 106) to cooperate with his superior, the *novus homo* consul Gnaeus Mallius Maximus.

The tribes' next move was evidently northwards, rather than south towards Italy; but in Rome, understandably, feelings of panic prevailed. News of the disaster at Arausio came not long after confirmation of Jugurtha's capture. So at the elections for the consulship of 104, with the war in Numidia now known to be over, Marius was elected in his absence and assigned the command in Gaul. For this purpose, the law of the late 150s permitting no more than a single tenure of the consulship had also to be somehow set aside; we do not know who took the initiative in doing this, or the means adopted. Even more remarkable is Marius' subsequent reelection as consul every year through 100, by which date he had held the office for five

Figure 5.1 *This bronze tablet—today in the museum of Cáceres (Spain)—displays the text translated as Source 5.1. It was found during excavation of a hilltop site known as Villavieja, near Alcántara, on the southern side of the Tagus river (Map 3.4). Because the right-hand end of the tablet has been shorn off and lost, the exact wording on each line must remain uncertain; but the general sense is never in doubt. Neither the Latin of this Roman document, nor the way in which it is inscribed, is especially elegant, but both are representative of their time.*

years consecutively and six in total. These reelections are a puzzle insofar as he might just as well have been continued in his command as proconsul. In all likelihood, however, there was an overwhelming desire on the part of voters to guard against any repetition of the standoff between Caepio and Mallius at Arausio; Marius was to remain in command without question.

In the event, the tribes' movement north in 105 gave Marius the precious breathing space he needed to restore the Roman army's strength with recruitment, training, and new equipment. To add to the strain, a force was also now needed in Sicily to suppress a second formidable slave rebellion there, which erupted in 104 (see Chapter Four and Fig. 4.4 for the first rebellion). By the time that the tribes did eventually turn south, Marius was able to defeat the Teutoni at Aquae Sextiae (modern Aix-en-Provence in southern France) in 102, and the Cimbri at Vercellae in northern Italy the following year. With the threat from the tribes thus removed, Marius was appropriately hailed as Rome's savior and offered two triumphs (he took only one); his election as consul for 100 reflected popular gratitude.

SOURCE 5.1: *The formal procedure for total, unconditional surrender* (deditio in fidem*) that Rome might traditionally demand from a defeated enemy (see Chapter Two) is well known from the historians Polybius and Livy. Only a single documentary record of an actual instance survives, however, on a partially preserved bronze tablet (Fig. 5.1). This deditio was made by an otherwise unknown people in Spain (the end of their name is lost too) in 104— proof that even after the wars there which ended with the capture of Numantia in 133 (see Chapter Three), challenges to Roman control still recurred periodically:*

In the consulship of G. Marius and G. Flavius:
The people of Seano … gave up themselves and theirs to L. Caesius, son of Gaius, *imperator* (commander). L. Caesius, son of Gaius, imperator, after he accepted them into his trust, referred to his *consilium* (council) what orders they considered should be issued to them. On the advice of his consilium he ordered that they hand over their arms, deserters, captives, stallions, and mares that they had taken. All these they handed over. Then L. Caesius, son of Gaius, imperator, ordered that they be free; he handed back to them the lands and buildings, laws and everything else such as then existed which had been theirs on the day before they gave themselves up, insofar as it should be the wish of the Roman people and senate, and he ordered that envoys should go [to somewhere: Rome?] concerning this matter. Crenus, son of …, and Arco, son of Cantonus, were the envoys…. (*AE* 1986. 304)

CHANGES IN THE ROMAN ARMY

Without question, the end of the second century saw changes not only to the recruitment of the Roman army (see next section), but also to its equipment, training, and battle formation (for training, see further Figure 6.1). More problematic, however, is just how extensive and sudden these changes were, as well as how far they were initiated by Marius himself (as our sources maintain). It may have been he who made the eagle a legion's principal standard, and who had javelins (*pila*; singular, *pilum*) produced with a weak rivet; once thrown, the shaft would buckle on landing and become useless to the enemy. It was evidently Marius, too, who required soldiers to carry more of their gear themselves than had been regular practice; hence the quip that they had become "Marius' mules" (*muli Mariani*). Less clear is the degree to which Marius reformed the army's battle formation. What we hear of battle formation from Julius Caesar's extensive descriptions in the mid-first century shows marked differences from Polybius' account in the mid-second. In particular, by Caesar's time there are no longer three distinct ranks of infantry identifiable by age and equipment, nor do Romans serve as cavalry or light-armed troops at this date. Instead, the two latter roles are now filled by allied auxiliaries, while the heavy infantry has become a uniform body of Romans grouped in larger formations (cohorts of four to five hundred men) than had been the norm a century earlier. Given Marius' urgent need to recruit widely and provide inexperienced men with fast, effective training to meet the threatened invasion of Italy from the north, it is tempting to speculate that he played some part in advancing these important changes, even if their introduction began earlier. What the army lost by them in flexibility, it gained in cohesive fighting power, and this was a vital boost after its series of demoralizing recent defeats.

MARIUS' CAREER IN ROMAN POLITICS

In the competitive atmosphere of Roman politics, multiple triumphs and consulships represented enviable distinction even for a noble of impeccably distinguished background. For a *novus homo* like Marius, they were honors beyond his wildest dreams. Now is the point, therefore, to review Marius' political career, with particular reference to appreciating its relationship to his military success and the resulting impact on the Roman state. Marius was born about 157 near Arpinum, a town sixty miles (96 km) southeast of Rome. His family had equestrian status, but was otherwise prominent only locally; even so, he was somehow able to serve under Scipio Aemilianus at Numantia, and he distinguished himself

---

SOURCE 5.2: *This sketch by Sallust of how Marius advanced himself to the point where he eventually dared to stand for the consulship may be uncritical, not to say exaggerated and inaccurate in certain respects. However, its tone is still instructive, as are the aspects selected for attention:*

Even prior to this stage [in 108], Marius had been obsessed by a powerful longing for the consulship, an office which he was amply qualified in every way to fill, except that he did not come from an old family. He was a hard worker, a man of integrity, and a highly capable soldier. He devoted his energies to warfare. His private life was unremarkable, and he was no slave to passion or riches; all he craved was glory. His birthplace was Arpinum, where he had spent all his boyhood. As soon as he reached the age to enlist, he had gone on active service, training himself in this way rather than by any course of Greek rhetoric or city polish. With this fine education his sound character soon matured. So on the first occasion that he stood for election as military tribune, even though many citizens did not know him by sight, they were sufficiently aware of his record that all the tribes voted for him. Thereafter he won one office after another, invariably shouldering his responsibilities in such a way that he was thought to merit the next higher one. Even so, despite the worth he had demonstrated thus far, he never—and I say this of a man who later would be ruined by overambition—dared to aspire to the consulship. This was still a time when plebeians might win other offices, but the consulship was handed down by the nobles from one of their own number to the next. For this distinction, a "new man" (novus homo)—no matter how famous he might be, or how outstanding his record—was considered unworthy, and even tainted. (*Jugurthine War* 63)

there. Not until after further military service, however, did he attempt to stand for office at Rome, and then only with the backing of a leading noble family, the Metelli. With this help he gained the quaestorship sometime in the late 120s, followed by the tribunate in 119. Thereafter he failed in his attempt to become aedile, and only just secured election as praetor in 115. His prospects for further political advancement were bleak; to build up the necessary wealth and influential support was a hard struggle. He did proceed to benefit financially, however, from a governorship in Further Spain, and was then able to make an advantageous marriage to Julia, whose family—the Julii Caesares—was an ancient patrician one, though not notably distinguished in the recent past (the famous Julius Caesar, born in 100, was to be her nephew).

In Spain, Marius had revealed a talent for guerilla warfare. This, and the family's previous relationship, prompted Quintus Metellus to make him his second-in-command when he set out against Jugurtha in 109. The two of them quarreled the following year, however, when Metellus denied Marius leave to go to Rome and stand for the consulship of 107. Allegedly, with a noble's condescension towards a novus homo, Metellus recommended the fifty-year-old Marius to wait until his own twenty-year-old son was ready to be a candidate too. Marius returned to Rome and ran for the office regardless, tapping his links with the equites (see Chapter Four), and stressing the need for a change from so much corrupt, ineffectual leadership by nobles. Scipio Aemilianus had successfully exploited such sentiments in earlier times of crisis, and Marius was now able to do the same. When the senate tried to thwart him by reappointing Metellus as commander in Numidia, the Plebeian assembly overruled it and appointed Marius (much as it had appointed Scipio to the command against Carthage).

Although authorized to draft men for his campaign in 107, Marius was wary of the difficulties he was likely to encounter if he attempted this. Instead, therefore, he limited himself to calling for volunteers, promising them rewards. He was even willing to take men of the lowest census rating, who would normally not be recruited because of their lack of property and, by extension, their presumed lack of commitment to the state's welfare. With hindsight, this step has been seen as the source of lasting harm, and Marius has been criticized for not anticipating the difficulties of rewarding his volunteers, as well as for not grasping the degree to which they might prove willing to advance the political ambitions of their commander. Even so, to expect such foresight of Marius or anyone else in 107 is hardly realistic. At that date neither he personally, nor the state generally, could afford to wait and rethink methods of army recruitment. The need for forces to defeat Jugurtha was too urgent, and the manpower available through the regular draft no longer adequate.

In the event, despite opposition, generous plots of land in Africa were readily assigned to the surviving volunteers as a reward in 103. The magistrate whom Marius had to thank for arranging this legislation was an ambitious tribune, Lucius Appuleius Saturninus; he was at odds with the senatorial establishment, and clearly drew inspiration from the example of the Gracchi. At the same time he was even less afraid of confrontation than they, and he cultivated Marius as a potentially valuable patron who would be able to provide military backing in a crisis, if required. It is likely, but not certain, that during 103 Saturninus also introduced a proposal that made Gaius Gracchus' grain distribution scheme more attractive in some way (and more costly for the treasury); if so, this may have helped gain voters' support for the assignment of land to Marius' veterans.

SIXTH CONSULSHIP OF MARIUS AND SECOND TRIBUNATE OF SATURNINUS (100)

In 100, Marius again needed help in rewarding veterans—this time those who had defeated the Cimbri and Teutoni—and he was again willing for Saturninus to act on his behalf. Saturninus was no less a controversial figure than before. He had also developed a working partnership with Gaius Servilius Glaucia. When censor in 102, Quintus Metellus (Marius' old commander) had proposed removing both men from the senate, but his colleague in office would not agree. Now, in 100, Saturninus was tribune again, and Glaucia praetor. Saturninus' legislative proposals were exceptionally wide-ranging, and it was quite predictable that they would provoke opposition. It was not just Marius' veterans that he wanted to settle (on land in Transalpine Gaul). He also proposed the foundation of colonies and allocation of land in Greece and Sicily for veterans of campaigns which had recently ended there (against invaders from Thrace and slave rebels respectively), as well as allocation of land in Cisalpine Gaul for Roman civilians. Such sweeping initiatives, if approved, were sure to make him a highly influential figure.

If this were not provocation enough, his opponents were offended by a clause which required all senators to take an oath to respect the law within five days of its passage; otherwise they would face a crippling fine and expulsion from the senate. The opposition also found fault with the right that Marius was granted to confer Roman citizenship on a small number of the settlers in each of the new colonies. This confirmed that not just Roman citizens, but also allies, were to benefit from the program, and it offered the chance to insinuate that Marius, in his sympathy for improving the allies' status, would next want to extend citizenship far more widely. Popular hostility to the extension of citizenship was again stirred up, just as it had been against Gaius Gracchus. Saturninus might conceivably have deflected it by including among his proposals something of special benefit to voters who lived in Rome itself or close by, in the way that he seems to have done in 103 by manipulating the grain distribution; but, for whatever reason, this time he took no such precaution.

The opposition did everything possible to prevent a vote on the proposals. Tribunes imposed vetoes, and calls were made to disband the assembly on religious grounds because thunder had been heard. Saturninus brushed all these obstacles aside. Once it was clear from the mood of the assembly that the proposals were likely to be rejected, Marius' veterans were deployed to keep hostile voters away by force, and they in turn reacted violently. In the event the veterans won the confrontation, but it took this ugly use of force to ram the proposals through. The immediate need for senators to take the oath embarrassed Marius and raised the tension still further; only Quintus Metellus refused, and he left Rome as soon as Saturninus proposed his exile.

Next Saturninus achieved his own reelection as tribune for 99, but he then overstretched himself in working to have Glaucia made consul. On election day, Marius as the presiding magistrate rejected Glaucia's candidacy since it did not meet the legal requirements. Saturninus then proceeded to have his followers beat a rival candidate to death, and tried to have a law passed permitting Glaucia's candidacy; but even with further resort to violence this attempt failed. The senate was now thoroughly alarmed by such disorder, and for the second time passed its "ultimate decree" (the SCU, first used in 121) instructing the consuls to secure the safety of the state. That step forced Marius to decide whether or not to remain loyal to his associates. He chose to take the lead in pursuing them, and their group soon surrendered to him after receiving an assurance that they would not be summarily executed. When Marius did no more than confine them in the senate house, however, a lynch mob quickly formed to take revenge for their violent treatment of fellow citizens. Men from the mob then climbed to the roof, tore off the tiles, and battered Saturninus, Glaucia, and the others to a gruesome death.

Subsequently, it would seem that the land assignments enacted by Saturninus were respected, but most of his colonies were never founded. The degree to which he was a responsible Popularis politician as opposed to just a manipulative self-seeker is hard to judge. Understandably enough, all the surviving accounts of his activity are hostile. Without question, his impact on political life at Rome was a damaging one. He had proved even more domineering a tribune than Gaius Gracchus, not least because he had grasped how effectively Marius' veterans could be deployed in political struggles. The danger of recruiting the poorest men as volunteers, and offering them rewards which their commander was not in a position to bestow himself, was all too starkly confirmed. The men themselves had nothing to lose by simply supporting their commander. The legality or morality of his ambitions were not their concern, and in any case they would seldom feel capable of evaluating such issues with confidence. As Sallust reflects (*Jugurthine War* 86.3): "If a man is ambitious for power, he can have no better supporters than the poor. They are not worried about their own possessions, since they have none, and whatever will put something into their pockets is right and proper in their eyes."

To be sure, Saturninus appreciated the special value of having veterans to call upon in the event of force being used against him by the senate—as it had been eventually against Gaius Gracchus, who lacked any such support of his own and was thus soon eliminated. But where Saturninus perhaps proved naive was in expecting Marius' continued support as alarm mounted within the senate. With hindsight, the argument could be made that Marius should have seized the opportunity to use his associates and his veterans to establish himself as supreme ruler and reformer of the state. To argue thus, however, would be to misunderstand Marius. He had no plans for reform. Rather, even as a *novus homo* of unprecedented distinction, what he craved most deeply was confirmation that the senatorial establishment now respected him as one of themselves rather than as still the outsider whom Quintus Metellus had so crushingly rebuffed in 108. Once Marius had at last woken to the realization that Saturninus was intent only on pursuing his own advantage in a more and more reckless way, the choice of whether or not to take his side became straightforward. Marius' overriding concern was to maintain the senate's esteem.

Its gratitude to him for decisive implementation of the SCU proved to be short-lived, however. He steadfastly opposed calls to restore Quintus Metellus from exile, and when such a proposal passed in 99 he left Rome for a year or two, claiming that he had a religious vow to fulfil in the East. On his return from there, he was politically active again, but never prominent until an extraordinary turn of events early in the 80s.

ADMINISTRATION OF THE PROVINCES

As explained above in Chapter Three, Rome's annexation of territories beyond Italy—which eventually comprised an "empire" of "provinces"—was a gradual, haphazard process. It is equally important to appreciate that the individual circumstances of an annexation, or the established character of particular communities and their administration, could lead to striking, permanent variations in their treatment. If existing arrangements for administration or taxation were acceptable to Rome, and functioning satisfactorily, there was no wish to overturn them for the sake of achieving uniformity.

Despite all the continuing variation, by the late second century norms for the administration of the provinces had taken shape, and can be outlined with some confidence. The underlying concerns were similar to those for Italy at an earlier stage in Rome's growth. Consequently, each provincial community or people was to continue locally autonomous, staying free from internal strife as well as from warfare with others. Tax (often agricultural produce rather than money) was normally payable to Rome, but there was no regular obligation to furnish manpower for the army. The fundamental components of a province and its organization were encapsulated in a "law of the province" (*lex provinciae*), which defined each community's form of constitution, its boundaries, its relationship with Rome, and its tax obligations. This law could be amended, but only by the senate and people in Rome. Naturally, it was every governor's ultimate work of reference; he was also obliged to adhere to all other relevant Roman legislation. To address matters of current concern, he issued his own edict (often merely repeating what one or other of his predecessors had prescribed).

Each governor had a quaestor assigned to him by the senate, whose special responsibility was to oversee Rome's financial interests in the province. The senate also assigned scribes, lictors, and other orderlies. It was for the governor himself to choose a handful of "legates" (*legati*), who were then officially recognized by the senate. Such men would be upper-class associates, or even relatives, of the governor (normally, but not necessarily, fellow senators), on whom he conferred authority as his deputies. Because their assistance could be of the greatest value, they were often chosen for some special skill or experience—in warfare, for instance. In addition, a governor would usually invite other friends (*amici*) or relatives to join his entourage (*cohors*). They would not have the legates' official status, although they might be included whenever the governor formed a *consilium* in the traditional way to seek advice on cases or issues calling for his decision. Last but not least, governors and their staffs were recommended (though not required) to leave their wives behind. At best, wives were reckoned not to have sufficient stamina for all the traveling required; at worst, their interference in official business was always to be feared.

A governor was supreme in his province. Everyone—civilian or soldier, Roman citizen or alien—was bound to obey his orders. In principle, Roman citizens had some right of appeal; in practice, however, this might prove difficult to exercise. The governor alone had the right of execution, so that cases liable to require a capital sentence had to be referred to him, along with certain other types of major charges. In addition, he could order instant execution, especially if he suspected a serious threat to Rome's main concern, the peace and security of the province.

Unless deterred by bad weather, or diverted by the need to go on campaign, a governor's customary routine would be to move from one major community to the next, checking on the welfare of each, and adjudicating the cases, petitions, and other matters brought to him. Inevitably, his checks could seldom be more than superficial; lack of time hampered him, as well as shortage of staff and limited expertise. For even the most conscientious of governors, this tour was a daunting challenge—encountering regions and cultures with which in all likelihood he had little or no prior acquaintance, and engaging with populations who were by no means necessarily well disposed to Rome. Because most provincials understood neither Latin nor Greek, and Roman interest in learning other languages was minimal, reliance upon interpreters was frequently essential. Appropriate behavior within societies where the giving and receiving of gifts was standard practice (as in the Greek East especially) posed a particular dilemma for fair-minded governors; to accept all gifts (or bribes) was clearly criminal, but to refuse everything might only cause offense.

Less responsible governors felt no such anxiety, and instead—with varying degrees of greed—exploited the opportunities which their situation offered. While the temptations were infinite, the term of office in which to indulge them was unlikely to exceed a single year. Many a governor had heavy debts to pay off, often ones incurred on the latest occasion that he had competed for office in Rome.

Although the senate allocated an ample lump sum for a governor's expenses, he received no salary. His orders and verdicts were not to be questioned, Rome was far away (from a distant province, messages could take weeks in summer, longer in winter), and for the most part provincial news attracted little attention there, so long as Roman interests were not under threat. It was not even necessary to be a notably venal judge. Instead, for example, how ungracious to refuse a gift spontaneously offered by a city requesting that troops be billeted elsewhere after the campaigning season. How easy, no less, to multiply the legal allowance for buying food when traveling. To claim this fixed cash amount from one community daily was permitted; yet if the claim were made in *each* community traversed during the day, which could refuse?

Some of the most painful dilemmas for fair-minded governors were likely to be created not by provincial subjects, but by the syndicates (*societates*) of private contractors, or *publicani*, who collected taxes on Rome's behalf. Whenever the tax contract for a major province was auctioned (Asia's five-year contract was the largest), a huge capital outlay was required to secure the winning bid. To operate effectively, a large tax-collecting syndicate had to maintain ships and branch offices, employ hundreds of staff (predominantly slaves or freedmen), and in many respects function as a bank. In addition, because it existed to deliver a profit to the partners who provided the capital, it could hardly afford to be patient or indulgent in its dealings with taxpayers. A governor too ready to lend a sympathetic ear to their complaints was by definition most unwelcome to a syndicate, and it would not hesitate to pressure him into rethinking his attitude by exerting its influence—often formidable—both in the province and at Rome. Accordingly, governors who persisted in strictness towards tax-collecting syndicates were exceptional, and they suffered for it. Otherwise provincials had little recourse against these syndicates' rapacity, and they deeply resented this helplessness. Worst of all was their plight in those instances where a governor unashamedly collaborated with a syndicate in fleecing taxpayers.

The senate, for its part, was acutely aware of Rome's dependence upon the tax-collecting syndicates for providing revenue; in consequence, efforts to discipline their operations too strictly would only prove self-defeating. This said, we should recognize that from the mid-second century there was an influential body of opinion in the senate eager to see members on a provincial assignment held to a high standard of conduct. As noted in Chapter Four, in 149 the novel step was taken of instituting a special jury court (*quaestio de repetundis*) to hear complaints lodged against such senators. Subsequently, Gaius Gracchus as tribune in 123–22, a member of the Cato family and others around 100, Sulla as dictator in 82–81, and Julius Caesar in his first consulship (59) were all responsible for legislation which sought to discipline governors and make them more accountable. Even so, adequate means of enforcement could not be found, while general principles which seemed admirable when advocated in Rome might well turn out more awkward to uphold under specific conditions in a province. Cicero, as governor in Cilicia (also see

Chapter Seven), would find himself faced with such dilemmas. Caesar likewise, both earlier in Spain and later in Gaul, blatantly ignored principles which his own legislation upheld. The convictions that Rome as a responsible ruler had obligations to the provinces, and that leading provincials who supported Roman rule should be treated as partners rather than mere subjects, were still not widely shared among senators at the end of the Republican period.

It is hard to determine how effectively the quaestio de repetundis acted to reduce misconduct by governors. The plain fact that no more than a limited number of the cases heard there led to conviction must have been heartening to those governors willing to risk prosecution. There was much else to give a defendant hope. A governor could be charged only after his term of office had ended. The court only sat in Rome, and its proceedings were all in Latin. Its jury comprised upper-class Romans exclusively (at different periods, senators or equites, or both), who would readily sympathize with a fellow Roman, and might also prove corruptible. Meantime, the provincials laying charges had to bear all the difficulty, risk, and expense of engaging advocates, assembling evidence, and producing witnesses. Even should they secure a conviction, there would be further uncertainty over whether they could successfully reclaim the cash or stolen items awarded to them; for example, it was easy enough for a convicted defendant to remove himself into comfortable, self-imposed exile beyond the reach of Roman jurisdiction.

We can surely conclude, then, that the prospect of a trial in the quaestio de repetundis was little or no deterrent to those governors willing to risk prosecution. Less easily quantifiable, by definition, is the proportion of governors averse to incurring the personal strain and exposure of a trial, no matter how favorable the prospects for evading conviction. Even so, it would be wrong to imagine that such men all governed honestly in consequence. For those who shrank from tangling with deep-rooted local disputes and rivalries, and sought a means of ensuring that they would not become the target of a prosecution, one practical safeguard was to identify the most powerful interest groups and then simply follow their guidance. In gaining protection of this sort, such a governor might well have to abandon any higher sense of responsibility to the province as a whole. But in all likelihood he had only been assigned there randomly by the lot, lacked any sense of commitment to the area, and saw no value in jeopardizing his own future prospects during a mere year's tenure.

TRIBUNATE OF LIVIUS DRUSUS (91)

Surviving accounts of the 90s are too fragmentary to give us adequate insight into the unfolding of political developments during that decade. At least it is plain that the existing tensions remained high. Moreover we know that the consuls of 95 went out of their way to provoke the allies by establishing a commission to investigate dubious claims to Roman citizenship, especially those accepted by the censors who had held office in 96. In 91, however, there emerged a tribune, Marcus Livius Drusus, with a wide-ranging program designed to overcome several of the principal difficulties. He was the son of the Livius Drusus who had opposed Gaius Gracchus, and like his father he acted in the interests of the Optimates. This may seem surprising at first sight, given that some of his measures were more characteristic of Populares. But the younger Drusus evidently acknowledged the pressing need to effect some major changes soon if serious conflict was to be avoided, and in these circumstances he wanted the initiative (and the credit) to belong to the Optimates.

So, in order to resolve the issue of whether the members of the jury courts should be senators or equites, Drusus proposed that they all be senators, but that 300 equites be made senators. He further proposed the foundation of colonies and the distribution of "public" land to poor citizens, and finally a grant of Roman citizenship to all Latins and Italians. Although some of these proposals seem to have been passed by the Plebeian assembly, each of the groups most affected by Drusus' program soon began to question whether their prospective gains would outweigh the losses. Some Optimate senators were not sure that they wanted the senate to be doubled in size. Equites regretted the loss of their distinctive role on the jury courts, and of their broader influence as a class which would now be permanently undermined. Rome's allies generally welcomed the grant of citizenship, to be sure, but at the same time the larger holders of "public" land among them did not relish the prospect of having to lose some of it to settle the poor. Eventually the opposition to Drusus' program asserted itself, led by the consul Lucius Marcius Philippus. He successfully maneuvered to have all of Drusus' legislation declared invalid. Shortly afterwards, when mingling with a crowd outside his house, Drusus died at the hands of an unknown assassin armed with a cobbler's knife.

SOCIAL WAR (91–87)

By seeking to please everyone, in the event Drusus pleased no one. Worse still, his efforts to reduce tension only raised it. In particular, many Italians—with their hopes of being awarded Roman citizenship dashed yet again—now began organizing to claim by force the status which Rome would not offer through legislation. Almost at once Rome was faced by just the threat that the structure of its alliance had been designed to eliminate, namely a confederation of member-states turning against their leader. Much of the initiative came from a Marsian (from near the Fucine Lake), Quintus Poppaedius Silo; hence the conflict is sometimes called the Marsian War as well as the Social or Allies' War (in Latin *socius* signifies ally). The peoples of the central and southern Apennines formed the largest concentration of rebels. In a display of remarkable speed and efficiency they established a confederate capital at Corfinium—which was evocatively renamed Italica—with

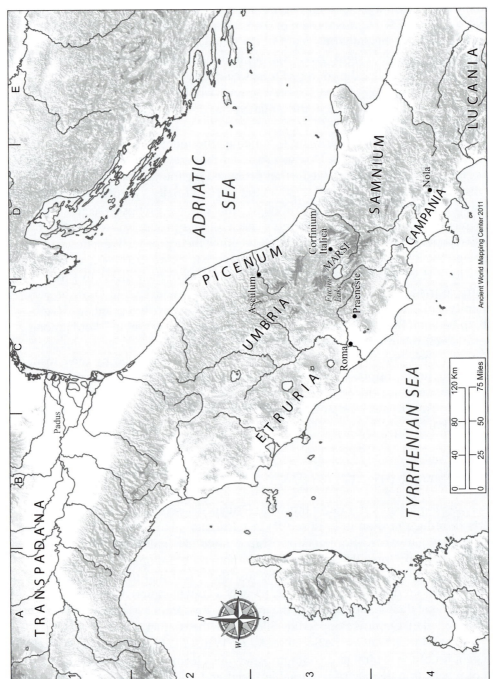

Map 5.2 *Social War*

TRANSPADANA

ADRIATIC
SEA

PICENUM

UMBRIA

Asculum

Corfinium/
Italica
MARSI

*Fucine
Lake*

ETRURIA

Roma

Praeneste

SAMNIUM

CAMPANIA

Nola

LUCANIA

TYRRHENIAN SEA

Padus

Ancient World Mapping Center 2011

0   40   80   120 Km

0   25   50   75 Miles

A   B   C   D   E

1   2   3   4

magistrates on the Roman model and a senate of 500 representatives from member-states. Their forces totaled perhaps 100,000 men, well acquainted with Roman methods.

It is important to recognize that many communities joined either only briefly at the outset (as in Etruria and Umbria, for example), or not at all. In particular, the Latin communities never joined (theirs was already the most privileged allied status), nor did central Campania; moreover even within predominantly rebel areas, certain individual communities chose to stay loyal to Rome. Altogether, without question, loyalist forces always outnumbered those of the rebels, and in the longer term, too, the financial and material resources that Rome could draw

Figure 5.2 *By the late third century, production of Roman coinage each year was normally made the responsibility of young men embarking on a career in public life. Within a further century it had become accepted that, in choosing types, these "moneyers" might take the opportunity to commemorate their place of origin or some special achievement by an ancestor. It was not yet typical Roman practice, however, to refer to contemporary events, as the rebels did during the Social War. Note their personification of "Italia," as well as the vignettes of eight warriors swearing an oath in front of a standard, and the (Italian) bull mounting and goring the (Roman) wolf; the language used on the second of these two coins is Oscan, which was widely spoken in southern Italy.*

upon would prove superior. Even so, the rebels caught Rome by surprise. During 90 they succeeded in capturing several Roman strongholds and inflicting some severe defeats, before Roman commanders were able to regain the upper hand. A vital lesson for each side emerged from the operations of this year.

To the rebels, these operations demonstrated that their ultimate defeat by Rome was inevitable. Any hope, say, of securing help from King Mithridates of Pontus (which was apparently tried, in vain), and overthrowing the Roman state, was just unrealistic. It would seem that only a minority of the rebels were so extreme in their thinking, notably the Samnites and Lucanians; the majority were fighting mainly for higher status within the Roman alliance.

To Rome, on the other hand, the rebels' effectiveness during 90 demonstrated that they had to be granted the advancement they had long sought. This realization made the tragedy of the war all the more poignant, because it was exposed as an entirely avoidable conflict provoked by the Romans' persistent inability to overcome their own shortsightedness. Years later Cicero recorded a telling piece of personal reminiscence from his late teens:

> The consul Gnaeus Pompeius [Strabo], son of Sextus, conferred with the Marsian commander, Publius Vettius Scato, between their two camps. I was there, serving as a recruit in Pompeius' army. . . . After Scato had greeted him, Pompeius asked, "How shall I address you?" "As a friend at heart," said Scato, "but by necessity an enemy." Everything about their discussion was calm, with no fear, no mistrust, not even notable hatred. For the allies were aiming, not to rob us of our state, but to be received as members of it. (*Philippics* 12.27)

During fall 90 Rome did in fact offer citizenship to all communities of allies which had remained loyal, as well as to those which had joined the rebels, but either had already abandoned hostilities or would do so by a specified date. This offer was not enough to prevent continued hard fighting during 89. Corfinium fell to the Romans, however, and eventually (in November) the rebels' last major stronghold at Asculum. The unashamedly pro-Roman historian Florus (2.6) later summed up this grim climax to the war: "Pompeius Strabo [cos. 89] made a universal waste by fire and sword, and set no end to the slaughter until by the destruction of Asculum he avenged the spirits of so many armies, consuls, and plundered towns." In addition to Cicero, among the very young men gaining their first military experience under Pompeius Strabo were Strabo's own son Pompey, and also Catiline (For their subsequent prominence, see later sections). Poppaedius died in battle. After 89 only a few rebel communities continued to hold out, including Nola in Campania. Meantime a second law was passed at Rome, which seems to have extended the offer of citizenship to those allies who were ineligible at the time of the previous grant in 90. Also in 89, communities directly north of the Padus River (in the "Transpadane" region, part of Rome's newly formed province of Cisalpine Gaul) were awarded Latin status.

It would be hard to overstate the importance of the Social War as a turning point with consequences stretching over the next several decades. It was Italy's first, sudden exposure to the traumas of full-scale civil conflict, a prelude (as it turned out) to successive, more prolonged bouts of similar horror over the next sixty years. It changed the administrative, political, and cultural complexion of Italy from the Padus River southwards. Communities which had run their affairs in accordance with a wide variety of constitutions of their own making now gradually abandoned these in order to become Roman municipia. Urbanization was encouraged for this purpose. At the same time, members of all allied communities gained the right to vote, and to run for office, in Rome itself. Last but not least, these changes fostered the spread of Latin and the disappearance of regional languages such as Etruscan, Oscan, Umbrian, and Messapic.

TRIBUNATE OF SULPICIUS RUFUS (88)

As we have seen, when Rome finally offered citizenship to the allies, this was done only under duress. There was a further respect in which the award can be regarded as either grudging or cautious, and in consequence the cause of violent reactions for several years to come. This was the restriction of the new citizens to a small number of newly created tribes (perhaps eight), which would all be called upon to vote only after the existing thirty-five tribes had voted. In other words, this arrangement would limit the influence that the new citizens could exert upon elections and legislation at Rome as a body; they would thus create minimal disturbance to established political patterns. It may be that the restriction was only meant as a prudent temporary precaution to guard against the unforeseen emergence of some sudden, unpredictable swing in voting behavior caused by the new citizens. On the other hand, it was also easy for sceptical new citizens, as well as enemies of the Optimates, to interpret the restriction as deliberate manipulation by the latter group; put another way, under duress Rome did award citizenship, but only with much reduced voting rights.

Inspired by the ideals of his predecessor Livius Drusus in 91, one of the tribunes for 88, Publius Sulpicius Rufus, pledged himself to gaining full voting rights for the new citizens. This would mean abandoning the creation of new tribes for them, and instead distributing them throughout the existing thirty-five tribes. While Sulpicius naturally anticipated opposition to such a proposal, he never expected that either consul would stand in his way. After all, one (Quintus Pompeius Rufus, only a distant relative of the Pompeius consul the previous year) was a friend of his, and he had helped the other (Sulla) win the election.

Lucius Cornelius Sulla had advanced far since we first encountered him in 107 as Marius' quaestor in the campaign against Jugurtha. He came from an old, but not recently distinguished, patrician family, and it was perhaps partly this background that had influenced the novus homo Marius to choose him. Certainly he served Marius well both in Africa and then against the German tribes, although later he increasingly provoked him by representing that he alone (and not Marius his commander) was responsible for contriving Jugurtha's capture. Recently, Sulla had been one of Rome's most successful generals in the Social War, and deserved his election as consul for 88. It was also appropriate that he was allotted a command against King Mithridates of Pontus, who (as we shall see in Chapter Six) was now posing a serious threat to Roman interests in Asia Minor. There was one further dimension to all this success which must have irked Marius, namely that Sulla enjoyed the support of the Metelli (once Marius' patrons), and proceeded to marry into their family.

In 88, when Sulpicius introduced his proposal to redistribute the new citizens among the thirty-five tribes, he was shocked to encounter fierce opposition, not just from the old citizens, but also from both consuls; they may have become apprehensive about the degree of change that such a radical step might unleash. Sulpicius, for his part, felt betrayed and desperate. If there was to be any hope for his proposal now, alternative powerful support was essential. One man was willing and able to provide this: Marius. He could rally influential equites in particular. But he also demanded an extraordinarily high price, which he and Sulpicius kept secret for the time being: Sulla's command against Mithridates must be reassigned to him. This maneuver would bring Marius double satisfaction; it would humiliate Sulla, and it would give Marius himself the chance to regain the military glory that his political ineptitude had so badly tarnished during his sixth consulship in 100. During the first year of the Social War he had accepted a command and proved effective against the rebels. Why he did not hold another in 89 remains unclear. Whatever the reason, his passion to reassert himself can only have been inflamed by the unique opportunity which Sulpicius now so fortuitously presented.

It is a further puzzle that Sulpicius, like Saturninus in 100, offered no proposal or concession designed to make voters more favorably disposed to his principal concern, the redistribution of the new citizens throughout the thirty-five tribes. Instead, he tried to use violence and intimidation to force this measure through, forming a bodyguard for the purpose. The consuls reacted by declaring a *iustitium* or suspension of public business. Sulpicius countered with a threat to use force against them if this ban were not lifted. Street fighting broke out, in the course of which Sulla found himself driven to seek sudden refuge in, of all places, Marius' house. In all likelihood, to save his own skin Sulla was then obliged to agree that the iustitium would be lifted. It duly was, and at the same time Sulla left for Campania to join his army, which was still besieging Nola, one of the last holdouts from the Social War.

After these developments, when Sulpicius put his redistribution proposal to the vote, it passed; its opponents evidently shrank from further confrontation. What came as a surprise and a shock, however, were two new proposals, which also passed. First, Pompeius Rufus was removed from his consulship; and second, the command against Mithridates was taken from Sulla and reassigned to Marius. Sulpicius had thereby fulfilled his bargain with Marius, but at the same time he also presented Sulla with an impossible dilemma. If Sulla accepted the reassignment, then he ruined all his hard-earned political prospects. On the other hand, if he attempted to fight it, he would be forced to take the law into his own hands. Personal interest aside, he was at least entitled to regard his predicament as insufferable. True, his reassignment had been legally enacted, but still there was no crisis at this date to justify a tribune arranging to take the Mithridatic command from a consul who was qualified for it in every way, and to bestow it upon a very elderly private citizen, even one renowned for his generalship (Marius was about seventy; Sulla was twenty years or so younger).

SULLA'S FIRST MARCH ON ROME (88)

Since only the use or the threat of force had allowed Sulpicius to pass his measures, it was natural enough for Sulla at this stage to contemplate introducing force on his own behalf. The means were ready to hand—the army of six legions now besieging Nola, which he had been due to lead against Mithridates. As he knew, from a constitutional viewpoint the very thought of bringing an army to Rome to seize by force what he could not secure by the appropriate vote in a citizen assembly was heinous; it was unheard of, and struck at one of the vital foundations of the Roman Republic. All politically active citizens in Rome were sure to be adamantly opposed to such a crime. Sulla himself realized the risk he ran in even broaching the possibility to his men. But he also had a sound appreciation of where their priorities lay, pointing out that if he simply accepted his removal from the command, then in all likelihood his replacement Marius would recruit other forces to take to Asia Minor, and these would become the ones to enjoy the rewards of easy victories there rather than themselves. This was an argument the men readily grasped, whereas the rights and wrongs of the constitutional and moral issues mattered less to them. In particular, poor citizens who had volunteered or been drafted when Rome suddenly needed recruits to fight the Social War had little incentive to consider those issues. A lucrative eastern campaign under Sulla was their brightest—indeed their only—prospect, and they would support him to secure it. So when officers sent by Marius arrived to take over command of the army, the men stoned them to death. All of Sulla's own officers, on the other hand, deserted him except one (Lucius Licinius Lucullus, on whose career see further below). In contrast to the men, they were sufficiently conscious of the illegality of a march on Rome not to want any part in it.

Sulla's anticipation of the reaction that his fateful step would provoke was largely accurate. There was never much doubt that he would gain control of Rome, because Sulpicius, Marius, and the senate were taken completely by surprise. It had never even occurred to them that Sulla would attempt this kind of coup (he would hardly have been allowed to leave for Campania otherwise), and they had no organized body of troops on hand. At the same time Sulla himself was not fully prepared for the desperate, even if makeshift, resistance that his army encountered from everyone in the city as it entered Rome, and he had to rally his men when their nerve came close to breaking.

Once in control of the city, Sulla immediately prevailed on the senate to declare a group of twelve—Sulpicius, Marius, his son of the same name aged about twenty-two, and nine others—enemies of the state because of their violent, seditious behavior. This maneuver created the impression that by contrast Sulla's own no less violent, seditious reaction was legitimate. It also—very disturbingly—made instant outlaws of Roman citizens without any trial, and let them be hunted down and killed. Next, Sulla cancelled all the measures passed by Sulpicius after the imposition of the iustitium. This meant that Sulla himself was now restored to the Mithridatic command, and Pompeius Rufus to his consulship; it also meant, however, that the new citizens were not to be redistributed among the thirty-five tribes. All this Sulla quickly achieved with his army still present in the city. To try to reduce the universal resentment felt towards him, he now sent it back to Campania. But its departure meant that, at the elections which followed, voters could take the opportunity to articulate their hostility. Neither of the candidates elected to the consulship for 87 was supported by Sulla, although afterwards he did successfully persuade both to swear that they would leave his measures intact. That done, he rejoined his army and proceeded to the East with it. Meantime, of the group outlawed by him, only Sulpicius had met his death as he fled. After some narrow escapes, Marius and his son had managed to reach Africa, where many of his veterans were settled.

CINNA'S RULE (87–84)

With Sulpicius now dead and Sulla departed to the East, there was some hope that 87 might turn out a less traumatic year than 88 had been. In fact it was not, because one of the consuls, Lucius Cornelius Cinna, was somehow persuaded to take up the cause of redistributing the new citizens among the thirty-five tribes. Evidently during the course of his election the previous year he had not declared any such concern, but he now became an implacable advocate of the cause. His fellow consul Gnaeus Octavius remained opposed to it, the tribunes were divided (some vetoed the proposal), and rioting ensued. Cinna then left Rome and traveled through Italy rallying support—behavior for which the senate removed him from office and declared him an enemy or *hostis*. Marius seized the opportunity to return from Africa and offer Cinna his assistance, which was accepted. Both sides took desperate measures to raise troops; slaves were offered their freedom in return for serving; and the Samnites (who were still stubbornly at war, having rejected Rome's concessions to the allies) in the end agreed to support Cinna. Eventually, late in the year, after a siege, Rome fell to Cinna and Marius. The consul Octavius refused to flee, and so was killed on the spot. Cinna and Marius then embarked on a bloody purge of their opponents and enemies, most of whom were dispatched without even the most perfunctory trial. Sulla was outlawed in his absence. Looting and killing by the freed slaves who had helped to capture

Rome was at first tolerated, but when they would not stop they were rounded up and massacred.

By some irregular means Cinna and Marius had themselves made consuls for 86, and duly entered office on January 1. Amid the widespread carnage and destruction Marius now felt a measure of gloating satisfaction. Finally he had overcome his enemies, as well as fulfilling a bizarre prophecy made to him as a young man that he would live to become consul seven times. He could also begin preparations to lead an army against Mithridates. By mid-January, however, he was dead, perhaps of pneumonia. It was a swift end for a man who had both saved the Republic and then in old age done much to undermine it. When Sulla had asked the senate to outlaw him in late 88, the courageous response of the *pontifex maximus* Quintus Mucius Scaevola was that a man with Marius' record could never be called an enemy of Rome (Valerius Maximus 3.8.5). Despite the political ineptitude that Marius had shown during his sixth consulship in 100, Scaevola's claim held up to 89. But it is quite impossible to justify the way in which Marius exploited the opportunity offered to him by Sulpicius the following year. To be sure, he was not solely to blame for the damage done to the Republic then, just as earlier in 107 he cannot reasonably be expected to have foreseen the disruptive political potential that his recruitment of poor volunteers would unlock. The fact is, however, that from 88 Marius discarded all sense of responsibility towards the state in favor of vengeful self-seeking at any cost. In consequence, his own reputation and the entire state both suffered irreparable harm.

Marius was replaced as consul by Lucius Valerius Flaccus, but leadership of the state remained with Cinna. In the short term, no major figure set out to oppose him. Everyone, after all, was bruised and exhausted by the recent conflicts, and preferred to wait and see how his plans might develop, as well as how Sulla might fare against Mithridates. In fact, the extent to which Cinna formulated plans for the longer term is unclear. All he could manage immediately was to tackle pressing crises, among which he did *not* include redistribution of the new citizens throughout the thirty-five tribes; they were still kept waiting. A financial crisis did receive attention, however. We only know the outcome, which was a law allowing debtors to pay back no more than one quarter of what they owed at that date—a devastating blow, in other words, to creditors, whose loan capital was drastically diminished. At least the law underlines for us the disruption and massive loss of confidence that affected everyone financially and economically.

Cinna's other immediate problem was to determine the attitude he now would take towards Sulla, whom he had made an outlaw. Formally, his decision was to treat Sulla as such; in consequence, his fellow consul Flaccus was dispatched to Asia Minor with two legions to take Sulla's place in the fight against Mithridates (this campaign is treated more fully in Chapter Six). At the same time there is reason to think that Flaccus was authorized to explore quietly whether Sulla would be open to reaching some kind of accommodation with Cinna. Sulla of course was not;

he placed no trust in Cinna or Flaccus. At least he did not proceed against Flaccus, any more than Flaccus contemplated trying to ally with Mithridates against him—a prospect truly frightening to Sulla. In fact, during the following year (85) Flaccus was killed in a mutiny fomented by his own subordinate Gaius Flavius Fimbria, previously Marius' associate and quaestor, and known for his ruthlessness. Fimbria then proceeded to corner Mithridates and evidently might even have captured him, had Lucius Licinius Lucullus, the quaestor in command of Sulla's fleet, responded to his pleas for assistance.

Sulla, however, felt no inclination to authorize help for Fimbria. Instead, it suited his purpose better to let Mithridates escape for the time being and to make peace with him; then Sulla attacked Fimbria and drove him to suicide. It is true that Mithridates was still a formidable foe, but had he been captured there was no one on his side of comparable stature to replace him. Really, we have to see Sulla's preference for missing this opportunity, and instead terminating hostilities in 85, as the product of his own selfish ambition to return to Rome with a minimum of delay. Granted, he did proceed to spend the next eighteen months reestablishing Roman control in the province of Asia, with many rich pickings, incidentally, to placate his soldiers, who had wanted to pursue Mithridates; but this was also a time to prepare for the fighting he was sure to encounter in Italy. At any rate, as we shall see in Chapter Six, Sulla's decision to give priority to his return, leaving Roman interests in the East open to renewed threat from Mithridates, was to have far-reaching consequences in the longer term. Meantime, it is true, Sulla's only viable prospect for his own future safety was first to emerge unscathed from this eastern campaign, and then to reestablish himself at Rome—a daunting double challenge, which in the end he only just surmounted.

Once news of Sulla's preparations for return reached Rome, Cinna and his handpicked colleague for the consulship of 85, Gnaeus Papirius Carbo, began rallying troops and resources against him. Both had themselves reelected consuls for 84. Their plan was to face Sulla in Greece, and they had already dispatched some advance contingents when Cinna was killed in the course of a mutiny at the port of Ancona on the Adriatic. There is no knowing how differently events might have unfolded if he had lived longer, or how a clash between him and Sulla would have turned out. It looks as if Cinna's reelection as consul through 86–84 had been simply an attempt to maintain control in a time of crisis, not any reflection of a rethinking of how the state should be ruled in the longer term. Our ability to assess Cinna suffers from the fact that the meager surviving information on him is uniformly hostile, but there is little reason to think of him as a potential savior of the state prematurely cut down.

After Cinna's death in 84, Carbo recalled the contingents dispatched from Italy, and decided that any stand against Sulla should be made there, not abroad. It was probably he, too, who at this critical juncture finally had a law passed providing for the redistribution of the new citizens in the thirty-five tribes. He may in addition have supported a decree of the senate that called for the disbandment of all armies.

SULLA'S SECOND MARCH ON ROME (83–82)

If this decree was intended to embarrass or deter Sulla, it did neither. As soon as he landed at Brundisium with his five legions in spring 83, he was joined by two men who both had reason to keep out of Cinna's way, Marcus Licinius Crassus, aged thirty-two and son of the consul of 97, and Gnaeus Pompeius ("Pompey") aged twenty-three, son of the consul of 89 who had captured Asculum in the Social War. Pompey had coolly raised three legions from his father's former supporters and veterans in Picenum, and now placed this private army at Sulla's disposal. In general, Rome and most of Italy were initially hostile to Sulla. The memory of his first march on the city in 88 remained a bitter one, and the new citizens could see little hope of redistribution throughout the thirty-five tribes if he were to gain control. In the event, however, the resistance to him suffered from divisiveness. Some commanders fought Sulla's forces, but others attempted negotiation, and there were many desertions to his side by troops for whom a prolonged struggle had no appeal. Moreover Sulla now offered an assurance that he would respect the redistribution of all the new citizens among the thirty-five tribes—except for the Samnites, on whom he refused to bestow any recognition at all. That naturally strengthened their opposition to him.

In Rome, too, there developed more deeply committed resistance in 82 with the election of Carbo as consul again (he had not been consul in 83), alongside Gaius Marius, the son of Rome's savior. Even the potency of Marius' name, however, could not prevent the city itself falling into Sulla's hands. "Young" Marius escaped to make a stand at Praeneste, twenty-three miles to the east (modern Palestrina). Gradually, the fighting that raged all over northern and central Italy during 82 came to center on this stronghold, from which "Young" Marius could be neither relieved nor dislodged. Eventually, fellow commanders of his, together with a Samnite force led by Pontius Telesinus, sought to relax Sulla's grip on the siege by making a diversionary attack on Rome from the north. On November 1, 82 they took up a position one mile outside the Colline Gate. Sulla dashed from Praeneste to confront them. When the battle began in the late afternoon, the left wing under his own command collapsed, but the right under Crassus broke the enemy. Very gradually, after a period of despair, the two men's forces at last gained the upper hand after nightfall. Telesinus was killed. If we can credit the account of the historian Velleius Paterculus, this "gallant man deeply imbued with hatred of the Roman name," knew full well how critical the battle was to the Samnite cause:

> Telesinus was everywhere among his men repeatedly saying that Rome's last day had come, and shouting that they must pull down and destroy the city: "The wolves who prey on Italian freedom will never disappear unless we wipe out the wood which is their lair." (2.27)

With Sulla's narrowly won victory at the Colline Gate, effective resistance to him in Italy came to an end. Praeneste soon surrendered, and "Young" Marius

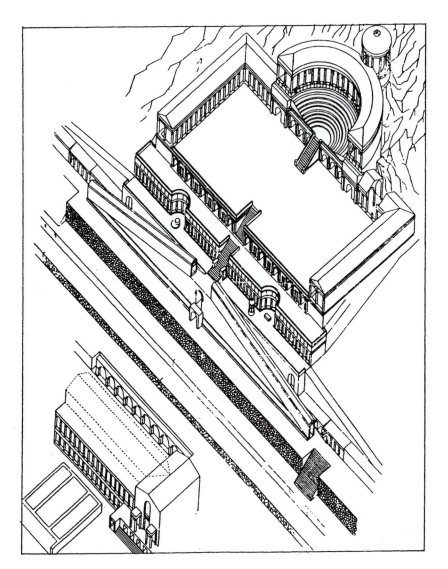

Figure 5.3 *Praeneste (modern Palestrina), situated on a spur of the Apennines east of Rome, was always appreciated as a cool refuge from summer heat in the city, and many wealthy Roman families had villas in its vicinity. It was also the site of an important sanctuary, the largest in Italy, dedicated to Fortuna Primigenia ("Firstborn Fortune"). The massive surviving remains reflect construction of the late second century B.C., with an amazing series of barrel-vaulted terraces ascending a steep hill-side on which the modern town is also built; ramps link the terraces. As the reconstruction shown here clearly demonstrates, architectural inspiration came from famous sanctuaries of the Greek world, such as those at Pergamum and Rhodes. The cult of the goddess drew not only men from Rome, Italy, and farther afield—especially those seeking success in politics or warfare—but also women eager for children. An additional attraction at Praeneste was an oracle associated with the cult; the responses made to those who consulted it took the form of inscribed wooden* sortes *(literally "lots").*

was killed. Elsewhere, Sicily and Africa were still in the hands of Sulla's opponents, but Pompey was sent to each of these provinces in turn, winning them back with a devastating efficiency that gained him the nickname "Young Butcher." One of his victims was Carbo, who had fled to Sicily after Sulla's victory at the Colline Gate. After these successful campaigns Sulla, who had already given his stepdaughter in marriage to Pompey, now instructed him to disband almost all his forces. Pompey wanted the further reward of a triumph, however, and so returned to Italy with his men for the purpose rather than disbanding them. Sulla tried to refuse on the technical grounds that Pompey was not a senator. But when reminded by Pompey that "more men worship the rising sun than the setting one" (Plutarch *Pompey* 14), Sulla gave way, and even addressed him by the name conferred by the troops in Africa, Magnus or "The Great." So as the climax to the first phase of his astounding career, Pompey, an eques not yet twenty-five, duly celebrated a triumph in March 81 with disregard for both the spirit and the letter of the law.

Meantime from November 82 Rome and Italy were at Sulla's mercy, resigned to whatever fate he had in store for them. Thanks to all the bloodshed, their conqueror in this latest bout of civil war now enjoyed a far tighter grip than Cinna or Marius had ever achieved. In addition, unlike his predecessors, he possessed a clear vision of the reforms required in his opinion to return the state to its old stability, as well as a steely determination to put them into effect. Even so, we may note at once that he did keep his promise to uphold the redistribution of the new citizens throughout the thirty-five tribes. Their repeated readiness to fight for these equal voting rights is impressive. Given that under normal circumstances few enough of them could ever hope to be in Rome at all frequently, their unwavering insistence upon the redistribution may seem as extreme as Romans' fear that the change might seriously upset established political patterns. But doubtless both sides' views of the principle and practice at stake stemmed from proud convictions no longer sufficiently clear to us. What we can appreciate is that, as a consequence of the extension of Roman citizenship and the redistribution of new citizens throughout all thirty-five tribes, the attendance at most citizen assemblies now became an even more inadequate reflection of the citizen body as a whole. However, no steps were ever taken to remedy this shortcoming. As the following chapter will demonstrate, Sulla radically rethought many of the ways in which the Republic functioned; but this was not one of them.

SUGGESTED READINGS

Dillon, Matthew, and Lynda Garland. 2005. *Ancient Rome from the Early Republic to the Assassination of Julius Caesar*. London and New York: Routledge. This extensive sourcebook, with its informed commentary, includes valuable chapters on women, Marius, and the Social War.

Evans, Richard J. 1994. *Gaius Marius: A Political Biography*. Pretoria: University of South Africa.

Goldsworthy, Adrian K. 1996. *The Roman Army at War, 100 B.C.–A.D. 200*. Oxford: Clarendon Press.

Kleiner, Diana E.E., and Susan B. Matheson. 1996. *I Claudia: Women in Ancient Rome*. New Haven: Yale University Art Gallery. An exhibition catalog, offering not only ample illustration and discussion of each object, but also concise essays on many key aspects of women's lives.

Lintott, Andrew. 1993. *Imperium Romanum: Politics and Administration*. London and New York: Routledge. Concise, informative overview and discussion of provincial government.

THE DOMINATION OF
SULLA AND ITS LEGACY

Our sources for Sulla's dictatorship and thereafter to the end of the 60s offer some improvement over the record of the preceding period and deepen our insight accordingly. Appian's account and *Lives* by Plutarch remain important, in particular the *Lives* of Sulla himself, also Lucullus, Pompey, Crassus, Caesar, and Cicero. A Greek historian of the early third century A.D., Cassius Dio, offers a narrative—uninspired, but useful—from 69 onwards. Above all, Cicero's speeches, dating from 80 onwards, are invaluable for the contemporary perspective they supply.

SULLA'S PROSCRIPTIONS (82–81)

For Sulla, victory at the Colline Gate on November 1, 82 was not enough. After so much fierce resistance, he needed to be confident of gaining undisputed control of Rome and Italy. For this purpose he instituted "proscriptions." In other words, he published lists of individuals who were thus automatically condemned to death without trial. Anyone could kill them, and then claim a reward. There were rewards, too, for informers, and penalties for those who helped the proscribed evade detection. A proscribed person's property was confiscated and auctioned off by the state, and his sons and grandsons were debarred from seeking any public office. The first proscription list was published very early in November 82, two more soon followed, and June 1, 81 was eventually set as the final day for publishing further names. Officially, Sulla's purpose in instituting proscriptions was to root out those prominent individuals—senators and *equites* especially—who had taken sides against him. The total number of individuals killed in this way is unclear because the figures given in different sources vary considerably; 500 seems the minimum figure, and it could have been two, or even three, times that. More important than the number, however, is the clear fact that Sulla's supporters cynically exploited the opportunity to instigate an indiscriminate witch hunt throughout Italy, to pay off old personal scores, to enrich themselves, and to acquire property at auction for a fraction of its true value. Names were improperly added to the proscription lists, and misidentified victims were killed "in error."

Sulla, insofar as he was even aware of these abuses, seemed not to care. He was sufficiently vengeful himself to order that Marius' bones be exhumed and scattered. We do not know what answer, if any, he gave to his loyal associate, the senator Quintus Lutatius Catulus, who had the courage to ask him whether anyone was to be left alive; at least the question highlights the helpless fear felt even by his own supporters (Catulus himself did in fact survive). Roman society had an ingrained respect for the law and for due legal process. Not surprisingly, therefore, of all the forms of violence that Sulla unleashed against his fellow citizens in the course of his career, it was the proscriptions which were remembered with the most lasting horror and revulsion. Moreover, by targeting men of wealth and initiative, as well as excluding their sons and grandsons from public office, the proscriptions caused severe social and economic disruption, and for too long deprived the state of talent that it could ill afford to lose. Not until 49, as it turned out, would the debarment from public office be lifted.

SULLA THE DICTATOR AND HIS PROGRAM (82–81)

Also in November 82, the senate recognized as legal all Sulla's past actions as both consul and proconsul. It officially conferred on him an additional name, Felix or "fortunate"; Sulla had always believed in his personal luck. Most important of all, the senate initiated the procedure which led to Sulla's immediate appointment as dictator charged with bringing order back to the state and formulating laws. The name and style of the office purposely recalled the traditional office of dictator, which remained familiar to Romans, although in fact no appointment had been made to it now since the end of the Second Punic War over a century earlier. In vital respects, however, Sulla's dictatorship departed from the traditional model. His appointment to it specifically validated all his actions in advance; thus he could execute anyone without trial, and was not required to submit any legislative proposal to a citizen assembly. In addition, there was no time limit to his tenure of this office.

Senate

The absence of such a limit, however, should not be taken as a sign that Sulla envisaged remaining dictator indefinitely. Far from it. Instead, he was committed to restoring the state to the stable condition which, in his view, it had enjoyed under the guidance of the senate a half-century and more ago, until Tiberius Gracchus and a succession of other ambitious leaders proceeded to upset its balance with increasingly damaging consequences. The senate's persistent weakness, as Sulla saw it, was that its predominance could readily be challenged. Moreover, most recently its numbers had been badly depleted in all the civil strife; perhaps no more than about 150 members still survived out of the normal total of around 300. Sulla therefore wasted no time in both making up this total and also introducing around 450 further members, so that altogether the senate now became double its traditional size, and its meeting place (the *curia*) on the north side of the Forum Romanum was enlarged. By definition, the new members came from the equestrian class, because this was the group of wealthiest Roman citizens outside the senate. Many equites had opposed Sulla, and had been proscribed. On the other hand, the most loyal of those who had supported him now gained this reward, at the same time further weakening equestrian identity and influence in the process. Even so, that was hardly a matter of regret to Sulla, since it diminished one potential source of challenge to the senate.

To help maintain a total of around 600 senators, Sulla raised the number of quaestors (the lowest senatorial magistracy) to twenty. Just how steep an increase this figure represented in the number being elected annually we happen not to know, but in all likelihood it was substantial, perhaps even a doubling. In addition, Sulla enacted that quaestors should become members of the senate immediately after their year of office, instead of having to wait until they could be enrolled at the next census (taken every five years).

At the same time, junior senators' advancement through the cursus honorum inevitably became a more competitive struggle, because Sulla increased the number of praetorships annually by only two (from six to eight), and he left the number of consuls at two. Orderly competition for office seemed essential to him, and to this end he revived certain old restrictions which had been either ignored or set aside in recent decades. These were, first, that only ex-quaestors were eligible for the praetorship, and likewise only ex-praetors for the consulship; and second, that these successive offices could not be held before the ages of thirty, thirty-nine, and forty-two respectively. Third, and very important, there must be a ten-year interval between holding any particular office again. In practice, this restriction would apply most often to the consulship, and make it impossible to repeat the electoral successes of Marius and Cinna above all.

Sulla evidently soon gained the chance to demonstrate his personal commitment to this set of rules. In 81, Quintus Lucretius Afella, who had finally dislodged "Young" Marius from Praeneste the previous winter and then sent his head to Sulla, as a reward demanded the privilege of standing for the consulship, although he was blatantly unqualified. The account given by the Greek historian Appian (*Civil Wars* 1.100–101) may be inaccurate in some of its details, but the general point is unmistakable:

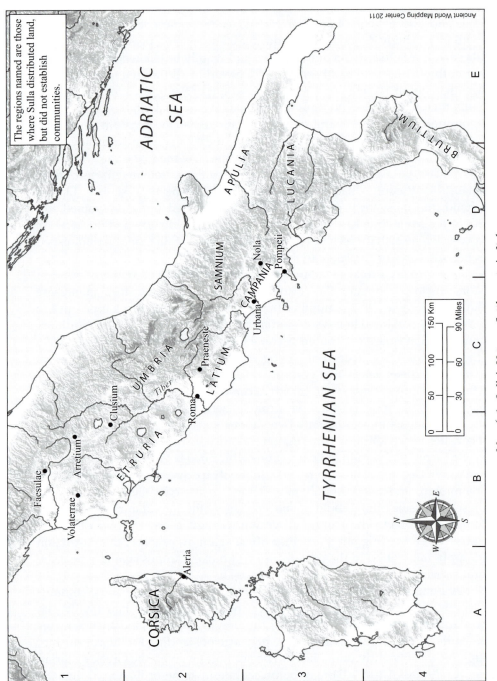

The regions named are those where Sulla distributed land, but did not establish communities.

ADRIATIC SEA

TYRRHENIAN SEA

CORSICA

Aleria

Faesulae
Volaterrae
Arretium
Clusium

ETRURIA

UMBRIA

Tiber

Roma

LATIUM

Praeneste

SAMNIUM

APULIA

CAMPANIA
Urbana
Nola
Pompeii

LUCANIA

BRUTTIUM

N
E
S
W

0   50   100   150 Km
0   30   60   90 Miles

Map 6.1 *Sulla's Veteran Settlements in Italy*

Sulla was a frightening man with a terrible temper. Quintus Lucretius Afella had captured Praeneste for him, and by his siege had beaten the consul Marius and put the final touch to Sulla's victory. Though still only of equestrian rank he wanted to become consul without having been quaestor and aedile, appealing by ancient precedent to the magnitude of his successes. Sulla tried to get him to change his mind, and when he failed in this, he killed Afella in the middle of the forum. Summoning an assembly of the people, he told them: "Know and learn from me that I killed Lucretius Afella because he disobeyed me."

Tribunate

The tribunate was the one magistracy that Sulla modified significantly, because he regarded the challenges to the senate mounted through it as particularly harmful. A man who served as tribune was now automatically debarred from standing for any further office, and tribunes' authority was drastically curtailed. Although the details are lost, it would seem that—at best—the only legislative proposals they might now bring to the Plebeian assembly were ones already approved by the senate. However, the tribunes' traditional right of exercising a veto may have remained intact. Even so, there is no question that Sulla deliberately set out to make the tribunate "a shadow without any substance," as the historian Velleius Paterculus (2.30) was to describe it; no office could now be less attractive to anyone with political ambitions.

Equites, Courts

Equites, as we have seen, lost much of their identity and influence as a class thanks to the violent deaths of many of their number, and the promotion of others to the senate. Sulla struck them a further blow by excluding them entirely from membership of the juries in the *quaestiones* (jury courts), and restricting these juries to senators only. The dominance of senators in this important sphere was made all the greater by Sulla's establishment of seven such courts on a permanent basis.

Citizens

Meantime citizen residents of Rome and its environs stood to lose by Sulla's abolition of the grain distributions instituted by Gaius Gracchus. He viewed subsidizing these as an unwarranted drain on the treasury, even more so when a Popularis tribune like Saturninus could gain favor with a proposal that raised the subsidy. Elsewhere in Italy, Sulla's two principal concerns were to find land for settling his veterans, and to discipline those areas which had opposed him. He addressed both concerns jointly by widespread confiscations from communities, especially in Etruria, Umbria, Latium, and Campania, and reallocation of the land to his veterans. The program's sheer size was unprecedented—there were perhaps as many as 80,000 men to settle—and its impact harsh and disruptive.

a

b

It was no accident that much of the settlement occurred within easy marching distance of Rome itself. Similarly, in remote areas, Sulla permitted his supporters to acquire large landholdings. He was severest of all in Samnium, as the geographer Strabo explains (5.4.11):

> Sulla's proscriptions did not end until he had destroyed or driven from Italy all who bore the Samnite name. When asked the reason for this terrible anger, he explained that experience had taught him that no Roman would ever know peace as long as they had the Samnites to deal with. So the towns of Samnium have become villages, and some have even vanished altogether.

Governors

Outside Italy, in Sulla's view, the state had most to fear from the commander who could persuade his troops to join him in attacking Rome, just as Sulla himself had done twice. The shorter a commander's term, the less time he would gain to cultivate his troops. Accordingly, Sulla's hope was that at the end of their original term of office as many consuls and praetors as possible would accept one-year provincial governorships, with their *imperium* extended as proconsul or propraetor. There was no law requiring such acceptance, however.

Sulla revived, and perhaps added to, the existing restrictions on a governor's activity within his province, which, like so much else, had been ignored in the recent past. These restrictions were that only with prior authorization from Rome could a governor make war or leave his province, either alone or at the head of his troops. In addition, he must leave the province within thirty days of his successor's arrival there.

Facing page

Figure 6.1a,b *Pompeii, famous as one of the Campanian cities overwhelmed by the volcanic eruption of Mt. Vesuvius in A.D. 79, preserves an amphitheater seating perhaps 20,000 spectators in thirty-five rows, surrounding an arena measuring 220 × 115 feet (67 × 35 m). An inscription dates the dedication of the structure to about 70 B.C., thus making it one of the earliest known amphitheaters to be erected in permanent stone form, and a marked advance on the temporary wooden structures which continued to be used in the forum at Rome and elsewhere. In addition, the dedication specifically identifies Pompeii's amphitheater as a structure commissioned for their own benefit by the veteran colonists who were settled there by Sulla within the previous decade, and who (as Cicero confirms) were for long resented by the established members of the community. Evidently the new, tougher, military training associated with Marius at the end of the second century incorporated gladiators' fighting techniques. In the likely event that the veterans at Pompeii had been among the recruits trained in this way, they might well have been eager to maintain an interest in gladiatorial combat. Moreover, the innovative erection of a permanent amphitheater in stone for the purpose acted as a stark warning to any hostile, ousted citizen that its builders' appreciation of effective fighting methods remained keen, and that they were here to stay. See further Plate 9b.*

After enacting his program, Sulla resigned the dictatorship by the end of 81, was elected consul for 80, and thereafter retired to a villa near Puteoli where he passed the time writing his memoirs, hunting, and drinking. Probably it was this last pleasure that killed him early in 78, when he suffered a major hemorrhage induced by acute liver failure.

VERDICTS ON SULLA'S PROGRAM

Because much of his program as dictator was to be dismantled so rapidly after his death, its shortcomings tend to engage our attention more than its strengths. The latter, however, are real, and should not be dismissed out of hand. Most striking is Sulla's reinforcement of certain Republican ideals as he saw them. The opportunity to subject Rome permanently to a sole ruler was easier for him to seize than it had been for Marius or Cinna earlier. Like them, however, he had no intention of going to this extreme, a restraint that Julius Caesar would later mock him for in a famous comment (see Chapter Seven). Sulla wanted to equip the state with stable, undisputed leadership, and he continued to regard the senate as the best agent for this key role. However, in his view, it now needed legal empowerment to exercise its once customary prerogatives. In addition, it must be boosted (doubled in size), and all possible sources of challenge eliminated—hence the regulation of competition for office, the supervision of governors' activity, the removal of equestrian jurors from the quaestiones, and the weakening of the tribunate. At the same time, thousands of veterans were settled within reach of Rome to lend their support as required. The mass of Sulla's opponents throughout Italy, rich and poor, were already eliminated anyway, and all descendants of proscribed opponents were to remain excluded from public life.

Figure 6.2 *Bust, possibly Sulla (see further Fig. 8.7).*

For all its cohesion and its adherence to certain Republican ideals, however, Sulla's program also reflected serious limitations, which he evidently overlooked or chose to ignore. Many groups of individuals, not to mention most of the controversial political and social issues of the past half-century, were simply set aside. Thus at a stroke the equites and the tribunate were eliminated as political forces along with the Plebeian assembly, and the monthly grain distributions in Rome were terminated. Proscriptions, as well as widespread land confiscation and resettlement, created huge social dislocation throughout Italy. Meantime, Sulla's program offered all those that it crushed nothing to hope for, either now or in the future.

In effect, any hopes could only be fulfilled by the enlarged senate. From the outset, however, there must have been grave doubt whether its members were capable of maintaining sufficient unity and sense of responsibility to provide the self-denying collegial leadership that Sulla somehow expected of them. When it came to a choice between resorting to force or respecting constitutional principle, his own example was quite appalling—memorable not only for its single-minded butchery, but also for the sheer success of resorting to such violence. It would be remarkable indeed if his newly recruited senators—themselves likewise the winners in civil strife—could prove consistently more restrained, especially when there was now sure to be increased competition for the top magistracies. As to the danger of another march on Rome, in the last resort Sulla's legal restrictions on governors could offer no more than paper protection. They were quite inadequate as the solution to a crisis all too likely to recur.

SOURCE 6.1: *Two passages from Cicero's successful defense of Sextus Roscius of Ameria in southern Umbria. This was one of his first major cases, conducted in 80 when he was twenty-six. Chrysogonus, a freedman of Sulla, accused Roscius of parricide. In fact his father had been murdered by others, and his name then added by Chrysogonus to a proscription list (after these had been closed) in order to justify the disposal of his property. Cicero gives his defense of the son broader significance by boldly arguing to the jury of senators that Sulla's new senate will lose public confidence if it tolerates the continuation of such disrespect for the law.*

(139) There was a period, of course, when the situation called for one man [Sulla] to be in complete personal control. But he has now re-appointed magistrates and passed laws restoring to each their traditional tasks and powers. And if the men appointed want to keep these powers, they can, for ever—but not if they indulge or acquiesce in acts of robbery and murder, or in such lavish expenditures as I have described. I do not want to bring bad luck to anyone by saying anything too harshly critical, gentlemen of the jury, but I must insist that unless the nobles show themselves the true guardians of the state, brave and merciful, they will be obliged to surrender the very powers they have so recently acquired to men who do have such merits.

(154, the conclusion) It is now the duty of all wise men of authority and influence such as yours to seek to remedy the ills which encumber the state. Every single one of you knows full well that the Roman people, whose clemency towards their enemies was once proverbial, is now itself the victim of self-inflicted cruelty. Blot out this cruelty, gentlemen of the jury, I implore you; do not allow it to endure a moment longer within the confines of the state. It is something evil and pernicious—so evil in fact, and so pernicious, that it has horribly destroyed innumerable citizens, and by inuring decent people to such calamities it has robbed them of all compassion.

Map 6.2 *Rome's Wars in Italy and Abroad, 78–63*

E F G

CASPIAN
SEA

Bosporus Phanagoria

CRIMEA

BLACK SEA

PONTUS ARMENIA

PROPONTIS PAPHLAGONIA Zela

BITHYNIA Tigranocerta

CAPPADOCIA

MACEDONIA

Cyzicus PARTHIA

Euphrates

AEGEAN
SEA Pergamum

A S I A CILICIA Antioch

ndisium

S Y R I A

Athenae

Rhodes

CRETA J U D A E A Jerusalem

INTERNUM MARE

Alexandria

Cyrene

AEGYPTUS

Nile

Ancient World Mapping Center 2011

LEPIDUS' UPRISING AND
ITS AFTERMATH (78–77)

In addition to expecting that the senate would act responsibly as a united governing body, Sulla left election procedures unchanged, so that there was no bar to candidates opposed to his program standing for offices and gaining them. There was the prospect of this occurring even while he was still alive, because Marcus Aemilius Lepidus won election to the consulship of 78, despite Sulla's open disapproval of his candidacy. Sulla was furious with Pompey for supporting Lepidus. It is unclear just why Pompey favored a figure who had earned a bad reputation for unscrupulously enriching himself during the proscriptions and then as governor of Sicily. Conceivably it was just a hunch that Lepidus might create trouble, which in turn could provide some opportunity for Pompey, who was otherwise unoccupied at this point.

If so, the hunch paid off. Soon enough, and possibly starting even before Sulla's death, Lepidus advocated increasingly sweeping measures—the repeal of Sulla's acts, the return of confiscated land to its former owners, the reintroduction of the grain distributions, and finally the restoration of tribunes' powers and a second consulship for himself. This heady crescendo motivated former owners in Etruria to attack the settlers placed on their land by Sulla. In its alarm, the senate sent both consuls to restore order, but Lepidus then proceeded to join the attackers and take charge of their rising himself. Fearing this challenge and dreading the prospect of new civil strife, the senate sought to placate him. Even so, he would not be deflected from marching on Rome early in 77. The senate conferred a command upon Pompey among others, and prepared to make a stand. In the event, Lepidus' ill-prepared assault was repulsed, his followers were pursued and many of them killed, and he himself died soon after seeking refuge in Sardinia.

Despite his failure, he had starkly exposed much of the discontent with Sulla's program, as well as the senate's vulnerability in such a crisis. He also turned out to fulfill Pompey's wish for further opportunities. After Lepidus' defeat, when ordered to discharge his troops, Pompey declined. In all likelihood, Quintus Caecilius Metellus Pius in Spain had already requested help to defeat Quintus Sertorius, the sole remaining opponent of Sulla and his regime outside Italy. It would, of course, be quite contrary to traditional practice (reinforced by Sulla) to dispatch a young private citizen for such a purpose instead of a senior officeholder. But neither of the consuls finally elected for 77 after Lepidus' defeat wanted such a dangerous and thankless assignment, and amid the general dearth of talent various other qualified senators were already committed elsewhere. Moreover, since Pompey already had a body of troops, it seemed only right to send him, and there was no other practical option anyway.

So Pompey departed for Spain in 77. Otherwise in Rome itself over the next few years the restoration of tribunes' powers seems to have been the most fiercely argued political issue, although the only concession made by the senate (in 75) was to remove the ban which prevented tribunes from holding any further office. In 73, monthly grain distributions were reintroduced for a moderate fixed price, on the Gracchan model. Finally, we know that towards the end of the 70s the regulation of governors' behavior and the restriction of juries in the quaestiones to senators again claimed attention, but no measures were taken yet. Instead, throughout the 70s, the state had to be more preoccupied with a formidable range of threats that emerged, or reemerged, in various areas of the Mediterranean as well as in Italy itself.

CHALLENGE FROM SERTORIUS IN SPAIN (80–73)

Among these challenges, we may note first Quintus Sertorius. An associate of Cinna, then Carbo, as ex-praetor he took up the governorship of Nearer Spain at the end of 83; but in 81 he was proscribed and expelled from there, and fled to the independent kingdom of Mauretania in Africa. The following year, however, the Lusitanians in the west of the Iberian peninsula, along with other anti-Sullan Roman exiles, invited him back to lead the rising which they had begun. He accepted, and by his rapid defeat of the governor of Further Spain prompted Sulla to dispatch there his consular colleague of 80, Quintus Caecilius Metellus Pius, son of the Metellus with whom Marius had clashed. Sertorius, however, continued so successful that by 77 almost all of Roman Spain, except the south, was under his control. At this stage he was joined by the survivors of Lepidus' uprising in Italy, led by Marcus Perperna Veiento; soon afterwards, on the other side, Pompey arrived to reinforce Metellus. For the next two years the struggle remained intense and inconclusive, with both sides gaining victories but also suffering defeats. Pompey in fact very nearly met his match in Sertorius. Early in 74, however, it was Pompey who finally galvanized the senate into furnishing greater support; if it were not forthcoming, he insisted, his army and the entire war in Spain would shift to Italy (see Source 6.2). Exactly what pattern of events he envisaged by this loose threat was left obscure, but the senate—itself short of funds—did now respond with supplies and reinforcements.

Meantime Sertorius successfully persuaded Mithridates to send him money and ships. Yet, by the time these arrived in 73, Pompey and Metellus had begun to gain the upper hand. Much of Sertorius' Spanish following fell away; finally his officers, led by Perperna, turned traitor and assassinated him. Soon afterwards (still in 73), Perperna in turn was easily defeated and then executed by Pompey; with his death, the prolonged and desperate rising in Spain came to an end. What Perperna and his fellow officers had expected to gain by their disloyalty to Sertorius remains a puzzle; just possibly they imagined that Pompey would reward them.

SOURCE 6.2: *Excerpt from Pompey's letter sent to the senate from Spain in 74, as it appears in a fragment (2.98) of Sallust's* Histories *written in the 30s. In accordance with the conventions of ancient historiography, this version with its readily identifiable rhetorical elements is likely to be Sallust's rather than Pompey's own; but it no doubt retains the drift of what the latter originally wrote.*

If it were against you [the senate] and my country and household gods that I had undertaken all the toil and dangers which have accompanied the many occasions since my early manhood when under my leadership the most dangerous enemies have been routed and your safety secured, you could have decreed no sterner steps against me—absent as I am—than you have been doing up to now. In defiance of the normal age limits, I have been thrust out to take part in a savage war against an enemy of proven quality [Sertorius]; and yet, so far as you are able, you have destroyed me by famine, the most miserable of all deaths. Was it in anticipation of this that the Roman people sent their sons to war? Are these the rewards for wounds and blood so often shed for the state? Weary of writing and sending deputations, I have used up all my private wealth and expectations, and you meanwhile over a space of three years have barely granted me the expenses of one. In heaven's name, do you think I am a substitute for the treasury, or that an army can be maintained without pay and provisions? . . .

Thus my army and the enemy's are in the same position. For neither of them gets paid, and both of them, if they win, can come to Italy. I call your attention to this, and ask you to take notice of it, and not to compel me to find a way out of my difficulties by abandoning the interests of the state for my own. Nearer Spain, insofar as it is not occupied by the enemy, has been devastated either by ourselves or by Sertorius with terrible carnage, except for the coastal cities; moreover these are a drain on our resources and money. Last year Gaul provided Metellus' army with pay and provisions; now, because of a bad harvest, it is hardly able to support itself. I have used up not only my property, but my credit as well. You are my last resort. If you do not help, my army—against my wishes and as I have predicted—will cross to Italy and bring with it the entire Spanish war.

Even harder to fathom is Sertorius' vision for the future. There is no question of his success in brilliantly inspiring and manipulating the native peoples upon whom he chiefly relied for support. They were impressed by the divine inspiration that he claimed to gain through a white doe, as well as by his military leadership, which included ingenious exploitation of guerilla tactics. At the same time he established a Roman school for aristocrats' sons, and acted like a Roman magistrate, even eventually forming his own senate. What larger end he had in view, however, remains elusive. He surely cannot have championed the expulsion of the Romans from the entire peninsula. On the other hand, it is difficult to believe that native peoples remained his loyal following for so long merely in order to insist that opponents of Sulla, rather than supporters, continue to be their rulers. To what degree, therefore, Sertorius deliberately misrepresented himself to the native peoples, or at what stage they finally acknowledged their aims to be irreconcilable with his, are issues that remain a puzzle.

SPARTACUS' SLAVE REVOLT (73–71)

With the elimination of Sertorius and Perperna in 73, the senate was relieved of one crisis at least. It was fortunate, therefore, that another developed only now. This occurred in Italy itself, when a group of seventy-four slaves led by a Thracian, Spartacus, and a Gaul, Crixus, escaped from a gladiatorial training school at Capua. In no time, the stronghold they established on Mt. Vesuvius attracted not only runaway slaves, but also free workers on rural estates, eventually 70,000 men and more in all. At first, the Roman forces hurriedly sent against them were defeated. Spartacus urged his followers to head north out of Italy, and to disperse back to their different lands of origin before Rome could prepare a major assault. Crixus countered by proposing that they loot southern Italy first, and this they proceeded to do until he and the force with him were wiped out by a Roman army in 72. Spartacus meantime did head north; but for some unknown reason he turned back after he had won a victory in Cisalpine Gaul, made for Rome itself but then thought better of it, and finally seized Thurii in the south.

Later in 72, after further Roman defeats, the senate decided to put Crassus—who had won the battle at the Colline Gate for Sulla in November 82, and had been praetor in 73—in sole charge of the offensive against Spartacus. He took over the consuls' four legions, and raised six more. Since the senate was still short of funds, he may have been chosen partly for his wealth; "rich" in his view was a description applicable only to someone with the means to maintain a legion out of his own pocket. With the forces he raised, Crassus drove Spartacus' force still farther south through Bruttium to the sea. Spartacus' hopes of crossing to Sicily were dashed when the pirates who had promised ships failed to provide them. His force was then hemmed in by Crassus, and it managed to break out only in 71 at the third attempt. Meantime Spartacus had tried in vain to negotiate with Crassus, and the senate in its continuing alarm had summoned Pompey back from Spain (where he was still helping communities recover), as well as the proconsul of Macedonia back across the Adriatic. Crassus naturally hoped that he could finish off the war alone, and he almost did so, winning a battle in Lucania in which Spartacus was killed, and then lining the Via Appia from Capua to Rome with 6,000 crucified captives. However, 5,000 slaves who managed to escape and flee northwards were caught and slaughtered by Pompey, who was therefore able to claim to the senate that *he* was responsible for finally ending the war.

CONSULSHIP OF CRASSUS
AND POMPEY (70)

This claim by Pompey merely increased Crassus' long-standing jealousy of him. Pompey, rather than Crassus, had been Sulla's favorite, and now he was awarded his second triumph.* For suppressing a slave revolt, on the other hand, Crassus was limited to the lesser distinction of an "ovation." Even so, now in 71, when both men contemplated running for the consulship, Crassus took the precaution of soliciting Pompey's support. Crassus' candidacy was unimpeachable; he was old enough, and had been praetor. Pompey, by contrast, was too young (only thirty-five), and he was not even a senator. He, like Crassus, had an army at his disposal in Italy and could have used it to demand high office. But it looks as if there was no difficulty over first securing exemption from the law for Pompey, and then in electing both men consuls for 70. That way, at least, Pompey's position was finally regularized. By this stage, nothing less than a consulship would be an appropriate reward for his service to the state, even if it did require the strict rules revived by Sulla to be swept aside. To insist that Pompey now run for no more than a quaestorship would have been impractical and insulting. Ideally, the prudent course would have been never to let such an exceptional figure advance unchecked in the first place; but having done so, Sulla's successors had largely themselves to blame for the consequences.

Once in office, Crassus and Pompey were soon on bad terms. They did cooperate, however, in proposing that the tribunate's full powers be restored, and evidently the law passed without disturbance. This need not mean that all opposition to the traditional powers of the office had evaporated since Sulla's dictatorship; it was more perhaps that doubters acknowledged the futility of making a stand on the issue at this date. Despite being former associates of Sulla, the two consuls had no scruples about unleashing the tribunate again.

Another, lesser blow to Sulla's program in 70 was the passage of a proposal to make equites two-thirds of the jury members in the quaestiones; the other third remained senators. Inevitably, the change further impaired the supremacy of the senate as established by Sulla, but it does at least seem to have ended the long-standing contention on this issue of jury membership. Crassus and Pompey between them neither obstructed the proposal nor showed any interest in it. After all, there seemed no prospect that they would gain or lose by it.

---

*A triumph could only celebrate the defeat of a foreign enemy; in this instance, therefore, the Spanish campaigns were declared to be against foreigners, not fellow Romans.

POMPEY FREES THE MEDITERRANEAN OF PIRATES (67)

At the end of 70, Crassus and Pompey staged a public reconciliation, but both ignored Sulla's hope that as senior magistrates they would agree to take up a command of some kind after their year in office. Routine governorships did not appeal to either of them, and otherwise at this date there was no immediate prospect of any specially attractive opportunity. One did arise for Pompey, however, in 67. By that date the widespread frustration felt throughout the Mediterranean at the Roman authorities' incapacity to suppress piracy had reached breaking-point. The problem itself was not new, nor had Roman efforts to control it been lacking. On the other hand, they had for long proven largely ineffectual, and pirates' depredations were becoming ever more damaging and outrageous. In the course of one pirate raid on Italy in 68, two Roman praetors traveling by road to Brundisium were even taken prisoner along with their magistrates' insignia, lictors, and entire entourage. Grain supplies to Rome itself were interrupted, and the maritime trade routes of the entire eastern Mediterranean had become altogether unsafe. There were no longer any strong powers there to keep piracy in check; Rhodes, Syria, and Egypt were now all weak.

The area most notorious as a pirate haven was the rugged coastline of the region of Cilicia in southeast Asia Minor. As praetor, Marcus Antonius, grandfather-to-be of the famous Mark Antony, was given a command to destroy the pirates there as early as 102, and their suppression recurs as one of the concerns of the law promoting better provincial government passed around that time (see Chapter Five). An ex-consul who was given a similar command in Cilicia during the early 70s campaigned there with some success. With a view to building on this, Marcus Antonius as praetor in 74 (son of the praetor of 102, above) was given a large fleet and a command encompassing the entire Mediterranean. As a result, he went some way towards eliminating pirates along the coasts of Spain and Sicily, but by the end of the 70s he had been defeated off the island of Crete, another important stronghold of theirs. One of the consuls for 69 then replaced him there, and was subsequently retained as proconsul; by the mid-60s, having established Roman control, he annexed the island as a province.

The threat from pirates, however, was far more widespread and even still growing; by now they were said to have as many as 1,000 ships. So in early 67 the tribune Aulus Gabinius responded to universal concern by proposing a three-year command that would equip Pompey with authority and resources to tackle the problem comprehensively. In particular, he would be a proconsul with authority throughout the Mediterranean and up to fifty miles beyond, equal but not superior to all other proconsuls; he would also have as many as twenty subordinate commanders or "legates," each with the rank of propraetor. This status made it possible for the legates to act independently, while still answerable to him. Gabinius' proposal aroused furious opposition from the substantial body of senators who asserted Sulla's principle that it was both unconstitutional and irresponsible to place so much authority in the hands of one individual. While recognizing Pompey's extraordinary generalship, at the same time they were naturally both jealous and fearful of him. As a climax to this bitter confrontation, the vote on Gabinius' proposal in the Plebeian assembly was obstructed by a fellow tribune's veto. Gabinius then proposed instead that this colleague be deposed. The clash between Tiberius Gracchus and Octavius in 133 seemed about to repeat itself, until after as many as seventeen tribes had voted for deposition (only one more was required for a majority) the colleague removed his veto, and Gabinius' original proposal proceeded to pass. Pompey himself took no part in this clash. He knew very well what a hero he was to the great mass of citizens, and he realized how it looked better to stand apart disingenuously awaiting exceptional invitations, rather than ignominiously scrambling for them like any other ambitious senator.

Once granted sweeping authority, Pompey wasted no time. He divided the entire Mediterranean into zones, each of them the responsibility of a legate, so that when their simultaneous offensive began there was nowhere left for pirates to run. Pompey himself tackled Cilicia, the coast with the greatest concentration of them. Thanks to this comprehensive strategy, the pirate menace was removed within three months. Rather than butchering the survivors, Pompey then proceeded to find land in Cilicia and elsewhere for them to settle. During the next unstable forty years or so, piracy did return to the Mediterranean, but never again does it seem to have attained the level of the early 60s.

THREAT FROM KING MITHRIDATES VI OF PONTUS

Once again Pompey had been offered the opportunity to deal with a major threat, and had succeeded where others before him had failed—in this instance, it is true, with the help of greater authority and resources than his predecessors had been granted. His unexpectedly rapid completion of this task in 67 meant that he seemed the obvious choice the following year when there was renewed pressure to appoint a commander who could end intolerably prolonged hostilities with a decisive victory. The opponent in this instance was the formidable King Mithridates VI of Pontus, who now needs to be properly introduced at last, and his previous engagements with Rome reviewed.

Pontus is the coastal region towards the southeast corner of the Black Sea. Its landscape is dominated by east-west mountain ranges and deep river valleys. At lower altitudes the climate is mild and damp, and the soil fertile. The country was noted for its superb timber, as also for its minerals; iron, copper, silver, and salt were all mined here. It was part of the Persian Empire until "liberated" by Alexander the Great. Thereafter, in the absence of any interest on the part of the leading powers, an aristocrat named Mithridates was able to carve out for himself a kingdom here at the beginning of the third century. His successors expanded it some way into both Paphlagonia to the west and Cappadocia to the south; during the same period they, along with the upper classes and the coastal cities, became hellenized. Their attitude towards Rome was cautiously cooperative, once Rome began to play a role in the affairs of Asia Minor from the early second century. This role was certain to become larger and more permanent following Roman annexation of the kingdom of Pergamum as the province of Asia in 129.

Mithridates, the older of two sons, was only eleven when his father was assassinated in 120. His mother Laodice then ruled as regent, favoring her younger son, until around 113 Mithridates (aged about eighteen) managed to oust them both and assert sole, personal control. His next concern was to raise both his personal standing, and that of his kingdom, which he did dramatically over the next few years by bringing the Crimea and the northern shores of the Black Sea under his control; these areas gave him immense material resources and manpower. He also pressed further and more aggressively than any of his predecessors into Paphlagonia and Cappadocia, eventually (about 101) even making his eight-year old son nominal king of Cappadocia. He tried to gain Roman recognition of these conquests, but can hardly have been surprised by growing Roman coolness towards him. When he and Marius (traveling in Asia Minor) met in 98, Marius is said to have advised him sternly "either to be greater than the Romans or to obey them" (Plutarch, *Marius* 31). Later, after a Cappadocian rebellion in the mid-90s, the senate ordered him to abandon that kingdom, and sent a governor (Sulla, in fact) to install a new ruler. Mithridates acquiesced in this instance, preferring to postpone the clash with Rome that seemed increasingly unavoidable. Around the same time (mid-90s), as it happened, he gained the notable advantage of an alliance with the major kingdom of Armenia to the southeast of his own; his daughter married its new king, Tigranes I. Then in 90, when Rome was preoccupied with the Social War in Italy, Mithridates caused the king of Cappadocia to flee, and expelled the young king Nicomedes from Bithynia, west of Paphlagonia. But, surprisingly, when a force of five Roman legions arrived, he agreed to withdraw.

At that point, however, the Roman commanders fatally miscalculated. They urged the newly restored kings of Cappadocia and Bithynia to take revenge, and to recoup their financial losses, by invading Pontus. Nicomedes did so, thus finally provoking Mithridates to action which he began to take in 89. That year and into the following summer of 88, Mithridates' westward sweep proved invincible.

Figure 6.3 *Once King Mithridates VI of Pontus had occupied the Roman province of Asia in 89, he showed no hesitation in issuing coins there with his image (modeled on Alexander the Great) on one side, and his name, title, and associated symbols on the other. The language used is Greek, and this example carries the date "Year 2" of a new era.*

His cavalry alone were sufficient to destroy Nicomedes' army when it entered western Pontus; the king himself was taken prisoner, and Mithridates' infantry never even struck a blow in this encounter. As he advanced west, three Roman commanders in succession were defeated next, none with difficulty. With resistance to him generally decreasing therefore, Mithridates soon had all of western Asia Minor under his control. In what had been the Roman province of Asia for the previous forty years, he was for the most part welcomed as a liberator.

He sought both to allow expression of hatred for Roman rule, and to reinforce his own position there, by secretly arranging for a horrific massacre of all resident Romans or Italians along with their families and Italian freedmen. It took place on a day in spring or early summer 88; the death toll was said to have been in the region of 80,000.

SULLA'S CAMPAIGN AGAINST MITHRIDATES (87–85)

By 88 Rome was less preoccupied than before by crises in Italy, and the Social War was largely won. So war was now declared against Mithridates, to be waged by Sulla with five legions. As we have seen, however, he had unusual difficulties to overcome in claiming this command and then arranging for his departure from Rome. This prolonged delay left Mithridates free to consider advancing still farther west, which he decided to do in 88 when invited to occupy Athens by opponents of Rome there. Once Sulla and his army finally set out in 87, therefore, it was Greece they made for. They did successfully take Athens and its port the Piraeus by siege, but Mithridates meantime dispatched to central Greece an army commanded by his general Archelaus that was perhaps three times larger than Sulla's. So it was here that the two decisive battles were fought in summer 86, at Chaeronea and Orchomenus (Map 5.1). Both were overwhelming victories for Sulla, and as a result almost all Archelaus' forces were wiped out. Sulla then offered terms: Mithridates should relinquish all his conquests since 90, and become an ally of Rome; at the same time he should give Rome eighty ships from his fleet, as well as 3,000 talents in compensation (equivalent to 72 million sesterces).

At this point, despite all the setbacks in Greece, Mithridates was disinclined to accept such terms, and it was hard for Sulla to pursue him further without a fleet, which he was only now beginning to assemble. Meantime control of the Aegean Sea remained with Mithridates. In Asia Minor, however, he had to deal with growing unrest, as well as with the unexpected menace posed by the two Roman legions of Gaius Flavius Fimbria. As we saw in Chapter Five, this was the force under Lucius Valerius Flaccus dispatched by Cinna in 86 to take over from Sulla in view of the latter's outlaw status. It had marched directly along the north shore of the Aegean and then into western Asia Minor, without diverting south to

Greece. So it did not encounter Sulla, but under the ruthless command of Fimbria—an officer who took the lead after a mutiny against Flaccus—it successfully closed in on Mithridates during 85.

In fall 85, therefore, as the threats to his control escalated, Mithridates finally agreed to accept the terms that Sulla had offered a year before. The two men met and reached agreement at Dardanus, on the Asian shore of the Hellespont. Both had much to gain by abandoning the struggle at this point. For his part, Mithridates had to acknowledge his inability to maintain the impact of the stunning blows he had delivered to Roman power in Asia Minor and Greece. On the other hand, the compensation he was called upon to pay for this havoc was light, and the whole area of his rule before 90—Pontus and the Black Sea—remained unscathed, and as productive as ever. The opportunity to fight another day might well return. He could be soundly prepared then, and there seemed every likelihood of the chance to exploit some future crisis facing Rome. It was precisely because of the current atmosphere of crisis there that Sulla, for his part, wanted to make peace and return home as soon as possible. It was not at all in his immediate interests to pursue Mithridates further, with or without Fimbria's help. All he was concerned to do first was to reestablish the Roman province of Asia. This he did with unwavering harshness, imposing among other burdens a demand for 20,000 talents in indemnity and tax arrears from the cities there; Mithridates by contrast had been asked for only 3,000. After doing terrible harm, Sulla and his army eventually left Asia in 84, spent the winter in Athens, and sailed to Italy in spring 83.

His decision not to pursue Mithridates further met with no favor among his men, and their view was shared by Lucius Licinius Murena, who was left as governor of Asia on Sulla's departure. Over the next two years Murena in fact acted independently in mounting three successive raids on Mithridates' territory. It was only the third of these that Mithridates dared resist, and once he had defeated and expelled Murena's force, an envoy from Sulla called an end to this fighting. Murena's action at least warned Mithridates that some Romans had no intention of leaving him in peace, but saw him as a threat to be eliminated at the first possible opportunity. Such Romans certainly supported the decision made around this time to station a commander regularly in southern Asia Minor. Officially his province was called Cilicia, because the initial priority was to suppress the pirate strongholds there, though in practice the first governors focused their attention on regions farther west. They could also keep watch on Mithridates to the north, as could the Roman governor of Asia from the west.

LUCULLUS' STRUGGLE WITH MITHRIDATES (74–67)

The sense of being hemmed in by Rome was only increased for Mithridates in 75, when Nicomedes of Bithynia died and bequeathed his kingdom to Rome. Rome's decision was both to accept the bequest and to resume the fight against Mithridates, regardless of the agreement reached at Dardanus. Lucullus, consul in 74, was made governor of Asia and Cilicia jointly, with five legions at his disposal. Before he advanced the following spring, however, Mithridates struck first by moving west from Pontus, through Paphlagonia, into Bithynia, where he laid siege to the key port city of Cyzicus on the Propontis. Surprisingly, the city held out, reinforced by Lucullus' land and naval forces, even though Mithridates had a larger army and navy. With the onset of winter he was no longer able to supply his forces, and so had to withdraw them back to Pontus. His mistake had been to concentrate so single-mindedly on the siege.

Lucullus, on the other hand, had achieved victory in 73 without risking a major battle. The following year he was bold enough to advance into Pontus, and penetrated more deeply there in 71. When Mithridates' cavalry attacked, the Romans repulsed it with heavy losses. Subsequently, when the king decided upon a withdrawal to the mountainous kingdom of Armenia, his infantry no longer had the cavalry's protection, and so incurred severe casualties from Roman pursuers. Tigranes, king of Armenia, respected his long-standing alliance with Mithridates to the extent of giving him refuge, but otherwise disappointed him by refusing to be drawn into the conflict between Pontus and Rome. Lucullus meantime, in his determination to overcome Mithridates, resolved to cross the Euphrates River and invade Armenia. This was a momentous and unauthorized step, since he had no instructions for extending his campaign in this way, and Armenia was a distant state which had previously lain quite outside Rome's orbit.

The further risk that an invasion of Armenia might in turn provoke its more powerful neighbor to the east, the Parthian empire, hardly seems to have struck Lucullus. In the event, he invaded Armenia in 69, and after a great battle captured and razed its southern capital Tigranocerta. Parthia—a huge kingdom extending beyond the Caspian Sea, but often unstable—declined to intervene. Tigranes and Mithridates both eluded capture, however, and the failure of Lucullus' energetic operations to pursue them finally provoked his troops to mutiny by late 68. The men were exhausted, in particular the two legions which had come to Asia Minor under Flaccus and Fimbria in 86, and had served there ever since. By chance just at the time of the mutiny, Mithridates managed to make his way back to Pontus with a small force. He stirred up revolt, and wiped out the main body of Roman troops stationed there at a battle near Zela in summer 67. Lucullus had already withdrawn from Armenia by then, but did not reach Pontus in time to prevent this unraveling of what he had achieved there; equally, he was unable to campaign further because of his men's refusal to cooperate. Dissatisfaction with him at Rome was only fueled by *publicani*. They resented his measures as governor of Asia to assist its communities in paying off the crippling debts incurred after Rome's repossession of the province.

POMPEY'S DEFEAT OF MITHRIDATES (66–63)

During the summer of 67, two new commanders arrived from Rome to take over Lucullus' huge sphere of command between them, but they had never expected to be faced by such a crisis, and it soon became clear that they were not equal to retrieving Rome's position. All Lucullus' success seemed to be reversed: Mithridates had recovered Pontus, and Tigranes had invaded Cappadocia. When this disastrous news reached Rome, it is no surprise that dismay and frustration led to pressure for more decisive action. One of the tribunes for 66, Gaius Manilius, consequently proposed that all the Roman forces in Asia Minor and the entire conduct of the war be handed to Pompey. Given his swift and total success against the pirates the year before (67), this solution seemed unarguable, and there was none of the fierce opposition that had resisted Gabinius' proposal the previous year. Yet again, therefore, Pompey was invited to take an extraordinary command to retrieve a situation where others had failed. This outcome left Lucullus embittered, because he had come so close to eliminating Mithridates. Lucullus was to resent Pompey as a successor who had deprived him of the victory that was largely his; no wonder that he is said to have compared Pompey to a "parasitical bird," whose habit was to settle on corpses killed by others (Plutarch, *Pompey* 31). Looking further back, we may reflect that this particular opportunity for Pompey, and the difficulties associated with it, need never have arisen in the first place had Sulla set himself different priorities in the mid-80s.

In 66, Pompey moved fast, as usual, to restore the Roman position. He now persuaded the king of Parthia not to help Mithridates or Tigranes, but instead to attack Armenia, a key development which forced Tigranes to abandon his invasion of Cappadocia. Pompey himself drove Mithridates to the far east of Pontus, and defeated him there. In consequence, Mithridates finally abandoned Pontus, and made his way overland round the Black Sea to the Crimean Bosporus, the last secure part of his realm. He reached here by summer 65. Pompey chose not to pursue him, but instead to secure the submission of Tigranes, which he did without difficulty by late 66. Tigranes was allowed to retain the core of his kingdom, but all the other territories he had acquired were now forfeited to Rome. Pompey then took the year 65 to suppress resistance in this distant region altogether, marching almost as far as the Caspian Sea, and demonstrating Roman power; the region was mostly divided among dependent rulers, however, rather than being annexed. In 64 Pompey was preoccupied with reorganizing part of Pontus as a Roman province, but late in the year marched south to annex Syria and then proceeded on to Judaea, where he captured Jerusalem after a three months' siege in 63. His justification for all this further unauthorized invasion and annexation was that effective, reliable rulers in the Roman interest were simply lacking here. In addition, although Parthia was not yet the obvious threat that it would later become, Pompey may have welcomed the chance to block the possible growth of its influence.

Predictably, Pompey was criticized at Rome for taking these other initiatives while Mithridates was still free. If Pompey had merely assumed that the king would be a spent force once he fled from Pontus, that may have been a mistake, because in fact Mithridates did set about vigorously building up power in the Crimean Bosporus once he reached there in 65. His troops, however, no longer shared his zeal, and it was a revolt on their part that led to his death in 63, either by suicide or possibly assassination; his son Pharnaces succeeded him (see Fig. 6.4). So finally died a king whose relentless struggle against Rome over a period of about thirty years forms an episode of exceptional importance for Rome's development. In this struggle he delivered stunning blows, gave hope to other enemies of Rome, and left a deep mark on Roman politics and outlook both during his lifetime and long after.

Figure 6.4 *The manly qualities—as a horse rider especially—shown by a concubine, later wife, of Mithridates were so outstanding that he was said to have called her by the masculine form of her name, Hypsicrates, rather than by the feminine Hypsicrateia. As a remarkable corroboration of this tale preserved by Plutarch (Pompey 32), Russian underwater archeologists diving at Phanagoria have recovered this impressive marble base for a statue inscribed in Greek "Hypsicrates, wife of Mithridates Eupator Dionysus, hail!" Phanagoria was an important city situated on an island on the eastern side of the Cimmerian Bosporus (modern Straits of Kerch), where the sea level has risen since ancient times. Phanagoria resisted Mithridates when he attempted to secure it as part of his final, desperate drive to mount a fresh offensive against Pompey in the mid-60s. 'Hypsicrates' could well have been killed in the fighting there then; her statue must have been erected later, perhaps in 48–47, when Pharnaces, Mithridates' son, briefly reasserted control of Phanagoria before his clash with Julius Caesar at the second battle of Zela (see Chapter Seven).*

ROLES OF CRASSUS AND
CICERO IN ROME (65–63)

Pompey's unbroken success and luck in the East aroused envy at home, as well as concern for how he might act on his return. In particular, would he seek sole power like Sulla, bringing further bloodshed and terror? No one brooded over these issues with greater jealousy and apprehension than Crassus. After his consulship in 70, we know next to nothing of his activities until he became censor in 65, but from then onwards we can detect him searching desperately to secure some kind of influence or authority with which to stand up to his former colleague. As censor, he proposed extending Roman citizenship to the Transpadana, the region of Cisalpine Gaul north of the Padus river; whoever carried out such a measure would automatically gain prestige and influence. Likewise he proposed accepting as genuine the dubious will of Ptolemy Alexander (who had died at least fifteen years previously), in which he bequeathed his kingdom of Egypt to Rome; again, whoever was sent to organize the annexation—and at this point it could hardly be Pompey—had much to gain. Crassus' colleague in the censorship, however, objected to both proposals, and the pair of them resigned their office with the census left unfinished.

The elections conducted in 64 for the two consuls who would hold office during the calendar year 63 were to have a particularly significant outcome. We know that seven candidates stood, but three dominated the race. Two were "nobles"— Gaius Antonius Hybrida, whose father had been consul in 99, and the patrician Lucius Sergius Catilina, better known today as Catiline. Both were suspect figures who had served under Sulla, and in very dubious circumstances had escaped conviction for major offenses; both were also in the typical senator's predicament of having seriously overspent in their competition for political office. At least they settled on the logical economy of cooperating against their main rival, the exceptional figure of Marcus Tullius Cicero. It was potentially to his disadvantage that he was a *novus homo*; thus no member of his family had previously been a senator, let alone consul. He was born in 106 to a wealthy family of Arpinum, southeast of Rome (Marius' birthplace, too), and made his mark as a brilliant advocate and orator. His most memorable case to date had been in 70, when against all the odds he had secured the conviction of Gaius Verres for extortion during his governorship of Sicily (see Chapter Seven). In 66 he had spoken in support of Manilius' proposal to give Pompey the command against Mithridates, and he continued to make Pompey's interests one of his principal political concerns.

The two noble candidates stressed that their background should favor them above the novus homo. But in the event this claim was not enough to dispel widespread doubt about their personal records. Cicero, by contrast, was a popular figure with a high reputation, as well as being a skilled electioneer who had cultivated support among aristocrats, equites, and other leading figures throughout Italy. So he came out on top of the poll, a remarkable achievement for a novus homo putting himself forward at the minimum age for the office, and with no military record of note to point to. In fact it had been thirty years since any *novus homo* had reached the consulship.

Antonius narrowly beat Catiline for the other consulship of 63. Cicero, as the leading figure, could hardly expect a calm year in office, and this became clear at once when a tribune Publius Servilius Rullus wasted no time in proposing the establishment of a major commission to take exclusive charge of the distribution of "public" land throughout Italy and the provinces. The commission would have funds to buy more land as required rather than resorting to confiscation (as Sulla had done), and to found colonies. In this way it could help relieve unemployment among the poor in the city of Rome by resettling them, as well as offer a fresh start to the huge number of people in distress throughout the Italian countryside. These included not only the many Sullan veterans who had failed as farmers for one reason or another and were now deep in debt, but also the landholders they had displaced in the first place. Altogether, there is no question that, thanks to Sulla, the level of debt and deprivation throughout Italy was alarming. One clear reflection of this predicament dating to 64 is the senate's disbandment of all associations (*collegia*) in Rome. Normally there was no objection to peaceful groups of any kind; neighborhood, religious, or trade associations were the commonest types. Recently, however, such groups in the city had been adding an unacceptable element of organized violence to political activity. To say the least, this was a frightening development in a community, like almost all ancient ones, with no regular police force.

In principle, therefore, the proposed land commission could do much to restore stability by reducing distress and the dangers it posed. There was also a less attractive side to the scheme, however. The ten senators elected to head the commission would become powerful figures, since they were to hold imperium for five years. With large funds at their disposal, they would have every opportunity for financial gain, and thus for paying off their own debts. Most ominous of all, Pompey on his return would have to apply to the commission if he was to secure land for the settlement of his veterans. These possibilities prompted Cicero to set aside any social concern he may have had, and instead to argue vehemently against Rullus' proposal. He represented it as designed more to benefit a narrow group of senators than the poor, and he also objected strongly to its stranglehold over Pompey. One danger for Cicero was a clash with Antonius over the whole matter, but he bought his fellow consul's silence by offering to exchange the provinces that they had each drawn in the lot; so Antonius now had the more lucrative opportunity to become governor of Macedonia rather than Cisalpine Gaul. In the end, Rullus withdrew his proposal.

Cicero faced his next notable challenge when another tribune prosecuted an elderly senator, Gaius Rabirius, for having taken a leading role in the gruesome episode long before in 100, where the tribune Saturninus and others were battered to death in the senate house by tiles flung from the roof. Rabirius personally was not the real object of attack. Rather, the point of the prosecution was to express strong disapproval of the senate's "ultimate decree" (SCU), and of any circumstances in which citizens were put to death without trial. Cicero joined in defending Rabirius. The case was deliberately conducted according to long-outdated procedures, and never reached a conclusion. This outcome hardly bothered the prosecution, because its point had duly been made to the authorities.

Two elections during the year 63 produced notable results. First, by chance, this was the time at which a new holder of the lifetime office of *pontifex maximus* was required. This leader of the priestly college of the *pontifices* was elected by seventeen of the thirty-five tribes, and the competition for such a venerable, prestigious position was normally just between elderly senators of the highest standing. Two such ex-consuls put themselves forward in this instance, but Gaius Julius Caesar (who was already a pontifex) had the nerve to compete also, and, thanks to heavy bribery which drove him deep into debt, he won. This was really the first achievement in his career that marked him out as exceptional. He was born in 100 into the most ancient of patrician families, but not one that had shown much distinction in the recent past, though it had gained some by association after Marius married into it. Caesar was favored by Cinna, whose daughter Cornelia he married. Later, he had the good fortune to be spared by his fellow patrician Sulla, and after Cornelia's death in 69 he married Sulla's granddaughter Pompeia. Eager to gain Pompey's favor, he supported the proposals of both Gabinius and Manilius, and thereafter when Pompey was out of Rome he also associated himself with Crassus; the potential for mutual advantage in their relationship was obvious to both. Caesar's election as pontifex maximus, as well as his election as praetor for 62, now made him a highly prominent figure.

CATILINE'S UPRISING (63–62)

The second election of note was for the consulships of 62, a race in which Catiline again competed and again lost. This was a grave blow to him, because he too had been risking bankruptcy in order to distribute more lavish bribes than ever. He owed his failure in part to Cicero, who demonstrated his personal distrust by having a bodyguard escort him to preside on election day in September, and wearing a breastplate visible under his toga. Catiline had already roused widespread alarm by championing the cause of those who were poor, in debt, or dispossessed, and calling for cancellation of debts and redistribution of land. Although he did attract a large following in this way, with several senators among them, these were altogether not the class of voter that carried most weight in the Centuriate assembly where consuls were elected; so it was understandable enough that the wealthier, more conservative voters should prefer less controversial candidates.

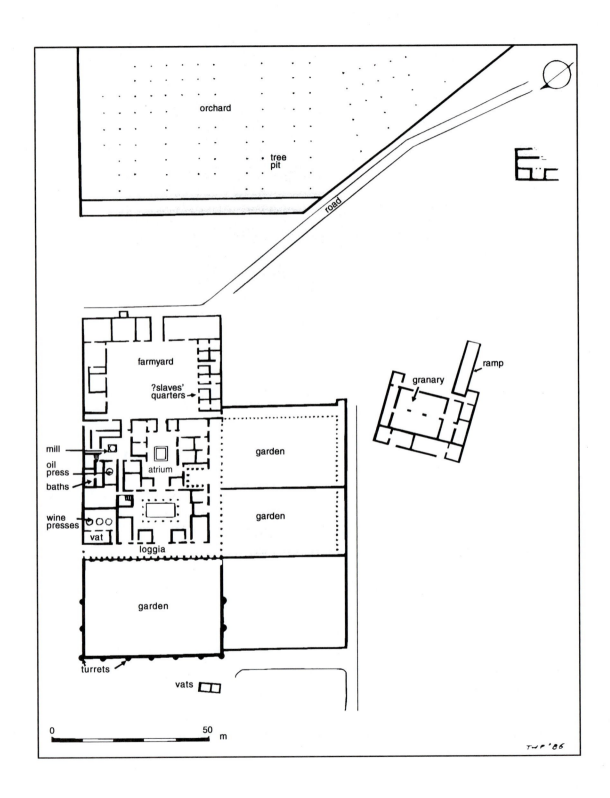

orchard

tree
pit

road

farmyard

?slaves'
quarters →

mill

oil
press

baths

atrium

garden

garden

granary

ramp

wine
presses

vat

loggia

garden

turrets →

vats

0   50 m

TWP '86

In despair at proceeding by legal means, Catiline and his associates now began to gather forces for an armed revolution and for other outrages such as arson and murder. It is unfortunate that the only accounts we have of Catiline's actions are uncompromisingly hostile. These are mostly speeches by Cicero, and a study by the historian Sallust written about twenty years later. Nothing survives from Catiline's side to bring some balance into the picture. Not everyone distrusted Catiline. So Cicero had to proceed against him with care, and above all secure condemnatory evidence that was unassailable. Once it was confirmed in late November that Catiline, taunted by Cicero and hounded by creditors he could not pay, had left Rome to take command of forces gathered in Etruria, the senate did declare war on him. Finally, at the beginning of December, the evidence that Cicero sought came into his hands from envoys sent to Rome by a Gallic people, the Allobroges. They had been invited to join Catiline and his associates—including a few senators, one of them currently praetor—in planning to set fire to Rome later in the month. At a meeting of the senate on December 3 Cicero was able to confront the associates with the letters bearing their own seals, obtain their confessions of guilt, and arrest five of them. This swung public opinion firmly behind him. Two days later, when he asked the senate what was to be done with the five, the decision after a tense debate was execution, a sentence which Cicero carried out at once.

Public opinion was soon sharply divided over this action, however. To his admirers, Cicero was now *Parens Patriae*, Father of his Country, a new founder of Rome. Opponents, by contrast, saw this summary execution of citizens without trial as illegal and unjustified. Even with the declaration of war against Catiline, there was some force to that argument, and later Cicero would be forced to confront it. For the moment, he was extravagantly proud of what he had done, and

Facing page

Figure 6.5 Settefinestre is the modern name for a grand villa in Etruria, not far inland from Cosa. Excavations here by a joint Italian–British team during the late 1970s/early 1980s have provided exceptionally important insight into the rural economy. The villa's construction dates to the mid/late first century B.C., and reflects to an uncanny degree the recommendations of Roman writers on estate management. It is both country residence and working farm. The owner's opulent living quarters—square in shape—were elegantly decorated, and the loggia, which extends along one entire side (145 ft/44 m long), overlooked an elaborate garden enclosed by a turreted wall resembling that of a city (Plate 5b). In addition, there was accommodation for an estate manager, and for slaves. The farm establishment included further gardens, a walled orchard, three presses for wine and one for oil, a large wine vat, and an even more impressive monumental granary. Clearly, several different crops were cultivated, with vines and grain representing the greatest investment. A port from which produce could be shipped out was ideally close (below Cosa), and it is quite possible that the grain was grown specifically for the city of Rome with its insatiable demand for staples. The villa's owners were by definition wealthy; they may have been a senatorial family, the Sestii.

Figure 6.6 *Bust of Cicero*

would in fact never waver from the view that he had taken the right course of action in the crisis. The executions aside, we may agree that his energy and resourcefulness did avert what promised to be a catastrophe for Rome. Meantime, however, he and others ensured that the deeper causes of so much discontent were not remedied. In the end, because he believed that it was now more important for him to remain in Rome, he did not take up the provincial governorship he had intended to.

The debate in the senate on December 5 gave further prominence to Caesar, who took the lead in opposing the execution of Catiline's associates, as well as to Marcus Porcius Cato, who successfully urged this extreme step. Cato was the great-grandson of Cato the Censor, who had been such a towering figure in Roman politics and culture during the first half of the second century. Born in 95, "Young" Cato was still a junior senator—about to become tribune for 62—but was already championing an inflexible devotion to conservative, Optimate principles in the tradition of his great ancestor. With Catiline's associates in Rome dead, his cause must have seemed hopeless. Early in 62, he and his forces in northern Etruria were trapped between two armies dispatched by the senate, and defeated. The casualties in this clash were high; Catiline's followers included many Sullan veterans as well as peasants, and all of them preferred to fight to the finish along with their leader.

The relentless civil strife of this period affected not just men, but also women and whole families. In line with the changes reshaping both private and public life, Sallust writes that many of Catiline's nefarious revolutionary plans depended upon audacious "debauched" women in Rome. By the first century there were apparently plenty of wealthy women who exercised effective control over their own wealth. Unless a woman had opted for the so-called *cum manu* form of marriage which was rare by this date (see Chapter Five), whatever she owned, acquired, or inherited was hers exclusively; in the event of divorce, even the dowry (cash or property, or both) that traditionally passed to her husband at marriage was returned to her father's family. Men's frequent absence from home (serving in the military, say, or hiding from political foes), together with the unpredictability of the judicial system, often led in practice to some relaxation of the formal requirements for control of property and wealth. In particular, the legal principle that most women could conclude major transactions only with the approval of a guardian (their father or, after his death, normally their closest adult male relative) was no longer rigorously upheld. Even without always seeking to act more independently in their domestic affairs, women from wealthy families did so to an increasing extent, and this capacity grew in importance (see Source 8.1, "Laudatio Turiae").

The last century of the Republic also saw more women engaged in public activities. Although relatively few are known to have been involved in public trials in this period, and even fewer contravened social convention by representing themselves at such hearings, Maesia, a woman from Sentinum in Umbria, along with a handful of others, won notoriety by advocating successfully in court. Such cases are associated with the Social War and similarly disruptive political and social changes. Equally, the few women known to have participated in assemblies and hearings did so because of the exceptional times. Around 100, Sempronia, the elderly widow of Scipio Aemilianus and sister of the Gracchi, answered a tribune's summons to appear on the rostra in the Forum at Rome, and there resisted intense pressure to acknowledge a man claiming to be her brother Tiberius' illegitimate son. Later, in 42, Hortensia, the daughter of a leading Optimate and orator, made a (successful) public speech against the imposition of a special emergency tax on 1,400 wealthy women; amid the same turmoil "Turia," a woman of comparable status, pleaded personally to secure justice for her exiled husband, and sustained severe injury in the process (Source 8.1). In short, Rome's instability acted to break down traditional barriers for women.

Not long after Catiline's death and the brutal suppression of his attempt at revolution, news arrived from Pompey that his work in the East was completed, and that he and his army were returning home. Suspense over the vital issue of what he would then do was about to reach its climax. Was Rome now about to acquire by violence, or alternative means, another strong leader and reformer on the model of Sulla? Would there be further civil war? Or was the state to remain divided and adrift, as it seemed to have been ever since Sulla's retirement? In this predicament, major threats abroad could only be tackled by resort to extraordinary commands, most conspicuously those created for Pompey himself. Meantime at home, the state was vulnerable to corruption, conspiracy, and rebellion, while little or nothing was done to relieve the miserable plight of the poor and the dispossessed both in the city of Rome and throughout Italy.

SUGGESTED READINGS

Badian, Ernst. 1968 (second edition). *Roman Imperialism in the Late Republic*. Ithaca, New York: Cornell University Press.

Beard, Mary, and Michael Crawford. 1999 (second edition). *Rome in the Late Republic: Problems and Interpretations*. London: Duckworth. Accessible discussion of major cultural, political, and social aspects, designed for readers who already have a grasp of the main framework of events and their geographical setting.

Keaveney, Arthur. 2005 (second edition). *Sulla: The Last Republican*. London and New York: Routledge.

Lacey, Walter K., and Brian W.J.G. Wilson. 1970. *Respublica: Roman Society and Politics According to Cicero*. Oxford: Oxford University Press. An extensive collection of extracts from Cicero's speeches and writings, with introduction and comments.

Nippel, Wilfried. 1995. *Public Order in Ancient Rome*. Cambridge: Cambridge University Press.

Rawson, Elizabeth. 1983 (revised edition). *Cicero: A Portrait*. Ithaca, New York: Cornell University Press.

Rosenstein, Nathan, and Robert Morstein-Marx (eds.). 2006. *A Companion to the Roman Republic*. Malden, Mass., and Oxford: Blackwell. Essays on a wide range of historical and cultural aspects, with marked attention to the challenges facing the Republic in the first century.

Seager, Robin. 2002 (revised edition). *Pompey the Great*. Oxford: Blackwell.

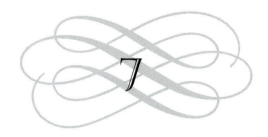

END OF THE REPUBLIC:

Caesar's Dictatorship

SOURCES

From the late 60s onwards, for a period of twenty years, the richness of our source material improves immeasurably because we have not only speeches and philosophical writings by Cicero, but also quantities of private letters that he wrote to friends and others, in particular the prominent *eques* Titus Pomponius Atticus, whom he had known from boyhood. Most of this correspondence was always intended to remain confidential, so that its commentary on current events and personalities is splendidly frank and indiscreet. Contemporary material of a very different type comes from Julius Caesar, who published narratives of his wars in Gaul and his civil war campaigns; in these, Caesar always strives to present himself in a favorable light. Among later works of importance, there are again many *Lives* by Plutarch (Pompey, Crassus, Caesar, Cicero, Lucullus, "Young" Cato, Brutus), and a very readable biography of Julius Caesar by Suetonius (Gaius Suetonius Tranquillus). He and Plutarch were contemporaries in the late first and early second centuries A.D. The significant growth and diversity of nonhistorical literature during the Late Republic is outlined in Chapter Eight.

POMPEY'S RETURN FROM THE EAST (62)

The dazzling wealth and glory with which Pompey returned from the East in 62 outclassed all previous Romans' conquests. There was truth in his own public boast that

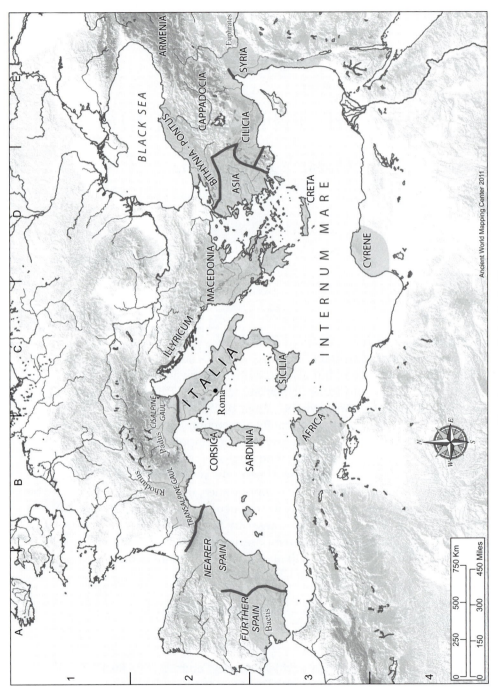

Map 7.1 *Rome's Empire in 60 B.C.*

ARMENIA

CAPPADOCIA

Euphrates

SYRIA

CILICIA

PONTUS

BITHYNIA

ASIA

BLACK SEA

CRETA

MACEDONIA

CYRENE

INTERNUM MARE

ILLYRICUM

I T A L I A

Roma

CISALPINE GAUL

Padus

SICILIA

Rhodanus

TRANSALPINE GAUL

CORSICA

SARDINIA

AFRICA

NEARER SPAIN

FURTHER SPAIN

Baetis

Ancient World Mapping Center 2011

250   500   750 Km

150   300   450 Miles

he had found Asia a frontier province, and left it at the heart of the empire (Pliny, *Natural History* 7.99). He had been courted by kings and princes, and offered god-like honors. He founded cities such as Nicopolis, "victory city," near the site of his final defeat of Mithridates in eastern Pontus. He took pos-session of Syria and made it a province. He enlarged the province of Cilicia, and reorganized Bithynia and part of Pontus into a single, combined province. Otherwise he entrusted eastern Asia Minor—most notably Cappadocia and Armenia—to rulers sworn to uphold Roman inter-ests; some even paid taxes to Rome. Only with Parthia does no pact seem to have been made, but he left strong Roman garrisons in both Cilicia and Syria to guard against any Parthian incursion there.

Figure 7.1 *Bust of Pompey.*

   The wealth that Pompey brought back from Mithridates' treasure stores and elsewhere was quite sim-ply staggering; inevitably it set rich and poor still further apart. Pompey delivered to the treasury 20,000 talents in gold and silver (equal to 480 million sesterces). To each of his soldiers he gave a minimum of 6,000 sesterces (a year's basic pay was 450). Officers were far more lavishly rewarded, and his own personal wealth now dwarfed that of Crassus. For the longer term, his conquests and annexa-tions in the East were reckoned to have raised Rome's annual revenues from 200 mil-lion to 340 million sesterces. His achievement there was to be epitomized in the theater complex begun in the Campus Martius after his magnificent triumph in 61, and ded-icated six years later in 55 (see Map 7.4). Rome had never seen anything like it. The the-ater itself was built in stone; linked with it was a vast portico containing a heroic, nude statue of Pompey himself holding a globe, the symbol of a world conqueror, and sur-rounded by personifications of the fourteen "nations" he had subdued.

POMPEY AND POLITICAL STALEMATE IN ROME

When Pompey finally reached Brundisium in late 62, he surprised everyone who feared and envied him by simply disbanding his army. It emerged that he had no intention of retaining it to march on Rome and seize power. Such restraint need come as no special surprise. After all, his political involvement had never been deep, he felt no particular attachment to any political group or set of ideas, and he had been away for the past five years or so. He might hardly be expected to match Sulla's passion for imposing a fresh political or social blueprint on Rome. It soon became apparent that his sole concerns were to see his arrangements in the East formally ratified by the sen-ate, and to secure land for the settlement of his veterans. Naturally enough, in view of his prestige, popularity, and achievements, he anticipated no difficulty on either count.

   As it turned out, however, he was to be robbed of this hope. One of his former legates was consul in 61, and so was expected to steer the necessary measures through the senate. Unfortunately, however, he proved ineffective, and the main focus of attention during the year turned out to be a frivolous scandal caused by the irresponsible patrician Publius Clodius Pulcher. His father (now dead) had been consul in 79, and he himself had just reached the quaestorship (so he must have been aged about thirty). His previous claim to notoriety was to have taken the lead in stirring the troops of his brother-in-law Lucullus to mutiny in 68 (see Chapter Six). Now, in December 62, he relished the risk of attending secret nocturnal rites in honor of the *Bona Dea* ("Good Goddess")—dressed as a woman, because males were strictly debarred from the ceremony. The special attractions for him were the venue—Caesar's house in Rome—and the hostess, Caesar's wife Pompeia, with whom he allegedly either had, or wanted, an adulterous relationship.

After Clodius was discovered at the rites, Caesar declared Pompeia innocent, but still divorced her on the grounds that his household (that of the *pontifex maximus*, after all) must be above suspicion. He took no action himself against Clodius, whom he regarded as a potentially useful associate for the future. The trial became a sensation offering extraordinary opportunities for bribery and political intrigue. Lucullus, among other enemies, no doubt lobbied against Clodius behind the scenes. Cicero was bolder, and rasher, by actually taking the witness stand to break the alibi that formed a vital part of the defense: Clodius claimed to be about ninety miles (145 km) from Rome on the day of the ceremony. In the end, even though Clodius' guilt in trespassing on the sacred rites was patent and serious, massive bribery of the jury determined the verdict, and he was narrowly acquitted. So Cicero's devotion to truth and principle here only served to create a dangerous, implacable enemy for himself. Otherwise among leading Romans any such devotion was largely subordinated to personal and political rivalry, to the lasting detriment of the senate in particular.

As it turned out, Pompey had to face the frustration of seeing his requests stalled not just in 61, but also in 60. Lucullus, Cato, and other Optimates took pride in being consistently obstructive. A tribune's proposal for major redistribution of "public" land (of the type made three years earlier in 63) was thwarted, as before, on suspicion that in practice it would serve to benefit the handful of senators placed in charge rather than Pompey's veterans and the mass of poor citizens in need of land.

By chance, during 60 two other unrelated requests arose which Cato took the lead in blocking. First, the syndicate that had won the major contract for collecting Rome's taxes in the province of Asia when this was last auctioned (possibly by the censors in 65) now found itself in difficulties. The amount of its winning bid—which had to be paid to the treasury in advance—was proving far larger than the syndicate found itself able to recoup through tax collection. Because it was now facing a heavy loss, it asked the senate to consider renegotiating the contract and thus, in effect, refunding part of the bid. The plea was hardly a strong one, given that syndicates entered bids at their own risk, and the state had no obligation to assist them if they miscalculated and overstretched. Even so, Crassus, who had himself been censor in 65, gave his strong support to the plea. Cato with equal vigor succeeded in blocking it, without regard to the fact that other equites with business interests would consequently take offense.

c

Figure 7.2a,b,c *A fashionable form of conspicuous consumption on the part of those made super-rich by Rome's imperial expansion during the second and first centuries B.C. was the construction of luxurious villas (Fig. 6.5, and Plate 5a). Among the most envied features of such an establishment was an artificial fishpond, so much so that Cicero (in a private letter to Atticus) could term the rich Optimates who so frustrated him as "fishponders" (piscinarii), while gossips spread tales of aristocrats who wept for the death of their favorite eels. Numerous such ponds are known from Italy in particular, although in many instances their design and development can be difficult to reconstruct in detail when those on or near the shore (using saltwater) have suffered sea damage, or when—as in the instance illustrated here—the pond underwent successive modifications and remained in use into the twentieth century. Even so, this pond north of Circeii (modern Circeo, about 60 miles/96 km south of Rome) offers excellent illustration of many typical features. Set within a rectangular terrace, it is a circle about 110 ft (33 m) in diameter and 7 ft (2 m) deep, with one central tank and four others (1–4) fanning outwards from it separated by walkways; two trapezoidal tanks (5–6), added later, extend beyond the circle. Openings (marked "a") interconnect the tanks. The pond was supplied by a link ("c") to a sea channel, as well as by a freshwater spring which bubbled up in tank 2; the sluice gate "b" made it possible to regulate the salinity of the pool water. A platform surrounded by a low parapet wall extends out over tank 1. It is carried on three parallel vaults, in which are set many amphora jars on their sides (the same feature occurs in tanks 5 and 6; see drawing); all of this is designed to provide shade and hiding places, especially suitable for eels. From the platform, the owner and guests could view the pond, and even dine there. There is unfortunately no evidence to uphold the tradition which makes the celebrated general Lucius Licinius Lucullus the owner of this pond, even though he was wealthy and a noted piscinarius. Such ponds were not necessarily mere decoration and self-indulgence. They were likely to produce more than a single establishment could consume, so fish could be either presented as gifts or sold; saltwater fish were valued over freshwater.*

he was prepared to overlook the widespread bribery that it entailed. Caesar had no such lavish help to hand, but he happened to be on good terms with both Pompey and Crassus, and he was keenly aware of how they too had been thwarted by Cato and the majority of senators. To date, Pompey and Crassus had been too estranged from each other to work together, but Caesar now arranged a reconciliation. He further arranged that the three of them would join to overcome the opposition and to achieve their goals; after all, their combined resources were formidable. Pompey and Crassus both had money and influence; Pompey could call upon his veterans, not to mention other clients and colonists in most areas of the Roman world; and Caesar could expect to gain a consul's authority. Pompey, the leading partner, stood to gain most at once; Caesar as the junior might hope to gain most in the long term; the potential gains for Crassus in the middle were less predictable.

Before the end of the year the three invited Cicero to join them, but after much anguished soul-searching he declined on grounds of principle. His hopes that all responsible members of society would work in harmony to keep the state stable (as they had rallied briefly against Catiline) were now thoroughly dashed. On a more personal level, he was dismayed, too, that his grandiose vision of a partnership between himself and Pompey—statesman collaborating with general, like Laelius and Scipio Aemilianus in the mid-second century (see Chapter Four)—had aroused no enthusiasm in the hero after his return from the East. This coldness was all the more hurtful to Cicero's vanity after his assiduous efforts to protect Pompey's interests previously. Cicero was well aware of the significance of the newly formed partnership. It is commonly referred to today as the First Triumvirate, but was soon branded more appropriately by hostile contemporaries as the "Three-Headed Monster." It was a secret pact at first, and only ever informal, but it could be expected to make a devastating impact.

At the same time, in growing isolation, Cicero felt as alienated as ever from Cato and the group of snobbish, bickering Optimate aristocrats who were his associates. He grasped that it was their shortsighted, unimaginative obstructiveness which had driven Pompey, Crassus, and Caesar together. Cicero protested in a letter to his friend Atticus around this time: "[Cato] with all his patriotism and integrity is sometimes a political liability. He speaks in the senate as though he were living in Plato's republic* instead of Romulus' cesspool" (21.8SB).

CAESAR'S FIRST CONSULSHIP (59)

On election day, Caesar and Bibulus were chosen as consuls for 59. So the fund to ensure the latter's election had fulfilled its purpose; but there was also point to the cruel joke that it ought to have been a double fund for two candidates, since Caesar had not been kept out. Once in office, he began by striving to be conciliatory, in

---

*A famous utopia conceived by the fourth-century Greek philosopher Plato.

particular over the proposal for land redistribution which he put forward first. This deliberately incorporated safeguards designed to overcome senators' objections to the previous schemes advanced by tribunes in 63 and 60. Even so, it was soon clear from the debate in the senate that Bibulus, Cato, and their supporters were not to be placated. They now resorted to filibuster tactics, declaring themselves opposed on principle to *any* land redistribution proposal. In his frustration Caesar therefore resolved to ignore the senate, and to bring the proposal directly to the Tribal assembly for a vote. Since both Caesar and his opponents could call upon tribunes for support, Bibulus believed that it would be more effective for him to give notice that on each day when it was lawful for an assembly to meet, he would be watching the sky for omens, which would automatically invalidate any assembly.

Caesar fixed a day for the vote regardless, and on it ugly scenes unfolded. Not only were the fasces of Bibulus' lictors smashed, but a basket of excrement was also flung over him. A tribune who tried to veto the proceedings was thrown from the platform, and several people were injured in the riot that erupted. Bibulus fled to safety, and Cato was expelled by force when he tried to make a speech. With this opposition removed, and some semblance of order restored, the proposal was voted through—to the benefit of Pompey's veterans, among many others. The following day, Bibulus failed in an attempt to have it invalidated by the now frightened senate, and as soon as he appeared in public to make a speech, an order for his imprisonment was given by a tribune on Caesar's side, Publius Vatinius. Even though protests by other tribunes ensured that this order was not carried out, it had become very dubious whether Bibulus could ever risk exercising his office in public again. Eventually, the course of action he settled upon was to stay at home, declaring that he was watching the sky for omens. This he intended as a means of invalidating any assembly that met, although controversy continued to surround the legal issue of whether such a declaration issued from his house, rather than at the assembly itself, was valid for the purpose.

To Caesar at least, the issue was immaterial, because from now onwards he just disregarded Bibulus anyway; the quip that the consuls of 59 were not Bibulus and Caesar, but Julius and Caesar, had point to it. His next step was a provocative demand that every senator swear an oath to respect the land distribution measure. This recalled Saturninus' demand during Marius' sixth consulship in 100, and, unlike on that occasion, every senator did eventually swear. Having asserted himself over the senate in this way, Caesar then proceeded to ignore it, and invite no more obstructions, by taking three key proposals direct to the Tribal assembly for voting. All passed. The first refunded to the tax-collecting syndicate for the province of Asia one-third of its overambitious bid; the second formally ratified Pompey's arrangements in the East at last. The third, also of special concern to Pompey, was a comprehensive measure to regulate the conduct of senators who governed provinces, including procedures for hearing charges brought against them and severe penalties for those found guilty. This important law both incorporated and expanded clauses in earlier such measures; over the succeeding centuries it would be modified, but never superseded.

In these ways Caesar duly repaid Pompey and Crassus for becoming his partners. Even so, the three of them were still nervous of opposition. Lucullus, for example, had tried to the last to block the ratification of Pompey's arrangements in the East. More significantly for the longer-term, when Cicero was rash enough to complain about the current political situation in a law court speech, Caesar took this as the cue to let Clodius have his remarkable wish—raised before, but rejected—of changing status from patrician to plebeian, and thus becoming eligible to stand for a tribunate. Caesar as pontifex maximus and consul presided at the ceremony, with Pompey's assistance as augur. It was carried out at once, so that Clodius could have the chance of being elected one of the tribunes for 58, which in due course he was, much to Cicero's dismay.

As the year progressed, the Triumvirs made further arrangements for their own benefit and for the continuation of their partnership. Pompey married Julia, Caesar's daughter by his first wife Cornelia, and the only legitimate child he would ever have. On Vatinius' proposal as tribune, Caesar was given a command in Cisalpine Gaul and Illyricum, with three legions, for five years; the senate's transparent pre-election maneuver of assigning supervision of the forests and tracks of Italy was merely ignored. Then on Pompey's proposal—after the premature death of another commander appointed here—the senate added responsibility for Transalpine Gaul and a fourth legion. While there was certainly serious trouble to be dealt with in Gaul, it must be doubtful whether this could justify a five-year term instead of the normal one year. Even so, that exceptional term would afford Caesar extended exemption from prosecutions that were sure to be brought against him for his conduct as consul, and the senate may even have felt relief at the prospect of his absence from Rome for so long. Vatinius at once accepted Caesar's offer to make him one of his legates in Gaul, and thus also escape immediate prosecution. Caesar made the same offer to Cicero too, but he declined on principle despite the obvious risks attached to his remaining in Rome during Clodius' tribunate.

Elections for the consulship of 58 were delayed, and this time the senate deliberately did not assign provinces in advance. The pair eventually chosen, however, were Aulus Gabinius (Pompey's friend, and proposer of his command against the pirates in 67), and Lucius Calpurnius Piso Caesoninus (Caesar's new father-in-law, on his marriage to Calpurnia in 59).

CLODIUS' TRIBUNATE (58)

To all appearances, therefore, it would seem that Pompey, Crassus, and Caesar were satisfied by the outcome of events in 59; the immediate hopes that each had when they formed their pact were broadly fulfilled. How far they could continue to work together was quite another matter. Their pact was now common knowledge, and it was resented not only by fellow senators, but also by many citizens who deplored its use of violence and its contempt for the law. At the same time as the three men experienced this drop in popularity, they began to have doubts about their mutual loyalty to one another. Now, however, if the earlier mistrust between Pompey and Crassus were to revive, Caesar would no longer be on the spot in Rome to calm them. In addition, all three men felt nervous at the prospect of Clodius as tribune. To be sure, he could prove a valuable ally, but he was also notoriously fickle and unreliable, quite capable of preferring to pursue his own unpredictable interests rather than theirs, and in those circumstances exceptionally hard to restrain.

True to form, Clodius made a marked impact with three proposals put forward as soon as he entered office. The first was an overhaul of the entire system whereby grain was imported to Rome from the provinces of Sardinia, Sicily, and Africa. At the same time, the monthly ration available to citizens in Rome for a fixed price would now become free. In other words, this grain would no longer just be partly subsidized by the treasury during months when the market price was high, as originally arranged by Gaius Gracchus; it would now be paid for in full by the treasury throughout the year. Needless to say, this was a huge additional burden for the treasury, although the recent steep increase in revenue won by Pompey could only act to reduce it. The second proposal, no less popular with citizens, was a removal of the ban on *collegia* and their activities that the senate had imposed in 64. The ban had been imposed to prevent associations contributing an element of organized violence to political life in the city. The danger that they would now do so again was still present; at the same time the proposal restored to ordinary citizens traditional opportunities for social interaction and community involvement which many must have missed. The third proposal narrowed the conditions under which watching the sky for omens could halt lawmaking activity; its clear intention was to discourage any future attempt to create obstacles by the same means that Bibulus had attempted.

Any proposer of the first two of these measures might well expect to encounter fierce opposition. But in this case the proposer was Clodius; meantime neither consul had yet been assigned a province, while Cicero knew what even a murmur of dissent might cost him. So votes passing all three proposals went smoothly. Clodius became extremely popular as a result. His aim of becoming the champion of the populace seemed to be fulfilled, and this made him still bolder. He did now arrange "rewards" for the consuls: Gabinius was assigned the governorship of Syria, Piso that of Macedonia. Clodius also succeeded in removing temporarily one senator he loathed, Cato. The opportunity had arisen for Rome to take over from Egypt the wealthy island of Cyprus, and a senator was needed to organize the annexation. What better choice for this special duty than Cato? He could be relied upon to enrich the treasury rather than himself, and above all he would be far from Rome. Fortunately, he accepted the invitation, and Cyprus was in due course added to the governor of Cilicia's responsibilities.

For Cicero, however, there was to be none of the consideration shown to Cato. Clodius had a proposal passed reaffirming the ancient principle that no Roman citizen should be executed without trial; anyone guilty of such executions must suffer exile. Although the measure made no reference to any individual or incident, Cicero recognized its purpose; his controversial execution of Catiline's associates on December 5, 63 had come back to haunt him. He was hardly surprised that neither consul would offer help, but stunned to discover that Pompey would do nothing for him, nor Crassus, nor Caesar. Caesar, who had argued against execution on December 5, 63, did make it clear that he disapproved of Clodius raking up the past in this way. Even so, he was not prepared to antagonize Clodius on the issue, especially after the rejection of his earlier offer to protect Cicero by making him one of his legates. Feeling deserted and isolated, therefore, Cicero lost his nerve and left Rome for Macedonia rather than awaiting prosecution. Clodius then had a measure passed officially declaring him an exile. It was in fact at this point, in late March 58, that Caesar finally left Rome to take up his command in Gaul.

Clodius' vindictive treatment of Cicero created widespread outrage which was only sharpened by his next moves, both of which suggest that he was now letting his popularity with the mass of citizens in Rome blind him to all other considerations. He provoked Pompey over aspects of Eastern policy, and when Pompey and Gabinius protested, he had the two of them physically assaulted by his supporters, and the consul's fasces smashed. He also called into question the validity of Caesar's acts as consul the previous year, even though one of these had been his own change of status from patrician to plebeian.

CICERO'S RECALL AND THE RENEWAL OF THE TRIUMVIRATE (57–56)

Pompey became so frightened for his personal safety that for a long period from mid-58 onwards he dared not venture out of his house in Rome. But he did encourage two of the tribunes of 57, Titus Annius Milo and Publius Sestius, to recruit gangs to combat those of Clodius. He also supported the senate's persistent efforts in 58, and again in 57, to arrange for Cicero's recall from exile. This issue became the centerpiece of opposition to Clodius. The recall was finally achieved by a vote of the Centuriate assembly at the beginning of August 57; large numbers of citizens from communities all over Italy answered Pompey's appeal to be present and thus overwhelm the hostility of voters from Rome itself.

Cicero reached the city about a month later to find it in the grip of a severe shortage of grain, and the senate deadlocked over how to resolve the problem. It was his motion for yet another extraordinary command that finally won acceptance—that Pompey be given control of grain supplies throughout the Roman world for five years. However, with the onset of winter, even Pompey could not immediately provide relief. By the following spring (56), therefore, his prestige had suffered, and he was harshly attacked in the senate by Cato, now back in Rome after successfully annexing Cyprus. Pompey suspected Crassus of supporting not only Cato, but also Clodius, whose gang warfare with Milo raged on unchecked. Meantime Cicero felt confident enough to work against the interests of the Triumvirate, and Lucius Domitius Ahenobarbus (who expected to be elected consul for 55) declared that he would press for Caesar's command in Gaul to be terminated.

With their enemies now poised to exploit any rifts emerging between them, the Triumvirs soon resolved to renew their pact with fresh measures for its security. In April 56, Caesar was free to take the lead at a meeting held at Luca (modern Lucca, in Italy), just within the southern border of his province of Cisalpine Gaul. Other senators were invited to attend too, and a strikingly large number of them came. The main item of agreement was that Pompey and Crassus would arrange to have the forthcoming elections postponed until after the campaigning season. They would then both stand for the consulship, and enough of Caesar's soldiers would come to Rome on leave to ensure that Ahenobarbus lost the vote. Thereafter, with the help of supportive tribunes, Pompey and Crassus would arrange major, long-term commands for themselves, and at the same time would extend Caesar's term in Gaul. More immediately, unequivocal loyalty would be demanded of Clodius, and Cicero would be reminded about the pledge of good behavior he had given on return from exile.

A crestfallen Cicero heeded the warning, and the rest of the agreement also took shape according to plan. The elections for the consulship were in fact postponed until January 55, so that an *interrex* was needed to hold them; Pompey and Crassus were the successful candidates. The Spanish provinces and Syria were assigned to them, each for five years, and Caesar was given the same extension in Gaul through 50 or early 49; our sources fail to preserve the exact terminal date. Because of his responsibility for the city's grain supply, Pompey had always intended to remain in Rome, and to administer his province through deputies ("legates"). He was content with Spain, therefore, while Crassus was delighted with Syria. It offered him the prospect of campaigning against Parthia, and thus of finally matching the glory which first Pompey and now Caesar had won by victorious military exploits in unknown lands.

Those hopes were not to be fulfilled, however. When Crassus eventually set off from Syria in 53, first the cavalry force commanded by his younger son pursued the Parthians too recklessly and was surrounded; then the main Roman army was trapped near Carrhae. Roman losses in this catastrophe exceeded 30,000 men, including Crassus himself and his son, along with the legionary standards. It was a final misfortune for a man who after his first consulship in 70 experienced persistent difficulty achieving the further distinction that he craved. He was jealous of Pompey's extraordinary achievements, and despite joining the Triumvirate he never adapted successfully to the changed political atmosphere.

CAESAR'S CAMPAIGNS IN GAUL (58–51)

During the winter following each of his first seven campaigning seasons in Gaul, Caesar wrote an account or "commentary," and then probably made it available for immediate circulation in Rome; his subordinate officer Aulus Hirtius subsequently added an account to cover the years 51 and 50. All eight accounts survive. While their clarity and detail are invaluable, there is equally no escaping their

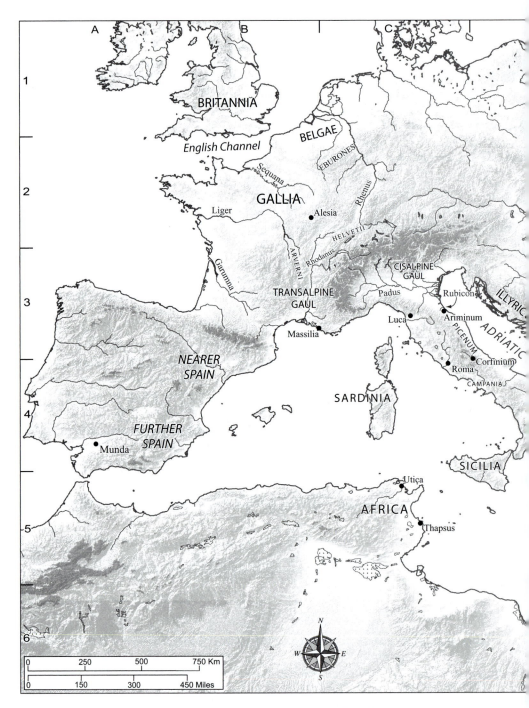

Map 7.2 *Campaigns of Caesar, Crassus, and Pompey, 58–45*

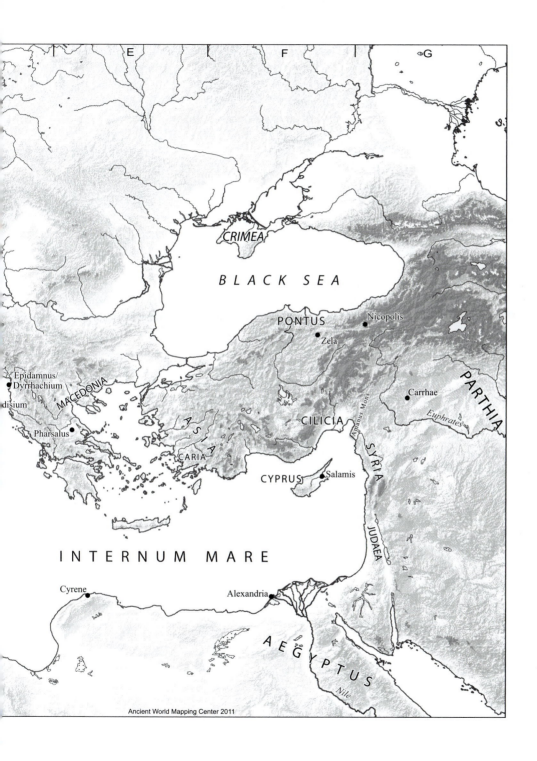

E   F   G

CRIMEA

BLACK SEA

PONTUS   •Nicopolis

•Zela

Epidamnus/
Dyrrhachium•
      MACEDONIA

disium

    A S I A   •Carrhae   PARTHIA

•Pharsalus

     CILICIA

    CARIA   Amanus Mons   *Euphrates*

    CYPRUS   •Salamis   SYRIA

I N T E R N U M   M A R E   JUDAEA

Cyrene•   •Alexandria

A E G Y P T U S

Nile

Ancient World Mapping Center 2011

bias in favor of Romans generally and Caesar himself in particular. Nor is there any other account with which to compare these, above all one that offers a more objective view of Caesar's opponents.

On taking up his command at the end of March 58, Caesar's urgent concern was to forestall the Helvetii, a Celtic people settled on the Swiss plateau, from embarking on a disruptive westward migration. This he soon achieved after major clashes, but his success at once drew him into struggles between peoples farther north. Another battle enabled him to break the control which the Germanic Suebi had been exerting within Gaul, and to drive them back across the Rhine River (Latin, Rhenus). By establishing winter quarters for 58–57 in northeast Gaul, Caesar alerted the peoples there to the prospect that he would next try to dominate them. Intertribal tensions led some to seek his friendship, but in 57 others made unsuccessful preemptive strikes, provoking clashes which brought most of today's northern France and Belgium under his control. Only the far northwest remained insecure, and this—together with the Atlantic coast—was subjugated in 56. By stages, therefore, Caesar unexpectedly found himself achieving Roman domination of Gaul's entire vast area. Granted, he had not engaged with the peoples in the center, but they were now surrounded, and at this point gave no cause for concern.

Rather, in 55 Caesar looked elsewhere to enhance his military reputation. He first drove more Germanic peoples out of northern Gaul across the Rhine River, marking it once again as the prospective limit of Roman control. Then he crossed to southern England, officially in order to cut off aid sent from there to his Gallic opponents, but no doubt also to gauge the prospects for a full-scale invasion. Although he did return to England in 54, from the following year onwards he was no longer free to do so. Suppression of risings in northern Gaul, by the Eburones and Belgae especially, preoccupied him during 53. A greater challenge followed in 52, however, when a fearsome coalition of peoples from central Gaul led by a prince of the Arverni, Vercingetorix, began a widespread revolt against Roman rule. Its timing was intended to worsen Caesar's political position, and it achieved that goal by compelling him to postpone the reentry to office in Rome that he had been hoping for. Eventually, however, Caesar's boldness, speed, and inexhaustible energy outwitted Vercingetorix, who was besieged at Alesia (modern Alise–Ste. Reine) and forced to surrender. Such resistance as remained to the imposition of Roman control throughout Gaul was suppressed the following year, 51.

It would be hard to overstate the damage shamelessly inflicted upon the entire plundered and devastated region and its peoples. Ancient estimates that, of the three million or so Gauls who fought Caeser, one million were killed, and another million enslaved, are credible. Caesar meantime developed his taste and talent for supreme command, while his army had no match for experience and fighting quality. There were financial rewards, too; for Caesar himself and his top officers these were so vast that the treasury in Rome received distinctly less than its due.

DEATH OF CLODIUS AND POMPEY'S SOLE CONSULSHIP (52)

Political life at Rome remained violent and disrupted. A climax came in January 52. Once again, magistrates had not been elected for the year ahead of time. Clodius was campaigning to be elected praetor, Milo to be consul. A major clash occurred between their gangs near Bovillae, ten miles (16 km) south of Rome on the Via Appia. Clodius was wounded and captured, and then finished off on Milo's orders. When his corpse was brought to the city, the populace was so distraught, and its mood so hostile to the senate, that it took up the outrageous suggestion of using the senate house itself as a funeral pyre. The whole structure and its furnishings burned too.

The sense that the city was slipping into anarchy now impelled the senate to pass its "ultimate decree" (SCU), to levy troops throughout Italy, and to adopt the novel expedient of making Pompey sole consul; a dictatorship was also discussed, but rejected. Even Cato was alarmed enough to give his support. Pompey quickly introduced measures that would bring to trial those responsible for the worst of the recent instances of bribery and violence—among them Milo, who was condemned and went into exile at the independent Greek city of Massilia (modern Marseille). Pompey also made it the law that, after any consul or praetor's year of office, five years must elapse before he could proceed to a governorship. This interval would allow time for any prosecution of misconduct during office. It would also drastically curtail a senator's opportunity to exploit an immediate governorship as the means of rapid repayment for heavy debts so often incurred during office or while campaigning for it; five years' worth of interest would prove a crushing burden. However, introduction of the new law did not deter Pompey from renewing his own absentee governorship of Spain for five years.

By unfortunate coincidence, it was around this time that Caesar first seems to have become seriously anxious about his future. Hopes he may have nursed previously of returning from Gaul well before serving out his full term there were now dashed by the need to subdue Vercingetorix's formidable rising. Once that was achieved, the terminal date of his command, in 50 or 49, would be coming into sight anyway. Timing aside, he knew that—after the turmoil of his consulship in 59—the normal procedure for a governor's return would be sure to lead to his political ruin. This procedure required him to become a private citizen again on recrossing the pomerium into Rome; and were he to seek further office, it would be with this private status that he would have to register in person as a candidate. Caesar fully expected that, no matter how short the period for which he became a private citizen again, his enemies would use it to bring charges against him. If he were to have any future in Roman public life, he had to gain exemption from the normal procedure, so that there would be no break between his serving as governor (with exemption from prosecution), and his immediately entering a new office (most naturally a consulship) with continued exemption.

To achieve such a seamless transition, however, Pompey's support would be essential, and at this stage his attitude to the issue of exempting Caesar from one or more of the legal requirements seems to have been ambiguous. The personal link between them provided by Julia, Pompey's wife and Caesar's daughter, had been broken prematurely in 54, when she died in childbirth aged about nineteen. Since then, Pompey had declined to pursue any proposal by Caesar for a further marriage bond. Instead he chose to look elsewhere, and early in 52 he married Cornelia, a member of the aristocratic Metelli family; it was in fact his new father-in-law that he arranged to have elected as his consular colleague in mid-year, once conditions were more stable.

In all likelihood there was nothing exceptional about the indecisiveness of Pompey's attitude towards Caesar at this stage. It simply reflected the broader lack of confidence which his participation in political life had shown ever since his return from the East in 62. That said, the question of his future relationship with Caesar was particularly delicate. On the one hand, less than a decade before, when the Triumvirate was formed, Caesar had been very much its junior member, and Pompey indisputably its senior one. Pompey can hardly have relished the prospect that now, by contrast, the upstart Caesar might soon be returning from Gaul not only with his prestige and wealth hugely enhanced, but also with a second consulship. On the other hand, Pompey owed Caesar gratitude for vital help in 59. If he were to do nothing in return for Caesar now, who else could he turn to for future support except Cato and the inflexible, condescending Optimates? Given their past treatment of him, they were not at all a group that he would otherwise choose to associate with. Moreover they would adopt him not so much as a leader, but as a partner in their own cause; in other words, they would gain the horrid satisfaction of feeling that he was finally in their control. With a choice to be made between two such unpromising alternatives, it need be no wonder that Pompey prevaricated.

PROSPECT OF CIVIL WAR (51–49)

It looked as if Pompey would be forced to clarify his attitude the following year (51), when one of the consuls gave notice that he would raise with the senate the question of replacing Caesar in Gaul. In fact the matter was postponed till September. Pompey's opinion then was that Caesar should relinquish his command in time for his provinces to be reassigned by the senate prior to the next elections for the consulship (in 50). The senate adopted this recommendation (which left Caesar's future open), and accordingly arranged for the matter to be raised again by the consuls in March 50.

Meantime disturbing news reached Rome in November 51 that two months previously a large Parthian force had crossed the Euphrates River. It was making for the Roman province of Syria, which had been left almost defenseless after Crassus' defeat at Carrhae two years before. It was clear that a senior commander ought to be dispatched here by the following spring, and speculation centered around Pompey and Caesar as the best choices. Naturally enough, in view of his previous experience, Pompey favored himself and, had he been sent, the potential impact on political developments at Rome in the short term could have been considerable. But in the event the senate left the matter hanging.

Early in 50 the figure who drew most attention at Rome was a tribune from an aristocratic family, Gaius Scribonius Curio, who had been a friend of Clodius and had subsequently married his widow Fulvia. With a zeal worthy of Clodius, Curio at once put forward an ambitious program of popular legislation, but he soon found himself blocked at every turn, by both consuls in particular. In an abrupt switch, therefore, he abandoned these aims, and instead from now on made it his principal concern to represent Caesar's interests. The switch was sufficiently remarkable to give rise later to the allegation (never proven) that Caesar himself had triggered it by paying off Curio's huge debts. It is at least certain that Curio was acting on Caesar's behalf by the time that the governorship of the Gallic provinces eventually appeared on the senate's agenda during April (rather than March). Nothing was resolved. Pompey made clear his disapproval of any arrangement whereby Caesar could proceed without a break from governorship to consulship. He did suggest that Caesar be permitted to relinquish his command as late as mid-November. But even this would still leave a month and a half before any fresh term of office in Rome could begin, and it was easily time enough to bring Caesar to court as a private citizen.

Pompey was again insensitive to Caesar's interests once the senate had finally resolved to reinforce Syria by requiring each man to contribute one of their legions to the garrison there. When Caesar needed extra troops urgently in 53, Pompey had "lent" him a legion. He now named it as his contribution to reinforcing Syria, so that his present strength in Spain would be unaffected, whereas Caesar would in practice lose two legions rather than just one. Moreover, unfortunately for Caesar, once he had sent the two legions, news came that the Parthians had withdrawn from Syria; so both legions were then kept in Campania, rather than being sent to the East.

With Caesar seeming defiant and Pompey increasingly unsympathetic to him, the alarming prospect of civil war began to loom. Pompey at last seemed ready to accept that challenge. When he fell seriously ill during the summer of 50, he was touched by the fervor with which communities throughout Italy prayed for him. His recovery further encouraged him to think he was being called upon to uphold stability and peace. To raise troops in Italy for his cause, he had only to stamp his foot, or so he imagined.

Curio meantime worked to achieve some degree of accommodation or compromise. In particular, at the beginning of December he proposed to the senate that both Caesar and Pompey should give up their commands (Gaul and Spain respectively) at a date to be determined. The vote was overwhelmingly in favor: 370 senators for, and only twenty-two against. So in principle, it seemed, the great majority of senators shrank from another bout of civil war. Both consuls, however, thought differently, and at once approached Pompey, giving him command of the two legions stationed in Campania, as well as authorizing him to raise such other forces as he thought necessary to defend the state against Caesar. Finally pressed in this way to declare himself unequivocally Caesar's opponent, Pompey accepted the consuls' commission.

Even so, the search for compromise continued, and Curio's concern for Caesar's interests was maintained by two of the tribunes for 49, Quintus Cassius Longinus (*not* Caesar's future killer) and Marcus Antonius (better known today as Mark Antony). On January 1, 49, Curio, now acting as Caesar's envoy, read the senate a letter in which Caesar proposed that he and Pompey lay down their commands simultaneously and submit to the judgment of the Roman people. This plea was ignored, however. Instead, the consul presiding called for a vote on a proposal that Caesar must disband his army by a specified date, or be automatically considered an enemy of the state; this vote was at once vetoed by the tribunes Cassius and Antony.

A few days later, other compromises were raised: Caesar should be permitted to try to proceed without a break to a second consulship, retaining meantime only Cisalpine Gaul and Illyricum with two legions, or even just Illyricum with a single legion. The degree to which these proposals represented sincere efforts to avoid a clash, rather than mere postures, is impossible to determine. Pompey at least was willing to consider such schemes, but any chance of their adoption was quashed by those senators (like Cato and at least one of the consuls) who were determined to force a confrontation with Caesar. On January 7, it was they who successfully persuaded the senate to pass its "ultimate decree" (SCU) again, instructing all magistrates in this instance "to see to it that the Republic suffers no harm." The tribunes Cassius and Antony were then warned that their safety could no longer be guaranteed if they chose to remain in Rome; so they and Curio fled north to Caesar.

CAUSES AND CONSEQUENCES OF CAESAR CROSSING THE RUBICON (JANUARY 49)

Pompey and his associates were unperturbed by their flight, and because of the winter season they expected no immediate developments. However, this mood of complacency at Rome was soon to be punctured by the shocking news that on or about January 10 Caesar had crossed the Rubicon, north of Ariminum, with one legion. Since this river formed the boundary between his province of Cisalpine Gaul and Italy, and he had absolutely no authority to bring troops across it, the significance of his action was plain. He had committed himself to civil war, and had done so with characteristic speed: "Let the die be cast," he is supposed to have said as he crossed the river (Plutarch, *Caesar* 32). All but one of his officers stayed with him, a striking reversal of Sulla's experience when he marched on Rome for the first time in 88 (see Chapter Five).

In part, Caesar justified his resort to civil war as a defense of the constitution which, he claimed, his opponents had abused by such means as resorting needlessly to the SCU and rejecting the legitimate rights of tribunes. At the same time Caesar did not hide particular concern for his own *dignitas*. In his view, it was disrespectful, petty, and inappropriate for the senate to dictate his future. He maintained that, as a senior senator and outstanding commander in Rome's service, he did not deserve to be faced with political ruin.

Caesar's opponents naturally disputed his view. They claimed to be safe-guarding the constitution against the extreme demands of a rebellious governor. To us at least, if not to many contemporaries, this devotion to constitutional propriety must have something of a hollow ring to it when Pompey of all people took a leading role. After all, his long career had time and again shown minimal respect for such lofty principles. On the other hand, it is only right to acknowledge that those who objected to Caesar remaining protected from prosecution had a valid point to make. Such a request to remain in effect above the law flouted one of the basic principles of the Republic, the more so when it was made by such an ambitious, unscrupulous figure. That said, a case for accommodating Caesar or compromising with him can also be recognized. To this extent, the outbreak of civil war in January 49 under such conditions was by no means inevitable. In view of developments since Sulla's dictatorship, however, compromise now could equally be regarded as just the postponement of an inevitable clash over some comparable challenge to the Republic sooner rather than later.

Cicero concluded that in the event both Pompey and Caesar were prepared to risk civil war because neither wanted to defer to the other; rather, each wanted to be supreme. This was certainly the kind of attitude reflected by many of their associates. Most notably, the Optimates were determined to cut Caesar down to size, and they saw Pompey as acting for *them*, rather than as they for him. Not surprisingly, their relationship with him remained uneasy, and this must be one reason why Pompey never brought the passionate personal commitment to his cause that Caesar was to display to such devastating effect.

Even so, it is important to recognize that at the outset most senators either stood with Pompey and the Optimates against Caesar, or had no wish to become involved. In particular, almost no ex-consuls took Caesar's side, and most of his senatorial associates were either young or disreputable or both. In Cicero's view, Caesar's cause had no moral or constitutional basis. At the same time he felt antagonized and disillusioned by the Optimates and Pompey, and in the end stayed with them only out of personal devotion to Pompey.

How the rest of society throughout Italy would react was hard to predict. In fact the general feeling turned out to be dread of more Sullan-style proscriptions and, in contrast to the 80s, a complete lack of engagement with the issues dividing the senate. Even the wealthy and better educated were indifferent to what they viewed as aristocrats' rivalries of no consequence to themselves. The poor meantime were for Caesar. They were keenly aware of how little the Optimates had ever cared for their plight, and they certainly did not rush to enlist under Pompey.

With hindsight, the formation, continuation, and then breakup of the First Triumvirate inevitably dominate our view of the 50s, and it is all too easy to conclude that it was the Triumvirate which "led" to the outbreak of civil war a decade later.

Such a view calls for further reflection, however. Potentially there were countless ways in which the Triumvirate might, or might not, have evolved, and the issue was never a major preoccupation for most contemporaries. For years, Caesar in Gaul was even more liable than Crassus to meet his death on campaign. Caesar seems not to have been seriously concerned about preparing a suitable return to Rome until as late as 52, and Pompey wavered over how to react to his requests in this connection for considerably longer. Between them, Pompey's eventual stand and Caesar's ultimate defiance did become the trigger for civil war, but this particular outcome was hardly predictable far in advance. The Republic was already beset by a formidable array of interrelated problems and pressures, both external and internal, at every level of society—issues that those in authority were no longer able or willing to tackle on an adequate scale. Willpower aside, they lacked the machinery, resources, and cohesion for the purpose. It is only realistic for us to believe that by now this highly dangerous predicament was liable to lead to breakdown or conflict of some kind. Within the broader, long-term context, it may seem largely fortuitous that the fatal clash arose in 49 over no more than a dispute concerning a single senator's future, one from which even many of his fellow members wished to distance themselves.

CICERO'S GOVERNORSHIP OF CILICIA (51–50)

Numerous letters written by Cicero during his governorship of Cilicia and Cyprus in 51–50 provide uniquely rewarding insight into upper-class Roman attitudes towards provincial administration during the late Republic (on this topic in general, see Chapter Five). Much of what he wrote was addressed to close friends and never intended for wider circulation, so that it preserves a frankness missing from his public statements. With his active involvements as politician and advocate at Rome, Cicero (like many of his fellow senators) had never taken the opportunity to govern a province, and he also declined the invitation to become Caesar's legate in Gaul in 58, even though it would have enabled him to shake off Clodius. However, Pompey's law of 52, requiring a five-year gap between holding office as praetor or consul and proceeding to a governorship, created a temporary shortage of senators eligible for appointment. In these circumstances Cicero was prevailed upon to go to Cilicia.

In view of his own past record, he knew that his performance there would attract special scrutiny. In particular, he had gained fame from publishing his remarkable speeches which in 70 led to the conviction of Gaius Verres. Cicero had served as prosecutor in this notorious case brought by the Sicilians whom Verres had robbed and exploited as governor. Verres' gains had been all the more outrageous because in the event his one-year tenure was twice extended to make a total of three years. So, as he liked to say, he would be able to keep the first year's profit for himself, pay his patrons and attorneys with the second year's, and then lavish all the third, most lucrative year's profit on the jury (1 *Verrines* 40). Cicero therefore set out for Cilicia determined not merely to act honestly and responsibly, but to be a paragon among governors for self-control, justice, approachability, and clemency (his own choice of merits, *To Atticus* 114.5SB). He expected the same of his staff too. They can hardly have been pleased when he insisted that they not even claim the regular, permitted allowances, and when he later refused to share out among them, in the customary way, what remained unspent of the senate's allocation for expenses; instead he scrupulously returned this surplus to the state treasury.

The provincials were surprised by Cicero's self-denial, and duly grateful. He found it harder to protect them from his fellow Romans. From summer 51 onwards, for example, his close friend Marcus Caelius Rufus kept pestering him to have some panthers trapped and sent to Rome for the games that he would be giving as aedile the following year. Cicero was willing to oblige, but as late as April 50 reports:

> About the panthers: Skilled hunters are, on my orders, hard at work looking for them, but they are in remarkably short supply and those there are grumble, I am told, because they are the only creatures in my province for whom traps are laid, and so, it is said, they are moving out of my province into Caria. However, the job is being energetically taken in hand. . . . (*To his Friends* 90.2SB)

Meantime Caelius casually asked Cicero to oblige a friend with a favor which is surely not quite as trivial as he represents it:

> I recommend to you Marcus Feridius, a Roman *eques*, the son of a friend of mine, a worthy and hard-working young man, who has come to Cilicia on business: I ask you to treat him as one of your friends. He wants you to grant him the favor of conferring tax-exempt status upon certain lands from which cities derive income—a thing which you may easily and honorably do, and which will put some grateful and sound men under an obligation to you. (*To his Friends* 82.4SB)

Another senator, Marcus Junius Brutus (best known for later conspiring to assassinate Julius Caesar), urged Cicero to help two businessmen friends of his recover a loan made to the city of Salamis in Cyprus. The more that Cicero learned of this matter, the more shocked he became. The interest rate on the loan had illegally been fixed at 48 percent. The businessmen had been allowed to use a squadron of cavalry to harass the city council for repayment; the cavalry had then confined the council members in their meeting place, starving five to death. Eventually, Brutus revealed that his "friends" were in fact his own agents, and that the loaned money was his, not theirs. To his credit, Cicero had the cavalry withdrawn at once, and then strove to persuade the businessmen to cut their losses by settling for repayment at the maximum legal interest rate (12 percent), which the Salaminians agreed to. This was not acceptable to Brutus, however, so Cicero could only leave the matter open.

In private correspondence Cicero time and again expressed delight that service as governor might boost his reputation, but declared that otherwise he gained no special satisfaction from the assignment, and longed to be back in Rome. As he wrote to Caelius Rufus near the end of his term,

> The city, the city, my dear Rufus, stay in it and live in its limelight. All foreign travel—as I have reckoned from an early age—is insignificant and degrading for men whose work could shine at Rome. Since I know this very well, I wish I had

stood by my opinion. To me, all the profit I make from the province can't compare with one little stroll together and one of our chats. (*To his Friends* 95.2SB)

From a later letter we learn that his legal profit from the governorship actually amounted to a cool 2,200,000 sesterces.

The fact that Cilicia's eastern border lay exposed to incursions from the Parthian forces which had already entered Syria alarmed Cicero, but also fulfilled his craving for achieving some military distinction. As it turned out, campaigning was to be his main preoccupation for the first five months (to the end of 51), and the news of his approaching force evidently did contribute to the Parthians' decision to withdraw. He then turned instead to attacking communities in the Amanus mountains, which were nominally part of his province, but had never acknowledged Roman rule. He created enough havoc here to be hailed "Imperator" by his men, and he then begged his friends in the senate to support the vote of a triumph; but in the end he was awarded only the lesser distinction of an "ovation." More seriously, he was alarmed from the outset by the ill-preparedness and low morale of the two legions in Cilicia. Even so, despite his urging and the continuing danger from Parthia, the senate did nothing to strengthen them.

On a more personal level, Cicero suffered from constant anxiety that, with the growing political tension at Rome, the senate would instruct all governors to remain at their posts beyond the expiry of the regular one-year term. For Cicero, such an extension would not only be unbearable in itself; but it would also rob him of the opportunity to contribute to critical debates in the senate for which, he argued to Caelius, he ought rather to be recalled early. In September 51, Caelius responded sympathetically both on this issue and on the risk of having to face the Parthians; at the same time he is too cheerfully cynical to share Cicero's expectation that Caesar's future will be settled at all soon:

> How worried you may be about the prospects for peace in your province and the adjacent areas I don't know, but for my part I am on tenterhooks. If we could so arrange it that the size of the war should be proportionate to the strength of your forces, and could achieve just enough for glory and a triumph while avoiding the really dangerous and serious clash, that would be the most desirable outcome. But I know that as matters stand any move by the Parthians will mean a major conflict; and your army is hardly capable of defending a single pass. Unfortunately nobody allows for this; a man charged with public responsibility is expected to cope with any emergency, as though every item has been put at his disposal in complete preparedness.
>
> Moreover, I see no prospect of your being relieved because of the controversy about the Gallic provinces. Although I expect you have settled in your own mind what you are going to do in this contingency, I thought that, since I see it coming, I ought to inform you, so that you may take your decision further ahead. You know the routine. There will be a decision about Gaul. Somebody will come along with a veto. Then somebody else will stand up and stop any move about the other provinces, unless the senate is given a free hand to pass decrees on all of them. So we shall have a long, elaborate charade—so long that a couple of years or more may drag by with these maneuvers. (*To his Friends* 83SB)

As events turned out, Cicero was free to leave Cilicia at the end of his year's service in the regular way (thus in July 50); the law may even have forbidden him to stay longer. There seemed no prospect that a successor would arrive at all soon, however. Consequently, Cicero was concerned about who should be left in temporary charge, but the reasons he offers for his eventual choice hardly reveal a lasting preoccupation with the long-term welfare of the province. His younger brother Quintus—a capable soldier, who had manfully served as his senior legate—seemed the natural choice. "But," as Cicero explained to Atticus,

> there are difficulties about my brother. First of all, I don't think I can persuade him to do it, because he can't stand the province, and I agree with him that nothing could be a more unpleasant bore. Then what sort of brotherly behavior would it be on my part, supposing that he didn't like to refuse me? Remember that a big war is thought to be on in Syria, it looks like overflowing into this province, there is no protection here, no extra funds have been voted. Is it an affectionate brother's job to pass this on to Quintus? Is it a thorough governor's job to leave it to a nonentity? (*To Atticus* 117.2SB)

Eventually, affection does prevail over thoroughness, and Cicero passes his authority to the newly arrived quaestor, who (it must be acknowledged) was the proper choice after Quintus. Even so, Cicero is defensive to Atticus: "I have put Coelius in charge of the province. 'But he's only a boy,' you'll say, 'and perhaps stupid, irresponsible, and lacking in self-control.' Quite. But there was no other way" (*To Atticus* 121.3SB).

CIVIL WAR CAMPAIGNS (49–45)

Having crossed the Rubicon River in January 49, Caesar soon dispelled fears that he would be a second Sulla or a vengeful Catiline. As he moved fast down the east coast of Italy, communities went over to him with little or no resistance, including even the entire region of Picenum, Pompey's own home territory. Lucius Domitius Ahenobarbus tried to make a stand with a substantial force at Corfinium (capital of the rebel Italian alliance forty years before), but Caesar quickly gained the advantage, and Ahenobarbus' own men forced him to surrender. The fact that even here Caesar released all captives, executed no one, and declined to take the state funds that came into his hands, made a decisive impression. Many of Ahenobarbus' men were now happy to enlist under Caesar.

In mid-January Pompey left Rome for Campania, and then in March made for Brundisium, from where he sailed to northern Greece with such forces as he had gathered. Without question, from a military viewpoint his situation in Italy was precarious. Psychologically, on the other hand, to abandon not just Rome, but Italy too, with almost no fight seemed defeatist in the extreme. His plan for subsequent reconquest sounded correspondingly brutal. With all his influence in East and West, he would recruit massive forces (even barbarians from beyond the Roman empire), control the sea, starve Italy, and then invade. "What Sulla could do, I can do," was his constant refrain, according to Cicero, who was horrified. (*To Atticus* 177.2SB)

Meantime the entire peninsula was left to Caesar within little more than two months after he had taken the great gamble of crossing the Rubicon. As Cicero in Campania wrote to Atticus at the beginning of March,

> But do you see what sort of man this is into whose hands the state has fallen, how clever, alert, well prepared? I truly believe that if he takes no lives and touches no man's property, those who dreaded him most will become his warmest admirers. Both town and country people talk to me a great deal. They really think of nothing except their fields, and their bits of farms, and investments. And look how the tables are turned! They fear the man they used to trust, and love the man they used to dread. I cannot think without distress of the blunders and faults on our side which have led to this result. (*To Atticus* 163SB)

After Pompey's departure from Italy, Caesar spent about two weeks in Rome before heading west to tackle the concentration of forces in Pompey's Spanish provinces. Reducing them was an obvious strategic priority, which Caesar successfully achieved by the fall. He was further detained by Rome's old independent ally, Massilia, making an unexpectedly strong stand against him; the city surrendered only after a long siege.

Caesar next turned almost at once to challenging Pompey himself, who had been assembling troops from all over the East. Even crossing from Brundisium to northern Greece was hazardous for Caesar, because Pompey's fleet dominated the Adriatic. Eventually, however, by the following year 48, Caesar's forces had all crossed, and they then blockaded Pompey's camp at Dyrrhachium (modern Durrës in Albania). However, Pompey's army broke out with such vigor that Caesar was forced to flee in order to escape being utterly routed. As he moved southeast, Pompey followed him. In August, under some pressure from his impatient Optimate associates, and against his own judgment, Pompey fought a set battle at Pharsalus in Thessaly—the type of major confrontation that he had seldom risked throughout his career. Despite having the larger army, he was defeated and fled. Caesar's self-justificatory reaction, as he surveyed this carnage of his opponents, was reported to be: "This is how they wanted it. I, Gaius Caesar, after all my great achievements, would have been condemned in the courts if I had not sought the help of the military" (Suetonius, *Deified Julius* 30.4).

Caesar offered to forgive any of the enemy who asked for mercy, as many did. Pompey's land and sea forces now dispersed. Cicero, who had remained at Dyrrhachium, returned to Italy. Cato and both Pompey's sons went to Cyrene in North Africa (annexed by Rome in the late 70s). Pompey himself had evidently made no plan for defeat, but now decided to seek refuge in Egypt, where he had enjoyed good relations with the authorities and thought that he might be safe. In fact, however, the advisers of the young King Ptolemy XIII had him cut down as soon as he landed at the end of September.

Caesar in pursuit reached Alexandria, the capital of Egypt, only a few days later. Since contrary winds would prevent him leaving at once, he chose instead to become embroiled in an ongoing war between members of the royal family—a dangerous venture, which left him trapped in Alexandria until relieved in March 47 by troops who came overland from Asia Minor and Judaea. While there, the ambitious royal princess Cleopatra (born in 69) became his mistress. By the time he eventually left Egypt in spring or summer 47 (the precise timing remains obscure), he had established her as ruler of the kingdom; and not long afterwards she gave birth to a son by him, Ptolemy Caesar, nicknamed Caesarion.

While still in the East, Caesar turned next to dealing with the threat now posed by King Pharnaces, who in 63 had been confirmed by Pompey as successor to his father, the infamous Mithridates, in the Crimea. Pharnaces had now taken advantage of the turmoil in the Roman world to reclaim his family's ancestral kingdom of Pontus. So Caesar challenged and defeated him at Zela—Roman revenge for Mithridates' surprise victory here twenty years before in 67. This was the battle of which Caesar wrote: "I came, I saw, I conquered" (*Veni, vidi, vici*, Plutarch, *Caesar* 50; cf. Suetonius, *Deified Julius* 37.2).

In September 47 Caesar was finally able to return to Italy. By this time, however, his opponents had regrouped in Africa, so he proceeded there at the end of the year. The campaign, which lasted till mid-year 46, was a difficult one. In the decisive battle, outside Thapsus, Caesar's troops disobeyed orders by attacking prematurely, but they achieved victory. Utica—at this date the principal city of the Roman province of Africa—then surrendered without a fight. Many of Caesar's prominent surviving opponents now felt their cause was lost, and preferred to commit suicide rather than face the prospect of owing their lives to him. Cato's suicide in particular quickly became a powerful symbol to those inspired by traditional Roman principles.

A few of the leaders, however, including Pompey's two sons, escaped to Spain, where they were able to raise such formidable forces that Caesar recognized the need for him to oppose them personally, rather than entrusting the campaign to others. He left Rome late in 46, therefore, and was to be in Spain till June 45. He himself acknowledged that the battle fought at Munda (near Urso) in southern Spain proved to be his toughest ever. Even so, it turned into a rout, with 30,000 of the enemy killed, and just one of their commanders escaping with his life; he was Pompey's younger son Sextus, in his early twenties.

Caesar returned from Spain through southern Gaul and northern Italy, and only reached Rome again in October 45. Altogether, his difficulties in overcoming the Pompeians, and the length of time it took him, are not to be underestimated. He had taken some extraordinary risks, and had repeatedly been on the verge of defeat. Just as in Gaul during the 50s, only an astonishing degree of perseverance and good fortune carried him through. Further campaigning lay ahead too. By fall 45 it had already been settled that he would leave Rome on March 18, 44 to lead a major campaign against the Parthians—who were continuing to threaten Syria—and avenge the disastrous defeat at Carrhae in 53. He clearly expected to be away for a considerable time, because by the time of his departure the holders of the annual magistracies for the next three years had been named.

CAESAR'S ACTIVITY AS DICTATOR (49–44)

At least during late 45 and early 44 Caesar had a breathing space in Rome, in which to address concerns other than military campaigns. As it turned out, this and the similar intervals between earlier campaigns would prove to be his only opportunities to offer an impression of a longer-term vision for the Roman world, and his own place within it, prior to his assassination on March 15, 44. Unfortunately, for these vital matters we lack his personal testimony, the limited insights in Cicero's correspondence are unsatisfactory, and otherwise the fullest source material dates to very much later. By then, all kinds of dubious traditions and misrepresentations had developed, both favorable and unfavorable. Contemporary coins and inscriptions contribute frustratingly little. The result is that many different shades of opinion about Caesar become possible, and the quality of his achievements and intentions remains highly controversial.

In discussing them, we should first be aware of how his official status developed. He held the dictatorship for a few days in fall 49 (on his first return from Spain) in order to preside over elections, in which he himself was made consul for 48; this was his second consulship, after the first in 59. In 48, after the victory at Pharsalus, he was made dictator for a year. It was with this authority that he held elections on his return from the East in fall 47, and was made consul for 46. After the victory at

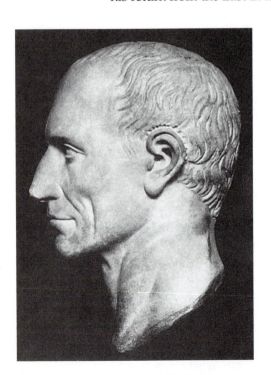

Thapsus that year, the senate voted him annual dictatorships for the next ten years, along with various other lavish and unprecedented honors, including the right to nominate the only candidates for some offices. While remaining dictator, Caesar was also sole consul for much of 45, until he resigned in the fall. In 44 he was consul again (for the fifth time), and from sometime in February he had his dictatorship converted into a perpetual one. We do not know the official purpose for making him dictator in any instance except the first, very brief one in 49, although it was presumably always to restore the state. As in Sulla's case, there seems to have been no particular concern to adhere to the traditional norms for this emergency office, especially the six-month time limit.

Caesar must surely win praise for his prompt, even-handed attention to pressing social problems. One of the most deep-rooted was that of debt, which had long affected all levels of society, as the widespread support for Catiline's uprising demonstrated. This already serious situation was then made critical by the outbreak of the civil war. As confidence evaporated, lenders began to demand repayment of their

Figure 7.3 *Bust of Julius Caesar.*

Figure 7.4 *Julius Caesar as dictator was the first living Roman with the audacity to permit his image to appear on coins. The issue shown here, by the moneyer Lucius (Aemilius) Buca in 44, dates to the final weeks of his life. It portrays him wearing a crown, and describes him pointedly as "perpetual dictator." Among the symbols on the reverse, the clasped hands affirm the trust between Caesar and his army, while the globe represents Roman aspirations to world power.*

loans, and real estate values collapsed. A serious shortage of coinage for circulation developed, because people hoarded whatever they had; in this society, after all, there was in effect no paper money, not to mention banks as we know them. Desperate borrowers began to agitate for a complete cancellation of debts. Lenders, by contrast, were appalled by the loss they would suffer if such an extreme solution to the crisis were adopted. It would be even more damaging than the measure implemented in the crisis of 86, which had cancelled three-quarters of all borrowers' obligations.

By early 48 at the latest, Caesar grasped the seriousness of the situation and both sides' fears. His approach was the moderate one of trying to offer some relief to each. Consequently, he ordered that property must be accepted for repayment at its prewar value, and he reintroduced an old law which prohibited anyone from holding more than 60,000 sesterces in cash. Coin held in excess of that amount (not huge by upper-class standards) would have to be spent in some way, and should thus find its way back into circulation. Even so, these measures were not enough to placate borrowers, some of whom raised an armed rebellion, which had to be put down by force after the senate had passed its "ultimate decree" (the SCU) for the purpose. Among the rebel leaders was even a praetor, Cicero's old friend, Marcus Caelius Rufus; he was killed in the fighting. Caesar did then act further to help borrowers by canceling interest payments due since early 49, for example, and permitting tenants to pay no rent for a year. Overall, it is true, he came nowhere near to eliminating the problem of debt, but he was responsive and creative enough to alleviate it in a balanced way.

Equally in need of attention was the calendar. The Roman civic year had only 355 days, with provision for an extra month to be inserted from time to time in

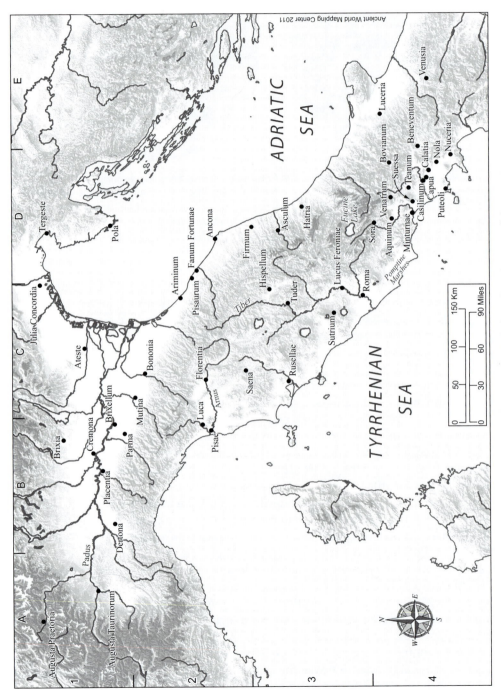

Map 7.3 *Settlement of Veterans in Italy by Julius Caesar and Augustus*

order to match the solar year. This "intercalation" had been so neglected in the recent past, however, that by the early 40s the Roman year and the solar year were about three months apart. Caesar therefore adapted the Egyptian solar calendar to Roman use. To catch up, the year 46 was lengthened to a unique 445 days, and thereafter each year would have 365 days, with an additional day to be inserted in leap years between 23 and 24 February (as a second 23 February; nothing was added at the end of the month). This "Julian" calendar was only to be modified again after another millennium and a half by Pope Gregory XIII in 1582, when it effectively attained the form still in common use today.

Caesar was naturally concerned to settle his veterans, and at the same time ready to dispel fears that he would proscribe and confiscate for this purpose as Sulla had done. In fact his attitude towards defeated enemies was typically one of forgiveness (*clementia*), and even though there does appear to have been some confiscation of land in Italy, it must have been on a limited scale. Not many veterans were settled there (15,000 perhaps) and, unlike Sulla's men, they were widely dispersed. Instead, most veterans, along with many of the poor from the city of Rome, were settled overseas—on land that either belonged to the Roman state already, or was confiscated from communities which had joined the fight against Caesar, in Spain, Africa, and the East especially. Caesar's two most ambitious settlement projects were perhaps the new colonies founded on the sites of Carthage and Corinth; both had remained undeveloped since their destruction a century earlier in 146. Like all Roman colonies, his foundations were certainly intended as centers of Roman strength and culture, but altogether there seems no cause to claim that he had in mind very specific ideas of either garrisoning or romanizing the empire when he selected their sites. Even the number of his colonies is unclear, given that few had developed far by the time of his death; others established later in his name may, or may not, have been among his plans.

There is the same uncertainty with regard to existing communities whose status Caesar is credited with raising. "Julian" in the name of a community with Latin rights or Roman citizenship could signify an award either by him or by the future emperor Augustus. Even so, in all likelihood there were some communities that he favored in this way, in Spain especially. Again, how far his motive here was to spread romanization, as opposed to express gratitude for support against the Pompeians, is impossible to judge. The grant of Roman citizenship to the Transpadana region by a law of 49—something that Crassus had proposed as censor in 65—certainly has the appearance of a reward for help during his Gallic campaigns. On the other hand, this seems a less likely explanation for his award of Latin status to the entire province of Sicily, all the more exceptional in that the island was predominantly Greek.

Altogether it may be possible to discern in Caesar's measures a new impetus to raise the status of approved provincials and to make them Rome's partners rather than merely subjects. Even so, to see this as a well formulated aim, consistently applied, would be excessive. His attitude to provincial government shows the same ambivalence. In line with his own law of 59 regulating it, he could act considerately.

In particular, we know that he abolished the oppressive system whereby a syndicate of *publicani* collected tax in Asia after making the winning bid at an auction in Rome; he now permitted the communities to collect it themselves. On the other hand, there is no sign that he planned any large reform of provincial government, and when he needed men and resources for his civil war campaigns he exacted them from provincials with much the same unfeeling ruthlessness as the Pompeians did, and as he himself had done during the 50s while in Gaul.

CAESAR'S IMPACT UPON THE CITY OF ROME

There was much in the city of Rome to claim Caesar's attention. To reduce unemployment, many of its poor were offered a fresh start in the new colonies overseas. Others who depended on the free grain available monthly to any Roman citizen (as instituted by Clodius in 58) were liable to suffer when Caesar limited these rations to a total of 150,000. Evidently as many as 320,000 citizens had been collecting them at that point. If he had contemplated cutting costs further by simply abolishing the free ration as Sulla had done, he no doubt concluded that the blow to his popularity would be too great. He did arrange for better supervision of the supply of grain to the city, and he is said to have been planning improved access to it generally from overseas, with a new harbor at Ostia and a canal from Tarracina.

Major new projects for public buildings also acted to reduce unemployment in the city. One of these, the Forum Julium (north of the original Forum Romanum), was sufficiently advanced for Caesar to dedicate it in 46; among its functions was the provision of more space for lawcourts. By contrast, work on another, the Saepta Julia, a huge enclosure for voting situated on the Campus Martius, was to be completed only in 26; the extensive use of marble in its construction was still unusual (see Map 7.4, opposite). However, after his firsthand experience of Alexandria, the greatest city of the Mediterranean, Caesar was all the more keenly aware of how unimpressive Rome seemed, and how bruised by the turmoil of the recent past. A new senate house was still needed to replace the one that had served as Clodius' funeral pyre in 52, and Caesar was authorized to build it. More generally, flooding by the Tiber in 54 had destroyed much mudbrick-built housing in low-lying areas of the city, and a major fire in 50 had caused further widespread damage.

None of these projects was finished in Caesar's lifetime, but they still demonstrate decisively how he intended both to enhance the city's appearance and to leave his own permanent mark on it. Such buildings, after all, would bear his name prominently, and have statues or other images of him in and around them. Supposedly, too, Caesar planned to add to the area of the city by diverting the Tiber. There were said to be other grandiose schemes for a huge temple of Mars, a theater to rival Pompey's, and a library on the model of Alexandria and other

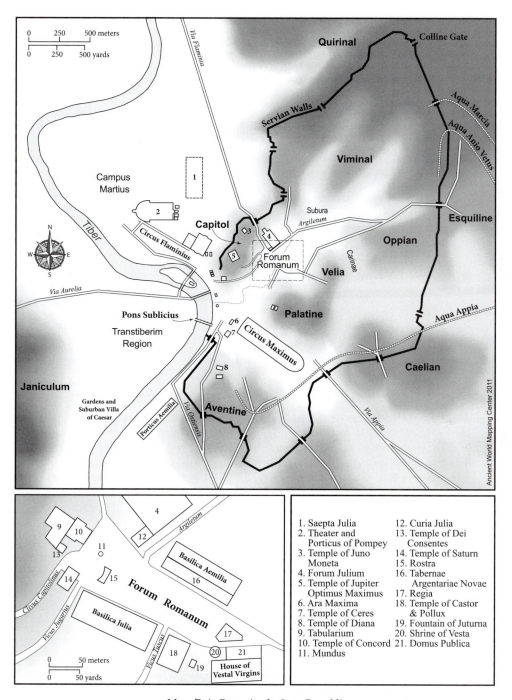

Map 7.4 *Rome in the Late Republic*

Legend:
1. Saepta Julia
2. Theater and Porticus of Pompey
3. Temple of Juno Moneta
4. Forum Julium
5. Temple of Jupiter Optimus Maximus
6. Ara Maxima
7. Temple of Ceres
8. Temple of Diana
9. Tabularium
10. Temple of Concord
11. Mundus
12. Curia Julia
13. Temple of Dei Consentes
14. Temple of Saturn
15. Rostra
16. Tabernae Argentariae Novae
17. Regia
18. Temple of Castor & Pollux
19. Fountain of Juturna
20. Shrine of Vesta
21. Domus Publica

Figure 7.5 *Part of the Roman Forum today, viewed from the Tabularium on the lower slope of the Capitoline hill. The extensive structure to the right, barely preserved above ground level, is the Basilica Julia, begun by Julius Caesar, completed by Augustus, and much used for lawcourt hearings. The trees in the background to the right are up on the Palatine hill.*

leading Greek cities. Temples to Concord and Clemency, two virtues that Caesar specially favored, were decreed by the senate in his honor.

Although all these latter schemes remain impossible to assess because Caesar never implemented them, it is quite plain that he wanted to make Rome a center of culture and education by attracting there leading intellectuals, doctors, and lawyers throughout the Mediterranean world. A plan to simplify and codify all of Roman law is even attributed to him. In his will he certainly did make a public facility of his villa and gardens across the Tiber, and the art collection there. From the measures he took, there can be no doubt that Caesar wanted to reward his supporters, and to glorify the city of Rome as well as himself. More broadly, we can see that he wanted to bring stability and prosperity to the entire Roman world. There seems little question that, in the limited intervals of time open to him, he did take encouraging steps in the right direction. Even so, there is no knowing how he would have continued, because he never gained the opportunity.

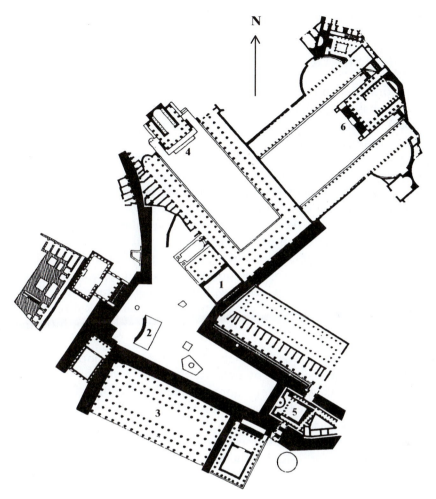

Figure 7.6 *From the mid-50s Caesar used huge sums he had gained in Gaul to fund new construction in the Forum Romanum and to purchase land for a new forum to the north. Once he became dictator, these projects were advanced and expanded. In the Forum Romanum he relocated and rebuilt both the Curia (1) and the Rostra (2), as well as replacing the old structures on the entire south side with a huge, new Basilica Julia (3) (see Fig. 7.5). The new Curia Julia (see Fig. 7.7) was integrated into his plan for a Forum Julium (or Forum Caesaris), dominated by a temple (4) to his family's divine ancestor Venus. As it turned out, most of what he had begun was still incomplete at the time of his assassination, and was finished only by Augustus. He in turn closed off the eastern end of the Forum Romanum with a new temple to Caesar as Divus Julius (5). In addition, he opened up a further forum (covering about 400 × 275 ft./122 × 84 m) beyond Caesar's; its shape at the northeast end had to remain irregular because the private owners there refused to sell their land to Augustus, and he declined to expropriate it. The focal point of this Forum Augustum was the magnificent temple (6) to Mars the Avenger (Mars Ultor), dedicated in 2 B.C., where Augustus instructed the senate to meet whenever wars or triumphs were on its agenda. Flanking the temple on either side were a colonnade and semicircle; into the rear walls of both were set niches containing statues of Rome's "great men" (summi viri) going back to earliest times. Altogether this forum serves as a potent symbol of Augustus' extraordinary achievements and of his concern to uphold and advance Rome's traditional greatness.*

POLITICAL PROSPECTS FOR ROME, AND FOR CAESAR

Caesar's work was cut short by his own closest associates, the senators. He seems not to have appreciated how badly he needed their continued support and respect. He did considerably increase the senate's size. Under him, the total membership of around 600 set by Sulla was expanded to 900. Inevitably, many of the new members were men he wished to reward, and they came from a somewhat wider variety of communities and social backgrounds than hitherto. Of course, traditionalists found fault, and exaggerated their grumbles. Among the ex-army officers introduced by Caesar were alleged to be some as low in rank as centurion. For certain, the new members must have included men from many Italian communities that had gained Roman citizenship only within the past forty years or so, and were seeing one of their own become a senator for the first time. There is no question, too, that Caesar did introduce a few members from Spain and Gaul as well, but contemporary jokes about their gaucheness—having to discard their pants for togas, and ask directions to the senate house—were simply malicious. Notably, Caesar did not introduce any Greeks.

To maintain the senate's size, and again to reward his supporters, Caesar doubled the number of quaestors set by Sulla from twenty to forty annually, and the number of praetors likewise from eight to sixteen. Inevitably, elections lost significance once Caesar gained, and used, the right to fill offices by nomination. By the same token, his dictatorships freed him from the need to pay attention to other magistrates, or to consult the senate except as a formality. Consequently, he poured scorn on Sulla for resigning the dictatorship, mocked the tribunate whose veto could not obstruct him now, and even dismissed the Republic itself as "nothing, a mere name with neither form nor substance" (Suetonius, *Deified Julius* 77). On one notorious occasion, he omitted the basic courtesy of rising from his seat when a senatorial deputation led by the consuls came to see him. His subsequent excuse—that he was too weak from diarrhea to stand up—failed to convince, since he later walked home. The senate itself—out of fear, or flattery, or even contempt—encouraged his growing arrogance by voting him a stream of ever more extraordinary powers and honors, most of which he accepted. By the beginning of 44 the image of his head was appearing on coinage, a distinction never before accorded to a living Roman (Fig. 7.4). Antony had also been chosen, though not yet instituted, as priest of a temple authorized by the senate for worship of Caesar as a god. Public worship of a living ruler was a Greek practice (see Chapter Nine), but it had no real precedent at Rome, and was completely contrary to the very concept of a republic.

Much the same may be said of kingship. Once again, it is unclear how far, if at all, Caesar wanted this distinction. The Greek world had indeed had kings, some of whom impressed Romans. Admittedly, too, elements of Rome's own archaic kingship had been carried over into the Republic. For Caesar to go as far as to take the title of *rex*, however, would be a giant leap, certain to offend almost everyone with any regard for the Republic. Early in 44, when some members of a crowd hailed him as king, he reacted by stating that he was Caesar, not Rex—a play on the fact that Rex is also a Roman surname (*cognomen*). Then, at a festival in mid-February (the Lupercalia), Antony made several attempts to crown him with a diadem of laurel as he sat on his golden chair, wearing a purple toga and gold wreath. Caesar rebuffed all the attempts, finally ordering that the diadem be taken to the temple of Jupiter, "who is the Romans' only king," on the Capitol. There is no knowing whether Caesar and Antony were deliberately colluding here to test popular reactions, or whether Antony was acting just on his own initiative (and if so, did he mean to bestow honor, or discredit?). Whatever interpretation be preferred, Caesar never did actually claim kingship, even though he may have toyed with the possibility. The fact that Cleopatra and her baby son Caesarion came to Rome in 46 and remained there can only have fuelled suspicions that Caesar had it in mind to found a dynasty.

By early 44, there was no further authority that fresh honors could confer on him. He already had absolute power. As he well knew, he was hated for that, and for the way he used it. After all, a dangerous consequence of his clementia was the survival of many of his enemies, plenty of them still in the senate. Even so, to him the Republic was dead, and he could see no secure alternative means of regulating the state's affairs for the future except through himself. His adoption of the title "perpetual dictator" during February 44 confirmed this conclusion. In any event, reform would now have to be put off until his return from the Parthian campaign to which he had long been committed.

To many senators, this new title and the prospect of Caesar's long absence marked the end of all hope, the final provocation. Naturally they resented the permanent removal of their own authority; beyond that, Caesar's complete and seemingly irreversible abandonment of all republican principle now became insufferable. They had to act before his departure on March 18, and so determined to kill him publicly in the senate at the last meeting he would attend, on the Ides (fifteenth) of March—just as Romulus had been killed when he became a tyrant, according to one tradition. The leaders of the sixty or so members in the plot were two praetors, Marcus Junius Brutus and his brother-in-law Gaius Cassius Longinus. Both had taken Pompey's side and been pardoned by Caesar. Both claimed descent from ancient families with a tradition of championing Rome's liberty; a celebrated Brutus had led the expulsion of the last king, Tarquinius Superbus.

Caesar fell at the foot of a statue of Pompey. Assassination by his peers was a tragic end for a man who had fought so long and hard to become unrivalled first man in Rome. But along with that insatiable ambition a certain naiveté was detectable. Somehow Caesar always seemed to imagine that, while he must be accorded special rights in deference to his dignitas, the rest of the state can, and

a

Figure 7.7a,b,c *This structure is today a prominent feature of the north side of the Forum Romanum. Once Rome's senate house, in the seventh century it became a church. Over time, with successive rebuildings and embellishments, the floor had eventually risen more than 20 feet (6 m) above the ground level in antiquity. Excavation in the forum at the end of the nineteenth century, however, showed that at least part of the ancient floor was still in place, and held out the tantalizing prospect that, if all later accretions were removed, much of the original structure might still be found intact underneath. An ambitious initiative during the 1930s did duly uncover and restore it; [a] shows the removal of additions to the rear and side in progress. The senate house thus revealed [b] had been erected after a fire in A.D. 283; the conspicuous horizontal openings either side of the front doors were for medieval tombs. It reproduced the design of the building commissioned by Julius Caesar as dictator and dedicated by Octavian as the Curia Julia in 29 B.C. (the very ancient senate house which this in turn replaced—enlarged by Sulla, and then torched as Clodius' funeral pyre in 52—had been situated nearby). The interior of the restored structure [c], viewed here from the front doors, is a tall, open chamber measuring 84 × 58 ft. (26 × 18 m). Only the floor now offers an impression of the fine marble that originally covered most of the walls too. Along either side are three broad steps where senators sat on benches; at the far end is a dais for the magistrate presiding. When the senate was in session, only members could enter, but the front doors had to remain open, allowing spectators a chance to follow the proceedings from there. So a chamber identical to the one seen here was the setting for memorable occasions which attracted immense (and audible) public interest, like the conclusion of Augustus' "First Settlement" (see Chapter Eight) or the trial of Gnaeus Calpurnius Piso the Elder (see Chapter Nine).*

b

c

will, continue to function around him in the regular, legal way. By early 44, however, even many of his supporters in the senate found it intolerable that they must all remain deprived of their dignitas for the foreseeable future. Hence they concluded that his personal interest could not continue to be so privileged above that of everyone else.

SUGGESTED READINGS

Griffin, Miriam (ed.). 2009. *A Companion to Julius Caesar*. Malden, Mass., and Oxford: Wiley-Blackwell. Thirty essays on Caesar's career, writings, and legacy to the present day.

Gruen, Erich S. 1995 (reissue of 1974 original, with new Introduction). *The Last Generation of the Roman Republic*. Berkeley, Los Angeles, London: University of California Press. This detailed, controversial account accords greater weight to the continuation of established institutions and practices during the period than to the elements that triggered change. The new Introduction offers an invaluable overview of the different approaches taken to the fall of the Roman Republic during the twenty years following the book's original publication.

Mouritsen, Henrik. 2001. *Plebs and Politics in the Late Roman Republic*. Cambridge: Cambridge University Press.

Rawson, Elizabeth. 1985. *Intellectual Life in the Late Roman Republic*. Baltimore: Johns Hopkins University Press.

Syme, Ronald. 1939 (and often reprinted). *The Roman Revolution*. Oxford: Clarendon Press. Classic treatment of the changes to state and society from the formation of the First Triumvirate to the death of Augustus (A.D. 14); a difficult, yet powerful, book.

Tatum, W. Jeffrey. 1999. *The Patrician Tribune: Publius Clodius Pulcher*. Chapel Hill and London: University of North Carolina Press.

Treggiari, Susan. 1996 (second edition). *Cicero's Cilician Letters*. London: London Association of Classical Teachers.

Yavetz, Zwi. 1983. *Julius Caesar and His Public Image*. London: Thames and Hudson.

8

AUGUSTUS AND THE TRANSFORMATION OF THE ROMAN WORLD

The surviving record for the period of not quite sixty years from the assassination of Julius Caesar to the death of Augustus is a notably mixed one. Speeches and letters by Cicero give a full, vivid picture of the turbulent initial phase. Thereafter Appian's civil war narrative is important until it ends with the death of Sextus Pompey in 35. Also essential is Plutarch's *Life* of Antony, though neither it nor any other source presents events from Antony's perspective, which is a serious obstacle to our understanding of the 30s. Cassius Dio's uninspiring year-by-year account composed early in the third century becomes vital from the mid-30s, especially for the Principate of Augustus; it is in fact our only such record for that entire formative period. The lively biographies of Augustus and Tiberius by Suetonius are valuable too, although the presentation is thematic and the focus primarily on each subject's background and character. From the time of Augustus onwards, many more documents come to be inscribed on stone or bronze, and there are some remarkable survivals from this varied body of materials. Among them, naturally, his own record of the achievements he wished to be remembered for occupies a very special position (see *Res Gestae* of Augustus, below).

REACTIONS TO THE ASSASSINATION OF CAESAR (44–43)

As soon as they had struck their blows, the senators who had conspired to assassinate Caesar hailed "liberty" and its senatorial embodiment, Cicero. They must have realized, however, that further obstacles to liberty's full return could well

Map 8.1 *Roman Campaigns, 44–30*

emerge. In the immediate confusion and panic, much would obviously depend on the attitude of Antony, Caesar's fellow consul, and of Marcus Aemilius Lepidus, the aristocratic former consul who was his deputy (*magister equitum*) as dictator and commander of the troops in Rome. When Antony summoned the senate two days later on March 17, 44, he gained its support for a compromise whereby no action would be taken against the assassins, but at the same time all Caesar's measures and appointments would remain valid. The intention was to heal divisions and prevent disruption of the state's management, but the effect was also to diminish the aim of the assassination. The compromise certainly failed to anticipate the mood soon shown by the people at Caesar's public funeral and the reading of his will, which left them his extensive property across the Tiber and bequeathed each individual 300 sesterces. There was now a mass outcry against the assassins, which Antony himself encouraged. It remained so intense that by mid-April the leaders Brutus and Cassius had been driven from Rome. Cleopatra returned to Egypt with her son without delay. Lepidus, too, left the city to assume command of troops in southern (Narbonese) Gaul and Nearer Spain, where Sextus Pompey was rebuilding his cause after the defeat at Munda in 45 (see Chapter Seven). Before departing, however, Lepidus—with Antony's support—first contrived to have himself made *pontifex maximus* in Caesar's place.

Meantime, as soon as he heard of the assassination from his mother, Caesar's eighteen-year-old grand-nephew Gaius Octavius left Apollonia (across the Adriatic from Italy, in Illyricum), where he had been studying, and sailed to Brundisium. He was accompanied by Marcus Vipsanius Agrippa, a friend of about the same age, but from an undistinguished family, who was to remain his close, loyal associate. Octavius' mother Atia was the daughter of Caesar's sister, Julia; his father Gaius Octavius was a first-generation senator (*novus homo*) who had been praetor in 61 and died two years later. Their son Gaius Octavius was born in September 63, and had accompanied Caesar on his Spanish campaign in 45 (see Table 8.1, below). Now, when he reached Brundisium, he learned that in a will drawn up the previous year Caesar had adopted him and made him his principal heir. Once in Rome, and against the advice of his stepfather, he formally declared his acceptance of the inheritance, and took the name Gaius Julius Caesar Octavianus, although he always preferred to omit Octavianus for greater effect. However, the modern convention used here is to refer to him as Octavian in order to distinguish him from the dictator Caesar.

In view of Octavian's youth and inexperience, Antony at first did not view him as a threat. But it soon became clear that Octavian was succeeding in his attempt to displace Antony as leader of Caesar's friends and supporters, especially among the city populace and the veterans. When asked by Octavian to release Caesar's money, Antony found various reasons not to, and Octavian then won tremendous popularity by selling off his own property in order to pay the bequest of 300 sesterces to each citizen. Thereafter too, amid the turmoil of the next few months, Antony increasingly lost ground to Octavian, who proved adept at attracting support with offers of money and appeals to Caesar's memory. Meantime in August, Brutus and Cassius decided to take advantage of an official reason to leave Italy altogether, offered by the senate when it made them governors of the minor combined province of Crete and Cyrene. By the end of November, Antony in turn chose to abandon his struggle to deprive Octavian of support in Rome, and instead to leave with an army for the province of Cisalpine Gaul that he had arranged to be assigned. He was to find, however, that the governor already in position, Decimus Junius Brutus Albinus (one of the conspirators, but not to be confused with Brutus the leader), was in Mutina (modern Modena) and refused to leave. Accordingly, Antony proceeded to lay siege to the city.

Cicero now seized the initiative in proposing that the senate at last assert itself by eliminating Antony, whom he persistently represented as a would-be dictator. This removal, after all, was a step which he and many others had long since come to believe ought to have been taken at the same time as the assassination of Caesar. Moreover, urged Cicero, for this purpose the senate could strengthen its own forces—under the command of the two consuls for 43, Aulus Hirtius and Gaius Vibius Pansa Caetronianus—by enlisting the help of Octavian and the large body of troops he had raised privately for himself. Consequently, in January 43 Octavian was offered, and accepted, authority (*imperium*) subordinate to that of the consuls, and membership of the senate with the right to be called on to speak among the ex-consuls. Attempts to reach a negotiated settlement with Antony failed, and when the decisive clashes occurred in April he was defeated and Mutina relieved.

EMERGENCE OF A SECOND TRIUMVIRATE (43)

Unfortunately for Cicero and the senate, however, both consuls were casualties of the fighting. Decimus Brutus and his troops were weak from their long siege, and so quite unable to pursue Antony effectively as he retreated westwards. Decimus Brutus was instructed by the senate to take over the deceased consuls' forces, but he received no support from Octavian, who declined to take orders from him. Octavian appreciated that he, too, had no prospect of eliminating Antony successfully at this stage. So Antony was able to make his way west and join Lepidus, who had so far been assuring the senate of his loyalty, but needed little persuasion by his own men and by Antony to switch allegiance. Meantime Octavian insisted that his immediate priority must be to secure appropriate rewards for his men from the senate; only his election to one of the vacant consulships, he told them, would ensure that these rewards were forthcoming. Predictably, the senate would not hear of permitting a nineteen-year-old to stand for that office, however remarkable he might be. Even so, they were forced to re-think in August when Octavian marched on Rome at the head of eight legions. Later that month he duly became consul with his relative Quintus Pedius, Caesar's nephew, who died later the same year.

Octavian now saw to it that Caesar's assassins were all formally condemned and outlawed; so too was Sextus Pompey, despite a settlement with him that the senate had approved in April. With Lepidus' mediation, Octavian also sought a reconciliation with Antony, the successful outcome of which was that the three men became "Triumvirs for the restoration of the state" (*triumviri reipublicae constituendae*) for five years. The arrangements they concluded at a meeting near Bononia (modern Bologna) were made law in Rome in November. Thus this so-called "Second Triumvirate" was formally legal, in marked contrast to its notional forerunner formed by Pompey, Crassus, and Caesar in 60–59 (see Chapter Seven). The Triumvirs—dictators in all but name—gained authority to make laws without reference to senate or people, to exercise jurisdiction without appeal, and to nominate all magistrates. In practice, however, some formal consultation of senate or people did continue, and some elections were held. As for the provinces, Antony was to take responsibility for Cisalpine and Transalpine Gaul, Lepidus for Narbonese Gaul and Spain, and Octavian for Africa, Sardinia, and Sicily. The Triumvirate's priority, however, would be to pursue and punish Caesar's assassins, and for this purpose Antony and Octavian were to have twenty legions each—amounting to perhaps two-thirds of the sixty legions under arms across the Roman world at the time. This is a staggering total, considering that when the First Triumvirate was formed the total number had been no more than about fifteen.

The Triumvirs lacked the means to pay such huge numbers of men (a legion comprised between four and five thousand) without rapidly acquiring land and cash on an extensive scale. This they now determined to achieve by resorting to proscriptions as Sulla had done (and as Caesar very deliberately had not). The number of victims was perhaps higher than in Sulla's time—supposedly as many as 300 senators and 2,000 *equites*—although it is clear that a considerable number of the proscribed escaped either to the East or to Sextus Pompey, who now moved with a fleet to Sicily. In the event, even the property of so many victims was insufficient for the Triumvirs' needs, so that they committed the further outrage of handing over to the military eighteen of the richest cities in Italy together with their lands.

Proscriptions by their very nature also offered the chance to remove political enemies, and so we may well believe that it was Antony who insisted on including Cicero in the list. He was caught and killed at a villa he owned near Caieta, about seventy miles (113 km) south of Rome, in December 43. He had hoped in vain that Antony's departure from Rome in late 44 would give the senate the opportunity to eliminate him. Thereby it would finally break free from the unbroken domination by one or more powerful individuals which had subverted its traditional control of the Republic ever since the formation of the First Triumvirate in 60–59. Cicero never anticipated the unlikely prospect that Antony would be defeated at Mutina, but still remain able to escape and join Lepidus. Even worse, however, he had quite underestimated Octavian's strength and his single-minded pursuit of power. In Cicero's own dismissive words, Octavian was merely a youngster "to be praised, honored, and disposed of" (*To his Friends* 401SB). Cicero, in his devotion to Republican principles, had not reckoned with Octavian's ability to switch the allegiance of the senate's own troops to himself, let alone with his demand for a consulship. Still more of a shock was the astonishing turnabout in Octavian's approach, from pursuing Antony as an enemy to making a partner of him in a Triumvirate dedicated to the pursuit of Caesar's assassins.

[margin note: why Caesar Fell & Octavian won]

BATTLE OF PHILIPPI (42)

At the beginning of 42 Julius Caesar was deified by the senate, and it was probably now that Quintilis, the month of his birth, was renamed Julius (July). Naturally, Octavian's prestige as "son of a god" (*divi filius*) was enhanced. He and Antony next began to move eastwards against Brutus and Cassius, leaving Lepidus in charge in Italy. The very real prospect of their Adriatic crossing being threatened by Sextus Pompey was eliminated when his fleet was severely damaged in a battle around the Straits of Messina. For many months past, Brutus had been gathering troops, funds, and other support in Greece and western Asia Minor, while Cassius had been doing likewise farther east.

The result of various delays was that not until late summer did Brutus and Cassius cross the Hellespont and jointly advance into Macedonia, where they encountered the forces of Antony and Octavian near Philippi. Each army comprised about twenty legions or 100,000 men, and in two successive battles about three weeks apart during October their fortunes were mixed. In the first battle, Brutus wiped out three of Octavian's legions and captured his camp, while the troops under Cassius' command were so decisively routed by Antony that he committed suicide. The second battle may also have begun well for Brutus, but in the end his entire front broke, and he too killed himself. It is really his death which marks the end of the Republican cause.

[margin note: Brutus & Cassius move on Antony & Octavian]

[margin note: Cassius & Brutus suicided]

Figure 8.1 *What was to prove one of Brutus' last coins (issued by the moneyer Lucius Plaetorius Cestianus in 42) shows his own head on one side, and "Ides of March" on the other, surmounted by two daggers either side of a "liberty cap" to symbolize the achievement of that fateful day in 44.*

SOURCE 8.1: Laudatio Turiae

This long Latin document, inscribed on stone at Rome, originally had two columns, of which only the second survives, and not all of it. It takes the form of a laudatio *or eulogy to be delivered at a funeral by an upper-class husband for his wife. We know the name of neither, although scholars have customarily (but erroneously) referred to her as Turia, since a literary source happens to preserve a story about a woman of that name which is comparable to part of this record. The wife praised here must have died around the beginning of the Christian era. For these extracts, the original paragraphing is retained, but no indication is given of the many instances where the text is badly damaged and has to be restored. For the wife's legal position and the nature of* cum manu *marriage, see "Changes in Roman Society" in Chapter Five. Among the many qualities which she exemplifies, note her care for the extended family, and her offer to divorce her husband because their inability to have children threatened the continuation of the family line.*

You were suddenly left orphaned before the day of our marriage when both your parents were murdered in lonely country. It was mainly due to you that the death of your parents did not remain unavenged, because I had already departed to Macedonia, and your sister's husband Gaius Cluvius likewise to the province of Africa.

You put so much effort into performing this sacred duty by insisting upon a prosecution and due punishment that, even had we been available, we should not have been able to do more. Rather, the credit is all yours, in partnership with that most respected of women, your sister.

While you were engaged with this duty, and the perpetrators had been punished, you immediately left your family home to safeguard your virtue, and moved to that of my mother, where you awaited my return.

You were then pressured to declare that your father's will, in which you and I were made heirs, was invalid on the grounds that he had taken his wife into a manus marriage. . . . This would have required you, and all your father's property, to revert to the guardianship of those pressing the point. Your sister stood to inherit nothing, because she had passed from the manus of your father into Cluvius'. Even though I was away, I am aware of how you reacted to these claims, and of the presence of mind with which you held out against them. . . .

Your resolution made them desist and not bring up the issue any further. As a result, you single-handedly accomplished the defense of your reverence for your father, the respect due to your sister, and your loyalty to me.

It is rare for a marriage to last so long, to be ended by death rather than broken by divorce; ours turned out to last forty-one years without upset. I only wish that it could have been my death which ended it, since it would have been fairer for me as the elder to go first.

Why should I mention your personal qualities? You were chaste, obedient, obliging, agreeable, an active wool-worker, pious but not to excess, in dress fashionable but not glamorous, and altogether discreetly elegant. Why should I speak of your affection for your relatives and your devotion to the family? You showed the same concern for my mother as for your parents, and provided the same restful retirement for both, displaying overall the countless qualities found in every matron who seeks to be well thought of. It is your own distinctive merits that I stress. Few men have encountered their like, and been able to make them known and vouch for them; human destiny has kept them rare.

Together we have taken care to preserve the entire inheritance received from your parents. You were not concerned to add to it, since you handed it all over to me. We shared responsibility such that I took care of your property, and you looked after mine. . . .

You demonstrated your generosity with regard to very many relatives, and especially in your devotion to the family as a whole. There are other noble women of whom the same might readily be said, but only one matched you in this respect, your sister. . . . Certain female relatives of yours you brought up in our household, and you equipped them with dowries so that they could attain a status worthy of your family. Gaius Cluvius and I put our heads together about these dowries that you had settled upon. While we approved of them, we did not want you to diminish your own inheritance, so we tapped our resources and used our property to pay them. . . .

You provided the greatest support for my flight [from proscription in 43/42], helping me with your jewelry in particular by handing me all the gold and pearls from your person. . . . You deceived our enemies' guards. . . . Even though your courage kept urging you to try and test the strength of the military, you restrained yourself. The clemency of those for whom you had such plans offered a better approach. Amid all this you had the resolution not to let slip any undignified remark. . . .

Caesar [Octavian] was right when he said that it was you who made it possible for him to restore me to my native land because, but for the arrangements you made for him to save me, even his promises of help would have been in vain. . . .

I will acknowledge, however, that your plight made for the most terrible event of my life. It was when I had been restored to my country—as a useful citizen of it still— by the generous decision of Caesar [Octavian], who remained overseas. His colleague [as Triumvir], Marcus Lepidus, who was in Rome, objected to my reinstatement. When you prostrated yourself on the ground at his feet, he did not just fail to raise you up, but you were caught and dragged along the way slaves are, your body was all bruised. Even so, you reminded him most resolutely about Caesar's edict with its congratulations on my reinstatement. After hearing his response and enduring his abusive, cruel insults, you openly denounced him as the person who should be known as responsible for all my perils. Later he suffered for his behavior. . . .

Once peace returned to the world and the Republic was restored [in the 20s], it was then a time of rest and contentment for us. We did long for the children that already for some time fate had begrudged us. If fortune in its usual caring way had allowed them, what would the two of us have lacked? Advancing age ended our hopes. . . .

Doubting your own fertility and distressed at my childlessness, you talked of divorce so that I—by remaining married to you—should not forfeit the hope of having children and be miserable as a result. You said that you would leave and hand over the household to another, fertile, woman—your sole aim being that, in line with the familiar harmony between us, you should seek out and arrange suitable circumstances for me. You insisted that you would regard these children-to-be as shared and as if your own. You would not make any division of our property, which to date had been shared, but it would continue to be under my control and, with my consent, adminstered by you. You would not regard anything as split or separated, but from then on your relationship to me and the respect you paid me would be that of a sister or mother-in-law.

I must admit to having become furious enough to be out of my mind; I was so aghast at your proposals that I could barely regain self-control. . . . (*ILS* 8393)

Figure 8.2 *Bust of Mark Antony.*

Antony's bold, skillful generalship was decisive in winning both these battles at Philippi, and he gained considerable military prestige as a result. As a reward, he was now able to assume the more attractive responsibility of remaining behind in the East to settle its affairs; this would include overseeing the discharge of several legions, among them the defeated forces of Brutus and Cassius. At the same time he retained his responsibility for Gaul, thus also controlling a strategic approach route to Italy from the West. In all likelihood he had not determined how long his stay in the East would be; it is most improbable that at this stage he envisaged staying there for an extended period.

Octavian by contrast had contributed little to the victories at Philippi, and so he was now obliged to undertake the settlement of discharged veterans in Italy. As it turned out, the land of the eighteen cities appropriated for this harsh purpose in 43 was nowhere near sufficient, and in the end perhaps as many as twenty-two more cities suffered confiscations. Inevitably, every part of the entire settlement process was plagued by injustices and inconsistencies; the misery caused throughout Italy was intense and long-lasting (see Map 7.3). At the same time Sextus Pompey had now rebuilt enough of a fleet to block grain imports to Rome from overseas, and this further pressure led to riots, which escalated into civil war. A short section of Appian encapsulates the desperate state of affairs (*Civil Wars* 5.18):

> Rome was suffering from famine, since no supplies reached the city by sea because of Sextus Pompey, and land in Italy was not being cultivated because of the warfare. In addition, the armed forces consumed such food as there was. At night, the ordinary people in the city took to theft, and disturbances more violent than theft took place, ones which were so bold that suspicion fell on the military. The civilian population shut its workshops and made the magistrates leave, declaring that they had no need of either magistrates or crafts in a starving and plundered city.

[Handwritten margin note: Octavian Dealt with V.A. Badly & Sextus Pompey Blocked Grain to Rome]

PERUSINE WAR (41–40)

Discontent against Octavian was coordinated by a consul for 41, no other than Lucius Antonius, Antony's brother; he was supported in turn by Antony's wife, Fulvia, the widow of Curio, who had been killed on campaign in 49. By the fall, Octavian had trapped both Antonius and Fulvia in Perusia (modern Perugia), which he besieged and eventually captured in spring 40. Antonius was then pardoned by Octavian, and Fulvia was allowed to depart for the East; both in fact soon died. Many Perusines, on the other hand, were butchered, and their city was looted and burnt. Ironically, Octavian's survival of this severe challenge, and his ability to reassert control in Italy, owed much to indecisiveness on Antony's part. Although far away, he was kept well informed of developments, but reckoned that he had most to gain by simply awaiting the outcome. Naturally it might not disappoint him if Octavian were to suffer defeat, yet at the same time he hesitated to act openly against him at this point. Because Antony sent no clear directives, therefore, several commanders in the West who were loyal to him chose not to engage their substantial bodies of troops. The fact is that, if they had, Octavian's chances of survival would have all but disappeared.

In summer 40 Octavian gave Antony further cause for concern by coolly taking over Gaul and its garrison, following the death of the governor there who had been loyal to Antony. Antony sought a meeting with Octavian, therefore, which took place at Brundisium in September. There was every likelihood that it would turn into a serious clash between both men's forces, but in the event the mood throughout their two armies was strongly for an agreement rather than further fighting. Agreement was duly reached, and sealed by the marriage of Antony and Octavian's elder sister, Octavia; both partners' previous spouses had recently died. Octavian in effect now took responsibility for the West, including Italy, and Antony the East; Lepidus, whose role had become increasingly insignificant, was assigned only Africa in his absence. Octavian was charged with ending the threat posed by Sextus Pompey, either by defeating him, or by making a settlement with him. There was some chance of the latter possibility, insofar as during the summer Octavian had agreed to marry Scribonia, the sister of Sextus Pompey's father-in-law, even though she was considerably older than he. It was her third marriage, and it lasted only a year. But by Scribonia Octavian had his only child, a daughter named Julia.

Inevitably the agreement reached at Brundisium encouraged Antony to confine his attention to the east of the empire; in fact, he was never to see Rome again after October 39. Octavian, meanwhile, had an invaluable asset in his possession of Italy, although he recognized that he would not be secure there until the threat presented by Sextus Pompey had been removed. For the time being, the impact of the latter's widespread raids and blockades made an agreement with him the only practical recourse. This was reached at Misenum in summer 39, with Sextus Pompey, Octavian, and Antony all present in person. Sextus Pompey undertook to abandon hostilities against the Triumvirate. In return, he was to retain control of Corsica, Sardinia, and Sicily, and gain that of the Peloponnese, all for five years; he was made an augur at once, and was promised a consulship in 33. Octavian had Antony to thank for help in reaching this pact, although of course he had no wish to adhere to its humiliating terms any longer than absolutely necessary. Antony, for his part, was concerned to see that the threat presented by Sextus Pompey did not extend eastwards.

ELIMINATION OF SEXTUS POMPEY AND LEPIDUS (39–36)

The extreme fragility of the agreement reached at Misenum was soon exposed. Sextus Pompey took offense when Octavian divorced Scribonia in fall 39, and again when Antony delayed handing over the Peloponnese to him. Meanwhile Italy was suffering from raids by pirates and their harassment of grain ships. These raiders may not have been under Sextus Pompey's control, but even so Octavian blamed him publicly for the distress created. Two major clashes between their fleets followed in spring 38—off Cumae, and in the Straits of Messina—both of which Sextus Pompey won decisively, although he then did not dare to follow up his advantage. His hesitation offered Octavian a respite, in which he begged Antony for help. Once again, Antony may not have been unduly dismayed by Octavian's plight. Eventually, however, at a long, tense meeting with Octavian at Tarentum (modern Taranto) in summer 37, the Triumvirate was renewed (probably to the end of 33), and Antony did consent to help him further, under certain conditions. In particular, Octavian was to postpone any new offensive until the following year, probably in order to synchronize with Antony's plans for the East. Octavian was also to send about 20,000 men there in return for being permitted to keep 120 of the warships accompanying Antony.

For Octavian, the advantage of this exchange was that the ships were immediately at his disposal, whereas his own commitment to provide men was only a promise for the future—which in fact he never honored properly. As consul in 37, Agrippa now took the lead in coordinating a supreme effort to deliver Sextus Pompey a knockout blow. Twenty thousand slaves were freed and trained as rowers. Lepidus even agreed to bring help from Africa—which he had not done in 38. He proved willing to contribute up to sixteen legions to a three-pronged attack on Sextus Pompey in Sicily during summer 36. It began badly, with many of Octavian's ships wrecked in storms, but thanks to Agrippa's leadership the enemy fleet was eventually annihilated in a series of naval battles which reached their climax offshore from Naulochus in north-east Sicily. Three hundred ships engaged on each side here, and only seventeen of Sextus Pompey's escaped. He himself then managed to reach Asia Minor, where he hoped that Antony's governors would welcome him. Soon, however, his efforts there to revive his cause seemed too much of a danger and an embarrassment, and he was pursued and executed in 35. The energy with which he had unflinchingly maintained the cause inherited from his father is remarkable, as is the degree of success that he achieved. With a little more boldness, in 38 especially, he might even have displaced Octavian.

Instead, as it turned out, Sextus Pompey's decisive defeat at Naulochus prompted Lepidus to conclude that *his* time to displace Octavian had arrived. He was, after all, very much Octavian's superior in age and family background, and no doubt deeply resented his exclusion from the crucial meetings at Brundisium, Misenum, and Tarentum. On the other hand, he had never matched Octavian's passion for power, let alone his willingness to take risks. So now, when Lepidus demanded that Sextus Pompey's land forces surrender to him, Octavian objected. The fierce argument was only resolved by Octavian brazenly entering Lepidus' camp and inviting all the troops—Lepidus' own and Sextus Pompey's—to recognize *him* as their commander. Not for the first time, his audacious personal appeal succeeded. As a result, Octavian was now able to humiliate Lepidus by removing him from the Triumvirate, taking control of Africa from him, and requiring him to live as an exile at Circeii about sixty miles south of Rome. Nominally, however, he was permitted to retain his membership of the senate and the office of pontifex maximus.

Octavian's victory at Naulochus thus became a doubly significant turning point for him, because it eliminated not only Sextus Pompey at last, but also one of his fellow Triumvirs. In addition, doubts about his military ability were now resolved; strictly speaking, the victory may have been Agrippa's, but the credit still went to Octavian. For the first time, too, undisputed control of Italy was within his grasp, together with the prospect of being able to begin its return to stability and prosperity.

ANTONY IN THE EAST
(42 ONWARDS)

This is the point for us to go back and trace developments in the East following Antony's victory at Philippi in October 42. Here there was much to occupy him over a vast expanse of territory. Funds had to be raised urgently for paying troops and settling veterans; disloyal local rulers had to be replaced; and consideration had also to be given to resuming the offensive against Parthia that Julius Caesar's assassination had forestalled. As part of all this activity, it made sound sense for Antony to establish good relations with the ruler of the richest independent state of the eastern Mediterranean, Cleopatra, Queen of Egypt. The meeting which he requested at Tarsus in Cilicia in 41 was probably not their first; they no doubt met previously when Cleopatra took up residence in Rome during Caesar's dictatorship.

a

b

c

Figure 8.3a,b,c   *Cleopatra's historical importance, and the inspiration still generated by her memory, make the quest for an accurate likeness of her only natural; but a satisfying outcome remains elusive. We see her [a] placed (remarkably) behind her son Caesarion on the rear wall of the Temple of Hathor at Dendera, presenting offerings to the gods (the miniature figure in between the two is Caesarion's "ka" or protective spirit); but these are by definition stylized images in the traditional forms of Egyptian religion. Coins minted in Alexandria [b] offer a more lifelike profile (compare Fig. 8.4). Several three-dimensional portraits have been identified by one expert or another, but in all cases the figure is not named. Only one [c] is widely thought to be Cleopatra. It is a marble head (with the nose missing) found in the Villa of the Quintilii family on the Via Appia near Rome; the hairstyle and the broad royal diadem match the coin portrait.*

Now, however, their relationship soon became personal. Cleopatra gave birth to twins only a year later, and Antony spent the winter of 41–40 with her in Alexandria. Even so, this is not to say that he abandoned his grip on affairs. His preference for letting Octavian's conflict with Lucius Antonius and Fulvia resolve itself was calculated, as we have seen. Meantime he did take various steps to help strengthen Cleopatra's rule (which was to Rome's advantage), and in spring 40 he departed to take the lead in stemming a major Parthian invasion of Syria and Asia Minor; this attack had come as a surprise amid Roman plans to attack Parthia. Very soon, however, Antony felt that instead the activities of Octavian and Sextus

Pompey demanded his presence in Italy; the repulse of the Parthians was therefore deputed to Publius Ventidius. He in fact achieved this so effectively over the
next two years (through summer 38) that there was little for Antony to contribute,
even though he did return to the East with his new wife Octavia in fall 39. The
spring and summer of 37 saw him back in Italy with a large fleet, however, with
the need to determine the most advantageous role to adopt in the worsening
struggle between Octavian and Sextus Pompey.

Octavia had accompanied Antony back to Italy, but she was left behind when
he returned to the East in fall 37; she had already had one daughter by him, and
would give birth to another early in 36. In Octavia's absence, Cleopatra now
joined Antony in Syria. At this stage he acknowledged paternity of the twins born
in 40, and in 36 she had another son by him. The nature of their relationship from
now onwards is hard to define. To Egyptians, it was evidently not quite a marriage, although they may have favored it as a sound step by Cleopatra to strength-
en her rule. There is no knowing how much Antony was influenced by a desire to
help her in this way, nor what private vision she may have had for her own future
and that of her kingdom. Maybe Antony had fallen too deeply in love to worry
about the consequences of the relationship, good or bad. Even if this is right, we
still have to wonder at his evident lack of concern for the impression made upon
his own wife Octavia, her brother Octavian, and Roman public opinion in general. Moreover, even should he divorce Octavia, as a Roman citizen he could never
contract a marriage recognized in Roman law with an alien like Cleopatra.

During 37 the Parthian king's decision to abdicate had led to the outbreak of
civil war there, and so created the ideal opportunity for a Roman counterinva-
sion. This Antony launched in 36 at the head of sixteen legions and many other
troops. He did penetrate successfully deep into Media, but at a critical point his
ally the King of Armenia panicked and withdrew vital cavalry support. Antony
was then driven back with the devastating loss of as much as one-third of his
great army. Roman opinion naturally contrasted his stunning defeat here with
Octavian's victories over Sextus Pompey in the same year, an extraordinary reversal of both men's military reputations to date.

CLASH BETWEEN ANTONY AND
OCTAVIAN (36–30)

From the fall of 36, the Roman world had just two rulers, Antony in the East and
Octavian in the West. The key issue now, we might imagine, was how long this
divided rule might continue. There need be no doubt that Octavian saw it as only
the prelude to a struggle for sole power. Thus the campaigns he undertook
against tribes in Illyricum between 35 and 33 were intended not only to enhance
his military reputation, but also to keep his forces in training. Meantime he intensified his hostile propaganda against Cleopatra and Antony.

Antony, by contrast, remained preoccupied with the tense situation on the eastern edge of his territory. We simply have no clue to why he took so long to react to the growing threat from Octavian in the West. It was no doubt unwelcome to him, but it was blatant, and he can hardly have thought it safe to ignore. As it was, he concentrated on subduing Armenia, partly to exact vengeance for its king's desertion in 36, partly to establish a strategic bridgehead for a further invasion of Parthia. This he did achieve in 35 and 34, despite being distracted in the first of these years by an acute embarrassment of Octavian's devising. He dispatched his sister Octavia to Antony with supplies and troops in token fulfillment at last of the exchange agreed in 37. After hesitation Antony accepted this aid, but he instructed Octavia not to proceed beyond Athens, and spent the winter of 35–34 in Alexandria with Cleopatra. The nature of his marriage with Octavia was now all the more perplexing, although still neither partner exercised their right to divorce the other.

Antony's behavior on returning to Alexandria in 34 seemed no less ill-judged. To celebrate the conquest of Armenia, he staged what might be viewed as a pastiche of a Roman triumph, and then in an extravagant ceremony—the so-called "Donations of Alexandria"—he distributed eastern lands (some of them Roman provinces) to Cleopatra, her three children by him, and her son by Julius Caesar, as each sat on a golden throne. To be sure, these actions amounted to little more than empty gestures, no doubt mainly designed to gratify Egyptians, but it is easy to see how a far more sinister construction could be placed upon them in Rome. They flaunted Antony's relationship with Cleopatra, drew attention to his appreciative reliance upon Egypt's resources and support, and left the impression that he meant to establish a powerful Egyptian dynasty.

By the following year, 33, however, Antony at last recognized that he must give priority to preparing for a clash with Octavian. He and Cleopatra moved to the Aegean, and set in motion a massive transfer of troops all the way from the eastern end of the Mediterranean to Greece. Some of his advisers urged that it would improve his image in Rome if she were sent home, but even so he acknowledged the impossibility of demanding that she leave, given all the ships and money she was providing. What could not be put off further, however, was Octavia's divorce. For all the bad impression it would create, Antony finally took this step in 32; to wait for her to take it, at her brother's prompting, would only look worse.

Octavian, for his part, was well aware that Antony still had many highly placed friends and supporters in Rome. No doubt it was deliberately to provoke them that, in 32, he attended the

Figure 8.4 *Coins of Antony and Cleopatra recall the "Donations of Alexandria," he on one side wearing a tiara and "Armenia Conquered" following his name, she on the other described "Queen of kings and of her sons who are kings."*

a

Figure 8.5a,b,c *The custom of leaving a commemorative monument or trophy at the site of a victory was a Greek one which spread to Rome. A striking example erected by Augustus is illustrated here. This is a 200-foot-long (61 m) podium wall [a] into which were inserted the prows (rostra) of thirty-four warships captured from Antony at the decisive battle of Actium in 31 (the rostra in the forum at Rome were so called because they were similarly decorated). The wall enlarged the precinct of an old temple of Apollo at the southern entrance to the Ambracian Gulf, where Antony had pitched his camp. From uncovering and measuring the wall sockets for the prows [b], archeologists have been able to deduce the likely size of the ship from which each came; some of the ships were clearly immense. For another Augustan victory monument, see Plate 6. Equally monumental in its way was the layout of the colony established in the Alps by Augustus at Augusta Praetoria (modern Aosta, Italy), part of which is seen here [c] from the air; the original colonists were 3,000 ex-Praetorian Guardsmen. Still today the city-plan reflects the original checkerboard pattern so characteristic of military camps and urban settlements established by the Romans. Following the subjugation of the implacably hostile people of the area, the Salassi, Augusta Praetoria was laid out in 25 B.C. as a walled rectangle measuring approximately 800 by 625 yards (724 × 572 m) and divided into sixteen main blocks. It was sited to secure an Alpine route of vital importance to Roman interests which forms the city's main thoroughfare (running left to right in the center of the view here). This route led from Italy (to the south-east) and then split into two branches, one continuing north through the Great St. Bernard pass, the other west, eventually reaching Lugdunum (modern Lyon, France) in Gaul through the Little St. Bernard pass.*

b

c

senate with an armed guard. In any event, both of the consuls and a large number of other senators (we lack a reliable figure) duly took offense, and fled to Antony. Even then, Octavian sought further means of justifying his cause. He actually descended to the shameless illegality of seizing Antony's will, which had been deposited with the Vestal virgins, and publicizing its alleged provisions. These supposedly included arrangements for burial in Alexandria, and lavish gifts to Antony's three children by Cleopatra. As a further, more solemn precaution, Octavian took the unusual step of arranging for civilians throughout the West to swear a personal oath of loyalty to him (compare Source 8.2, "Oath," below) in the war that was declared against Cleopatra. This declaration was made against her alone, not Antony too; all suggestion of civil conflict was studiously avoided.

Once the two sides' large forces encountered each other, at Actium in western Greece in 31, the ensuing action proved surprisingly undramatic. Throughout the summer each side sought to trap and blockade the other, much as Caesar and Pompey had done at Dyrrhachium in 48. Antony was forced more and more on the defensive. Eventually, at the beginning of September, he ordered a major breakout by his fleet. In the brief clash, both he and Cleopatra did burst through successfully with their squadrons, but for some reason they then sailed on—she back to Alexandria directly, he via Libya first. That left the rest of the fleet, and their entire land forces, at Octavian's mercy. All quickly gave up the fight.

The following year, 30, after elaborate preparation, Octavian mounted a full-scale assault on Alexandria, by land from east and west simultaneously. In the event, however, the city fell at the beginning of August with almost no resistance. Antony's fleet deserted, and he committed suicide, perhaps in reaction to a false report that Cleopatra had done so. In fact she was captured and spared; but then she, too, took her own life nine days later, possibly to avoid the humiliation of being paraded through Rome in Octavian's triumph. Caesarion, her son by Julius Caesar, was executed. Egypt's wealth came into Octavian's hands, and the kingdom was annexed as a Roman province. Octavian at once recognized how valuable an acquisition it could be to anyone aiming to rival him. Consequently, from the outset, the top Roman officials and commanders sent to Egypt were all equites, and no senator could even visit there without permission.

OCTAVIAN AS SOLE RULER (30 ONWARDS)

So, at the age of only thirty-three, Octavian had finally achieved the undisputed control of the Roman world which had been his unwavering ambition through fourteen years of civil war. To this end, he had been responsible for death, destruction, confiscation, and unbroken misery on a scale quite unmatched in all the previous phases of Roman civil conflict over the past century. Time and again he had returned from the brink of disaster, thanks to his skill as a propagandist, his ability to attract able associates, and his willingness to sacrifice any principle to one overriding purpose. Now, after this utterly amazing outcome, it became his concern to maintain the supremacy he had gained. The fact that he was also to do this successfully over a period of forty-four more years is hardly less miraculous than his elimination of all rivals to date.

Among the challenges of every description facing Octavian after his restoration of peace in 31–30, the nature of his own official position for the future was a particularly delicate and pressing issue. There had been no renewal of the Triumvirate after its lapse, probably at the end of 33. In practice, however, he continued to exercise a Triumvir's sweeping powers, even after beginning to hold a consulship annually from 31 onwards. Nobody was in a position to contest such irregularities, especially after the oath of loyalty had been sworn in 32. Even so, Octavian wanted a more secure footing for the long term. The fundamental question was the nature of the regime that should now rule Rome. Two possibilities were surely to be avoided. The first was Caesar's style of autocracy; with its contempt for traditional forms of government, and its leanings towards dynasty and divinity, it had only led to his assassination. A second, related possibility would be to develop some form of sole rule that relied primarily upon the army. Octavian's civil war experience must have warned him against attempting this; he had seen too often how fickle and undisciplined soldiers could be. Rather, he believed that from the traditional republican framework itself could emerge a way forward which would both satisfy the upper classes' desire to reestablish the supremacy of the senate, and at the same time enable him to keep control. However, to restore the Republic without retaining some form of personal control can never have struck him as a serious option. The outcome of such an attempt by Sulla—when he was almost twice Octavian's age—offered no encouragement.

Octavian signaled his choice of approach in 28 by acknowledging for the first time that he and his partner in the consulship, Agrippa, were coequals. Then, at a carefully staged meeting of the senate in January 27, he handed back all his authority to the senate and people. To calm members in their alarm, he at once consented to remain consul, and to take responsibility for Spain, Gaul, Cilicia, Cyprus, Syria, and Egypt for ten years, on the grounds that these areas were in particular danger from invasion or revolt. Wherever it should become safe to do so within ten years, however, he undertook

Figure 8.6 *This coin is a gold piece, from an issue not known until 1992, probably minted in the province of Asia. It dates to Octavian's sixth consulship (28 B.C.), and its reverse shows him wearing a toga, sitting on his magistrate's chair, holding out a scroll, with the words (in Latin) "he restored to the Roman people their laws and rights." This remarkable find underlies the perception that the changes we term the First Settlement were not all made at a single meeting of the senate in January 27, but instead began in 28 as a series of steps.*

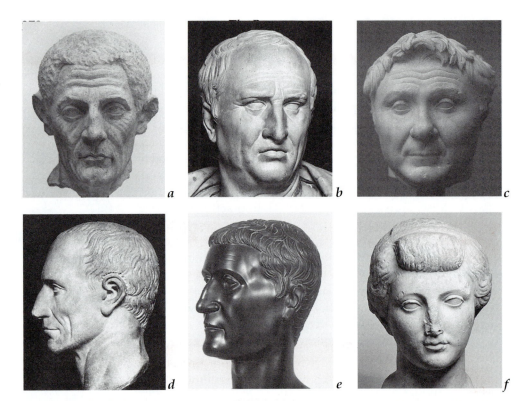

Figure 8.7a,b,c,d,e,f *By the first century* B.C., *intensified competition in public life made leading Romans more eager to promote themselves. As a result, images of many such individuals were created during their lifetimes in one medium or another, and also copied later. No living Roman appeared on a coin, however, before Julius Caesar in the 40s. At least coin portraits (whether contemporary or posthumous) are usually named. By contrast, that is seldom the case for busts or gems, for example, so that there is almost always some degree of doubt about their identification. In addition, of course, it may be naïve to assume that even a securely identified portrait accurately reproduces its subject's appearance. It would be more typical for it to reflect the way in which whoever commissioned the portrait (the subject personally, or an admirer) wanted the subject to be seen and remembered. This appearance may still be instructive, therefore, but unlikely to be true to life. Despite the stark features, identification of a travertine head [a] as Sulla must remain insecure. Among several busts portraying the same elderly man, one bears the name* CICERO, *and this is regarded as a genuine ancient identification; the example shown seems likely to be a later copy of an original made in his lifetime [b]. A marble bust [c] found in the tomb of the Licinii family near Rome is likewise convincingly identified as Pompey. It, too, is probably a later copy of an original made in his lifetime, and matches posthumous coin portraits as well as descriptions of his appearance (including the "crest" of hair especially associated with Alexander the Great). Moreover, Licinii in the first century* A.D. *are known to have taken pride in a family connection with Pompey. Because the man portrayed by another marble head bears a close resemblance to Caesar as he appears on coins, this bust [d] has been identified as his. A green basalt bust found near Canopus (close to Alexandria) in Egypt [e] may well be Antony—portrayed with a trim, reflective appearance that (on coins, at least) changes during the 30s to a heavier, less reflective one (Fig. 8.4). The last bust shown [f] can confidently be identified as Livia. Her surviving portraits suggest that she wished to be portrayed only as a young, ideal Roman matron, who never aged. Her hairstyle—also favored by Augustus' sister, Octavia—is a novel one; its elegant simplicity may be a pointed rejection of the more elaborate, sectioned style worn by Cleopatra (Fig. 8.3b).*

to hand the area back to the senate sooner. Clearly, he could not govern all of them personally, still less command the troops stationed there, so he was granted authority to appoint deputies ("legates") to serve for whatever terms he should fix. The expectation was that he would continue to be reelected consul himself. Governors of all other provinces would now once again be chosen by lot from ex-consuls and ex-praetors to serve for one-year terms in the traditional manner.

Along with this grant, often referred to today as the "First Settlement," the senate bestowed upon Octavian the new name Augustus, and also renamed the month of his birth, Sextilis, in the same way. With the sense of "revered," this name has a semireligious connotation, and was deliberately intended to symbolize Octavian's decisive break with his violent past. The times were now to be normal, with peace and the Republic restored.

"THE REPUBLIC RESTORED"

How genuine is this claim? Certain ancient writers much later, looking back with the advantage of hindsight, represent it as a sham, because they are keenly aware of how authoritarian the rule which dates from this point would become over time. It is vital to appreciate, however, that contemporaries enjoyed no such insight into the future. Their comparison would be to the past. By this measure, there is no question that the First Settlement allowed the Republic's traditional institutions and offices to function with a degree of independence and stability unknown since, say, the formation of the First Triumvirate in 60–59. Augustus wanted a return to the rule of law, and sought a legitimate, regular position within such a framework. Those who had no grasp of constitutional issues might refer to him as *imperator* (hence "emperor"), but he represented himself as no more than *princeps*, a bland, informal term signifying merely "leading figure." Previously there had been many *principes* (Caesar, Cicero, Crassus, Pompey, and others), whereas now there was to be only one. Hence this new phase in Rome's history is termed the Principate. Even this single Princeps might in time relax his hold further. The First Settlement, after all, was made for no more than ten years. To this extent there was cause for hope. There was also now the realization, unlike in 44, that another assassination would not of its own accord serve to make the senate supreme again. Rather, there would be another vicious power struggle, as well as popular outrage even fiercer than the hostility which Caesar's death had aroused; both prospects were unbearable so soon after the horrors of the long Triumviral period.

For his part, Augustus understood, as Caesar had not, how vital the senate's support was to his control of the Roman world. He further realized from Caesar's experience that an ostentatious display of authority—by means of special titles, and dress, and other trappings—was counterproductive; it gave offense without bestowing more power. Instead, Augustus believed that the authority he could exercise within the traditional republican framework was sufficient. He had no wish to be constantly intervening in every sphere, and he positively encouraged the senate to determine many matters without reference to him. Even where he had an interest, he typically chose to advance it, not by open exercise of authority, but through his personal, unofficial *auctoritas* or "influence." In other words, a private suggestion from Augustus, or even a gesture, could suffice to ensure, say, that a particular action was taken or a proposal dropped. In the same way, he might informally encourage friends to steer through legislation on an issue of concern to him, without ever promoting it himself.

Augustus' auctoritas was unmatched—just as that of the senate itself had once been—and contemporaries were certainly aware of how the noun and his new name share the same root. His quiet, skillful use of auctoritas served as a formidable reinforcement of his official authority. He even used it to extend that authority, however, and this was more disturbing insofar as it undermined his own representation of his position after the First Settlement. In particular, he caused governors outside his own assigned sphere to take steps (even make war) which no individual consul had the right to authorize without consulting his partner in office or the senate. If Augustus wished to act in this way, then he would have to alter the formal basis of his position. At the same time he shared the growing sense that it would not be truly republican for him to continue holding the consulship year after year; when Marius had done so, after all, it was only under special circumstances in a crisis. Nobles moreover were sure to become increasingly frustrated that from now on they could compete for only one of these prized consulships annually, rather than two. Last among the manifestly unrepublican features of the First Settlement was the sheer size of Augustus' sphere of command. No consul had ever had been assigned one so large; the arrangements made for Pompey in the late 50s were at least of comparable type, but their scale was not.

SECOND SETTLEMENT (23)

The First Settlement was unavoidably experimental. Augustus' experience with it convinced him that he needed to make his formal authority more sweeping, as well as less obtrusive. A plot by senators that was fortunately detected at the planning stage may have prompted him to act; a near-fatal illness in mid-23 certainly did. The changes he now made were threefold, and are often referred to today as the "Second Settlement." First, on July 1, 23, he resigned the consulship, and never held the office again under normal conditions. He had realized that he could just as well retain only its authority. Accordingly, he kept his provinces and the all-important *imperium* (now of a proconsul, strictly speaking) to govern it. Moreover—the second change—his imperium was made "greater" or *maius* by the senate. In other words, it was now specifically recognized as superior to that of all other officials everywhere, and could therefore be the legitimate basis of instructions to them. Third and last, he took a further power without office, that of a tribune (*tribunicia potestas*), and was in fact to renew this annually until his death, so that the years of his rule from 23 can be counted in this way. Since Caesar had made him a patrician, he could not hold the tribunate itself, nor would he specially welcome such a commitment. Even the powers of the office [see Chapter Two] added little to authority he already had, although they did make him sacrosanct, and they conveniently permitted him to summon the senate and to impose a veto, should the need arise. The uniquely special appeal of "tribunician power," however, was its modest, popular image as provider of protection for ordinary citizens. It therefore became the power that Augustus paraded; by contrast, attention was never drawn to his *maius imperium*.

[margin: New Role]

Although the Second Settlement offered every prospect of eliminating the flaws in the First, Augustus evidently did not anticipate the strength of the reaction to his withdrawal from the consulship. The people had no understanding of the Settlement's subtleties. Rather, they were bewildered by Augustus' failure to stand for the top office as usual, and feared that as a result they were losing their greatest benefactor. In 22 they evidently begged him to accept a life consulship, which he declined; in both 21 and 20 they rioted and refused to elect more than one candidate, thus leaving the other place for Augustus. Eventually, in 19, the senate permitted Augustus to wear a consul's insignia when he appeared in public; the fact that he now looked like a consul seems to have soothed widespread fears.

[margin: Peoples Response]

Thereafter his official position underwent little further alteration. No doubt it was awareness of the offense given by Caesar in February 44 which cautioned Augustus against accepting powers or offices for life; they might be renewed for a further term after the initial grant, but none was to be regarded as fixed indefinitely, with no prospect of change. The only exception was the religious office of pontifex maximus, always held for life anyway, which Augustus finally took in 12 after Lepidus' death following almost a quarter-century of exile. The title (rather than office) of *Pater Patriae*, "Father of his Country," bestowed on Augustus in the senate in 2, was likewise naturally for life.

[margin: Took Religion Rule & "Pater Patriae"]

THE ROMAN FAMILY IN THE AUGUSTAN PERIOD

Augustus' designation as "Father of his Country" was celebrated on coins and inscriptions, and it marked his role of father of the Roman family and state. He had already demonstrated active interest in these matters. He felt that Rome, and the upper classes in particular, no longer showed sufficient respect for marriage and its vital role in rearing children to maintain families and the community as a whole. In Augustus' view, too many respectable Roman men were choosing to remain bachelors; some men who did marry made unsuitable matches, or condoned adulterous behavior by their wives; and married couples capable of producing children were deliberately remaining childless. We cannot ascertain the accuracy of these perceptions, but there is no doubt about the strength of Augustus' lasting concern to remedy what he considered to be a crisis. He promoted some complex legislation for this purpose in 18/17, and had it revised as late as A.D. 9.

[margin: Restores Marriage Laws]

First, in one law, penalties were introduced for both men and women who remained unmarried, or who married but for whatever reason failed to have children, between the ages of 25 and 60 for men, and 20 and 50 for women. Second, members of the new senatorial class (see "Senate and *Equites*" below) were debarred from marrying any ex-slave or anyone not regarded as respectable (an entertainer, for example). And third, all validly married couples who did have children were rewarded, on an ascending scale (the more children, the more benefits). In another law, a husband who became aware of adultery by his wife now had to divorce her and then prosecute her (the same did not apply in the case of an adulterous husband, but his wife could still divorce him). Even if the husband (or his father-in-law) caught the wife in the act of adultery, he could not treat her violently, although under certain conditions the male partner could be killed on the spot. However, for the husband not to prosecute his divorced wife within two months was itself an offense, and a third party could then prosecute (it would have to be a private individual, since Rome never had public prosecutors). On conviction for adultery, a woman stood to lose half her dowry and one-third of her other property; she also faced exile to an island, and could never remarry. Her male partner, if still alive, could likewise be prosecuted and punished.

The striking feature about all these measures is the way in which they regulate by law for the first time a wide variety of spheres that Romans had always regarded as entirely private. In many respects, the measures represent blunt, disruptive interference, and—despite Augustus' commitment to the values underlying them—there is no sign that they were particularly successful in altering society's behavior or attitudes. Indeed, although Augustus' own daughter Julia had five children with her second husband Agrippa (some twenty-five years her senior), she resented the third marriage expected of her (to Tiberius) within a year of Agrippa's death in 12 (see Table 8.1). Later, in 2 B.C., she was exiled for adultery and treason. Similarly, her daughter Julia (born in 19) was exiled for adultery in A.D. 8. As *Pater Patriae* Augustus was conscious of having to set an example, and as *pater familias* he took the disobedience of his daughter and granddaughter very hard.

Some women may equally have chafed at the pressure to marry and bear children. Wives were held to a higher standard of behavior than husbands. Married men's involvements with other women could largely be tolerated so long as they were not blatant, and not with married women of supposedly respectable background; men's affairs with slaves and others of low status, of either sex, were usually condoned. A wife, by contrast, who became involved with any other man, especially one of lower social status, could not expect the same tolerance, and the Augustan laws outlined above expanded the legal ramifications. Either partner to a marriage, however, could initiate divorce. In Roman law, marriage itself was a purely private act, which required no formal ceremony—although a celebration was often held—nor any certification by the state. Rather, a relationship where both partners were eligible (neither could be a slave, for example), and behaved towards one another as husband and wife, constituted a legally valid marriage. By the same

token, either marriage partner could formally mark the termination of the relation- **Divorce Law**
ship with a divorce by simply informing the other—even through a third party,
without necessarily stating a reason. Once again, this was a purely private matter.
As already mentioned, a husband contemplating this step would need to consider
his obligation to return all (or, in some circumstances, part) of the dowry; he could
be sued if he did not. The wife, for her part, if she had borne children, would have
to weigh the likelihood that after a divorce they would remain with their father,
since they were regarded as belonging to his family, not hers. Typically, little stigma
attached to divorce or remarriage. To some wives, however, the ideal was to be *uni-
vira*, in other words, never to have more than one husband, even if they were wid-
owed and were in a position to remarry. This traditional ideal—upheld by Cornelia,
mother of the Gracchi brothers, for example (see Chapter Four)—seems at odds
with Augustan legislation encouraging remarriage and procreation.

How far women could control their childbearing remains unclear. Without
question, Roman women shared—mainly just by word of mouth—a rich store of
information about both contraception and abortion. The effectiveness of these
procedures is hard to determine, but surviving texts show that many were downright dangerous for the woman. The preference of wealthy women to hire wet-
nurses for their babies could accelerate the birth rate for a fertile woman like
Augustus' daughter Julia, who bore Agrippa five children in eight years. On the
other hand, maternal mortality was high, and the young age at which an elite
woman could be married—in her lower teens—made childbearing even more
risky for her in the first years of a marriage. In any event, few women eager to
rear children to adulthood would limit their family's size. So many children were **Raising**
likely to die either at birth or as infants (see Fig. 9.7 and Chapter 11) that as many **Kids**
as three out of five might never reach adulthood. Poor understanding of infant
nutritional needs, ignorance about germs, and lack of skilled medical help were
among the factors limiting family size; the lower the parents' place on the social
and economic scale, the less chance there was for a child's survival. Children were
not even given a name until several days after birth. Despite the ubiquity of child
mortality, however, epitaphs poignantly express parents' grief at the loss of a son
or daughter. Even for those children who did reach adulthood, life expectancy
remained low. A bride in her late teens would be lucky if she had even one grand-
parent still alive to attend the wedding; the chance that her mother would still be
living was no better than 60%, and her father 50%. Given the traditional, long-
standing importance of family to the Romans, many couples must have wished
for as many children as they thought they could raise.

SUCCESSION

From the First Settlement of 27 onwards, despite his claims to have restored
Rome's traditional constitution, Augustus in practice infringed a basic principle

Table 8.1 The Julio-Claudian Family

*This family tree is a deliberately selective one, omitting certain individuals and marriages. The abbreviations b., d., cos. signify respectively born, died, consul (in the year stated). All dates given are certain, or almost certain; dates A.D. are in **boldface**. Names **bolded** are those normally used for the individuals concerned; descriptors in italic (e.g. the younger) offer additional identification. Emperors' names are in CAPITALS.*
= signifies a marriage; the figure above = gives the date of the marriage, where known. The figure in parentheses immediately before or after the name of an individual who married more than once specifies this marriage's place in the sequence.

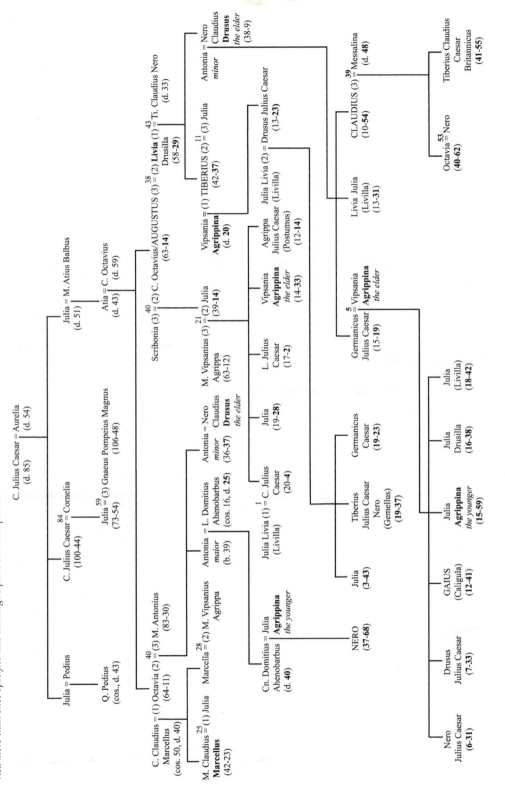

of any republic by quietly wielding a quite disproportionate amount of personal authority. From an early stage too, he developed another highly unrepublican preoccupation by planning to pass on his position to a capable successor of his own choosing, and if at all possible a blood relative. To uphold both his family's interests and those of the state for the purpose was certain to prove an extraordinary challenge. But most Romans would surely have agreed that a power struggle after Augustus' death was to be avoided at almost any cost. Moreover, given the depth of family pride in Roman society, his passionate desire to install a successor of his own blood must at least have met with some understanding, even on the part of contemporaries opposed to such a plan. That said, for him to gain the acceptance of any successor was still extraordinarily delicate, not only on grounds of principle, but also because he only ever had one child—a daughter Julia, from his short-lived marriage to Scribonia. His wife thereafter, Livia Drusilla, whom he married in 38, never had children by him, despite having produced two sons by her first husband Tiberius Claudius Nero—Tiberius (born in 42) and Drusus (born in 38).

In view of the fact that work on Augustus' huge mausoleum in Rome's Campus Martius began in the early 20s, he must have been giving his death and its possible consequences some thought even at that date. Only in 25 was anyone singled out who might seem destined as a possible successor, when Julia married Marcus Claudius Marcellus (born in 42), son of Augustus' sister Octavia by her first husband. Julia and Marcellus produced no children, however, and he died prematurely in the fall of 23. Moreover, a few months earlier when Augustus himself had expected to die, it was to his loyal associate and contemporary Agrippa that he gave his signet ring, not to young Marcellus. That desperate gesture demonstrated the embarrassing absence of viable plans for any succession at this stage. Had Augustus died then, it seems very dubious whether Agrippa could have taken over at all smoothly. He held no office (and thus had no legal authority), he was not a family member (and thus would not be one of the principal inheritors of Augustus' wealth), and he was viewed as an upstart by aristocratic senators. Rivalry between them would surely have erupted into civil war.

Fortunately for the stability of the Roman world, Augustus did not die in 23, and in fact his persistently poor health even improved thereafter. But this crisis now stirred him to make adequate arrangements for the succession. Since he had no remaining male blood relatives, he again turned to Agrippa, prevailing upon

Figure 8.8 *Bust of Livia.*

a

c

b

Figure 8.9a,b,c,d *Surviving images of Augustus can be numbered in the hundreds—a sign of how ubiquitous they must have become—and considerable development can be seen in their style and variety over his lifetime. For the early years, as Octavian struggled for sole control of the Roman world, coins are our most instructive guide. They* [a] *show him bearded (to signify vengeance or mourning) and stress his relationship to his deified "father," Julius Caesar; later in the 30s the beard is removed and the focus directed more sharply towards himself. An outstanding example of what became a standard, idealized image from the 20s (when all Augustus' rivals had been eliminated) is the large bronze head* [b] *excavated in 1910 at Meroe, capital of the independent kingdom of Kush on the Nile River (in modern Sudan). In the years immediately following Rome's annexation of Egypt, relations with Kush to the south were hostile, and the head was no doubt*

d

booty from a Meroitic raid into the new province. Notably, it was then buried below the steps leading up to a royal temple of Victory, so that anyone approaching the shrine would have the satisfaction of treading it underfoot. A full-size statue [c] with a head of similar type and a fold of the toga covering it, found in Rome, presents Augustus as the most pious of citizens. Another, from Livia's villa north of the city, renders him as military leader. The central scene on his breastplate [d] depicts the Parthian king's return of Roman standards to a Roman soldier (or possibly the god Mars), in other words the climax of Augustus' successful diplomacy in 20. The wider array of gods above and below confirms that Augustus has achieved the right relationship with them too, and that his sway extends far beyond territory directly controlled by Rome.

him in 21 to divorce Marcella (his second wife, Marcellus' sister) and marry Julia. Agrippa already had imperium bestowed on him for a mission in the East. In 18 this was renewed (perhaps even made *maius*), and *tribunicia potestas* added. Agrippa was the first person with whom Augustus shared this latter power, and it became the mark of a designated successor. Augustus was overjoyed that the marriage of Agrippa and Julia had already produced a son, Gaius, born in 20. A second, Lucius, followed in 17; both were adopted by Augustus as his own sons the same year.

Gaius and Lucius were still only children, however, when Agrippa died unexpectedly in 12, aged about fifty. Augustus now therefore looked to his elder stepson Tiberius for the first time. He in turn was asked to divorce his wife Vipsania Agrippina (Agrippa's daughter by his first wife, Caecilia Attica) and marry his stepsister Julia. He did so with great reluctance, not least since it was only the previous year that Vipsania had given birth to a son, Drusus. The new marriage became a failure, and the son it produced died in infancy. Tiberius was granted imperium and tribunicia potestas for five years in 6, but soon afterwards he evidently felt so alienated by the efforts to advance Gaius—who was now about to enter public life—that he withdrew to become a recluse on the island of Rhodes. His official position was not renewed, and he only returned to Rome in A.D. 2, still out of favor. Julia by contrast had not left Rome, but in 2 B.C. Augustus felt obliged to exile her for scandalous sexual misconduct with several partners, including Iullus Antonius, a son of Antony and Fulvia.

Augustus' dynastic ambitions now brought him greater grief than ever when both adopted sons died young, Lucius in A.D. 2 and Gaius two years later. In 5 and 2 B.C. respectively, Augustus had even occupied the consulship to introduce each to public life, the only times he ever took that office after 23. Gaius became consul himself in A.D. 1; his marriage to Livia Julia (Livilla) the previous year remained childless. Augustus had so fervently desired one or both these young men to succeed him that their deaths were the most cruel blow; he wanted it remembered that "Fortune snatched them from me when they were young" (*Res Gestae* 14.1). By A.D. 4 his only practical option was to turn back without enthusiasm to his elder stepson Tiberius (the younger stepson, Drusus, had died in 9 B.C.). At last, Tiberius was no longer merely a stopgap for others. He was now adopted by Augustus as his son, and had imperium and tribunicia potestas conferred on him for ten years; when those powers were renewed in A.D. 13, his imperium was specifically made equal to that of Augustus.

So against all the odds, when Augustus died the following year 14, there duly occurred the smooth, undisputed transition to a capable new Princeps that he had so long planned for. Fate had by no means permitted him to secure his top choice of successor, let alone a blood relative. Nonetheless Tiberius was reliable, experienced, and faced no obvious rival (by contrast, what if Gaius and Lucius had both lived? or if Tiberius and Julia had had sons?). Beyond that, a sound foundation was laid for Augustus' broader concern to maintain the regime which he had developed for the long-term benefit of the Roman world.

SENATE AND *EQUITES*

In a prayer, Augustus once referred to his regime with studied vagueness as the "best condition," *optimus status*. If we now turn to reviewing some of its most important aspects, it is appropriate to begin with the senate and its members. No other group stood to lose so much by any shift away from the traditional form of the Republic. Caesar had demonstrated this all too starkly. Augustus not only wished to avoid his fate, but he also recognized how much reliance his restored Republic placed upon senatorial support. A strong, active senate, comprising an outstanding elite of wealthy statesmen, was therefore at the center of his vision for the future. So in order to remove unworthy members, he conducted two major reviews himself—acting like a censor for the purpose, although this office was not revived on a regular basis either now or later. The first review, as early as 29, reduced the senate from about 1,000 to 800, with Octavian placed at the head of the roll as *princeps senatus*. The second review, in 18, removed a further 200. This left a body of about 600 members (the size that Sulla had made it), to which the normal means of entry was by election as one of the twenty quaestors annually—again a reversion to Sulla's number, which Caesar had doubled. By the time of the second review, Augustus had further elevated the senate as a new, exclusive social class to which members and their families belonged. He also made 1,000,000 sesterces the minimum level of wealth for any senator; previously, none had been specified beyond the 400,000 required of an eques. It is hard to believe that the new minimum made much practical difference, when senatorial membership had always been known to demand a lavish outlay among other qualifications; but the intention to reinforce exclusivity is clear.

Generally speaking, Sulla's rules regulating a senator's rise through the *cursus honorum* were once again observed. Elections were conducted freely, too, although Augustus did intervene in some key respects. It became his prerogative to fix the number of praetors to be elected each year, and both for this office as well as lower ones he seems to have recommended a certain number of candidates, whose election was thus in effect assured. To what extent, if at all, he acted likewise for the consulship remains obscure. He certainly did introduce an important change for it from 5 B.C. onwards, whereby the pair who entered office on January 1 resigned midyear, thus requiring "suffects" to replace them. Since it was above all the honor of attaining the top magistracy that senators sought—with length of tenure a matter of indifference—this new practice was a brilliant means of satisfying more aristocrats' ambitions, while still maintaining the tradition that only a pair of consuls should be in office at any time.

Even if a senator about whom Augustus had reservations did rise through the cursus honorum, that was little cause for alarm; a senior magistrate's scope for action was now severely limited. Rather, the practical value of a praetorship or consulship was the eligibility it conferred for holding the empire's top military or administrative positions. Most such appointments were for the Princeps to make, and he did little to depart from the tradition that senators alone should be chosen to fill them. Hence in practice ambitious senators needed to cultivate and maintain Augustus' favor, however much he might protest that they were free to do as they pleased. Already in 27, at the time of the First Settlement, most legions were stationed within his provinces, and by his death only one (in Africa) was not. Thus almost all legionary commanders were his legates (ex-praetors, or sometimes less senior senators), as were the governors of the provinces where these forces were stationed (ex-consuls or ex-praetors, corresponding to the significance of the region). Within Rome and Italy, senior senators also came to be given administrative responsibilities in spheres of greater concern to Augustus than they had ever been to the Republican senate. They supervised the distribution of free grain rations in Rome, for example, as well as the upkeep of the city's aqueducts and public buildings, and the main roads of Italy.

It need be no surprise that the morale of the senate as a corporate body seems generally low throughout the reign. Plenty of old families had faded during the civil war period, many members survived only to be removed, and the remainder had to adjust their outlook and expectations. The same applied to new entrants, whom Augustus (himself the son of a novus homo) followed Julius Caesar in cautiously encouraging from Italy and the Latin-speaking West. But for any senator aspirations of emulating Gaius Gracchus or Cicero were now unimaginable, naturally. The dilemma, rather, was how best to act in an environment where the Princeps' opinion had always to be respected, and nothing that he requested or supported could be denied. Augustus went out of his way to attend the senate, to consult it respectfully, and to encourage debate; he even formed a committee of members to determine the agenda in advance of meetings. However, this step only sharpened the sense that the senate now met primarily to approve what had already been decided in private elsewhere, especially with regard to such key issues as state finances, foreign affairs, and the disposition of the army. Augustus strove to improve attendance by a variety of means—among them, quorums, fixed dates for meetings, fines for absentees—but these, too, only reinforced the fear or resentment felt by disenchanted members. Others meanwhile resorted to flattery, and almost all hesitated to articulate opinions. Really, it was not until Tiberius' reign that the senate's morale was boosted by the adoption of some important new functions. Even then, inevitably, the basic issue of the relationship between Princeps and senate was to remain tense and unresolved.

In contrast to senators, equites had no cause to feel immediately threatened by Augustus' development of the Principate. Rather, because the Roman Republic had done almost nothing to tap their particular managerial and financial talents in its service, equites were gratified when Augustus took the novel step of seeking out their assistance. He significantly increased the number of officer positions in the army reserved for them, and it became understood that such service was normally expected of any eques hoping to hold a civil post in the Princeps' service. The sphere where Augustus particularly enlisted equites was in managing all the various properties which came under his control by one means or other, and in representing him in the courts in this connection. Soon enough, no doubt, he must have had such equestrian "procurators" in every province of the empire (the Latin noun *procurator* simply means "agent").

Strictly speaking, they were all just his private staff. Even so, procurators within his own provinces gradually came to be entrusted with assignments in the public domain—handling tax payments, for example, commanding troops, and even governing an entire province. In this latter connection, the most outstanding example was Egypt where, from its annexation in 30, all the top Roman officials and commanders were equites exclusively. Security was surely the reason here—equites would not share senators' political ambitions—and it again must have been what prompted Augustus to place his own guardsmen, the Praetorian Guard, under the command of a pair of equestrian prefects from 2 B.C. onwards. Some years later, in A.D. 6, a disastrous fire in Rome prompted him to form a patrol force of "watchmen," or *vigiles*, to combat such outbreaks, under the command of an eques. Then soon afterwards, following a severe grain shortage, he recognized the need for permanent monitoring of its supply to the city, and asked another eques to undertake this responsibility. He certainly could as well have chosen senators in these two last instances, and we can only speculate on why he decided not to. Maybe it was simply that the individual he considered most suitable for appointment in each case just happened to be an eques. At least, the explanation that he was deliberately aiming to develop an "equestrian division" of a "civil service" should be rejected. His employment of equites was extremely limited, and never more than a succession of unstructured responses to pressing needs.

ARMY

Augustus' bitter experience during the long civil war period had demonstrated the importance of the army to his rule, yet also the many dangers that it posed. He had himself encouraged disloyalty on the part of his opponents' troops, while also needing to combat it among his own men. Now he had to secure the entire army's unshakable loyalty, as well as to reform the traditional Republican arrangements for recruitment and discharge. For some decades past, these had been far from satisfactory. In particular, the old model of the army as a militia into which citizens with property were drafted for relatively short periods had long broken down.

After his victory at Actium, Augustus' immediate concern was to discharge at least 140,000 men from both sides, and perhaps more; Egypt's wealth enabled him to buy them land instead of confiscating it, and to give them a little cash (see Map 7.3 and Fig. 8.5c). This left a standing army of twenty-eight legions (each about 5,000 infantrymen), which must represent the size of force that Augustus regarded as strategically adequate for the long term, and at the same time affordable. Not until 13, however, do we hear of new conditions of service. The changes were radical. In principle, henceforth all legionaries would be volunteer citizens who committed to serving for a fixed number of years, at the end of which—if they stayed loyal and survived to be honorably discharged—they would receive a fixed bounty payment. During their service they could not legally be married; Augustus was no doubt eager to keep his forces mobile, and he perhaps wanted to avoid all claims by dependents. In cash, the bounty equaled about thirteen years' pay (thus sufficient to support most veterans to the end of their lives), although we find some instances where it comprised land with proportionately less cash. Initially, a legionary's term of service was set at fifteen years with a further four as reservist, but various setbacks forced Augustus to raise those figures to twenty and five respectively, and even then it seems that men might be held longer. Finding the necessary funds for such substantial bounties was evidently enough of a struggle that in A.D. 6 Augustus established a special "military" treasury, the *aerarium militare*, administered by ex-praetors, for this sole purpose. He funded it himself initially, and for the future made the proceeds of a sales tax and an inheritance tax payable to it. For citizens, therefore, from 13 onwards military service became a lifetime career choice, and the army a professional force. For the great majority, the end of drafting, not to mention the general atmosphere of peace, were a marked and very welcome change.

Julius Caesar had already doubled soldiers' pay, and—except in the singular case of his own Praetorian Guard—Augustus did not seek to buy their loyalty by raising it further. Nor was he eager to continue the civil war practice of bribing soldiers with "donatives." Only certain contingents had benefited from these special payments, and even they had by no means invariably received all that was promised by rival leaders. As sole leader, Augustus, by contrast, now limited himself to infrequent, modest donatives, paid to the entire army. He did, on the other hand, quite deliberately give a huge boost to the regular pay of centurions (legionary officers), who now received anything from thirteen to over fifty times the basic rate depending upon rank and seniority. Previously, the pay differential between officers and men had been small. So, as Augustus had seen during the civil wars, when mutiny broke out centurions had in some instances sided with the men, and thus provided leadership which would otherwise have been lacking. Now, however, Augustus rewarded centurions so handsomely that they would be much less likely to identify with mutineers.

With increasingly rare exceptions, all top army officers (senators and equites) were Augustus' own legates, appointed by him and serving for whatever period he might determine. For a long time, from fear of rivals, he chose not to entrust large groupings of legions to the command of aristocrats, preferring either members of his own family or "new men" (as his own father had been). More broadly, he ensured that it was now he and his family to whom all soldiers swore their oath of loyalty—not to their officers, who were only his deputies. Just how solemn a regard soldiers would have for this oath is impossible to gauge, but the deliberate focus of all loyalty on the single figure of the Princeps does seem to

Figure 8.10 *This tomb monument was erected by the brother of a centurion, Marcus Caelius—said here to be originally from Bononia (modern Bologna) in northern Italy—who died in what is referred to as "Varus' war," in other words the massacre in the Teutoburg Forest in A.D. 9 (see Fig. 8.11). The inscription specifically gives authority for Caelius' bones to be placed in the monument subsequently—unlikely prospect though that was (compare Fig. 9.6 for the issue of reusing a tomb). Caelius is presented as the model of a successful career officer in Augustus' reshaped professional army. His age (53) and high status as a centurion of the first rank are specified. As part of his uniform, he wears a very distinguished set of decorations for valor—an oak-leaf "civic crown" (corona civica) for saving a fellow citizen's life, torques hanging from his shoulder straps, medallions on his chest, and bracelets on each wrist. In his right hand he grasps the dreaded stick of vine wood (vitis), with which all centurions maintained discipline. The sense of his proud status is enhanced by the inclusion of a freedman either side of him; whether they were with him, their patron, at the time of his death is left unclear.*

have been successful in creating a strong bond. Mutinies and strikes against the established regime remained a very real concern throughout Augustus' rule and far beyond. In general, however, his efforts to maintain the army's loyalty proved remarkably successful over the long term.

THE EMPIRE AND ITS EXPANSION

The army was to be used both to protect Rome's empire and to expand it. Augustus saw no contradiction when he sought praise both for bringing peace and for making conquests even more extensive than those of Pompey or Caesar. In his own words, his peace was one "secured by victories" (*Res Gestae* 13, "parta victoriis pax"). It is hard to define his various goals for the expansion of Roman power. There is no question that in any case these underwent changes over such a long period of rule, and there were plainly major disappointments and failures too. Moreover his geographical grasp was nowhere near as complete or accurate as ours.

SOURCE 8.2: Oath of Loyalty

It was specifically to Augustus and his family that soldiers came to be required to take a regular oath of loyalty. Despite no more than a random scatter of evidence, it is clear that Augustus also used oath-taking as a means of promoting civilians' loyalty to himself— even if not necessarily on the same regular basis, or with quite the same degree of legal compulsion. In practice, however, it is hard to imagine many individuals declining the "opportunity" to take such an oath when "offered" one, as civilians in the West were as early as 32. Here follows the text of a Latin oath sworn by the magistrates, senate, and people of Conobaria, not far north of Gades (modern Cádiz) in southern Spain, probably in connection with the introduction of Gaius Caesar to public life in 5 B.C. Note that Marcus Agrippa (Agrippa Julius Caesar), Agrippa's posthumous son by Julia born in 12, is named here among the members of the imperial family; later, however, in A.D. 6 Augustus removed him from the family, allegedly for some mental disability or character flaw. The text survives on a bronze tablet with holes drilled top and bottom so that it could be posted in public.

In all sincerity I avow my concern for the safety, honor, and victory of imperator Caesar Augustus, son of the Divine Julius [Caesar], pontifex maximus, and of Gaius Caesar, son of Augustus, Leader of Youth [Princeps Juventutis, a purely honorific title], consul designate, pontifex, and of Lucius Caesar, son of Augustus, and of Marcus Agrippa, grandson of Augustus. I shall bear arms, and shall hold as friends and allies the same ones I understand to be theirs. I shall consider as my enemies, too, those whom I observe in opposition to them. And should anyone take action or make plans against them, I shall pursue him to the death by land and by sea. (*AE* 1988. 723)

It is possible that for a long time he had "world conquest" somehow in mind, along the lines claimed by his great Republican predecessors. This could certainly furnish some explanation for expeditions ordered in the 20s south from Egypt and far into the Arabian peninsula, as well as for his determination to subdue the huge area between the Rhine and Elbe rivers. To stretch so far in each of these instances proved a failure in practical terms. The image they fostered was still a glorious and exotic one, however, which diplomatic dealings with rulers as far away as Britain and India only reinforced (but no further expedition was sent to Britain to resume Caesar's initiatives there).

Meantime Augustus was aware after Actium that several areas within the empire were not secure, and that from a strategic viewpoint it was altogether a badly fragmented whole (compare Map 7.1). Its Latin-speaking West and Greek-speaking East were so far apart from one another that for each to split off under its own ruler was quite conceivable. During the mid 30s this is possibly what Antony assumed would happen, and it eventually did from the fourth century. Moreover, with the empire so vulnerable to outside threats throughout the civil war period, it was sheer good fortune that no such invasion occurred then.

Augustus himself devoted considerable time during the 20s to imposing Roman control throughout the Iberian peninsula, especially its rugged northwest, which had never been subjugated previously. At the same time he authorized others to embark upon the immense task of extending Roman control northwards in central and eastern Europe as far as the Danube River. This led to the creation of the provinces of Raetia, Noricum, Dalmatia (an expansion of Illyricum), Pannonia, and Moesia, and meant that there was now Roman territory linking the empire's western and eastern halves. A related initiative, long overdue, was to bring the entire area of the Alps under Roman control. As late as the teens B.C., tribes there could threaten southern Gaul and northern Italy with their raids (see Plate 6).

In the East, there was much less campaigning, and in general Antony's administrative reorganization remained in place. Apart from Egypt, the two notable additions to the empire were the large region of Galatia in central Asia Minor in 25, and Judaea in A.D. 6; both were former "client kingdoms." Several other states maintained this status; as such, they were not ruled by Rome, but respected Roman interests. Augustus' major concern in the East was to forge a viable long-term relationship with Parthia, the one state on any of the empire's borders which had demonstrated the potential to be a serious threat. To exact some form of vengeance for the defeats of Crassus and Antony seemed essential. On the other hand, Augustus felt unable to spare substantial forces to guard against Parthian incursions, and he was still less enthusiastic about mounting his own major offensive there. Since he also appreciated that it was the exception rather than the norm for Parthia to act as a well-organized, aggressive military power, he risked relying upon tough diplomacy rather than force. By this means, in 20, he did achieve the return of legionary standards captured from Crassus and Antony, and gained

Map 8.2 *Expansion of the Empire in the Age of Augustus*

CASPIAN SEA

BLACK SEA

Tomis

SIA

ARMENIA

BITHYNIA-PONTUS

Amaseia

zantium

Ancyra

MESOPOTAMIA

PARTHIA

GALATIA

Euphrates

phesus

ASIA

CILICIA

Antioch

RHODES

SYRIA

CYPRUS

CRETA

JUDAEA

ARE

ARABIA

Alexandria

AEGYPTUS

Nile

RED SEA

KUSH

Meroe

Figure 8.11a,b,c *Finds from the Germans' massacre of three Roman legions in the Teutoburg Forest,* A.D. *9. Excavations undertaken since the late 1980s at Kalkriese, not far north of modern Osnabrück, Germany, have finally identified the site of this catastrophic defeat. The long Roman column was evidently ambushed as it passed through a narrow defile in a sandy area at the forest edge. Makeshift ramparts of turf and sand erected by the Germans even began to collapse during the fighting, thereby concealing some items that might have been expected to attract looters subsequently. Altogether, as might be expected, the finds are scattered over a wide area, and include more than 1,000 coins. Shown are: [a] three iron components for an otherwise largely wooden shield—boss (5.5 in/14 cm diameter), grip, and edge binding; [b] a bronze decorative disk (1.5 in/3.8 cm diameter) with head of Augustus; [c] a mule's bronze bell (6.5 in/16.5 cm long without handle) and iron clapper, found stuffed with straw to silence it. For the tomb monument of a senior centurion who died in the ambush, see Fig. 8.10.*

agreement to the principle that the king of Armenia should acknowledge Roman overlordship.

Skillful presentation of these diplomatic achievements created confidence that Syria and the entire region west of the Euphrates River were adequately secured. As events turned out, too, Parthia did not become a threat. Instead, it was in the West that such shocks occurred. In A.D. 6 chiefs of peoples in Dalmatia and Pannonia acted upon the realization that Roman rule across this vast expanse was inadequately consolidated, and raised a major rebellion, which Tiberius had to spend three years suppressing. At the time of the outbreak he was about to launch a strike against the powerful Marcomanni in modern Bohemia, north of the Danube River, but this had to be abandoned indefinitely. Suppression of the rebellion brought no respite either, because in the same year, A.D. 9, German tribes ambushed and massacred three Roman legions as they marched through the "Teutoburg Forest," just to the northwest of modern Osnabrück. Their commander, the governor of Roman territory east of the Rhine River, Publius Quinctilius Varus, committed suicide. Here, too, Roman rule had not been adequately established, and in fact it never would be. Augustus authorized some reprisals east of the Rhine, but no more full-scale efforts to annex any of this area. He was devastated by the loss of Varus' legions, as well as by the fact that the German leader responsible, Arminius, chief of the Cherusci, had previously served in the Roman army, and had even been awarded Roman citizenship.

Bad loss in Nord

Augustus never recovered from these severe blows, and it is natural enough that when he died in A.D. 14 he advised Tiberius against any rash further expansion of the empire. By then, too, it had clearly reached various natural boundaries of sea or desert, and the three great rivers, Rhine, Danube, Euphrates. This said, Augustus' warning to Tiberius need not mean that he would have been opposed to all future attempts at expansion. As it is, he delighted in the glory and respect that he gained for doubling the empire in size, which thus made him the greatest conqueror in all Roman history. At the same time, by forging a territorially unified whole for the first time, he gave Romans a new conception of empire and their imperial mission, as well as new pride in the achievement of peace through victories.

LATIN LITERATURE IN THE LATE REPUBLIC AND AUGUSTAN AGE

Latin literature, which flourished in the Late Republic and Augustan Age, has two fundamental aspects that create difficulties for many modern readers: literary patronage and "creative imitation." At Rome, as in other societies without mass print communication, it was impossible for authors to earn a living from book sales. Instead, they had to be independently wealthy, or to be supported and rewarded by one patron, perhaps more. The obligations imposed by the latter situation must have varied widely, but even the notion raises skepticism among readers familiar with the intense propaganda campaigns and "disinformation" disclaimers of the modern world. Similarly, the special value that has been placed on originality in art and literature ever since the development of cheap copying technologies makes many today suspicious of Roman authors' "borrowings" from Greek literature. But it would be simplistic to deny originality and independence to great writers, a group that includes almost all those Roman authors whose work has been preserved through the centuries.

That said, some literature of the Late Republic was openly political and biased. Beginning in the late second century, Quintus Lutatius Catulus, Sulla, and certain other prominent figures wrote autobiographical works; Sulla's was even in Greek. Julius Caesar's surviving *Commentaries on the Gallic War* and *Commentaries on the Civil War* give us the flavor of this type of autobiography, which presents information in a way overwhelmingly favorable to the author. Powerful men were also the objects and recipients of flattering historical works or biographies: Theophanes of Mytilene, who received Roman citizenship from Pompey in gratitude, wrote about Pompey and his achievements, and particularly played up his likeness to Alexander the Great. Yet authors could equally well refuse to write for their influential friends, as we know happened when Cicero asked the poet Lucius Lucceius to commemorate his exploits during Catiline's conspiracy. Cicero consequently resorted to composing an epic poem himself, *On His Own Consulship*, from which only a few verses survive.

Given the limitations of mass communication, even authors whose work did not have a marked political character were associated with a patron or "circle." One such author is Lucretius (?94–51), whose Epicurean philosophical poem, *On the Nature of Things,* is addressed to the senator Gaius Memmius. Memmius is also linked to a very different type of poet, Catullus (?84–54). Better known because of the striking immediacy of his love poems, he served on Memmius' staff when the latter governed Bithynia in 57–56. Even so, politics are a marginal concern in the poetry of both Lucretius and Catullus. The fact that Catullus became a friend of Caesar, despite having previously attacked him and his companions in some poems, warns us not to attach undue significance to political elements in the literature of the time.

More important for Lucretius, Catullus, and others was the development of Latin literature, particularly the refinement of its formerly unsophisticated language into one capable of philosophical, lyric, and other kinds of expression. Catullus is identified with a movement now called "neoteric," whose adherents embraced Hellenistic culture and poetry in a search for new forms and content. As we noted when discussing the literary sources for early Roman history in Chapter One, Rome's relative slowness in developing literature, as well as the broad attraction of Greek culture, meant that Latin authors of all types tended to turn consciously to Greece for their models. This trend further advanced once the booty reaching Rome included libraries. For example, when Sulla brought Aristotle's library to Rome as loot from his capture of Athens, he provided a rich stimulus for Latin works on philosophy and natural science. Cicero's vast output included works of both types, and he, Lucretius, and others consciously strove to make the Latin language more expressive and precise. From the second century, Roman libraries had developed first privately and then publicly with sponsorship from Julius Caesar. By the end of the Republic, Latin authors were also turning back to earlier Latin works for inspiration and material.

Thus, Vergil's epic poem, the *Aeneid*, is a multilayered work. As Vergil (70–19) charts one of the foundation myths of Rome—the establishment of the Roman race in Italy by the Trojan hero Aeneas—he skillfully weaves in references to Homer's *Iliad* and *Odyssey*, as well as to Ennius (one of Rome's first poets), Lucretius, and others. At the same time Vergil constantly alludes to and even mentions Augustus, whom he knew from belonging to the circle of the eques Gaius Maecenas, one of Augustus' close associates. Yet the *Aeneid* is neither a pastiche of earlier writings, nor mere propaganda for Augustus. Vergil makes the material his own, whatever its source, and any biases he may have felt are expressed with sufficient nuance to contribute to the entrancing complexity of the epic.

Two other poets considered classic and representative of the Augustan Age are Horace (65–8) and Ovid (43 B.C.–A.D. 17). Horace, the son of a freedman but also part of Maecenas' circle, has a charming self-deprecatory persona in much of his writing. However, this persona does not obscure his brilliant crafting of different meters and genres, as he fashions new types of Latin poetry on earlier Greek models, in his *Odes* especially. Horace's work, too, is no simple translation of Greek forerunners, and he couples innovations derived from Greek literature with his own sentiments. Nor is Horace Augustus' spokesman, despite his personal connection to him. At times his skepticism is almost painful, as when he searches to discern what is noble and valuable in Rome after the bloody excesses of the civil wars.

Ovid was supported by the leading senator Marcus Valerius Messalla Corvinus. Yet Ovid was ambivalent about the Principate. In A.D. 8 Augustus banished him far from Rome to Tomis (modern Constanta, Romania) on the west coast of the Black Sea. Ovid was never to be recalled, even though he wrote two series of poems from there, which contained both general appeals and ones directed specifically to the Princeps. Altogether, Ovid's extensive output reflects wide interests, from love (such as the didactic *Art of Love* written around 1 B.C.) to myth (*Metamorphoses* or "Transformations," composed in epic hexameters), and even the Roman year (*Fasti* or "Calendar," which charts Roman religious rituals and legends day by day). Although he wrote mainly in elegiac couplets, he turned to many kinds of Greek literature for inspiration and material. For all his debt to these models, his poems are strikingly original and dazzling, even disturbing at times.

CITY OF ROME

It was essential that Rome itself be worthy of its status as the empire's capital. As early as the 30s, Augustus began to improve the city's amenities and services, as well as to restore its dozens of temples and public buildings, and to construct a stunning array of new ones (compare Maps 7.4 and 8.3). The latter included a senate house (Curia Julia, begun by Julius Caesar and finished in 29; see Figure 7.7), an entire new forum dominated by a great temple of Mars the Avenger (vowed at Philippi and dedicated forty years later in 2 B.C.; see Figure 7.6), and extensive development of the Campus Martius. Augustus' mausoleum and the Altar of Augustan Peace are among the monuments constructed in the latter area.

There were multiple benefits to these initiatives. All served to glorify Augustus' rule and to boost his popularity; he himself bragged that "he found Rome a city of brick, and left it one of marble" (Suetonius, *Augustus* 28). The construction work provided employment for the free poor in huge numbers. Perhaps as many as 1,000,000 inhabitants were now crammed into the city. Improvements to services were tangible daily reminders of a concern for this population that had been absent during the Republic. For example, thanks to Agrippa's efforts in particular, three new aqueducts were built, and a permanent organization established to maintain the entire water supply system. No aqueduct had been built since the 120s, when the city's population had been nowhere near so large. Also, after an alarming grain shortage, Augustus arranged in 22 that the monthly distributions of free grain should be supervised by four senators (ex-praetors). Since these free rations went to no more than about 200,000 recipients, the population as a whole was still heavily reliant upon commercial suppliers (Figure 6.5). So sometime after A.D. 7, in response to more shortages, Augustus took the further step of appointing an eques to oversee the entire import of grain to the city, most of it shipped from Egypt and Africa.

Rome became a safer place with the establishment of three "urban cohorts" (perhaps 1,500 men in total) to maintain law and order; their commander, the City Prefect, was a senior senator. In practice they were reinforced first by the three (out of nine) cohorts of Augustus' own guardsmen, the Praetorian Guard, that were regularly stationed in the city (one such cohort comprised at least 500 men); then also, from A.D. 6, by the force of 3,500 or so "watchmen," or *vigiles*, of freedman status, whom Augustus recruited to try and reduce the devastation caused by fires.

Last but not least, Augustus knew the value of providing the people of Rome with memorable entertainment. It need be no surprise that when recording the achievements he wished to be remembered for, he included the shows he had sponsored—eight gladiatorial games, three athletic games, twenty-six beast hunts, one mock naval battle, the special "Secular Games" of 17 B.C. symbolically inaugurating a new age (*saeculum*), and twenty-eight other shows. These events could involve the participation of thousands of people.

ATTITUDES OUTSIDE ROME

In Italy and the provinces, too, Augustus' rule was widely welcomed. He made little change in the established pattern of provincial administration. It may be that his novel step of slowly taking a census of the entire empire region by region

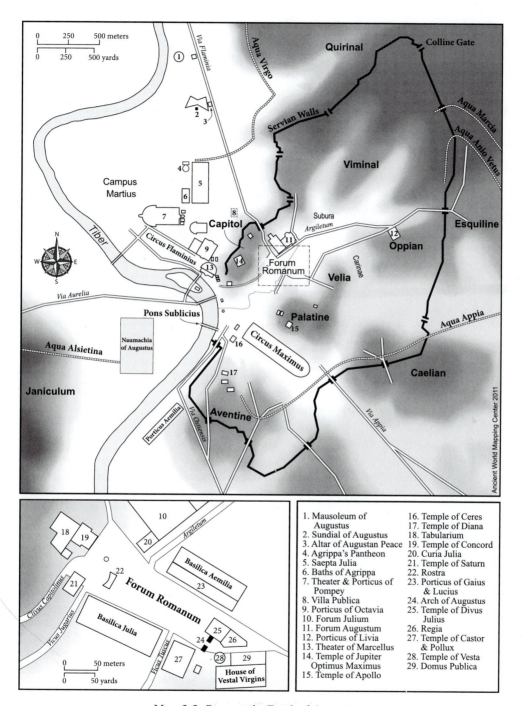

Map 8.3 *Rome at the Death of Augustus*

1. Mausoleum of Augustus
2. Sundial of Augustus
3. Altar of Augustan Peace
4. Agrippa's Pantheon
5. Saepta Julia
6. Baths of Agrippa
7. Theater & Porticus of Pompey
8. Villa Publica
9. Porticus of Octavia
10. Forum Julium
11. Forum Augustum
12. Porticus of Livia
13. Theater of Marcellus
14. Temple of Jupiter Optimus Maximus
15. Temple of Apollo
16. Temple of Ceres
17. Temple of Diana
18. Tabularium
19. Temple of Concord
20. Curia Julia
21. Temple of Saturn
22. Rostra
23. Porticus of Gaius & Lucius
24. Arch of Augustus
25. Temple of Divus Julius
26. Regia
27. Temple of Castor & Pollux
28. Temple of Vesta
29. Domus Publica

Ancient World Mapping Center 2011

Figure 8.12 *South frieze of the Altar of Augustan Peace (Ara Pacis Augustae), Rome. Augustus himself records (Res Gestae 12.2) that this altar was voted by the senate to mark his return to Rome from Spain and Gaul in 13, and that an annual sacrifice was to be performed there. Surrounding it was a walled precinct (38 × 35 ft/12 × 11 m), with reliefs in marble on the two longer sides depicting a religious procession of the imperial family and many other participants (all about three-quarters life-size). The effect is to convey a lasting impression of Augustus' concern for peace, inclusiveness, and religious devotion. Discoveries of the relief panels have been made ever since the late sixteenth century, although there was no effort to assemble them until the late 1930s, when this was done hastily and without sufficient regard to the restorations which they underwent even in antiquity. For this reason alone, all identifications of individual figures should be made with greatest caution. That said, the tall male figure towards the left of the section shown is often taken to be Agrippa, accompanied by his young son Gaius; equally, the female at the center here, facing back (see detail), may be Antonia minor, with her young son Germanicus. In any event, close examination of her dress has led some scholars to believe that the join immediately to her left is a mistake, and that these two panels should not abut one another.*

increased the burden of Roman taxation. Even so, this was made bearable by the return of peace and stability, as well as by the sense that now, at last, there was a responsible, approachable ruler in control who was personally concerned to remedy distress and injustice. Moreover he funded construction work all over the empire, especially the building and repair of roads on a massive scale, and the foundation of colonies. The latter—twenty-eight of them in Italy alone, according to Augustus himself (*Res Gestae* 28.2; see Map 7.3)—were primarily, although not exclusively, for the settlement of veterans.

In the East, the sheer extravagance of the devotion shown by Greeks actually became a cause of concern to Augustus at an early stage. Ever since the fourth century, there had been public cults of rulers as benefactors in the Greek world, Alexander the Great especially. Once Rome became involved there from the second century, cults sprang up to *Roma* as well as to individual Roman commanders, including Antony. Augustus welcomed similar devotion to himself with some caution. He stipulated that Roman citizens should only worship "Roma *and* Augustus," thus discouraging any development of a personal cult. This would be sure to offend conservative Roman sentiments, as the experiments during Caesar's dictatorship had confirmed (see Chapter Seven). With the same reasoning Augustus gave no encouragement to any such cult of himself in Rome itself, Italy, or the more romanized of the western provinces. On the other hand, he did promote it at Lugdunum (modern Lyon) in Gaul and at Ara Ubiorum (modern Köln/Cologne) in Germany as a means of fostering loyalty. Its effectiveness in these more recently annexed regions was mixed; Gauls or Germans who resented the imposition of Roman rule were only alienated further by it.

This selective promotion of what we generally refer to as an "imperial cult" is in fact just one means among many by which Augustus exploited religion to strengthen his own position. People of widely differing status and wealth were called upon to participate, across the entire empire. For example, in each town or city, formation of a group of freedmen was encouraged, who would maintain a cult of Augustus' *genius* or "vital spark." These *Augustales* thereby enjoyed a public role which their slave origin otherwise denied them. At a higher social level, delegates from each community in a province had the honor of forming a "council"—*koinon* in the Greek East, *concilium* in the Latin West—to celebrate the imperial cult. In legionary barracks, Augustus' image was placed with the standards, and associated with the cult that these received.

RES GESTAE OF AUGUSTUS

Augustus left a personal record of his "achievements" (*res gestae*), which was read out in the senate after his death. He had evidently begun its composition long before, and had thereafter updated it at least partially from time to time. Its format and style recall the autobiographical inscriptions left by earlier great Romans, although Augustus' record is doubtless more extensive than theirs had been. This said, with no more than thirty-five paragraphs, most of them short, it can hardly be considered a lengthy document. It was to be inscribed on bronze pillars at the entrance to his mausoleum in Rome, and copies must also have been set up for public view throughout the empire. The text happens to be known to us only through three such copies, all by chance from communities in Galatia. By far the most complete of them is still to be seen, with a Greek translation, on the walls of a temple dedicated to "Roma et Augustus" at the provincial capital, Ancyra (modern Ankara, Turkey).

Augustus' primary concern in formulating the document was to make a deep, immediate impact on admiring readers or hearers. Despite the relentlessly monotonous presentation in the first person singular, such an audience could only be impressed by so many incomparable achievements and honors, the solemn devotion to duty documented by a stream of remarkable statistics, the bountiful public expenditures (in Rome itself, especially), and the rapid blur of names for individuals, places, peoples, and regions, plenty of them marvelously exotic and unfamiliar. Fittingly enough, the climax of the work is its final paragraph, commemorating the bestowal of the title Pater Patriae, "Father of his Country," upon Augustus by the senate, *equites*, and people in 2 B.C.

Perhaps inevitably, given its traditional nature and purpose, the work does not stand up well to more critical approaches, rewarding though it can prove to attempt them. It is easy to see that the scope and presentation of material are unashamedly selective, in particular, wherever the long period before Augustus became sole ruler is concerned. Consequently, no rival or enemy in those struggles is ever mentioned by name, whether Roman (Brutus, Cassius, Lepidus, Antony) or foreign (Cleopatra); the clashes with Sextus Pompey are merely said to have been with pirates (25.1). Later, too, the defeats eventually suffered in Germany are ignored, so that no modification is made to the claim: "I brought peace to the Gallic and Spanish provinces as well as to Germany, throughout the area bordering on the Ocean from Gades [modern Cádiz] to the mouth of the Elbe River" (26.2). As vital an element to Augustus' control as his possession of *maius imperium* from 23 is never mentioned either; by contrast, he states unequivocally that no one rivaled him in auctoritas (34.3).

An overriding concern of the work is to illustrate the responsibility and restraint with which Augustus faithfully served the Roman people throughout his life. The honors and recognition that he received in return are duly recorded too, along with explicit reminders that—despite his constant responsiveness to senate and people—he declined anything which might seem excessive or untraditional. Extra triumphs he declined, therefore (4.1), as well as dictatorships (5.1), a perpetual consulship (5.3), and usurpation of the office of pontifex maximus (10.2); in short, "I would not accept any office inconsistent with the custom of our ancestors" (6.1). No less vital to the work's purpose is the sense conveyed that Augustus is a leader who acts honorably, spends his own money for the public's benefit, and is devoted to peace. So if his enemies seek pardon, he spares them whenever possible, even in a civil war (3.1–2); under his rule, the temple of Janus is closed with unprecedented frequency (13; traditionally signifying a time when Rome was waging no war); he duly pays for land on which to settle his veterans (16.1), and gives them and others cash from his own pocket (17–18); his good faith encourages more foreign peoples than ever to make offers of friendship with Rome (32.2). Meantime, as the latter part of the work fully demonstrates without any sense of contradiction, Augustus has spared no effort to recover (27.3), expand, and consolidate Roman territory by force of arms: "I extended the territory of all those provinces of the Roman people on whose borders lay peoples not subject to our rule" (26.1). Altogether the clear intention is to reinforce respect, gratitude, and loyalty not merely to the deceased Augustus for his past achievements, but also by extension to his successor for the future.

AUGUSTUS: FINAL ASSESSMENT

Augustus' goal as Princeps was to involve all sections of society and gain their lasting support. In one form or another his name and image were prominent everywhere, even on coins. There remains the ugly fact that a large measure of his success stemmed from the death and destruction he had previously ordered through fourteen years of civil war. After this ordeal—only the latest of several during the previous half-century—everyone was desperate for peace, stability, and reconciliation. Among the politically active upper classes, many of the most energetic were dead, and there was grudging acknowledgment that some form of monarchy was the only practical safeguard against the recurrence of ruinous personal rivalries which, among much else, blocked large-scale social or economic change. The rest of society was indifferent to the loss of whatever political role it had ever had, since this had become increasingly meaningless. The upper classes were irked by Augustus' novel, and repeated, attempts to regulate by law a range of private moral and social matters such as marriage, childbearing, and adultery. On the other hand, they were gratified by Augustus' studied respect for them, as well as by his continued exclusive reliance on them for commanding the army and administering the empire along traditional lines. Senators and their families were now marked out more distinctively than ever, and equites were offered a role in administration for the first time.

Both Augustus' transformation of the city of Rome and his largely successful desire to expand Roman power by force of arms brought him much popularity. Peace within the empire was counted the greatest blessing, along with the end of any draft for citizens. A "professional" army with a clear focus of loyalty was a development welcomed universally. Welcome, too, were his manifest concern for everyone's welfare, his basic respect for the rule of law, and his reluctance to flaunt supreme authority, let alone exercise it hastily. There is no question that he learned much from the prior experience of Sulla, Pompey, Caesar, Antony, and other leading figures. Gradually he came to appreciate, as they had not, that it was possible for him to retain control *and* at the same time restore the institutions of the Republic along with much of its outlook. Many changes could thus be linked to the past and tradition, and several were represented as an overdue return to neglected past practice. Altogether, by appealing to conservative sentiments which he shared himself, and at the same time instituting a new, personal style of long-term, responsible leadership, Augustus saved and reshaped the Roman world. As he claimed himself, "By new laws passed on my proposal I brought back into use many exemplary practices of our ancestors which were disappearing in our time, and I personally transmitted exemplary practices to posterity for their imitation" (*Res Gestae* 8.4). For him to succeed in this way, rather than by introducing more visible change—as Antony might conceivably have done in his place—was by no means natural or inevitable; but it worked.

By A.D. 14 it was at least clear that Augustus had used his sole power beneficially, whether or not this could ever become sufficient justification for all the blood spilled to gain it. That aside, in his all but sixty years as a public figure, there had been setbacks, failed experiments, and disappointments of all kinds, which he felt keenly to the end. In his old age, the major challenges to Roman control in Dalmatia, Pannonia, and Germany, and the huge losses they brought, were painful blows. A source of more prolonged personal sorrow was the gradual extinction of every hope of passing his position to a blood relative, despite successive bright prospects. Nonetheless, the *optimus status* or "best condition" which he forged for the revival of the Roman world was an astonishing achievement, even if it did ultimately value peace and security above freedom. How far his prayers for its endurance would be answered, only time could tell.

SUGGESTED READINGS

Campbell, Brian. 2002. *War and Society in Imperial Rome, 31 B.C.–A.D. 284.* London and New York: Routledge.

Cooley, Alison E. (ed.). 2009. Res Gestae Divi Augusti: *Text, Translation, and Commentary.* Cambridge: Cambridge University Press.

Earl, Donald. 1968. *The Age of Augustus.* London: Elek Books. A concise, perceptive overview, incorporating an extensive set of superb illustrations.

Favro, Diane. 1996. *The Urban Image of Augustan Rome.* Cambridge: Cambridge University Press.

Morton Braund, Susanna. 2002. *Latin Literature.* London and New York: Routledge.

Osgood, Josiah. 2006. *Caesar's Legacy: Civil War and the Emergence of the Roman Empire.* Cambridge: Cambridge University Press.

Roller, Duane W. 2010. *Cleopatra: A Biography.* Oxford: Oxford University Press.

Wallace-Hadrill, Andrew. 2008. *Rome's Cultural Revolution.* Cambridge: Cambridge University Press.

Wells, Colin. 1992 (second edition). *The Roman Empire.* Cambridge, MA: Harvard University Press. This wide-ranging survey spans the assassination of Julius Caesar to the early third century.

Zanker, Paul. 1988. *The Power of Images in the Age of Augustus.* Ann Arbor: University of Michigan Press.

9

THE EARLY PRINCIPATE
(A.D. 14—69)

*The Julio-Claudians, the Civil War of 68–69,
and Life in the Early Empire*

SOURCES

Most literary sources for this chapter center on members of the imperial family, now called the Julio-Claudians because of their relation by blood or adoption either to Augustus, who was adopted into the Julian family by Julius Caesar's will, or to Livia, whose sons had been born into the Claudian family (see Chapter Eight). Reading the lively portrayals of political manipulation and human frailty in the biographies of Suetonius, the *Annals* of Tacitus, and Cassius Dio's *History*, it is easy to forget the rest of the Roman world, especially the countless individuals whose labor supplied the food, services, and materials essential to those at the top. Tacitus' *Histories*—which begins at Nero's death, covers the civil war of 68–69, and breaks off in 70 while discussing the Germano-Gallic revolt of Civilis (see Chapter Ten)—similarly tends to focus on Rome's elite. Plutarch wrote biographies of Galba and Otho, two of the contenders in 68–69, and his information largely corresponds with that preserved by Tacitus and Cassius Dio. The latter's history survives primarily in abbreviated or excerpted form after 46; we cannot identify the presumed common source. Taking its lead from our literary sources, therefore, the first part of this chapter offers a chronological account of civil government and military affairs in the early Principate.

Information for the chapter's second half—wider social history and matters outside of Rome—comes from nonhistorical literature, such as the poems of Ovid (see Chapter Eight). In addition, papyri, coins, and archeological material— including silverwork, tombstones, and historical reliefs, as well as more mundane pottery and glass—provide vivid details overlooked by the authors. Inscriptions supply valuable insights into laws and procedures in Rome and other communities (see Source 9.1, which gives part of the senatorial decree concerning the elder Gnaeus Piso). *Acts of the Apostles* and other parts of the New Testament offer a fascinating glimpse into the incipient Christian religion in Judaea and the eastern Mediterranean; Jewish life is reported in the *Jewish Antiquities* and the *Jewish War*, both by Josephus. Philo, a Jewish philosopher from Alexandria, documents Jewish-Greek tensions there, as well as attempts made from Egypt to engage the attention of the Princeps, in this case Gaius. Papyri illuminate daily life in Egypt and, to a lesser extent, a few other areas. The relatively new invention of glass blowing, together with the proliferation of workshops manufacturing fineware pottery, provides durable evidence of increased access to higher-quality goods. Between them, the surviving materials illustrate many changes throughout the Roman world, including growing prosperity for the political elites in cities and those who served them.

THE JULIO-CLAUDIAN EMPERORS: CIVIL GOVERNMENT AND MILITARY CONCERNS

The relations between each emperor and his subjects encompassed dealings with the highest orders, that is, senators and *equites*, and with the masses comprising the populace of Rome itself and Roman subjects elsewhere. Julius Caesar's assassination had revealed how dangerous it was for a Roman ruler to shame or humiliate his supposed peers in any way. Augustus had deliberately opted to portray himself as a princeps who was *primus inter pares*, first among equals, rather than as *rex* or *dictator*, thus emphasizing civil rather than military power.

The personal tone of his relationships with individuals had disguised or mitigated his transformation of Rome's institutions; further, the civil upheavals of the end of the Republic had brought many new men into the upper orders. Through Augustus' genius, charm, and diplomacy, not to mention his deceitfulness and bribery, they had been convinced to work with him for the good of the state. Congeniality and accessibility (*comitas, civilitas*) were among the imperial virtues. Augustus' immediate successors came from his extended family so that, although the principle was never enunciated, a single dynasty ran the Roman empire from 14 to 68. Yet Augustus' virtues were not genetic. The political difficulties of his successors usually stemmed from neglecting civil consensus and from alienating Rome's traditional political and military elite.

Equally vital for success or failure was the emperor's relationship to the army and Rome's military traditions. The yearly oaths of allegiance to the Princeps and imperial family were by no means the armed forces' only ties to the imperial house. The feast days of deified emperors and empresses—first Augustus; next, ephemerally, Gaius' sister Drusilla; then Livia and Claudius—were holidays for the camps. The emperor was commander-in-chief of all armed forces by virtue of his *maius imperium.* Restriction of the right of a full triumph to him or a member of his family after 19 B.C. underlines his military preeminence. Men outside the imperial house could and did still receive "triumphal ornaments," which included some of the symbols of a triumph, but not the right to enter the city in a triumphal procession. Alternatively, they could be awarded an "ovation," a procession in which the victorious general entered the city on foot or on horseback rather than in a triumphal chariot. But neither of these accolades was as impressive as the traditional triumph.

The state's military traditions meant more than armed men loyal to Rome. As its history amply confirms, the army and imperial growth were two of Republican

Figure 9.1 *"Sword of Tiberius." This silver relief—from a commemorative scabbard found in Germany, and now in the British Museum—depicts a young general in military costume presenting a small, winged statuette of Victory to an emperor, enthroned and represented as Jupiter. A shield inscribed* Felicitas Tiberi *("the Good Fortune of Tiberius") leans against the throne. The gods Mars Ultor and Victory flank the two mortals, and Victory carries a shield inscribed* Vic(toria) Aug(usti) *("the Victory of Augustus"). The scene has been interpreted as Tiberius offering to Augustus a victory that he gained in the Alps in 16–15 B.C., but it is perhaps better to see it as Germanicus offering to Tiberius his German victory of A.D. 14–16/17. In either case, the smaller stature of the general, his deferential gesture, and the iconography of the emperor as Jupiter all emphasize the primacy of the Princeps as supreme commander-in-chief. The difficulties in identification highlight the similarities marking portrayals of Augustus and the Julio-Claudians, a feature that suggests dynastic continuity.*

Rome's key elements. Social, political, and religious rituals, as well as the economy, sustained Rome's militarism at the same time as they depended on it. But the political and social turmoil of the last century of the Republic, as well as the limited technology and communications of the time, brought into question Rome's indefinite expansion. Augustus is said to have advised in his will that the empire be kept within its boundaries. Borders are conceptual rather than real, however, and the frontier was permeable everywhere, especially in the north and east. Moreover, borders were constantly renegotiated in Rome's vital yet shifting treaties with kings at the empire's edges, most notably with the kingdom of Armenia that separated the Romans and their most organized enemy, the Parthians. The fifty-four years of Julio-Claudian power after Augustus' death witnessed different ways of dealing with the army and with the ideological and practical ramifications of militarism and its renunciation. Military revolts in 14 strikingly underscored the necessity of military support for imperial power. At the end of the Julio-Claudian dynasty, this truth was revealed again by the revolt of Julius Civilis and the wider military dissatisfaction of 68.

TIBERIUS (14–37)

Although at Augustus' death in 14 Tiberius hesitated to don the mantle of ruler, declaring his reluctance and inadequacy before the senate, he immediately assumed control of the Praetorian Guard; it was imperative that someone take this step. His authority as Augustus' heir also stemmed clearly from his tribunician power, his adoption by Augustus, and Augustus' bequest to him of most of his estate as well as the name Augustus. Yet Rome's armies in Pannonia and on the German border saw Augustus' death as an opportunity to mutiny. They clamored for higher pay, more humane treatment, fixed terms of enlistment, and no recalls to service. Tiberius sent his own son Drusus the Younger to Pannonia, and dispatched to Germany his nephew and adopted son Germanicus. The revolts were quelled primarily by capitulation to the soldiers' demands, which were reasonable enough. Among other concessions, legionary service was fixed at twenty years, although it was later restored to twenty-five—a saving to the state, since many fewer men would survive to receive their discharge bonus.

   Tiberius had spent much of his adult life away from Rome before becoming Princeps, and he did not have many personal friends in the city. After an auspicious start in public life at Rome itself, he had then spent many years elsewhere on military service. His brilliant exploits during this period (see Map 8.2) have been obscured by the hatred he later aroused among senators, the authors of most Roman histories. In 20 B.C. he had advanced into Armenia in a show of force against the Parthians; in 15–14 he had campaigned in the Alps to secure Raetia and Noricum; from 12 to 9 he had fought insurgent tribes in Illyricum; and from 9 to 7 B.C., as well as again from A.D. 4 to 6, he had led strikes against Germanic tribes. From 6 to 9, he was again in Illyricum to take command during the bloody Dalmatian-Pannonian revolt, which was quelled only by the virtual extirpation of the tribes south of the Dravus River (modern Drava). From 6 B.C. to A.D. 2, however, he had withdrawn to the Aegean island of Rhodes. His eight-year stay there allowed him to deepen philosophical, astrological, and other intellectual interests, and to escape his failed marriage to Julia (see Chapter Eight).

Largely absent from Rome itself, therefore, for the thirty years between his twenties and his fifties, Tiberius had never developed the easy familiarity with his peers that Augustus enjoyed. His personality only aggravated the situation. From all accounts he seems to have been a secretive, even suspicious soul, reticent, introspective, and cautious. He did have some trusted senatorial and equestrian confidants and friends, such as Gaius Sallustius Crispus (related to the historian Sallust), to whom he turned for advice. But he was made uneasy by the blunders that individual senators committed when dealing with him. Unused to Tiberius, and unsure of how far he really wanted to be treated as an equal in his role as Princeps, at times they spoke too familiarly and apparently disrespectfully, while at other times they seemed sycophantic. Tiberius' interactions with senators only worsened as treason (*maiestas*) trials increased during his rule. By this date—although no formal enactment was ever issued—charges of treason could be made on the grounds of conspiracy against the Princeps' life, libel and slander against him, or adultery with a member of the imperial family; those laying successful charges received a portion of the convicted person's estate.

Tiberius' general distrust, combined with his military background, led him to rely on the Praetorian Guard. Between 19 and 23 he built this force of about 9,000 a huge barracks at the edge of Rome itself (see Map 10.3). This step ensured that all future emperors would have a personal bodyguard there, and over the next two centuries these troops did often influence the choice of emperors. Gaius, Claudius, Otho, and Didius Julianus all came to power through their support; Septimius Severus, however, broke their grip in 193. The prominence of these special troops, underscoring the military and personal basis of imperial power, subverted the value of civil consensus and contributed to the difficulties of Tiberius' Principate. By the early 20s, Lucius Aelius Sejanus was sole Praetorian Prefect, and he exploited Tiberius' trust and confidence to advance himself. Treason trials proliferated. In 23, Sejanus may even have masterminded the death of Tiberius' own son, Drusus the Younger. Sejanus' influence increased after Tiberius' move to Capri in 26, since thereafter it was he who controlled communications with the Princeps. Although Sejanus' unscrupulous intrigues finally brought about his own denunciation and execution in 31, Tiberius looked at the individual and not the weakness of the system. The equally dissembling Quintus Sutorius Macro then took over as Praetorian Prefect, restricting access to the Princeps just as closely as had Sejanus.

Despite his early military successes and the construction projects in Rome sponsored by him or in his honor—such as the Porticus of Livia which he and his mother Livia dedicated in 7 B.C.—Tiberius never developed a close relationship with Rome's populace. The popularity once enjoyed by Gaius and Lucius was replaced at the beginning of Tiberius' rule by even more fervent approval for Germanicus, the son of Tiberius' deceased younger brother Drusus (see Table 8.1). A vivid impression of the public outcry at Germanicus' premature death is offered by a recently discovered senatorial decree concerning the elder Gnaeus Piso (see Source 9.1). As Princeps, Tiberius proved generally apathetic about providing Rome with monuments and amenities; other than the Praetorian barracks, he sponsored only the Temple of the Deified Augustus (which has yet to be located) and a new stage for Pompey's theater. His restraint may have stemmed from fiscal concern, since maintaining the pace of building and other expenditure set by Augustus would have beggared the treasury; even so, the change marked an unwelcome break with Augustan precedent. Tiberius did respond quickly to public calamity, yet he chose not to highlight his generosity; for instance, he is the only Princeps not to assume the honorific title *Pater Patriae*. When twelve cities in Asia were devastated by an earthquake in 17, he remitted taxes and gave other aid, perhaps even sending architects to the province. In 33 he lent 100 million sesterces at low interest to defaulting debtors, and in 37 he spent another 100 million sesterces to rebuild houses and apartment blocks destroyed by a fire on Rome's Aventine Hill. Yet none of this liberality improved his reputation.

We have no way of knowing how Rome's citizens reacted to such events or to the transfer of consular and praetorian elections from the Centuriate assembly to the senate in 14. By this time the Roman populace was accustomed to communicating its likes and dislikes at gladiatorial games and other public spectacles in the Forum Romanum and similar public spaces. Augustus had encouraged this behavior by his constant attendance at public gatherings, by the creation of new public spaces such as the Forum Augustum, and by the embellishment of traditional gathering spots like the Forum Romanum and the Saepta Julia (both formerly voting sites). In contrast, Tiberius rarely attended public games: he had actors expelled from Italy in 23, and limited the number of gladiators. After twelve years as Princeps, in 26 he moved to the island of Capreae (modern Capri) in the Bay of Naples. He never returned to Rome, not even for the public funeral of his mother, Livia, in 29. His absence meant that he had no direct contact with anyone there, and his relationships with both the elite and the populace remained at a low ebb to his death in 37.

Most of Tiberius' energies went to military and administrative matters. In 14, after Germanicus had quelled the uprising of the troops stationed in Germany, Tiberius ordered him to go on the offensive along and beyond the Rhine. These strikes against the Germans from 14 to 16–17 were ostensibly to avenge the great disaster of 9, when the Germans had cut down Varus' three legions in the Teutoburg Forest; but they also suggest Rome's customary use of external war to encourage internal harmony. Germanicus did not succeed in establishing a new border north of the earlier one at the Rhine, and Tiberius recalled him in 16–17. After a great triumph in Rome, he next sent the young general east with maius imperium (but subordinate to his own), since the Parthian king had just expelled the Roman nominee from the throne of Armenia. Amid his dealings with Armenia, the newly organized province of Cappadocia, and the recently annexed territory of Commagene (Map 9.1), Germanicus visited famous sights. His tour included Egypt, although Augustus had declared this province off-limits to senators without express imperial permission. Then, in 19, Germanicus sickened mysteriously and died, allegedly poisoned by Gnaeus Calpurnius Piso the Elder, the governor of Syria, who had quarreled repeatedly with him (see further Source 9.1).

To display Rome's military might, Tiberius also turned to his own son Drusus, two years younger than Germanicus, as well as to other men of less renown. It was Drusus the Younger who was dispatched to the rebellious legions in Pannonia in 14. Upon returning to Rome he held a consulship in 15, then from 17 to 20 served in Dalmatia, another area of Tiberius' own early successes. The progression of

---

SOURCE 9.1: Senatorial Decree Concerning the Elder Gnaeus Piso

In 20, the year after Germanicus' death, Piso and his associates were tried in the senate. Even though Piso committed suicide before his formal condemnation, the senate still published its final verdict and recommendations. As the inscribed copies of these measures state, it was decided that: "this decree of the senate, inscribed in bronze, be posted in the most frequented city of every province and in the most frequented place of that city; and likewise . . . it should be posted in the winter quarters of each legion near the standards" (lines 170–72). The document is fascinating in many particulars. The passage reproduced here illuminates the dynamics between Princeps and senate:

Whereas Tiberius Caesar Augustus, son of the deified Augustus . . . referred to the senate for decision: how the case of the elder Gnaeus Piso had seemed, and whether he seemed to have taken his life with due cause, and . . . CONCERNING THESE MATTERS THEY DECREED AS FOLLOWS:

> THAT the senate and Roman people, before all else, expressed gratitude to the immortal gods because they did not allow the tranquility of the present state of the Republic—than which nothing better can be desired, and which it has fallen to our lot to enjoy by the favor of our Princeps—to be disturbed by the wicked plans of the elder Gnaeus Piso; then to Tiberius Caesar Augustus, their own Princeps, because he made available to the senate everything necessary for seeking out the truth; and THAT the senate admired his fairness and forbearance on this account also, because, although the crimes of the elder Gnaeus Piso are most manifest and Piso himself had exacted punishment from himself, nonetheless he wanted Piso's case to be tried, . . .

(lines 4–20, excerpted from the translation by Cynthia Damon in *American Journal of Philology* 120.1 [1999], pp. 15–17).

honors that Drusus continued to receive—a triumph when he returned to Rome in 20, a second consulship in 21, and the grant of tribunician power in 22—signify Tiberius' preference for the military in his conception of the Principate. But Drusus' premature death in 23, allegedly by poison at Sejanus' agency, ended his career. Tiberius also relied on men who were not his relatives. He entrusted to Marcus Furius Camillus, governor of Africa in 17, the suppression of a chieftain's rising; in 22 renewed disturbances there were tackled by Quintus Junius Blaesus, the uncle of Sejanus. In 21 Gaius Silius and other generals suppressed a rebellion in Gaul. Problems in Thrace in the early 20s were finally resolved by Gaius Poppaeus Sabinus (grandfather of Poppaea, the later wife of Nero), who received triumphal ornaments for his success. Altogether, the number of commanders employed, as well as the readiness with which Tiberius authorized the use of force, demonstrated Rome's military preparedness and the emperor's willingness to associate others with himself in the empire's defense.

Tiberius also monitored the activities of provincial governors closely. Ironically, his habit of extending the tenure of good governors for more than the customary single year may have discredited him at Rome; some men who had hoped for such a position possibly felt deprived of one by this practice. His death at the age of seventy-seven in 37 was generally welcomed in Rome itself. His standing in the provinces is harder to gauge. As Princeps he neither traveled through the empire nor, after the death of his son Drusus the Younger in 23, did he send family members out of Italy. Though this lack of mobility prudently spared communities the enormous costs of hosting an imperial visit, at the same time it significantly diminished opportunities for provincials to forge a personal link with the Princeps. Yet his rule did generally better the empire. How perceptible such benefits were, however, is hard for us to discern.

GAIUS (CALIGULA) (37–41)

Tiberius' grandnephew and successor Gaius is known by the nickname Caligula given him for the miniature military boots (*caliga*) that he wore as a toddler while living in military camps with his parents, Germanicus and Agrippina the Elder. He had a glorious lineage, directly descended from Augustus through his mother and from Livia through his father; he advertised this ancestry when, aged only seventeen, he gave a public funeral oration for his grandmother Livia in Rome. But he had a difficult childhood, and suffered severe bouts of epilepsy throughout his life. When he was seven, his father died amidst malicious rumors; as a teenager, he saw the exile and execution of his mother and brothers voted by the senate under apparent pressure from Tiberius. When eighteen he was summoned to Capri, where his companions for the next six years or so were an ill-assorted group—his cousin, Tiberius' young grandson Tiberius Gemellus; royal hostages from Rome's bordering states; astrologers; and Tiberius himself, by then in his seventies. Gaius had no familiarity with his peers from the senatorial and equestrian orders, and although he was elected pontifex in 31 and quaestor in 33, he was not permitted to fulfill the duties of either position.

At Tiberius' death the Praetorians' favor for Gaius, rather than for Tiberius' grandson Tiberius Gemellus (made coheir by Tiberius), seemed suspicious to some. But Gaius' arrival in Rome from Capri was celebrated with high hopes, and the senate immediately conferred imperial power on him. After all, he was the son of the wildly popular Germanicus, a connection he paraded. Among his first acts was the rehabilitation of his mother's and brothers' memories and the public burning of their correspondence, with oaths that he had not read any of it. Further, he undertook both to restore senatorial prestige, by granting the senators full authority to make decisions, and to overturn the secrecy of Tiberius' later years, by publishing an imperial budget. Gaius attended races in Rome, and showed himself accessible to the people. He was interested in Italian roads and other utilitarian constructions, and in Rome he began two new aqueducts as well as the Vatican circus (later completed by Nero and famous as the site of St. Peter's martyrdom). The new Princeps' level of public activity contrasted favorably with that of Tiberius.

Yet within a year Gaius fell seriously ill, perhaps with a brain fever, and, although he recovered, his erratic behavior escalated. By 38 he executed Tiberius Gemellus and the Praetorian Prefect Macro. By 39 he had quarrelled violently with the senate, and was ruling more and more autocratically. His insults ranged from the political, as when he allegedly planned a consulship for his favorite racehorse Incitatus, to the moral and religious, as when in 38 he had his sister Drusilla deified. He was rumored to have had incestuous relations with her before her death that year; she was the first Roman female to be deified (Livia was deified only later by Claudius). Gaius appeared in public in the dress of various gods, notably that of Castor and Pollux. He had a huge golden statue made of himself, and he evidently wanted a special temple of his own. In Rome he performed as charioteer, gladiator, and singer, pandering to the populace but shocking and insulting senators and *equites*. As part of this showy self-promotion, he even drove a chariot over a bridge of boats from Baiae to Puteoli, resplendent in the breastplate of Alexander the Great. Such horrendous stories reveal the fear and anxiety caused by an emperor unconcerned to mask his autocratic power.

Yet Gaius also attended to the army and to foreign affairs, though in ways that often appear erratic. He launched small expeditions against Germany and Britain during the winter of 39–40. His other foreign and provincial activities cannot be dated with the same precision. At any rate, in Mauretania he had the king Ptolemy deposed and executed, thus prompting a revolt and Claudius' later annexation of the region as a province. Otherwise Gaius' attention was directed eastward. He dethroned the king of Armenia, triggering problems here that lasted through the rule of Nero. In 38 he restored the territory of Commagene to its king, Antiochus IV, only to depose him later (in 41 Antiochus was reinstated by Claudius and ruled until 72, when Vespasian incorporated Commagene into the province of

Map 9.1 *Roman Empire in* A.D. *69*

E   F   G

Legionary base (normally a single legion)
Principal settlement with legionary base adjacent
Not all legions' bases are known.

BLACK SEA

Viminacium
Oescus Novae Odessus
MOESIA   Amastris
THRACIA   BITHYNIA-PONTUS
                Ancyra   CAPPADOCIA
Perinthus   Nicomedia   GALATIA
MACEDONIA   Caesarea (Mazaca)   COMMAGENE
Thessalonica   Euphrates
        Pergamum   ASIA   Cyrrus
        AEGEAN   CILICIA
        SEA Claros   Antioch
        Ephesus Aphrodisias   SYRIA
ACHAIA Corinth   LYCIA   Raphaneae
                        Myra
Gythium   RHODES   CYPRUS
                Paphos
                CRETA
        Gortyn   Caesarea   JUDAEA
                                Jerusalem
INTERNUM MARE   Dead Sea
                                Masada

        Alexandria
Cyrene

AEGYPTUS   RED SEA

                Nile

Ancient World Mapping Center 2011

Syria). Gaius appointed Agrippa I, the grandson of Herod the Great, to rule part of Judaea. For reasons that elude us, he also insisted that his own statue be installed in the Temple in Jerusalem and other synagogues. Although this order was countermanded following his death on January 24, 41, it contributed to the unrest which resulted in the First Jewish Revolt in 66.

Gaius' megalomania, unpredictability, and religious arrogance alienated many. He could harm even the masses in Rome, as when he shut down the public granaries and let the people go hungry. He traveled only to Gaul and the Rhine regions (in 39–40), in both instances at great cost to local communities. His isolated upbringing and illnesses added to his estrangement from his peers and from many of Rome's traditions. Unsuccessful though it was, the conspiracy in 39 of Gnaeus Cornelius Lentulus Gaetulicus, commander of the troops on the Upper Rhine, suggests the unease of generals and troops alike in the face of such instability. Gaius' deficient military leadership was the root cause of his assassination by members of the Praetorian Guard, whom he had relentlessly humiliated. Few mourned his passing.

CLAUDIUS (41–54)

Gaius' uncle, Claudius, had been born at Lugdunum (modern Lyon, France), as the youngest son of Drusus the Elder and Antonia; he was Livia's grandson and Tiberius' nephew. In his youth he had endured various illnesses, perhaps including cerebral palsy, and he was deaf in one ear as well as lame. Military and political preference had always gone to Germanicus, his older and more charismatic brother. On the other hand, Claudius had a scholar's mind and training, and the historian Livy was one of his tutors. Before becoming Princeps in 41, Claudius had held some high positions, serving as augur under Augustus and as consul with the new emperor Gaius for the latter part of 37. But he had exercised no real power. He had survived the lethal years of Tiberius and Gaius by playing the fool and keeping out of the public eye as much as possible. In a society that valued appearances so highly, Claudius' "deformities" or disabilities discredited him among the elite, and Suetonius (*Claudius* 3–4) preserves some particularly nasty words about him from Livia, Augustus, and even his own mother Antonia. The shame accorded his physical challenges consigned him to the inner rooms of the palace and the company of women and imperial freedmen, most untraditional companions for Roman leaders. This stigma was to disadvantage him throughout his life, as did his lack of ease in addressing his nominal equals.

Claudius' imperial power was due to the Praetorians. Suetonius comically narrates that after Gaius' assassination Claudius hid in the imperial palace, to be accidentally discovered there by a Guardsman who hailed him as Princeps. The senate had already convened in order to "restore the Republic," but as their deliberations dragged on, the people began to demand Claudius as Princeps. Claudius was thus emboldened to let the Guards acclaim him as emperor. Once in power, however, he reduced his reliance on the Praetorian Guard, and loosened its grip by appointing two Praetorian Prefects rather than one. But he had already alienated the senators, and he angered them further when he paid each Praetorian 150 gold pieces (*aurei*).

As princeps, Claudius took his imperial duties seriously, and treated the senate with respect. He consulted it frequently and involved himself actively in

---

SOURCE 9.2: Claudius' Speech on the Admission of Gauls to the Senate

By a rare chance, we have two versions of a speech that Claudius made in the senate concerning the admission of prominent citizens from the Gallic provinces to that body. The version here is part of the actual speech as he delivered it in 48 during his censorship, which was copied and then "published" on a bronze inscription at Lugdunum (ILS 212). The other surviving version, not reproduced here, is a paraphrase by Tacitus (Annals 11.23.1–25.1). Comparison of the two offers instructive insight into Tacitus' aims and methods as a historian.

. . . Granted, my great-uncle, the deified Augustus, and my uncle, Tiberius Caesar, were following a new practice when they desired that all the flower of the colonies and municipalities everywhere—that is, good, wealthy men—should sit in this senate house. You ask me: Is not an Italian senator preferable to a provincial? I shall reveal to you in detail my views on this matter when I come to obtain approval for this part of my censorship. But I think that not even provincials ought to be excluded, provided they can add distinction to this body. . . .

The time has come, Tiberius Caesar Germanicus [here Claudius addresses himself], now that you have reached the furthest boundaries of Narbonese Gaul, for you to unveil to the members of the senate the direction of your speech.

All these distinguished youths whom I see here will no more give us cause for regret if they become senators than my friend Persicus, a man of most noble ancestry, has cause for regret when he reads on the portraits of his ancestors the name Allobrogicus [an honorific one derived from the Allobroges, a Gallic tribe presumably defeated in battle by an ancestor of Persicus]. But if you agree that this is so, what more do you want, when I point out to you this single fact, that the territory beyond the boundaries of Narbonese Gaul already sends you senators, since we have men in our ranks from Lugdunum and do not regret it? It is indeed with hesitation, members of the senate, that I have gone beyond the borders of provinces with which you are routinely familiar, but I must now unreservedly plead the case of Gallia Comata [the part of Gaul conquered by Julius Caesar]. In this connection, if anyone observes that these people engaged the deified Julius in war for ten years, let him set against that the unshakable loyalty and obedience of the past hundred years, tested to the full in many of our crises. When my father Drusus was subduing Germany, it was these Gauls who by their passivity afforded him a safe and securely peaceful rear, even at a time when he had been summoned away to war from the task of organizing the census, which was still new and unfamiliar to the Gauls. How difficult such an operation is for us at this precise moment we are learning all too well from experience, even though the sole purpose of the census is to create an official record of our resources.

military and administrative affairs, even reviving the old Republican office of censor in 47–48. Yet his tone, as it emerges from surviving documents, often appears introverted and almost fussy. He considered it his task as Princeps to take part in all sorts of trials. Senators, however, saw this judicial activity as meddling with their prerogatives and dignity, especially because his judgment was liable to prove erratic. When he began to recruit a few wealthy men from the western provinces into the senate, a process that ultimately contributed to imperial Rome's strength, he further estranged senators from Rome and Italy. Despite frequent consultation with the senate, for most advice Claudius relied on imperial freedmen rather than equites or senators. His choice is understandable in view of his previous circumstances in the imperial household, but it antagonized Rome's elite, who felt that their power and prestige were being handed to social inferiors.

Claudius also seemed to be susceptible and credulous with women. In 39 he married his third wife, Valeria Messalina, a second cousin about thirty years his junior who bore him two children, Octavia and Britannicus. Claudius did not notice or care that she became unfaithful to him. When she conducted a mock marriage in 48 with Gaius Silius, however, her infidelity took on a political dimension. She was descended from Augustus' sister Octavia, and Silius was due to become consul the following year. Yet only with difficulty was Claudius persuaded to denounce her (leading to her suicide). His own niece Agrippina the Younger then schemed successfully to marry him in 49. Within a year she had greater public visibility than any other woman, and received the honorific title Augusta. By 53, she had secured the succession of her own son, Nero, who married Claudius' thirteen-year-old daughter Octavia and superseded the slightly younger Britannicus. Claudius' apparent inability to take charge in his own home only sharpened the resentment felt by many in Rome when he assumed the censorship and conducted public, but characteristically erratic, reviews of individuals' lives.

Claudius was much more active militarily than his two imperial predecessors; rather, he shared Augustus' concern to expand the empire. He temporarily overcame unrest in Judaea by granting local rule to the Jewish king Agrippa I, but he interfered more intrusively with other provinces and adjacent areas. In 43 he directed the invasion of Britain, emulating Julius Caesar's exploits there and going to the island personally for the climax of the campaign. This annexation of Britain was celebrated in various ways. In particular, the honorific name Britannicus was bestowed on the son born in 41 to Claudius and Messalina, and a temple to Claudius was begun in the new provincial capital Camulodunum (modern Colchester) in the east of the island. In 43 he annexed Mauretania as a province, and in 46 Thrace. When Agrippa I died in 44, most of Judaea reverted to the status of an imperial province run by procurators. Claudius even launched exploratory expeditions into Germany in 47. The expansion of Roman power must have seemed inexorable. Claudius received as many as twenty-seven official salutations as *imperator*, underscoring the importance he attached to gaining and maintaining a military reputation.

Figure 9.2 *Claudius subdues Britain. This marble relief was found at Aphrodisias in the province of Asia (modern Geyre, Turkey), a city that took pride in its special relationship with Rome in general and the family of Julius Caesar in particular. The relief is one of a series depicting the Julio-Claudian emperors and embellishing a centrally located sanctuary (sebasteion) of the imperial cult, which was begun in the rule of Tiberius and completed early in that of Nero. Here we see Claudius almost life-size, heroically costumed only in helmet, military cloak, and sword belt, about to strike down the female personification of Britain (his sword and most of his right arm are missing). He pins her down with his right knee, and with his left hand draws back her head, exposing her throat. The island's submission is emphasized by rendering Britannia as a woman, unarmed, and with her right breast exposed. The composition is based on earlier Greek models of the slaying of a female Amazon warrior ("Amazonomachy"), thus transcribing the Roman imperial theme into iconography familiar to a local audience in the province of Asia.*

Claudius unpretentiously enjoyed races, gaming, and dicing, pleasures that he shared with the majority of Rome's inhabitants (see Chapter Ten). His many celebrations of military achievements brought in booty and created memorable festivities for the city. He was particularly alert to Rome's grain supply. When a grain shortage incited a mob in the Forum to pelt him with crusts and stale rolls, rather than punishing the rioters Claudius devised special inducements for merchants to import grain during the winter. His public buildings and renovations tended to be utilitarian, such as the new aqueduct for Rome, Aqua Claudia, and the new port just north of Ostia (Portus; see Fig. 11.2). Claudius seldom traveled far from Rome, but his constant military activity kept his name before the empire's inhabitants. Even so, his widespread popularity never overcame the resentment felt towards him by senators. His reputation in the literary record is mixed at best, despite his deification at death.

NERO (54–68)

Nero was not yet seventeen when he succeeded Claudius. At his accession in 54 he promised good relations with the senate, equites, and army, and one late

Figure 9.3 Nero and Agrippina in 54. This gold coin (aureus) was struck in the first year of Nero's rule. On the "obverse"—a coin's more important side, seen left—are depicted Nero and his mother Agrippina the Younger, face-to-face and of equal size. This is the first time that anyone had appeared on the obverse of a Roman coin with a current emperor. The surrounding text ("legend") translates: "Agrippina Augusta, wife of the deified Claudius, mother of Nero Caesar." Nero is referred to as the ruling Princeps only on the reverse of the coin, which depicts an oak wreath (symbolizing the protection of citizens), encircled by the words: "To Nero Caesar Augustus, son of the deified Claudius, Germanicus, Imperator, with tribunician power," and within the wreath: "In accordance with a decree of the senate." The image and texts evidently reflect Agrippina's dominant role in the transfer of imperial power to her son, and perhaps also the senate's hopes for a harmonious working relationship with the new Princeps.

source even reports praise of a golden five-year period until 59 (Aurelius Victor, *Caesars* 5). At first, without doubt, Nero did heed his two tutors—Lucius Annaeus Seneca, a brilliant philosopher, author, and senator hailing from Corduba (modern Córdoba, in southern Spain), and Sextus Afranius Burrus, a learned eques from Narbonese Gaul, who was one of the Praetorian Prefects. Agrippina also tried to exercise power through her young son, but her behavior was more scandalous than seriously detrimental to the empire. Meantime Nero's own interests were in the arts and showmanship rather than in government and the military, and he became more headstrong as he grew older.

In 59 Nero staged the Juvenalia festival marking the official shaving of his beard and whiskers for the first time, and in the same year he had his mother Agrippina killed in an elaborate ruse involving a staged shipwreck. In 62 his unlimited spending, together with protracted military actions in Britain and Armenia, caused him to devalue coinage and to revive the laws of treason. He forced Seneca first into retirement, and then to suicide three years later in 65. In 63 Burrus died, supposedly poisoned on Nero's orders; the Praetorian Prefect who succeeded him, Ofonius Tigellinus, seemed as venal and corrupt as Nero himself. Some senators, such as Publius Clodius Thrasea and Publius Helvidius Priscus, were suspect to Nero simply because they refused to adopt their fellow members' servility towards him, and adhered to Stoic philosophical principles. Other senators and equites actively colluded against him, however. The crucial but abortive Pisonian conspiracy of 65, which Tacitus (*Annals* 15.48–74) describes in some detail, drew on hatred of Nero shared among different levels of society. By the end of his rule he was boasting that he would dispose of the entire senate. In 68, as reports streamed in about revolts in Gaul and Germany, and as Nero vacillated between terror and nonchalance, the senate finally disowned him, declaring him a public enemy or *hostis*. Terrified by the penalty—to be publicly stripped, tied to a stake, and scourged to death—Nero committed suicide.

Even so, his death was generally mourned by the people of Rome, for he was the most popular of the Julio-Claudians. Both as spectator and as performer he loved exhibitions and performances of all kinds. He considered himself a great actor, charioteer, and singer. He followed the Juvenalia of 59 with other extravagant games, including the Neronia of 60. He wrote poetry, and his literary circle at first included Lucan, who won a prize at the Neronia for a poem praising him. As time went on, and particularly after 59, Nero adapted his public image ever more to Rome's masses, and ever less to the senators and equites. His shows and productions often demeaned members of the upper classes by forcing them into ridiculous or humiliating situations in public. He was fickle in his friendships. For example, by 63 or thereabouts he had banned Lucan from reciting his poetry publicly and from speaking in the law courts, perhaps because of the poet's growing popularity.

Similarly, Nero's relationship with the populace in Rome was not always smooth. In 62, they reacted violently against his divorce and murder of Octavia, Claudius' daughter, and they were hostile to his subsequent marriage with Poppaea. He was rumored to have caused the great fire of 64, which damaged eleven of Rome's fourteen regions, because he then appropriated much of the devastated land for his immense Golden House (compare Plate 9a). The scandal persisted even after he proposed a rational plan for rebuilding the city to reassert its primacy as capital of the empire, and permitted the dispossessed to camp in his imperial gardens. When he tried to provide a scapegoat by attacking a new sect, the Christians, his plan backfired because the horrible tortures inflicted on the accused provoked widespread sympathy. By 66, however, when he crowned Tiridates as king of Armenia in Rome, he seems to have regained public favor in the city.

Outside of Italy Nero's reputation was high in Greece, the sole part of the empire that he visited during his fourteen-year rule. During his tour of the Panhellenic sanctuaries in 66–67, he declared the province of Achaia exempt from taxes. But public favor in Rome and Achaia did not help him allay the problems of Judaea, where the First Jewish Revolt broke out in 66. Nor did such popularity secure Nero support against the generals and governors of the western provinces, who began to rebel in 67. There were many causes for the dissatisfaction. Nero was uninterested in military matters and never visited any Roman troops. Despite being served by some capable commanders, he was unable to solve the provincial and foreign problems created by Gaius' mismanagement and Claudius' expansionism. Upon accession in 54 he sent Gnaeus Domitius Corbulo to the client kingdom of Armenia, where the Parthian monarch had installed his own brother Tiridates as king in place of Rome's nominee. Corbulo's military successes in the region eventually paved the way for a diplomatic resolution whereby both sides moderated their stances, but extensive campaigning by two or more legions had been required, often year-round and under difficult conditions. Moreover the settlement itself in 66, a visit to Rome by Tiridates, was an extravagantly expensive affair. The gala at which Tiridates received his crown from Nero in an opulent public celebration dazzling with gold was reported to have cost 8,000 *aurei* a day—in other words, more than the average annual earnings of about 2,000 workers.

Some expansion of the empire occurred uneventfully under Nero when two former client kingdoms were now annexed. Part of the mountainous area of southeast Gaul became the small province of Alpes Cottiae around 58, and the area of Pontus not yet annexed became a province in 64. But such gains were offset by difficulties beyond those in Armenia, not to mention Nero's general indifference to provincial and foreign affairs. Despite Claudius' conquest, Britain was still far from secure, and Roman rapacity, embezzlement, and cruelty led to a revolt there in 60, headed by the queen of the Iceni, Boudica, and supported by other native leaders. Much of its impetus came from the Druids, dynamic female and male priestly leaders, and one of the war's first casualties was the temple of the Deified Claudius in Camulodunum. The costs of resecuring the province were high; each side is said to have suffered some 80,000 casualties. In 66 the first Jewish Revolt broke out as the combined result of Roman mismanagement and Judaea's internal problems. In February 67 Nero sent Titus Flavius Vespasianus to take command there, a solid military man who had risen from a successful command in Britain under Claudius to a consulship in 51. Vespasian's unpretentious ancestry and relative obscurity may have protected him from Nero's paranoia in the later 50s and 60s. No one suspected that such a first-generation senator would use initial victories against Jewish rebels as a springboard to the Principate.

CIVIL WAR IN 68–69: GALBA, OTHO, VITELLIUS, AND VESPASIAN

While touring Greece in late 67, Nero summoned to him Corbulo and the two consular commanders of the armies in Upper and Lower Germany; on suspicion of conspiracy, he then compelled all three generals to take their own lives. The same year saw the revolt of Gaius Julius Vindex, governor of Gallia Lugdunensis. Vindex was a senator of Gallic descent, from a family granted Roman citizenship by Julius Caesar. Although ineffectual, this insurrection precipitated Nero's downfall and a civil war. Vindex did at least gain the support of Servius Sulpicius Galba, the governor of Hispania Tarraconensis, who promised the single legion under his command. Nero, when recalled back to Rome from Greece, did nothing to address the growing crisis, and by the time Vindex's modest force was defeated in Gaul, the senate declared Nero a public enemy. In his place, it recognized as Princeps the seventy-one-year-old Galba, who came from a most distinguished patrician family. Nero committed suicide on June 9, 68, in a villa on Rome's outskirts. The Julio-Claudian dynasty ended with him.

The civil war that filled the next eighteen months was particularly devastating both for northern Italy, through which various rival armies passed on their way to Rome, and for Rome itself; many non-combatants inevitably suffered, daily life was disrupted, and property rights were overturned. Yet, as Tacitus remarked (*Histories* 1.4), the events of the period revealed "the secret of the empire . . . emperors could be made elsewhere than at Rome." Nero's indifference to military matters had opened the way for any commander with willing troops to bid for the imperial power. Of the four men declared emperor in 68–69, only Galba could boast that he was selected by the senate and the people of Rome. Yet, as his downfall showed, military support might not prove sufficient for a general to retain power once in Rome; at that point, maintaining authority depended upon securing the active goodwill of society as a whole.

Accompanied by Marcus Salvius Otho, the governor of Lusitania, Galba slowly made his way to Rome by October 68, but there he openly alienated a significant part of the army and failed to win the favor of the Praetorians or the populace. While still on the outskirts of the city he massacred as many as 7,000 men he thought loyal to Nero. He refused to pay a donative to the Praetorians, who had deserted Nero for him on their Prefect's promise of a lavish reward. Perhaps also in misguided anxiety about money, Galba suspended public games. Worst of all, he did not placate the troops on the Rhine, who felt insufficiently rewarded for their suppression of Vindex's revolt. So on January 1, 69, the four legions of Upper Germany took the oath of allegiance in the name of the senate only, omitting Galba's name. The next day, at the urging of the ambitious legionary commanders Aulus Caecina and Fabius Valens, the four legions in Lower Germany declared their new general, Aulus Vitellius, as emperor, and were then seconded by the four legions in Upper Germany. Vitellius, the undistinguished son of a father who had made a brilliant career at the Julio-Claudian court, accepted his new role but brought little energy to it.

Galba was by now attempting to strengthen support for himself by adopting a successor. He again misstepped, however, since his choice was the relatively unknown aristocrat Lucius Calpurnius Piso Frugi Licinianus, rather than the more popular Otho, who had already rendered him valuable service. Otho's reaction was to seek the Praetorians' backing for himself through bribes and promises. This he quickly achieved, so that on January 15, 69, both Galba and Piso were slaughtered in the Roman Forum in full sight of the populace. Cowed by the Praetorians, senate and people then declared Otho emperor.

As news of these developments at Rome spread, neither Vitellius nor the troops elsewhere were satisfied. In April, the armies of Otho and Vitellius clashed decisively in northern Italy, first at Cremona, where casualties were reckoned to number 40,000 on each side, and then at Bedriacum, where Otho committed suicide. Once in Rome, however, Vitellius seemed incapable of making political or military decisions.

On July 1, 69, the troops in Judaea declared their general Vespasian emperor, seconded by the Syrian legions led by Gaius Licinius Mucianus. Vespasian immediately won the allegiance of Tiberius Julius Alexander, Prefect of Egypt. Since the latter controlled not only two legions but also the ample Egyptian grain supply, Vespasian's position was extremely strong. The troops in Pannonia also declared for him and, led by their commander Marcus Antonius Primus, marched to Italy. In October, they defeated Vitellius' forces in a second battle at Cremona and sacked the unfortunate city. By December Primus' men stormed Rome itself. Vitellius was killed in the fierce fighting that destroyed many sectors of the city, including the temple of Jupiter Optimus Maximus. Senate and people declared Vespasian emperor, and order was restored upon the arrival of Mucianus a few weeks later. Vespasian himself entered Rome only the following

October (70). In the meantime, Mucianus took charge of the city, aided by Vespasian's younger son Domitian, who had survived by hiding and disguising himself as a follower of Isis.

The catastrophe of 68–69 revealed the disunity of the empire in general, and of the troops in particular. Much of Gaul had rebelled against Italy; the armies in Germany, and then those in the East, had threatened Rome; and each side had attacked the other. Who was at the center: the senate, Praetorians, or Roman people? The senate had exerted some authority. When it had declared Nero a public enemy and named Galba emperor, Nero had killed himself in despair. On the other hand, Galba's failure to win support among Rome's populace and the Praetorians undermined the senate's decision. Otho's elevation once again underscores the power of the Praetorians in Rome. Yet this elite corps proved to be no match against more numerous troops from elsewhere. The declarations for Vitellius and Vespasian highlight the importance of the officers heading the various forces. Of the four contenders of 68–69, only Vespasian proved himself enduringly capable once in power, and his bid to gain it was the best prepared.

This turmoil made it clearer than ever that the dynastic principle instituted by Augustus was unable to guarantee the best ruler for the Roman world. His unique coordination of charismatic *auctoritas*, responsible vision, and military loyalty was simply not one that could be passed down by blood or adoption. Even so, Romans' ingrained respect for family, the slow pace of change, the widespread sense of obligation to the Julio-Claudians, and the benefits bestowed by Tiberius and Claudius, together enabled Augustus' extended family to continue his rule for just over half a century. Meantime the coincidence of minimal civil strife and no pressing external threats was a rare blessing for the empire.

ECONOMIC AND SOCIAL CHANGE: ARMY

Archeological and documentary evidence confirms that the Julio-Claudians' continuation of Augustus' Principate is associated with profound changes for the empire. Above all, peace now extended across the Mediterranean and over the areas under Roman control. One could denounce Augustus as a military despot, but still the concentration of power into his hands had allowed him to demobilize the huge armies of the Triumviral period. After the loss of three legions in Germany in 9, the army was maintained more or less steadily at about 150,000 legionaries and an equal number of auxiliaries. These land-based forces were supplemented by marines in naval squadrons stationed at Misenum on the Bay of Naples, Ravenna, Forum Julii (modern Fréjus, France), and other ports to curb piracy and aid military communication. Although it was expensive to pay the armed forces and to offer the discharge bounties instituted by Augustus (see Chapter Eight), these costs could be foreseen and budgeted for; in the first century legionary pay was 900 sesterces annually, and auxiliary pay no doubt less, although perhaps not by much. The general peace of the period possibly freed up some funds allocated for equipment and materials. Peace may also have allowed both legions and auxiliary units to be slightly undermanned, further cutting costs. In addition, the growing tendency to recruit soldiers, especially auxiliaries, from the areas in which they were stationed must have reduced movement costs. Most of the Julio-Claudian emperors' military activity took place along the frontiers, so that civilians elsewhere were now largely freed from armies marching through their territory and requisitioning supplies except whenever civil war broke out again.

The simple fact of creating a standing, state-funded army, with its requirements of steady pay and supplies, encouraged the monetarization of the Roman state, the production of surplus goods, and trade. Imperial mints were established in Rome and Lugdunum, striking gold, silver, bronze, copper, and other alloy coins (*aurei, denarii, sestertii,* etc.). Local coinage in nonprecious metals continued to be minted, in the West until Claudius' time, and in the East right up to that of Diocletian in the late third century. Important as this coinage is for the insight it provides into individual cities, it was only used for local, low-level exchanges, and not for larger, empire-wide transactions. The establishment of the imperial army helped break down barriers created by Rome's hitherto pervasive subsistence farming economy. To be sure, an agrarian economy still continued to characterize the Roman world; but a commodity economy also grew up. Towns, military camps, and other centers all needed and wanted finished products like shoes and boots, lamps and other pottery, glassware, cloaks, and other manufactured goods. This demand encouraged some economic mobility, and with it social and political change.

The "imperial peace," *pax Augusta,* was due not only to the cessation of internal strife, but also to the general absence of external conflict. Difficulties with Parthia over Armenia were mostly confined to a local level until Nero's Principate, although enduring Roman distrust is demonstrated by the permanent presence of four legions in Syria. Persistent stereotyping of the Germanic tribes and Transdanubian groups as pitiless, lawless barbarians helped justify a buildup of troops along the Rhine and Danube rivers. Border skirmishes and Roman incursions across the Rhine continued even after the Teutoburg disaster in 9 (see Chapter Eight). More concerted efforts came in 15–17 under Germanicus, fruitlessly in 39–40 under Gaius, and in 47 under Claudius. In the Julio-Claudian period, thirteen of Rome's twenty-five legions were stationed in the provinces along the Rhine and Danube. Three legions were in Spain, whose northwest region had been pacified only under Augustus; one was in Africa. The approximately 300,000 armed men along the empire's borders and elsewhere changed the economic, social, religious, cultural, and political lives of the areas they occupied, although Roman military groups could and often did also act as societies unto themselves.

ECONOMY

The general halt to expansion after the Teutoburg disaster in 9 altered Rome's economy by precluding new sources of income. Perhaps this limitation may account for the financial crisis of 33, an issue of liquidity that we hear about elliptically in Tacitus, Suetonius, and Cassius Dio. Possibly in an attempt to encourage cultivation in Italy, it was decreed that individual senators should invest two-thirds of their wealth in land there. But they were unable to comply, because when they called in the money owed them in order to purchase Italian land, their creditors did not have it. Banks, as we know them, did not exist; rather, wealth had been loaned by individuals to other individuals, and perhaps to associations, with no guarantees. To resolve the resulting panic and crisis, Tiberius made a loan of one hundred million sesterces free of interest for three years. Our understanding of the crisis is hampered because—like many other aspects of the Roman economy—the ancient authors present it to illuminate the moral qualities and political dynamics of individuals. For example, Cassius Dio (58.21.4–5) writes:

> About this time, however, a certain Vibullius Agrippa, an *eques*, swallowed poison from a ring and died in the senate-house itself. Nerva [not the later emperor], who could no longer endure any contact with the emperor, starved himself to death, chiefly because Tiberius had reaffirmed the laws on contracts enacted by Julius Caesar, which were sure to result in great loss of confidence and financial confusion; even though Tiberius repeatedly urged him to eat something, he declined to make any response. Tiberius then modified his decision regarding loans and gave one hundred million sesterces to the treasury, with instructions that senators should lend this money for three years without interest to those who needed it. He also ordered that the most disreputable of those who were bringing accusations against others should all be put to death on a single day.

Although the treasury had a surplus of thirty-seven million sesterces at Tiberius' death, almost all this sum was used up in the four years of Gaius' Principate. Some new resources were gained through Claudius' expansion of the empire, but not so much as might have been hoped. Rome's heavy-handedness in the new province of Britain, for example, precipitated almost constant revolts there through the 80s, confirming the geographer Strabo's earlier prediction (4.5.3) that as a province the island would cost more to administer than could be gained there in tribute and taxes. While Claudius' annexations of Mauretania and Thrace went relatively smoothly and did create income through new taxes, the reannexation of Judaea in 44 only served to inflame this volatile area. Roman tax collectors were frequently brutal and inflexible, and their marked favoritism towards municipal elites widened the divide between rich and poor in the provinces.

Offsetting any economic gains that may have accrued from Claudius' rule, Nero's unbridled wastefulness worsened the imperial finances. In 64, the year when much of Rome was devastated by fire, Nero began building his lavish Golden House, raised taxes, and debased the coinage, reducing the weight of the silver denarius without diminishing its nominal value. These actions should also be seen in the light of trade abroad. Pliny the Elder in the 70s criticizes the drain of Roman wealth to the East, where it was exchanged for pepper and spices, silks, incense, perfumes, gems, and other expensive but relatively lightweight items. Quantities of Roman gold and silver coins have been found in archeological contexts across South India and Sri Lanka, and also as far east as South Korea, testifying to the extent of Roman commerce. Some of the trade was maritime, coming from India with the monsoons up the Red Sea and then through Egypt, but much merchandise also passed overland through western Asia in caravans.

Pliny and other moralizers may deplore Roman extravagance and the drain of money to the East, but these trends also demonstrate a general rise in the economy. Although taxes were now exacted from the provinces more systematically, they were also assessed more regularly and fairly than during the Republic. When some governors recommended increasing provincial taxes, Tiberius is said to have retorted, "A good shepherd shears his flock; he does not flay them" (Suetonius, *Tiberius* 32).

INTELLECTUAL LIFE

Rome's controversial drain of wealth for luxuries and the reckless spending by certain emperors should not be permitted to overshadow the vitality of intellectual life during the first century. Widespread recognition of Roman abilities in these spheres is shown by Tiridates' return from Rome to Armenia with many Roman artists, and by Domitian's dispatch of Roman engineers to Dacia in 88. The high level of building activity boosted Roman technology and engineering. Intellectual activity was altogether intense. Though some poets refined an ever more elaborate style—like Lucan and his friends, who traded verses with Nero—others used their poetry to explain natural phenomena. It was a sign of status, and a further mark of prestige, to write literature and to be surrounded by authors and literary connoisseurs. Emperors themselves wrote, as did other members of the imperial family, and all literary genres and types were popular. Germanicus, for example, wrote comedies in Greek, Greek and Latin epigrams, and a Latin translation of *Phaenomena*, a third-century Greek astronomical poem. Claudius produced books on Etruscan and Carthaginian history, an autobiography, and a history of Augustus' Principate, as well as an essay on dicing. Agrippina the Younger wrote memoirs, a work that Tacitus consulted (*Annals* 4.53) and that many historians today would love to have. Men successful in politics could also reach literary eminence, although it is not clear which quality brought them first to notice. In particular, Seneca the Younger, who advised the young emperor Nero until 62, was also a philosopher and a dramatist, although his personal Stoicism may now seem at odds with his sensationalist plays such as *Thyestes*.

Alongside the polished writings of poets and the imperial court, this period also saw a vast outpouring of prose. Some works were compendia, like the two-volume Roman history by Velleius Paterculus (died around 31) which spans earliest times to 29. Despite the summary nature of its coverage, it presents Sejanus in a most favorable light (2.127–28), and repeatedly praises Tiberius, in whose German campaigns Velleius himself had served; his flattery, although much criticized by modern scholars, illuminates power relationships in early imperial Rome (compare Source 9.1). Valerius Maximus' *Memorable Doings and Sayings*, dedicated to Tiberius as emperor, preserves many classic Roman vignettes; these include stories that illustrate the power of censors during the Republic, and Cornelia, mother of the Gracchi, identifying her children as her "jewels" (4.4). More obviously practical is the agricultural treatise of Columella (from Gades in Spain), written between 60 and 65 to offer advice on rural labor, crops, vines, managers' duties, and other matters. Pliny the Elder, an *eques* from Comum (modern Como, Italy) who served extensively in the military and died in 79, wrote various specialized works now lost and a 37-volume *Natural History* that survives. Its range is encyclopedic, and its learning quite remarkable, showcasing Roman control and exploitation of the world's peoples, lands, animals, plants and other natural resources, including the rarest and most exotic.

Grammar and rhetoric flourished, as witnessed by Suetonius' treatises devoted to the great teachers of both types of education, by papyri from Egypt preserving school exercises (see further Chapter Ten), and by the books entitled *Controversiae* and *Suasoriae* by Seneca the Elder (father of Seneca the Younger); these he wrote, apparently during the 30s, to report outstanding orators' treatments of set-piece declamations and other rhetorical exercises. Such intellectual endeavors contributed to greater literacy, as did increasing travel and communication, more widespread use of monumental inscriptions, and emperors' encouragement of schools and (in Rome itself) of state libraries. While the vast majority remained illiterate and bound to subsistence labor, still the 15–20 percent of the population estimated to be resident in cities gained greater access to literacy and to an intellectual life than ever before.

"BENEFICIAL IDEOLOGY"

While peace had been gained by Augustus' elimination of his rivals, it was maintained by the threat of force and by a "beneficial ideology." In other words, the Roman emperors were expected to care for their subjects, even if not necessarily to a uniform degree or in every sphere. Of the Julio-Claudians, for example, only Claudius followed Augustus' example of funding construction in the provinces, although the range of his building types and their distribution fell far short of those of Augustus. Claudius also considered it appropriate to legislate for the disadvantaged; for example, his laws bettered the plight of slaves, albeit only slightly. In Rome itself, imperial beneficence was regularly expressed in the provision of cheap food and lavish entertainments for the populace, the "bread and circuses" (*panem et circenses)* made famous by the Roman satirist Juvenal (10.80). Emperors also distributed money, food, and other goods. Even emperors deemed miserly did not entirely neglect such public munificence, as we saw with Tiberius' swift alleviation of the calamity caused by a fire in Rome in 37. Emperors were typically generous with aid to communities struck by disaster.

Imperial liberality touched individuals as well as communities. The Julio-Claudian period, particularly Claudius' Principate, witnessed imperial encouragement of equites and senators from outside of Rome and its immediate environs (see Source 9.2). New entrants to Rome's small ruling elite came from north Italian and provincial cities—the latter in southern France and southern Spain especially, where colonization and settlement by Romans and Italians extended far back to the second century B.C. Rome's expansion had stimulated some upward social and political mobility in the Late Republic. Mobility thereafter resulted not only from the decimation of the nobles at the end of the Republic, but also from Augustus' evolving policy of coopting fresh blood into the Roman elite. The Republican stigma of being a first-generation senator (novus homo) was considerably lessened, although it still had some force, as in Vespasian's case noted above.

The number of equestrian and senatorial offices—the nearest equivalent that Rome had to a bureaucracy—rose in the Julio-Claudian period and faster thereafter, although never to a particularly high level. It is estimated that only between 150 and 350 elite officials oversaw the civilian government in the first century A.D., at most one for every three hundred and fifty to four hundred thousand subjects. Equestrian administrative positions were paid at fixed levels from Augustus' time. The equestrian and senatorial orders had great prestige, although more respect traditionally went to senators. Tacitus (*Annals* 16.17) recounts as a sign of Neronian "perversity" that Seneca's brother Lucius Annaeus Mela chose to remain an eques rather than enter the senate. Mela allegedly believed that he could enrich himself more easily as an eques in the emperor's service, and thereby match the authority of ex-consuls. The imperial freedmen who rose to prominence and extraordinary wealth under Claudius and Nero became the targets of far blunter snobbery. Ability and culture were the prerequisites to success, but even these talents could rarely overcome the stigma of a slave or freedman past. In any case, the political elite of Rome, whatever their origin, made up only a minuscule fraction of the empire's population.

CITIES AND PROVINCES

As established by Augustus, the empire relied not on bureaucracy imposed by the central government, but on communities' self-administration. Throughout Italy and the provinces, local magistrates and councilors were responsible for the collection of taxes, census registration, supply of men for the army when volunteers were lacking, provision of hospitality and transport animals for travelers on official business, and shelter, equipment, and supplies for any military units passing through. Such obligations to the central government coexisted with a high degree of local autonomy. As a general rule, individual cities were left to oversee their own public buildings and cults, the maintenance of their water supply and baths, local law and order, and embassies to Roman officials, including to the Princeps himself.

The empire, which encompassed perhaps fifty to sixty million inhabitants during the first and early second centuries, depended on cities. Achaia, Asia, Crete and Cyrenaica, southern Gaul, and eastern and southern Spain had long been urbanized along their coasts and waterways. Other provinces had different forms of social and political organization. In the interior of Gaul and the Iberian peninsula, for example, warrior elites commanded tribal groups, usually either nomadic or scattered in farmsteads and villages. Between them, Julius Caesar and Augustus established some seventy-five veteran settlements in the provinces, and over forty in Italy. They were located primarily in north Italy, southern Spain, north Africa, coastal Illyricum and Greece, and southern Turkey. In Italy they often supplanted communities that had been on the losing side during the Triumviral period; elsewhere, too, they could be just as disruptive to the local inhabitants. In addition, stationing troops on the borders of the empire encouraged the development of towns there, as well as along the roads leading to them, although such placement of garrisons could cause hardship too, diverting food, timber, and other resources from local populations to the camps.

The new foundations and centers, like older cities in the Roman world, consisted of an urban nucleus and dependent agricultural land. The urban centers were quite small by modern standards. Most had a maximum of only five to fifteen thousand inhabitants, comprising local citizens (including freedmen and freedwomen) and their "families" (including slaves); nonlocal citizens, such as traders; and public slaves and other dependent labor. It was essential that cities govern themselves by some version of the tripartite system traditional to Rome: magistrates, advisory council, and citizen body. Even during the Republic (and sometimes with Rome's direct influence), municipal governments associated with Rome tended towards timocracy, in particular requiring magistrates to possess a certain level of wealth. This trend increased during the Principate. The common basis of landed wealth strengthened the bonds between municipal elites and Roman officials. Yet the urban conglomerations themselves offered various possibilities for financial gain and prestige. In cities, the imperial peace encouraged at least limited social mobility. Freedmen and freedwomen could engage in small businesses and gain some wealth and respectability for their children; as we saw in Chapter Eight, freedmen even could hold a priesthood as *Augustales* (note Figure 9.7 for one such individual). Descendants of former slaves often gained municipal offices and other priesthoods, sometimes even within a generation.

The growing number of cities in the Roman world was made possible not only by peace, but also by the Roman engineering responsible for urban amenities such as a forum, aqueducts, fountains, streets and sidewalks, temples, baths, spectacle buildings like theaters and amphitheaters, and multistoried dwellings. Some of these structures were built when new cities were founded; Agrippa, for example, sponsored the famous Pont du Gard and the entire long aqueduct carrying fresh water to Colonia Augusta Nemausus (modern Nîmes, France; see Figure 10.9). However, our

Figure 9.4 *This funerary monument from Mogontiacum (modern Mainz, Germany) dates to the first century* A.D., *and provides an intriguing tale. A lengthy, roughly metrical inscription is the main focus of this "talking stone," whose ornate top includes motifs relating to the practice of placing flowers and plants at a tomb. The scene below the inscription shows a shepherd, a ram and four sheep, and a dog; two graceful trees add to the bucolic setting. The inscription reads:*

The shepherd Jucundus, freedman of Marcus Terentius. As you pass by, whoever reads this, stop, traveler, and look at how I lament in vain, unworthily snatched away. I could not live more than thirty years, for a slave stole away my life and then threw himself headlong into the river. The Moenus River took from this one [the slave] what he stole from his master [life]. My patron erected this monument with his own funds.

Although on first reading the inscription may seem to demonstrate a patron's affection for his freedman, it can also be interpreted as a means for the patron, Terentius, to proclaim his erudition, wealth, and control of others' lives.

vision of the "typical" Roman city took time to evolve in the provinces (see Chapter Ten). The urban model was Rome itself, upon which Caesar, Augustus, and many subsequent emperors lavished attention. Although by the early third century the empire had attained a degree of urbanization not to be matched again in the West until the nineteenth century, the limitations of its preindustrial technology and science meant that many areas still remained scarcely urbanized. Cities were mostly found along coasts, rivers, and major inland routes. Inaccessible hinterlands were more desolate, and were normally left undisturbed so long as their few inhabitants did not cause problems.

One major type of imperial benefaction initiated by Augustus and resumed by Claudius was the building and maintenance of roads and harbors. Generally speaking, land transport cost at least five times more than water transport, and bulky commodities such as grain, timber, and fine stone were conveyed long distances only for the army or for the city of Rome itself. Yet archeology increasingly documents long-distance trade for luxury and semi-luxury goods too. The technologies essential to blown glass and to highly polished, molded ceramic bowls, lamps, and other pottery objects had been invented by the end of the Republic. In the Augustan peace such technologies disseminated quickly, spreading the availability of these and similar personal items. Once a technology reached a region, regional variations developed. Nonetheless, it is still possible to distinguish a "Roman" material culture. One gauge of an area's Romanization is the proliferation in its graves of Roman-style goods, such as glass perfume bottles, ceramic lamps, iron objects like needles and strigils (curved scraping instruments used for personal hygiene), worked-bone pieces like combs and even dolls, and similar accessories. Such items were bought and exchanged in towns by increasing numbers of individuals who attained status and prestige through various possible types of service to their own communities or to Rome, or both. Even so, as we have already noted, Roman urban culture never extended to the great majority of the empire's inhabitants.

WOMEN

The material remains from the early Principate demonstrate increasing public visibility for women in Rome and in Italian and provincial cities. Although Roman women had long before gained some financial and legal independence (see Chapter Five), the very institution of the Principate, with its stress on family, thrust the imperial women into the limelight. Augustus' sister Octavia and his wife Livia had unprecedented visibility and patronage. Upon Augustus' death, Livia, now renamed Julia Augusta, became the first priestess of the cult of her deified husband *divus Augustus* (see further below on the imperial cult). The newly significant dynastic role of the Julio-Claudian family's women, together with the apparently limitless resources at their disposal (note Plate 7), made them more powerful than most men, and a conceivable threat. Agrippina the Elder, for example, was never allowed to remarry after the death of her husband Germanicus; Tiberius, her *pater familias* as the heir and stepson of Augustus, perhaps feared the influence that her status as Augustus' grandchild would give a second husband. She and other early imperial women tended to stay out of the public eye unless they were appearing in a familial role such as the procession depicted on the Ara Pacis (see Fig. 8.12). Agrippina the Younger was much less retiring (see Fig. 9.3 and Plate 10a), and we find her criticized for such presumptuous behavior as sitting on a tribunal in front of military standards when British prisoners paid homage to Claudius in Rome in 51 (Tacitus, *Annals* 12.37).

Whatever the causes may have been—the example of imperial women perhaps, or Augustus' stress on procreation (see Chapter Eight), not to mention the general increase in opportunities and prosperity offered by the *pax Augusta*—growing numbers of women were now commemorated by statues, relief sculpture, and inscriptions as patronesses of towns or organizations, model wives or priestesses, or both (see Fig. 9.5). Elite women in the cities of Italy and adjacent areas of the Latin West began to hold prestigious

Figure 9.5 *Statue of Eumachia. This statue from Pompeii depicts a woman in the pose and costume of a respectable matron. She modestly shields her chest with her right hand, and covers her head and most of her arms with a heavy cloak. A dedicatory inscription (not shown) reads: "To Eumachia, daughter of Lucius, public priestess of Pompeian Venus, from the fullers." The statue was found in a covered gallery at the back of the 'Building of Eumachia,' a spacious, opulent building donated by Eumachia in the first half of the first century A.D. alongside Pompeii's Forum. An inscription over one entrance confirms that she was the sole benefactor: "Eumachia, daughter of Lucius, public priestess, with her own money and in her own name and that of her son Marcus Numistrius Fronto, built the vestibule, the covered gallery, and the portico, in honor of Augustan Concord and Piety, and dedicated them." We know neither the specific use of the building, nor the source of Eumachia's wealth, although her father's family were noted producers of wine, amphoras, jars, and bricks. Both the rendering of Eumachia herself and the decoration of the building reflect the influence of models to be found in the city of Rome; the same may be said of Eumachia's public generosity and visibility.*

religious positions, as they had already long been doing in cities of the Greek East. Women had now greater mobility too, although it was sometimes contested; only after a long and emotional debate in the senate in 21 were wives of governors given the right to join their husbands in the provinces. Women's activity is also attested for less highly placed individuals; in the New Testament, for example, Paul shows women as important participants in early Christian congregations. Although the number of women celebrated or denounced in various ways never equals that of men, sufficient evidence survives to allow us some insight into this aspect of the rapidly changing social history of the early Principate.

DIVERSITY: LOCAL LANGUAGES AND CULTURE

Despite an increasing similarity of material culture, the empire still retained great diversity. Many different languages were spoken in the various provinces, even though Latin dominated in the army and official correspondence. In the Greek East—the region where already for centuries the common language of educated people had been Greek—Roman administrative correspondence was written in Greek. Instances of parallel texts in Greek and Latin, especially for records of important decisions, are numerous too. We also find bilingual texts apparently aimed at two different audiences (see Fig. 9.6).

Even so, indigenous languages and dialects persisted alongside these official languages for a variety of reasons—communities' autonomy in local affairs, the large number of static rural dwellers on their subsistence farms, the relatively low level of bureaucracy, the uneven spread of the military, and the absence of extensive mass communications. For similar reasons, local cultures remained dynamic, and still maintained a hold even when Roman material culture spread to a region. In Judaea, for example, Aramaic was used in daily transactions, but study of the Bible was usually in Hebrew or Greek. Our understanding of regional and cultural diversities within the empire has notably increased over the last generation, as archeological research and tools have become more sophisticated and sensitive. For instance, faunal bone analysis at excavations in Hungary has revealed the persistence of local diets even after Roman legionary camps were established in Pannonia.

RELIGIOUS PRACTICES AND PRINCIPLES

Rome's diversity, and its limits, are perhaps reflected most strikingly in the wide array of religious beliefs and practices of the polytheistic empire. Such an array reflects an empire gained by military conquest (primarily during the Republic), yet then consolidated and for the most part ruled by the cooption and collaboration of its indigenous peoples during the Principate. Thus the traditional Egyptian zoomorphic gods later decried by Christians as "dog-headed" could be, and were, worshipped with their traditional rites even after Egypt was annexed as a Roman province in 30 B.C. In Gaul, various powerful female

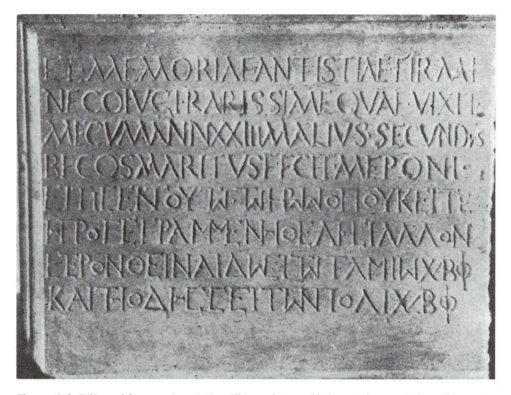

Figure 9.6 *Bilingual funerary inscription. This modest marble inscription comes from Odessus in the province of Lower Moesia (modern Varna, Bulgaria). It probably dates to the second half of the second century* A.D. *The top four lines are in Latin, recording Malius Secundus' installation of the tomb for the departed shades and memory of his "most rare" wife, Antistia Firmina. Malius also specifies here that he is a special attendant on a man of consular standing. The bottom four lines, in Greek, state the financial penalties payable to the treasurer and people of Odessus by anyone who should have the temerity to place another body in the tomb. The two texts are saying quite different things, therefore. As the husband of a properly dutiful "Roman" wife and the holder of a desirable military position, Malius begins with Latin to impress others like him with his control of resources and his assimilation of Roman ways. The use of Greek for the subsequent warning implies that the local population, on the west coast of the Black Sea, was more familiar with Greek than Latin.*

deities, often called "mothers," were venerated alongside other gods less alien to the Romans, such as Jupiter sky gods. Silvanus, a god of the woodlands, was worshipped in the heavily forested areas of the northern empire. In Achaia and Asia the customary Olympian gods received dedications and temples, some even from Roman emperors. The famed oracle of Apollo at Claros (Asia) figured among the sites that Germanicus toured, and later in the first century oracles revived powerfully, continuing to thrive into the third century. Hero cults revived too, like that of Achilles on the shores of the Black Sea. The ancestral

Figure 9.7 *This votive relief of the late second or early third century is dedicated to the Nutrices, protective "nursing" deities found in many northern provinces. The relief comes from a well-attested shrine in Poetovio, Pannonia (modern Ptuj, Slovenia), and is damaged on its upper right and lower left corners. On the right is a Nutrix, seated on a low chair; she holds a baby in swaddling clothes to her left breast. To her right is an altar over which a woman holds a naked child; this toddler rests its left leg on the altar, and extends its arms towards the Nutrix. At the relief's left edge, a woman (perhaps a servant) in a long dress holds on her head a basket with two ribbons. Below the image, an inscription states in Latin: "Sacred to the Augustan Nutrices. Lucius Fuscinius Exsuperatus, Augustalis of the colony of Poetovio, and Aelia Honorata, discharged the vow made for the health of their son, Fuscinius Honoratus." The cult of the Nutrices is apparently Celtic in origin. The description of Poetovio's Nutrices as "Augustan" reflects one means by which local cults were linked to the imperial house. The strength of this cult at Poetovio during the Principate suggests high infant and childhood mortality in the area, an all-too-common phenomenon in antiquity.*

gods of the hearth were venerated in Italy, and deities without images received
worship in the interior of Asia.

Testimony to this great diversity of gods, deities, and religious experience
comes from inscriptions, shrines and temples, literature, paintings and other visual arts, coins, and the like. Although some of the evidence may appear remarkably pious, in fact we have merely the vestiges of individual and communal
religious activity. It is impossible now to gauge the depth of anyone's belief.
However, there is no doubting the apparent ease with which many individuals
participated in disparate religious practices, nor the wide range of religious dedications, even within a single town or sanctuary. This latter phenomenon was
aided by what Romans termed *interpretatio*, the assertion of some form of equiv-
alence between a foreign deity and a Roman one (as with Mars Belena). Romans
and their subjects could believe as they pleased, so long as they did not actively
reject religious rituals that had been made part of the state religion. In some
instances syncretism occurred, as when a local deity or abstraction had
"Augustan" added to its name (see Fig. 9.7).

In general, no belief was forced on citizens or subjects. Instead, Rome often
accepted a foreign deity and rites even after recognizing its distinctive alien
nature. This acceptance might occur after the ceremony of *evocatio*, by which the
Romans called upon a deity to desert his or her town (as Juno from Veii in the
early fourth century B.C.), or following a decision by the *quindecimviri sacris faciundis*, the board of fifteen men in charge of ritual observances (as when the
Magna Mater was brought to Rome in 204 B.C.; see Chapter Three). But not all
non-Roman gods became part of the state religion. In some instances we know of
a deity simply because some soldier or local notable spontaneously recorded a
dedication.

The few exceptions to the Romans' generally tolerant polytheism arose when
a religion seemed to pose a political threat. For example, since Druidism functioned as a source of resistance to Rome in Gaul and Britain, Claudius and his
successors apparently undertook to extirpate it, killing its priests and priestesses and destroying Druid shrines. Judaism, with its exclusively monotheistic
belief, gave continuing problems because of the number of its adherents, their
spread throughout the Roman world, their strict lifestyle, and the antiquity of
their doctrines. Various accommodations were reached, as when Claudius
issued a special edict in favor of the Jews of Alexandria, and a general one guaranteeing Jews throughout the empire the undisturbed practice of their religion.
But such arrangements would fail to prevent three successive Jewish revolts
(see Chapter Ten).

The Christians, who first came to notice under Tiberius, ultimately posed an
even more intractable problem. Roman authorities and intellectuals did not
know what to make of this new religion. Like Jews, Christians were exclusively
monotheistic, and they included the Jewish Old Testament among their sacred
books. The earliest Christian adherents came from the Jewish geographical and

social world. But Christians distinguished themselves from Jews. Initially, therefore, Romans considered the new religion to be simply a sect of Judaism but without the authority of antiquity, much like the sects documented by the Dead Sea Scrolls or other contemporary evidence. Thus the debate about Jesus Christ was seen as a dispute of merely local concern. According to the earliest accounts of Jesus' life and death, the governor of Judaea, Pontius Pilatus, did not know what to do with the man denounced to him as a popular and potentially dangerous religious leader. Following a tumultuous examination rather than a formal trial, Pilate decided to have him executed, apparently capitulating to traditional Roman fears of subversive provincials and to pressure from the Jewish authorities and the crowd. After his death, the religion mostly dropped from Rome's official consciousness. The growing body of Christian literature seems to have been completely unknown to writers in Rome, and when Pliny, Suetonius, and Tacitus mention Christ and Christians, they are confused and puzzled.

Christian monotheism, however, was sharply at odds with the polytheism prevalent throughout the empire. Thus Nero fixed on the Christians when he needed a scapegoat after the great fire of Rome of 64. His brutality created some of Christianity's first martyrs, possibly including St. Peter, and unintentionally strengthened the new religion. By around 120, key features of Christianity had taken shape—an organized priesthood; the scriptures or sacred writings; an insistence on revelation (Jesus was revealed as Christ, "the anointed one" or God, and the scriptures were revealed to the faithful); initiation at baptism and subsequent stages; and a belief in salvation and the afterlife. The Epistles of Paul and the Gospel of Mark were probably written between 50 and the 70s, and by 130 the other scriptures were completed. The roughly contemporary Book of Revelation and slightly earlier Dead Sea Scrolls similarly manifest the religious ferment of Judaea and the Greek East. Christianity spread in cities before the countryside, as indicated by the name "pagan" used for non-Christians (*paganus* denotes someone from the countryside). But we should always bear in mind that during the early Principate Christianity was merely one of what may now seem a bewildering number of religions.

IMPERIAL CULT

Christianity, Judaism, and a few other monotheistic religions aside, the imperial cult cut across all the varied beliefs and practices. This religious and societal phenomenon provided one of the strongest unifying forces for the diverse Roman empire. Imperial cult could be practiced on the personal level: Ovid in exile (*Letters from Pontus* 4.9) claims to have offered incense and prayers daily at a "shrine of Caesar" in his house. This shrine included images of Augustus, Livia (now priestess of the deified Augustus), Tiberius, and other imperial family members. Since the cult was principally public, however, there is much fuller evidence for it at the municipal and provincial levels and at Rome itself.

Roman imperial cult evolved from Hellenistic Greek and Republican Roman precedents and, like them, it was intrinsically tied to military and political power. Beginning with Alexander the Great, dominant kings (and later their queens) had commanded cults with temples or altars, priests, public sacrifices, and games—visible signs, in short, of their unmistakable power over their subjects. Rituals were enacted periodically at the cities where the shrines stood (see Chapter Two). As Rome became involved in the Greek East from the end of the third century B.C., certain Roman generals received extraordinary, quasi-divine honors there to mark their popularity or military success. In the West, too, leading figures could find it advantageous to exploit divine associations: Marius had sought guidance from a Syrian prophetess, Martha, and Sertorius gained inspiration from a white doe (see Chapter Six). In Rome itself great charisma accrued to triumphing generals, who were dressed like the Capitoline statue of Jupiter Optimus Maximus as they paraded through Rome on a chariot pulled by four white horses. Increasingly during the last century of the Republic, the senators responsible for minting featured heroic ancestors in the designs for their coins. Julius Caesar advanced his claim to be descended from the goddess Venus both on coins and by building a temple to her in his new Forum in Rome. In what was to be the last year of his life, Caesar even had a temple for himself authorized by the senate, and Antony appointed as his priest (although these measures were never implemented). Later, the people of Rome spontaneously established a shrine where Caesar's body had been cremated in the Forum; the appearance of a meteor shortly thereafter reinforced the belief that he had ascended to heaven. The authority of the Triumvirs, and of Octavian in particular, was boosted when the senate eventually ratified Caesar's deification early in 42 B.C.

Designation as "son of a god" (*divi filius*) was only one of many divine associations that Octavian assumed over time, despite discouraging any cult that seemed too closely tied to his own person (see Chapter Eight). His position as *pontifex maximus* after 12 B.C. placed him as intermediary between the Roman people and the gods. Thereafter each Princeps until Gratian in the late fourth century took this leading priesthood on accession. The divinity that the senate ratified for Augustus after his death was only one of many such posthumous honors. These tributes, as well as an apparently more personalized cult, spread rapidly. In 15 the province of Tarraconensis successfully sought permission to establish a temple and *flamen* (priest devoted to a specific deity) to Divus Augustus in Tarraco (modern Tarragona, Spain). Although the senate had to give its permission, the emperor was also consulted—as demonstrated by a letter from Tiberius to Gythium in southern Greece concerning its measures honoring the deified Augustus, Tiberius himself, and his mother Livia. Even so, at this early date it was evidently the senate's permission that was essential before a city or provincial assembly could add imperial cult rituals to its public religious ceremonies. These rituals involved the apotheosis of dead emperors and veneration of the living one, specifically prayers for his preservation.

The imperial cult spread after Augustus. Although Tiberius steadfastly refused the organization of any cults to himself and was not deified after his death, Gaius assiduously pursued religious associations, as noted earlier in this chapter. Claudius promoted Livia's deification by the senate; he, too, was deified (see Plate 10a). Later the emperor Vespasian was to quip on his death bed, "Dear me! I must be turning into a god!" (Suetonius, *Vespasian* 23) Activities identified with the imperial cult will be discussed in the following chapter. Here, however, it is important to stress Rome's incipient imperial cult as an expression of the ambiguous relationship between the Princeps and his subjects. Individual cities and provincial assemblies voluntarily petitioned for permission to profess, through public rituals, their homage to the living emperor. Especially in its early stages, the cult often matched the emperor with Rome itself, whose personification as a female warrior underscores the military basis of the empire. It was common to assimilate emperors and members of their families to gods by pose or by attributes added to representations (note Figs. 9.1 and 11.4), or by coupling their name to that of another deity (Fig. 9.7). As "good" emperors and their relatives were deified at their deaths, their veneration too was included in a community's rituals. Gold and silver images of them were added to the processions, for example, and animals were sacrificed on their behalf as *divi*. When the senate authorized a community's establishment of an imperial cult, it ostensibly claimed its customary role in power negotiations. At the same time, however, members of the senate were demonstrating their compliance with the extraordinary and superhuman domination of Augustus and his successors.

SUGGESTED READINGS:

Barrett, Anthony A. 1990. *Caligula: The Corruption of Power*. New Haven and London: Yale University Press.

Champlin, Edward. 2003. *Nero*. Cambridge, Mass., and London: Harvard University Press. A provocative attempt to interpret Nero's extreme behavior as highly intelligent and calculated to appeal to widespread social attitudes of the time.

Erdkamp, Paul. 2005. *The Grain Market in the Roman Empire: A Social, Political and Economic Study*. Cambridge: Cambridge University Press.

Erdkamp, Paul (ed.). 2007. *A Companion to the Roman Army*. Malden, Mass., and Oxford: Blackwell.

Greene, Kevin. 1986. *The Archaeology of the Roman Economy*. Berkeley, Los Angeles, London: University of California Press.

Harl, Kenneth W. 1996. *Coinage in the Roman Economy, 300 B.C. to A.D. 700*. Baltimore: Johns Hopkins University Press.

Lefkowitz, Mary R., and Maureen B. Fant, (eds.). 1992 (second edition). *Women's Life in Greece and Rome*. Baltimore: Johns Hopkins University Press.

Levick, Barbara. *Tiberius the Politician*. 1999 (new edition). London and New York: Routledge.

Levick, Barbara. *Claudius*. 1990. New Haven and London: Yale University Press.

Oleson, John P. (ed.). 2008. *The Oxford Handbook of Engineering and Technology in the Classical World*. Oxford: Oxford University Press.

Price, Simon R.F. 1984. *Rituals and Power: The Roman Imperial Cult in Asia Minor*. Cambridge: Cambridge University Press. Despite its focus on Asia Minor, this book is of wider significance for understanding the imperial cult.

Rowe, Greg. 2002. *Princes and Political Cultures: The New Tiberian Senatorial Decrees*. Ann Arbor: University of Michigan Press.

10

INSTITUTIONALIZATION
OF THE PRINCIPATE

*Military Expansion and Its Limits,
the Empire and the Provinces (69–138)*

SOURCES

Although we lack a continuous historical narrative for this period (Cassius Dio exists only in excerpts after 46), many authors provide extended analysis of individual aspects. Suetonius' imperial biographies continue through the death of Domitian. Pliny the Younger, Suetonius' contemporary and friend, offers many details about the lives of senators and *equites* in his ten books of letters. Moreover, his tenth book—correspondence he exchanged with Trajan while serving as a special imperial legate in the province of Bithynia-Pontus around 111—offers invaluable insights into provincial administration, relationships between emperor and official, and the province itself. Josephus' *Jewish War* has special significance because the author, a prominent Jew, was personally involved; he led his fellow countrymen against the Romans before defecting to the Roman side and ultimately receiving Roman citizenship from Vespasian. Pausanias, Plutarch, and lesser known writers reveal the concerns of Rome's intelligentsia in both Latin West and Greek East over such matters as ethics and philosophy, image and standing in one's own city, and the proper relationship with Roman power. Early Christian writings also grapple with this last question, among matters more directly relevant to the new religion. But Rome itself still dominates in most literature, in contrast to the subsequent period when authors such as Apuleius and Tertullian focus more on local problems and politics.

The first part of the chapter weaves together military and civil topics, looking specifically at military expansion and its limits, and at the relationship of the central government to the provinces. Our understanding of social and cultural history,

347

the subject of the second part of the chapter, is advanced by documentary and material evidence. The era's relatively abundant inscriptions give us a fuller picture of individuals' lives, careers, hopes, and aspirations. Public inscriptions illustrate the nature of imperial power and local governance. From the latter half of the first century and from the second come astonishing archeological finds, such as those at Pompeii and other Campanian sites buried by the eruption of the volcano Vesuvius in 79. The assembled data reveal growing urbanization through the early third century. This development seems tied to the "beneficial ideology" of the Principate, which held that the emperor both demonstrated his aptitude for the position and justified his *auctoritas* through his generosity (see Chapter Nine). In the later first and second century, such benefits often went to cities other than Rome itself. It is striking that the benefactions by Hadrian listed at a shrine in Athens are gifts of all types (temples especially) to non-Roman cities (Pausanias 1.5.5).

Other evidence for increased attention to Rome's provinces comes in ever more frequent imperial grants of the city status of *municipium* and *colonia*, and in military attention to peripheral regions such as the Danube lands. Both steps spurred the growth of cities. Yet they and more well-established ones could flourish only with surplus wealth dependent on Roman peace and the conquests of Trajan. Peace made possible the preoccupation with local priorities such as civic rivalry (often tied to the imperial cult), the exaltation of a glorious past in the Second Sophistic, and other cultural activities. These features were particularly notable in North Africa and the Greek East. But the picture should not be construed too positively, for as the Principate became more institutionalized it also took some steps towards autocracy. The delicate balance between beneficial paternalism and harmful interference surfaces in this chapter, and will emerge more clearly thereafter.

INSTITUTIONALIZATION OF THE PRINCIPATE

One of the earliest and starkest signs of the Principate's institutionalization is the law now called the *lex de imperio Vespasiani*, passed some time in 69–70. A substantial part of it—specifying various powers and rights of the emperor—survives on a bronze inscription now in Rome's Capitoline Museum. Ratified by the Roman people upon presentation by the senate, this law indicates the continuing significance both of popular support for the Princeps and of concern for Rome's governmental processes. Yet it also makes clear that the emperor's authority was no longer a nebulous auctoritas centered on the individual himself (as with Augustus) or on family loyalty (as with the Julio-Claudians). Rather, the document clearly defines various powers and prerogatives, justifying them by specific imperial precedent. Here we may note both Romans' respect for their past and their pragmatism; this law made custom binding. From now onwards, when the senate and people of Rome ratified the choice of a Princeps, not only was an individual being approved, but also the powers that he could legally wield. The lex de imperio Vespasiani seems to have been passed before Vespasian actually

Figure 10.1 *This relief, and a counterpart (not shown), both about 7 ft/2 m tall, once decorated an altar base and are known as the "Cancelleria reliefs" from their find spot in Rome; they are now in the Vatican Museum. Here we see Vespasian's arrival in Rome in 70; he is the first full figure on our right. With his right hand he touches his son, Domitian, who had been in Rome during the civil strife of the previous year. Behind and flanking Domitian stand two personifications, the "genius" of the senate (a mature, bearded man) and the "genius" of the Roman people (a youth with a cornucopia). Secular power is symbolized by the leftmost figure seen here, a lictor with fasces, the bundle of rods signifying the power of the magistrate he accompanies. Further to our left (but not shown here) stand the goddess Roma, personified as a female warrior with her right breast bared like an Amazon's, and a Vestal virgin. Domitian's central position in this scene, which commemorates Rome's unanimous welcome of the Flavians and stresses their civilian roles by depicting them in togas, is one reason why the reliefs are dated to the 80s (he became emperor in 81).*

arrived in Rome in October 70. That sequence contrasts with the timing of earlier constitutional innovations like Caesar's novel powers in 46–44, or the prerogatives granted to Augustus in 27 and again in 23 B.C., when extraordinary laws were passed in the presence of the new, indisputable leader.

Another sign of the institutionalization of the Principate is the adoption of *Imperator* by Vespasian and subsequent emperors as a first name (*praenomen*). As such, it now becomes a mark of the office held by the emperor. Imperator originally designated a man who legally held *imperium*, the right of life and death over Roman citizens first expressed in military contexts. It is hard for us to determine whether or not its use now as a personal name should be taken to mark a renewed consciousness of the military basis of imperial power.

The Principate's civil underpinnings were reestablished by a greater use of senators and equites, rather than freedmen, in the imperial service. This change, perhaps induced by loathing for Claudius' presumptuous freedmen and Nero's toadies, sent a clear signal that to rule the Roman world was not the exclusive prerogative of one individual or family. Added involvement of equites and senators in administration began with Vespasian and gained momentum in the second century. More subjects than ever actively participated in their own government, filling a quantity of prestigious positions hierarchically arranged. This social and political mobility seemed to confirm the Augustan ideal that equestrian and senatorial posts—from the prefecture of a cohort to administration of a great province like Asia—were open to any man of good birth, merit, and the requisite financial standing.

Such upward mobility was tied to the emperor's advancement of individuals to magistracies and special posts, one of the rights specified in the lex de imperio Vespasiani. Vespasian used this right most strikingly during the censorship that he held jointly with his elder son Titus in 73. Between them, they restored the senate to its former total of 600 from a low of about 200 caused by Nero's treason trials and the civil war of 68–69. As a further enhancement of prestige, the emperor could also bestow patrician status. To judge by inscriptions and other evidence, many of the "new men" in the Flavian senate came, as before, from north Italy and the nearer western provinces, especially Narbonese Gaul and Spain. By the end of the first century, Rome also saw senators whose hometowns were in North Africa, Greece, or Asia. The newcomers, like Pliny the Younger (from Comum), Tacitus (from Cisalpine or Narbonese Gaul), and Marcus Ulpius Trajanus (father of the later emperor Trajan, from Italica in southern Spain), were typically quick to embrace such traditional Roman values as service to the state (*virtus*) and thrift.

At the same time, imperial promotion of senators and equites, and increased use of both orders in administration, tightened the ties of imperial patronage even while sustaining the new political institutions. Pliny the Younger can exemplify the deference created by such a system. His *Panegyricus* is an expanded version of the customary speech of thanks that he delivered to Trajan in the senate in 100 on the occasion of taking up the consulship. Most modern readers, however, find it unbearably sycophantic. The many letters exchanged later between Pliny and Trajan about the affairs of Bithynia-Pontus betray similar insecurity concerning the boundaries between the powers of imperial functionaries and those of emperor (see further Chapter Eleven and Source 11.5).

Another gauge of the Principate's institutionalization is the spread of the imperial cult, which is explored at the end of the chapter. The second half of the first century witnesses the appearance of more priests and priestesses of the cult in cities and in regional or provincial gatherings in Asia, Spain, Gaul, and (more rarely) North Africa and elsewhere. Vespasian was ready enough to exploit others' superstitions in his rise to power, although he had few illusions about his own mortality and human failings.

Much of Vespasian's imperial imagery, especially on coins, marks him as the founder of a new Rome, and as a new Romulus. There is some truth to the latter identification: Vespasian was first and foremost a military man, like Romulus the son of Mars. Further, Vespasian struck a royal note in his commitment to dynastic succession, declaring to the senate: "Either my sons succeed me, or nobody" (Suetonius, *Vespasian* 25). His willingness to make this regal claim, which Augustus had studiously avoided, signals increasing acceptance of the Principate and its monarchical base. Although dynastic succession was resented by some—especially Stoics, Cynics, and traditionally minded senators—Vespasian's legacy of imperial power to his two sons, Titus and Domitian, ensured political continuity for twenty-seven years. Moreover, the underlying organization of the Principate was not to change for the next century. It allowed for much discretion on the part of the Princeps. When an emperor conformed to the role of first among equals, more or less as did Trajan and Vespasian, the government ran smoothly at all levels. But when rulers like the harsh Domitian and the aloof Hadrian were less concerned to mask their power, friction arose between the emperor and his notional peers, the senatorial and equestrian orders. How much impact such unhappiness made on the wider Roman world, however, it is difficult to discern. Material and documentary evidence indicates a generally rising prosperity in this period.

VESPASIAN (69–79)

Vespasian was an unpretentious man from Reate in north-central Italy. His family, the Flavii, had been respectable tax gatherers and custom agents of equestrian rank, with none of its members ever advancing to the senate before his elder brother and himself. Vespasian's special strength was his military acumen, demonstrated outstandingly in Germany, Britain, and Judaea. It was through the army that he came to power. His talents as a civilian leader, on the other hand, were unknown. Yet both aspects of the imperial position were demanded in 70. The Jewish and Germano-Gallic revolts had still to be suppressed, while Rome and Italy meantime needed to regain normalcy after the destructive civil strife there.

The first problem that Vespasian had to face was the Jewish revolt, also known as the First Jewish War (66–73). The Jews conducted their desperate struggle against the Romans as a kind of guerilla war, and within the Jewish population there was much dissension, especially between Pharisees and Sadducees. The revolt had not yet been completely crushed when Vespasian, who had been sent to Judaea by Nero, was declared emperor by his troops with the support of Gaius Licinius Mucianus, the governor of Syria. Vespasian left Titus, his eldest son, as his legate in charge in Judaea; he and Mucianus departed for Rome, he via Alexandria and Egypt, Mucianus by the northern route. In 70 Titus stormed Jerusalem. To the Romans, the destruction of its great Temple signaled the end of the revolt, although pockets of resistance held out a few years longer. Of these, Masada is the most famous, thanks to Josephus' dramatic account (*Jewish War* 7.9. 389–406), and the enduring symbolic importance of the site. Its Herodian palace-fortress fell only in 73, after the self-immolation of almost every one of the 390 men, women, and children besieged there for years by the Romans.

The revolt was extremely damaging for the Jews. It decimated Judaea's population, and in Jerusalem caused the deaths of the High Priests and the destruction of their Holy of Holies. Worship and sacrifice ceased at the site of the Temple. From now onwards, the tax previously paid to the Temple was earmarked for the temple of Jupiter Optimus Maximus in Rome. Jews were prohibited from proselytizing to gain new converts. A few concessions were made, however, in recognition of the antiquity of the Jewish religion; those born in the faith could worship in it, and Jews were evidently not forced to participate in the imperial cult. The suppression of this Jewish revolt furthered the Jewish diaspora and contributed to the distinction of Christians from Jews.

More immediately important for Vespasian, the fall of Jerusalem furnished the occasion for a huge triumph in Rome, lasting thirty days. This celebration advertised that Vespasian and his family had restored order in the Roman world; it simultaneously diverted attention from the bloodshed in Italy and Rome that had accompanied his accession. To exhibit the booty seized from the Jews as well as the public statuary reclaimed from Nero's private appropriations, Vespasian built

---

Facing page

Figure 10.2 *The triumphal procession of Vespasian and Titus in 71 (see Josephus,* Jewish War *7.121–158) was memorialized in various relief panels on the marble Arch of Titus. Since the main arch also contains a panel depicting the apotheosis of Titus (not shown), its completion must postdate his death in 81. Here we see part of the triumphal procession as it goes into Rome through an ornate city gate or arch. Soldiers wearing laurel wreaths (the symbol of victory) carry litters on which are displayed some of the booty seized in Jerusalem: (left to right) a menorah, the table of the Shewbread, and the silver trumpets. The placards carried by the soldiers may originally have offered painted identifications of the booty, or of the military units responsible for the victory. Such displays would precede the triumphing general himself, who was in a special chariot drawn by four white horses. The lower panel represents Titus as* triumphator, *but substitutes Roma (left) and allegorical figures for some of his escorts.*

the Temple of Peace on land in central Rome previously appropriated by Nero's Golden House. Nearby he started the great amphitheater known today as the Colosseum, paying for it with booty (presumably from Jerusalem and Judaea), and using Jewish slaves as laborers (as newly found inscriptions indicate). He embarked on other huge building projects that emphasized peace, Jupiter Optimus Maximus, and his own role as re-founder of the city and state.

In 69–70 Vespasian also had to attend to the Germano-Gallic revolt. It had developed from Vindex's revolt against Nero in 68 and the ensuing civil war. After Vitellius and his supporters had marched most of the eight legions from the German border towards Rome, the Gallic chieftain Gaius Julius Civilis roused the local tribes and locally-recruited auxiliary soldiers. The German tribes, the first to rebel, were quickly joined by Gallic ones. Although the insurrection was quelled by spring 70, it plainly demonstrated the perils of recruiting men locally to serve as auxiliary soldiers in their native areas. The Flavian emperors now ended this practice, as well as breaking up large concentrations of troops such as the eight legions stationed in close proximity along the Rhine. By Domitian's death in 96, a policy of stretching out legionaries and auxiliaries along Rome's borders had been implemented. In addition, legionary recruitment was extended from Italy alone to Roman citizens in Gaul and Spain too. Discharge certificates (*diplomata*) and other documents suggest that it now became standard practice to station individuals other than where they had been recruited, although exceptions still occurred. These military policies helped to counteract the centrifugal force of regionalism in the empire, as did the use of Latin as the official language of the army everywhere.

In line with Vespasian's military background, the Flavian emperors attended to Rome's borders and troops by other means too. Domitian involved himself personally in such activity much more than his father and his elder brother, Titus, perhaps because he came to power without having gained close familiarity with the troops. Under Vespasian and Domitian, and again in the second century, attempts were made to acquire and fortify the re-entrant angle between the upper Rhine and the Danube: Roman control of this area, the so-called *Agri Decumates*, would allow troops to move more swiftly between Rhine and Danube. In Gallia Belgica (probably around 90), Domitian differentiated two new provinces along the Rhine, Germania Superior and Germania Inferior (Upper and Lower Germany), so as to separate this more militarized zone from the civilian populations farther west and south. Also during Domitian's rule, the Romans advanced farther into Britain under the leadership of Gnaeus Julius Agricola, in campaigns documented in his biography written by his son-in-law Tacitus. The Danube region was more problematic. During Nero's Principate, after a governor of Moesia had complained of encountering previously unknown enemies, Rome established diplomatic relations with the Dacians and other tribes of the region. Our limited sources indicate that Roman goodwill gestures included settling 100,000 Transdanubian men, women, and children within the province of Moesia. The area was not fully pacified, however, and the lower Danube called for renewed attention from Domitian.

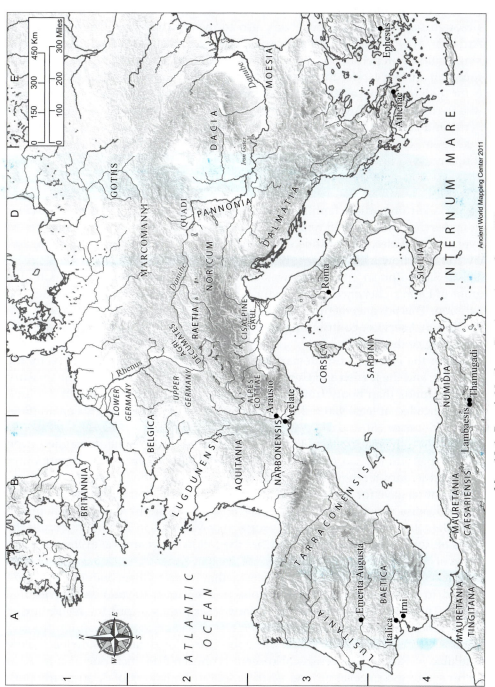

Map 10.1 *Rome's Northern Provinces Around* A.D. 100

Ancient World Mapping Center 2011

Vespasian and his sons also consolidated affairs in the East (Map 10.2). Citing continued discontent in Judaea, they increased the number of troops in Syria, although part of their purpose was also to oversee the Roman protectorate of Armenia. This "client kingdom" was experiencing incursions from tribes that its king could not repel. In addition, Parthia, southeast of Armenia, was a constant source of anxiety. Under the Flavians many roads were built in the East, primarily for military purposes like guarding the crossings of the Euphrates. Cappadocia was garrisoned. In 72 Vespasian annexed Commagene as part of the province of Syria, and Lesser Armenia as part of the province of Cappadocia.

One source of Vespasian's success was his ability to balance military and civil concerns. He and his sons gave "Latin" status (*ius Latii*) to about 350 cities in the Iberian peninsula. This privilege, which recognized the communities as Latin *municipia*, offered Roman citizenship to individuals who undertook local magistracies; their immediate families gained the same status too. Although the communities themselves could retain the styles of self-government they had evolved over the centuries, the various extant city charters documenting the change of civic status show a strong assimilation of local laws and procedures to those at Rome. Since Roman citizenship was considered advantageous at this date, the grant of Latin rights encouraged individuals to assume positions in local administration. This advancement then opened the way for local notables to move into the imperial service, contributing to the renewal of the system discussed at the beginning of the chapter.

Under the Flavians, a fresh start was essential. The extravagance of Nero, the civil war, and the Jewish and Germano-Gallic revolts had all drained the treasury of more funds than booty from Judaea could repay. Vespasian himself declared that he needed at least 400 million sesterces to set the state to rights again (Suetonius, *Vespasian* 16), and one of his first acts was to rescind the tax exemption that Nero had granted to Achaia. Flavian public building at Rome demanded even more expenditure. Also costly were benefactions like Vespasian's exemption of most elementary teachers from the civic burden of billeting troops, and the endowment he gave for two professorships of Greek and Roman rhetoric at Rome. Titus likewise provided funds to alleviate the catastrophe caused to Pompeii, Herculaneum, and environs by the eruption of Vesuvius in 79, and to rebuild the areas of Rome destroyed by a major fire the following year. One of the few criticisms of Vespasian reflected in the literary sources targets his avaricious desire for income regardless of its origin. The census that he and Titus conducted in 73–74 helped to ensure a soundly based collection of taxes throughout the Roman world. Their work was far-reaching. Many inscriptions record the restitution of public lands to communities. Pliny the Elder's exact numbers of communities and buildings in his *Natural History* reflect the extent of detailed knowledge now available at Rome. This census also seems connected to such documents as an archive plan, on marble, of land distribution at the colony of Arausio (modern Orange, France).

All of this work helps to account for Vespasian's high standing in the ancient sources. Peace was restored. Although taxes were raised, they were assessed and collected less capriciously than under Nero. In turn, Roman rule dispensed benefactions such as road building or repair. Vespasian himself was accessible, hardworking, modest, and diligent in his attention to the senate and the state. At the same time, the monarchical foundation of the Principate was plainly strengthened by the institutionalizing processes discussed above. Vespasian banished philosophers and astrologers, and the resistance by Stoics and Cynics to his open dynastic intent led to at least one expulsion of Stoics from the senate. The year 75 even saw the execution of the Stoic senator Helvidius Priscus, who had survived a moral stand against Nero. The powers accruing to Vespasian help to account for the autocratic rule of his younger son, Domitian.

TITUS (79–81)

Before Domitian, however, his elder brother Titus was to serve as Princeps for no more than two years. Despite sporadic opposition to Vespasian, on his death in 79 the dynastic principle helped ensure Titus' succession. Titus was well groomed for the position. He had taken a leading role in the suppression of the Jewish revolt, and by 79 he had served as Praetorian Prefect, consul seven times, and censor. He held tribunican power and *maius imperium* every year after 70. He was popular and proven by experience when the senate and people ratified his position as Princeps after his father's death; moreover, once emperor he demonstrated Roman dutifulness by renouncing his mistress Berenice, a descendant of Herod the Great, who had joined him in Rome after the Jewish revolt. Titus' unexpectedly brief tenure of power is marked by two disasters: the eruption of Mount Vesuvius in 79, and a devastating fire in Rome in 80. In good imperial fashion, he worked immediately to mitigate losses. Further, signaling a desire for a smooth relationship with Rome's upper orders, he banished informers from the city and refused to hear *maiestas* cases. What else he would have accomplished, however, will never be known, because he died prematurely and still unmarried in 81.

DOMITIAN (81–96)

Power passed smoothly to Vespasian's younger son, Domitian, with strong Praetorian backing that was encouraged by a distribution of 1,200 sesterces to each Guardsman. Domitian differed from his father and brother in many ways. He had no military experience, and he had held few positions in Rome other than six consulships that all seem to have been sinecures. Compared to Titus, he had been ignored; there had been no expectation that he would ever become emperor. Once he was, he somehow never gained the self-confidence or the patience to develop a satisfactory working relationship with the senate. In part, the alienation resulted from his tactless accumulation of offices. From 82 through 88 he held the consulship every year, and in 84–85 he became "perpetual censor." His neglect or contempt for the senate contrasts with his devotion to the army and his concern for the people of Rome and the provinces.

Many in Rome's highest circles were estranged by Domitian. Although he seduced his niece Julia and caused her death by a forced abortion, in his censorial role he had three Vestal virgins executed for immorality, and subsequently had another Vestal entombed alive. He was supposedly suspicious to the point of lining the walls of his palace with mirrors of dark, highly polished marble veneer. He encouraged treason trials, hearing cases both privately and in the senate. Tacitus and others who lived through his rule speak of the servility they assumed, and the fear they felt of their peers and potential informers. Early in 89 Lucius Antonius Saturninus, commander of the troops in Upper Germany, led a conspiracy against Domitian. Although it was quickly suppressed by Marcus Ulpius Trajanus (the future emperor Trajan) and the legion under his command, Domitian's relations with the senate deteriorated sharply thereafter. Adherents of Stoic philosophy were banned and even put to death. By 93, Domitian apparently insisted on being addressed as *dominus et deus* ("lord and god"), and another unsuccessful conspiracy occurred. He wore triumphal costume in the senate, offending traditional sensibilities. These actions and others that emphasized his supreme prerogatives shattered the illusion that the Princeps was first among equals. Yet the length of Domitian's rule indicates that he had an inner circle of support among senators and equites—the senators including the two men who in turn would succeed him as Princeps, not to mention rising "new men" like Tacitus and Pliny.

Domitian's power rested not only on such supporters and his family's general popularity, but also on continuing approval by the populace of Rome and the troops. In Rome itself, Domitian intensified the building and reconstruction programs initiated by his father and brother, providing work for many. He added two teams, the Gold and Purple, to the existing four in the popular chariot races. His "Capitolia," Greek-style games with musical, equestrian, and athletic events first celebrated in Rome in 86, added to his heavy expenditures. These increased further when he raised legionaries' annual pay by as much as one-third (to 1,200 sesterces). Beginning in 83, he embarked on campaigns across the Rhine, for which he received the honorific name Germanicus. He crossed the central Danube to attack the Quadi and Marcomanni to its north; farther east he went into Dacia. As the first emperor since Claudius to go on campaign personally, Domitian reasserted the military character of the Principate. He was generally successful; by 88, despite initial setbacks, Roman forces had defeated the Dacian king Decebalus.

Military support, however, did not make Domitian's autocratic style any more acceptable. His increasing paranoia turned him against many senators, and finally his own family. In 95, he killed his great-nephew Flavius Clemens, Clemens' wife, and others on charges of "atheism" (perhaps for Christian practices, although this is uncertain). The conspiracy that killed him the following year may have involved his wife Domitia (daughter of Nero's great general, Corbulo), as well as the two Praetorian Prefects. Even Rome's city populace was allegedly not stirred by the news of his assassination.

A NEW, BETTER ERA?

Domitian's death in 96 ushered in an era which would last to 180, and later be praised by the eighteenth-century English historian Edward Gibbon as "the period in the history of the world, during which the condition of the human race was most happy and prosperous." All the emperors of this period made a point of deferring to their peers, who gained more marks of status. Ever more responsible administration was linked to peace and prosperity; child support schemes, seemingly aimed at bettering the lives of those of lower status, were established; urbanization was liberally encouraged; and the judicial system was standardized. The period was free of the state-ordered persecutions of Christians that were to scar the history of the third century, and it also had the good fortune to be spared lengthy warfare with external foes.

Gibbon based his assessment on the ancient literary sources. As usual, these reflect the opinions of those in the emperor's circle, and they focus on life at the highest social level. Since Domitian's record was so tainted by poor relationships with senators and equites, by failed conspiracies and recurrent treason trials, it is not altogether a surprise that subsequent rulers are represented as splendid in comparison. Pliny the Younger, for example, stresses the concord of emperor and subjects, the absence of strife, the peace and prosperity of all. These themes are echoed by Cassius Dio, and form the background to the works of Pausanias, Aelius Aristides, and others (see Chapter Eleven). The (self-)congratulatory tone of such writings is all the more striking when compared to Tacitus' dark and cynical portrayal of first-century history. Even Tacitus himself seems to approve of the early second century. At the beginning of his *Agricola*, written in 98, he notes that the accession of Nerva marks the dawn of a most happy era, which sees two elements once considered incompatible now thriving together—liberty and the Principate.

Gibbon was not as familiar with the nonliterary evidence—the coin designs featuring imperial benefactions, the laudatory inscriptions, and the spacious buildings, fine sculptures, and exquisite reliefs that reflect widespread wealth. Had he known this material, however, his assessment might only have been urged with even deeper conviction. Altogether, such evidence paints the picture of a kind and benevolent government, characterized by harmony, and by a principle of the adoption of the most meritorious as emperor. It is no wonder that a scholar like Gibbon, deeply immersed in the ancient historical writers, would come to the conclusion that he did. This said, modern sensibilities are more aware that his evaluation is incomplete. It downplays, among other events of this period, internal discord manifested in the second and third Jewish revolts as well as in local, but violent, persecutions of Christians. It also overlooks the plight of the vast majority of the population, whose destitute lives left little or no trace in the historical record but whose labor sustained the empire and its elites.

NERVA (96–98)

Very few individuals participated in the plot to assassinate Domitian, although he was widely hated in Rome. The Praetorian Guard, in particular, mostly had little notion of what was being planned or by whom. At all levels of society, there must have been many who recalled with dread the dire aftermath of Nero's death in 68. When the senate met after the assassination, it officially condemned Domitian's memory (*damnatio memoriae*), and chose as his successor Marcus Cocceius Nerva, a senior ex-consul aged sixty-six. His seniority was what counted. Otherwise he lacked military distinction, and had passed through perilous times unscathed. He had been rewarded by Nero after the suppression of the Pisonian conspiracy in 65, and later served as consul with Vespasian in 71, and again with Domitian in 90, the year after Saturninus' revolt. Now, in 96, he was confirmed as emperor and given the honorary title Pater Patriae. He took an oath in the senate not to execute any senator. The first coins struck for him by the imperial mint emphasize virtues and admirable concepts: Equality, Liberty, Safety, and Justice.

 corn source

Nerva devoted special attention to Italy during his two years as Princeps. He gave sixty million sesterces to buy land for distribution to citizens who had none, especially those living in Rome; the acquisition and assignment of this land was deputed to senators. Nerva also seems to have been the emperor who established the so-called *alimenta*. This complex child-support scheme—known almost exclusively from inscriptions—enabled emperors to furnish the principal for low-interest loans to Italian landowners. The interest paid by these borrowers funded monthly distributions to children. More boys are attested as recipients than girls, though this may simply be because only parents without eligible sons would put forward daughters for the scheme, since boys received higher payments. The scheme is often interpreted as an attempt to increase the birthrate in Italy and the amount of land under cultivation there. If so, however, we cannot gauge its effectiveness in either respect, nor can we be sure that these were its ultimate purposes.

Despite these benefactions, Nerva lacked the support of the Praetorians and of the army, who still remembered the favor shown to them by Domitian. By 97 the Praetorians were demanding the execution of Domitian's assassins. Dissatisfaction persisted even after Nerva gave his consent. Worse consequences were only precluded by an unexpected move on his part. In late October 97 he adopted Trajan, the newly appointed governor of Upper Germany (now with a garrison of three

Figure 10.3 *Thamugadi (modern Timgad, Algeria), a colony established by Trajan in 100. This view, from the interior of the city towards the west, shows in the foreground a well-paved street which forms part of the regular checkerboard grid. In the middle distance, dominating the smaller remains of houses and streetside porticoes, stands the triple arch that marks one of the principal entrances to the colony. Like most of the other large and imposing public monuments, this "Arch of Trajan," dating to c. 200, was erected only when the local economy allowed. Although they are not visible in this photograph, Timgad also came to boast a theater (begun c. 160) and, of course, a forum. A temple and city council building both opened onto the forum's central open space, which accommodated public meetings, processions, religious rituals, and other communal events.*

legions) and the son of a brilliant soldier-governor. Born and raised at Italica in southern Spain, and forty-four years of age at the time of his adoption, Trajan was to be the first emperor from the provinces. Nerva marked him out as successor by conferring the title "Caesar" on him, and by securing his election as consul for 98. Already in 97 the senate had conferred on him tribunicia potestas, maius imperium, and the title Imperator. When Nerva died a natural death on January 25, 98, Trajan's succession as Princeps was ratified despite his absence from Rome. He remained away until October 99, inspecting the frontiers along the Rhine and Danube. The maintenance of consensus of Rome at this time is a remarkable achievement, because it allowed the empire to survive Domitian's assassination without further civil war. The smooth transfers of power to Nerva, and then Trajan, offer a memorable contrast to the turmoil that erupted following the death of Nero and that was to resurface in the late second century.

TRAJAN (98–117)

In 99 Trajan entered Rome on foot and in a civilian toga rather than military uniform; he was welcomed by every segment of the population, according to Pliny's *Panegyricus*. Indeed, Trajan is one of the few Roman emperors who successfully combined the goodwill of the army and harmony with the senate. He was involved in many civilian initiatives, yet was decidedly eager to expand the empire. He has come down in the tradition as *Optimus Princeps*, "Best Princeps," a term appearing on coins and inscriptions beginning in 103.

Source

From the start, Trajan acted independently despite conscientious consultation with others. He executed or discharged the mutinous Praetorians who had demanded the execution of Domitian's assassins. Moreover, contrary to the habit of new emperors to give ever bigger donatives to the Praetorians, Trajan actually halved the normal donative. He could do so because of his prestige among the regular rank and file of the army, whose size he was to increase by raising the total of legions to thirty. In Rome in 99 and 100 he was much praised, notably in 100 by Pliny's speech in the senate later revised as the *Panegyricus*. Trajan held his fourth consulship in 101. Thereafter, he never took the office again, no doubt conscious of the negative impression created by Domitian's continual tenure of it. Trajan aimed to strike the note that he was Princeps, not *dominus*, Rome's first among equals and not its monarch. Nevertheless, his accessibility was coupled with an iron will. His preeminence is underscored by Pliny's use of dominus ("lord") when writing letters to him.

Trajan expended much energy on civil matters. He remitted the "crown tax," a contribution that communities were expected to send to each emperor on his accession. In Rome itself he was responsible for distributions of cash to the populace on three occasions—in 99 (300 sesterces a head), in 102, and again in 107 (an astonishing 2,000 sesterces a head; a legionary's annual pay was now 1,200).

Figure 10.4 *Two bands of the marble relief on the Column of Trajan in Rome, dedicated in 113. The Column's continuous relief portrays events in the Dacian Wars of 101–102 and 105–106. Juxtaposed here are two significant motifs: Roman military superiority, and the farseeing supremacy of Trajan. Below, Romans defend themselves against a Dacian attack on their camp. The bearded Dacians fight bravely, but are no match for the better-organized and equipped Romans. Above, Trajan, followed by troops, is reunited with a legionary contingent at a fortified locale (in the background). Soldiers and officers meet him with a bull decorated for sacrifice and attendants for the ritual. Behind them are two bandsmen playing curved horns, and three military standards. These reliefs are sufficiently detailed to distinguish between Roman auxiliary troops, depicted in fringed overshirts and neckcloths (below), and legionaries depicted in their sturdier armor (above right). As always, Trajan appears calm, somewhat larger than other figures, and in full control.*

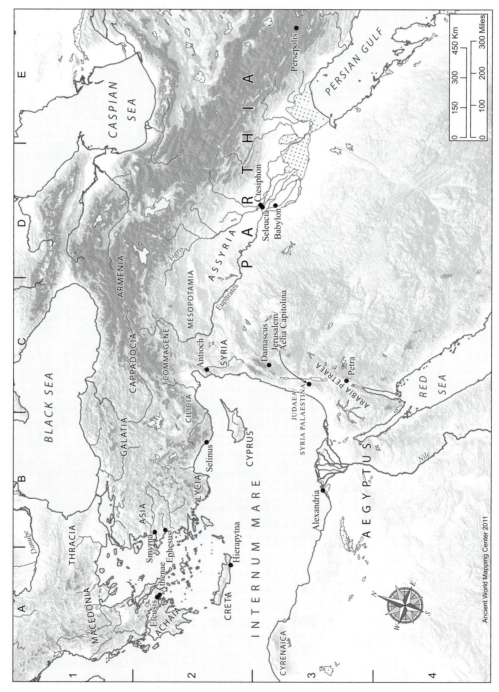

Map 10.2 *Eastern Expansion of the Empire in the Early Second Century*

Ancient World Mapping Center 2011

Distributions of grain went to more recipients, too. Trajan gave lavish and frequent spectacles, celebrating the end of the Second Dacian War, for example, with 123 days of games spread over three years. With his support, the alimenta schemes begun by Nerva were extended in Italy. In addition, some of the last veteran colonies established by Rome are Trajan's initiatives. A prime example is North African Thamugadi (modern Timgad, Algeria), whose orthogonal planning, handsome public monuments, and evident prosperity seem to embody the effects of the "beneficial ideology" at the local level (see Fig. 10.3).

In response to local difficulties Trajan made special appointments to oversee cities and whole regions for limited periods. These troubleshooting caretaker officials (*curatores*)—including Pliny the Younger, dispatched to Bithynia-Pontus in 111–112—reported directly to the emperor; how their tasks meshed with those of the regular officials is far from clear. At least we can see how this innovation breaks with the traditional principle of cities' autonomy which all emperors from Augustus onwards had consistently upheld. Yet the work of such caretakers (who had seldom been appointed previously) seems to have been beneficial, and Pliny's letters to Trajan certainly document the concern with which both the emperor and his special representative approached the task of solving local problems (see Chapter Eleven and Source 11.5). Finally in this connection, Trajan was responsible for numerous public works that featured opulent buildings of all types in Rome, as well as roads in Italy and the provinces.

Funds for these extensive benefactions came primarily from the Dacian Wars, which Trajan waged in 101–102 and 105–106. From the time of the Late Republic onwards, Rome had dealt intermittently with the Dacians of the Transylvanian plateau and the Carpathian Mountains—rich in gold, silver, and iron mines—above the loop of the lower Danube. Relations had intensified in the late first century, when the Dacian king Decebalus had consolidated power and fought against the Romans until his recognition as a "friendly king" by Domitian in 88. But Decebalus had then in fact renewed his bid for expansion, triggering further war with the Romans. Rome's victories are said to have yielded about 225 tons of gold, double that amount of silver, and 50,000 slaves. These spoils financed the great Forum of Trajan in the heart of Rome—its dimensions of 606 × 984 feet, or 185 × 300 meters, making it almost as large as all the other imperial fora combined (see Map 10.3). Dacian spoils also funded many other monuments in Rome, Italy, and elsewhere. After Decebalus' death and the destruction of much of Dacian culture, the Romans annexed the land. Dacia's mineral wealth prompted many immigrants to move there. Other newcomers were the soldiers from various parts of the empire who were stationed in the new province. Its more exposed location, beyond the well-defined Danube River boundary, shifted the weight of Rome's garrisons east from the Rhine to the lower Danube and to Dacia itself.

It was possibly the sheer success of the Dacian Wars that spurred Trajan to further expansion. In 105–106, during the second Dacian War, he annexed Arabia Petraea, "rocky Arabia," previously called Nabataea. This new province was wealthy because of its incense, spices, gold, and gems, as well as its active role in Roman trade with India. Almost immediately, Trajan marked the area as Roman by commissioning a great road from the Red Sea to Damascus in Syria. But the creation of the province destabilized an area already unsettled by the death of the king of Parthia to its east (probably in 105). In 110 problems surfaced in Armenia, when the new Parthian king replaced the Roman vassal king there with a noble of his own choosing. This action provoked the Parthian War, which was to occupy Trajan until his death in 117.

In October 113, Trajan set off to the East to command the war in person, and perhaps to explore the possibilities of advancing beyond Armenia. Mesopotamia, which was ruled by a land-owning military aristocracy under a king, was characteristically volatile. Its annexation would give Rome a very rich province as well as access to the Persian Gulf. Literary sources also cite Trajan's emulation of Alexander the Great, who had traversed this area on his famous eastern march. By 114, Trajan had captured Armenia and reduced it to a province. In 115 he made the lands between Armenia and the upper reaches of the Tigris into the province of Assyria; northern Mesopotamia was then reduced, and annexed as the province of Mesopotamia. Trajan was awarded the title "Parthicus" in 116, and the thirty legions now under his command must have seemed invincible. But they were also a heavy burden on Rome's economy and society, and the war itself was exacting. Long stretches of desert and semi-arid land obstructed communications. The Roman troops were unused to the harsh climate, and supplies were hard to obtain. Disasters, both natural and manmade, exacerbated the difficulties. In winter 114–115 a devastating earthquake hit Syrian Antioch (modern Antakya, Turkey). Although Trajan himself was spared, and also his distant relative Publius Aelius Hadrianus accompanying him, many other men of high rank died, as did soldiers assembling at Antioch for the following year's campaign against the Parthians. The city was wrecked, and it must have seemed to some as though the gods were trying to warn the Romans. In addition, later in 115 the second Jewish revolt broke out, diverting attention from the expansionist Parthian war to internal discontent.

In 115, Jewish communities in Cyrenaica, Egypt, Cyprus, and perhaps Judaea itself rebelled against the Romans. The outbreaks may have been coordinated. At the least, the exasperated Jews of the diaspora, exploited and scorned for years by gentile neighbors, took advantage of the authorities' preoccupation with the Parthian War. By 116, the unrest had spread to Mesopotamia, disturbing the new province. The crisis was not finally brought under control everywhere until late in 117. Repression of the Jews was especially brutal in Egypt, where a virtual pogrom extirpated all traces of them from the country outside of Alexandria. In every area of discontent, rebellious Jews attacked garrisons and destroyed towns. Trajan heard of the revolt at Babylon in 116 while sacrificing to the spirit of Alexander, and he had to dispatch forces immediately to the rebellious areas. But this Jewish revolt was not the only internal turmoil of the time. In 117, disturbances on the

Plate 9a Domus Transitoria decoration *Although Nero's sprawling Golden House – built after the great fire of Rome in A.D. 64 (see Chapter Nine) – was notorious for its luxury, even more opulent traces survive from its short-lived predecessor, Nero's Domus Transitoria on the Palatine hill. This fragment of a fresco from one of its halls is thought to show a scene from Homer's* Odyssey, *the type of learned reference commonly found in Roman wall and ceiling frescoes. Two far more unusual and lavish features seen here are the semi-precious stones embedded into the plaster (as the centers of the vine rosettes), and the gilding on the beaded border of the panel.*

Plate 9b Riot at Pompeii fresco *Relatively few surviving frescoes depict historical subjects. This one, from the peristyle garden of Pompeii's House of Actius Anicetus, illustrates a riot in Pompeii's amphitheater (see Figure 6.1a,b) so notorious that Tacitus recorded it in his* Annals *(14.17). The occasion was a gladiatorial show in A.D. 59, during which Pompeian spectators came to blows with visitors from the nearby rival town of Nuceria; it may be that recent settlement of veteran soldiers at Nuceria had heightened tensions about landholding. In any case, the riot was so injurious (especially to the Nucerians) that the Roman senate banned gladiatorial shows at Pompeii for ten years. The bird's-eye depiction of the amphitheater shows in addition Pompeii's Large Palestra or exercise ground (with painted inscriptions) and the city walls (with two gates), as well as trees and what seem to be temporary stalls. Only part of the massive linen awning over the amphitheater (to provide shade during shows) is depicted, so as to allow a view into the structure.*

Plate 10a Agrippina as priestess *This grey basalt statue (6 ft/1.8 m tall) depicts Agrippina, wife of Claudius and mother of Nero (see Chapter Nine), in a pose derived from a Greek prototype of the fourth century* B.C., *and used for women of very high rank. The pose also denotes someone at prayer, especially a priestess. The statue was found in pieces in Rome near the Temple of the Deified Claudius, and the likelihood is that it once depicted Agrippina as priestess of the imperial cult for Claudius. The grey basanite stone resembles silver, adding to the luster of the piece. As seen here, it is a reconstruction: today the head is in the Ny Carlsberg Glyptotek, Copenhagen, and the body in the Centrale Montemartini Museum, Rome.*

Plate 10b Roman-period mummy with portrait *Roman-Egyptian mummy (4.5 ft/1.33 m long) dating to around* A.D. *100–120, from Hawara, southeast of the Fayyum, today in the British Museum, London. A striking feature is the inserted panel portrait of an adolescent youth, one of about 900 "mummy portraits" known from Roman Egypt, some even still in their original mummy casings (as here). The practice derives from Egypt's longstanding funerary traditions, and attests to the persistence of indigenous customs there under Roman rule. Such portraits were usually painted in tempera or encaustic (pigmented hot wax) on a thin sheet of wood. The wrapping of this mummy resembles a common image of Osiris, the consort of Isis, and it is further elaborated with gold studs in the diamond-shaped hollows made by the linen.*

Plate 11 Colle Oppio fresco, Rome *Excavation under Rome's Oppian hill in 1997 brought to light the wall of an unidentified late first century A.D. structure on which a large fresco was painted (about 33 sq ft/10 sq m). Despite its imperfect preservation, it clearly depicts a walled city in bird's-eye view, with buildings represented in perspective. Identifiable features include a street-grid, theater, forum, temples, and statues. There is also a fortified harbor area, but nowhere (it seems) are human figures to be seen. Such a cityscape is unparalleled among surviving landscape frescoes, which take rural scenes as their subject. No convincing identification of this city with an actual one of the time has been made, however, and it seems more likely to be an idealized one, symbolizing the artist's conception of how a great city of the Roman world ought to be imagined at a period when such communities were flourishing (see Chapter Ten).*

Plate 12a Staffordshire Moorlands pan *The so-called Staffordshire Moorlands pan – unearthed by a metal detector in England's Midlands during 2003, and now in the British Museum, London – would seem to be a souvenir produced for a Roman soldier who served on Hadrian's Wall (see Chapter Ten). It is 1.85 ins (4.7 cm) in height, and its diameter extends to 3.7 ins (9.4 cm). The form of the pan is a familiar utilitarian one. Even though it now lacks a handle or base, it could never have been serviceable. Rather, its remarkably well preserved enamel inlay and inscription are more appropriate to a memento than to a cooking vessel. The pan's entire outer surface is decorated with a band of Celtic-style curvilinear ornament in several colors. Above runs an inscription inlaid with turquoise enamel. The unbroken letter sequence lists four forts at the western end of the Wall, followed by three or four words apparently referring to the Wall itself.*

Plate 12b Palmyra funerary relief *Palmyra, situated on the eastern border of the Roman province of Syria, was a powerful and prosperous oasis (see Chapter Twelve), whose art forms drew upon Parthian, Semitic, Greek, and Roman elements. Palmyrene limestone funerary reliefs are especially distinctive. This bust (21.5 by 16 ins/55 by 40.5 cm) from one such relief – dated to around A.D. 200, and now in the Ny Carlsberg Glyptotek, Copenhagen – commemorates an elegantly dressed wealthy woman. Originally, the bust was backed by a slab that fitted it into a tomb monument; traces of the slab can be seen behind the woman's shoulders. She wears profuse jewelry highlighted by paint, including thick bracelets, multiple chains with pendants, a large round brooch on her left shoulder, earrings, and an elaborate headdress. Her hair and lips are also painted. Her multi-layered garments include a veil, which she pulls forward with her left hand as a gesture of modesty* (pudicitia), *a standard convention in Roman female sculpture.*

Plate 13a Water-organ, third century A.D. *An ingenious Greek invention and the world's first keyboard instrument, the water-organ (hydraulus) became very popular in the Roman world, fascinating the emperor Nero among many others. Even in the less stable and prosperous conditions of the early third century, a gift of one was made to a trade association's social center at Aquincum (modern Budapest, Hungary) in 228. So attests the dedication-plate recovered by archeologists in 1931 along with the organ's mass of metal parts. Their relative completeness has inspired efforts to build reconstructions, one of them pictured here in the Aquincum museum, with a photograph of the parts recovered in the background top right. Just how water was delivered to pressurize the air that made the organ's pipes sound remains uncertain (no wooden or leather part survived); the relative placement of the keyboard and pipes is not in doubt, however. What music was played on water-organs can only be imagined.*

Plate 13b Gold-glass, third century A.D. *The economic decline and consequent impoverishment that occurred during the third century* A.D. *were far from universal. Some luxury objects continued to be produced, and in the case of glassware the delicate technique of "gold-glass" became more widespread. This medallion, 2 ins (4.9 cm) in diameter, probably made in Italy, typifies the period's craftsmanship. Its base disk is deep blue glass, onto which gold foil and paints were applied first, followed by a colorless cover glass; the medallion was then heated in a kiln until the glasses fused, and finally it was ground and polished. A woman is portrayed, with a word of Latin either side of her head: "Anatolius, rejoice!"; her face and shoulders are encircled by running ivy rendered naturalistically. The unexpected juxtaposition of female portrait and male name suggests that the woman was Anatolius' wife or companion.*

Plate 14 *Notitia Dignitatum* **illustration**   *The top-level administration for the entire later empire is laid out in schematic form in the* Notitia Dignitatum *(Roster of Offices), a book kept by the emperor's "Chief Notary". It survives only in medieval copies, but these offer a tantalizing reflection of the make-up of the fourth- and fifth-century bureaucracy (see Chapter Twelve). An illustration – like the one here depicting the insignia of the western Count of the Sacred Largesses – accompanies the text of each section, which lists the subordinate officers who worked for each high official. The Count of the Sacred Largesses was charged with the collection of money taxes and the production of coins and other precious metal objects, many of which appear here. On either side of the table, observe gold and silver leaf for appliqué and embossed gold belt-buckles, given as a sign of office and produced in workshops managed by the Count. Below, note plates full of gold coins (marked* LAR[G]ITIONES, *"largesse", since they were "in the gift of the emperor"); in the foreground, vessels filled with gold coins, a gold coffer, and a locked strong-box. The text that follows (not illustrated) lists eighty-one high-level officials grouped into ten divisions (for example, accountants, treasurers, and mint supervisors); each division could employ hundreds of bureaucrats.*

Plate 15 Sol Invictus medallion *Immediately after experiencing a vision of the sun god Apollo-Sol in 310 (see Chapter Thirteen), Constantine began minting images of this deity on his coinage. The most striking example is this gold medallion, weighing one-eighth of a Roman pound (1.4 oz/40 g), which features Constantine's head beside that of the deity, to whom he bears a striking resemblance. The emperor's shield shows the sun god riding his chariot into the heavens. Also notable here is the change that Constantine made to his official titulature, which reads: "Unconquerable (Invictus) Constantine Greatest (Maximus) Augustus." Maximus reflects his claim to have been greatest among the ruling emperors after he defeated Maxentius in 312; Invictus was the epithet regularly applied to the sun god since the third century.*

Plate 16 Jerusalem in a mosaic map, Madaba, Jordan *See Map 14.3b, page 513.*

Plate 17 Apse mosaic, church of Santa Pudenziana, Rome   *From the fourth century onward, emperors, their officials, and private citizens all poured vast wealth into the construction of churches (see Chapter Fourteen). The level of artistic achievement attained can be gauged from this fine apse mosaic installed in the fairly modest church of Santa Pudenziana, Rome, around 390. It depicts Christ enthroned, very much in the manner of an emperor, and surrounded by his apostles. The four winged creatures in the sky above him represent the four evangelists, and the city beneath them is Jerusalem; some scholars have even speculated that the mosaic offers an accurate depiction of the buildings constructed there by Constantine. At either side in the foreground are the apostles, with two female figures (perhaps personifications of the Church and the Synagogue) standing behind them and crowning the martyrs Peter and Paul. Restorations of the mosaic in the sixteenth century removed two apostles on the outer sides and considerably altered the appearance of some of the remaining ten.*

lower Danube required the transfer there of the outstanding general Gaius Julius Quadratus Bassus, who had been governor of Syria since the beginning of the Parthian War. Trajan now appointed Hadrian to replace him in Syria. He also concluded his Parthian campaigns, and embarked on his return journey to Rome.

However, in the course of this journey, Trajan died unexpectedly at the port of Selinus in Cilicia. Just before he died, he adopted Hadrian as his heir. The latter was aged forty-one at the time, and was still in Syria. In his youth, Trajan had been his guardian. Like Trajan, he came from Italica in southern Spain. In 100 he had married Trajan's grand-niece, Sabina, and later served him in different capacities—as speechwriter, for example. Despite these close links, however, Trajan did not clearly mark him out as his successor until the adoption. Cassius Dio and others insinuate that this was really arranged by Trajan's wife Plotina, who was close to Hadrian. Yet Hadrian was amply qualified to become Princeps. He had held many administrative and military positions, serving in Pannonia as well as Syria, both of them strategically vital provinces. He had been a member of Trajan's entourage in the first Dacian War, and was already designated to hold the consulship in 118. As a cultured and prominent senator, he combined military and civil talents.

Trajan's rule marks a delicate moment in Roman history, particularly with regard to Rome's traditional imperialism. From some perspectives at least, Trajan's expansion into Dacia may seem glorious and beneficial. Huge amounts of wealth fell into Roman hands, and the emperor and his army performed amazing feats like bridging the Danube below the "Iron Gates" rapids. The society created in Dacia after its conquest may seem to demonstrate a constructive type of Romanization. Only one legion and some auxiliary troops were stationed there, and the Romans developed the province's mines, attracting immigrants from the eastern provinces in particular. During what was to be a relatively brief period of Roman control—from 106 to 270, when the emperor Aurelian abandoned the area to the Goths—Dacia saw the introduction of the Latin language, Roman religion and rites, and cities in the Roman style. Still today, the Romanian language is heavily Latinate. In short, the new province seems to have been made a flourishing part of the empire, rather than simply remaining territory to be exploited.

There is a strong contrast between Trajan's expansion into Dacia and his involvement with Parthia. The East provided luxury goods for the Romans, and the Parthians were their most organized and formidable foe. Involvements with Parthia predated Roman contact with Dacia, and they had generally not been advantageous; the defeats of Crassus and Antony in the first century B.C. had been particularly severe (see Chapters Seven and Eight). But the rich and exotic East apparently always beckoned. The pull here of Rome's traditional imperialism may have been strengthened by memories of Alexander the Great's attempted world conquest. To this extent, it is not hard to see why Trajan decided for a Parthian war. However, it was not as easy to win as to begin. It vastly overextended Roman troops and energy. It diverted Roman attention from provinces elsewhere, opening

Table 10.1 The Antonine Family *The presentation follows the style of Table 8.1, explained there.*

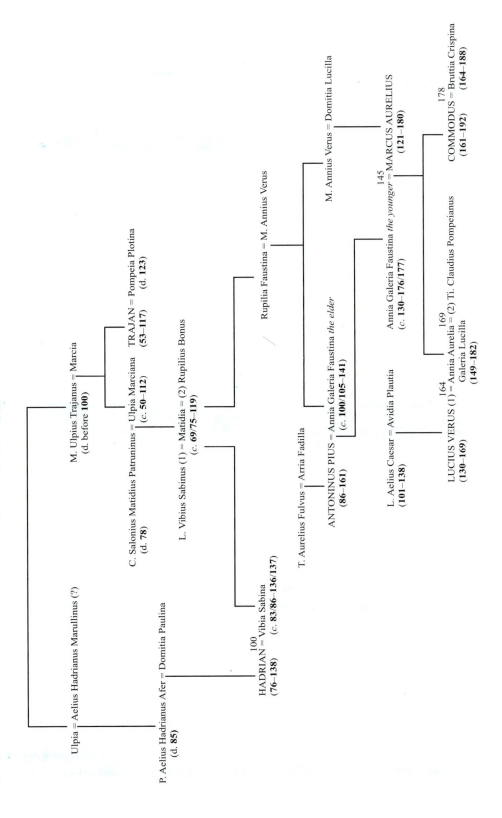

the way to revolts and invasions. Very soon, Trajan's eastern conquests had to be abandoned, and in hindsight we can appreciate this war's negative consequences for Romans and Parthians alike. The withdrawal is attributed to Hadrian by many authors, because in antiquity's schematic view of Roman history and its leaders, Trajan was unanimously and unequivocally praised. A large part of his fame was his military achievement, represented as always successful. Hadrian was to acquire a decidedly more ambivalent reputation.

HADRIAN (117–138)

With Hadrian's accession in 117, the focus both in Rome and the provinces shifted from expansion to consolidation. As it turned out, Hadrian spent more than half of his twenty-one-year rule outside of Rome in travels throughout the empire, visiting cities, natural wonders, and troops along the frontiers. His activity centered on bettering the empire internally in various ways: improving material and administrative infrastructure (including communications), boosting municipal elites as well as the senatorial and equestrian orders, invigorating religious practices, and encouraging cultural activities, especially those of a literary and ritual kind. An inward turn is detectable in other ways. Hadrian himself painted, designed buildings, and wrote poetry as well as speeches and an autobiography. He appreciated aesthetics deeply and actively. He had a mystical bent—expressed in his rising as high as the "second level" in the Mysteries at Eleusis, in his involvement in other types of mysteries and oracles, and in his heroization of his lover, Antinous, when the young man drowned in 130. None of these preoccupations would have been possible without widespread peace. Peace was further secured by the smooth transmission of power in this period, thanks to imperial adoptions and the fortuitous longevity of the emperors, from Trajan to Marcus Aurelius.

Hadrian ruled from 117 to 138. One of his many accomplishments was to settle the succession for the next two generations, although he had no children of his own (see Table 10.1). Towards the end of his life, in 136, he adopted Lucius Ceionius Commodus (renamed Lucius Aelius Caesar); but when he died within a year, Hadrian turned to others. At the beginning of 138 he adopted Titus Aurelius Fulvus Boionius Arrius Antoninus (later known as Antoninus Pius), and since Antoninus had no son, he had him adopt two younger men. One, the seventeen-year-old Marcus Annius Verus, was to become the Princeps Marcus Aurelius. The other, the seven-year old son of the deceased Lucius Aelius, would later rule as Lucius Verus jointly with Marcus Aurelius. All three of Hadrian's choices belonged to a circle of friends and relatives with ties to southern Gaul and Spain, typical of the senatorial and equestrian orders in early second-century Rome. Their family connections and the Roman custom of adoption may together have made the dynastic arrangement's political purpose more acceptable. In any event,

Hadrian's foresight in this regard certainly preempted the suspicions surrounding his own deathbed adoption by Trajan, and contributed to the unusual stability of the second century.

Trajan's death in Cilicia in 117 led to countless rumors—as was only to be expected when a beloved ruler dies far from home—and Hadrian's choice of a circuitous route to Rome through Dalmatia and Pannonia only encouraged the spread of gossip. The principle of meritocracy—which had surely been the basis of Nerva's adoption of Trajan—may have influenced at least a few senators to think themselves more worthy than Hadrian to succeed Trajan. Before Hadrian returned to Rome in 118, four influential men had been condemned to death by the senate on charges of conspiracy. Although Hadrian swore that this had been done without his knowledge, the deaths tainted his first years. His own mercurial, sometimes difficult, personality increased senatorial animosity against him, as did the forced suicides of two distant relatives near the end of his life. Overall, the literary tradition is hostile to Hadrian. Yet his earlier career, including his appointment as governor of Syria, suggests Trajan's confidence in his abilities, loyalty, and military acumen. This confidence was repaid over the twenty-one years of his Principate.

Some innovations can be credited to Hadrian; other changes are not due to him alone. One of his first acts was to complete Rome's decisive withdrawal from Trajan's farthest conquests, allowing Armenia, Mesopotamia, and Assyria to return to their previous forms of rule. The cessation of costly hostilities and the abandonment of military occupation in the East allowed Hadrian to cancel debts due to the treasury in 118, to make lavish donations in Rome and the provinces (especially from 118 to 121), and to excuse communities from the "crown tax." These benefactions, acclaimed on inscriptions and even in literature, may have resulted in greater public confidence in the economy, and an increase in public spending by affluent city elites and by the Princeps himself. Widespread confidence was also spurred by Hadrian's travels, during which local notables throughout the empire could meet him personally. In his first great journey, from 121 to 127, he visited Gaul, the Rhineland regions, Britain (where he began "his" Wall), Spain, Asia, Greece, and Sicily. He returned to Rome for less than a year, and then visited Africa briefly in 128. After returning to Rome again, at the end of 128 he embarked on his second great journey, which lasted until 131. In these years he visited Athens, and many regions of Asia, Syria, and Egypt. Sometime during this trip he may have visited Judaea, where his decision to settle a veteran colony at the site of Jerusalem (Colonia Aelia Capitolina), combined with his prohibition of circumcision, led to a major revolt.

The third Jewish revolt, also known as the Bar Kokhba War after the Jewish leader Shim'on bar-Cosiba (nicknamed Bar Kokhba, "Son of a Star," by a rabbi), lasted from 132 to 135. It devastated Judaea and exacted a heavy death toll from Jews and Romans alike. Cassius Dio summarizes the destruction: fifty Jewish outposts and 985 villages razed, 580,000 rebels slain; many more civilians perished by famine and fire, and numerous Romans fell (69.14). Afterwards, in what now seems an attempt to eradicate Judaism, Judaea was renamed Syria Palaestina, and Jews were forbidden entry into Jerusalem. The Jewish diaspora intensified, and Christians were more obviously differentiated from Jews and Jerusalem.

Hadrian plainly encouraged well qualified individuals to participate in administration, where his rule was less damaging. His Principate sees increased prominence of equites like the biographer and intellectual Suetonius, who was placed in charge of imperial correspondence. Hadrian accorded special respect to the emperor's traditional group of private advisers that dated back to Augustus' time (*consilium principis*), and he invited not only his friends (*comites*) to serve on it, but also legal experts ("jurists") approved by the senate. As a result, these senators and equites gained an influential role in decision-making and in adjudicating appeals referred to the emperor.

Another innovation by Hadrian—the appointment of four judges known as the *Quattuorviri consulares,* all of them ex-consuls— underscores the difficulties that now face us in determining emperors' motivations. These four judges heard cases and adjudicated disputes in

Figure 10.5 *Statue of Hadrian from Hierapytna, Crete. Hadrian wears full parade-dress military costume, including a large laurel crown. His magnificent breastplate includes a depiction of Romulus, his twin brother Remus, and the she-wolf (below its central figure) that is said to have rescued and nursed them (see Chapter One). Hadrian triumphantly rests his left foot on the back of a captive barbarian boy. Some scholars have dated the image to between 120 and 125; others suggest that the boy is Jewish, which would date the statue to the third Jewish revolt (132–135) or (less likely) to the end of the second (117). The statue—originally set up in an imperial cult shrine on the island of Crete—embodies the merciless violence that the Romans inflicted on those who opposed them.*

Italy, which was divided administratively into four regions for the purpose. Previously, Roman citizens in Italy had to come to Rome itself to have appeals heard, or for cases of more than local significance; cases involving senators would be heard in the senate. Although Hadrian's innovation addresses the burdens and inequities caused by the earlier system, it was apparently thought to be treating Italy too much like a province. It has been interpreted as indicating a long-standing desire to streamline administration and legal proceedings, as well as an ecumenical vision of the Roman world as one in which all regions deserved equal respect. On the other hand, it was a step that apparently caused rancor in the senate, whose corporate prestige may have seemed diminished. The new office was to be dropped by Antoninus Pius, although later revived by Marcus Aurelius.

The blurring of legal and administrative functions for the Quattuorviri consulares is indicative of Hadrian's Principate, in which civil administration seems ever more concerned with judicial questions. The daily activities of the emperor centered on hearing cases and appeals. Hadrian's well-organized mind had a legal bent. Among his achievements is codification of the set of legal procedures and types of proceedings that praetors would allow in office. Previously, individual praetors, often advised by jurists, could choose or modify the rules and procedures they would follow, although already by the Augustan period the various praetorian edicts were more or less standardized and permanent. The same principle was followed by governors and other magistrates with judicial authority. Now, in the late 120s, Hadrian asked the jurist Salvius Julianus to compose a revised version of the Praetorian edict, which would be permanent. In 131 the senate ratified the document, and from the early third century the codification was to be known as the "Edictum Perpetuum." From now onwards, the procedures of civil law at Rome could be changed only by the Princeps or by decree of the senate. Although emperors tended to monopolize this prerogative, Hadrian also declared that in court cases the unanimous opinion of authorized jurists could count "as if it were law" (Gaius, *Institutes* 1.7). He thus signaled that others could make law as well as himself.

Hadrian worked hard to show that he was approachable and cordial, but with mixed success. At his accession he had forbidden treason trials; he visited senators and equites when they were sick; he consulted frequently with his comites. His concern went beyond Rome's highest ranks. He bettered the condition of slaves by requiring that an owner obtain the approval of a state magistrate before killing any slave who had committed crimes. The alimenta scheme was expanded; more curatores, and of several types, were appointed to oversee various communities. In addition, Hadrian engaged in an enormous program of building and other benefactions throughout the Roman world. He personally mingled with the people of Rome and the provinces. His constant travels proclaimed his accessibility and his care for all, and because he journeyed with the apparatus of the central government (still small in this period), important decisions were often made outside of Rome.

SOURCE 10.1: Hadrian Inspects Troops at Lambaesis, Numidia

When Hadrian visited North Africa in 128, he reviewed the troops of the province of Numidia at their Lambaesis headquarters (modern Lambèse, Algeria). The garrison later inscribed excerpts from his five addresses to the men (ILS 2487, 9133–35). The sections below give a flavor both of the troops' mundane tasks and of their military training; they also show Hadrian at work as commander-in-chief:

[To a cavalry cohort] . . . Defenses which others take several days to construct, you have completed in one. You have completed the lengthy task of building a strong wall—the type typically erected for permanent winter quarters—in not much more time than is needed to build a turf wall. For that type of wall, the turf is cut to a standard size and is easy to carry and to handle; its erection presents no problems because it is naturally pliable and level. But your wall was built of large, heavy, uneven stones which no one can carry or lift or position without them catching on each other because of their uneven surfaces. You cut a trench straight through hard coarse gravel, and made it smooth by leveling it. Once the job had been approved, you entered the camp speedily, and got your rations and your weapons. . . .

[To the cavalry of the Sixth Cohort of Commagenians] It is difficult for cavalry attached to a cohort to make a good impression even on their own, and still harder for them not to incur criticism after a maneuver by auxiliary cavalry—they cover a greater area of the plain, there are more men throwing javelins; they wheel right in close formation, they perform the Cantabrian maneuver in close array; the beauty of their horses and the splendor of their weapons are in keeping with their level of pay. But, despite the heat, you avoided any annoyance by doing energetically what had to be done; in addition you fired stones from slings and fought with javelins. On every occasion you mounted briskly. The remarkable care taken by my distinguished legate Catullinus is evident from the fact that he has men like you under his command. . . .

Hadrian's military background matches with his acute concern for the empire's security. Despite renouncing further expansion, he took a keen interest in the army and military matters. His rule sees greater attention to frontiers, where he attempted to impose fixed borders. The great wall in northern England, "Hadrian's Wall," was established after 121. It cut through the lower of Britain's two narrow necks, from modern Bowness to Newcastle, a distance of 73 miles or 118 kilometers; Roman troops were also stationed both north and south of it (see Plate 12a). In all likelihood it was during Hadrian's rule, too, that the German-Raetian frontier came to be defined by a continuous high wooden barrier. Overall, he ensured that the army was well prepared and well disciplined. He frequently reviewed training exercises, and maintained the practice of employing troops on civil projects like aqueducts and roads during intervals between military activity.

Hadrian's most pressing military concerns were internal. The second and third Jewish Revolts mar the beginning and end of his rule, and further insurrections in Britain and Mauretania occurred around 117. Hadrian may have aimed his provincial benefactions at preventing discontent, but he apparently could not conceive that provincials might reject the Greco-Roman culture he so fervently promoted. As already noted, his blunders with the Jews in the 130s provoked one of the fiercest revolts that the Romans ever experienced. Hadrian thereafter slowed his activity and became more isolated. His suspicions caused the suicides of two of his distant relatives; his choice of Lucius Aelius as successor was unfortunate and unpopular; in 137 his wife, Sabina, from whom he had been distant ever since 122, died. In 138 Hadrian himself died, "hated by all" (*Historia Augusta, Hadrian* 25.7), and his deification earned its proposer, his successor Antoninus, the cognomen "dutiful" (Latin *pius*).

ROMAN CITIES AND
THE EMPIRE'S PEOPLES

In size and population the Roman empire was at its peak between the reigns of Vespasian and Hadrian. Its vast expanse—from modern England, the Atlantic Ocean, and Germany, across to Syria, Armenia, and the Nile Valley—was studded with cities on the coasts and rivers (for an idealized image, see Plate 11). There were perhaps fifty to seventy million people living in Roman territory, with probably some 20 percent of these in cities (one million people in Rome itself). The percentage in cities is relatively large. At the end of the twentieth century, 47 percent of the world's people were living in cities, according to United Nations calculations. But this extraordinary proportion is possible only because of recent technological advances like refrigeration, heating and cooling, antibiotics and other advances of public health, gas-fueled transport, agriculture, and the like. In the Roman world, there were probably as many as 2,000 cities, perhaps more.

After the great push by Caesar and Augustus, the numbers of veteran colonies settled by subsequent emperors dropped. Such colonies were extremely intrusive when imposed on earlier settlements, and the need for them was lessened by the establishment of a standing army. Some emperors reinforced towns by adding a group of discharged soldiers to its citizen rolls, as Nero did in 60 to Tarentum and Antium (modern Taranto and Anzio, Italy). But the period of Trajan and Hadrian marks the virtual end of veteran settlements. Instead, emperors encouraged cities by other means both direct and indirect—through grants of colonial or municipal status, remissions of taxes, personal visits, and funding construction. Better communications and the necessity of supplying the Roman army assisted commerce, agriculture, and the creation of some surplus capital. Small-scale commerce and artisan work advanced, providing individuals with occupations other than simply agricultural ones. The provincial cities were above all where social and political mobility could take place. There, freedmen could gain some local prestige and wealth, opening doors for their descendants to rise still higher in the social and economic scale. Soldiers honorably discharged from the legions or auxiliary forces commanded great respect in the towns where they retired, and they often served as town patrons or in some other political capacity. Even working women are documented in Roman cities as greengrocers, midwives, and shopkeepers, besides the more customary but disreputable professions of prostitute or barmaid.

Rome's cities were linked to one another and to Rome itself by roads and harbors, to which the Flavian emperors, Trajan, and Hadrian, paid much attention. Individuals might travel to nearby towns for games devoted to the imperial cult, local festivals, or visits from the provincial governor or some other Roman official. The relatively modest inns and taverns that have been found at Pompeii and elsewhere catered to such travelers. Long-distance travel was undertaken by ambassadors from cities to the emperor, and by troops on the move; both types of traveler would have been accommodated overnight by individuals either voluntarily or (for troops) under compulsion. Merchants and sailors also covered long distances, as did athletes and other performers for periodic games celebrated at Rome and elsewhere, especially in the Greek East. There is evidence—such as an inscription from Puteoli attesting a "station of the Tyrians"—to indicate that ethnic groups sometimes took care of their own travelers. But the Roman world's vast majority, whose horizons were limited to the land they tilled and to towns within a day's walk, can never have traveled far.

To this vast majority, did it really matter who ruled at Rome? In the early fifth century, a cultured bishop and philosopher from the coast of modern Libya suggested that even educated provincials were indifferent to, perhaps ignorant of, the ruling emperor (Synesius of Cyrene, *Letters* 148). Such must have been the case throughout Roman history for the mass of Rome's subjects, struggling to eke out a living from land prone to drought, flood, and other natural disasters. But during times of relative peace and prosperity, those inhabitants of the empire fortunate enough to live in or near a city probably had some inkling of the emperor, perhaps even of some benefaction from him. How did such people know of the emperor and other high-placed, almost untouchable individuals, and with what effects? These are obvious questions, but challenging ones when we take into account the absence of extensive mass communication.

THEATERS AND PROCESSIONS

One way that the imperial family affected Roman citizens and subjects was through the demonstration of their images at almost every event. As in the well-preserved theater of Emerita Augusta (modern Mérida, Spain; Fig. 10.6), for example, care was taken to exhibit statues of the emperors and their relatives at

Figure 10.6 *Theater at Emerita Augusta (modern Mérida, Spain), as restored in the early twentieth century. Originally commissioned by Agrippa in 16–15 B.C., this theater was remodeled in the early second century A.D. to include a shrine (*sacrarium*) for the imperial cult in the lowest part of the seating (the area now lacking seats in the rising semicircle). In the photograph can be seen reproductions of some of the statues originally placed between the columns of the stage's backdrop, commemorating local notables, members of the imperial family, and gods and goddesses. Also visible are traces of the marble that once covered the backdrop's structural elements, contributing to the public opulence and sense of urbanity.*

public gathering places. Theatergoing was a favorite pastime of the Romans. A later, fourth-century calendar found in Rome designates 102 days a year as "theater days," and there is little reason to think that the total was much less during the three previous centuries. Behind their stages, Roman theaters characteristically exhibited an elaborate and unchanging architectural backdrop (*scaenae frons*), whose many niches were filled with statues of gods, heroes, and the imperial family. Theaters—dating predominantly after the mid-first century A.D.—are found throughout the Roman world, about ninety of them in the area of modern France alone, for example. Typically seating some 5,000 spectators, but often much larger than seems warranted by just their city, they must also have accommodated countryfolk and visitors from neighboring towns alongside the local citizens. Spectators included men and women, slave, freed, and free. Although theatrical performances varied, invariably each "theater day" opened and closed with sacrifices and prayers on behalf of the Princeps, the imperial family, and the senate and people of Rome.

Theaters in the Greek East staged at least selected parts of the classic Greek plays like *Oedipus Rex*. The Latin West favored performances that could be described as mime or vaudeville, with stock characters in silly situations. "Atellan" farces, for example, featured a glutton, a fool, and a hunchback. Ironically, given the popularity of theatrical spectacles, professional actors and actresses were considered disreputable; in Roman law they were under certain restrictions, such as not being permitted to receive legacies. In both East and West actors usually wore masks. Among the details recounted by Suetonius (*Nero* 21) to demonstrate Nero's unsuitability as Princeps, is the point that when he appeared in operatic tragedies as a hero or god, or even a heroine or goddess, he wore masks modeled on his own face or on that of whichever woman happened to be his current mistress. Masks may have helped to amplify actors' voices, and amplification was also increased by building technology. Comprehension of what was being staged was aided in addition by some standardization of the plays and performances; the stories would have been immediately obvious and familiar.

Religious and civic processions often began or ended at theaters. Such processions were an essential part of the public and official religion of Rome and its cities. A few are known in detail from inscriptions like that recording the foundation instituted by Gaius Vibius Salutaris at Ephesus early in the second century. On festal days the city's priests and priestesses would parade precious metal images of gods and goddesses, deified emperors and empresses, and personifications of civic groups through a city, stopping at various points for public prayer. Often a local notable would pay for a public distribution, feast, or additional performance such as a singing contest, further enhancing the appeal of the day and simultaneously forging a personal link with the gods and emperors. Distributions were typically angled towards the privileged, and often given out hierarchically—for example, with the town magistrates and councilors receiving the most, then the Augustales, then the mothers of leading citizens, and finally free citizens in general. Seating in theaters was similarly arranged, with the seats closest to the orchestra reserved for those with the most prestige. On the other hand, at least the processions were open to all, and no business could be transacted on "theater days." Events staged in theaters clearly underscored the connections between leisure (*otium*), culture (*urbanitas*), official religion, the municipal elite, and the emperor and imperial house.

CIRCUSES AND CHARIOT RACING

Such connections were also obvious for circus races, another favorite diversion of the Romans. Again, the fourth-century calendar from Rome is illuminating; then, at least, sixty-four days a year were designated for circus races at public expense. The most famous circus is Rome's Circus Maximus. It was supposed to date to the city's earliest times. According to tradition, at its site Romulus and the first

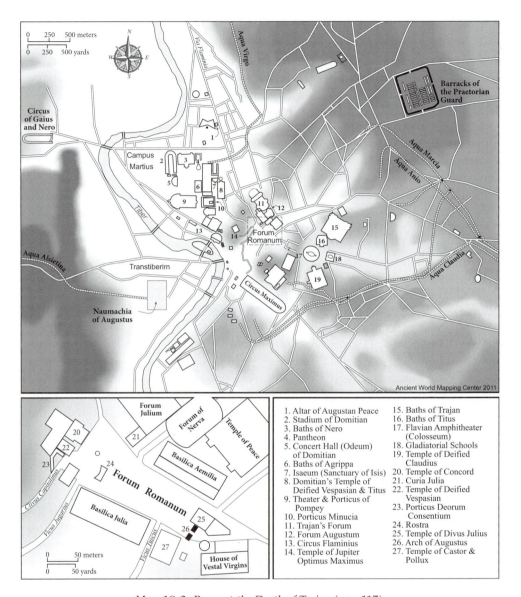

Map 10.3 *Rome at the Death of Trajan* (A.D. 117)

The following labels appear on the map:

0 250 500 meters
0 250 500 yards

N W E S

Via Flaminia
Aqua Virgo
Aqua Marcia
Aqua Anio
Aqua Claudia
Aqua Alsietina

Barracks of the Praetorian Guard

Circus of Gaius and Nero

Campus Martius

Tiber

Forum Romanum

Circus Maximus

Transtiberim

Naumachia of Augustus

Ancient World Mapping Center 2011

Forum Julium
Forum of Nerva
Temple of Peace
Basilica Aemilia
Forum Romanum
Clivus Capitolinus
Vicus Jugarius
Basilica Julia
Vicus Tuscus
House of Vestal Virgins

0 50 meters
0 50 yards

1. Altar of Augustan Peace
2. Stadium of Domitian
3. Baths of Nero
4. Pantheon
5. Concert Hall (Odeum) of Domitian
6. Baths of Agrippa
7. Isaeum (Sanctuary of Isis)
8. Domitian's Temple of Deified Vespasian & Titus
9. Theater & Porticus of Pompey
10. Porticus Minucia
11. Trajan's Forum
12. Forum Augustum
13. Circus Flaminius
14. Temple of Jupiter Optimus Maximus
15. Baths of Trajan
16. Baths of Titus
17. Flavian Amphitheater (Colosseum)
18. Gladiatorial Schools
19. Temple of Deified Claudius
20. Temple of Concord
21. Curia Julia
22. Temple of Deified Vespasian
23. Porticus Deorum Consentium
24. Rostra
25. Temple of Divus Julius
26. Arch of Augustus
27. Temple of Castor & Pollux

Romans had abducted the Sabine women from their fathers and brothers. The site was then said to have been monumentalized by the king Tarquinius Priscus, with an Etruscan flair for civil engineering. It was rebuilt a few times during the Republic. Its popularity attracted Julius Caesar and Augustus, who both undertook renovations and additions. In Augustus' day it was claimed to hold between 150,000 and 180,000 spectators, men and women, slave and free; in *The Art of Love* (1.135–162), Ovid recommends the Circus as one of the best places for singles to meet. Almost every Princeps left some mark there, such as an embellishment of the central dividing island (*spina*), or improvements to the starting gates. After

Figure 10.7 *A Roman charioteer. This top of a four-sided marble funerary monument shows a Roman charioteer much as he would have been dressed in a race. Over his tunic—which would probably have been painted the color of his team (green, red, blue, or white)—is wrapped a corset of leather cords to provide protection for his rib cage from the jarring ride. The palm tree at the front corner of the monument recalls the palms of victory that were given to the winners. On the side can be seen a racehorse. The monument is dated to Hadrian's time by the beard and hairstyle of the charioteer, as well as by the general carving technique, including the excised pupils of his eyes; previously, pupils on marble statues would be painted.*

Trajan made repairs and additions at the beginning of his Principate, as many as 250,000 spectators could be accommodated.

Circus racing remained popular even into Late Roman times, when it provided an important venue for public demonstrations in Constantinople. But gatherings at Rome's Circus Maximus, just as those at theaters and amphitheaters, had always allowed the populace to express their opinions to emperors and other figures in authority. This function of the Circus Maximus was reinforced by the location of Augustus' house on the Palatine overlooking it, and by the later extension of Domitian's palace towards it. Biographies and histories often note interaction between emperor and subject at the races, so that Tiberius' infrequent attendance at the Circus only added to his unpopularity. Other features of circus spectacles also remained constant. In the standard arrangement, four-horse chariots lapped at least seven times, for a total distance of 5.25 miles (8.4 km). Each race took about fifteen minutes, and twenty-four different races were usually staged in a day. The contenders were traditionally divided into four teams—Reds, Whites, Blues, and Greens (Domitian's innovation of additional Gold and Purple teams did not outlive him). Competition was fierce, and successful charioteers were richly rewarded. Racing—not to mention betting—was extremely popular. Mosaics and terracotta lamps depicting the Circus Maximus have been found throughout the Roman world, and charioteers were much acclaimed in their communities.

The potential use of circuses elsewhere—other than at Rome and, later, Constantinople—to express political dissatisfaction was also recognized, to judge by surviving regulations on the status of impresarios and the annual number of races in Italy and the provinces. The senate heard complaints about communities that had not offered appropriately good seating to senators and others of high status. Even so, like other festivals, circus races staged outside of Rome opened and closed with rituals celebrating the emperor and imperial family, and the gods that formed part of the state religion.

THE AMPHITHEATER, AND GLADIATORIAL GAMES

Similar rituals were integral to spectacles at the amphitheaters. Although these are perhaps the most notorious feature of Roman civilization, they were not held as often as is commonly assumed. The fourth-century calendar from Rome lists only ten days a year devoted to games in the amphitheater. Gladiatorial and beast fights are documented there as early as the third century B.C., but the earliest known permanent amphitheater was built only around 70 B.C. (see Figure 6.1 and Plate 9b), and the first permanent amphitheater in Rome dates to the Augustan Age. Both Roman and modern amphitheaters are commonly called "Colosseum" after the great Flavian amphitheater that rose in place of the lake of Nero's Golden

Figure 10.8 *Scenes from the amphitheater, as shown on a mosaic from Zliten, Tripolitania, now in the Archeological Museum of Tripoli, Libya. These two mosaic bands formed part of a larger floor, which depicted on its edges numerous scenes from gladiatorial and other shows exhibited in the amphitheater. From left to right, here we see (above) condemned criminals' public slaughter in the arena by wild beasts* (damnatio ad bestias); *various wild beast hunts* (venationes; *compare Plate 8b); (below) a fight between a man on foot and a man on a horse (the unhorsed rider's left arm and leg can be seen on the left); a fight between a bear and a bull; and one man whipping another towards lions. The mosaic perhaps dates to around 200, and the room from which it came was probably used for banquets or receptions.*

House. The name in fact derives from the adjacent colossal 120-foot-tall (36 m) statue of Nero, which the Flavians then modified to resemble Titus or the sun god, Sol. This Flavian amphitheater is a marvel of engineering, harmoniously proportioned, designed to maximize visibility and audibility, and structured so that it could be emptied of its 50,000 or so spectators in five minutes. Its sumptuous embellishment included water fountains for the spectators. Its design, which also rendered it fairly impervious to earthquakes, set the standard for all later amphitheaters throughout the Roman world. These structures were more prevalent in the West than in the East, although many remain in both halves of the empire.

Together with mosaics, gems, lamps, and inscriptions commemorating events in amphitheaters, these arenas attest to a Roman liking for "blood sports" that shocks many modern sensibilities. Spectators in the amphitheater watched men fighting against men, almost always in individual pairs except on extraordinary occasions funded by the emperor. Other events pitted men against wild beasts, various types of beasts against each other, and also beasts against unarmed men or even women, as when an individual found guilty of a capital crime was condemned "to the beasts" (*ad bestias*; see Fig. 10.8). This latter punishment has become notorious because it was often used for those who were condemned to death after refusing to renounce their Christianity (see Chapter Eleven); Ignatius, bishop of Syrian Antioch, was thus martyred in Rome some time before 117. Gladiatorial costumes and weaponry were standardized, and gladiatorial training schools were usually maintained at public expense. Most gladiators began as slaves; men of good repute and high social standing were to be spectators, not actors, in the amphitheater. A few female gladiators are documented, but this was primarily a male sport. Many rich men financed games in the arena in a display of public benefaction as well as a conspicuous sign of their wealth and power. The search for exotic beasts—whose display reflected the extent of Roman rule—contributed to emptying North Africa and other regions of indigenous fauna.

Although gladiatorial and wild beast fights were relatively rare in most years, the pace could be accelerated by individual emperors. For example, during the many celebrations that Trajan offered to the people of Rome from 106 through 114 to commemorate his Dacian Wars, some 11,000 beasts were slain, and 10,000 pairs of gladiators fought in the Colosseum, according to Cassius Dio (68.15). Such spectacular shows were deeply ingrained in Roman life. Gladiatorial fights were banned only by the emperor Theodosius II in 407, after almost a century of Christian emperors, and wild beast fights continued in Rome's Colosseum until 523.

Recent interpretations of amphitheater spectacles have stressed their use for social control and manipulation; thus the demonizing of gladiators and victims here strengthened the unity of the Roman citizens watching them.

Other interpretations have focused on the martial aspects of the gladiatorial fights, and on the virtuous bravery that men were expected to show in the very face of death. As every spectacle day at an amphitheater included public prayers to the gods and public homage to the emperor, we again find the same peculiarly Roman amalgam of imperial transcendence, public leisure, and the creation of consensus that was standard in the theater and circus.

Figure 10.9 *The Pont du Gard. This span, 330 feet (49 m) in height, is part of a larger aqueduct system that Agrippa sponsored to carry water to Colonia Augusta Nemausus (modern Nîmes, France) from a source 31 miles (50 km) away. In fact most of this aqueduct, like others, was underground, which was a safer and more economical method of construction. But because gravity was responsible for water flow, and siphons were generally unreliable and expensive, the water channel of an aqueduct would be carried directly across gorges, often at a considerable height, as here. This aqueduct is estimated to have had a flow of some 30,000 cubic meters a day, and to have cost up to 100 million sesterces.*

OTHER URBAN AMENITIES

The culture described above was furthered by the urban amenities of Roman cities. Aqueducts—apparently an essential component of veteran colonies established by emperors, and extremely expensive—began to be built in other cities, too, by the end of the first and the beginning of the second century, particularly in the East. Hadrian, for example, sponsored the construction or restoration of at least twelve aqueducts. Thanks to the Romans' engineering and the strength of their concrete, the remains of many Roman aqueducts can be seen today. In a few places, some of the inscribed lead pipes which divided and channeled water after its arrival at a city have even escaped being melted down, and so are able to provide particulars about workforces and water users.

Archeology and topography supplement detailed information provided by Sextus Julius Frontinus, whom Nerva appointed in 97 to be Rome's superintendent of aqueducts. Frontinus describes strict rules for the allocation of water brought to a city through a public aqueduct. Water went first to the public fountains, which either gushed water continuously or let a smaller volume trickle out more slowly. They were often ornamental, as well as functional in bringing clean water to a city's inhabitants. After the public fountains, water was supplied to the public baths. Runoff water was channeled to the baths' toilets or neighboring public ones before being carried out of the city through sewers. Only after public uses had been satisfied could private individuals pay to have water brought to their houses, where it served the usual domestic purposes, as well as ornamental fountains, and sometimes even private baths. Prices were high, and the powerful often tapped into water lines surreptitiously. Frontinus notes steep penalties for such illegal siphoning.

Although Roman baths were created by the end of the Republic, their great heyday came during the Principate, and particularly from the later first century into the third. Bath design did not become standardized until the time of Nero and his ostentatious public baths in Rome's Campus Martius; the great imperial baths of Rome were created first by Titus and then Trajan. There is no city in Italy and the provinces that could provide space for a bath of more than forty rooms; local patrons could hardly afford to install and embellish such spacious structures. Smaller and more intimate baths were built in almost every city, however, and many cities boasted more than one: Thamugadi had at least fourteen, Athens twenty. After undressing in a foyer, individual bathgoers would typically go first to the *tepidarium*, then to the *sudatorium* (sweat room), and then to the great cool pool of the *frigidarium*. As the water was not completely drained nor continually replenished, those who came later in the day might find less hygienic conditions than those who came early. Some open ground was also provided, where people could roll hoops, throw balls, sprint, or do other exercise. Peddlers hawked their wares in the baths, and teachers and poets often used the larger rooms and courtyards to teach or declaim.

Pompeii and a few other cities preserve evidence for separate baths catering to each sex. Elsewhere—to judge from a few inscribed bath regulations—the two sexes may have used the same facilities at different hours. We do not know if individuals bathed in the nude or with some modest covering, although Roman paintings and sculptures suggest a deep-seated aversion to total nudity. Baths were one of the most accessible places that the ordinary individual could go to be surrounded by opulent architecture and embellishment evoking Rome's majesty; statues of the imperial family were frequently displayed in them. Baths were extremely popular, therefore. They were good meeting spots. Often found near taverns, they had something of a racy reputation. As a famous epigram of the second century holds:

> Baths, wine, and lovemaking destroy our bodies,
> Yet lovemaking, wine, and baths make life worth living.
> (*Palatine Anthology* 10.112)

EDUCATION

Integral to Roman culture was the Roman system of education. Schooling and literary culture were based on a thorough knowledge of the past, and the skill to reshape the past for the present. There was little emphasis on innovation of a technological sort. Memorization was essential, and students had to learn by heart speeches of Cicero and long passages of Vergil, for example. The first three lines of the latter's *Aeneid* have been found incised on a first-century roof tile made in Spain, presumably by a bored worker or manager waiting for the clay to "cure" before firing; such a graffito demonstrates that literature was far from being the sole prerogative of the elite. The most famous Roman libraries were those at Rome and Alexandria, but smaller ones were to be found in Athens, Ephesus, Comum, Thamugadi, and other cities. Vespasian and subsequent "good" emperors encouraged education by offering teachers immunity from public duties, and by funding professorships of rhetoric at Rome, Athens, and elsewhere. By the second century, girls could also participate in classes offered by publicly funded teachers in cities, at least through the basics of reading, writing, and grammar. Some elite women such as Balbilla, one of Sabina's companions, could even be as highly educated as their brothers and husbands.

The cultural and literary movement termed the Second Sophistic, which lasted from around Nero's time into the third century, reached its peak in the Antonine period. Public speakers like Dio Chrysostom, Polemo of Smyrna, Aelius Aristides, and Herodes Atticus thrived under the emperors from Trajan through Marcus Aurelius. Their speeches and essays—deeply imbued with nostalgia for the classical Greek past, yet keenly aware of present political realities—dazzle with rhetorical flourishes. Thanks to the *Lives of the Sophists*, written by Philostratus in the early third century, the best known participants in this movement are those from the Greek East or men like Favorinus of Arelate (modern Arles in France), who wrote in Greek. Orators and writers in Latin, however, also won great acclaim and public standing through rhetorical bravura. For all a reader's or translator's expertise, the surviving texts can scarcely convey the excitement of the mass gatherings that hung on these speakers' displays of learning and brilliant turns of phrase. Wealthy, ambitious young men flocked to study under the leading sophists, above all at Athens, Ephesus, or Smyrna. Such esteemed teachers were often active, arrogant public figures in their communities, as well as effective envoys to provincial governors or the emperor himself. Philostratus (*Lives* 535) admiringly comments that Polemo, for instance, "conversed with cities as his inferiors, emperors as not his superiors, and the gods as his equals."

STATE RELIGION AND IMPERIAL CULT

Religious practices show the empire at its most diverse, but even here there was a common thread, the acknowledgment of Roman state religion. As previously noted, apart from a few cults considered threatening to public order, individuals generally could do as they pleased in terms of religion. Many religious practices and beliefs initially considered "un-Roman" or alien were later acknowledged by the Roman state and made an official part of its religion. For example, despite Tiberius' expulsion of worshippers of Isis from Rome, Domitian disguised himself as an acolyte of Isis and evaded Rome's street fighting during the civil war of 69. Once Princeps, he magnificently rebuilt the Isaeum in Rome's Campus Martius, linking it to the imperial cult and featuring it on his coinage.

During the Principate the touchstone of Roman state religion was the imperial cult. So long as men and women participated in it by means of their community's rituals, the authorities generally paid little attention to their other religious acts and beliefs. Beginning with the Flavian period, we find ever more priests and priestesses of the cult in cities and provincial (or regional) gatherings in the Spanish and Gallic provinces, North Africa, and Asia. Similarly, the first appearance of more than one imperial cult temple in a single province of the Greek East dates to the 80s. The imperial cult spread elsewhere in the second century. Its prestigious priests and priestesses, titled *flamen, flaminica, archiereus* and the like, administered to their communities the annual oath of allegiance to the emperor and his family and the senate and people of Rome. They oversaw community-wide celebrations on the emperor's birthday, and on the birthdays of earlier deified emperors and empresses. They organized city festivals for military victories and the suppression of revolts, and for special events in the imperial family like the birth of a child. Today, the pervasiveness of television, the Internet, and other forms of electronic personal entertainment makes it hard to grasp the impact of a community's games, processions, sacrifices, and prayers. Such days of public festivity must have been particularly welcome to the working poor, like the Egyptian weaving apprentice whose contract allowed him only "twenty holidays a year on account of festivals without any deduction from his wages." The monotheistic beliefs of Jews and Christians discouraged them from participating. As a result they may have been conspicuous by their absence on public feast days, but so long as state authorities did not demand sacrifice and public prayer, lack of involvement was no crime.

It is important to stress that the imperial cult itself was never imposed on a community by Rome. Individual cities and assemblies applied to the senate and emperor for permission to erect sanctuaries. If this were granted, the community usually chose its own priests and determined the statues to be paraded in processions, the order of the parades, and even the type of games to be performed. As a way to gain extra prestige, the patron or community might reapply to the emperor and senate for ratification of its decision. Although again the initiative had to be a local one, games organized in the emperor's honor likewise needed ratification by the emperor. Such procedures inevitably meant that the imperial cult took many different forms throughout the empire. In one city festivities might include contests of verse and prose panegyrics praising the emperor; in another, the celebration might be less highbrow, centered instead on animal sacrifices and offerings of incense and wine. The unifying thread was public awe and acknowledgment of imperial power. As we shall see in the following chapter, this is precisely why Christianity posed such a challenge to the Roman world.

SUGGESTED READINGS

Aldrete, Gregory S. 2008. *Daily Life in the Roman City: Rome, Pompeii, and Ostia*. Norman: University of Oklahoma Press.

Bennett, Julian. 2001 (second edition). *Trajan: Optimus Princeps*. London and New York: Routledge.

Birley, Anthony R. 1997. *Hadrian. The Restless Emperor*. London and New York: Routledge.

Boatwright, Mary T. 2000. *Hadrian and the Cities of the Roman Empire*. Princeton: Princeton University Press.

Bowersock, Glen W. 1969. *Greek Sophists in the Roman Empire*. Oxford: Oxford University Press.

Evans, Harry B. 1994. *Water Distribution in Ancient Rome: The Evidence of Frontinus*. Ann Arbor: University of Michigan Press.

Fagan, Garrett G. 2011. *The Lure of the Arena. Social Psychology and the Crowd at the Roman Games*. Cambridge: Cambridge University Press.

Goodman, Martin. 2007. *Rome and Jerusalem: The Clash of Ancient Civilizations*. New York: Knopf.

Jones, Brian W. 1992. *The Emperor Domitian*. London and New York: Routledge.

Levick, Barbara. 1999. *Vespasian*. London and New York: Routledge.

Potter, David S. (ed.). 2006. *A Companion to the Roman Empire*. Malden, Mass., and Oxford: Blackwell. This large volume's broad scope encompasses the different sources of our knowledge; government; religion; social, economic, and intellectual life.

Rives, James B. 2007. *Religion in the Roman Empire*. Malden, Mass., and Oxford: Blackwell.

Wallace-Hadrill, Andrew. 1994. *Houses and Society in Pompeii and Herculaneum*. Princeton: Princeton University Press.

ITALY AND THE PROVINCES

Civil and Military Affairs (138–235)

SOURCES

For the period covered in this chapter—at least until about 220—inscriptions, papyri, archeology, coins, and legal treatises and opinions reflect general prosperity and marked attention to justice and law. Ulpian, Paulus, and other jurists flourished at the beginning of the third century, encouraged by the *constitutio Antoniniana* of 212 that granted Roman citizenship almost universally within the empire. Ulpian, for example, wrote 200 books to explain Roman law to the new citizens. Such initiatives must be kept in mind when reading the literary sources for this period, which tend to be critical of all the emperors except Antoninus Pius and Marcus Aurelius, and to paint a picture of general decadence.

Cassius Dio's record now draws upon personal experience and oral testimony. A senator from Bithynia, Dio rose to high civil and military positions under the Severan emperors, almost losing his life around 228 in a military insurrection while governor of Lower Pannonia. He usually portrays the Severans and their predecessor Commodus as hostile to individual senators and senatorial freedom, and he comments at the death of Commodus' father Marcus Aurelius, "Our history now descends from a kingdom of gold to one of iron and rust, as did the Romans' situation at that point" (71.36.4). Herodian, also writing in Greek in the early third century but serving in lower civil administration, describes events from 180 to 235 in eight books divided by individual rulers. He is a moralizer, and the rhetorical nature of his work can make it seem shallow, but he also furnishes vivid details that illuminate Rome's culture and society, like the funeral rites for Pertinax (see Source 11.3). Later and less reliable is the *Historia Augusta*, a set of imperial biographies beginning with Hadrian, composed at the end of the fourth century. Its unknown author delights in salacious anecdotes about emperors' immorality and capriciousness, and shares a common perception of their growing neglect or mistreatment of the senate. Further, the apparent power of imperial women greatly increased with the Severans, creating another source of irritation for traditionalists. Overall, the historical texts for this era are fragmented, focused on the imperial court, and generally biased against individual emperors.

Further literature, less directly concerned with political and military events, sheds light on a wide variety of cultural and other aspects. Marcus Aurelius, a philosopher as well as Princeps, wrote *To Himself* (now called *Meditations*) in Greek, a startlingly personal exploration of his own conceptions of the Good and his place in human society. The *Metamorphoses* (now commonly called *The Golden Ass*), a picaresque Latin novel written by Apuleius (c. 125 to after 170, from North Africa), describes the adventures of a young man magically transformed into an ass, the lowliest of creatures, before Isis returns him to human form. Many scholars see the last book of the novel as a conversion story that brilliantly illuminates the cult of the Egyptian goddess Isis and its powerful attraction. Besides offering a fascinating tale, it is a good example of the recondite style of the Latin writing fashionable at that date. Numerous authors represent the Greek Second Sophistic: for example, Aelius Aristides (born in 118 in the province of Asia) wrote his *To Rome* around 144 (Source 11.1). A very different set of preoccupations is seen in the trenchant works of the first Christian apologists, including Tertullian (160s to 240s, from Carthage). These sources provide much information about social history. In addition they elucidate Christian attempts to define the new religion both for non-Christians and for themselves; even from the beginning, there were wide variations in how Christians understood their religion. Tertullian's *On the Games*—a fierce denunciation of the shows in circus, theater, and amphitheater, and their ties with the Roman gods—incidentally preserves rich detail about these significant occasions.

The first half of the chapter discusses the rulers of the period, and its volatile political and military events. The second half treats three broad topics that now come to assume increasing importance: Roman law, Roman citizenship, and religious practices and beliefs, including Christianity.

ANTONINUS PIUS (138–161)

Hadrian's successor Antoninus Pius never left Italy during the twenty-three years of his rule. He was much less involved with the military than were his predecessors and successors. Yet he maintained the appearance of military preparedness and encouraged good officers. A governor of Britain, Quintus Lollius Urbicus, reconquered southern Scotland. This advance was consolidated by the Wall of Antoninus, a turf wall on cobble foundations some hundred miles north of Hadrian's Wall; even so, for reasons no longer identifiable, Antoninus' Wall was abandoned not long after his death in 161, and Hadrian's Wall was then regarrisoned

Figure 11.1 *The dynastic hopes of the Antonine family. The obverse of this bronze coin, a* sestertius *struck in the last year of Antoninus Pius' rule (160–161), depicts the emperor with a laurel crown of victory. The legend translates: "Antoninus Pius, Father of the Fatherland, with tribunician power for the 24th time." The legend on the reverse reads: "To Augustan Piety. Consul for the fourth time," and also carries S C, denoting that the coin was issued with the senate's authority. The standing woman with four children on the reverse is to be identified with Faustina the Younger, Antoninus Pius' daughter, who by now had presented her husband Marcus Aurelius with four daughters (Lucilla, Cornificia, Fadilla, and Annia Faustina). Among other values, the coin highlights Rome's concern for population increase.*

(Map 11.1). Other military action, apparently overseen by Marcus Gavius Maximus (Praetorian Prefect from about 139 to 159), included a show of force against the Parthians at the beginning of Antoninus' rule, repulse of invading Moorish tribes in Mauretania and Numidia (145–150), minor skirmishes in Dacia, and a modest extension of Roman territory along the Rhine.

Under Pius, no far-reaching legal changes were enacted, nor were there notable administrative changes other than the withdrawal of Hadrian's consular judges in Italy. This latter step, like many other actions by Antoninus, contributed to harmony between emperor and senate, one hallmark of his Principate. Another characteristic of the time is the firm stress on family and the imperial dynasty, which has meant that the era is often called the "Antonine" age. Although Antoninus may seem the most unmemorable of emperors, the sheer uneventfulness of his rule reflects both the accomplishments of the preceding half-century and his own capability. Antoninus' time seems to mark the empire's climax as an organized, benevolent, and self-assured form of rule. The diverse forces that would undermine its stability were already present—unrest along the borders, inequities at home—but the vast majority of the empire's inhabitants still accepted their present condition more or less willingly.

SOURCE 11.1: A Greek Provincial Praises Roman Citizenship

The panegyric To Rome, *also known as the* Roman Oration, *was written around 144 by Publius Aelius Aristides, a Roman citizen of Greek origin from a town founded by Hadrian in the province of Asia, who became one of the leading practitioners of the Second Sophistic. In true sophistic style,* To Rome *demonstrates its author's deep engagement with history and philosophy, while placing Roman rule in the most favorable light. It provides an instructive glimpse into the mindset of wealthy, well-connected provincials during the empire's heyday and the elite's enduring belief in meritocracy.*

. . . You sought the expansion of your Roman citizenship as a worthy aim, and you have caused the word Roman to be the mark, not of membership in a city, but of some common nationality, and this not just one among all, but one balancing all the rest. For the categories into which you now divide the world are Romans and non-Romans. . . . Since these are the lines along which the distinction has been made, many in every city are fellow-citizens of yours no less than of their own relatives, though some of them have yet to set eyes on this city [Rome]. There is no need of garrisons to hold their citadels, but the men of greatest standing and influence in every city guard their own fatherlands for you. And you have a double hold upon the cities, both from here [Rome] and from your fellow citizens in each. No envy sets foot in the empire, for you yourselves were the first to disown envy when you placed all opportunities in view of all, and offered those who were capable a chance to be governed no more than they in turn governed. Neither does hatred steal in from those who are not chosen. . . . All the masses have as a share in the constitution the permission to take refuge with you from the power of the local magnates. Indignation and punishment from you will come upon these magnates immediately, if they dare to make any unlawful change independently. . . . What previously seemed to be impossible has come to pass in your time: maintenance of control over an empire—a vast one, too—and at the same time firmness of rule without severity. (63–66; translation based on that of James H. Oliver, *The Ruling Power. A Study of the Roman Empire in the Second Century after Christ through the Roman Oration of Aelius Aristides*. Philadelphia: American Philosophical Society, 1953)

MARCUS AURELIUS (161–180) AND LUCIUS VERUS (161–169)

Antoninus Pius was deified immediately after his death. Power then passed smoothly to Marcus Aurelius and Lucius Verus, as Hadrian had arranged in 138 by having Antoninus adopt both. Ties among their families had been strengthened further since then (see Table 10.1). The marriage of Marcus Aurelius and Antoninus' daughter, Faustina the Younger, produced perhaps as many as fifteen children—a model demonstration of the importance attached to the family at this period. One of their daughters, Lucilla, was betrothed, aged eleven, to Lucius Verus. The marriage took place at Ephesus in 164, when she was fourteen and he (aged thirty-four) was based at Antioch to prepare for war against the Parthians.

Figure 11.2 *This marble votive relief dates to around 200, and gives pride of place to a ship sailing into the harbor built to the north of Ostia by Claudius. The V and L on the sail probably represent the words V(otum) L(ibens) [S(oluit)] ("He/she repaid the vow willingly"). Meantime, wine-shipping containers are being unloaded from a smaller ship, already moored, at bottom right (compare Plate 8a). So the relief seems to be a dedication from a wine merchant at Ostia's temple of the wine god Liber. To the left, the larger ship has just entered the harbor; at the stern, it is presumably the shipowner and his family who are celebrating a sacrifice for their safe arrival. Duplicated on the sail is the powerful Roman symbol of the she-wolf with Romulus and Remus; nearby an eagle flies through a wreath of victory, a symbol of imperial Rome. To the right of the ship's prow stands Neptune, god of the sea, holding his trident. Behind the prow can be seen the famous four-storied lighthouse; the statue on its third story may represent either Claudius, who began the construction of the harbor, or his successor Nero, who completed it. The two colossal statues with cornucopias and wreaths seem to represent the city of Ostia (the female with the lighthouse on her head) and the harbor itself (her male companion). On the right, an arch bears a chariot drawn by four elephants and driven by an emperor; far right stands Liber, god of wine, with two of his distinctive attributes, a wand (thyrsus) and a panther. The relief conveys both the pervasiveness of religious activity and icons in daily life—note the large "evil eye," believed to avert bad fortune—and the ubiquity of imperial statues and buildings in important cities. Trajan dug an inner, six-sided basin to extend the capacity of Claudius' harbor.*

Despite the inevitable difficulty of sharing authority, Marcus Aurelius and Verus ruled from 161 to 169 as joint Augusti with equal powers. Only Marcus Aurelius' position as pontifex maximus marked him as the senior emperor and acknowledged his greater *auctoritas*. The two demonstrated their cooperation by immediately quelling minor insurrections in Britain and Germany that had erupted upon news of Antoninus' death. For much of the time, they divided their energies and attention, Verus commanding in the East against the Parthians from 162 to 166, and Marcus Aurelius ruling in Rome or, after 167, often on the northern frontiers. The double threat to East and North led to the creation of two new legions in the mid 160s.

Verus' Parthian war was prompted by the Parthians' seizure of Armenia and invasion of Syria in 161. In 162 Verus went to Antioch to organize the Roman counteroffensive, which was boosted by three legions and additional troops dispatched to the East from the Rhine and Danube. Much of the actual fighting was undertaken for him by others, however. In 165–166 Gaius Avidius Cassius, then governor of Syria, won conspicuous victories in Mesopotamia, destroyed Seleucia, and razed the Parthian king's palace at neighboring Ctesiphon (near modern Baghdad, Iraq). The Parthians sued for peace, relinquishing part of northern Mesopotamia to Roman control, and Verus celebrated a triumph in Rome jointly with Marcus Aurelius. This brief offensive against Parthia underscores the deadlocked, evenly matched strength of the two empires. Parthian forces were well organized and equipped, and Avidius Cassius' victories would turn out to be short-lived.

Roman troops returning from the East brought back with them a violent infectious disease, perhaps smallpox. After 166, it spread through the empire for some twenty-five years. More than a fifth of the inhabitants of Alexandria are said to have perished, other cities were decimated, and military camps were particularly hard hit. Heavy mobilization of troops for the campaigns against the Marcomanni in the North must have increased the death toll. Even rural areas were afflicted, so that suffering was then exacerbated by ensuing famines. Only the interior of North Africa may have escaped the epidemic. Given the rudimentary understanding of germs and disease, this plague must have been terrifying as well as devastating. It may have contributed to increasing tensions between Christians and the polytheistic majority, which had already led to mob violence against Christians at Smyrna (modern Izmir, Turkey) during the 150s. Another such outbreak, at Lugdunum in Gaul, occurred in 177. The decrease and demoralization of the military and urban populations—that is, the skilled individuals who undertook defense, commerce, and administration—undoubtedly weakened the empire. It is true that in the city of Rome itself, as well as in those provinces not directly affected by warfare, literature, monuments, art, and architecture all continue to convey the impression of a comfortable urban elite through the beginning of the third century. By then, however, we also begin to hear more frequent complaints about difficulties in filling municipal administrative positions.

Life-threatening epidemic disease was a regular feature of the ancient world. We cannot identify precisely the closest modern equivalent for each "pestilence" reported by our sources, but smallpox, malaria, tuberculosis, typhus, measles, and

SOURCE 11.2: Morbidity and Mortality in the Roman Empire

Other contemporary authors note the effects of the Antonine plague, but the sophist Aelius Aristides gives a vivid description of its effects on him personally. Even the short excerpt below allows us to discern misunderstandings about communicable diseases and the lack of proper medicines:

I happened to be in the suburbs at the height of summer [165]. A plague infected nearly all my neighbors. First two or three of my servants grew sick, then one after another. Then all were in bed, both the younger and the older. I was the last to be attacked. . . . The livestock, too, became sick. And if anyone tried to move, he immediately lay dead before the front door. . . . Everything was filled with despair and wailing and groans, and every kind of difficulty. There was also terrible sickness in the city . . . I was attacked by the terrible burning of a bilious mixture and prevented from taking nourishment. . . . The doctors gave up, and announced that I would die immediately . . . [But after seeing visions of the divinities Asclepius and Athena,] I took goose liver and sausage, and little by little with trouble and difficulty I recovered. The fever did not leave me completely until the most valued of my foster children died. (*Orations* 48.38–44, excerpted from P. Aelius Aristides, *The Complete Works*, translated into English by Charles A. Behr, Leiden: Brill, 1981–)

leprosy were almost certainly common. Ironically, epidemics were spread and made more devastating by the general peace that encouraged travel, long-distance transport, and concentration of populations in cities and military camps. To judge by the limited evidence available, the young were particularly susceptible to disease and ill health. Our understanding of Roman mortality patterns depends on 100,000 or more inscribed epitaphs (mostly dating between 50 B.C. and A.D. 235), over 300 census returns surviving from Egypt, human skeletal remains, and an excerpt from the *Digest* (35.2.68.pr) that concerns inheritance taxes. Despite many problems with this material, some facts emerge. Without question, there was very high infant and childhood mortality. Perhaps 33 percent of all children born in a given year died before reaching their first birthday, and 55 percent before reaching their fifth. Once a teenager passed the fifteen-year-old threshold, however, he or she might expect to live to be at least thirty-six; even so, in view of infant and child mortality, the median age of the population was only about twenty-five years. No more than about 8 percent of the Roman population lived to be more than fifty years old.

These general patterns are very broad, and ignore many distinctions. Military medicine was excellent in its provision of doctors, quarantine wards, fresh water, and medicinal herbs to the troops. But such advantages were certainly offset during warfare, since there were no antibiotics. Rural civilians living far from a port or a major Roman road would be less exposed to epidemics; on the other hand, they surely suffered from malnutrition, polluted water, and overwork, unless they were part of the small wealthy minority. Ample running water brought by aqueducts must have made the Roman cities supplied in this way least vulnerable to

Map 11.1 *Campaigns of Marcus Aurelius and the Severan Emperors*

Legend:

☐ Legionary base (normally a single legion)
◼ Principal settlement with legionary base adjacent
Not all legions' bases are known.
Bases and provinces (boundaries, names)
around A.D. 200 are shown.

SARMATIANS

DACIA
Potaissa
pulum
Sarmizegetusa
gidunum
GOTHS
Viminacium
Novae
Durostorum
LOWER MOESIA
PPER
OESIA
THRACIA
BLACK SEA
Danube
incum
ES

Amastris

BITHYNIA-PONTUS
ARMENIA
Satala

Byzantium
Nicomedia
Ancyra
CAPPADOCIA
Amida
MESOPOTAMIA
Tigris

Perinthus
Nicaea
GALATIA
Melitene
Samosata
Resaina
Singara

ACEDONIA
Cyzicus
Caesarea
(Mazaca)
Carrhae
OSROENE

hessalonica
LEMNOS
Pergamum
Faustinopolis
Issus
Sura
Ctesiphon

PIRUS
LESBOS
Mytilene
ASIA
Tarsus
Antioch
Oriza
Euphrates
Seleucia

ACHAIA
Smyrna
LYCIA
CILICIA
Raphaneae
SYRIA
COELE
Palmyra
PARTHIA

olis
Ephesus
Emesa

Corinth
Myra
CYPRUS
SYRIA
PHOENICE

Paphos
Berytus

CRETA
Gortyn
Tyre
Caparcotna
Bostra

Caesarea
5

Aelia Capitolina

ARE
RE
Alexandria
ARABIA PETRAEA
Petra

Cyrene
Nile

AEGYPTUS

Ancient World Mapping Center 2011

water-borne disease. But at the same time the amenities and opportunities offered by cities must have led to the kind of crowding that admitted more air- and vector-borne disease. Even the rich, who could enjoy the indisputable advantages of roomy living space, a varied, plentiful diet, and clean water, were exposed to ills that have come to be recognized in modern times: lead poisoning both from the water pipes to their residences and from women's cosmetics, and inadvertent poisoning from abortifacients and other medicines.

The Romans' decision to end the Parthian war in 166 coincides with growing problems along the Danube, caused in part perhaps because one key legion and auxiliaries had been removed from the forces here. Beginning in 166, the German Lombards, Marcomanni, and Quadi, as well as the eastern Sarmatians and Iazyges, crossed the middle Danube into the Pannonian provinces and Dacia, and then pushed farther south. Both Marcus Aurelius and Verus went north to engage them in 168; when Verus died of a stroke in 169, Marcus Aurelius continued as sole Princeps. In fact he was to spend most of the rest of his life fighting in the north, and in his *Meditations* he steels himself to carry through his obligations even though he considers warfare contrary to philosophy and the Good (10.9). Before 170, the Marcomanni and Quadi reached Aquileia, an important port on the Adriatic Sea. Although they were then both turned back in hard fighting, other tribes joined the assault meantime. These persistent hostilities divide into the First and Second Marcomannic Wars (166–173, 176–180). At some stage during them, the Romans evidently felt sufficiently successful and confident to envision the creation of two further provinces north of the Danube that would be named Marcomannia and Sarmatia.

Roman success depended in part on Marcus Aurelius' acceptance of trans-Danubian migrants within the borders of the empire as *dediticii*. He is known to have settled more than 11,000 of them in the German provinces, Pannonia, Dacia, Moesia, and possibly even in Italy too. The precise nature of their status is controversial, since the key document—a papyrus recording part of the *constitutio Antoniniana* (see Caracalla, below)—is damaged. It seems, however, that they were permanently debarred from full integration into the Roman state. Even so, their settlement within its borders satisfied their land hunger, and made them responsible for protecting Rome's assets and land, even though they were perceived as "barbarians." Archeological evidence—mostly grave goods and tombstones, but also domestic and religious structures—indicates that at least some dediticii did assimilate Roman culture. In practice, the distinction between Roman and non-Roman was not as sharp as literature and some of the visual arts represent it to be (see Fig. 11.6). Archeology also reveals the presence of Roman forts and outposts across the Danube within barbarian territory (*barbaricum*).

Marcus Aurelius' great fame rests not on his military victories but on his frank, and apparently genuine, commitment to Rome's "beneficial ideology." In line with his own philosophical interests, he endowed professorships of rhetoric and philosophy at Athens. Rather than increase taxes to fund the two new legions

Figure 11.3 *This white marble relief panel from a lost monument in Rome shows part of a religious ceremony. In the background, the temple of Jupiter Optimus Maximus is depicted frontally; to its right is shown one of the many covered walkways (or colonnades) on Rome's Capitoline hill. Marcus Aurelius, the large, individualized figure just left of center, offers a libation at a portable altar; he has pulled a fold of his toga over his head ritually. Next to him, a boy holds an incense box, and a bearded man (shown small because of his low social status) plays music to accompany the ritual and to mask any ill-omened sounds. The bare-chested man with the axe is a* victimarius, *a specialized religious attendant who slew a bull (as here) or other victims in blood sacrifices. Behind Marcus Aurelius stands a tall senator identified as Tiberius Claudius Pompeianus, his close friend and later son-in-law (see Table 10.1). The emperor appears as the intermediary between humans and gods, and as the preserver of Rome and its order.*

raised in the 160s, he auctioned off imperial jewels and finery. His council of advisers worked well, with its members in Rome handling routine administration while he was far away on campaign. When he reinstated four consular judges for Italy (Hadrian's initiative, dropped by Antoninus), there was no protest by leading figures in Italy or in Rome itself.

Only one significant civil disturbance marred the general atmosphere of harmony under Marcus Aurelius. It occurred in spring and summer 175, and reveals some fundamental tensions in the empire, although our disjointed source material leaves the background obscure. Avidius Cassius, the general largely responsible for the successful Parthian War of 162–166, was appointed governor of Egypt in 171, where he suppressed an uprising of desert peoples. Later, probably in early March 175, he announced to his troops that Marcus Aurelius was dead, but that he himself was willing to assume imperial power. Duly acclaimed emperor, he ruled in the East for almost four months. He was then killed by a subordinate, just as Marcus Aurelius was making his way to the East with his wife Faustina and the fourteen-year-old Commodus, their sole son to survive childhood.

According to some versions of these events, Avidius undertook his coup only after receiving a report that Marcus Aurelius had died. In other versions, however, he is said to have been encouraged to revolt by Faustina, either on sheer impulse or because she feared for her husband's health and wanted to ensure the succession of her son. The first variant highlights the empire's inadequate communications; the second, the deep-seated mistrust of women, especially those in power, and the perpetual problem of imperial succession. A final striking aspect of Avidius Cassius' rule over Egypt, Syria, and most of Asia Minor is that it reflects the underlying division of the empire. Without mass communication and rapid transport, it was inherently difficult to maintain political unity over Rome's wide expanse of territory and cultures.

After personally reestablishing his imperial authority in the East, Marcus Aurelius returned to Rome in 176. Faustina died in Cappadocia on the return journey; the senate deified her, and the city where she died was renamed Faustinopolis. Together with Commodus, Marcus Aurelius then celebrated a great triumph over the northern barbarians. Commodus received further honors, the consulship and acclamation as Augustus. But by the end of 176, father and son, now joint Augusti, were in Pannonia and Raetia to confront renewed threats from the North. When Marcus Aurelius died of natural causes in early March 180 at Vindobona (modern Vienna, Austria), nineteen-year-old Commodus was acclaimed sole emperor. It is not clear whether he had personally participated in any battles or major military decisions yet, but his father had always surrounded him with the best tutors and a loyal, capable group of advisers. In the ancient sources, Marcus Aurelius' designation of his son to succeed him as Princeps is the one blot on his reputation. Yet his choice was in line with Rome's traditional emphasis on kinship, and even most of the adopted emperors in fact had family links to their predecessors.

COMMODUS (176–192, RULING AS SOLE AUGUSTUS AFTER 180)

During the first five months of his sole rule, Commodus concluded the Marcomannic wars, and abandoned the plans for the prospective new provinces of Marcomannia and Sarmatia. Although Herodian and the *Historia Augusta* maintain that his decision ran completely counter to his father's aims as well as the opinion of his advisers, some scholars today believe that by now Marcus Aurelius himself had decided to abandon these campaigns to extend Roman control across the Danube. Protracted difficulties in Pannonia had already highlighted the limits of Roman communications and manpower, and Commodus' peace treaty with the Marcomanni and Quadi may have included the one-time recruitment of a large number of their young men. Yet once again—just as in 117 after the abandonment of Trajan's eastern conquests— many observers regarded the preference for peace and the consolidation of borders as inglorious expedients, and they criticized Commodus accordingly.

Commodus returned to Rome and another triumph, and the Column of Marcus Aurelius (still a prominent monument today; Map 12.2) was erected at Rome to mark the wars' end and Rome's invincibility. Although Commodus did take some initiatives in the provinces, he never came close to matching his father's exceptional concern for the empire. Rather, Commodus' council of advisers was entrusted with much of the administration, and successive Praetorian Prefects exercised great power. Commodus behaved erratically towards the senate, and conspiracies soon began. In 182, his sister Lucilla (once married to Lucius Verus) was implicated in a failed assassination plot involving one of the Praetorian Prefects and other highly placed men; many were executed. Disorder in Rome itself increased, with the Praetorians lynching their Prefect, Sextus Tigidius Perennis in 185. Commodus then fell under the influence of Marcus Aurelius Cleander, his freedman servant whom he promoted to be Praetorian Prefect.

To judge by the accounts in our sources, Commodus' own major concerns were his personal gratification and that of Rome's masses. He made many distributions in

Figure 11.4 *Commodus as Hercules. This bust, dated to around 190, was found in Rome in an underground walkway (cryptoporticus) of a luxury garden belonging to the imperial family. The face is that of the adult Commodus as it is known from other portraits, but he is portrayed as Hercules. He wears the lion skin over his head, and carries a club in his right hand. In his left he holds apples, recalling another of Hercules' legendary labors—taking the apples of the Hesperides. The bust is balanced on an Amazonian shield whose corners are fashioned as imperial eagles, and on the tops of two cornucopias. All these elements rest on a small globe that symbolizes the entire world. Two Amazons (one now completely missing, the other without her head) flanked the support, looking upwards in homage to the hero. The bust corresponds to ancient writers' claims that Commodus "accepted statues in the costume of Hercules, and sacrifices were made to him as a god" (Historia Augusta, Commodus 9.2). Its remarkable preservation suggests that it was carefully hidden after Commodus' violent death.*

the city, and restructured its grain imports. Like Nero before him, he frequently appeared in untraditional public roles. He fancied himself a great gladiator and wild beast hunter (*bestiarius*). With his own hands he supposedly killed many thousands of animals, including elephants and ostriches. He is also said to have fought as a gladiator 365 times during his father's rule, and so often during his own Principate that he won a thousand gladiatorial crowns just by defeating or killing "net-fighters," quite apart from other types of gladiator (*Historia Augusta, Commodus* 13.1).

From 185 to 192 the situation grew grimmer for everyone, the populace included. Cleander's fall from power in 190 was marked by rioting, and authority then passed to Commodus' mistress and one of his servants. In 192, he sponsored two full weeks of gladiatorial games in which he personally performed. He planned to take up the consulship on January 1, 193, dressed as a gladiator rather than in the traditional toga, and to rename Rome "Colonia Commodiana." His dangerous instability finally provoked his assassination on December 31, 192, and the senate then immediately condemned his memory (*damnatio memoriae*).

The chaos that followed stems from Rome's lack of constitutional means either to expel unworthy emperors or to ensure an orderly succession. This deficiency was to cause two more serious internal crises within the next half-century (in 193–197 and 217–221), and ever more frequent ones after 235. From the turmoil of 193 emerged the dynasty known as the Severans (Latin, *Severi*), and an apparent renaissance for the city of Rome, the northern provinces, North Africa, and the East. The Severans are named after Lucius Septimius Severus, who seized power in 193. All subsequent rulers until 235—even the eques Macrinus and his ten-year-old son Diadumenianus who ruled briefly in 217–218—either were, or claimed to be, related to Septimius Severus or to his wife, Julia Domna (see Table 11.1).

CIVIL WAR AND THE RISE OF SEPTIMIUS SEVERUS (193–211)

Upon Commodus' assassination, various groups vied for power—the senate, the Praetorians, and the army, or rather three different divisions within the army that each promoted its own commander. Each group proved strong enough to bring a candidate to imperial power, but only one of these, Septimius Severus (promoted by the troops along the Danube), was then able to maintain and expand his control. As happened after the coup that removed Nero, many uninvolved civilians became caught up in these power struggles and lost their lives as a result. In this instance, however, the damage occurred mainly in the provinces (Asia, north Syria, and Gaul in particular), a reflection perhaps of how Italy and Rome were now losing their prime importance for the Principate.

The first Princeps to be proclaimed in 193 was Lucius Helvius Pertinax. A sixty-six-year-old senator who had loyally served Marcus Aurelius in military and civil positions, Pertinax was the senate's choice. His position as City Prefect in 192 gave him command of the Urban Cohorts in Rome. The Praetorians, however, acclaimed him only reluctantly, despite being paid a donative of about 12,000

Table 11.1 The Severan Family *The presentation follows the style of Table 8.1, explained there.*

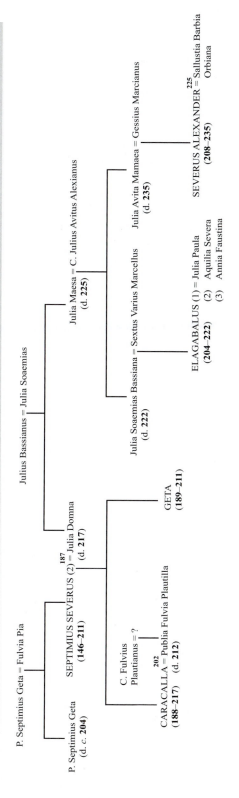

sesterces per man. Pertinax vowed to respect the senate, and to restore the imperial finances ravaged by Commodus' extravagant games and luxuries. To raise money, he auctioned Commodus' property, cut back on expenditures, and announced other reforms. He promised full ownership and ten years free from taxes to those who would settle and farm abandoned land; this initiative would bring back into cultivation acreage no longer cultivated because of the plague and the losses in Rome's northern and eastern wars of the previous generation. But Pertinax never could enlist the Praetorians' wholehearted support, and at the end of March 193 they murdered him in the palace. To judge by Cassius Dio's comment that Pertinax had "failed to comprehend that one cannot safely reform everything at once" (73.10.3), it was not just the Praetorians who were becoming dissatisfied with Pertinax. Nonetheless, it was they who determined Rome's next emperor.

The ensuing episode is reported with disgust by Herodian and others. After assassinating Pertinax, the Praetorians proceeded to auction off the Principate at the gates of their barracks in Rome. Two senators were in the bidding: Titus Flavius Sulpicianus, the City Prefect and father-in-law of Pertinax, and Marcus Didius Severus Julianus. The latter won with his promise of 25,000 sesterces per man, more than double what Pertinax had given three months earlier. Cowed by the Praetorians, the senate ratified their choice. The Roman populace rioted throughout the city and staged an all-night protest in the Circus Maximus.

But the armies outside of Rome, who vastly outnumbered the Praetorians, had already declared emperors of their own. The three legions in Syria declared for Gaius Pescennius Niger, and seven other legions in the East followed their lead. Britain's three legions and auxiliary troops declared for their own commander, Decimus Clodius Albinus. The legion at Carnuntum in Upper Pannonia (modern Petronell, Austria) acclaimed as emperor their commander and governor, Lucius Septimius Severus; his support then spread to the other legions on the Danube and the Rhine, sixteen in all. Severus was the shrewdest of the three claimants, according to Cassius Dio. He set off for Rome immediately, and reduced the threat from his rivals by appointing Albinus "Caesar" over Britain, Gaul, and Spain. As the Praetorians' loyalty to Didius Julianus began to waver, the senate sentenced him to death, and acclaimed Septimius Severus instead. Didius Julianus was killed at the beginning of June 193. A week later, Septimius Severus entered Rome as Princeps.

Septimius Severus was as politically astute as he was militarily brilliant. He entered the city as a civilian in a toga, as had Trajan, but he did not disband the cavalry and infantry forces accompanying him. He had the damnation of Commodus' memory cancelled, and Pertinax deified; the senate confirmed his own assumption of the name Pertinax. The purpose of these measures was to link himself to recent emperors, and to forge a tie with the senatorial favorite Pertinax. In order to break the excessive power that the Praetorians had been wielding in the city, he dismissed this fickle body of troops, and replaced them with legionaries selected for their valor and loyalty. He stationed a legion about thirteen miles (21 km) southeast of Rome at Castra Albana (modern Albano Laziale), and increased the size of the city's "watchmen" units (*vigiles*) and the Urban Cohorts. These additional forces there

---

SOURCE 11.3: Deification Ceremonies for Pertinax in Septimius Severus' Rome
Cassius Dio, as an eyewitness, describes Septimius Severus' honors for Pertinax in 193. The following excerpt shows the awesome elaboration of the ceremony, as well as some of the ways in which divine attributes and trappings were bestowed upon emperors.

Upon establishing himself in power, Septimius Severus erected a shrine to Pertinax, and commanded that Pertinax's name should be mentioned at the close of all prayers and all oaths; he also ordered that a golden image of Pertinax should be carried into the Circus Maximus on a chariot drawn by elephants. . . . In the Roman Forum a wooden platform was constructed next to the marble rostra, upon which was set a shrine made of ivory and gold. In it there was placed a bier of the same materials adorned with coverings of purple and gold. Upon the bier rested an effigy of Pertinax in wax, laid out in triumphal costume; there was a handsome youth keeping the flies away from it with peacock feathers, as though it were really a person sleeping. . . . There moved past, first, images of all the famous Romans of old, then choruses of boys and men, singing a dirge-like hymn to Pertinax; next followed all the subject nations, represented by bronze figures attired in native costume, and then groups within Rome itself—lictors, scribes, heralds, and the like. . . . Behind these were the cavalry and infantry in armor, the racehorses, and all the funeral offerings sent by the emperor, by us [senators] and our wives and the more distinguished *equites*, as well as by communities and by associations in Rome. Following them came an altar gilded all over and decorated with ivory and Indian gems. [After a eulogy by Septimius Severus, the bier was taken in procession to a funeral pyre built like a tower in the Campus Martius. Then, after the offerings had been thrown onto the pyre, and soldiers had performed some further pageantry around it,] at last the consuls applied fire to the structure, and when that had been done, an eagle flew up out of it. In this way Pertinax was made immortal. (75.4.1–5.5; translation excerpted and adapted from the Loeb edition)

---

offset the extraordinary power that the Praetorians had wielded. No legion had ever been stationed far from a war zone or disturbed area before, let alone in Italy.

With Rome secured and Albinus placated, Septimius Severus next marched east against Niger, who had moved north into the province of Asia. He proceeded to chase after Niger's army, clashing with it at Byzantium, Cyzicus, Nicaea, and finally Issus. At Issus alone, the casualties were said to have been so heavy that the nearby river ran red. In further pursuit, Septimius Severus seized Antioch, the leading city of Syria, and Niger was killed fleeing farther east. The cities that had supported him now had to pay enormous indemnities as well as suffer other punishments: Antioch and Byzantium, for example, were no longer permitted to administer their own affairs, and Byzantium's famous city walls were pulled down. Looking to the future, Septimius Severus then acted on the lesson that he had learned from Niger's strength. He divided the large province of Syria into two smaller ones, Syria Coele and Syria Phoenice, thus reducing the number of troops under the command of any single governor.

To boost his image and to deflect attention from civil war, Septimius Severus campaigned against the Parthians in 194–195 and again in 197–199, claiming first that they had offered to help Niger, and then that they had seized Roman territory. In these offensives, he annexed northern Mesopotamia as a Roman province (as had Trajan briefly), and also created the province of Osroene. Both campaigns were heralded as glorious triumphs, and were celebrated on the Arch of Septimius Severus that is still a prominent feature of the Roman Forum today (Map 12.2). Cassius Dio (75.3.3), however, deplores the conquest of Mesopotamia as "a source of constant wars and great expense to us," seeing it as an overextension of Roman power. It is true that these new provinces did set off a chain of events which weakened the Parthian kingdom, ultimately causing it to fall by 226 to a new group, the Sasanians, a Persian dynasty from the south. The Sasanian empire proved notably more aggressive than its Parthian predecessor, and better able to coordinate the resources of the large area under its control. Moreover, the Sasanians combined their rule with a monotheistic religion, Mazdaism, encouraging fierce loyalty and unity throughout their empire.

Between the two Parthian wars Septimius Severus eliminated his rival Albinus, and had himself and his family adopted posthumously into the family of Marcus Aurelius. This latter step, confirmed by the senate, was intended to claim for Septimius Severus a dynastic relationship with the quintessential "good" emperor. When Septimius Severus at the same time renamed his eleven-year-old son Septimius Bassianus as Marcus Aurelius Antoninus and elevated him to the rank of Augustus, he demonstrated yet again the primacy of family at Rome. This son is better known by his nickname "Caracalla," derived from the Latin word for the long overcoat used by Roman soldiers stationed in the north. Caracalla's designation as Caesar called into question his father's earlier grant of that title to Albinus, and in fact by 196 Severus had turned west to face his rival there. The two-year campaign against Albinus (196–197) was conducted primarily in Gaul, culminating in his defeat at Lugdunum. Casualties on both sides were high, and Albinus' defeat in this battle also led to the elimination of many senators who had supported him in Rome.

Despite such appalling loss of life, Septimius Severus enjoyed great popularity among the troops. Like Trajan, he fought alongside them and shared their hardships on campaign. He readily engaged in warfare. In addition to his Parthian wars and civil conflict, he fought in Britain from 208 until his death there in 211, trying to deter invasions from the north or perhaps attempting to conquer Caledonia (Scotland). He also enacted many far-reaching military reforms. He further increased the number of legions by three (making a total of thirty-three), stationing one of them near Rome itself as noted above, and the other two in the new province of Mesopotamia. He improved the terms of military service. Around 200, he permitted soldiers to be married while in service, removing the ban on such marriages imposed by Augustus (see Chapter Eight). Soldiers no doubt appreciated this official recognition of the army as a way of life; documentary evidence shows that veterans' sons were already making up a large proportion of recruits. Septimius Severus increased the pay for legionaries from 1,200 to 2,000 sesterces a year, with corresponding increases in the stipends of auxiliary units. Herodian and others denounce these substantial pay increases and other military reforms as blatant attempts to buy the army's favor, but on the other side it is important to recognize that, despite inflation, there had been no increase in military pay since 84, over a century earlier. The personal nature of Septimius Severus' ties to the military is demonstrated by the spread of the title "Mother of the Camp(s)" (*mater castrorum*) for his wife Julia Domna.

Our literary sources contrast Septimius Severus' generosity to the army with his rough handling of the senate and individual senators. His violent rise to power prompted numerous treason trials which he and his close advisers heard rather than the senate as a whole. The sentences handed down were arbitrary and usually harsh; on one occasion, for example, Septimius Severus released thirty-five senators charged with having supported Albinus, but killed twenty-nine others. He reduced the number of administrative posts open to senators, and gave more prestige and positions to equites. Equites now held almost all the great prefectures as well as new salaried positions created specifically for them. Both the City Prefect and Praetorian Prefects extended their administrative and military duties to include judicial ones, and the former's jurisdiction was extended to a one-hundred-mile limit. All three of Septimius Severus' new legions were placed under equestrian rather than senatorial commanders, and the army's command structure was reformed, making it possible for equites to rise all the way through the ranks. Within a generation, the equestrian officer Macrinus had done precisely this (see Macrinus, below).

Our fragmentary, biased literary sources make it impossible to date most of Septimius Severus' reforms at all precisely or, more important, to assess their aims with confidence. Cassius Dio and others admit that he was a Princeps who had a brilliant, wide-ranging mind, and that he diligently attended to all the business of Roman government and law. He was closely associated with outstanding jurists like Aemilius Papinianus, who wrote extensively as well as taking charge of petitions to the emperor (the post of *a libellis*) and later becoming Praetorian Prefect; by the fourth century, Papinian was widely considered the greatest Roman jurist. Despite his heavy spending, Septimius Severus left a surplus in the treasury. He clearly had a talent for manipulating public opinion. He lavishly praised Cassius Dio (73.23) for writing a "little book about the dreams and portents which had given the emperor reason to hope for the imperial power"; marks of divine favor towards him are frequently noted. He built and restored temples and other monuments in Rome. Very notably, the "Septizodium," which he dedicated at the corner of the Palatine Hill in 203, was a multistoried, multicolored marble façade that displayed statues to visitors approaching Rome from the south; the figure of Septimius Severus himself dominated it (Map 12.2). In 202, on the tenth anniversary of his accession, he gave the Praetorian Guard and the Roman populace *aurei* amounting to two hundred million sesterces—more than any other single donative had ever totaled. He frequently presented public displays, including the spectacular funeral arranged for Pertinax in the Roman Forum and Campus Martius (Source 11.3). Meantime he by no means neglected the empire outside the city of Rome. In the course of his rise to power and his travels as emperor—to Syria and Egypt in 199–202, to North Africa in 202–203, and to Britain in 208-211—he visited most of the Roman world, and evidently did so with a genuine sense of duty.

Even when all this is said, the overall picture remains incoherent. Septimius Severus is undeniably one of Rome's great reforming emperors. Like Augustus and Hadrian, he profoundly changed many Roman institutions. Unlike the rule

Figure 11.5 *This painting on wood depicted Septimius Severus, his wife Julia Domna, and their two sons Caracalla and Geta; Geta has been defaced, however. The painting dates to soon after 198, when Geta was awarded the title "most noble Caesar," and his older brother Caracalla was made Augustus with their father. Here, Septimius Severus and Caracalla wear gem-studded gold crowns, and Julia Domna wears a smaller, opulent diadem on her head; Geta, too, presumably wore some sort of crown. The three males also carry scepters. This image of a happy, united family is belied by a history of persistent discord between the two brothers. Although on his deathbed Septimius Severus is said to have advised his sons, "Stay partners, enrich the soldiers, and don't care about anyone else at all" (Cassius Dio 76.15.2), within a year Caracalla had ordered his brother's murder. Geta's name and image were then erased from all public records* (damnatio memoriae). *As in the present instance, however, such erasures themselves were often prominent, a striking reminder of the power of public opinion.*

of these two predecessors, however, his was not followed by prosperity and general peace. Instead, his successors were so politically incompetent and militarily inept that their failures damage Severus himself and his reforms. Further, his years as Princeps—unlike those of Augustus, by contrast—were not long enough to efface his use of civil war to gain power. The senatorial bias of the literary sources, our relative ignorance of much of the wider context, and Rome's subsequent history all combine to leave Septimius Severus with less than his due.

CARACALLA (198–217, RULING AS SOLE AUGUSTUS AFTER 211)

Caracalla (officially Marcus Aurelius Antoninus), a less charismatic and more brutal personality than Septimius Severus, followed his father's deathbed advice to show special concern for the military, and even raised legionary pay further from two to three thousand sesterces a year. It may have been the need to fund this substantial increase that caused him to issue the *constitutio Antoniniana* in 212, known from a fragmentary papyrus, Ulpian, and Cassius Dio. By this decree he granted Roman citizenship to virtually all the free inhabitants of the empire. Cassius Dio (77.9–10) says that he did this to gain revenue, and various other motives have been advanced as well. Only Roman citizens had been liable to pay the 5 percent inheritance tax that had been earmarked for legionaries' discharge bonuses ever since the time of Augustus; Caracalla's decree made many more liable for the tax. But if the aim of the universal grant of citizenship was to raise money, it failed. Around the same time as he made the grant, Caracalla issued a new coin, the "Antoninianus," that was nominally worth twice the silver denarius and eight times the bronze sestertius (four sesterces = one denarius). Even at its issue, however, the Antoninianus contained only half as much silver as the denarius. It later became more debased, which led to inflation.

Caracalla needed the goodwill of the soldiers, since the empire's borders were increasingly under attack and he spent most of his Principate on campaign. In 213–214, he campaigned against Alamanni and Goths in Germany, where he defeated some tribes and settled other difficulties by diplomacy. In 215 he moved to Armenia in order to tackle problems caused by his father's Parthian wars. He traveled there through the Danubian regions, and this was where he mobilized his army. By 216, he had successfully battled through Armenia to points farther east and south in Parthia. In 217, however, he was assassinated at Carrhae. His officers feared his erratic paranoia, and his troops were disgruntled at seemingly endless campaigns in desert conditions.

MACRINUS (217–218)

The leader of the coup, now saluted as Augustus by the troops, was Marcus Opellius Macrinus, an *eques* from Mauretania who had held the position of

Praetorian Prefect under Caracalla since 212, but had never been made a senator. He thus becomes the first Roman emperor without senatorial rank. Although he had plotted Caracalla's assassination, he quickly saw the need to associate himself with the Severan family because of its widespread popularity among the military. He adopted the name Severus for himself, and added "Antoninus" to the name of his young son Marcus Opellius Diadumenianus, whom he also designated as Caesar. He was unsuccessful in continuing the campaign against the Parthians, and caused outrage among his troops when he negotiated a treaty, because this was seen as a cowardly attempt to buy off the enemy. Even more damaging were his decisions to make reductions in army pay, and to keep the Danubian troops in the East. In 218 the increasingly dissatisfied troops were approached by Julia Maesa, the sister of Septimius Severus' wife Julia Domna, who claimed that Caracalla was really the father of her fourteen-year-old grandson, Varius Avitus Bassianus (see Table 11.1). As a result, the army eagerly saluted him as Marcus Aurelius Antoninus. Macrinus and Diadumenianus were then hunted down and killed by the same troops who had supported their supplanting Caracalla as emperor only a year before.

ELAGABALUS (218–222)

The four-year rule of Marcus Aurelius Antoninus—or Elagabalus (alternatively Heliogabalus) as he preferred to be called—was one of the strangest that Rome ever experienced. Elagabalus differed from all previous emperors. His advancement resulted not from his own ambitions but from those of his grandmother, Julia Maesa, and his mother, Julia Soaemias Bassiana. His name derived from the god he worshiped as hereditary priest, Elah-Gabal, the sun god of Emesa (modern Homs, Syria). This god was represented not in human form but as a "betel," a sacred black stone. Although some other deities in Rome likewise lacked anthropomorphic representations—the Magna Mater, for example, brought to the city in the late third century B.C.—many Romans were antagonized by the conspicuous orgiastic rites for Elah-Gabal, as well as by Elagabalus' fervid promotion of his own religion. When he arrived in Rome a year after his acclamation in 218, it was religious rituals and spaces that preoccupied him, not government. He built two temples for his sun god, one of them in the imperial palace on the Palatine. When he "married" his sun god to the Carthaginian deity Juno Caelestis, he divorced his own wife to marry a Vestal Virgin, Aquilia Severa, in a parallel "sacred marriage" that appalled traditionalists. He then made "the Unconquerable God, the Sun Elagabalus" (*deus invictus Sol Elagabalus*) the main deity of Rome. Novel and shocking choice though this was for Romans, Elagabalus' promotion of monotheism does at least correspond to other sentiments of the time (see "Rome and Christianity" below).

The senatorial authors, stung by Elagabalus' indifference to administration, depict him as a freakish tyrant, and maintain that everything was entrusted to his mother and grandmother. In 221 his grandmother, Julia Maesa, certainly forced him to adopt his cousin, Gessius Alexianus Bassianus, as Caesar. Thereafter the power play intensified. The following year, Julia Avita Mamaea, Elagabalus' aunt and the mother of his cousin, bribed the Praetorians to murder both Elagabalus and his mother, Julia Soaemias, Mamaea's own sister. His cousin Alexianus was then acclaimed emperor as Marcus Aurelius Severus Alexander.

SEVERUS ALEXANDER (222–235)

Although only fourteen years old at his accession, Severus Alexander ruled with some success for the relatively long period of thirteen years. Part of the credit must go to his mother, Julia Mamaea, whose title "Mother of Augustus, and of the Camps, and of the Senate, and of the Fatherland," indicates, however conventionally, that attention was directed to military and civil matters alike. But Severus Alexander also gained by his ostensible deference to the senate. He placed some senators in advisory positions, and entrusted the key post of Praetorian Prefect to senators rather than equites—fresh prestige for the former, which may have masked the continued equestrian control of most administrative positions. Severus Alexander's rule was a time of great legal advances, the heyday of the outstanding jurists Domitius Ulpianus and Julius Paulus. Severus Alexander was also alert to economic and social concerns, reducing taxes, aiding the grain supply of Rome, and subsidizing teachers and scholars.

His relationship with the military was more problematic. In 223 the Praetorians revolted, killing their Prefect the jurist Ulpian. In contrast to Trajan's execution of rebellious Praetorians in 98, Severus Alexander failed to punish this outrage. Nor could the young emperor identify with rank-and-file soldiers in the way that, say, Trajan and Septimius Severus had been able. Soldiers apparently despised him as a weak general, and this disgust only led to further military uprisings, in one of which Cassius Dio was nearly killed. In 231, generalship was demanded of Severus Alexander when the aggressive Sasanians under King Ardashir I—now dominant in the former Parthian empire—invaded Mesopotamia. Accompanied by his mother Julia Mamaea, Severus Alexander went on campaign from Antioch, and did recover Mesopotamia by 232. The following year, he returned to Rome to celebrate a triumph, but by 235 he had to go on campaign again, this time against German invaders in Raetia. When he proved unable to defeat them in battle and began negotiations instead, the army again interpreted this as a cowardly attempt to buy peace. As a result, mutinous soldiers murdered both Severus Alexander and his mother, and acclaimed as emperor their ringleader, an equestrian general of Thracian origin, Gaius Julius Verus Maximinus. He was to be the first of the so-called "soldier-emperors." His rule marks the beginning of a turbulent half-century in which the empire suffered severe pressures on all sides as well as increasing impoverishment.

ROMAN LAW

Roman law remains fundamental to European law, and to our own. Ulpian, the great jurist who served as Severus Alexander's Praetorian Prefect, sums up law as follows: "Justice is a steady and enduring desire to give every man his due.

The basic principles of the law are these: to live honorably, not to injure any other person, and to render to each his own. Jurisprudence is the knowledge of things divine and human, the science of what is right and wrong" (*Digest* 1.1.10). Another jurist of the early third century, Herennius Modestinus (a pupil of Ulpian), offers a slightly different formulation: "Law and right derive from consent, necessity, and custom" (*Digest* 1.3.40). Such concepts are central to modern systems of justice too. As is equally true today, in practice Roman law did not always live up to its ideals. Romans and others, however, have justifiably regarded Roman law as one of their civilization's greatest achievements.

Roman law can be divided into private (civil), public (administrative), and criminal law. It is generally agreed that criminal law and procedure developed slowly, and never attained the importance of private law and procedure; since the nineteenth century, scholars have focused their attention on private law. From the "Twelve Tables" onwards in the mid-fifth century B.C. (see Chapter Two), the Romans recorded their laws, and several inscriptions found in recent years have increased the number of public laws now known to us (at least in part) in their original form rather than solely through references by ancient authors. Some of these inscriptions transform our understanding of important laws of the second and first centuries B.C., for example. Others, like the late first-century A.D. bronze tablets from Irni in southern Spain, record town charters and illuminate life far from Rome itself. Besides actual laws, legal opinions of all types were also recorded beginning in the late second century B.C. From the late second century A.D. onwards, jurists wrote specialized works on various offices: Ulpian, for example, wrote ten volumes on the duties of a provincial governor. Roman law and jurisprudence flourished during the empire, notably from Augustus to the death of Severus Alexander.

One of the essential rights and privileges of being a citizen in Republican Rome was active participation in Roman voting assemblies, whose decisions were legally binding. These citizen assemblies primarily passed public laws and some criminal ones. Yet from Claudius' Principate onwards these assemblies became much less active as lawmaking bodies, and the last known laws passed by one or other of them are relatively insignificant ones dating to the end of the first century A.D. By contrast, resolutions of the senate (*senatus consulta*) in practice gained the force of law during the Principate. Those resolutions attested from this period typically concern public order and matters of private status and standing. As such, they demonstrate the continued functioning of the senate, and the attempts of "good" emperors to collaborate with their ostensible peers.

Magistrates charged with administering justice, particularly praetors and governors, could make an impact upon the law by their choice of which legal means they would use while in office to recover a right, or to prevent or redress a wrong. Such procedural power allowed them in effect to recognize new rights, and to deny or abolish ones previously recognized. Legal innovation of this type was most active during the second and first centuries B.C., but seems to have become rare by the time that Hadrian commissioned the "Perpetual Edict" (see Chapter Ten). Since Gaius in the second century A.D. wrote a treatise *On the Provincial Edict*, it appears that by this date the legal procedures used by provincial governors were also standardized. But there was always room for doubt about the applicability of specific laws and procedure to any individual case. For legal advice, administrators of justice, including the Princeps himself, turned to jurists (sometimes called jurisprudents). These men, specialists in the analysis and interpretation of law, first came to prominence in the third century B.C., and their importance rose steadily thereafter. By the early third century A.D., the notable jurists Papinian and Ulpian served as Praetorian Prefect, an office whose judicial role had become just as important as its military one.

Roman law did not develop widely until the second century B.C. The distinctively Roman institution of patronage may have inhibited the advancement of law for a long period after the Twelve Tables. It has been convincingly argued that the vast increase of citizens after the Social War made a major contribution to the growing sophistication of Roman law, particularly private law. More cases were being heard, including many that resulted from property seizures during the war and its aftermath, and many new citizens must have lacked powerful Roman patrons. The Roman legal system was forced to become more sophisticated, and its procedures more standardized. Earlier, the phenomenal expansion of Rome's interests and activities during the third and second centuries B.C. had led to comparable growth in Roman public law.

Such growth of both private and public law accelerated under the emperors, not least because Augustus, Hadrian, and others considered their personal involvement with law to be integral to their role as Princeps. Emperors' legal activity mostly took place in public—Hadrian, for example, used the interior of the Pantheon as a law court (a remarkable temple in Rome, rebuilt during his reign, and still intact today); decisions were publicly commemorated in inscriptions "to be posted in the most frequented place of the city" (see the senatorial decree concerning the elder Gnaeus Piso, Source 9.1). An emperor's *maius imperium* gave him the right to interpret and execute the law, and his decisions were regarded as definitive. He often judged private and public law cases in person. In addition he heard appeals from citizens, noncitizens, and communities even outside the areas of the empire for which he was primarily responsible. Provincial magistrates also turned to him for legal advice, as Pliny did to Trajan from Bithynia-Pontus; time and again, imperial letters from the first to third centuries urge that matters be settled locally rather than referred to the emperor.

Emperors made law, too; their rulings were generally termed constitutions (*constitutiones*, singular, *constitutio*). These included *rescripta* and *epistulae*, responses to petitions (*libelli*) on points of law sent not only by prominent officials but also by private individuals, especially humbler folk, women, freedmen, and even alleged slaves. Some modern experts maintain that Roman private law can be detected as becoming gradually more liberal and humane; slaves, for example, are increasingly recognized as having some rights, and women gain more legal independence. More sweeping were the measures that the emperor issued as either *decreta*, sayings or pronouncements with the force of law; or *mandata*, instructions to governors and other officials; or *leges*, laws enacted by means of the emperor's tribunician power.

Emperors thus made law and influenced it in numerous ways, so much so that contemporary writers tend to emphasize the sole agency of individual emperors as lawmakers. But an emperor could not respond single-handed to the crush of legal questions directed to him. We know that when Augustus, for example, had to determine questions relating to wills and inheritance, he often assembled a group of jurists, asked their opinion, and then added his authority to their response; even so, no Princeps was bound to accept the majority view of such a group. Later, however, Hadrian seems to have affirmed the ability of jurists to lay down the law if acting unanimously (Gaius, *Institutes* 1.7). One mark of a virtuous emperor was his consultation with jurists, and his respect for them—behavior which stressed the importance of civil consensus in the Principate.

The variety of ways in which legislation could be enacted begs the question of where actual laws were kept, and who had access to them. Some collections were in Rome, in the Record Office (*tabularium*) constructed in the early first century B.C. at the western end of the Forum Romanum, as well as in various archives, including one in the emperor's palace; other collections were kept in provincial capitals, the main seats of governors. Individual cities, too, kept archives of their own. Yet people did not always trust the ability of the Roman state, or even of their own city, to store and retrieve laws and legal decisions. For example, papyri from the province of Arabia in the early second century A.D. document the personal collection of legal decisions pertaining to a woman named Babatha and her legal difficulties. In addition, as it happens, Babatha's archive underscores a growing tendency for Roman law to eclipse local law: although Babatha seems not to have been a Roman citizen, she turned for legal redress to the court of the Roman governor at Petra (in modern Jordan). Free persons within the Roman world who were not Roman citizens—that is, the majority of provincials until the *constitutio Antoniniana* of 212—could use the law of their indigenous community when the case did not involve a Roman citizen. Yet Babatha's documents and other evidence, like the incomplete Flavian municipal laws found at Irni and other Spanish communities, reveal the spread of Roman law in the provinces.

What we know of Roman private law is mostly due to the astonishing efforts of the emperor Justinian and his jurists in 528–534. In an attempt to reassert imperial control in the fragmenting empire of his day, Justinian decided to revive the judicial experience and wisdom in classical writings and imperial rescripts, and to make all this material more accessible. He commanded his minister of justice, Tribonianus, and legal committees in Berytus (modern Beirut, Lebanon) and Constantinople (modern Istanbul, Turkey) to collect the great legal writings in the empire, and to synthesize them into three different works. With a team of helpers, Tribonian reduced roughly three million lines of text to about 150,000, arranging them in three main parts. The resulting "Collection of Civil Law"

(*Corpus Iuris Civilis*) thus comprises: a textbook for students (the *Institutes*); a collection of imperial constitutions (the *Code*); and a collection of the opinions of jurists (the *Digest*). Taken as a whole, these parts separate the law into three main categories: (1) persons—law relating to one's personal status (e.g., free or slave) or to corporations (*collegia*), which gained some legal recognition in the mid-second century A.D.; (2) things—law relating to property, including inheritances, obligations (like contracts), and what today might be called torts; and (3) actions—civil procedure encompassing how, where, and why to file a lawsuit. Laws are often quoted in the original form that emperors issued them, sometimes with a jurist's interpretation added.

Roman criminal law has important distinctive aspects of its own. There was no public prosecutor. Instead, every case had to be instigated by a citizen who assumed the role of accuser by denouncing the wrongdoer and filing a charge against him with the head of the competent criminal court (the procedure is *delatio nominis*, and the accuser a *delator*). Beginning in the second century B.C. all citizens of good repute had the right to bring an indictment and to conduct a prosecution, but this opportunity was never open to slaves or anyone disgraced as *infamis* (see next paragraph), and it was considered most improper for a woman to be personally involved in proceedings. If the accuser proved his case, he could receive some part of the accused's property in proportion to the type of crime. Frivolous prosecutions were discouraged. For example, if an accuser was found guilty of having made an accusation in bad faith, he was to be branded on the forehead with the letter K (for *kalumniator*, slanderer). If an accuser were not himself of high status, and not even connected in some way to someone who was, he was likely to experience difficulty in initiating his case, because the praetor or another magistrate with appropriate jurisdiction had first to be convinced that the case should be heard. Further, Roman criminal cases, like civil ones, often depended not so much on legal issues like the validity of the evidence, but on the reputation and status of the accused, the accuser, and even their advocates.

Status and prestige loomed large in Roman law, as indeed in our own. A common penalty was *infamia*, a political and social stigma that could remove, for example, a citizen's right to vote or to bring an accusation, or an individual's senatorial or equestrian status. Some scholars argue that by the early second century A.D. Roman citizens were in practice divided into two groups, *honestiores* and *humiliores*. The honestiores ("more honorable") are reckoned to comprise senators, equites, town councilors, and veterans, together with their families; the humiliores ("more lowly") were everyone else. Honestiores were exempt from harsh and demeaning penalties, in particular any form of corporal punishment; instead, if convicted of a serious crime, they were likely to be fined or sent into exile. Humiliores, by contrast, would in all likelihood be punished for the same offense by assignment to the quarries or mines (tantamount to a death sentence), to hard labor on roads, to public servitude, or to being thrown to the beasts in the amphitheater. However, it always seems to have been at the discretion of the court to determine the status of the accused in each individual case; status is not defined explicitly in the surviving laws.

Some other features of criminal procedure underline its severity. Torture was commonly used in cases involving non-Romans, and was mandatory in ones involving slaves, since it was believed that only under duress would slaves tell the truth. A prison sentence was seldom imposed. Instead, prisons were used only for holding persons briefly, pending trials: Romans were less interested in penitence and rehabilitation than in deterrence and retribution. Many Roman officials had authority to hear criminal cases and impose sentences; in so doing, they were likely to involve a group of advisers, but they were not obliged to follow any recommendations it made, nor was there any jury. In Rome itself during the Republic the *tresviri capitales* constituted a board of three with oversight of capital punishment. During the Principate, criminal cases would be heard there by the City Prefect, Praetorian Prefects, or Prefect of the "watchmen" (vigiles). In the provinces, a community's own magistrates would administer justice locally according to its own laws, although, as mentioned above, we can discern an increasing resort to Roman law. Moreover, in the provinces capital crimes and other major cases could be judged only by the governor, not by any local court.

Papyri and legal sources preserve evidence of numerous appeals, suggesting widespread belief in the possibility of commuting a sentence. Roman citizens had the right of appeal, originally to the Roman people assembled in the Centuriate assembly, but later to the emperor himself. A famous instance of appeal is that of St. Paul who, as a Roman citizen, was brought to Rome for a hearing in person before the emperor. Vestal virgins and emperors' wives—who, after Octavia and Livia, had the rights of the Vestals—could absolve and free individuals. Sacred temples (*asyla*) offered sanctuary to individuals who fled there to escape punishment. Despite the persistence of slavery and dependent labor, not to mention the ingrained concept of "womanly weakness" that continued to disadvantage women legally, Roman jurists often expounded a belief in basic human equality, as indicated in the quotations at the start of this section. Even clearer is the confidence that jurists and emperors display in the rationality and merit of Roman law. That conviction seems to be reinforced by the countless appeals and the sheer amount of legal material recorded from the period of the Principate.

ROMAN CITIZENSHIP

Roman law is central to the original concept of Roman citizenship, which was tied to rights (including access to Roman law), duties, and privileges. This tripartite division is common to all ancient societies. A feature peculiar to Rome, however, was the automatic incorporation of freed slaves into the citizen body (albeit with some restrictions in the first generation), and the ease with which individuals and whole communities of outsiders could be admitted. The grant of Roman citizenship to a slave upon manumission by a Roman citizen continued during the

Principate. But even before the *constitutio Antoniniana* of 212, this period witnesses four additional ways to gain citizenship. Two are connected with military service, which had also been integral to Roman citizenship at its inception. The other two reflect the dominant position of the Princeps in the Roman world.

The first new means to gain citizenship is known primarily through bronze tablets, the *diplomata* that record the grant of citizenship at honorable discharge to provincials who had served in the auxiliary forces; the earliest known diplomata date to the Principate of Claudius. By the early second century, another means had evolved informally, and reflects the continued primacy of the soldier-citizen. Since the legions were supposed to be manned by Roman citizens, individuals who enrolled in them were awarded citizenship upon enlistment if they did not already have it. A third means to Roman citizenship was a direct grant by the emperor to individuals, and even to whole communities. During the Republic, the Roman people in one of their assemblies had sometimes made such grants, as had a general like Pompey, too, very occasionally. Thereafter, however, the Princeps alone could award such a generous benefaction (*beneficium*; see Source 11.4). A fourth, less direct means was the Princeps' grant of "Latin" status (*ius Latii*) to a non-Roman community, a promotion which in turn conferred Roman citizenship on those who served the community politically. This means reinforced the original link of citizenship to political duty and privileges.

The rights of Roman citizens to vote in elections and on legislation, which caused such great conflict at the end of the Republic, became defunct early in the Principate. Citizen elections for senatorial magistracies were abandoned in Tiberius' time and, as already noted, assemblies ceased passing laws by the end of the first century. At the same time, on the other hand, the onerous military duty of Roman citizens was greatly lessened by the general shift to a volunteer, professional army. Roman citizens were liable for various taxes, particularly the 5 percent inheritance tax that funded the "military" treasury. Roman citizens in Italy, however, would remain immune from payment of land taxes until the end of the third century. Most important to the functioning of the empire—since Rome relied so heavily on cities for local administration—Roman citizens as well as all others had to serve their local communities. Each Roman had obligations to his town of origin (*origo*), as well as to Rome itself. Every individual's origo was an essential part of his political and social identity. Roman citizens enjoyed extra privileges, however, like joining a legion, or (at the top level) seeking equestrian or senatorial status at Rome; altogether, without question, they had the greatest social and political mobility. They might also expect easier access to the emperor—by custom, if not always by law—when appealing a sentence, say, or requesting some exemption from civic obligations. In the early Principate, Roman citizenship seems to have been attractive to non-Romans; it was no doubt seen as the pathway to power and privilege.

However, inscriptions and other items of evidence suggest that by the end of the second century Roman citizenship was losing its allure. Among municipal elites we find increasing instances of men unable or unwilling to serve their com-

SOURCE 11.4: Grant of Roman Citizenship (*Tabula Banasitana*)

Inscriptions, such as the following part of a bronze tablet dating to around 168 (AE 1971.534), proudly record imperial grants of citizenship, and allow us to see specific instances of the emperor conferring such benefits. This document comes from Banasa in southwest Mauretania (modern Sidi Ali bou Jenoun, Morocco), where Augustus had settled a veteran colony; the Zegrenses were a local tribe. Note that the male members of the family have Latin names, but Ziddina does not—reflecting a trend found in provincials' nomenclature elsewhere in the empire. The last phrase in the wording of the grant is an important warning that a beneficiary's new status as a Roman citizen does not supersede his former civic identity, nor exempt him from local obligations. Dual citizenship of this type can be seen as a strength of the empire, but both the imperial authorities and local ones were keen to ensure that such privileged individuals did not seek to stop supporting their community of origin on this account.

Copy of the letter of our Emperors Marcus Aurelius and Verus, Augusti, to Coiiedius Maximus [governor of Mauretania Tingitana, who had forwarded Julianus' request for citizenship]. We have read the petition of Julianus the Zegrensian attached to your letter, and although it is not usual to give Roman citizenship to men of that tribe except when very great services prompt the emperor to show this kindness, nevertheless since you assert that he is one of the leading men of his people and is very loyal in his readiness to be of help to our affairs, and since we think that there are not many families among the Zegrenses who can make equal boasts about their services—whereas we wish that very many be impelled to emulate Julianus because of the honor conferred by us upon his house—we do not hesitate to grant Roman citizenship, without impairment of the law of the tribe, to himself, his wife Ziddina, likewise to their children Julianus, Maximus, Maximinus, Diogenianus.

munity politically—participation that by tradition had been seen as an enviable privilege, not a burden. Local political service was essential to the functioning both of individual cities and of the empire as a whole, and by the second century the city councils (whose members are termed "decurions") were the most powerful local political figures. Men paid a sum of money, the so-called *summa honoraria* (usually 20,000 sesterces), upon being elected magistrate or coopted into the city council. Among other duties, a city's officials were responsible for local law and order, public contracts, religious rituals, and entertainment; they also supervised the collection of the tax quota demanded from their community by Rome. Roman, as opposed to local, administration could accordingly be relatively lean (see Chapter Ten). The obligations of a city's council and magistrates were offset by their relative autonomy, an underlying principle of the Principate. But this civic autonomy would function successfully only so long as the empire's cities were willing and able to regulate themselves. Various developments, such

Figure 11.6 *Tombstone of the mid-second century from Gorsium, Pannonia (near modern Székesfehérvár, Hungary). This monolithic tombstone combines decoration in the Greco-Roman style—such as the grape-vine spiraled columnettes—with local elements. The two women portrayed are wearing "native" dress, with heavy turbans, prominent pendant necklaces, and large pins on their shoulders. They are framed, however, by two elegant herm figures. At the foot of the stone, two servants are shown frontally under a curved border characteristic of art from the region, but these plain figures are flanked by sinuous Bacchanalian dancers. The beautifully cut Latin inscription translates, "To the spirits of the dead. Publius Aelius Respectus, city councilor of the municipality, while alive made this for himself and for Ulpia Amasia, his wife. Aelia Materio, their daughter aged ten, is placed here. The parents put up this monument for her memory." The names indicate that the family are all Roman citizens, and the father specifies that he is a city councilor in his community, although without naming it. The unusual "Amasia" and "Materio" apparently maintain the area's indigenous names, as does the women's dress. This tombstone represents the creative interaction of Roman and provincial cultures; compare Plates 10a and 12b.*

as the appointment of "caretakers" from Rome (*curatores*; see Chapter Ten), acted to alter the balance between Rome and its cities.

Even by the early second century, some of the distinctive privileges of Roman citizenship had begun to erode, as we saw with the enlistment of non-Romans in the legions and the two-tiered treatment of Roman citizens in the courts. At the lowest levels of Roman society, however, such legal disparities were always almost meaningless. Whether someone from the rural poor or urban homeless—who had few or no possessions, and no education—was freeborn, freed, or even slave, probably made little difference to the authorities in court or elsewhere, because the elite were so superior in every way to such powerless individuals. The latter themselves were hardly likely to be much preoccupied by the question of their legal status, when it was a constant struggle for such poverty-stricken people just to stay alive.

It is against this background that we must set Caracalla's grant of Roman citizenship to virtually all free inhabitants of the empire. What functional and ideological difference did it make? And what constituted being "Roman" at this date? Septimius Severus and his family may illuminate these difficult questions, at least at the top of the social scale. His origo was Lepcis Magna, an important city founded by the Carthaginians on the coast of what is now Libya. Although Latin sources call Septimius Severus "Italic"—descended from Italian emigrants—his Punic background was at least as strong. His grandfather served as chief magistrate of Lepcis Magna, an office which still retained its Punic title *sufes* even long after the city had become a Roman municipality. Septimius Severus himself allegedly never lost his provincial accent when speaking Latin, although his Greek was excellent. The origo of his wife, Julia Domna, was Emesa in Syria, and

Figure 11.7 *View of Lepcis Magna, Tripolitania (75 miles/120 km east of modern Tripoli, Libya). Lepcis Magna was developed as a Phoenician trading settlement from around 600 B.C., using a harbor at the end of a stream bed, from where a route led far inland to sub-Saharan Africa. Later, the settlement also derived prosperity from its rural territory, which produced olive oil in great quantities. By the late first century B.C., Lepcis Magna was shipping three million pounds of olive oil annually to Rome. By the end of the first century A.D. it had become a* municipium, *and then under Trajan its city status was raised to that of a colony. Later, Septimius Severus, who was from Lepcis himself, patronized it lavishly, although it could already boast handsome buildings. He sponsored an enormous forum—whose ruins are prominent here—flanked by a public hall or "basilica" (behind the high wall on the right); an adjoining, long colonnaded street (partly visible in the right foreground); and a multistoried, elaborate fountain that marked the shift in the city's street grid. The fountain is often compared to the Septizodium in Rome (see "Civil War and the Rise of Septimius Severus" above). Altogether, the ruins of this magnificent city—preserved by the silting-up of its harbor and subsequent disuse—represent dramatic testimony to emperors' wealth, and to the potential power of imperial patronage.*

Greek and Syriac were her first languages. Thus what we might consider ethnicity apparently mattered little as a constituent of Roman identity.

On the other hand, those identifying themselves as Romans aspired to adopt Greco-Roman culture and its devotion to, among other tastes, Latin and Greek literature, rhetoric, art, and city life. Although as emperor, Septimius Severus never attempted to mask his reliance upon the military, he participated fully in the Greco-Roman cultural ideal. One of his most spectacular accomplishments was the magnificent rebuilding of Lepcis Magna. Julia Domna is said to have regularly met with members of the intelligentsia, including the orator and physician Galen, and Philostratus, author of the *Lives of the Sophists*. Thus at the beginning of the third century, the imperial family—despite its origins—conspicuously embraced traditional values of Greco-Roman culture, providing a model for the rest of the empire. Some have argued that a key factor in the emergence of changed forms of government and society in the empire from the third century onwards was a shift of individuals' attention from such traditional values to a new focus on individual salvation and personal belief. This prospect leads to the next section.

ROME AND CHRISTIANITY

Renewed cautions about our sources are essential when we discuss religion in the Roman world, and particularly the development of Christianity. Religion is notoriously difficult to investigate, because it combines practice, or ritual, with belief, or faith. Rituals, which are enacted periodically, are transient even with the best of documentation, such as a movie; participants are caught up in the moment, and observers are disconnected from the experience. Roman rituals are known by various means—descriptions in literature, which are invariably incomplete; depictions on coins, reliefs, mosaics, pottery, wall paintings, and other artifacts, which present only a snapshot of the action; notices in calendars; and incidental references in other documents. As for beliefs, we cannot measure the sincerity of what we read in the stylized writings of the Romans, or even in the public proclamations of belief made in inscriptions, graffiti, or other documents. At the same time, however, we should not dismiss all such declarations as hollow just because they are not statements of Christian or other religious belief as understood today. We should bear in mind that the Roman authorities were to make repeated attempts to eradicate Christianity during the third and early fourth centuries, and that later Christian emperors would likewise seek to obliterate polytheism and Judaism. It is no wonder that the relationship between Rome and Christians was an uneasy one, and that the literary sources for early Christianity are radically polarized.

The close connection between religion and politics in Roman society helps to account for the vehemence of the interchange. As we have seen, religious ceremonies preceded all Roman political activity. The same individuals frequently held political and religious positions at Rome, and minimal specialized training or knowledge was required for most of the latter. At the same time, the Roman state seldom sought to impose any particular religion, concerning itself mainly with the appropriate performance of public cult and the prohibition of any human sacrifice. This apparent laxity is clear even in the most salient instance of religious and political linkage, the imperial house. From 12 B.C. onwards, each Princeps assumed the position of *pontifex maximus* and also became a member of all the other major priestly colleges, making him the head of Roman religion. The institution of an imperial cult made various deified emperors and empresses—even the living emperor at times—the object of public religious rituals. Although individuals might not believe that an emperor was a god, this did not matter as much as the participation of Roman citizens and provincials in state cult.

But Christian belief demanded absence from polytheistic state rituals. There was a fundamental difference between Christian and polytheistic religious sensibilities. The Christians' religious affiliation provided them, individually and collectively, with an identity distinct from that of city, tribe, or family. By contrast, for polytheistic Romans, religious rituals and practices were integral to all civic and familial activities, and religious roles overlapped with political ones. Romans and their subjects could "believe" as they pleased, so long as they did not actively reject rituals that had been made part of the state religion. Through revolts and legislation, the monotheistic Jews and Rome gradually worked out a compromise during the final decades of the Republic and over the first two centuries of the Principate, which allowed Jews to be excused from participating in state cult rituals. Initially, the Romans regarded Christianity, too, as a sect of Judaism. But once it became clear that Christians claimed a distinct identity, they became more problematic for the Roman state.

Widespread incomprehension about Christians in the first century met with a range of reactions in the second. From about 120 to 220, Christians struggled to formulate their own hierarchy, and to explain themselves to non-Christians. In part, this attempt came in response to sporadic "persecutions" that were launched spontaneously by non-Christians. We are told of outbreaks of violence against Christians during the rule of Domitian in Rome, under Trajan in Bithynia-Pontus (see Source 11.5), in Smyrna during the 150s, in Lugdunum in 177, and in Carthage and Alexandria at the beginning of the third century. To defend Christianity, Clement of Alexandria, Tertullian, and other "apologists" wrote brilliant tracts that are strikingly sophisticated in their rhetoric and philosophical argument. These authors aimed not so much to convert non-Christians as to persuade them that they had no good cause to fear Christians or persecute them. It is important to note that brutal treatment suffered by Christians at this period was not initiated by the state.

Pliny's ignorance partly reflects the limited spread of Christianity by his time. Although he states that its adherents were "of every age, every rank, and also of both sexes," no contemporary of his own high rank is known to have been a Christian. Until the second half of the second century, most Christians lived in cities in Judaea and elsewhere in the Greek East, and in a few large cities such as

SOURCE 11.5: Pliny, Trajan, and Christians

This celebrated exchange between Pliny and the emperor Trajan regarding Christians in Bithynia-Pontus around 112 (Pliny, Letters 10.96–97) provides valuable insight into the Roman state's reaction to Christians. It also sheds light on the rituals associated with imperial cult, and the economic and social ramifications of state religion.

[Pliny to Trajan] It is my practice, my lord, to refer to you all matters about which I have doubts. For who is better able to resolve my hesitation or to inform my ignorance? I have never been present at trials of Christians. So I do not know what offenses it is the practice to punish or investigate, and to what extent. And I have hesitated considerably over whether there should be any distinction on account of age, or no difference between the very young and the more mature; whether pardon is to be granted for a change of mind, or, if a man has once been a Christian, it does him no good to have ceased to be one; whether the name itself, even without offenses, is to be punished, or only the offenses associated with the name.

Meanwhile, in the case of those who were denounced to me as Christians, I have observed the following procedure: I asked them personally whether they were Christians; those who confessed, I asked a second and a third time, threatening them with punishment; those who persisted, I ordered to be executed. For I had no doubt that, whatever the nature of their admission, their stubbornness and inflexible obstinacy surely deserve to be punished. There were others gripped by the same folly; but because they were Roman citizens, I assigned them to be transferred to Rome.

Soon accusations spread, as usually happens, because of these proceedings, and several incidents occurred. An anonymous document was published containing the names of many persons. My view was that I should discharge those who denied that they were or had been Christians, when they called upon the gods in words dictated by me, offered prayer with incense and wine to your image (which I had ordered to be brought in for this purpose, together with statues of the gods), and in addition cursed Christ—none of which actions those who genuinely are Christians can be made to take, I am told. Others named by an informer declared that they were Christians, but then denied it, asserting that they had been but had ceased to be, some three years before, others many years, some as much as twenty years. All these individuals also worshipped your image and the statues of the gods, and cursed Christ.

They declared, however, that what their fault or error amounted to was that they were accustomed to meet on a fixed day before dawn and sing alternately among themselves a hymn to Christ as to a god, and to bind themselves by oath, not to some crime, but rather not to commit fraud, theft, or adultery, not to commit a breach of trust, nor to deny a deposit when called upon to restore it. After doing this, it was their custom to depart and to reassemble to consume food—but of an ordinary, harmless type. Even this, they said, they had stopped doing after my edict by which, in accordance with your instructions, I had banned associations. Accordingly, I believed it all the more essential to find out what the truth was by torturing two female slaves who were called "attendants." I discovered nothing further except depraved, excessive superstition.

I therefore postponed the trial and hastened to consult you, since I felt the matter warranted consulting you, especially because of the number of people at risk. For many persons of every age, every rank, and also of both sexes are and will be exposed to danger. The contagion of this superstition has spread not only to the cities, but also to the villages and farms. But it seems possible to check and cure it. It is certainly quite clear that the temples, which had been almost deserted, have begun to be thronged again, that religious rites are being resumed after a long interval, and that the meat of sacrificial victims is on sale everywhere, even though up to this point almost nobody could be found to buy it. So it is easy to realize what a mass of people can be reformed if they are given a chance to change their minds.

[Trajan to Pliny] You have observed appropriate procedure, my dear Pliny, in sifting the cases of those denounced to you as Christians. For it is not possible to lay down some general rule to serve as a kind of fixed standard. They are not to be sought out; if they are denounced and proved to be guilty, they are to be punished, with this reservation, that whoever denies that he is a Christian and quite clearly proves it— that is, by worshipping our gods—he shall gain pardon because of his change of mind, despite having been under suspicion in the past. But anonymously posted accusations ought to have no place in any prosecution, since they set the worst precedent and are unworthy of our times.

Rome and Carthage in the West; even by 200, Christians as a whole can have represented no more than the tiniest fraction of the empire's population. The third Jewish revolt of 132–135 and its aftermath unequivocally differentiated Christians from Jews, and Christians began to be found among the municipal elite a generation or so thereafter. The increasing sophistication of the church is reflected in the formation of a church hierarchy in Rome, and in the growth of the concepts of heresy and orthodoxy in a debate apparently evolving in the third quarter of the second century. In the Severan period, Christianity evidently gained its first adherents in the equestrian and senatorial orders. These were women. But it remains difficult to say with any certainty who was Christian, and in what numbers, since few publicly professed their adherence. As Pliny's exchange with Trajan makes all too plain, anyone identifying with Christianity was liable to denunciation before Roman officials, as well as exposure to mob violence and fear.

From the mid-third century, into the early fourth, the Roman state actively persecuted Christians. They were labeled a menace to society, and officially sponsored efforts were made to extirpate their cult. In the first state persecution (249–251), an empire-wide requirement of sacrifice to the Roman gods allegedly resulted in thousands of deaths, many at the hands of mobs. All who duly offered sacrifices were issued certificates (*libelli*), which in the case of Christians served to record their renunciation of Christianity. The second state persecution (257–260) initially targeted clergy, but then widened to eliminate upper-class men and women who refused to renounce their faith; their property was to be seized, and they themselves were to suffer execution, exile, and other severe penalties. Finally, the third "Great" persecution, initiated by the emperors Diocletian and Galerius in 303, targeted Christian meeting places for destruction, deprived

Christian honestiores of their legal privileges, and finally required sacrifice to the Roman gods as a test of loyalty. Although Diocletian ended this persecution in the West as early as 305, in the East it continued until Galerius' Edict of Toleration in 311, and was even briefly reauthorized during the following decade or so. Christians were fairly easy to identify, because they refused to participate in state cult. As a result, they could not serve in the army, where religious ritual was an integral part of the routine. By the same token, they faced difficulty in taking up municipal or state positions. A major reason for the hostility shown to Christians may well have been their general refusal to assist the community in a civil or military capacity during a period when such help was urgently needed.

The persecutions created a category of persons known as "martyrs" from the Greek word for "witness," since these individuals were considered to have witnessed their faith through their public refusal to deny it. When ordered to sacrifice and to curse Christ, the martyrs refused, even though they were aware that this would lead to torture and death. Some Christians bewildered and irked the authorities by presenting themselves voluntarily for martyrdom. Altogether, the persecutions actually strengthened Christianity. They provided inspiring examples of brave Christians whose faith was unshakable, and they encouraged Christian self-perception as a beleaguered, suffering minority. "Martyrologies," stories of the martyrs, were widely circulated, often in an embedded form; thus the early third-century *Martyrdom of Perpetua* contains a martyr's retelling of another martyr's tale as a way to strengthen conviction and faith.

Christianity was appealing in other ways, too. The martyrologies and scriptures promised victory over death. Even in this life Christianity could be powerful, as when Christian churches offered aid to widows, orphans, and other marginalized or dispossessed individuals. In the mid-third century, for example, 1,500 widows and needy people were said to be receiving aid from the bishop of Rome alone (Eusebius, *History of the Church* 6.43). This form of charity contrasts sharply with the distributions given by the Princeps or by wealthy individuals, which were sporadic and almost invariably directed more towards prestigious recipients. The egalitarian community based on Christian love (*agape*) ignored differences of legal, social, or political status. This alternative approach attracted many individuals excluded from Rome's elites. Women were welcome in the Christian community, too, and they seem to have played important roles as organizers and proselytizers in the early church.

For these and other reasons, there developed the impression that Christians rejected Roman order and society. Their scriptures advocated peace. Many of their rites and customs were misunderstood. Their "eating the body and drinking the blood of their Savior" was called cannibalism, and their habit of addressing one another as "brother" and "sister" was taken to signify incestuous promiscuity. The high proportion of lower-class Christians must have alienated elitist Romans, with their established hierarchical institutions and their concern for social and political standing. But Roman order and society had been changing from the beginning of the Principate. The age-old self-identification according to political and social distinction was shifting. From the second century onwards, it is possible to identify a growing phenomenon, which may be termed "conversion": deliberate and public acts of religious commitment that often acknowledged psychological change. These are mostly associated with what have been termed "mystery" or oriental religions, like those of Isis, *Magna Mater*, and Mithras. Christianity shares some characteristics with these cults insofar as it, too, is based on a revealed doctrine, and features initiation, a dedicated priesthood, the promise of an afterlife, and community on earth. Yet Christianity differs from mystery religions in its greater openness to converts (one of the most widespread mystery religions, Mithraism, excluded women altogether), its proselytizing, its monotheism, its emphasis on scripture, and its stress on belief and behavior.

These distinctions became more marked during the state persecutions, which were episodes that also made the numbers and whereabouts of Christians more obvious. Perhaps 5 to 10 percent of the Roman world was Christian in the early fourth century. This seemingly low number is offset by the fact that many of these individuals lived in cities, and were thus among the fortunate. By now, Christians really could be found among all sections of Roman society; at its pinnacle, the emperor Diocletian's own wife and daughter were at least Christian sympathizers, if not practicing Christians. Even so, before the rule of Constantine in the early fourth century, there was no good reason to predict that within less than another century Christianity would emerge as the most powerful religion in the Roman world.

SUGGESTED READINGS

Birley, Anthony R. 1987 (revised edition). *Marcus Aurelius: A Biography*. New Haven and London: Yale University Press.

Birley, Anthony R. 1988 (revised edition). *Septimius Severus: The African Emperor*. New Haven and London: Yale University Press.

Bowman, Alan K. 1994. *Life and Letters on the Roman Frontier: Vindolanda and Its People*. London and New York: Routledge.

Gardner, Jane. F. 1986. *Women in Roman Law and Society*. Bloomington: Indiana University Press.

Gardner, Jane F. 1993. *Being a Roman Citizen*. London and New York: Routledge.

Hekster, Olivier. 2002. *Commodus: An Emperor at the Crossroads*. Amsterdam: Gieben.

Hekster, Olivier, with Nicholas Zair. 2008. *Rome and Its Empire, AD 193–284*. Edinburgh: Edinburgh University Press. Concise discussion of the period's historical developments, followed by extracts from key sources in translation.

Lendon, Jon E. 1997. *Empire of Honour: The Art of Government in the Roman World*. Oxford: Oxford University Press.

Lieu, Judith M. 2004. *Christian Identity in the Jewish and Graeco-Roman World*. Oxford: Oxford University Press.

Mattern, Susan P. 1999. *Rome and the Enemy: Imperial Grand Strategy in the Principate*. Berkeley, Los Angeles, London: University of California Press.

Riggsby, Andrew M. 2010. *Roman Law and the Legal World of the Romans*. Cambridge: Cambridge University Press. A clear, wide-ranging introductory treatment.

THE THIRD-CENTURY
CRISIS AND THE TETRARCHIC
RESTABILIZATION

SOURCES

Difficulties with our sources contribute to the controversies and confusion attending most of the events covered in this chapter. The political and military history of the third century is itself chaotic, and the lack of surviving contemporary literary accounts makes it all the more elusive; the relatively well documented first and second centuries may appear "normal" by comparison, although we must realize that in fact their stability was unusually fortuitous. Fourth-century authors are quite selective about the information they include. Several, such as Aurelius Victor and Eutropius, who wrote in the mid-fourth century, offer abbreviated historical summaries that give broad outlines but few details. They focus on the emperors, especially their personal merits and faults, but offer little insight into social, economic, or cultural history. Zosimus' Greek *New History*, composed around 500, covers the entire period but must be used cautiously. Though it is based on earlier, reliable sources, it abbreviates and distorts them. The *Historia Augusta* (see Chapter Eleven) likewise prefers to moralize rather than to analyze, and its concluding *Lives* of third-century emperors are remarkably fallacious and sensationalist.

The late third and early fourth century is a relatively well documented period, although problems abound here too. Nine imperial *Panegyrics* offer crucial insights into the contemporary portrayal of state affairs but remain frustratingly vague about specific events. Historical information in *On the Deaths of the Persecutors*, by the Christian Lactantius (written around 315), is colored by his determination to emphasize the horrible end of all who persecuted Christianity, especially the emperors of his own day. Thereafter the figure of Constantine dominates. For the most part, the ancient authors who write about him divide sharply over the key issue of his adherence to Christianity. His contemporary and biographer Eusebius, bishop of Caesarea in Palestine, wrote a *Life of Constantine* that mixes biography and panegyric. Though it can be highly tendentious, it remains valuable for its preservation of many authentic documents issued by Constantine himself. In addition, Eusebius invented a variation on the traditional narrative history. He called it *Ecclesiastical History*—that is, the history of the Christian church. His extant version of this new genre, completed in 324, though primarily of interest for religious matters, offers useful information about political and military events. Here, as in his *Life of Constantine*, he quotes imperial documents in their original form, an invaluable tool for the historian.

Coins and inscriptions provide insight into the chosen images of various rulers and usurpers. But the general decrease in the number of Roman inscriptions, especially ones commissioned by private individuals, reduces information for social history. Archeology reveals an overall impoverishment of material culture in many areas, though not all (Britain, southern Asia Minor, and most of North Africa seem to have thrived). Nevertheless, the empire's political fragmentation makes it hard to determine how representative the evidence from any one region may now be; this problem diminishes the potential value of the relatively abundant documentary records from third- and fourth-century Egypt, Palestine, and Mesopotamia. Legal codes, which record imperial pronouncements for the third century in previously unparalleled numbers, go some way toward providing a remedy. Nevertheless, it is frequently impossible to discern the various stages of important developments, or who initiated them and why. This chapter first discusses the mid-third century by topic, rather than by ruler, and then turns to the important emperors of the later third and early fourth centuries. The narrative ends with Constantine's consolidation of the entire empire under his sole rule in 324.

MID-THIRD CENTURY

The years from the assassination of Severus Alexander in 235 to the acclamation of Diocletian in 284 witnessed rapid, often violent political change. In less than fifty years, at least eighteen emperors took power with their legitimacy confirmed or ratified by the Roman senate. Even more men claimed to be Princeps without such sanction. The list of would-be emperors, most of whom were initially appointed by armies on the borders, includes sons appointed to hold office with their fathers, usurpers, and pretenders; most met a violent death. The senate had little power, no longer provided political stability, and must have seemed obsolete when Marcus Aurelius Carus was accepted as emperor in 282 without even applying to it for validation. Though the period is often called the Age of Crisis, there was at the time a strong stress on continuity with the past and the promise of a bright future. The leaders proclaimed the timelessness, imperturbability, and transcendence of the empire in coins and inscriptions. For example, despite a devastating loss to Persia, ongoing internal insurrections, and invasions by trans-Danubian Carpi and Goths, Rome's thousandth anniversary in 248 was celebrated with great pomp by the emperor Philip "the Arab" (who came from the region of Damascus). Imperial inscriptions and coins insistently cite *Roma Aeterna* (Eternal Rome) and describe emperors as *Invictus* (Unconquerable) and the like. There seems to have been a greater resistance to innovation, to judge from the empire-wide Christian persecutions of the emperors Decius (249–251) and Valerian (253–260) (see Chapter Eleven), which were resumed in the early fourth century.

Just as shortsighted and futile were the efforts of various emperors to assert their supremacy over rivals, rather than to address systematically the problems that the empire faced on its northern and eastern borders. These were the areas of the greatest external dangers. The jagged northern boundaries—for the most part, the great rivers of the Rhine and Danube—divided the empire from various Germanic and other tribes. But the separation was never complete. Commercial, social, and cultural interaction regularly occurred in times of peace. During hostilities, the rivers were by no means impenetrable barriers. Not only could they freeze over to become passable in winter, but also even in summer they constituted as much a means of transport and an avenue of communication as they did a line of demarcation or a bulwark of defense. By the mid-third century, when Rome's river frontiers had been more or less fixed for two centuries, the peoples beyond these frontiers had undergone substantial changes from the days when the empire first encountered them. In large part as a response to their Roman neighbors, these "barbarian" peoples had grown more economically powerful and their societies had coalesced into more complex, hierarchical groupings. Rome no longer seemed so formidable or overwhelming, especially to those barbarians who had served as allies with its armies. Furthermore, new peoples were constantly pushing against the old, creating pressures for borderland groups to enter the empire or to strengthen themselves against threats from both sides by forming coalitions. It is over the course of the third century that we first encounter new confederacies of barbarian groups, not empires like Rome's nor even quite kingdoms, but alliances capable of standing up to Roman armies and even defeating them.

By the mid-third century, the Rhine and Danube were being crossed repeatedly by these groups, including Franks, Alamanni and Juthungi, Vandals, and Sarmatians. Franks and Saxons crossed the English Channel to harass Roman Britain, too, which also suffered attacks from the north by tribes in Scotland. The middle Danubian provinces—Noricum, Upper and Lower Pannonia, Dacia, and Upper and Lower Moesia—saw recurrent fighting and military threats. This general region, often termed Illyricum, was famous as a source of fearless soldiers. It provided many of the emperors of the mid-third century; these men, like all "Illyrians," were stereotyped as semi-barbarian but valiant protectors of Rome. The Roman provinces along the lower Danube were often attacked by Goths, a Germanic people who by this time had migrated and settled beside the Black Sea. Their coalition achieved some degree of unity under a king named Cniva, who

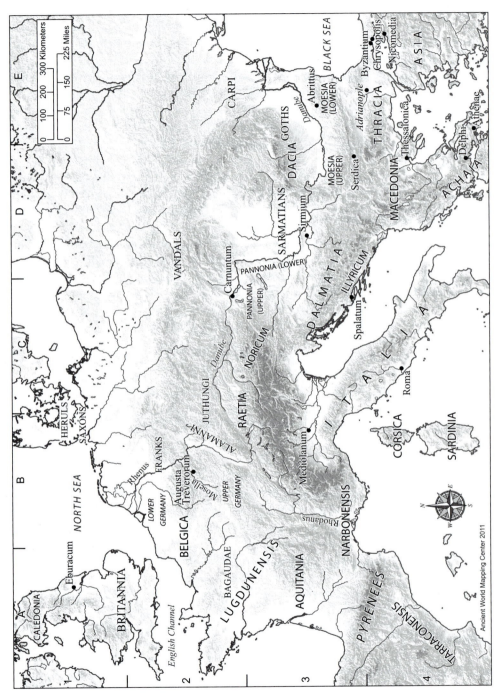

Map 12.1 *The Empire's North and West in the "Age of Crisis"*

Ancient World Mapping Center 2011

invaded the territory of Thrace in 250 and sacked many Roman cities. When the emperor Decius marched against them the following year, they were able to surround his army at Abrittus (in the marshy territory of northern Moesia) and kill him and his son, whom he had appointed co-emperor. This was the first time Rome had ever lost an emperor in battle against a foreign foe. The Goths later went on to assault Roman provinces in northern Asia Minor, sacking Trapezus (modern Trabzon, Turkey) in 256. Again in 267, Goths and Heruli invaded the Balkans, and sacked Athens, Delphi, and other Greek centers, necessitating the creation of local militias to deal with the problem in the absence of imperial support.

In Persia a new, more aggressive dynasty called the Sasanians had supplanted the Parthians in the 220s and had begun challenging Rome on its eastern border. Under their King of Kings Shapur I (242–272), they reached Antioch (modern Antakya, Turkey) in Syria, sacking it in 253 and again in 260. In the latter year, Shapur even captured alive the emperor Valerian at Edessa (modern Urfa, Turkey) in Osroene. Valerian lived out his remaining days serving as the footstool—literally—of the Persian king, a humiliating blow to Roman pride. This military effectiveness was possible because the government of the Sasanians, centrally controlled under its King of Kings, was strikingly different not just from the less cohesive, shifting groups encountered by the Romans on their borders elsewhere, but even from their Parthian foes of the first century B.C. and following. The Sasanians' political sophistication, and the relative difficulty of maneuvers through the dry lands separating them and the Romans, led the latter to use diplomacy as well as force to settle or prevent problems in the East. The two empires were often in conflict, however, and the crisis provoked by the capture of Valerian led to internal fragmentation within the Roman empire.

Foreign invasions and pressure were not the only causes of Rome's political instability. The Principate had never evolved a clear system for the succession. No recognized hierarchy was ever established among the positions below that of emperor, so that the governors of the major provinces, for example, were all notionally equal rather than ranked. Consequently, when a ruling emperor was assassinated or died on the battlefield—common enough occurrences in the mid-third century—anyone could be selected, and there was no impartial way to distinguish between claims. Under Gallienus, who ruled from 253 to 268 (jointly with his father Valerian from 253 until 260), senators may actually have been barred from military commands. Few senators are known to have held positions of military and administrative influence after this time. They did not serve as governors of the many provinces with military garrisons, since a governor's duties included the command of the troops in his province. Yet because effective military leadership and good administration require different sets of personal and managerial skills, the empire's response to the turmoil of the third century may have been weakened by its lack of a professional bureaucracy.

The shameful capture of Valerian in 260 surely represented the nadir of Rome's political and military disarray. His son and co-Augustus, Gallienus, did not attempt to avenge his father; he faced too many other invasions and revolts elsewhere in the empire. His response to these crises was shrewd, but ultimately represented the

Figure 12.1 *The Sasanian King of Kings Shapur I (242–272) took great pride in his many victories over Roman emperors. At Naqsh-i Rustam Shapur described these in a detailed trilingual inscription, across from which he had this monumental relief carved in a cliff face. Here Shapur, seated atop his horse, lords it over two emperors, both shown in military capes* (paludamenta) *with laurel wreaths as marks of their office. It is not absolutely certain which emperors are depicted, but this can be surmised with a high degree of probability. Philip I the Arab, who suffered a major defeat near what is today Fallujah (Iraq) and was forced into a humiliating peace, kneels in deference before the King of Kings, and the figure who stands with his upraised hands held by Shapur is almost certainly Valerian, whom Shapur claims in his inscription to have captured "with his own hand" in a battle of 260. To the right we see a bust of the priest Kartir, a powerful figure in the Zoroastrian religion, which was harnessed by the Sasanians to promote unity within their empire.*

need to make a virtue of necessity. He let others take charge of the East and West unopposed, while he secured Italy, North Africa, Egypt, the Danubian provinces, and Greece. Septimius Odenaethus, a noble from the powerful oasis of Palmyra (modern Tudmur, Syria), received the unusual titles *dux* ("leader") and *corrector totius Orientis* ("overseer of the entire East") in recognition of his protection of the area between the Sasanians and Romans. On his death in 267, his widow Zenobia continued his rule in the name of their young son, Septimius Vaballathus, and remained unchallenged until the 270s. Under her leadership, Palmyrene control ultimately extended to Syria, Palestine, Arabia, Egypt, and much of Asia Minor. In the West, the former military commander Marcus Cassianius Latinius Postumus controlled Gaul, Spain, Raetia, and Britain as a usurper. From at least 260 to 269, and without official recognition by Gallienus, Postumus collected taxes in these regions, coined money, levied soldiers, and protected the populace from incursions over the Rhine. He thus functioned as a sort of territorial emperor, but in rivalry rather than cooperation with the authority of the emperor in Rome.

To the north and northeast, the Romans apparently continued to settle *dediticii* (enemies who had surrendered to Rome) within the empire's borders, although this was not enough to stem the wave of invasions. In response, Gallienus made greater use of Rome's cavalry. This step marks the start of a gradual shift (that continued into the fourth century) to a twofold defensive system relying on a mobile field army and a more stationary frontier force. Gallienus suspended the Christian persecution begun by his father Valerian and attempted other reforms, but in 268 he was killed while trying to suppress a mutiny at Mediolanum (modern Milan, Italy). As a general rule, the cities in the north and east of the empire gained greater political and economic importance from the need for third-century emperors to be based closer than before to the vulnerable frontier areas.

Depopulation deepened the empire's problems. The scanty evidence for the mid-third century indicates a twenty-year plague in Italy and cities elsewhere. There were said to have been 5,000 deaths a day at Rome in 262, and two thirds of the population of Alexandria supposedly perished. Famine could arise from transport difficulties, and the frequent diversion of food and supplies to the army. Emperors' attention to their rivals and to the borders led to neglect of roads and harbors, not to mention public amenities like games and baths. Local communities and their resources came under intense pressure. The established pattern of "beneficial ideology" that we have noted in Chapters Nine to Eleven slowed considerably in the third century. Indeed, emperors now felt the need to begin issuing laws and instructions designed to force municipal elites to maintain the services their cities had come to expect, or even simply to prevent members of this social group from attempting to escape appointment to their city councils altogether. Civic problems were further exacerbated by the growing scale of Christian persecutions. Although these had begun in part as a way to increase cohesion, they resulted in neighbors and families turning against themselves. Municipal elites were hard hit, with especially devastating effects in North Africa, where the anti-Christian legislation of Decius and Valerian was harshly enforced in the mid-third century.

Another manifestation of the instability of the period is the constant debasement of Rome's coinage. One modius of wheat (about 8.6 dry liters) cost two sesterces around A.D. 150 but 400 sesterces around A.D. 300; its nominal price thus increased two hundredfold in a century and a half. A different gauge of inflation and the debasement of Rome's currency can be seen in the comparison of silver denarii from different Principates. Under Nero, who first debased imperial coin so that its silver content was less than its face value, the denarius was reduced to 90 percent purity; under Marcus Aurelius it was at 75 percent and under Septimius Severus only 50 percent. Caracalla's "Antoninianus" (see Chapter Eleven) further confused monetary values. By the 260s it had become the standard "silver" coin, but at its most debased it had an actual silver content of less than 2 percent; the remainder consisted of bronze. This third-century debasement reflects larger economic woes brought on by the perfect storm of problems witnessed in the period: external warfare, which fueled internal crises of leadership, which led to usurpations, which demanded rapid and sizeable payments to soldiers, which forced emperors and claimants to mint more coins by debasing them with bronze, which created inflationary pressures, which drained taxpayers to the breaking point, which reduced tax revenues and thus weakened the empire further. Although the economic problems were real, we must be careful not to exaggerate them. Strangely enough, the periods of most pronounced inflation occurred only later in the third century after Aurelian and other emperors began taking steps to tackle debasement and restabilize the coinage. Moreover, while the archeology of the period shows a definite trend toward stagnation, there is little evidence of decline and no sign of total collapse (note Plates 13a and b).

AURELIAN (270–275)

The emperor Aurelian (Lucius Domitius Aurelianus), an Illyrian commander who ruled from 270 to 275 after acclamation by his troops, illustrates the times. His nickname, "Hand-on-Sword," emphasizes the military prowess that was the basis of his accomplishments; although he did not focus exclusively on military problems, they demanded much of his attention during his brief rule. His first step was to defeat northern invaders who had made their way into Italy. He then applied himself to regaining control over those parts of the empire which had fallen from the dominion of the central state. Zenobia of Palmyra had profited from the assassination of Gallienus to expand into Egypt and deep into Asia Minor. She had also begun to style herself "Augusta," and her young son Vaballath "Augustus," a clear sign of her growing power and ambitions. In two campaigns conducted in 272–273, Aurelian defeated her and restored all her territory to Roman rule. What he perhaps overlooked was that, in removing her, he was also removing a valuable buffer between the Roman empire and the Sasanians. In 274 he likewise brought an end to what is sometimes called the "Gallic empire" by defeating the last successor of Postumus, who had himself been murdered in 268; as a result, Gaul and other parts of the West once again came under central control after fourteen years of local autonomy.

Aurelian tried to reform Rome's coinage after an eightfold rise in prices between 267 and 274. To tighten the emperor's control, he closed down local mints in the East and abolished the senatorial one at Rome. In their stead he introduced a number of new imperial mints which now struck coins that had a guaranteed silver content, low though it was. In the city of Rome, he imposed state control on the *collegia* (associations) that were responsible for such services as construction and baking bread. He also tried to extend his religious authority by encouraging a monotheism centered on the cult of *Sol Invictus* (the Unconquered Sun). The god of the sun had long been worshipped, but became particularly popular in the third century. We have already seen that the emperor Marcus Aurelius Antoninus took his nickname Elagabalus from the Syrian version of this deity (Chapter Eleven), whose cult he promoted in Rome. Aurelian built an enormous temple in Rome to Sol Invictus, as well as establishing a new priestly college of Pontiffs and a series of games in honor of the Sun. He also styled himself as the vice-regent of Sol Invictus, featuring on coins and inscriptions the title *Dominus et Deus natus* ("born Lord and God").

Two other steps taken by Aurelian are important. First, he abandoned the province of Dacia, regarding its exposed position north of the Danube as no longer tenable in the face of persistent onslaughts throughout the previous century. Removing all Roman forces stationed there to the south bank of the Danube, he carved out a new province also named Dacia from parts of Upper and Lower Moesia, and Thrace. It is unclear how many civilians followed the army south, since no mass emigration is suggested by archeology, religious practices, or linguistics. Aurelian issued coins proclaiming *Dacia Felix* ("Fortunate Dacia"), but his withdrawal from north of the Danube was an acknowledgment that Rome could no longer maintain control of all its territory.

Second, in 271 Aurelian ordered a twelve-mile-long (20 km) brick wall to be built around the city of Rome. Beginning in the mid-third century, and notably in Gaul, Spain, and the East, an increasing number of cities had devoted resources to building or repairing walls. But Aurelian's wall around Rome was the most uniform set of defenses erected there since as long ago as the fourth century B.C. and the largest ever. The changed conditions to which it was a response seem a far cry from the confidence felt by Aelius Aristides only a century before Aurelian's time, when Aristides praised Rome for not having walls around the city itself—"as if you [Rome] were hiding or fleeing from your subjects"—but only at the edges of the empire (*To Rome* 80; see Chapter Eleven).

Like many of his predecessors, Aurelian was killed by his own soldiers. His assassination in 275 ushered in ten more years of political and military strife that ended only in 284 with the acclamation of Diocletian. Apart from the feckless Gallienus, he was to be the first emperor in half a century who would maintain power for more than a few years. He would also be the first to abdicate voluntarily, in 305.

DIOCLETIAN, THE TETRARCHY, AND THE DOMINATE (284–305)

Diocletian was a man with absolutely no dynastic claims to power. Indeed, the murky history of his early life would indicate that he was either a freedman or, more likely, the son of a freedman. What he lacked in pedigree, however, he made up for in talent and ambition. Like so many third-century emperors, he was born in Illyricum, probably in the Dalmatian town of Spalatum (modern Split, in Croatia). By the time he came to power he had served in several military units in the West and was acting as commander of the *protectores,* a new unit of imperial guardsmen who served at the emperor's side (most of the old Praetorians were now cocooned in Rome as a sort of glorified police force). Prior to accession his name had been the Greek-sounding Diocles, but as emperor he altered this to the Latinate Diocletianus, proving early on that he was open to change. From the beginning he also proved himself brutally decisive, for his predecessor Numerian had died under mysterious circumstances, and in the ceremony at which he was acclaimed Diocletian is said to have murdered the man he blamed for Numerian's death, the Praetorian Prefect Aper. Even with this act, however, Diocletian was not free of rivals, for Numerian's brother Carinus was still ruling in the West. Diocletian's first military expedition was thus aimed at him, and although Diocletian suffered defeat in battle along the Danube, in a bizarre turn of fortune Carinus was assassinated by his own men, leaving Diocletian sole ruler.

Figure 12.2 This group portrait of the four tetrarchs (ca. 300) was originally mounted on a column in Constantinople. In the foreground, the senior Augustus is bearded, and grasps his Caesar with his right arm. Otherwise Augustus and Caesar are identical to each other and to their mirror images, the other two tetrarchs. All four wear the identical military cloak (paludamentum) fastened at the right shoulder; abrasion suggests that a metal brooch or a stone of a different color was fixed here originally. Each man's breastplate is held in place by an elaborate military belt. Each also carries an eagle-headed sword in a rich scabbard, and wears a Pannonian cap, the front of which was originally ornamented with a jewel or stone in its center. In rendering all the tetrarchs alike and positioning them so closely together, this group portrait embodies the unanimity that the four men were resolved to uphold. Their furrowed brows indicate their concern for the empire. But at the same time their elevation above their subjects is conveyed by the gems they wear, as well as by the use of porphyry—a rare, hard, reddish-purple stone reserved by this time exclusively for emperors and their families. During the Middle Ages, this statue was taken from Constantinople to Venice, where it now stands at the southwest corner of St. Mark's Basilica.

The elimination of Carinus in mid-285 makes it seem strange that, within a matter of months thereafter, Diocletian appointed a co-emperor with the title *Caesar* named Maximian. Diocletian knew well, however, that the empire had grown too large for a single ruler and, in contrast to Carinus, Maximian was an old friend and fellow Balkan soldier whom he could trust. Indeed, Maximian, despite an impulsive character, would remain unswervingly faithful to Diocletian for the next twenty years, thus providing the key to the imperial stability that would distinguish Diocletian's reign. To further cement their relationship, the two emperors assumed parts of one another's nomenclature, so that they were officially known as Gaius Aurelius Valerius Diocletianus and Gaius Galerius Valerius Maximianus. They also advertised themselves as "brothers" in official propaganda despite having no blood relationship. Above all, beginning in 287 they each adopted divine protectors in the traditional gods Jupiter/Jove (king of the gods) and Hercules (Jupiter's son, the archetypal strongman), and each began using the additional titles *Jovius* and *Herculius*. These names they applied to everything from military units to new provinces; they also propagated images of their two protective gods on coins and in art.

Immediately after his accession in late 285, Maximian was dispatched to Gaul to deal with an uprising of the Bagaudae, rural insurgents under local, indigenous leadership. His successes there induced Diocletian to promote him to full Augustus in April 286, making the two equals in rank, even if Diocletian remained the dominant ruler. Later that same year Carausius, one of Maximian's commanders, launched a revolt with the North Sea fleet and occupied Britain and northern Gaul. Maximian would struggle with this revolt for the next seven years, both because of Carausius' skill as a leader and because of other pressing military difficulties caused particularly by Germans along the Rhine. Meanwhile, in 285 Diocletian had been able to return eastward to campaign against the Sarmatians— an Indo-Iranian people who inhabited the territory north of the lower Danube— and, in 287, to appoint a new king for Armenia. The following year he returned to the West, where he and Maximian executed a brilliant pincer movement against tribes in Germany. By 290 he was back on the eastern frontier fighting yet another enemy new to Rome, the Saracens. These were Bedouin Arab tribes who would come to play an increasingly important role, sometimes as allies and at other times as enemies, along the desert edge of Syria and Palestine.

With all of this jockeying back and forth from east to west, Diocletian soon realized that even two emperors were not enough to handle Rome's military situation, so he took the decision to expand the leadership to four. On March 1, 293, he appointed a partner who was now to be named Galerius Valerius Maximianus to support him in the East, and Maximian appointed Flavius Valerius Constantius in the West. These new partners—both fellow Illyrians—were given the title Caesar rather than Augustus, indicating their subordination to their more senior colleagues, and, as is evident, both assumed parts of their colleagues' nomenclature. In addition, each was linked by marriage to his respective Augustus: Galerius married Diocletian's daughter Valeria, and Constantius married

Theodora, the daughter of Maximian, under whom he had already been serving as a general (Table 13.1).

This four-man system of rulership, which scholars since the nineteenth century have termed the "tetrarchy," has often been characterized as a carefully crafted system of joint rule with two senior emperors exercising authority over two juniors, who were intended to replace them after a period of service. However, the level of forward planning and systematization involved has been questioned. It seems most likely that some degree of conscious planning was indeed present to promote merit and symmetry over the traditional randomness imposed by the old dynastic principle of rule and succession, but traditional elements of dynasty—like intermarriage—were certainly exploited too.

Diocletian had thus doubled the size of the imperial "college," a term we have already encountered in the context of professional "associations" and one which the tetrarchs applied to their own association of emperors. As we might imagine, the application of this system of joint rule to the military and political arena produced dramatic results. Already in 293, Constantius was able to defeat the usurper Carausius in battle and retake northern Gaul. This led to Carausius' assassination and replacement by a subordinate, Allectus, whom Constantius also crushed after crossing the English Channel and invading Britain in 296. Maximian, meanwhile, passed through Spain and across to Mauretania in North Africa in 297 in order to defeat a dangerous tribal group known in Latin sources as the Quinquegentiani. By 298 he entered Carthage, then crossed back into Italy and celebrated a triumph in Rome in 299. While there he undertook construction of the largest baths Rome had ever seen, named after his colleague Diocletian (Map 12.2). From this point forward, Maximian seems to have remained in Milan, poised near the frontier but inactive, relying on his younger colleague to continue the defense of the northwestern frontier.

In the East, Diocletian remained in Sirmium (modern Sremska Mitrovica, Serbia) near the Danube while Galerius was sent to the eastern frontier to guard against the new Sasanian King of Kings, Narses. In 296, Narses invaded Armenia, provoking Galerius into a hastily prepared campaign during which the Caesar was defeated near Carrhae (modern Harran, Turkey) in early 297. Ashamed, Galerius returned to Antioch to meet Diocletian, who punished him by forcing him to run in full imperial garb for over a mile alongside his chariot. Anxious to impress his superior, Galerius gathered a new force and surprised Narses by marching into Armenia that same fall. Narses fled, and Galerius captured his baggage train and extensive harem before continuing into Persia and taking its capital Ctesiphon (near modern Baghdad, Iraq) early in 298. Narses was forced into a humiliating peace which required him to surrender control of northern Mesopotamia in its entirety (including the impregnable fortress of Nisibis) as well as his suzerainty over several Armenian dependent territories. Thus Galerius' campaign not only won back for Rome the whole area sacrificed to Persia in the wars of the mid-third century, but it also gained new territory. This was an iconic event in the tetrarchic regime, and as such was commemorated on the arch that Galerius erected in Thessalonica.

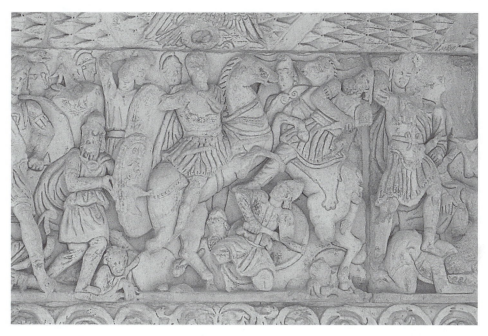

Figure 12.3 *The emperor Galerius (293–311) constructed an elaborate palace complex in the city of Thessalonica in northern Greece, a regional capital and major transportation hub. Through the city runs the Via Egnatia, the most important east–west artery across the southern Balkans. Astride this road and on axis with his palace, Galerius constructed a massive and ornately decorated three-bay arch which was covered with bands of sculptural reliefs depicting important events from his reign. In this scene, Galerius is shown on horseback (left) attacking the King of Kings Narses (293–303), characterized as Persian by his pants and beard, who reels back in defeat. Around these central figures, Persians—also wearing pants and distinctive pointed caps—cower in defeat as they are trampled by conquering Romans. Above Galerius, an eagle prepares to crown him with a victory wreath. The scene is an idealized version of events; Galerius and Narses never actually met on the field of battle.*

The perfect test of Diocletian's tetrarchic system occurred even as Galerius was invading Armenia. In 296 a usurper named Domitius Domitianus seized much of Egypt, a threat that would have placed the empire in grave peril if Galerius had been sole emperor. Instead, Diocletian was able to march south and subdue the revolt by late 297, while Galerius remained engaged in Persia. When in Egypt, Diocletian even took the opportunity to advance up the Nile, where he renegotiated a treaty with the Nobatae on the southern border of the province. The tetrarchy had clearly worked, proving itself a system that was at once tightly knit and flexible, with the capacity to respond effectively against all military threats, external and internal. As the tetrarchs would soon learn, however, there remained the problem that, in the absence of a strong leader like Diocletian, old habits of dynasticism and infighting would quickly reappear and once again prevail over the elegant, but also sterile, symmetry that he had imposed.

The one major misstep Diocletian can be said to have taken was the choice to initiate a series of persecutions against minority religious groups, and especially the Christians, after he had been ruling for almost twenty years. Since 260 the Christians had largely been left in peace by the imperial administration. A whole generation had grown up in relative calm; the emperor Aurelian had even allowed himself to become involved in settling internal disputes among the Christian clergy. Diocletian, however, was extremely conservative as a religious leader, as his choice of patron deities for the tetrarchs, the old Roman gods Jupiter and Hercules, demonstrates. Probably in 302 (though possibly earlier), this sentiment manifested itself in a brutal decree issued against the Manichaeans, a religious group that combined elements of Judaism, Christianity, and Zoroastrianism. The decree accused the group of acting as a Persian fifth column inside the empire and of introducing dangerous innovations; its leaders were to be burnt alive together with their books, and all imperial officials among its followers were to be sent to the mines (*Collation of the Laws of Moses and Rome* 15.3). This harsh attack was a precursor to Diocletian's efforts against the Christians, which were initiated the following year.

Diocletian's conservatism was in some ways characteristic of religious belief throughout the Greek and Roman world. In contrast with a modern outlook, those who lived in this world did not prize innovation in their lives, and particularly in their religion. On the contrary, they feared it as impious and dangerous. As a religion that began in the first century A.D.—and with the public execution of a criminal, its critics argued—Christianity was innovative and revolutionary. Diocletian had already expelled Christian soldiers from the army in 299, but a series of failed sacrifices followed by a mysterious fire at his palace in Nicomedia (modern İzmit, Turkey) stoked the flames of his rage to new heights. On February 23, 303, he ordered his soldiers to destroy the sizeable Christian church of Nicomedia, and on the following day he issued an edict ordering churches across the empire to be pulled down and scriptures confiscated and destroyed. Christians of rank were stripped of status and imperial freedmen re-enslaved. Later in 303 he issued a second edict ordering the arrest of Christian clergy, who could be freed only if they demonstrated their apostasy by offering sacrifice. Two further edicts followed in 304, ordering that all the empire's subjects demonstrate their loyalty by sacrificing in public.

This series of laws and their enactment constitute what modern scholars refer to as the "Great Persecution." The heavier hand of Diocletian's government allowed him to enforce his wishes with more systematic pressure than in any previous state persecution (see Chapter Eleven). While the two western tetrarchs, and particularly Constantius, seem to have enforced the decree only very haltingly, in the East Diocletian demonstrated that the same brutality he had used to pacify the barbarians could also be used against Christian citizens of the empire. Although, much to his chagrin, the Great Persecution did not have the effect of stamping out Christianity, it did leave its mark in the form of a heightened

Christian ideology of resistance and martyrdom. It also provoked considerable infighting among Christians over their various reactions to the pressure of this persecution, including outright apostasy. The rifts caused by such strife were to send shockwaves through the Christian church for the next century and more.

DISSOLUTION OF THE TETRARCHY (305–313), AND THE RISE OF CONSTANTINE (306–324)

Increasingly ill, Diocletian retired in 305 from his capital in Nicomedia to a palace he had constructed earlier at Split. During the twenty-one years of his rule, he had established what could have seemed a reliable new means of regulating the succession. Diocletian's abdication in the East presumed that his own Caesar, Galerius, would move up to become Augustus. At the same time he forced retirement upon Maximian, his fellow Augustus in the West, elevating Maximian's Caesar, Constantius, to Augustus there. To Galerius and Constantius were now subordinated new Caesars in the persons of fellow Illyrian soldiers of a younger generation: Maximin Daia for the East, and Severus for the West. Both these men were friends of Galerius, and Maximin Daia was actually his nephew, an indication that family and influence were still important in their selection.

The whiff of patronage and dynasticism behind these appointments no doubt contributed to the almost immediate disintegration of this plan. In the East, the relatively unknown Valerius Licinianus Licinius, who had also served under Galerius, was eager for power. In the West, Severus was little known, and he had many rivals for his position as Caesar there. Meanwhile Maximian did not want to retire, and his son, Maxentius, had ambitions of his own despite being ignored in the deliberations. Further, Constantius' son, Constantine, had been marked as an imperial favorite by being trained at Diocletian's court and had already proven himself a talented army officer; but he, too, had been overlooked in the succession. The ambitions of these rivals were fed by their knowledge that the empire's subjects, and above all its soldiers, retained a strong preference for dynasty.

In 305, an aging Constantius summoned his son, Constantine, then at Galerius' court, to help him fight the Picts in Scotland. When Constantius fell ill and died at Eburacum (modern York, England) in July 306, the troops there promoted Constantine to replace his father with the title of full Augustus. Their initiative represented a direct affront to Galerius' authority as the sole remaining Augustus in the tetrarchic system. It also challenged that very system and its succession scheme, according to which Severus would move up to senior Augustus in the West. At first Galerius was understandably furious, but knowing that there was little he could do about affairs so far away, he compromised by insisting that Severus be promoted to Augustus while Constantine could be made his new Caesar. Meanwhile Constantine kept command of his father's troops and during the next few years used them successfully in the Rhine borderlands.

a

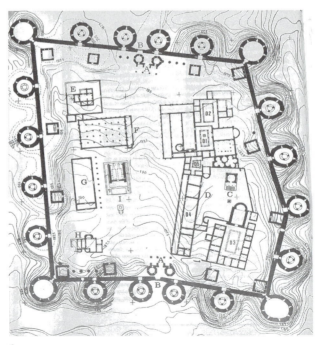

b

As early as October 306, however, this fragile compromise was threatened when the populace of Rome, in league with the Praetorian Guard, promoted Maxentius to be yet another emperor in the West. In contrast with the rulers of the previous forty years, he chose to reside in Rome and to commission new public monuments there in an attempt to revitalize a civic patriotism that had long been on the wane (Map 12.2). In 307, Severus advanced against Maxentius in Rome but was deserted by his own troops—they were, after all, the former army of Maxentius' father. Severus was captured and eventually forced into suicide. Maxentius also repelled an attempt on Rome by Galerius, once again by threatening to undermine the loyalty of Galerius' troops. The power of dynasty was clearly greater than the tetrarchs had reckoned. Meanwhile, Maxentius' father, Maximian, long resentful at being forced to retire at the same time as Diocletian in 305, was scheming to reclaim his earlier supreme position as Augustus in the West.

In November 308 Galerius tried to shore up the faltering tetrarchy by calling a conference at Carnuntum in Upper Pannonia (modern Petronell, Austria). Here Diocletian was urged to resume power but refused, saying he preferred to cultivate the garden at his retirement palace. He had grown weary and lived on only until around 311. However, Diocletian did lend moral support to the arrangements reached, which reaffirmed Galerius as supreme Augustus and Maximin Daia as his Caesar in the East. Galerius' friend and associate, Licinius, was now made Augustus in the West, even though he had never held the position of Caesar. Maxentius and his father Maximian were excluded from these arrangements, which assumed their elimination. By 310 Maximian had been killed by Constantine, but Maxentius, though considered a usurper, continued to reside in Rome and to control Italy and Africa, effectively limiting Licinius to no more than Illyricum. Maximin Daia, resentful that Galerius had promoted Licinius directly to be Augustus, had induced his own troops to proclaim him Augustus, while Constantine was also now openly styling himself Augustus. By 310, therefore, Diocletian's tidy tetrarchic scheme was well on its way to unraveling; four emperors still ruled together, but only with great friction.

Throughout this period Constantine generally restricted his movements to Gaul, campaigning against the Franks and Alamanni on the Rhine in 309 and 310. Nevertheless, his larger ambitions are indicated by an anonymous Latin pane-

Facing page

Figure 12.4a,b *The tetrarchic Villa Romuliana. Excavations conducted since the 1950s at modern Gamzigrad, Serbia, have revealed a massive fortified villa complex identified as the luxury palace of the emperor Galerius (293–311). The villa was surrounded by walls outfitted with round towers, and it contained a palace with many rooms (D on the plan), two temples (C and I), and two large meeting halls (F and G). An inscription and a reference in a text attest that Galerius built this villa in honor of his mother Romula; both were buried in twin mausolea found outside the walled perimeter. This style of fortified villa became popular across the empire in the period. Diocletian himself built a similar palace on an even grander scale and retired there after his abdication in 305. Located on the coast of Dalmatia, its walls—which still stand—formed the basis for the construction of the medieval town of Split in modern Croatia.*

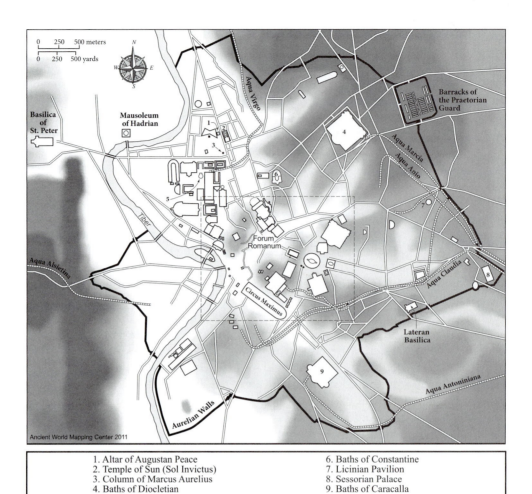

Map 12.2 *Rome in the Age of Constantine*

1. Altar of Augustan Peace
2. Temple of Sun (Sol Invictus)
3. Column of Marcus Aurelius
4. Baths of Diocletian
5. Pantheon
6. Baths of Constantine
7. Licinian Pavilion
8. Sessorian Palace
9. Baths of Caracalla

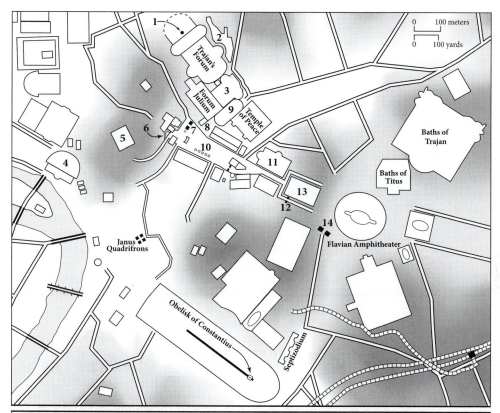

1. Column of Trajan
2. Trajan's Markets
3. Forum Augustum
4. Theater of Marcellus
5. Temple of Jupiter Optimus Maximus
6. Porticus Deorum Consentium
7. Arch of Septimius Severus
8. Curia Julia (rebuilt under Diocletian)
9. Forum of Nerva (Forum Transitorium)
10. Five Column Monument of Diocletian
11. Basilica of Maxentius and Constantine
12. Arch of Titus
13. Temple of Venus and Rome
14. Arch of Constantine

SOURCE 12.1: Galerius' Edict of Toleration (April 311)

Galerius' "Edict of Toleration" survives in two sources, Eusebius' Ecclesiastical History
(8.17) and Lactantius' On the Deaths of the Persecutors, *the first in Greek and the second in Latin. Although the two sources are independent, both reproduce the same text with
only slight variation. This match attests both to the new Christian historiographical fashion
for copying the precise wording of imperial pronouncements—rather than just paraphras-
ing them, as earlier historians had done—and to the widespread dissemination of the edict
made possible by the new tetrarchic bureaucracy.*

Among all the other arrangements which we are always making for the advantage
and benefit of the state, we had earlier sought to set everything right in accordance
with the ancient laws and public discipline of the Romans, and to ensure that the
Christians, too, who had abandoned their ancestors' way of life, should return to a
sound frame of mind. For in some way such willfulness had overcome these same
Christians, such folly had taken hold of them, that they no longer followed those practices of the ancients which their own ancestors perhaps had first instituted; but simply
following their own judgment and pleasure, they were making up for themselves the
laws which they were to observe, and were gathering various groups of people
together in different places. When finally our order was published that they should
devote themselves to the practices of the ancients, many were subjected to danger,
many too were struck down. Very many, however, persisted in their determination,
and we saw that these same people were neither offering worship and due religious
observance to the gods, nor practicing the worship of the god of the Christians.
Bearing in mind, therefore, our own most gentle clemency and our perpetual habit of
showing lenient pardon to all, we have taken the view that in the case of these people
too we should extend our speediest leniency, so that once more they may be
Christians and restore their meeting places, provided they do nothing to disturb good
order. . . . Consequently, in accordance with this leniency of ours, it will be their duty
to pray to their god for our safety and for that of the state and themselves, so that from
every side the state may be kept unharmed, and they may be able to live free of wor-
ries in their own homes.

(Lactantius, *On the Deaths of the Persecutors* 34; translation based on J. L. Creed,
Lactantius, De Mortibus Persecutorum, Oxford, 1984, p. 53).

gyric of 310, which claims that in a vision he saw the gods Apollo and Victory,
who each predicted triumphs and long rule for him (*Panegyric* 6.21.4). At this time
his coins begin to display Sol Invictus, the Unconquerable Sun, Aurelian's
favorite image, suggesting a conscious shift away from the tetrarchic system and
its promotion of Jupiter and Hercules (see Fig. 13.3a). Meanwhile Constantine—
and indeed Maxentius—had also abandoned Diocletian's policy by calling an
official halt to the persecution of Christians in the West. This shift was in sharp
contrast to the situation in the East, where Galerius and Maximin Daia had

revived the persecutions with a vengeance. Only in 311, shortly before his death, did Galerius finally come to see that his efforts, far from eliminating Christianity, had merely furthered discord among the population. Before his death that same year, he issued an Edict of Toleration that revoked the ban on Christian worship and grudgingly granted Christians the right to meet. But this prolonged period of persecution in the East left deep scars, which would be reopened again first by Maximin Daia, and later by Licinius.

Galerius' death in May 311 could only unsettle whatever stability had been achieved. Rifts opened instantly between Licinius and Maximin Daia over control of Galerius' former territory in Thrace, Greece, and Asia Minor. In summer 311, the two agreed that the Bosporus should divide their realms, but Licinius was detained there working to ensure the arrangement would stick. Meantime, his absence from the West allowed Constantine to concentrate his efforts on eliminating Maxentius, whom he denounced as a "tyrant." In summer 312 he first defeated Maxentius' forces in northern Italy, and then proceeded down the peninsula to Rome. The decisive battle occurred in October near Rome, outside the walls. Maxentius had unwisely abandoned their protection to face Constantine's superior forces. When he attempted to re-cross the Tiber back into the city after his defeat, he was caught by a booby trap he himself had set on the Milvian Bridge (Map 14.3), and drowned in the river along with many of his men. The next day Constantine swept into the city with Maxentius' head on a pike. Our sources emphasize his triumphal welcome and his restoration of the liberty that Maxentius had abolished. One of his first measures was to disband forever Rome's Praetorian Guard, whose support had been so vital to Maxentius. These men Constantine replaced with a new special force named the *scholarii* ("staff guards"), who—together with the *protectores* once commanded by Diocletian himself—accompanied the emperor wherever he went.

Constantine's victory over Maxentius at the battle of the Milvian Bridge has been glorified by Eusebius, Lactantius, and many others as the pivotal episode leading to his acceptance of Christianity and his subsequent emergence as sole emperor. Before the battle, we are told, he received an omen of his coming victory. Eusebius and Lactantius differ on its nature—either a dream or an apparition in the sky—but they agree that it was understood as coming from the Christian god. Constantine allegedly saw a cross over the sun, and heard the militant encouraging words, "Conquer in this sign" (Greek, *en touto nika*). Modern scholars, too, are divided over the nature of this vision and sign, although most agree that Constantine's conversion was more of a process, perhaps extending back to his vision of Apollo in 310, rather than a single event. The sources agree, however, that in 312 Constantine entered battle after having his men decorate their shields with an emblem resembling a Christogram (☧). This symbol creates a monogram of chi [Χ] and rho [Ρ], the first two letters of the name "Christ" in Greek (compare Fig. 13.3b). The victory Constantine won outside Rome, and his subsequent successes under the same emblem, persuaded him of the power of the Christian god.

The military and political realities were less straightforward, however, as reflected in deliberate official vagueness about just what "divinity" had inspired Constantine. Thus, on the arch dedicated to him by the senate and people of Rome in 315 (Fig. 13.1), the inscription opaquely proclaims that he triumphed over the "tyrant" and all his "faction" by "divine stimulus and greatness of mind." Moreover, although the Christogram features prominently in Christian sources, it rarely appears on official media (coins, art, and inscriptions) before the mid-320s. It is certainly true that already in late 312 Constantine began granting extensive favors to Christians and acting as arbiter in their disputes, but outside the Christian community he gave only vague hints of his new religion and often muddled these with continuing nods to his interest in other deities like the Sun God.

Although it must have been clear by 312 that the tetrarchy was irretrievably broken, there were still two other claimants to power along with Constantine. He now held Italy, North Africa, and the West; Licinius held Illyricum and the rest of the Balkans; and Maximin Daia held the East. At this date most of the army and much of the West were non-Christian, and even hostile to Christians. While religion did play a part in the ensuing struggles for control, Constantine was well aware that he could not promote Christianity too openly. Above all, at this point, he seems to have seen Christianity as a guarantor of victory, a means toward military success against his opponents.

Despite Galerius' Edict of Toleration in 311, Maximin Daia had resumed the persecution of Christians in his eastern territories. By refusing to end it, despite a request from Constantine, he gave Constantine and Licinius cause to ally against him. In 313, the latter two met at Mediolanum, where they jointly issued a decree—known today as the Edict of Milan—which proclaimed freedom of religious expression and ordered the return of confiscated properties to the Christian church. Their united front was strengthened by Licinius' marriage to Constantine's half-sister, Constantia. Meanwhile Maximin Daia took advantage of Licinius' absence in the West to steal a march into his territories in Thrace. Licinius countered, defeated him at Adrianople (modern Edirne, Turkey), and later forced him into hiding in Cilicia; here Daia went insane and soon died. By the end of 313, therefore, Constantine and Licinius were the only leaders remaining who claimed supreme command. Accordingly, they now divided the empire between them, with Constantine ruling the West and Licinius the East, including Illyricum and the rest of eastern Europe.

Their dual rule as Augusti was to last eleven years (to 324), but it was not a harmonious partnership. The two quarreled repeatedly, and even faced one another in open battle in 316. Constantine proved the winner, and took the opportunity to expand his territory as far east as the borders of Thrace. In a peace arranged in early 317, both men named their sons as Caesars, indicating individual dynastic plans rather than a commitment to joint rule. Their estrangement widened when Licinius resumed the persecution of Christians in the East around 320. By this time Constantine was expressing his Christianity more openly, and had begun to portray himself as a champion of believers—a stance that also provided excellent cover for his political ambitions. When Constantine entered Licinius' territory in 323 to counter an invasion by the Goths, Licinius declared war. In 324 he was defeated three times, at Adrianople, at Byzantium, and, after crossing into Asia, at Chrysopolis (modern Üsküdar, Turkey). With Licinius eliminated in this way, Rome's forty years of organized experiments in shared rule were abandoned. Constantine now had sole control of a unified empire.

ADMINISTRATIVE REORGANIZATION UNDER THE DOMINATE

Scholars refer to the period beginning with Diocletian's reign as the "Dominate," a designation which distinguishes it from the "Principate" established by Augustus. The term is modern, but it traces to Diocletian's use of the designation *dominus* ("lord," or even "master") to reinforce his claims to authority. Such claims filtered throughout the central government in ways that show a much stronger desire and ambition on the part of this late Roman ruler and his successors to govern actively. This development was made possible in no small part by Diocletian's increase in the size of the imperial college to four active members. The growth in the emperor's power and his desire to extend his reach more systematically are also evident in inscriptions, for we have numerous examples of tetrarchic decrees attested in multiple copies from across the empire; these show how the emperor worked to impose his laws upon all his subjects with heavy and evenly distributed pressure.

The period also witnessed a change in imperial manners. The affected *civilitas* of an Augustus now gave way to considerably more pomposity. Numerous sources note that the emperor placed himself above his subjects, and began wearing more grandiose trappings such as a purple mantle, a crown, and shoes studded with gems. His subjects were now forced to prostrate themselves in his presence and kiss the hem of his cloak; his court was forced always to stand in his presence, hence its designation as the *consistorium* ("standing room council") rather than the *consilium* ("advisory council") familiar from the Principate. Eunuch chamberlains first became prominent in court politics in this period; and the emperor's appearance also took on a new look, with hair cropped and beard short in the fashion of a soldier. Indeed, the entire court assumed a more military air under these soldier emperors, so much so that even civilian officials now wore a *cingulum* (military belt) as a mark of their bureaucratic service, which they referred to as *militia* (akin to our word "service," with its double connotations). There was more ceremony, too, as the emperor encouraged the veneration of himself and his court. In this vein, the word *sacer* (sacred) came to be virtually synonymous with "imperial" in many official contexts.

With his concern for system and order, Diocletian undertook a number of major reforms in the apparatus of government and the organization of the empire that would essentially lay the foundations for the remainder of its history in the West. The changes he introduced were generally adopted and often elaborated upon by Constantine. It is worthwhile to take stock of them, therefore, keeping in mind that what follows describes developments begun in the 290s but fully realized only over a span of fifty years. Overall, the changes were characterized by an increase in the size of the government, an increase in hierarchy and professionalization, and an increased differentiation between military and civilian functions.

As to size, it has been estimated that the late Roman bureaucracy grew to the point that there were around 30,000 to 35,000 bureaucrats on the imperial payroll, as opposed to the few hundred senatorial and equestrian officials and about 10,000 slaves who administered it in the first century A.D. This increase necessarily demanded a growth in bureaucratic hierarchies, a fact which can be confirmed in the elaborate lists of offices cataloged in the early fifth-century *Notitia Dignitatum* (see Plate 14). The growth was fueled from the bottom up, for most of the new bureaucrats, even those in lofty positions, were not senators but equestrians or even decurions. They were trained in the increasingly powerful law schools at Rome and, as the fourth century wore on, Berytus (modern Beirut, Lebanon) and Constantinople.

One key change occurred in the organization of the imperial court. The late empire's very mobile officials were often referred to as the *comitatus* (retinue) because they traveled in the emperor's company. They consisted of six or more chief officials, many new to the period, each with staffs numbering in the hundreds. The six were: 1) the Chief of the Sacred Bedchamber, who was responsible for the eunuchs and palace staff; 2) the Count of the Sacred Largesses, a sort of minister of finance charged with the collection of money taxes and the minting of coin; 3) the Count of the Privy Purse, who oversaw the emperor's extensive private properties; 4) the Quaestor of the Sacred Palace, an official first attested under Constantine who was charged with the drafting of laws; 5) the Master of the Offices, a catch-all who supervised the imperial secretaries, handled embassies, managed the public post service, and oversaw state arms factories; and 6) the Praetorian Prefects. These last underwent considerable transformation first under the tetrarchs, who granted them even greater judicial powers, and then especially under Constantine, who stripped them of all military authority and made provisioning the army their primary responsibility. These changes removed the threat that Praetorian Prefects once posed to the emperor's own security, and allowed them to act as a check on the ambitions of potentially rebellious generals. By the end of his reign Constantine had also increased the number of Praetorian Prefects from two under the tetrarchs (one for each Augustus) to four, one for each major region of the empire.

The introduction of regional Praetorian Prefectures was made possible by changes to the organization of the provinces that were also initiated by Diocletian. The Christian Lactantius states that Diocletian "chopped the provinces into bits" (*On the Deaths of the Persecutors* 7.4), a hostile way of saying that he divided the fifty or so

Figure 12.5 *This imposing structure at Augusta Treverorum (modern Trier, Germany) was just one part of a larger palace complex constructed by Constantine in the early part of his reign when he made his capital here. It was completed by 310 and consists of a massive covered hall, lined with arched windows, and closed with an apse at one end. It would have served as a meeting chamber in which the emperor could grant audiences and dispense justice. Such grand buildings were typical of the tetrarchs' style and the new "capitals" which they established in cities across the empire.*

provinces existing at the beginning of his reign into over one hundred smaller ones. These he put under the charge of governors called *praesides*, whom he also stripped of military power. Later, probably in 313/314, Constantine and Licinius regrouped the newly divided provinces into larger units termed "dioceses" (originally twelve in number), a step that earlier scholarship long attributed to Diocletian. Each diocese was placed under the charge of a new official termed a Vicar (literally "substitute," i.e. for the Praetorian Prefect), whose job it was to ensure the smooth collection of taxes levied in kind. Part of this process also represented a major departure from policy in force ever since the second century B.C., as Italy was split into provinces and incorporated into this system. It was now ruled by provincial governors, albeit with grander titles, and was forced to pay taxes. Only Rome itself was left out of the system, for it had its own Urban Prefect who was answerable directly to the emperor. In many ways the change here reflected the reality that, by this date, neither Italy nor even Rome was the center of the empire any longer. The tetrarchs only rarely visited Rome, and the very isolation which shielded the Italian peninsula from invasions also made it unimportant strategically to a new kind of emperor focused primarily on the frontiers. Instead, the tetrarchs introduced the policy of reconstructing the major cities in the provinces frequented by them into "capitals" with elaborate

Map 12.3 *Roman Empire of Diocletian and Constantine*

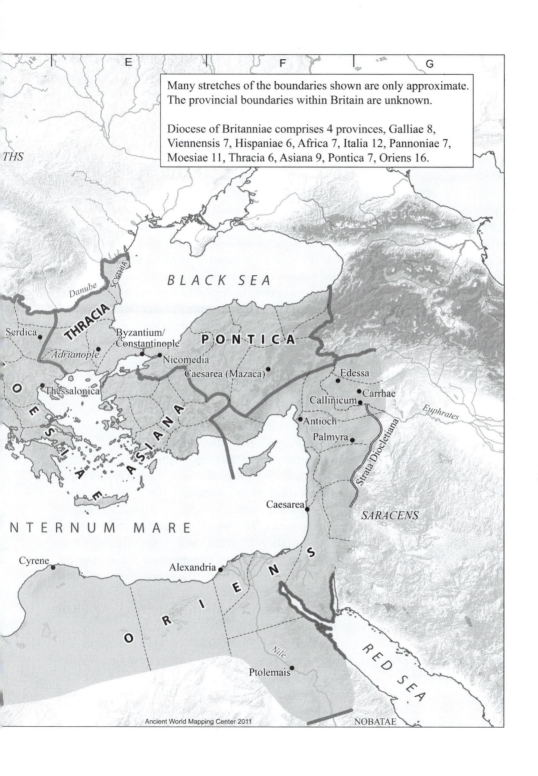

Many stretches of the boundaries shown are only approximate.
The provincial boundaries within Britain are unknown.

Diocese of Britanniae comprises 4 provinces, Galliae 8,
Viennensis 7, Hispaniae 6, Africa 7, Italia 12, Pannoniae 7,
Moesiae 11, Thracia 6, Asiana 9, Pontica 7, Oriens 16.

THS

BLACK SEA

Danube SCYTHIA

THRACIA

Serdica

Adrianople

Byzantium/
Constantinople

Nicomedia

P O N T I C A

Caesarea (Mazaca)

Edessa

Callinicum • Carrhae

Euphrates

Thessalonica

MOESIA

A S I A N A

Antioch

Palmyra

Strata Diocletiana

Caesarea

SARACENS

INTERNUM MARE

Cyrene

Alexandria

O R I E N S

Nile

RED SEA

Ptolemais

Ancient World Mapping Center 2011

NOBATAE

palaces, hippodromes, baths, and even mausolea. Thus Augusta Treverorum (modern Trier, Germany) in Gaul, Milan in northern Italy, Serdica (modern Sofia,
Bulgaria), Sirmium and Thessalonica in the Balkans, and Nicomedia and Antioch in
the East, were all rebuilt to accommodate the tetrarchs.

The late empire also saw tremendous changes to the army. Just as he did with
the provinces, Diocletian carved the old-fashioned legion into much smaller units
which averaged around 1,000 men. These were easier to mobilize and better able
to respond to the multiple crises so characteristic of the period. Though the units
shrank in size, the total size of the army grew. Lactantius claims Diocletian
quadrupled the army, but this is surely an exaggeration (*On the Deaths of the
Persecutors* 7.2). An effective strength of 600,000 soldiers, perhaps double the size
of the first-century army, is much more likely. Recruitment was now organized
annually along strict guidelines, and the sons of soldiers were required to enlist to
fill the vacancies left by their fathers. Because provincial governors no longer controlled troops, a new class of regional generals was invented called *duces* ("dukes")
and *comites* ("counts"). These leaders were better equipped to deal with the heightened insecurity of the period because they regularly held authority over territory
stretching across multiple provinces, now grouped as security districts.

Diocletian continued the trend initiated by Gallienus of developing units of
soldiers not bound to a particular territory—that is, a mobile field army.
Nevertheless, it was Constantine who went further by introducing large bodies
of *comitatenses* ("retinue troops") that followed the emperor or his generals
wherever they went. By the mid-fourth century we hear of comitatensian
armies numbering upwards of 60,000 men who traveled with the emperor as a
massive expeditionary force. To lead them Constantine also developed a new
supreme commander called the *magister militum* ("Master of the Soldiers"), who
often had his own field army in addition to that of the emperor. These comitatensian troops came to be distinguished from so-called *limitanei* ("border
troops")—generally considered second-class soldiers—who guarded the edges
of the empire from stationary emplacements. The limitanei tended to be based
in a new type of fortification much smaller in scale, but more abundant in
number, than the old legionary fortresses. Diocletian constructed these in great
numbers along the river and desert frontiers. His most famous series of such
installations was used to fortify a strategic roadway, the Strata Diocletiana,
located at the edge of the empire's eastern desert and stretching from Azraq in
modern Jordan north to the Euphrates River (Map 12.3).

Finally, Diocletian also undertook sweeping fiscal and economic measures. By
the time he came to power, the empire effectively had no silver coinage, for the
old denarius had been reduced to an extremely debased bronze coin. Ever the tra-
ditionalist, Diocletian tackled the problem by reintroducing a monetary system
that looked very much like that of the Julio-Claudians. With characteristic thoroughness, he imposed it across the entire empire through the introduction of
enough new mints for there to be one in almost all twelve of the dioceses created

SOURCE 12.2: The Tetrarchs Introduce Their Edict on Maximum Prices

The Edict on Maximum Prices is preserved in almost forty copies in Greek and Latin, more than for any other decree from antiquity. Nevertheless, all of these derive from the East, where Diocletian ruled. While there is evidence that the decree was intended for the West too, the lack of western inscribed copies underlines the point that the tetrarchs did not always operate in perfect unison in promulgating—and enforcing—Diocletian's legislation. The edict's preamble, parts of which are translated here from a Latin copy (ILS 642), includes bombast and moralizing typical of late Roman legislation. This rambling text was then followed by a list of over a thousand prices for services and goods ranging from beers to beasts—including, as an extreme example, lions.

As we recall the wars which we have successfully fought, we must be grateful to the fortune of our state, second only to the immortal gods, for a tranquil world that reclines in the embrace of the most profound calm, and for the blessings of a peace that was won with great effort. . . . Therefore we, who by the gracious favor of the gods previously stemmed the tide of the ravages of barbarian nations by destroying them, must now fortify the peace which we established for eternity with the necessary defenses of justice.

If the excesses perpetrated by persons of unlimited and frenzied avarice could be checked by some self-restraint . . . or if the general welfare could endure without harm this riotous license by which, in its unfortunate condition, it is being very seriously injured every day, the situation could perhaps be faced with excuses and silence, with the hope that human restraint might relieve the cruel and pitiable situation. But the only desire of these uncontrolled madmen is to have no thought for the common welfare. . . . Therefore we, who are the protectors of the human race, are agreed, as we view the situation, that decisive legislation is necessary, so that the long-awaited solutions which mankind itself could not provide may—through the remedies provided by our foresight—be applied for everyone's good.

It is our pleasure that anyone who resists the measures of this statute shall be subject to a capital penalty for daring to do so. And let no one consider the statute harsh, since there is at hand a ready protection from danger in the observance of moderation. . . . We therefore call for everyone's loyalty, so that a regulation instituted for the public good may be observed with willing obedience and due diligence, especially when it is seen that by a statute of this kind provision has been made, not for single municipalities and peoples and provinces, but for the whole world.

by Constantine and Licinius. Beginning in the 290s he initiated a regularly minted gold coin which he struck at 60 to the pound, like the old Roman aureus. He also minted a nearly pure silver coin, the argenteus, at 96 to the pound, just like the old Neronian denarii. Because of his limited supply of bullion, however, Diocletian continued to rely heavily on bronze coinage to pay his troops, and his attempts to dictate an artificially low price for the precious metals led to ongoing problems with inflation. For this reason he was forced to attempt to re-tariff the coinage in 301 by claiming that his bronze coins were now worth double their face value. When this provoked a crisis among creditors, he tried a different approach of characteristically sweeping proportions. In November 301 he issued an Edict on Maximum Prices which dictated in minute detail price levels for over a thousand goods and services and threatened those who overcharged with dire penalties. The sincerity of his efforts, and the reach of Diocletianic government, can be measured in the fact that fragments of the inscription posting the decree have been found in almost forty copies from across the eastern empire. As might be expected, however, even Diocletian's outsized bureaucracy was in no position to dictate the laws of the marketplace, and the Prices Edict soon failed and was repealed. It fell to Constantine to stabilize the economy further, which he did by the introduction of a new gold standard (see Chapter Thirteen).

The currency crisis of the mid-third century had led to a much heavier reliance on taxes paid in kind. The single biggest fiscal expense was always army pay, and because the coinage had inflated so wildly, it made sense to collect taxes in grain, which was then distributed directly to the soldiery. Diocletian preserved this practice, but also rationalized it by introducing a new form of tax collection called the *iugatio vel capitatio* ("acreage or headcount"). Where the old system had attempted to collect a percentage of each year's produce, Diocletian's new plan collected fixed amounts based either on the total acreage owned by a taxpayer or on the total number of producers in his household, or both. Because not all acreage is equally productive, Diocletian created a standard taxation unit called the *iugum* (literally "yoke") and assigned it to various lands proportional to their expected level of productivity. Similarly, the head tax was now apportioned to individuals according to formulas for their productive value depending on age, gender, and status. This rationalized system permitted the government to predict annual revenues more accurately and thus to undertake some sort of advance budgeting. It also led to a much stronger desire on the part of the state to oblige people to remain on the land where they were registered. Diocletian's new fiscal system thus contributed to the process whereby tenant farmers (*coloni* in Latin) were eventually "bound" to the land on which they were born, a precursor of medieval serfdom.

For all of his conservatism, Diocletian was thus an innovator on the grand scale. He reinvented the face of government, giving it a more magisterial appearance and feel. He greatly increased the size and complexity of the bureaucracy, and thereby extended the reach of government into the lives of the empire's citizens. He rearranged imperial offices by increasing their responsibilities and separating civilian and military functions. He reorganized the provinces into smaller units, which were subsequently tied to intermediate jurisdictions with the creation of the diocesan system. He also shrank the size of military units, but enlarged the army and its command structure. Moreover, he undertook major economic and fiscal reforms that improved the collection of taxes, and he began the process of stabilizing the coinage. These administrative measures made an excellent fit with the new tetrarchic system of government which he devised. By increasing the number of emperors to four, he was finally able to gain the upper hand in the border crises that had threatened Roman security, as well as in the civil wars that had so weakened the empire during the third century. This stabilization, internal and external, was perhaps his single greatest achievement, because it furnished the empire with a renewed solidity that ensured prosperity for another century to come. His providence as a military leader and administrator was not, however, matched by equal foresight in the realm of religion. By the time the tetrarchy had completely dissolved in 324, the Christian religion that Diocletian was so eager to suppress had taken the lead. It is to the credit of his successor Constantine that this new religious wave could be absorbed into the powerful state that Diocletian had engineered, and could be given the necessary impetus to outlive the Roman empire.

SUGGESTED READINGS

Brown, Peter. 1971. *The World of Late Antiquity from Marcus Aurelius to Muhammad.* London: Thames and Hudson. Classic introduction to the period emphasizing the cultural transformation that moved society from Antiquity to the Middle Ages.

Corcoran, Simon. 2000 (revised ed.). *The Empire of the Tetrarchs: Imperial Pronouncements and Government, AD 284–324.* Oxford: Oxford University Press. Detailed survey of the massive data for lawgiving under Diocletian and the tetrarchs.

Dodgeon, Michael H., and Samuel N.C. Lieu. 1991. *The Roman Eastern Frontier and the Persian Wars (AD 226–363).* London and New York: Routledge. A history of Rome's wars with Persia told through the sources.

Mitchell, Stephen. 2007. *A History of the Later Roman Empire: AD 284–641.* Malden, MA and Oxford: Blackwell. Comprehensive survey of institutional history with an emphasis on the East.

Nixon, C. Edward V., and Barbara S. Rodgers, 1994. *In Praise of Later Roman Emperors. The Panegyrici Latini.* Berkeley, Los Angeles, London: University of California Press. Translation with commentary of speeches which provide some of the best contemporary evidence for the tetrarchy and the age of Constantine.

Potter, David S. 2004. *The Roman Empire at Bay: AD 180–395.* London and New York: Routledge. Excellent survey of political and military history.

Rees, Roger. 2004. *Diocletian and the Tetrarchy.* Edinburgh: Edinburgh University Press. Concise discussion of key themes, followed by extracts from sources in translation.

Watson, Alaric. 1999. *Aurelian and the Third Century.* London and New York: Routledge.

13

THE RISE OF CHRISTIANITY
AND THE GROWTH OF
THE BARBARIAN THREAT
(324—395)

SOURCES

The relatively spotty source record for the third century is balanced by a much fuller picture for the fourth. The narrative sources can be broken down into two groups, ecclesiastical and secular. The fourth-century Latin *Ecclesiastical History* of Rufinus as well as the early fifth-century Greek histories of Socrates and Sozomen offer much useful information. Eusebius' *Life of Constantine* (see Chapter Twelve) continues to be important for the final years of that emperor. Meanwhile, traditional secular, or as it is sometimes called "classicizing," historiography continued to be written. Zosimus' *New History* covers the entire period, but because of factual distortions must be used with caution. Much more dependable is Ammianus Marcellinus, who wrote in Latin, very much in the tradition of Tacitus. Although his *Histories* originally consisted of thirty-one books, only the last seventeen survive, leaving us with a detailed narrative that covers the years 353 to 378. As a military officer Ammianus was personally involved in many of the events he narrates, and is thus able to offer a uniquely vivid account. In all histories of the period, whether Christian or not, a marked tension over the rise of Christianity and the eclipse of traditional paganism now emerges.

The fourth century is extremely rich in official material composed by emperors and their chanceries. The writings of the pagan emperor Julian, for example, survive extensively, including official letters, philosophical treatises, and even satires. Pride of place, however, goes to the *Theodosian Code*, compiled in 438, which collects laws issued by emperors from Constantine onward. This invaluable source affords a rich understanding both of the administrative workings of the empire and of the regulations governing social relations. It is also a goldmine of data for political events; its thousands of documents preserve precise dates, places of issue, and names of official addressees, allowing historians to assemble lists of who was doing what, when, and where. We also learn much about politics as well as social relations from letter collections, which survive in abundance. Those of the Roman senator Symmachus and the Greek intellectual Libanius are particularly informative. Libanius' speeches are preserved too, including many directly relevant to politics and religious affairs, and his are only a few of the many imperial panegyrics from the period that can be used almost like modern press releases to measure the official "spin" that was placed on events.

Documentary sources like inscriptions and papyri, while still plentiful, are less abundant than in the early empire. This gap is compensated for by the rise of Christian literature. Because the copyists of the Middle Ages were more interested in preserving Christian authors than pagan, they have transmitted many more texts from this period than earlier centuries. Many of these so-called "patristic" sources are of use only for religious history, but a number bear directly upon social and political matters. A source like the *Confessions* of St. Augustine, to take just one example, is unique in the ancient world for presenting us with an autobiography of the experiences—and indiscretions—of a young man growing up in Roman North Africa and Italy. Overall, the sources for the fourth century indicate an empire that had recovered from the "Crisis of the Third Century" and show remarkable continuity with earlier centuries. They also reveal a world undergoing tremendous religious, political, and social change.

CONSTANTINE: A CHRISTIAN EMPEROR

After gaining sole control of the empire in 324, Constantine modified his style of rule in measurable ways. Up to this point he had given at least nominal consent to the system of shared rule initiated by the tetrarchs, but he had never found it satisfactory since it ignored the longstanding tradition of dynastic succession in favor of a system of power transfers that remained too schematic. As a remedy, Constantine took what was good about the tetrarchy, its principle of shared rule, and grafted it onto the stronger stock of the family tree. In so doing, he devised a hybrid system that would prevail for the rest of the century. Already in early 317 he had proclaimed his two sons Crispus and Constantine II Caesars, in step with Licinius, who did the same with his own son Licinius II. These promotions resulted in a system of five-man rule with two senior and three junior emperors that mimicked the tetrarchy. With the elimination of Licinius in 324, Constantine promoted his third son, Constantius II, to Caesar and, in 333, his fourth son, Constans. Dynasty was thus used to backstop shared rule, providing the advantage of imperial birth to legitimize anticipated successors, as well as the benefit of family ties to reduce the chances for discord—at least in theory. To distinguish himself from his sons,

Figure 13.1 *South side of the Arch of Constantine (Map 12.2). This monument was built along Rome's triumphal route by the senate and people soon after Constantine's victory over Maxentius in 312. Much of the enormous edifice is reused material. For example, the bearded statues above the columns were taken from Trajan's Forum, and the round reliefs over the side-arches are from a monument of Hadrian's time. The arch represents the beginning of a trend toward the strategic reuse of earlier material (sometimes called* spolia) *in new monuments in late antiquity. The narrow, horizontal reliefs running below the roundels, by contrast, were commissioned under Constantine and represent his battles with Maxentius and his triumphal entry into Rome; the left band features Constantine's siege of Verona, and the right band the battle of the Milvian Bridge. The depiction of victory in civil war was unusual, but was justified in this instance by Constantine's claim that Maxentius was a "tyrant."*

Constantine held the titles *Maximus Augustus* and *Invictus* ("unconquerable"), a designation he shared with his favorite pagan deity, the Sun God.

Constantine's projections of heavenly rulership fed directly into his claims to be God's representative on earth. This is a role that he had begun to play already in the wake of his victory over Maxentius when he started showing signs that he now favored the Christian church. In 313 he granted special exemptions from mandatory government service to Christian clergy and offered Christian churches a share in imperial revenue. Jointly with Licinius he issued the "Edict of Milan," guaranteeing a final end to persecutions. Indeed, the "Great Persecution" had been so thoroughgoing in certain parts of the empire that it had opened sizeable rifts in the church itself. In North Africa, where Christianity had grown strong by the mid-third century, the persecutions had been particularly harsh and had led some Christians, even those in positions of authority, to lapse from the faith by denying their Christianity or turning over sacred scriptures to the persecutors. After the attacks had ceased in 306, those Christians who had remained rigorous in their defense of the faith quarreled bitterly about what penalty should be imposed upon those among the "lapsed" who sought readmittance to the church. The rigorists came to be known as Donatists after one of their early leaders, Donatus. They refused communion with the more lenient church establishment, and repeatedly appealed to Constantine in hopes that he would affirm their claims to be the legitimate representatives of the North African church. In response, Constantine organized two councils, the first at Rome in 313 and the second at Arelate (modern Arles, France) the following year; at both, the Donatists' case was rejected. However, this rebuff did not bring the matter to a close, because they refused to accept the councils' judgment, and the schism continued into the sixth century, with a number of violent episodes. The emperor had long been the final arbiter of disputes, but up to this point Christians had largely avoided imperial intervention in their own affairs. The Donatist appeal offers the first in a long line of instances where the emperor was pulled directly into ecclesiastical politics.

Upon gaining control of the east, Constantine faced a similar controversy that arose not so much over questions of leadership as of theology, though the boundary between the two was always blurred. A priest in Alexandria named Arius had hypothesized that Christ, though truly the son of God the Father, had been created by the Father and was thus posterior to him in time and inferior to him in status. The logic of this theory appealed to many, and a party of supporters soon formed around Arius. To his superior Alexander, bishop of Alexandria, the theory was rank heresy. When both parties appealed to the emperor in hopes of gaining support, Constantine at first rebuked them both for debating such imponderables, but soon realized that here too he must intervene. In May 325 he organized a council at Nicaea (modern İznik, Turkey)—the first "ecumenical," or world, council of the church—at which he essentially dictated that Christ was indeed "one in being with the Father" (in Greek *homoousios*). This wording, together with the broader Nicene Creed that was formulated around it, continues to be repeated in Christian churches today. Here again, however, Constantine's arbitration did little more than fuel further controversy which lasted down to 381, when Arianism was, at least theoretically, laid to rest in favor of a staunch affirmation of the Nicene Creed at the second ecumenical council held in Constantinople. Meanwhile, Constantine also favored the church in any number of other ways that will be discussed below. To mention just one here, he legislated that Sunday should become an official day of rest each week, another change with repercussions enduring up to the present.

From at least the mid-nineteenth century, and arguably stretching back to antiquity, people have questioned the sincerity of Constantine's conversion. There are good reasons for this doubt, because Constantine always left ample room for ambiguous interpretations of his person and reign. At times he appears downright pagan in his self-presentation, as when he was portrayed side by side with the Sun God on coins and medallions. He is known to have worshipped this deity prior to his conversion, and it was even claimed that he had witnessed an epiphany from the Sun God in 310 (see Chapter Twelve). The same deity appears on his bronze coinage down to 325 with the legend SOLI INVICTO COMITI ("To his Companion the Unconquerable Sun"; see Fig. 13.3a and Plate 15). Such a choice of wording might be excused as an appeal to his non-Christian subjects in the period prior to the elimination of Licinius, were it not for the fact that Constantine erected a statue of himself portrayed as that same Sun God on a massive porphyry column in his new capital of Constantinople, dedicated in 330 (Map 14.2). Indeed, as late as 337 he permitted an imperial cult temple to be built to his family at the Italian city of Hispellum (modern Spello), provided there be no blood sacrifice performed there. While some historians have seen in this ambiguity a crypto-paganism or, worse yet, a cynical willingness to play all sides to his advantage, it seems fairer to say that Constantine was striving to discover what it meant to be the first Christian emperor in a period when it was not yet clear where the lines between old and new religious traditions should be drawn.

Nevertheless, the significance of Constantine's conversion to Christianity is hard to deny in the light of his own statements about his faith, preserved in great abundance, and also by the monumental church-building program he initiated across the empire. This program is most evident in the two cities of Rome and Jerusalem. Prior to 312 Rome's churches were the so-called *tituli*, usually the homes of Christians that had been turned over to the church to use as places of worship (Map 14.3a). Probably already in November 312, Constantine began construction in Rome of a massive new purpose-built "basilica," a word formerly used of royal audience halls that now came to designate large churches. Constructed inside Rome's walls on a property called the Lateran, this basilica was meant to serve as the seat of Rome's bishop, the Pope, a role it still plays today. Constantine also founded some nine other churches, most designed to mark the burial sites of martyrs (*martyria*) outside Rome's walls. Among the nine was a church of St. Peter on the far side of the Tiber at the Vatican Hill, a site that came to serve as the Pope's residence in the Middle Ages. Constantine thus established the architecture of Christian Rome, and as such helped bridge the gap

Figure 13.2 *Fragments of colossal statue of Constantine. This colossal head (8.5 ft/2.6 m tall) and hand, together with other marble fragments, were found in the massive basilica ("royal audience hall") which Maxentius had begun and Constantine completed in the center of Rome (Map 12.2). They formed part of a monumental seated image made of a composite of marble (for body parts) and bronze (for drapery). The head is typical of Constantine in mid-career with its clean-shaven, square jaw, its "Trajanic" locks (much fuller than the crew cuts of the tetrarchs), and its large upraised eyes. This gaze was interpreted by Eusebius (Life of Constantine 4.15) as a sign that Constantine was looking up to heaven, but a comparable gaze can also be traced to pagan rulers of the Hellenistic age. Similar ambiguity arises from the pose of the statue; it is seated and semi-nude, like cult images of Jupiter, but its hand bears a square cutting which—we can deduce from Eusebius (Ecclesiastical History 9.9)—may have held a Christian cross.*

between Antiquity and the Middle Ages, for it was as a Christian capital that the city of Rome survived the fall of the empire.

A similar story can be told in the East. Following Titus' sack of Jerusalem in 70, the city had become something of a backwater, and had even been renamed Aelia Capitolina by Hadrian. Shortly after gaining control of the East, however, Constantine sent his mother Helena to the Holy Land in an effort to reestablish its religious identity, but now along Christian lines. While there, she helped to initiate churches at the reputed site of Christ's nativity in Bethlehem, and on what was believed to be the site of Christ's tomb, the Church of the Holy Sepulcher (Map 14.3b). Not least because of these new churches, Jerusalem became a destination favored by Christian pilgrims, who began to travel there in substantial numbers already in the 330s, and still do so today. The impact of Constantine's conversion was thus profound and lasting.

In other respects, too, the empire's balance was being tilted eastward by Constantine. No single act of his had a greater impact in this respect than his establishment of a new capital on the Bosporus at the site of the city formerly known as Byzantium. His new city, dedicated under the name Constantinople in 330, was designed for a population of about 80,000 and was provided with baths, an imperial forum, and a massive palace connected to an extended hippodrome for chariot-racing. The city was established quite consciously as a "Second Rome" with fourteen districts, its own subsidized grain supply, and above all a new senate. Constantine embellished his city with famous statues taken from around the eastern empire—many of them former cult statues which he pilfered from their original religious contexts for display in secular settings like the hippodrome. He also confiscated gold and silver cult statues, but rather than rededicate these, he simply melted them down into bullion and reminted them as coinage. This measure served the dual purpose of diminishing the power and wealth of the traditional cults and increasing his money supply.

Indeed, the measure fitted well with a larger monetary reform that Constantine almost stumbled into, one which had a profound impact on the development of the late Roman economy. Already in 309, faced with the need to pay his growing army from a limited supply of bullion, Constantine introduced a new gold coin weighing only 4.5 grams in contrast to the traditional *aureus* of 5.4 grams. This *solidus*, as it was termed, represented primarily a way to squeeze more coin out of a limited metal supply, but because Constantine promoted the *solidus* as the new monetary standard in his territories, it quickly became the official unit of exchange and taxation. His takeover of the entire empire in 324, combined with the massive influx of gold confiscated from the temples, allowed him to convert the economy to a new gold-based system. This change would have major economic consequences, because while it permitted tremendous stability in the upper ranges of the economy, it also widened the gap between rich and poor. Those who could not afford to deal in gold became dependent upon their wealthier superiors for conversion of their bronze coins, now all but worthless, into gold. Nevertheless, the economy flourished throughout the fourth century in most parts of the empire. Indeed, survey archeology has revealed that many areas—particularly North Africa, central Asia Minor, and Syria—thrived to a quite unprecedented extent.

Upon his death in 337, Constantine left a prosperous empire to his heirs. After a thirty-one-year reign, the longest since Augustus, he had placed the empire on a firm footing and had established his own dynasty solidly enough that it would endure for the next twenty-six years. Already in the final years of his rule, however, there were signs of troubles to come. In 332 he faced a threat from the Goths and was forced to send his son Constantine II into their territory to defeat them and impose peace. So, too, in the last years of his reign the Sasanian Persians began persecuting Christians in their empire, and eventually they invaded the territory of Armenia, long a bone of contention between the two superpowers. Both Goths and Persians would inflict major defeats on the Romans in the decades to come. Thus, when Constantine set off to battle the Persians in 337, he was about to spark a conflict that would endure for the next half-century. Even so, he did not progress far before succumbing to illness on May 22 near Nicomedia. Shortly before dying, he was baptized a Christian. In this period, the choice to wait for baptism until the approach of death was common, but it was also of particular benefit in the instance of an emperor, who was obliged to fight battles and order executions, and who thus had added motivation to postpone a sacrament meant to cleanse sin. Few other Roman emperors had a more lasting impact on the course of world history. With his conversion to Christianity, his foundation of a new capital and senate, his establishment of the Holy Land as a site of Christian pilgrimage, and his construction of a Christian Rome, Constantine opened the way to a new epoch. Like Augustus, he was a truly revolutionary figure, who left his mark as much through the imposition of his personality on history as through the execution of his policies.

THE SONS OF CONSTANTINE (337–361): THE POWER OF DYNASTY

When Constantine died, his dynasty should have been on a sound footing. He had left three sons, previously appointed Caesars, to resume the tradition of joint rule that he had preserved from the tetrarchy. Constantine II, the eldest, was to rule Gaul, Spain, and Britain; Constans, the youngest, held Italy, Africa, and the Balkans; and Constantius II, the middle son, took Asia Minor and the East. But Constantine's growing taste for the grandiose at the end of his life had led him to appoint two further co-rulers, his nephews Dalmatius and Hannibalianus. In the summer of 337 Constantius had these nephews murdered, along with a host of other relatives who might pose dynastic claims. Such familial violence was not new to the dynasty: Constantine himself had ordered the execution of his own son Crispus in 326 after suspecting him of adultery with his wife Fausta, Crispus' stepmother, whom he also executed. In September 337, the three remaining

TABLE 13.1 **The Constantinian Family** *The presentation follows the style of Table 8.1, explained there.*

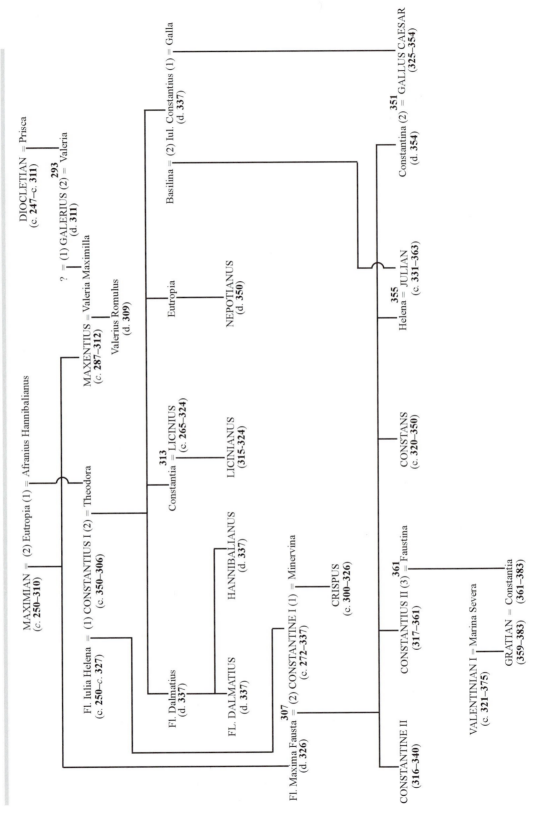

brothers had themselves promoted to full Augustus, and were thus meant to rule in concord as equals. In summer 340, however, Constantine II began laying claims to the territories of his younger brother Constans and eventually invaded northern Italy. As it turned out, Constantine II was himself defeated near Aquileia and killed in battle. In this way Constans became master of the entire western empire.

Constans' reign is not well documented, but he is known to have defeated the barbarian Franks in northern Gaul as well as the tribes in Britain. By January 350, however, the army in Gaul turned against him and proclaimed its own general Magnentius in his stead. Constans was executed, whereupon a cascade of usurpations ensued, with a general named Vetranio being proclaimed emperor in Pannonia, and Nepotianus, a relative of Constantine I, staking his claim in Rome. Meanwhile Constantius II, the lone surviving son of Constantine, had been preoccupied in the East with the aggressive Sasanian King of Kings Shapur II, who was assaulting Roman fortresses. Rather than come to their rescue, Constantius was compelled to return west to Sirmium, where he succeeded in persuading Vetranio to abdicate. Meantime Magnentius suppressed Nepotianus, hoping he would thereby be able to secure an accord with Constantius that might give him control of the West. But Constantius would have none of it and instead pursued Magnentius, whom he defeated in a bloody struggle at Mursa (Osijek, in modern Croatia) in central Pannonia in September 351, and eventually forced to suicide in Gaul in 353 (Map 13.1).

The later empire was thus continuously plagued by civil war, a problem it had faced so often since the mid-third century. The empire was large enough, and the foes on its borders fierce enough, that multiple emperors were required; nevertheless, these often turned on each other, causing Roman armies to slaughter one another. Even when legitimately proclaimed emperors were in place, as with Constantine's sons, the dangers of usurpation and conflict still loomed large. Constantius, thinking to resolve this mix of difficulties using the power of dynasty, appointed his cousin Gallus as Caesar for the East in March 351, while he marched west to suppress Magnentius. Gallus was the son of Constantine I's half-brother, whom Constantius had murdered in the summer of 337. Unsurprisingly, Gallus was less than fully cooperative, and by 354 their relationship had deteriorated to the point that Constantius had Gallus executed. With external troubles continuing to roil in East and West, Constantius felt forced to try a second dynastic appointment. This time he chose Gallus' brilliant half-brother Julian, a man equally resentful toward Constantius, but one whose abilities as a general and devotion to the empire made him a true asset. Julian was proclaimed Caesar in November 355, and sent north to Gaul to regain control of this territory, which had been overrun by barbarians in the aftermath of Magnentius' usurpation. Over the next five years, Julian would systematically travel the Rhine frontier, driving back the Franks in the north and the Alamanni in the south. His most spectacular victory came at Argentorate (modern Strasbourg, France) in 357 when he defeated the Alamannic king Chnodomarius and his force of 35,000 men, ample testimony to the scale of the external threat that Rome faced in this region.

Map 13.1 *Major Battle Sites of the Fourth Century*

The map includes the following labels and legend:

Regions and peoples: PICTS, SCOTS, BRITANNIA, FRANKS, GALLIA, ALAMANNI, HISPANIA, MAURETANIA, AFRICA, QUAI[DI], PANNO[NIA], Brigetic

Sites: Trier, Parisii, Argentorate, Solicinium, Aquileia, Frigidus, Cibalae, Siscia, Turin, Milan, Verona, Susa, Arles, Roma, Carthago

Rivers: Rhine

Compass rose: N, W, E, S

Legend:
- • Site
- ⊗ Site of civil war
- × Site of external war
- ⊠ Site of both civil and external war

Scale:
0 — 250 — 500 — 750 Km
0 — 150 — 300 — 450 Miles

Civil wars (dates of battles)
Adrianople A.D. 313, 316, 324
Aquileia 340, 388
Byzantium/Constantinople 324
Chrysopolis 324
Cibalae 316
Cyprus 334
Frigidus River 394
Mursa 351
Nacoleia 366
Parisii 383
Propontis 324
Roma 307, 3[?]
Siscia 316, 3[?]
Susa 312
Turin 312
Verona 312

Many campaigns known from the period, particularly ones against northern
barbarians, can no longer be associated with proximity to a specific city or
geographical feature; hence they are not shown here.

ALANS

HUNS

GREUTHUNGI

MATIANS
FALI   GOTHS

TERVINGI   BLACK SEA   Bagawan ×
m   *Danube* SCYTHIA   ARMENIA
              MINOR
THRACIA   Byzantium/   Tigris
Adrianople Constantinople   Amida   Nisibis
              Chrysopolis   GALATIA   SASANIAN
                                            Singara ×   EMPIRE
              Nacoleia
                                                    Euphrates   Pirisabora
                                                                Maiozamalcha
              Ephesus   Antioch
                                            SYRIA   Ctesiphon

                        CYPRUS

INTERNUM MARE
                        Caesarea
                        Bethlehem
                                        PALESTINA
              Alexandria

                                        Nile

                                                    RED SEA

                                Thebes

External wars (dates of battles)
ianople A.D. 378   Pirisabora 363
da 359   Scythia Minor 377
entorate 357   Singara 348
awan 371   Solicinium 368
siphon 363   Taifali 330
hs 332, 367-369   Thrace 322
ozamalcha 363
bis 338, 346, 350

Ancient World Mapping Center 2011

Meanwhile Constantius and his generals were also regularly compelled to engage in military campaigns. When he inherited the eastern empire in 337, Constantius had to face the Persian threat stirred up by his father. From then until 350 he based himself in Antioch, parrying the various attacks of the aggressive Shapur II who besieged Nisibis (modern Nusaybin, Turkey) no less than three times and fought Constantius to a stalemate in a famous night battle at Singara in 348. During the 350s Constantius shifted his attention to eliminate the usurper Magnentius. Toward the end of this decade, however, the Persian threat re-emerged when Shapur launched a massive expedition into Roman territory in 359 and sacked the Roman fortress town of Amida (modern Diyarbakır, Turkey) on the River Tigris. This loss drew Constantius east again, and compelled him to request that Julian send detachments from his Gallic armies in support. The request stirred up unrest among Julian's soldiery, who insisted on promoting him to full Augustus in early 360. Constantius was outraged, and threatened military action if Julian did not renounce this new title. After a year of tension, the much younger and more able Julian stole a march on his cousin and reached the middle Danube by late 361. Meanwhile Constantius extracted himself from the eastern frontier and headed west to face Julian in battle. Instead, he fell ill and died en route in November, but only after suppressing his enmity and proclaiming Julian his successor. The empire had narrowly avoided yet another civil war.

JULIAN (361–363): A TEST OF THE CHRISTIAN EMPIRE

After learning of Constantius' death, Julian continued east to Constantinople, where he spent the early part of 362. As a member of the Constantinian line, Julian had been raised a Christian, but in the course of his formative years he had developed an aversion to the religion of the dynasty which had wiped out most of his immediate family. At the age of twenty (in 351), he explains in a letter (47 [434D]), he abandoned Christianity and "apostatized" to paganism, although he revealed his convictions only to a small inner circle when he was serving as Caesar under Constantius. Earlier, during the period of his education, Julian had been especially influenced by Maximus of Ephesus, who practiced a version of Platonist philosophy that advocated not just contemplation of the divine, but also its worship through ritual, above all sacrifice. From early in 362, Julian invited Maximus and other pagan intellectuals to join his court, and began offering blood sacrifice openly. As a symbol of his commitment to philosophical paganism, Julian also grew his beard out long, a novelty not seen since the Severan period, after which emperors had worn only short beards or none at all. When he advertised this new look on his coinage, it provoked mockery from his Christian subjects, a reaction which he answered in kind with a satire called *Beardhater*.

Julian's support of traditional paganism and his disdain for Christianity also played out on the practical level. He began issuing a series of decrees revoking

a *b* *c* *d*

Figure 13.3a,b,c,d *Fourth-century coins. These four specimens illustrate the power of coinage to convey imperial messages to the citizens of the empire, who encountered their imagery every day. The first two, minted under Constantine, show the conflicting religious propaganda he disseminated. The reverse of one [a] depicts a nude image of his favored pagan deity "Unconquered Sun" (SOLI INVICTO), whom Constantine styles his "Companion" (COMITI). The other [b] shows his new Christian battle standard, the* labarum, *piercing a snake (a symbol of Satan and, by extension, Licinius) and surmounted by a Christogram (an X crossing a P, the first two letters of the name "Christ" in Greek). The third coin [c] shows Julian the Apostate with his long beard, characteristic of pagan philosophers. The reverse features a bull and two stars, pagan symbols over whose interpretation modern scholars differ. Julian's contemporary Christian subjects interpreted this coin as a promotion for animal sacrifice, and they were outraged. The fourth [d] depicts on its reverse Valentinian and his brother Valens enthroned side by side holding a globe with Victory behind them. This image emphasized the concord between the two brothers and their shared hopes for military glory. Below their feet can be read TR for Augusta Treverorum, the city where the coin was minted, and OB for Obryzum ("pure gold"), a quality mark on gold coins after Valentinian's coinage reform of 367.*

privileges granted to Christian clergy by Constantine and his sons, and even declared that Christians should no longer be allowed to teach classical literature—authors like Homer and Vergil—for the very reason that they did not believe in the gods who featured so prominently in these works. Julian also recalled most bishops exiled by his predecessors. Although he could claim this to be a philanthropic gesture, he knew well that it would maximize discord, for most of the exiles had been sent away to minimize infighting among the clergy. Seeing that Christianity had considerably more appeal than paganism among the masses because of its organizational structure and charitable institutions, Julian diverted imperial resources to build the same sorts of administrative hierarchies and systems of distribution in pagan cult. Being a philosopher, Julian also undertook an intellectual

SOURCE 13.1: Julian attempts to bring paganism into line with Christianity
Emperor Julian composed this letter (22 [429D-430D]) in 362 to Arsacius, who was serving as high priest in Galatia. It highlights his awareness of the appealing advantages of certain aspects of Christianity, which he disparages as "atheism," over "Hellenism," as he and his contemporaries termed paganism. These advantages included a greater concern with public displays of respectable behavior and, above all, free-handed charity to those in need regardless of their beliefs. With this letter Julian was launching a rearguard action to promote similar behavior among pagan priests, even offering to pay for it out of imperial funds.

Why then do we not observe that what increases atheism the most is charity toward strangers, concern for the tombs of the dead, and the fiction of holiness in their lives? I think we ought to strive to imitate all of these things. And it should not be sufficient for you alone to behave thus, but literally all the priests in Galatia must do so. Either shame them or persuade them to strive for this, or remove them from priestly service if in visiting the gods along with their wives, children, and servants they should allow these same servants, children, or wives to be impious toward the gods, or even to prefer atheism to piety. Then, too, persuade priests neither to attend the theater, nor to drink in a tavern, nor to oversee any craft or labor that is shameful and disreputable. Honor those who obey, and expel those who do not. Establish many hostels in every city in order that vagrants may enjoy hospitality from us, nor just those who are members of our community but also whoever else should be in need of money. I have come up with a plan so that you may have sufficient funds. I have commanded that 30,000 measures of grain and 60,000 pints of wine be donated for the whole of Galatia annually. I order that a fifth of this be used for the poor who serve the priests, but the rest should be allotted to travelers and to those who make requests from us. For it is shameful if no Jew must beg, and if the impious Galilaeans offer food both to their own people and to ours, but ours appear to be lacking in care even from us.

campaign against Christianity by writing a lengthy tract entitled *Against the Galilaeans*, in which he scorned Christianity as a heretical splinter group from Judaism. To drive the point home, he ordered one of his officials to begin rebuilding the Jewish temple in Jerusalem, which had been in ruins since its destruction by Titus in 70. The project foundered after explosions occurred in the foundations.

Julian also had other motivations to terminate this costly rebuilding effort. He needed all the resources he could muster to fund his most grandiose undertaking yet, a full-scale invasion of Persia. The Sasanians had been disturbing Rome's eastern frontier ever since the death of Constantine, and Constantius had been planning to engage them in battle in 361 before he was forced to move westward to confront Julian. Upon gaining sole power and uniting his own army with that of Constantius, Julian felt ready to face the challenge himself and organized an invasion of Persia for 363. He carefully prepared his expeditionary force—some 65,000 men—at Antioch in winter 362/363. While he was there, rioting broke out, both because of the food shortages caused by the added burden of an imperial army in the vicinity, and because of Julian's attempts to restore the shrine of Apollo at Daphne, just outside the city. The temple and oracle there had become derelict after Christians had transferred the bones of the martyr Babylas to the site. Julian's attempt to revive the cult met with staunch resistance from Antioch's powerful Christian populace, who (it seems) felt no shame in setting the temple ablaze. Public opinion thus strongly opposed his efforts to halt the progress of Christianity.

In the event, Julian left the city in a rage and moved his army into position to invade Persia down the River Euphrates. Initially the Persians offered little resistance, allowing him to capture and sack a number of important cities. Even so, by the time he reached the capital at Ctesiphon, resistance had stiffened. Julian's generals advised against a protracted siege in the face of guerilla assaults from the enemy. However, for reasons that are not entirely clear, Julian ordered the boats carrying his supplies to be burned, and he was eventually compelled to retreat northward along the River Tigris under constant attack. Ever the impetuous general, he sallied out to engage some skirmishers in June 363 without putting on his armor, and a spear pierced his side. He was brought back to his tent, and died later that night.

Julian was to be Rome's last openly pagan emperor. His efforts to revive the traditional religion had been valiant, but may well have been self-defeating. Following a late antique trend, Julian strongly associated his pagan revival with the defense of Hellenism ("Greekness"). By the late fourth century, Hellenism and paganism were considered synonymous, with the consequence that the Christian establishment began drawing into question not just traditional Greek religion but also some elements of Greek culture. Had he lived longer, Julian might actually have succeeded in at least transforming paganism into an effective rival to its new challenger. Ultimately, however, his premature death instead seems to be symbolic of the fate of a religious tradition which had come to rely too heavily on the support of the ruler.

JOVIAN, VALENTINIAN I, AND VALENS (363–378)

Julian's death put the army in grave danger, and his reversal of Constantinian religious policy had created massive rifts among the highest court officials, the *consistorium*, who were responsible for choosing his successor. Their squabbling in fact opened the way for the soldiers to preempt them by putting forward a candidate of their own. This man, Flavius Jovianus, was from the Balkans, and an officer in the imperial guard unit of *Protectores*. His election revived a pattern familiar from the third century, when Balkan-born guardsmen had so regularly been made emperor by the army. From the start of his rule, Jovian was faced with the challenge of negotiating a settlement with the Persians that would permit him to extricate his army from their territory. Despite his position of severe disadvantage, he concluded a compromise that ceded only half of the territory formerly held by Rome along the Upper Tigris. The treaty equalized power between Rome and Persia in this strategic region, and helped to minimize conflict between the two powers over the next century and a half. As regards religion, Jovian was Julian's opposite. He was both a Christian and a moderate. He reestablished Christianity as the religion of the court, and revoked Julian's law that forbade Christians to teach. What further plans he may have had, we cannot know, because he died on his march to reach Constantinople in early 364.

The *consistorium* was not prepared to let its chance to elect a successor slip by again, although their choice, after reaching Nicaea, was another guardsman from the Balkans, Flavius Valentinianus. Valentinian was proclaimed on February 24, 364, and a little over one month later he made his brother Valens co-emperor with the rank of full Augustus. In so doing, he was continuing the tradition of dynastic co-rulership perfected by Constantine (Fig. 13.3d). After the two had divided up the army and administration, Valentinian set off for the West, leaving his brother to manage the East.

Ammianus (26.4.5-6) tells us that Valentinian and Valens were instantly faced with the collapse of all frontiers to barbarian invaders, and while this may be an exaggeration, it is certainly true that military operations dominate this period. From the first year of his reign, Valentinian struggled against the Alamanni and himself defeated them in a battle at Solicinium (modern Schwetzingen, Germany) in 368. To bolster Roman control in the region, he began an extensive fortification program along the Rhine—the last systematic construction of defensive works along this frontier. Valentinian's choice to locate some forts inside Alamannic territory, however, provoked conflicts which persisted for the rest of his reign. His general Theodosius also faced, and subdued, the Picts, Attacotti, and Scots in Britain. This success won him promotion to Master of the Cavalry, and in 373 he was sent to suppress a revolt in North Africa led by Firmus, a Mauretanian chieftain. Again Theodosius was successful, which only makes it more mysterious that Valentinian should order his execution in 375, the victim of court intrigue. By this point, however, Theodosius' son of the same name was in a position to replace his father as a talented general. He first proved himself in 374 in battles with the Sarmatians and Quadi, who had invaded Roman territory along the middle Danube when Valentinian gave orders for forts to be built in their land too. The following year, Valentinian crossed the Danube and subdued both peoples. In the course of the negotiations that followed, however, he became so enraged that he had a stroke and died at Brigetio (modern Szöny, Hungary) in November 375.

Valentinian's tireless efforts to defend the empire's frontiers are mirrored by his unflagging attention to its administration. He reformed the collection of taxes, the distribution of military supplies, the operations of the public post, and the management of Rome's grain supply; he even created a new local officer, the *defensor civitatis* ("defender of the city"), to protect common citizens against local and imperial officials. One of his most striking reforms involved a complete restructuring of the collection of money taxes that resulted in a new standard for minting pure gold coins from 367 onward (see Fig. 13.3d).

In the east, Valens was equally competent as an administrator, though much less so as a military leader. Already in the second year of his reign he had to face an attempted usurpation by Procopius, a relative of Julian. This challenge he did suppress in 366, but he remained incensed that the Goths had sent military support to Procopius and therefore undertook two expeditions north of the Danube against them (367–369). Valens' forces also fought in Armenia, where they drove out an invading Persian army at the Battle of Bagawan (371). By 376 he was preparing an expedition to invade Persia in hopes of recovering territory lost in Jovian's treaty of 363.

Such ambitions were abandoned, however, in the wake of an uprising by the Goths in the Roman territory of Thrace. These barbarians had entered the empire after suffering attacks by the Huns, a nomadic people from the Asian steppe, whose lightning military tactics were to make them almost invincible for nearly a century to come. Unaware of the scale of this threat, Valens permitted a small group of Goths to cross the Danube for resettlement inside the empire in 376. This concession, however, only served to encourage many more Goths and other barbarian peoples, who poured into Thrace and eventually broke into revolt. After failing to contain the uprising in 377, Valens' generals in Thrace urged him to return from the Persian frontier with his army. However, by the time he actually arrived in spring 378, the Gothic forces had gained the upper hand, and they soon defeated the Romans near Adrianople (modern Edirne, Turkey) in August 378. This disastrous battle cost Valens his life and resulted in the massacre of two thirds of the eastern field army, about 26,000 of an original 40,000 men. The setback was a grave one. Not only did the eastern empire now lack a fighting force capable of defending it, but it was also encumbered with a large and hostile group of Goths who had no home to which they could return.

GRATIAN, VALENTINIAN II, AND THEODOSIUS I (379–395)

Valens' death did not leave the empire without an emperor. In fact, he had ruled conjointly with not just his brother but also his nephew, Gratian, whom Valentinian had appointed as a second co-emperor in 367, when Gratian was just eight years old (see Table 14.1). Gratian's immediate promotion to full Augustus, rather than to the lesser grade of Caesar, established a precedent of appointing child emperors that endured into the late fifth century. Indeed, the next to follow was Gratian's younger half-brother Valentinian II. Valentinian I had moved to the Danube in 375 (leaving Gratian in Trier to guard the Gallic frontier), and when he died that same year, the army accompanying him proclaimed Valentinian II Augustus at the tender age of four. Needless to say, this initiative did not please the current reigning Augusti, Valens and Gratian, but they were forced to accept it.

After the death of Valens at Adrianople, Gratian was himself faced with the rebellious Goths. Emboldened by their victory, they had spread out and gained effective control over the entire central Balkans. Aware of the challenge they posed, Gratian resolved to appoint an experienced military commander as co-Augustus. Not surprisingly, he chose Theodosius, son of Valentinian's most successful general, who had a formidable record of his own. Theodosius took office early in 379 and quickly set to work repelling the invaders, who were quite fragmented at this point and could be attacked piecemeal. Although today they are referred to collectively as "Visigoths," they were in fact a multi-ethnic group of Gothic Tervingi and Greuthungi, as well as Taifali, Alans, and Huns. These peoples had crossed the Danube separately in 376, but in response to Roman hostility they were forced to coalesce around the leadership of the Goths—the strongest group numerically. As a result, however, when Theodosius wished to attack or negotiate, he had trouble identifying the main leaders.

After four years of frustrating guerrilla actions, Theodosius made an uneasy compromise peace in October 382, which required the Goths to fight in Roman armies, but also granted them the right to settle under their own leadership in northern Thrace. In effect, therefore, Theodosius had created a semi-autonomous barbarian state inside the bounds of the empire; the consequences were to prove devastating (see Chapter Fourteen). Fortunately the eastern frontier was much calmer. The aggressive Sasanian king Shapur II died in 379, and a series of weak successors followed. In 387, during this period of reduced tension, Theodosius and Shapur III reached an agreement to divide control of Armenia between them.

Otherwise, two successive usurpation attempts were Theodosius' primary military concern. The first arose in Britain, where the general Magnus Maximus had himself proclaimed emperor in early 383, and then moved into Gaul to defeat Gratian near Paris and kill him. Maximus believed that he could win recognition as western Augustus from Theodosius in Constantinople, and thus sent embassies to both him and Valentinian II, whose court was in Milan. Valentinian was able to use Ambrose, bishop of Milan, to negotiate a peace that granted Maximus recognition from Theodosius on condition that he left Valentinian (still just eleven years old) undisturbed. Three years later, however, Maximus broke this agreement by marching into Italy and forcing Valentinian to flee to Theodosius. In retaliation Theodosius defeated Maximus in a series of engagements in Pannonia, and eventually captured and executed him at Aquileia in northern Italy in summer 388.

Theodosius remained in the west down to mid-390, helping Valentinian reestablish his rule. Theodosius' son Arcadius (already appointed Augustus in 383) was left in Constantinople to manage affairs. Theodosius himself returned there in mid-390, but only two years later trouble arose once again in the West. Theodosius had left Valentinian II to rule here under the regency of the Frankish general Arbogast—establishing another pattern, regency by barbarian generals, that would recur in the years to come. Valentinian, by now just over twenty, was so thoroughly dominated by Arbogast that when he attempted to dismiss him in 392 and was defied, he was reduced to desperation and committed suicide. Arbogast then proclaimed a court official, Eugenius, as Augustus. Theodosius' reaction was

Figure 13.4 *Obelisk base from the Hippodrome of Constantinople (Map 14.2). Following an ancient tradition, Theodosius erected an obelisk in the center of the Hippodrome of Constantinople after his victory over Magnus Maximus. On its base, pictured here, he is shown in the imperial box at the race course, which was attached directly to the palace. He presides at the circus races holding a crown for the victor and surrounded by court officials, senators, and bodyguards. Beneath him are the assembled masses, and below them acrobats and musicians, including organ-players. The circus races grew in importance during late antiquity, and offered the emperor a powerful symbolic venue for demonstrating his beneficence to his subjects and his rule over them.*

a very decisive one. He proclaimed his second son Honorius as Augustus in January 393—a sign that there would be no recognition for Eugenius—and in summer 394 he marched west to eliminate the usurper. The two armies met in September at the River Frigidus (in the foothills of the Tirol, east of Aquileia) and fought for two days. On the first, Arbogast and Eugenius had the upper hand, though they succeeded only in killing large numbers of Theodosius' Visigothic auxiliaries. On the second, a tremendous wind came up in the face of the rebel forces and turned the battle in Theodosius' favor. Christian authors portray this as an act of divine intervention on his behalf, and there certainly was an element of pagan–Christian conflict in this battle. In seeking to shore up his cause, Eugenius had courted favor from the aristocrats of Rome by allowing them to revive many traditional cults that had been suppressed under the harsh religious policies of Theodosius. While the degree to which this conflict represented a last-ditch effort to revive paganism has surely been exaggerated by the sources, the battle at the Frigidus reflects a change nonetheless; it was the last time that a large body of pagans would win military support from an emperor, albeit a usurper.

In the aftermath of the battle, Theodosius remained in Italy and even visited Rome in an effort to crush any remaining support for the rebel cause. In January 395 he succumbed to a hard life of campaigning, and died in Milan. His death marks the end of an era. He was the last in a long line of emperors—stretching back to the days of Marcus Aurelius—who participated actively in military affairs. For the next century and a half, all western and most eastern emperors would leave military action to their generals, and confine themselves to administrative and courtly activities.

NEW ELITES FOR THE EMPIRE

The administrative changes introduced by the tetrarchs, together with the new priorities and values of a Christian world, combined to alter the nature of the ruling elite in the fourth century. In many ways late antiquity represents the period when the multifarious regions of Rome's empire reasserted their unique identities with new vigor; yet at the same time this period witnessed a massive homogenization of elite culture that pulled against fragmentation and served to hold an aging empire together. The growth in the imperial bureaucracy introduced by the tetrarchs and Constantine set the stage for this process. The empire of the second century had functioned with a very bottom-heavy government. At that date there were never more than 600 or so senators, and the senate exercised little practical authority as a governing body, although its individual members had tremendous power as liaisons between the emperor and his subjects. However, their role declined markedly after the Severan period and reached its nadir under the tetrarchs, who favored equestrians and above all military men for appointment to offices.

Constantine, by contrast, began a revival of the senate which reinvigorated it in the fourth century, yet he did this while making fundamental changes to the senatorial career. His single biggest alteration was the creation of an entirely new senate in Constantinople. By 359 his son Constantius II had increased its membership to nearly 2,000, and had graced the new capital with its own Urban Prefect, an office equal in status to that of Praetorian Prefect. From the time of Constantine the senate in Rome had been increased to a similar size, meaning that the empire now had a senatorial elite about six times larger than what it had been two centuries earlier. This expansion was made possible because Constantine had drafted primarily men of eastern provincial origin, especially former city councilors, for the Constantinopolitan senate; by this means he opened the way for these formerly low-level aristocrats to come pouring in. In addition, emperors from Constantine onward used senatorial status as the ultimate reward for service in the greatly expanded new bureaucracy, or on retirement from it.

The consequences of this expansion are evident in a series of laws issued by Valentinian I from 372, which bestow senatorial status on the holders of a variety of imperial offices. These same laws also draw distinctions between three grades of senators: *clarissimi* (mid-range governors and some bureaucrats); *spectabiles* (high officials such as the most prestigious governors and mid-level generals); and *illustres* (top officials and military officers such as Praetorian Prefects, Consuls, Masters of the Soldiers). Immediately striking about this list is its combination of traditional senatorial titles, new bureaucratic offices, and military rank, any one of which could now serve as the gateway to senatorial status. Equally striking is the fact that now, with a senatorial order of some 4,000 members, there was a perceived need for additional gradations to mark out the loftiest senators appropriately. Finally, this expansion and ranking gave emperors increased control over access to elite status, especially because two of the channels feeding into it—the army and the bureaucracy—were routed through the imperial hierarchy. The consequent effects on the religious status of the elite were tremendous. With only a single pagan emperor in power from 324 to 395, imperial offices in both the civic and military realm came to be dominated by Christians.

Much of this growth in the eastern and western senates occurred at the expense of local city councils. The order of *curiales* ("town councilors," formerly termed "decurions") had traditionally been the bedrock of local administration, because they had voluntarily managed city finances, coordinated building projects, resolved minor legal disputes, and overseen the collection of taxes. Many of these duties continued in the late empire, but increasingly they came to be seen as burdens, in particular when other career opportunities were now available that entailed exemption from curial duties. These opportunities were normally accessed through education, making the elite of the late empire less of an aristocracy than it had once been and more of a meritocracy. Hence there arose a new fashion for the study of the law that encouraged students to bypass the traditional rhetorical and literary training so important in the early empire, and to move straight to a subject that offered direct access to the imperial chancery. Many took this path. Although there were still probably around 250,000 curiales in the mid-fourth century, emperors were so keenly aware of the decline in their numbers that the single longest section in the *Theodosian Code* (12.1) lists 192 laws designed to prevent the loss of curiales to other careers.

As the imperial service drew local talent away into bureaucratic and senatorial offices, yet another new elite group was forming: the army. The early empire's professional army of citizen soldiers was now no more than a fading memory. To be sure, citizen soldiers continued to enlist or to be drafted into the ranks, but they could not fill the manpower needs of the fourth-century army, which had grown to as large as 600,000 soldiers. The Roman authorities thus turned increasingly to barbarians to fill the ranks. Use of non-citizens in the military was of course nothing new; such auxiliary forces had made up about half of Rome's fighting force during the Principate. But the status accorded to barbarian soldiers in the late empire was unheard of even a century earlier. Thus while the emperor's elite Praetorian Guards had once been not mere Roman citizens but even men of exclusively Italian origin, the *scholarii* formed by Constantine to replace the Guard were for the most part barbarians, especially Germans. The same can be said of the officers, about half of

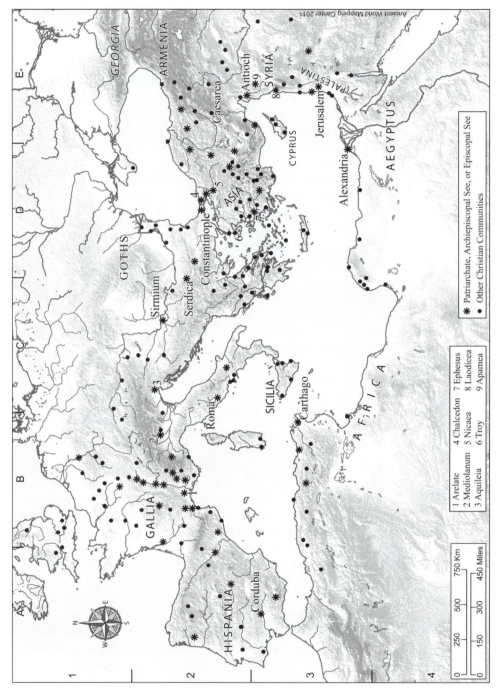

Map 13.2 *Christian Congregations Attested by 325*

Legend:

✳ Patriarchate, Archiepiscopal See, or Episcopal See
● Other Christian Communities

1 Arelate	4 Chalcedon	7 Ephesus
2 Mediolanum	5 Nicaea	8 Laodicea
3 Aquileia	6 Troy	9 Apamea

GEORGIA
ARMENIA
Caesarea
Antioch
SYRIA
PALESTINA
Jerusalem
CYPRUS
Alexandria
AEGYPTUS
ASIA
Constantinople
Serdica
Sirmium
GOTHS
SICILIA
Roma
Carthago
AFRICA
GALLIA
HISPANIA
Corduba

0 250 500 750 Km
0 150 300 450 Miles

whom were non-Roman. Nor were such officers excluded from participating in imperial government. On the contrary, over the course of the fourth century figures like Valentinian II's Frankish general Arbogast became virtual regents. The Vandal Stilicho, who succeeded to Arbogast's role in the next generation, was even welcomed into the imperial family when he married Theodosius I's niece Serena. This late Roman "military nobility," as it has been termed, even came to dominate imperial politics during the fifth century, when figures like Aetius and Ricimer became highly influential powers behind the throne. It would be wrong to assume, however, that such "foreign" generals precipitated the "fall of the Roman Empire." Since they had been fully acculturated to Roman military life, they constructed their identities very much along Roman lines rather than barbarian ones, and they usually remained steadfastly loyal to the empire.

Any description of elite groups in late antiquity must inevitably include a new class of leaders whose power had been minimal in the second century: the bishops. The resilience of the church in the face of the persecutions had stemmed in no small part from the strength of its organizational structures. By constructing itself as an entity independent of the Roman state, the Christian church had been able to resist Rome and survive. At the heart of this organizational structure was the bishop, a title going back to the earliest days of Christianity that had come to characterize the head of an urban Christian community. By the early fourth century there were bishops for every major city in Italy and for many minor ones, as well as for areas in heavily Christianized regions like North Africa and parts of Syria and Anatolia. Thus by 325 Syria had nearly 30 bishops who headed the church in cities like Antioch, Apamea, and Laodicea. The most famous bishop for westerners was the bishop of Rome, whom we now call the Pope, a figure who already in the mid-third century could boast a staff of 46 priests, 14 deacons or subdeacons, 42 acolytes, 52 exorcists, and who subsidized living expenses for no less than 1,500 needy people. By the fourth century, the bishopric of Rome was an office so sought after that fights would erupt over the succession; on a single day in 366 some 137 people lost their lives in riots over a disputed papal election. Most bishoprics were, of course, considerably less powerful, but with the rapid spread of Christianity during the fourth century, the bishop grew in power as the premier local leader, eclipsing the curiales to the point that by the mid-fifth century he had taken their place as community leader.

The bishop's power stemmed not just from the growth of his congregation but also from the many powers and privileges accorded him by the emperors. Constantine, for example, granted bishops the right to receive some revenues generated by imperial estates; he allowed them exemption from taxes and curial service; he regularly allowed them to use the imperial post-horse system; he granted them the right to sit in judgment over civil suits; he also granted them the right to manumit slaves in their churches. These privileges made the bishop into a local powerbroker *par excellence*. His authority is also reflected in the rise of Christian architecture; just as bishops replaced curiales as civic leaders, so too Christian architecture replaced traditional civic architecture as the standard expression of local prosperity and pride of place (Plate 17).

In many ways, however, bishops also assumed the role of a counterweight to imperial power in late antiquity. The sources on this point must be interpreted with care, because typically they are Christian and thus prone to inflate the role of the bishop as a champion of truth against supposedly tyrannical emperors. Nevertheless, a bishop's ability to resist imperial authority is attested in numerous instances, and tellingly illustrates how the church was growing into an alternative source of power. Perhaps the best example comes in the person of Ambrose, who became bishop of Milan in 374. His father had been a Praetorian Prefect, and he had himself served as a provincial governor before he was unexpectedly tapped for this bishopric. Shortly after his consecration, the child emperor Valentinian II took up residence in Milan, and the pagan senators of Rome believed they could convince the boy to restore an altar to the goddess Victory that had been placed in their senate house by Augustus, but removed by the Christian emperor Gratian. When Ambrose heard of the senators' embassy, he wrote two menacing letters to Valentinian that convinced him not to give in to these demands. Ambrose also crossed swords with the much stronger emperor Theodosius I. In 388, after a group of Christian zealots destroyed a Jewish synagogue at the eastern frontier city of Callinicum, Theodosius ordered them to rebuild it at church expense. With a letter that signals the growing power of anti-Jewish rhetoric in the period, Ambrose convinced Theodosius to withdraw his demand. Then in 390, after the citizens of Thessalonica had killed one of Theodosius' generals during a riot, the emperor unleashed his soldiers on a rampage that massacred as many as 7,000 people in the city's arena. Ambrose, emboldened by his earlier success, openly rebuked Theodosius (then resident in Milan) for this slaughter, and made him do penance for months before accepting him back into communion in his church. Thus, less than eighty years after the close of the Great Persecution, Christian bishops were able to force the emperor to acknowledge their superior authority in religious matters.

PAGANISM AND CHRISTIANITY

Modern scholars use the word "paganism"—cautiously and uncomfortably—to describe the collectivity of practices that characterize ancient, non–Judeo-Christian religions. In fact ancient pagans had no one word with which to designate their religion, nor would they have conceived of themselves as a unified group in any period prior to late antiquity. The Latin *paganus* has the sense of "rustic," and was first employed by Christians in the late fourth century as a derogatory designation for those who followed the traditional religious practices. The reason for this ambiguous terminology is that ancient paganism was a fundamentally decentralized phenomenon, best expressed at the local level, with only very weak forces drawing its varied manifestations together into anything that might be recognized today as a single religion. Each community had its own deities, rituals, and festivals—a diversity that emperors generally tolerated, even fostered (see Chapter Nine).

Among the cults to benefit from this tolerance was Christianity. While it endured periods of persecution that grew increasingly intense through the early fourth century, it was largely left alone to develop and spread. During the century after Constantine's death its marginal situation was transformed. It not only gained the ascendency as the religion of the majority and of the state, but it also persecuted, and all but extirpated, paganism. This is not to suggest that paganism was somehow moribund when Constantine converted in 312. On the contrary, pagans in all likelihood represented around 90 percent of the Empire's population, and they still controlled religious practices and politics at the local and imperial levels. By the mid-fourth century, however, Christianity had probably reached a demographic tipping-point in cities (the centers of regional power), and it now had the advantage of inertia on its side. Unfortunately no census numbers exist, but a witness like Firmicus Maternus, an aristocrat from Sicily, illustrates the trend. In the final years of Constantine's reign he wrote a lengthy treatise on astrology steeped in pagan belief. A decade later he had converted to Christianity and composed a blistering book *On the Error of the Profane Religions*. Conversion was thus fashionable in a period during which the emperor had converted and was promoting his new faith with the one hand while repressing the old religions with the other. Studies have shown that as early as the 340s emperors began showing preference for Christians in making official appointments. By the 390s very few pagans are attested in office, and by 415 they were legally debarred from holding administrative posts (*Theodosian Code* 16.10.21). In this environment, as one can imagine, some conversions were less than sincere, as people trimmed their sails to the prevailing religious winds. For example, when the young Julian visited the historic city of Troy, its bishop Pegasius showed him altars and statues of the old gods that he still lovingly revered even though now a Christian leader.

Julian himself offers strong proof of pagans' awareness that they were now on the defensive. His efforts to bring paganism into line with Christianity represent a rearguard action, too little and too late to compete with a religion that better suited the needs of its time. Not only did he introduce new systems of charitable distribution and insist that pagan priests follow stricter codes of morality, but he and fellow pagan intellectuals also undertook a campaign to reformulate pagan myth and ritual to suit prevailing philosophical notions. They promoted henotheistic theology based on supreme deities like the Sun God or the so-called "Highest God." They integrated the old gods into a Platonic cosmology that accounted for their plurality by describing them as intermediate divinities between the supreme god and man. They formulated rationalizations for blood sacrifice and idol worship using sophisticated phenomenological arguments. While these explanations carried weight among the intellectual elite, they were often too abstruse to appeal to the masses, who found the pithy slogans of Christian leaders more compelling. Had Julian lived longer, there is no telling what might have happened to both paganism and Christianity, but his premature death and his replacement by Christian emperors closed off any further chance for a successful pagan revival.

Already under Constantine Christianity began to inflict some of the same violence on the pagans that it had itself received at the hands of pagan emperors.

After assuming control of the East in 324, Constantine ordered the destruction of a handful of temples in Cilicia, Syria, and Palestine. He also appears to have issued a law against sacrifice, although we have only allusions to it in various sources and not the law itself; its enforcement must have been limited. His son Constantius is more firmly attested as having banned sacrifice. While Julian repealed all such laws, they were reactivated with a vengeance by Theodosius, most notably in 391 (Source 13.2). Around the same time he also began permitting the destruction of pagan temples, both through his eastern Praetorian Prefect Cynegius and on the local initiative of bishops and "holy men," Christian leaders whose authority stemmed from their ascetic lifestyle rather than official recognition by the church. One outstanding instance was the destruction of the massive temple of Serapis in Alexandria, a showpiece of architecture and major center of worship. After the local bishop Theophilus staged a scene of public mockery

---

SOURCE 13.2: The end of pagan sacrifice

These two laws illustrate both how closely we can trace imperial legislation on religious worship in late antiquity (note their detailed headings and subscriptions), and how many gaps still remain in our knowledge. In the first text, Constantius II orders the first firmly attested ban on pagan sacrifice. He also mentions a sacrificial ban instituted by Constantine, yet no such law is preserved in the Code, *and other sources on the matter offer contradictory testimony. The second text is a more explicit and wide-ranging law issued in 391, not just cataloging forbidden activities but also showing how imperial officials were coerced into enforcing it. It, too, has a subtext. A parallel version (CTh 16.10.11) issued four months later was directed to the Prefect of Egypt at precisely the period when a Christian mob incited by Theophilus, bishop of Alexandria, was besieging the temple of Serapis. Though the law does not explicitly authorize the destruction of temples, the Christian Alexandrians eventually wiped out this massive shrine.*

Theodosian Code 16.10.2. Emperor Constantius Augustus to Madalianus, Vice-Praetorian Prefect. Let superstition cease, let the insanity of sacrifices be abolished. For whoever should dare to celebrate sacrifices in contravention of the law of the divine Emperor my father and of this command of Our Clemency, let a fitting punishment and immediate sentence be passed against him. Received when Marcellinus and Probinus were Consuls (A.D. 341).

Theodosian Code 16.10.10. Gratian, Valentinian, and Theodosius to Albinus the Praetorian Prefect. Let no one pollute himself with sacrificial animals, let no one slaughter innocent victims, let no one approach shrines, visit temples, and admire idols formed by human labor, lest he become subject to divine and human sanctions. This order should also bind governors so that, if any of them is devoted to profane rites and should enter a temple anywhere for purposes of worship, whether along a road or in a city, he should be compelled to pay fifteen pounds of gold immediately, and his staff should pay the same sum with equal speed if they do not resist the governor and report him immediately with a public attestation . . . Given on February 24, in the consulship of Tatianus and Symmachus (A.D. 391) in Milan.

against pagan images in 391, the city's pagans rose up in revolt and barricaded themselves in the temple precinct. Their action ignited a street war between pagans and Christians; many on both sides were killed, and the Christians eventually obliterated the temple. This was just one of many such instances where Christian zealots attacked pagan holy sites with utter impunity.

As a fundamentally decentralized, largely local phenomenon, and one heavily dependent on sacred buildings and objects, paganism had difficulty recovering from these blows. Moreover, the removal of imperial subsidies for local cults from Constantine's reign onward eliminated the means by which rituals could be conducted, as well as severing ties to the local communities that had once been fed and feted at civic religious festivals. Once the shrines were closed or destroyed and the festivals discontinued, paganism could survive only in isolated local contexts, especially in the countryside where it had always thrived, and in a limited number of obstinately traditional cities. To be sure, certain pagans did continue to practice their religion well into the sixth century, but only in radically altered form, some by maintaining a very low profile, others by intellectualizing their theology and limiting its enactment to an arcane inner circle. Even these, however, were ferreted out after the emperor Justinian closed the Platonic Academy in Athens in 529. By this date paganism was becoming a distant memory, surviving less through active practitioners and more in Christian practices adapted from the ancient pagan forms.

Meanwhile, Christianity had exploited the conversion of the emperor to strengthen the unity that had always been its primary advantage. As a monotheist religion and a religion of the book, Christianity was also able to develop a more coherent theology. Nevertheless, as a mass movement it, too, was plagued by division from the beginning. Disputes arose sometimes over leadership (a matter of fundamental concern to the Donatists in North Africa, for example) and at other times over dogma, as in the Arian controversy. The former type of controversy is usually referred to as *schism*, the latter as *heresy*. In both instances the rival Christian communities typically sought the emperor's immediate intervention as mediator and, from Constantine onward, he readily obliged. Rarely, however, did his authority bring matters to a close, since both sides in any given debate usually regrouped and came back for renewed engagement, with the previous loser sometimes then winning in the end. Engagement persisted because much more was at stake than principled discussion about pious behavior and the nature of God. Theological controversies were often thinly veiled excuses for power plays between the bishops of rival cities or even rival bishops within a single city. The church, after all, was always divided by geography, with each region following its own traditions and each major city—especially Alexandria, Antioch, Ephesus, Constantinople, and Rome—claiming the right to impose its own doctrine and ritual. Thus, although Theodosius theoretically put a stop to ecclesiastical bickering over Arianism at the Council of Constantinople in 381, quarrels soon resumed over other issues, like the role of Mary as mother of God, or the admixture of human and divine qualities in the person of Jesus. These questions demanded further ecumenical councils at Ephesus in 431 and Chalcedon in 451, and they continued to create fissures in church unity that persist to the present day.

All of this discord would seem to speak against the unifying power of Christianity as an imperial religion. "No beasts are as harmful to people as most Christians are savage to each other," the pagan Ammianus (22.5.4) once quipped. But this would be to oversimplify. Christianity had grown up independent of imperial support and had developed its own leadership structures, its own infrastructure, and its own set of values and beliefs, all of which made it what Edward Gibbon in the eighteenth century famously termed "an independent state at the heart of the Roman empire." But once Christianity allied itself with the emperor, it became increasingly intertwined with the state to the point that, by the sixth century, the two formed a seamless web of power. Theological controversies were thus all part of the dynamics of power, providing channels for the expression of rivalries that the emperor himself could control. Christianity also offered a conduit through which he could extend his influence beyond the frontiers. Thus, around the time of Constantine's conversion, the leadership of the kingdoms of Armenia, Georgia, and Axum (Ethiopia) also converted. It is no surprise that the emperors embraced this fortunate situation to widen their political reach. Christianity soon spread—often with active support from the emperor—to the Saracen Arabs, to the Goths, and to other Germanic peoples, and here too it provided common ground (see Fig. 14.3). This trend not only boosted the power of the emperor beyond his territorial borders, but it also remained one of the empire's most lasting legacies.

SUGGESTED READINGS

Cameron, Averil, and Stuart G. Hall. 1999. *Eusebius*, Life of Constantine. Oxford: Oxford University Press. Model introduction, translation, and commentary on this pivotal source.

Curran, John R. 2000. *Pagan City and Christian Capital: Rome in the Fourth Century*. Oxford: Oxford University Press. Surveys the development of Rome's architecture and topography in this period of change.

Chuvin, Pierre. 1990. *A Chronicle of the Last Pagans*, trans. B. A. Archer. Cambridge, MA: Harvard University Press. Brief introduction to paganism's struggle for survival in a Christian empire.

Heather, Peter, and John F. Matthews. 1991. *The Goths in the Fourth Century*. Liverpool: Liverpool University Press. Excellent sourcebook documenting the arrival of this new people.

Lee, A. Douglas. 2000. *Pagans and Christians in Late Antiquity. A Sourcebook*. London and New York: Routledge.

Lenski, Noel, ed. 2006. *The Cambridge Companion to the Age of Constantine*. Cambridge: Cambridge University Press.

Matthews, John F. 1975. *Western Aristocracies and Imperial Court, AD 364–425*. Oxford: Oxford University Press. Invaluable treatment of the ongoing importance of the senatorial aristocracy in late antiquity.

Matthews, John F. 1989. *The Roman Empire of Ammianus Marcellinus*. London: Duckworth.

Rapp, Claudia. 2005. *Holy Bishops in Late Antiquity: The Nature of Christian Leadership in an Age of Transition*. Berkeley, Los Angeles, London : University of California Press.

14

THE FINAL YEARS OF
THE WESTERN EMPIRE AND
ROME'S REVIVAL IN THE EAST

SOURCES

The sources for the final period of Rome's empire in the west are rich in social and cultural detail, but comparatively poor in narrative. Zosimus provides a continuous account through the 410s. After this date, we must rely on the fragments of classicizing narrative histories by Olympiodorus, Priscus, and John of Antioch, all in Greek, and on the quirky Latin history of Orosius. Interesting detail on contemporary events around the year 400 derives from the panegyric poet Claudian, who wrote for the court of the emperor Honorius in Latin, and from the wickedly biting satirist Synesius, who wrote in Greek under Honorius' brother Arcadius. As the fifth century wears on, however, we are compelled to fall back on the jejune testimony of chronicles and chronographers; while both types of work arrange events year by year, the former comprises mere lists, while the latter includes narrative. Although the Greek chronographic tradition of authors like John Malalas or the *Paschal Chronicle* sometimes provides considerable detail, it was not contemporary writing; the Latin chronicles by contrast were often composed during the period, but their testimony is so brief that it can raise more questions than it answers.

The ecclesiastical historians Socrates and Sozomen provide quite accurate information on events through the 430s. So, too, saints' lives ("hagiography") and the patristic sources discussed at the start of Chapter Thirteen continue to be preserved in abundance. The two writers whose works survive in greatest volume from all of antiquity, Augustine who wrote in Latin and John Chrysostom in Greek, both derive from this period. Their letters, sermons, biblical exegesis, and philosophical investigations are of absorbing interest to the political, social, cultural, and above all religious historian, as are the many other works by the numerous Christian writers of the period. Inscriptions become even scarcer, as do papyri, but both media then see a revival in popularity in the sixth century. Their absence is compensated for to some degree by the survival of imperial laws in the *Theodosian Code* and *Justinianic Code*.

Perhaps most interestingly, the late fourth and fifth centuries saw the efflorescence of literatures written in languages other than Latin and Greek, and from contexts other than the centers of imperial power. Using these resources, we can begin to gain a wider perspective on the ancient Mediterranean and the peoples who surrounded it. Hebrew, the language of Judaism, had of course been written long before the arrival of the Greeks and Romans in the Near East, but in the later empire it came to be used much more widely with the rise of Rabbinic literature. In the early fifth century, a script was first invented for the Armenian language, spoken in the mountains of eastern Anatolia; a rich tradition of literary writing, especially historiography, soon followed. So, too, the Georgian language from the southern Caucasus began to be written in the fifth century. The transmission of Egyptian (which had been written since the fourth millennium B.C.) also underwent fundamental changes at this time. Even in the early empire, Egyptians had begun composing their texts using Greek rather than hieroglyphic characters. After the addition of a handful of unique characters for distinctly Egyptian sounds, this practice became standard by the fourth century A.D. when this new form of Coptic Egyptian was elevated to the status of a literary language. Perhaps most important, the northern Aramaic dialect known as Syriac began to be written as a literary language in the third century A.D., then flourished in the fourth and became wildly prolific in the fifth. Many of these developments were connected with the activity of the Christian church, not just because Christianity was fast becoming the predominant religion in all these regions, but also because Christianity, as a religion of the book, placed great emphasis on the transmission of sacred knowledge through the written word. To a lesser degree, we find parallel developments in the West. A script was invented for the Gothic language by a fourth-century bishop (see Fig. 14.3). Sources also come to be written in Latin from a non-Roman perspective, most notably the *Gothic History* of Jordanes, composed in the sixth century. The emergence of such literatures and histories contributed in turn to the rise of regional identities among the empire's former subjects and, at the same time, to the fragmentation of the empire.

THE THEODOSIAN DYNASTY DOWN TO THE FIRST SACK OF ROME (395–410)

Theodosius I is widely revered for having turned Rome's fortunes around in his sixteen-year reign. He had assumed the throne in the chaotic aftermath of the disastrous battle of Adrianople (378). Using a combination of force and diplomacy, he reached a compromise with the Goths that put them to work in the empire's service. When he died in January 395, there was also hope for continued stability because he left behind two sons as legitimate successors. Unfortunately, the seeds of trouble were already sown in both of these arrangements. While the Goths had been pacified, they were by no means subdued. Their presence as a semiautonomous group operating inside Roman territory allowed them to build momentum against the empire until they eventually sacked the city of Rome in 410, and went on to secure the surrender of the region of Aquitaine (in Gaul) into their control in 418. All this occurred during the reigns of Theodosius' sons, Arcadius and Honorius, who succeeded to power in 395 at the ages of 18 and 11 respectively. Both had been Augusti since early childhood, but both failed to master the art of rulership in the manner exhibited by their father. They never took to the field on campaign, nor did they become strong managers of affairs at court.

Historians have often regarded 395 as the beginning of the definitive split between the eastern and western halves of the empire. After this date East and West were never again ruled by a single emperor. In truth, however, the division was only gradually worked out over the course of Arcadius' and Honorius' joint reigns, and much of the very real tension that arose between East and West under their rule stemmed from ongoing assumptions that the two halves were and should remain fundamentally one. The gradual development of the division makes it useful to treat the two emperors together in the first part of this chapter, which will then move into separate treatments of West and East in the sections to follow.

Because of their youth upon accession, and because neither ever grew into a strong leader, both Arcadius and Honorius were controlled by a succession of officials who managed affairs for them. For Honorius, the longest lasting and most successful of these was Stilicho, the son of a Vandal cavalry officer, who had risen to become Master of the Soldiers in the last year of Theodosius' reign. Upon his death in 395, Stilicho gained effective control of both the eastern and the western field armies, because the two had been united by Theodosius at Milan following his victory at the battle of the River Frigidus (394). Furthermore, a number of sources indicate that Theodosius had left Stilicho with oversight over both of his youthful sons. However, this claim was not universally credited and, as can be imagined, it caused offense at the eastern court. Here, in the eastern capital of Constantinople, Arcadius had been nominal ruler since 392, when his father had left him in charge during the war with Eugenius. In 395, Arcadius' Praetorian Prefect Rufinus took control of the court, and instantly began to quarrel with Stilicho. Tensions first arose over the Visigoths, who were angry at the heavy losses they had suffered while serving as auxiliaries on the front lines in battle at the River Frigidus. They broke into revolt in the Balkans, forcing Stilicho to intervene with soldiers he brought from the West. Arcadius and Rufinus saw his intervention as an encroachment into eastern territory and ordered him to surrender

TABLE 14.1 **The Theodosian Family** *The presentation follows the style of Table 8.1, explained there.*

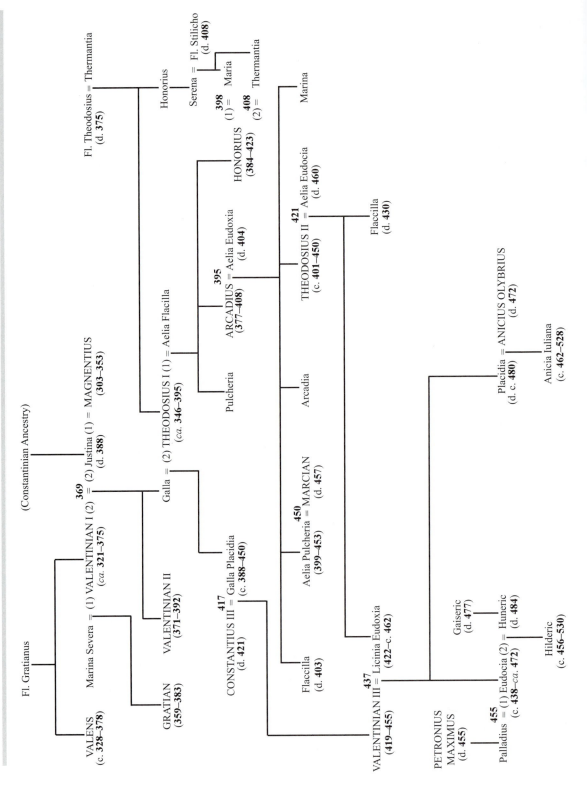

command of part of his army before he had fully subdued the Visigoths. Stilicho's reaction was to obey, sending the troops to Constantinople under his Count Gainas; but he also ordered Gainas to murder Rufinus upon his arrival.

Rufinus was in turn succeeded by another powerbroker named Eutropius, the chief imperial eunuch. He, too, quarreled with Stilicho over the same issues, because Stilicho intervened against the Visigoths a second time after they invaded Greece in 397. Once again Stilicho failed to subdue these barbarians fully, nor did he receive any military aid from Eutropius, who was preoccupied with fending off a force of Huns that had descended from the Caucasus into Cappadocia and Syria. After this success, Eutropius placated the Visigoths by granting their leader Alaric the Roman military title "Master of the Soldiers for Illyricum." He also began to exert pressure on Stilicho, who was declared a public enemy by the senate of Constantinople. On Eutropius' recommendation, Arcadius even responded favorably to a proposal by Gildo, the Count of Africa (part of the western empire), to transfer his territory to the control of the East. Such a transfer would present a tremendous threat to the city of Rome, given its dependence on African grain. Nevertheless, Stilicho again gained the upper hand. He promptly eliminated Gildo in 398 and refused to recognize Eutropius' claim to the consulship of 399 in the West by contending it was an unthinkable distinction for a eunuch and former slave.

Figure 14.1 *Diptych of Stilicho and Serena. Late Roman grandees advertised major events, like appointment to an office or the celebration of a wedding, by having commemorative diptychs—two facing writing tablets—produced in ivory. This example shows the general Stilicho, a man of mixed Vandal and Roman heritage who rose to become Master of the Soldiers under Theodosius. Stilicho married Theodosius' niece Serena, portrayed on the left together with their son Eucherius, who is dressed as a young Roman noble. The contrast with his father, who styles himself as a barbarian general by wearing a full beard and pants, reflects the intermingling of Roman and Germanic families and customs at this period. Stilicho remained steadfast in his loyalty to Theodosius' sons, the emperors Arcadius and Honorius, whose portraits can be seen on his shield. He even betrothed both of his daughters in turn to Honorius, but was eventually executed by the emperor in 408.*

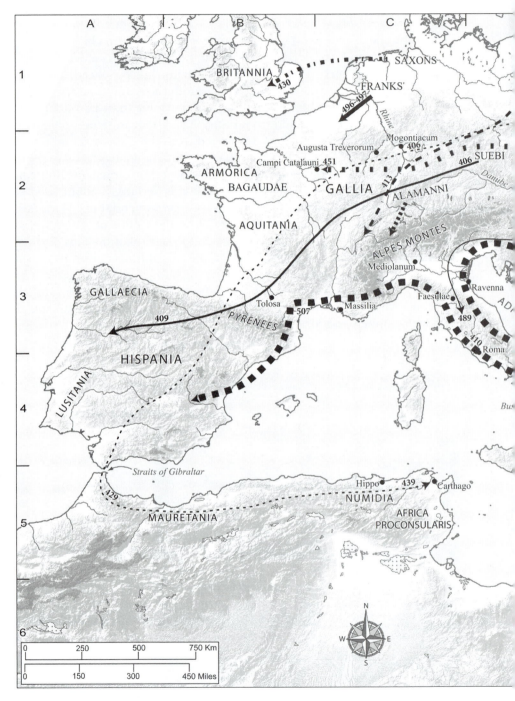

Map 14.1 *The Barbarian Invasions*

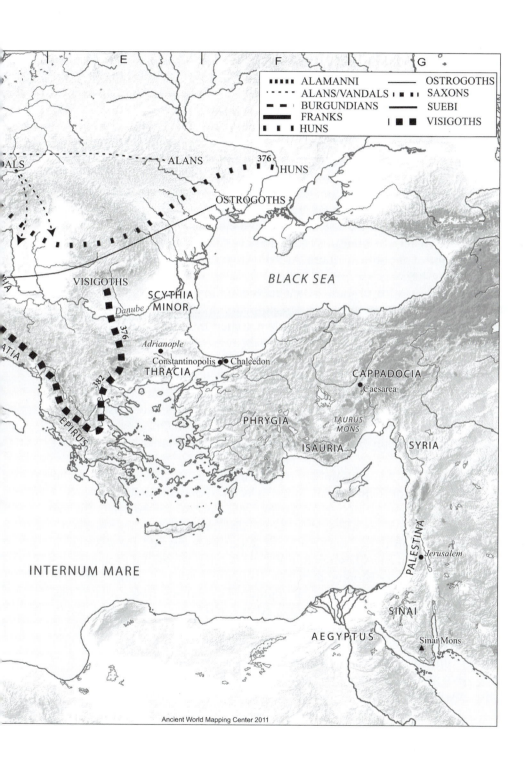

E   F   G

ALAMANNI   **OSTROGOTHS**
ALANS/VANDALS   **SAXONS**
BURGUNDIANS   **SUEBI**
FRANKS   **VISIGOTHS**
HUNS

ALS

ALANS   376
HUNS

OSTROGOTHS

BLACK SEA

VISIGOTHS

SCYTHIA
MINOR

Danube

Adrianople

Constantinopolis ● ● Chalcedon

THRACIA

CAPPADOCIA

● Caesarea

PHRYGIA

*TAURUS
MONS*

ISAURIA

SYRIA

EPIRUS

PALESTINA

● *Jerusalem*

INTERNUM MARE

SINAI

AEGYPTUS

▲ Sinai Mons

Ancient World Mapping Center 2011

Eutropius ran into further trouble this same year when a revolt erupted in Phrygia under the leadership of a barbarian general, Tribigild. He commanded yet another group of Goths settled inside Roman territory, and when Gainas (himself a Goth) was sent against him, the two soon joined forces. Gainas and Tribigild then occupied Constantinople, and demanded Eutropius' removal from power in 400. This they achieved, but the people of the city resented the barbarian force in their midst and expelled it, in the process burning alive a huge number of Goths in a church. In the years that followed, the eastern court became much warier of turning to barbarian generals and troops to fight its battles. In some ways it benefited from circumstances, because in fact it was to be another twenty years before another serious threat arose on the Danube. The Persians too—whose King of Kings Yezdegerd I was unusually friendly to Rome—were not to attack the eastern frontier until 421. However, far from seizing this relative quiet to gain control of political affairs, Arcadius remained a weak figure down to his death in May 408.

Arcadius' eastern court to some extent succeeded in avoiding defeat by shifting its barbarian problems westward. This appears to have been the case in 401 and 402, when Visigoths led by Alaric twice marched into Italy; both times they were driven back by Stilicho, but only at a heavy cost to the western army. During the 402 invasion, Honorius had even felt compelled to withdraw his court from Milan to the city of Ravenna, on Italy's Adriatic coast. Because Ravenna is surrounded by an almost impenetrable swamp, the transfer of the court there was designed to insulate the emperor from threats, but it also had the effect of isolating an already disengaged ruler from action. Once established in Ravenna, the court remained sequestered there for the remainder of the western Empire's history.

The years 405 and 406 saw an unprecedented wave of incursions into the empire. The reasons for them are not entirely clear, but may be related to the displacement of more settled barbarian groups from beyond the frontiers by the arrival of new groups of invaders, Huns especially. Late in 405 a large multiethnic barbarian coalition under the Ostrogoth Radagaisus crossed the Alps from Pannonia and invaded Italy. Though they succeeded in overcoming Roman resistance initially, to ease provisioning they soon split into groups; the largest of these was cornered in central Italy at Faesulae (modern Fiesole) and massacred in 406. Another multiethnic invasion of Vandals, Alans, and Suebi crossed the lower Rhine on New Year's Eve 405—or some argue 406—sacked Trier and other cities, and proceeded into southwestern Gaul. Also in 406, groups of Alamanni and Burgundians invaded across the upper Rhine. As had often happened before when western regions were faced with crisis, a local leader was proclaimed Augustus in response. In this instance the usurper was a general named Constantine (sometimes called "III"), who came out of Britain but moved into Gaul, and promptly began to challenge Honorius for the western throne. By late 406, then, all of Britain and most of Gaul were outside of Honorius' control.

Meanwhile, closer to Italy, Alaric's Visigoths also began to agitate again. Stilicho had asked them to march into Epirus, where he promised to deploy them to help him take back this region from the eastern court. Delayed by the collapse of the western frontier, however, he failed to join the Visigoths in Epirus, and their anger over this slight was placated only when the senate paid them an indemnity of 4,000 lbs of gold. In the face of such chaos, resentments grew, as did suspicions that Stilicho was favoring the Goths and behaving disloyally to the empire. In mid-408, in a scene of high court intrigue tinged with more than a little ethnic tension, Stilicho was arrested and executed by Honorius. This was one of the few decisive acts of Honorius' career. Many of Stilicho's barbarian followers resident in Italy were then set upon and massacred, together with their families. Those followers that remained—as many as 30,000—were instantly driven into the hands of Alaric, whose Visigoths they now joined as allies.

With this swollen force, Alaric grew bolder. In autumn 408 he marched on Rome and besieged it, but relaxed the siege after an agreement was reached with Honorius, still isolated in Ravenna, to pay another massive ransom of 5,000 lbs of gold, 30,000 lbs of silver, and sundry luxury goods. When Honorius began holding back on payments, a second siege of Rome ensued in late 409 that ended with Alaric creating a usurper of his own in Rome named Priscus Attalus. Alaric's plan simply to take control of the western throne faltered, however, when Africa's governor stopped sending grain supplies to Rome. Consequently, in the summer of 410, Alaric deposed Attalus and then marched on Rome again, this third time with no intention of settling for any compromise. On August 24, 410, the Visigoths entered the city—some sources claim they were let in by the starving population—and proceeded to loot for three days. During the rampage, Honorius' sister, Galla Placidia, was captured. Although damage was limited and most lives were spared, the symbolic impact of this first "sack of Rome" was massive. Citizens across the empire were made aware of the devastating event. Jerome, living far away in Palestine, lamented, "the Roman empire was decapitated, and the whole world perished in one city" (*Comm. in Ezech. Praef.*).

THE FALL OF THE WESTERN EMPIRE (410–476)

After leaving Rome, the Visigoths marched south, hoping to sail on to Sicily and Africa, but storms wrecked their ships. Late in 410 Alaric died. The Goths paused long enough to offer their great leader an elaborate funeral in which they diverted the river Busento, placed Alaric's body in the riverbed, then flooded it over again to seal him in a watery grave—along with the captives who had dug it. The Goths were then compelled to return north, now under the leadership of Alaric's brother-in-law, Athaulf. By 412 they crossed the Alps into the chaos that was Gaul in this period. Meantime the usurper Constantine (III) had allowed the coalition of Vandals, Suebi, and Alans who had entered the empire in 406 to gain control of Gallaecia and Lusitania (northern Spain and Portugal). Constantine himself was eliminated by Honorius' general Constantius in 411, which led to further usurpation attempts. After suppressing these, Constantius turned his attention to the

---

SOURCE 14.1: The Gothic King Athaulf's Shifting Attitude Toward Rome

Paulus Orosius (c. 375–418) was from Gallaecia in Spain, but eventually moved to Africa and then Palestine, where he came to know St. Jerome. Around 417 he composed a History against the Pagans, *in which he argued that the disasters Rome was experiencing in his day paled in comparison to those it had experienced prior to the appearance of Christianity. In this passage (7.43), he discusses a conversation with a confidant of the Gothic king Athaulf. Although the religious program explicit in Orosius' work invites skepticism about his credibility, nevertheless his history remains useful. This passage is striking for its claims to eyewitness testimony, and for the influence it attributes to the captive princess Galla Placidia, whom Athaulf married in Narbo on January 1, 414. It epitomizes the changes afoot in power relations and the adjustments being made in expectations on both sides of the Roman–barbarian divide.*

Athaulf ruled over the Gothic people as king at that time. In the period after the capture of Rome and the death of Alaric, as I said, he married Placidia the captive sister of the emperor, and succeeded Alaric as ruler. As rumor had it and even as his own final end proved, he was a quite zealous champion of peace, and preferred to fight faithfully for the emperor Honorius and use the forces of the Goths to defend the Roman state. For I myself even heard a certain man from the province of Narbonensis [southern Gaul], who had done honorable service under Theodosius and was religious as well as prudent and serious, report to the blessed priest Jerome in the town of Bethlehem that he was quite close friends with Athaulf at Narbo and that he often heard, under oath to God, what Athaulf used to say when he was still strong in mind, body, and intellect: At first he longed ardently to wipe out the Roman name, and to make all Roman territory into an empire of the Goths, as he would call it; he wanted what used to be "Romania" to become "Gothia," to put it in layman's terms; he wanted Athaulf himself to become what Caesar Augustus used to be. But when he discovered through long experience that the Goths were in no way able to obey laws because of their unrestrained barbarity, and that a state ought not to be deprived of laws (without which a state is simply not a state), he decided that at least he should seek glory for himself by restoring the Roman name to its original condition and by augmenting it using the forces of the Goths, and that he should be considered the originator of Rome's restoration among posterity, since he was not able to be its transformer. For this reason, he strove to avoid war and to pursue peace, being especially softened by the persuasion and advice of his wife Placidia, a woman of incredibly sharp intellect and admirable religion. But while he was adamant about seeking and offering this peace, he was killed at Barcino in Spain (modern Barcelona) by the treachery of his own people, it is reported.

Visigoths, and by 415 trapped them at the southern tip of Spain. From here they wished once more to reach Africa, but again their hopes were dashed by the destruction of a fleet. In desperation, they negotiated with Honorius. As a result, in exchange for supplies and a treaty, they agreed to fight on the emperor's behalf, and even to return the princess Galla Placidia, whom they had held captive since 410. Going on campaign almost immediately, they all but annihilated the Alans, as well as one of the Vandal groups in Spain. Afterwards, in small part as a reward but more because there was no better solution for their relocation, these Goths were granted the right to settle the territory of Aquitania in southwestern Gaul in 418. Because the information about this arrangement is poor, there has been considerable debate over its precise nature. In the opinion of some scholars at least, the Romans actually agreed to divide up existing estates with the Visigoths and to permit them the right to rule in this territory even though it was well within the empire's borders—a new and dangerous step.

The same process of settlement was occurring elsewhere around the same time, but with less overt sanction from the Roman state. Information about other barbarian groups at this period is even spottier, so that we can only guess at the precise nature of the ongoing changes; even so, a broad summary is possible. Britain was abandoned already in 410 when, in the midst of the chaos surrounding the sack of Rome, Honorius told its leaders in a letter that they would have to look after their own defenses. At some point in the course of the fifth century, Britain's eastern shores began to be settled by the Germanic Saxons from what is today Denmark, who had already been raiding there for over a century. Meanwhile Spain became a battleground between the Vandals, Suebi, and Alans who had entered the region in 407, and a variety of Roman generals and usurpers, at great cost to the local Roman population. Southeastern Gaul (Savoy) was overrun by the Burgundians, who were then settled there on terms similar to those received by the Visigoths in the early fifth century; the Alamanni invaded further to the north (Alsace). At the same time northeastern Gaul, over which the Romans had always had weak control, was beginning to fall under the dominion of the Franks and Saxons. In northwestern Gaul the Roman state also clashed regularly with the Bagaudae (see Chapter Twelve). Our sources brand this shadowy group as bandits, but it seems more likely that they were local residents dissatisfied with Roman rule.

Most costly of all was the loss of North Africa. Since the reign of Theodosius it had been subject to usurper generals, and eventually it fell prey to some of the Vandals previously settled in Spain. Under their masterful king Gaiseric, they crossed the Straits of Gibraltar in 429 and quickly overran the territories of Mauretania and Numidia (modern Morocco and Algeria). The most famous victim of their attacks was St. Augustine, bishop of Hippo (modern Annaba, Algeria), who died during the siege of his city in 430. Having little choice in the matter, Valentinian III (see below) at Ravenna acknowledged the Vandal claim to western Africa in hopes of retaining the more prosperous province of Africa

Proconsularis and its capital Carthage. But this hope soon vanished when Gaiseric took Carthage in 439, and forced both eastern and western emperors to sanction his actions. Gaiseric's power continued to grow as he came to treat the western Mediterranean as a giant hunting ground for his plundering naval forces. These essentially ruled the western seas in this period, giving rise to the modern term "vandalism." In 455 Gaiseric was even able to land a force in Italy and sack Rome a second time, carrying off countless treasures, including, it is said, the menorah taken from the temple in Jerusalem by the emperor Titus (see Chapter Ten). Already the Vandals had weakened the city immeasurably, now that their control of Africa had deprived it of its largest source of grain. The city's population declined dramatically; by the early sixth century it cannot have been more than about 50,000, one twentieth of its size during the early empire.

Among the prizes Gaiseric took from Rome in 455 were the empress Licinia Eudoxia and her daughter Eudocia; the latter he married to his son Huneric. Licinia Eudoxia was the wife, and Eudocia the daughter, of the emperor Valentinian III, who had succeeded to the western throne in 425. This, then, marks the appropriate point to turn to a discussion of the imperial court in the West, stepping back for that purpose to the death of Honorius in August 423.

Valentinian III was the son of Honorius' sister Galla Placidia, famous for her long captivity among the Visigoths. When Honorius died, Valentinian III and his mother were living in Constantinople rather than the West. In their absence, a non-dynastic successor named John attempted to claim the throne in Ravenna, but the eastern emperor Theodosius II (see below) determined to support Valentinian instead. Theodosius sent a huge force from Constantinople to Italy, which defeated John, and imposed the young Valentinian. This was the first in a long series of examples of the eastern court's new primacy over the West; from now onward, the West looked to Constantinople for political support rather than vice versa.

At the time of his accession, Valentinian III was only six years old, making him the next in the series of child emperors of the Theodosian dynasty. Like his predecessors, he also turned out to be a weak ruler who was easily manipulated. The principal power behind his throne was his Master of the Soldiers, Aetius. Relying above all on Hunnic auxiliaries, Aetius won a series of victories over the Franks, the Visigoths, the Burgundians, the Bagaudae, and the usurper Boniface, who controlled Africa immediately prior to the Vandal invasion. Aetius even planned a joint strike together with the eastern navy against the Vandals for 441, but it had to be abandoned when eastern troops were withdrawn to face the Huns under Attila; he now threatened the Roman East from just across the Danube.

Indeed, Aetius' most glorious moment came in 451 when he defeated Attila at the battle of the Catalaunian Plains (modern Champagne, France). After expelling the Gothic leadership from what is today Romania in the 370s, the Huns had gained control of this eastern territory and gradually built a surprisingly centralized and powerful kingdom there. Behind their success lay Attila, who defeated eastern imperial armies again and again. In 450, he decided to march west. Skirting the northern edge of the Danube, he crossed the Rhine near Mogontiacum (modern Mainz), and attempted to gain support from the barbarian kingdoms of Gaul and even to control them. In the event, Aetius was able to convince them (Visigoths, Franks, Saxons, Burgundians, and others) that Rome better served their interests than the Huns. In this way he assembled a coalition capable of halting Attila's advance. Although the Huns moved south against Italy the following summer, Attila was again turned back—according to legend, by the diplomacy of Pope Leo I, who traveled to northern Italy to plead in person for mercy. More probably Attila had learned that the eastern emperor Maurice was taking advantage of his absence to attack the Hunnic homelands. Attila raced his weakened army back north of the Danube, but died in 453, having succumbed to a brain hemorrhage during sex.

In spite of his skill as a general and diplomat, or perhaps because of it, Aetius did not escape resentment from his emperor. In September 454 Valentinian III chose to assassinate him, but within six months was himself murdered by Aetius' former bodyguards. The succession dispute that ensued led to the final collapse of Roman imperial control in the west. In the absence of a strong dynastic claimant, the contest for the throne fell to an extensive list of contenders with support from a variety of interested groups: the eastern imperial court, the Roman senate, the Council of Gaul (a group of Romano-Gallic aristocrats who began meeting in southern Gaul after 418), the armies of Italy and Dalmatia, and even various barbarian groups (especially the Visigoths, Burgundians, and Vandals) all vied to influence the choice of successors. Predictably enough, none lasted long. In the last twenty-one years of the western empire, nine rulers claimed the throne, only three of whom lasted into a third year. Once again the relative weakness of their positions made them reliant on barbarian generals, in particular Ricimer, of mixed Suebic and Visigothic background, and Gundobad, a Burgundian.

Ultimately, however, the western throne was becoming an irrelevancy, for it no longer bestowed much more than titular power. As the West had begun to shed territories to barbarian challengers and to local self-autonomy in the early fifth century, it had simultaneously lost tax revenue, since it no longer controlled the lands and peoples that once filled its coffers. In consequence it was less and less capable of paying for armies and indeed of fielding them, because the loss of territories also diminished the size of its recruiting pool. This reduction in turn led to an ever-growing reliance on barbarian military manpower, which simultaneously strengthened Rome's barbarian contenders and weakened Rome's own capacity for self-defense. This vicious cycle ground down the state to the point that, by the time of Valentinian III's death in 455, the western empire was little more than a rump of what it had been just half a century earlier. In effect it controlled just Italy and a slice of southeastern Gaul. Thus, when a boy emperor was imposed once again on the rickety western throne in October 475, it took less than a year to topple ruler and throne together. His name was Romulus Augustus, but because of his youth he was referred to in the diminutive as Augustulus. Rome's last emperor thus bore the name of its first king *and* first emperor. When he refused to reward his barbarian auxiliaries, he was deposed and exiled by a general of mixed barbarian race, Odoacer, in September 476. Rather than set up another puppet, Odoacer had the senate of Rome write to the eastern emperor Zeno to report, "they had no need of a separate empire, but a single common emperor would be sufficient for both territories" (Malchus fr. 14). The statement was of course filled with irony, for Odoacer had no real intention of submitting to eastern authority. The Roman Empire had ceased to exist in the West.

THE GROWTH OF A BYZANTINE EMPIRE IN THE EAST (408–491)

Turning now to the eastern court after the death of Arcadius in 408, the first point to note is that, like his father before him, he had the good fortune of a son to succeed him, and the bad fortune that this son, Theodosius II, was only a child of seven at the time. Like Arcadius himself, Theodosius II was forever subject to the powerful influence of courtiers. Indeed, in his instance this weakness was compounded by his indifference to politics and his passion for matters intellectual and religious. His court witnessed the blossoming of a religious and literary culture that would come to characterize Byzantine rule in the centuries to come. Theodosius II never participated in military campaigns, and is notorious instead for having focused on personal piety. This devotion was encouraged by his older sister Pulcheria, who played an important role in the conduct of state affairs. Following a trend common for pious women of the age, she had dedicated herself to virginity and so helped to foster a court atmosphere which some contemporaries likened to that of a monastery. It does not follow, however, that Theodosius II was entirely impractical. He did organize the first systematic effort to codify Roman imperial law ever yet undertaken, an effort which resulted in the appearance of the monumental *Theodosian Code* in 438. He also reorganized the grain supply for Constantinople, where the population had grown. In addition, he equipped the expanded city with a new set of walls, which formed a nearly impregnable bulwark.

Fortunately for Theodosius II, relations with Persia were relatively stable throughout the forty-two years of his reign. Despite small wars in 421–422 and again in 440, the eastern frontier was to remain largely at peace until 502. The same atmosphere did not prevail on the Danube, however. Here, as we have seen, during the late fourth century the Huns had come to unite the disparate peoples in what is today Romania, and from the 420s onward they had begun to pose a serious threat to the empire. Under their king Attila, who came to power in 434, this threat became acute as they made a series of attacks on the Balkans that were calculated to win concessions from the eastern court in the form of annual tribute as high as 2,100 lbs of gold. Theodosius II and his general Aspar gladly paid this tribute rather than face the uncertainty of battle. To be sure, the eastern empire was

Figure 14.2 *Theodosian Walls of Constantinople. By the early fifth century Constantinople had more than outgrown the walls built for it by Constantine. To protect its population (which grew to half a million by the sixth century), Theodosius II ordered a new set of walls to be built between 408 and 413. These stretched almost four miles (6.4 km) from north to south along the western edge of the peninsula on which the city was built, and consisted of a taller inner wall (40 ft/12.1 m high and 16 ft/4.8 m thick—seen in the background) with 96 towers separated from a shorter outer wall (28 ft/8.5 m high and 7 ft/2.1 m thick) by a wide terrace. In front of the lower wall a moat offered the first line of defense. On all sides but the west, the city was surrounded by water, so it was diffi-cult to attack in an era when amphibious military landings were nearly impossible. This remarkable bulwark, some of which still survives, prevented the city from being overcome by siege down to 1453, when the introduction of gunpowder allowed the Ottomans to take it.*

not entirely hamstrung on the military front. But it focused its energies on the west-ern empire instead, intervening four times during Theodosius II's reign: in 410 (against Alaric), in 424–425 (to impose Valentinian III), in 431 (against the newly arrived Vandals), and in 441 (during an abortive expedition against the Vandals).

Chief among Theodosius II's concerns was the orthodoxy of his subjects. He was thus easily convinced of the need to call the third ecumenical council in 431, when disputes arose between Nestorius, the bishop of Constantinople, and his rival Cyril, bishop of Alexandria, over the nature of Christ's humanity and, by extension, the proper designation for the Virgin Mary: was she Theotokos (the "God Bearer"), as Cyril contended, or merely Christotokos (the "Messiah Bearer"), as Nestorius asserted? Today, such disputes seem arcane and often futile, but they constituted the intellectual and cultural spaces within which the ecclesiastical heavyweights of late antiquity wrestled. Theodosius II convened the council at Ephesus, where

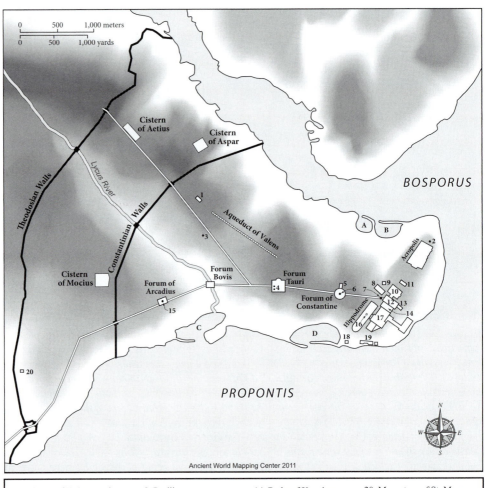

Map 14.2 *Constantinople in Late Antiquity*

1. Church of Holy Apostles
2. Column of Tyche
3. Column of Marcian
4. Arch of Theodosius
5. Curia
6. Column of Constantine
7. Milion

8. Basilica
9. Church of St. Maria in
   Chalcoprateis
10. Church of St. Sophia
11. Church of St. Eirene
12. Augusteion
13. Curia (Magnaura)

14. Baths of Xeuxippus
15. Column of Arcadius
16. Obelisk of Theodosius
17. Great Palace
18. Church of Sts. Sergius
    and Bacchus
19. Palace of Justinian

20. Monastery of St. Menas

A. Neorion Harbor
B. Phosphorion Harbor
C. Harbor of Theodosius
D. Harbor of Julian

Nestorius was defeated and exiled. But the issue boiled over again later in the reign, leading to a second council at Ephesus in 449. Here the level of pious bullying was so intense that this meeting has won the nickname "Robber Council." Though the rival parties agitated for yet another council, Theodosius II resisted down to his death, which occurred in July 450, after he fell from his horse.

Theodosius' successor was a retired general named Marcian, who no doubt owed his elevation to the powerful general Aspar. Marcian promptly married the empress Pulcheria, by now fifty-one years old and still a committed virgin; the arrangement supplied an air of dynastic legitimacy to an otherwise undistinguished candidate. Despite his low birth, however, Marcian played his role as emperor well. He benefitted from Attila's choice to turn his attacks westward, and from Attila's death in 453. It was at once followed by infighting among Attila's sons and then the complete collapse of the Hunnic empire. Marcian added to the Huns' difficulties by withholding any further payments of tribute to them. He also addressed the still-gaping rifts in the church by organizing the fourth ecumenical council at Chalcedon (modern Kadiköy, Turkey) in 451. It restored the Constantinopolitan bishopric to prominence, and issued a new formula describing Christ's nature as consisting of two parts, divine and human, indistinguishably commingled. Although the western church promptly rallied to this new formula—in whose composition Pope Leo had played a major role—it met a chilly reception in Syria and Egypt. Rather than follow the imperial church, these regions went their own way, forming what came to be called a Monophysite ("one nature") theology that endures in the Christian churches of Egypt and Syria down to the present. This important split in church union constituted a major stumbling block to imperial unity for the remaining years of Byzantine control of the Near East down to the seventh century.

Marcian died in 457 with no heir. Yet another undistinguished officer, Leo, was chosen to replace him. Leo maintained both the findings of the council of Chalcedon and the eastern interest in managing affairs in the West. He even saw to the imposition of the general Anthemius on the western throne in 467, and coordinated with him a massive expedition against the Vandals the following year. To both men's dismay, it turned into a disaster. The Vandals, using fire-ships, succeeded in destroying the Roman fleet before it ever reached the coast of Africa. The loss cost 64,000 lbs of gold, probably more than a year's revenue for the entire eastern empire, and ultimately it cost Anthemius his throne as well. This level of outlay underlines the extent to which Constantinople continued to contemplate rebuilding the tattered Roman empire.

Leo's reign witnessed the rise of a new group of Goths in the Balkans. In the wake of eighty years of ongoing devastation, the provinces of Thrace and Pannonia along the Danube had been left open to barbarian settlement by two separate groups of Ostrogoths. The powerful general Aspar had used the Thracian Ostrogoths as *foederati*—independent peoples bound by treaty (*foedus*) to serve in Roman armies in exchange for payments. Wishing to free himself of Aspar's heavy hand, Leo found an alternative pool of military support in the

Figure 14.3 *The* Codex Argenteus *(Silver Codex), now housed in the library of the University of Uppsala, Sweden, has been radio-carbon dated to the sixth century. It contains a translation of the four Gospels into the Gothic language using Gothic script, an alphabet based closely on Greek characters. It was written in silver lettering on fine vellum (calfskin) that was dyed purple, a color associated with royalty. Given the book's lavish production techniques, its dating, and its language, it is likely to have been produced for the court of Theodoric the Ostrogoth in Ravenna. Gothic script was invented in the fourth century by the bishop Ulfilas ("Little Wolf"), a child of Christian Greeks who were taken to Gothic territory as captives in the third century. Ulfilas created the script in order to translate the Bible into Gothic. His translation played a major role in helping convert the Goths to Christianity, and thus in spreading this aspect of the Roman legacy to Rome's successors. The page seen here, the first one extant from the manuscript, features* Matthew 5:15-48.

Isaurians. They were a people living in the Taurus highlands of southern Anatolia, well within the empire's geographical boundaries. Because of the mountainous inaccessibility of their homeland, however, they had long been able to resist Roman control. Like so many peoples of the period, they could be classed neither as fully Roman nor entirely independent. Leo tapped the Isaurians as a counterweight against the Thracian Ostrogoths, who rebelled in 471 after he finally eliminated their long-time patron Aspar. Leo even went so far as to marry his daughter Ariadne to the Isaurian general Zeno.

Upon his death in 474, Leo was succeeded by the child of this marriage, his grandson Leo II, who died after only ten months in office. But Leo II had appointed his father Zeno as co-Augustus, thus allowing Zeno to continue in power as sole emperor down to 491. Because of his Isaurian background, Zeno was often treated as an outsider in Constantinople, and faced no less than three usurpation attempts. The third of them, instigated in 484 by another Isaurian leader named Illus, was the most significant. Zeno was forced to turn to the Pannonian Goths and their leader Theodoric to crush this uprising by his fellow countryman. Theodoric proved to be a formidable military and political leader, uniting all the Ostrogoths under his authority, and eventually marching them west at Zeno's request to retake Italy from Odoacer. After achieving this in 489, Theodoric ruled on as "king of the Romans," in principle holding Italy for Zeno but in practice establishing an independent Ostrogothic state. The Ostrogoths were to maintain control here with Constantinople's consent until the 540s, when the emperor Justinian began a long and bloody war that eventually led to Italy's brief return to "Roman" control.

In a perilous world, Rome's eastern empire had thus developed a formula for survival and prosperity that would serve it well in the centuries to come. Rather than exterminate the peoples who challenged it for power, it put them to work fighting each other or, whenever possible, sent them west. This game was always a dangerous one, but the Byzantines raised diplomacy to a finely tuned art that achieved remarkable results. In no small part their diplomatic skill explains the success of a state which flourished as the largest empire of Christendom through the Middle Ages and into the early modern period.

A CHRISTIAN CULTURE

From the mid-first century, Christian communities had shown a remarkable ability to reproduce themselves with rapidity and relative uniformity. Like an embryonic organism, the church began as a tiny series of cells which by division and subdivision continuously developed in form and function to suit changing geographical or temporal circumstances, but always retained the same basic genetic code. It was able to achieve its surprising continuity and uniformity in large part because it was a religion of the book. While disputes about the canon of Christian texts arose almost immediately, the rough outlines of a Christian Bible were becoming clear by the mid-second century, and its final form was definitively laid out by the ecclesiastical establishment of the mid-fourth. Like its scriptures, Christianity's basic organizational modules were also relatively uniform, consisting of a bishop, a clergy, a *laos* ("congregation" or "people" in Greek, our word "laity"), and a building in which to worship. These were all, of course, subject to local variation, but by the sixth century the basic outlines could be found in communities from as far east as Sogdia in central Asia to as far west as Ireland. Schoolchildren from across this vast expanse studied the same scriptures, clergy preached from the same body of tenets, and all Christians saw themselves as subject to one law and religion. In some regards, then, the most uniform cultural artifact bequeathed to posterity by the Roman empire, and the one that had the greatest worldwide impact, was Christianity.

All Christians believed first and foremost in a message of sin and salvation. All saw themselves as subject to the snares of evil manifested in sins provoked by the devil and his demons, but all also assumed that belief in the power of God as manifested in Christ could permit any Christian to overcome these challenges and win access to eternal life. This was a radically egalitarian message, for none who had been baptized had any inherently stronger claim to divine access than any other. Yet it was also always clear that some Christians more obviously counted as the saved than others. Chief among them were of course the martyrs. After the conversion of the empire and the end of persecutions, however, the surest way to battle sin and guarantee salvation was through *askesis* (literally "practice" in Greek). This involved spiritual and physical training of the body—much like the work of an athlete—in order to overcome sinfulness. Asceticism had long been a part of Mediterranean religious traditions, particularly in pagan Neoplatonic schools, but Christian asceticism differed both in the scale of the renunciation it demanded and in the breadth of the audience it reached. Indeed, it was in no small part because Christians argued that all believers, rather than just a select cadre of holy men and women, had access to salvation that asceticism became so significant as a means to mark off the holiest Christians. The late fourth and early fifth centuries represented the revolutionary turning point during which new modes of worship and new ways of living involving radical self-denial and mortification went from seeming exotic to being normal.

This golden age of late antiquity witnessed what one prominent scholar has termed the "rise of the Holy Man." The quintessential representative of this phe-nomenon is also one of its earliest: St. Antony of Egypt (*c.* 250–356). He had grown up in a moderately wealthy farming family in the Egyptian Fayyum. At about twenty years of age he was so moved by the scriptural passage exhorting believers to "sell all you have, give it to the poor, and follow me" (*Matthew* 19:21) that he liquidated his estates and moved out to the eastern desert. Egypt's geog-raphy is marked by a thin ribbon of cultivable land along the Nile River, on either side of which is a nearly endless expanse of desert. Over the course of the remain-der of his life, Antony gradually moved deeper and deeper into this waste, living on almost no food, denying himself marriage, sexuality, and family, and doing constant battle with the demons he believed surrounded him. Despite his renun-ciation of the world, however, Antony was anything but isolated, for he was reg-ularly visited by those seeking healing or advice, and he even attracted the atten-tion of the emperor Constantius and the Alexandrian bishop Athanasius.

Upon this holy man's death, Athanasius composed a *Life of Antony* that became an instant "bestseller" across the Roman empire. Though written in Greek, it was quickly translated into Latin, and circulated as far away as Gaul by the early 370s. By then, the story of this social radical was winning converts to a new way of life across the entire spectrum of Christian believers, from the poorest to the richest. This new "philosophy," as they termed their lifestyle, demanded no elaborate education and no comfortable standard of living, but was open to any who could endure self-denial in excruciating doses. Moreover, because of the desert stamp of Antony's peculiarly Egyptian asceticism, Christian ascetic practice also took on a fascination with the desert, not just as a symbol of solitude but also as the nor-mative setting for spiritual action. The very word "hermit," coined in this period to describe solitary monks, derives from the Greek word for desert. Even in cli-mates and landscapes that were anything but desert, *anachoresis* (withdrawal) into the wilderness came to mark off Christian asceticism and to characterize its lan-guage. We thus find western ascetics in the snowy Alpine mountains around Geneva who conceive of their refuges as "deserts."

Antony was by no means the first or only holy man of late antiquity. Indeed, by the time of his death a veritable wave of anchoretic asceticism had swept across the eastern empire, not just in Egypt but also in Syria, where one could witness an even stauncher renunciation of the world and more intensive mortification of the flesh. Nor was Antony's lifestyle as a solitary hermit the only acceptable approach to ascetic living. His contemporary Pachomius (c. 292–347) pioneered a form which included hierarchy (with a leader and a prescribed rule) and community (with individuals living in a walled complex of rooms termed "cells"). This "cenobitic" style—from the Greek *koinos bios* (common life)—was also initiated in Egypt (in the Thebaid), but soon spread beyond it. Termed *monachoi* (solitary ones), from which our word monk derives, these spiritual separatists soon began to appear in Palestine, Cappadocia, and Constantinople.

Athanasius' *Life of Antony* was revolutionary not just because of the lifestyle it championed, but also because it represented a new genre of literature, called hagiography—that is, the writing of the lives of saints. The *Life of Antony* was soon followed by a spate of such biographies, which in their turn were promptly translated into the range of languages common in late antiquity—Greek, Latin, Syriac, Coptic—and disseminated throughout the Mediterranean. Such literature brought a wave of travelers to Egypt and Syria to visit the holy men and spread word of their accomplishments. Prominent among these publicists were figures like Jerome, a man from Dalmatia educated in Rome, who visited Syria and then returned to Rome, preaching the virtues of virginity and fasting to aristocrats there. Later he moved to the Holy Land, where he founded a monastery of his own. So too John Cassian, a Greek from the territory of Scythia Minor (the modern Dobrudja, in Romania), carried his experiences of Egyptian monasticism to Massilia in southern Gaul around 415. As monasticism spread, increasingly elaborate codes were developed and collated, culminating in the sixth-century *Rule of St. Benedict*, which mandated firm governing hierarchies, stern rules of behavior, a regimen of work and prayer, and a strict division of the day according to liturgical "offices" involving set prayers and the singing of psalms. Benedict's rule became the foundation for an institution which would dominate many aspects of religious practice throughout Christendom in the Middle Ages.

Monasticism was only one major development in Christian culture at this time. Late antiquity also saw the rise of what is now called the cult of the saints. Having begun as care for the corpses of those who had been martyred in the persecutions, this practice grew into a new mode of worship focused on the bodies of those whose life or death marked them off as holy. Saints' bones or other body parts were lovingly preserved and venerated in elaborate purpose-built churches. Such "relics" came to be treated as talismans imbued with religious power that offered access to God through the "patron" saint from whose body they derived. Nor were bodies the only source of relics; rather, any object touched by holiness could offer access to God—a fragment of the True Cross, for example (Source 14.2), or a piece of clothing. Yet another development in Christian religion during this period was pilgrimage to the Holy Land. From Constantine's reign onward, it came to be the premier travel destination for Christians, who regarded it as a site of particular spiritual power. At the same time late antiquity also saw the emergence of new attitudes toward the poor and needy. Roman culture had long advocated the feeding and entertainment of the

a

b

masses by wealthy members of the elite at public festivals. Christianity, by contrast, removed the civic focus of such benefactions and extended the obligation to give freely much lower down the social ladder. It was now incumbent upon all Christians, not just local notables, to give alms as part of their pursuit of salvation.

Many of these developments represent significant departures from earlier Roman practice. Even so, despite its introduction of revolutionary new cultural ideals and practices, in most ways Christianity was a strong force for the preservation of Roman traditions. Indeed, this contradiction is rooted in the Christian gospels, which are by turns both radical and conservative. As a mass movement, Christianity could play to either strain, so that even as Christian radicals introduced an unheard-of new fascination with worldly renunciation, other Christian leaders worked hard to amass power and wealth along more traditional lines. Basil (died 379) of Caesarea (modern Kayseri, Turkey), who played a crucial role in the development of eastern monasticism (see below), was himself a rather traditional bishop from a wealthy background, who worked hard to promote the political and economic power of his congregation. Similar stories are even more common in the West, where the political chaos of the barbarian invasions made the church into something of a refuge for *Romanitas* ("Romanness"). Fifth-century Gaul saw the development of a virtual ecclesiastical aristocracy, in which the office of bishop was passed literally from father to son. Such bishops had at their disposal stores of wealth, landed estates, impressive complexes of buildings, and above all power over cities with walls—bastions for the preservation of life and the continuation of prosperity. These same bishops also had access to education and to Latin texts, which they fastidiously preserved as part of their patrimony from the Roman past. In their hands, and the hands of a growing monastic establishment, Roman culture survived the economic and military turmoil of the barbarian invasions and the early Middle Ages.

A similar story could be told with slavery. Since the nineteenth century some scholars have argued that Christianity had a mitigating effect on this characteristically Greco-Roman institution, which receded in importance in certain parts of the empire in late antiquity. Other researchers, indeed the majority, have denied the influence of Christianity. They have attributed the decline of slavery to a reduction

---

Facing page

Figure **14.4a,b** *Simeon the Stylite. Simeon Stylites spent almost 40 years (until 459) living in the open air on top of a series of pillars (in Greek,* styloi*) at Telneshe in Syria. The tallest of these reached over 40 ft/12 m into the air. This silver plate [a] shows him on a pillar being tempted by a demonic snake. Simeon became an extremely influential holy man, devoted not only to private prayer and fasting but also to a very public role by resolving disputes, offering cures, and advising pilgrims and even emperors. By the end of the fifth century his style of asceticism was imitated by others across the East. Upon his death, the emperor Zeno constructed an elaborate complex which consisted of four basilicas placed back to back in the shape of a cross around his last pillar (which rested atop the base just visible through the doorway in [b]). The site, which also had a massive monastery and guest houses for pilgrims, stands in ruins in northern Syria, where it is referred to in Arabic as Qal'at Sim'an ("the Mansion of Simeon").*

SOURCE 14.2: Holy Land Pilgrimage and the Cult of Relics

The fashion for traveling to the Holy Land grew wildly in late antiquity following Constantine's opening of new churches there, in particular the church of the Holy Sepulcher, reputed to occupy the site of Christ's crucifixion and burial (Map 14.3b). By the mid-fourth century there were people who believed that they had found the True Cross on which Christ was crucified—as attested in sermons by bishop Cyril of Jerusalem, and in the Latin inscription below which marked the dedication of a church by a veteran officer in a coastal city of Mauretania in North Africa in 359. This man had commanded a crack unit with a characteristically late Roman name, the "Junior Armbearing Cavalrymen."

Having brought and placed a piece of the holy wood of the cross of Christ our Savior here, Flavius Nuvel, former commander of the *Equites Armigeri Iuniores*, son of Saturninus *vir perfectissimus* [an official title granted to high-ranking equestrians], a former Count, and of Colecia, a very honorable woman, grandson of Elurus Laconicus, dedicated this basilica, which he had promised in a vow and offered together with his wife Nonnica at his own expense. (Ernst Diehl [ed.], *Inscriptiones Latinae Christianae Veteres* [Berlin: Weidmann, 1925-1967], 1822)

There is also abundant evidence of travel from west to east to visit the Holy Land and other regions associated with Biblical history or the rise of monasticism. One of the earliest and most extensive accounts of such journeys was written by a woman—probably named Egeria (the heading of her work does not survive)—who traveled from the Rhone valley in Gaul to Palestine, Syria, Egypt, and the Sinai peninsula in the 380s. This passage (3.1–8), from the beginning of her extant travelogue, describes her arrival at Mt. Sinai (where Moses received the Ten Commandments) and the hospitality she experienced from the monks there. Not only is this early evidence for a monastic community that endures to this day at Sinai, but it is also precious testimony from a woman, who was reporting her findings back to a group of fellow female ascetics in Gaul.

We reached the mountain late on the Sabbath, and came upon some hermit-cells where the monks who live there received us quite warmly, offering us great hospitality. There is also a church with a priest. We stayed that night there, and then early on the Lord's Day we began to climb the individual mountains with the priest and monks who live there. Those mountains are extremely difficult to climb, since you do not go up bit by bit in a circuit or, as we say, in a spiral, but you go straight up as if it were a wall, and then you must go straight down each of the mountains until you come to the base of the one in the middle which is actually called Sinai. [On reaching the summit of Mt. Sinai, she is greeted by an ascetic priest who manages the small church there.] After we had read everything from the book of Moses there, and made an offering in proper order, and shared in communion, we went out from the church..... Then I began to ask them to show us the various places. And the holy men agreed immediately, for they showed us the cave where holy Moses was when he climbed the mountain of God the second time in order to receive the tablets again after he had broken the first ones because of his sinful people, and the rest of the places. And I want you to know, honorable ladies and sisters, that from the place where we stood on the circuit of the walls of the church and from the summit of that same central mountain, these mountains which we had barely been able to climb seemed to us like tiny hills next to that middle one where we stood, even though they were so large that I had thought at one point that I had never seen taller ones, except that the central one surpassed the others by so much. But from there we seemed to see beneath us Egypt, and Palestine, and the Red Sea, and the south-eastern Mediterranean which extends up to Alexandria, as well as the vast territories of the Saracens, so that I could scarcely believe it. And those holy men showed us all the details.

in the slave supply after the end of Rome's wars of conquest, and to the rise of alternative modes of bound labor like the "colonate" (see Chapter Twelve) which resembled medieval serfdom; the collapse of a pan-Mediterranean market economy from the fifth century onward made an impact too. In some sense, both sides of the argument carry conviction. The decline of slavery had multiple causes, and economic factors always played a paramount role. But Christian ideology, which came to permeate all aspects of Mediterranean culture by the fifth century, also had an effect, albeit an ambivalent one. Christian prohibitions on sexual exploitation and the murder and abuse of slaves, coupled with notions of the equality of all humans before God, began to influence Roman slave law already under Constantine, and led to radical reductions in the freedom of masters to exploit slaves by the sixth century. By the same token, however, Christian injunctions that slaves be obedient to their masters and the notion that slavery was a natural result of human sinfulness helped to perpetuate slavery. Ultimately, the barbarian invasions that split the empire also seem to have resulted in a split in slaveholding practice. In the East, where the central state apparatus remained dominant and came to be intimately connected with the church, agricultural slaveholding on a large scale disappeared by the sixth century, and alternative forms of exploiting semi-dependent labor came to predominate. In the West, by contrast, the barbarian peoples who inherited Roman territory were responsible for an increase in captive-taking due to renewed warfare, as well as for new cultural practices which sustained large-scale agricultural slaveholding down to the eighth century. In both instances, Christian principles were used to justify, and equally to condemn, the underpinnings of slavery, because on this issue like so many others Christian thinking was always complex and could fall back on alternate strains to reinforce social practice or instead to change it.

WOMEN'S POWER IN LATE ANTIQUITY

Much of the pattern for women's lives remained in late antiquity as it had been in the early empire. A large part of the reason was the demographics of a world where so few children were likely to reach adulthood (see Chapter Eight). This cruel fact of nature compelled women to endure multiple pregnancies, and also encouraged the marriage of girls early in their teens. If anything, marriage commitments occurred at an even younger age in the late empire, for the practice of legally enforceable *sponsalia* (betrothals) at around the age of seven became much commoner in this era of heightened sensitivity to sexual morality.

The Christian church, which had always been stricter regarding sexual restraint than Roman or Greek society, also began to exert its influence on ancient law and social practice. In addition to the strictures on sexual behavior laid down by Augustus' legislation, the church began enforcing its own standards of conduct. Abortion and infant exposure were strictly forbidden by the church, which used excommunication and periods of penance to enforce its rules. As church and state became increasingly intertwined, the state in turn introduced its own

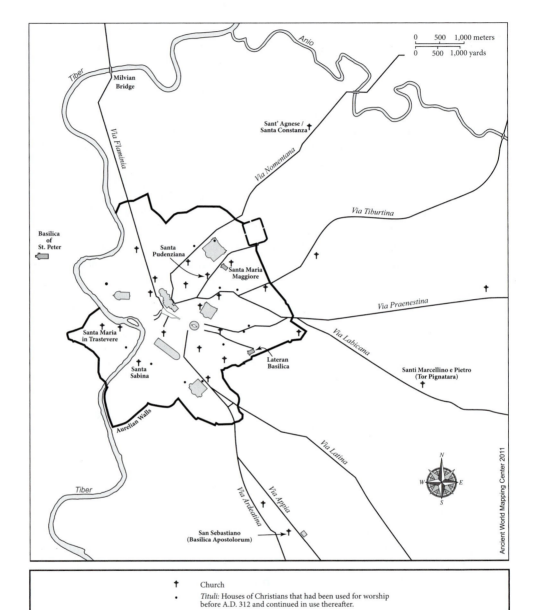

Map 14.3a *Churches in Rome by the Late Fifth Century*

Map 14.3b *This representation of Jerusalem is based on a mosaic map of the Holy Land found on the floor of a church in Madaba, Jordan (see Plate 16). It offers our most detailed, if also very schematic, image of the late antique city, which is shown surrounded by an oval wall (in fact it was roughly rectangular). The top of the map is oriented east. Thus the main road, or* cardo *(A), running north-south through the city was flanked by two covered colonnades that have recently been excavated. It culminated in a massive gate on the north that opened onto a square with a monumental column (1) erected by Hadrian after his capture of the city (see Chapter Ten). There was also a secondary colonnaded* cardo *(B). The most prominent buildings shown are the Church of the Holy Sepulcher (2) and the "Nea" Church (3). On the summit of Mt. Zion, at the south end of the city, is to be found the Church of Holy Zion (4).*

regulations against both practices; it also at times allowed charges of treason to be brought against adulterers. Similarly, in contrast with earlier Roman society's tolerance of a double standard with regard to male and female fidelity to the marriage bond, during the late empire husbands who committed adultery faced considerable criticism from church leaders. As may be imagined, social practice did not always fall in line with these stricter codes of conduct, but the change in attitude gradually had the effect of making infidelity seem a serious risk rather than a matter of slight consequence. So too with divorce, which the Roman state had always permitted but the church staunchly condemned. In 331 Constantine forbade divorce except in cases where both husband and wife consented to it, and subsequent rulers introduced further regulations. Earlier, in 320, Constantine had also removed Augustus' restrictions on celibacy (see Chapter Eight). These laws had long represented an unwelcome interference in people's private lives, but the Christian taste for ascetic celibacy seems to have offered an additional motivation. Constantine was not simply offering the freedom to remain unmarried, he was eliminating a major legal impediment to the life of holy virginity.

By modern standards it may seem rather shocking that the Church's interest in sexual morality led society to prize the renunciation of things physical and even the mortification of the body. However, this was not how the ancients saw it, and particularly not women. At the very least, the church's official refusal to countenance double standards of sexual behavior put women on a more equal footing in the family. Moreover, the new emphasis on asceticism brought with it an acknowledgement that women were just as capable of this form of virtue as men. Their ability became most evident in the period of radical social and religious reform witnessed by the late fourth and early fifth centuries. Single examples from the eastern and western empires may illustrate the point.

Macrina, born into one of the wealthiest families of Roman Cappadocia (central Turkey) in 327, was betrothed to a fellow aristocrat, but when her fiancé died before the marriage, she resolved to live the rest of her life as a virgin. She even established a community of fellow virgins—ranging in background from former slaves to the wives of court politicians—that constituted one of the first female monasteries. Indeed, Macrina's community served as a model for a men's monastery founded by her brother Basil, bishop of Caesarea, which in turn became the model for monasteries in the Greek Orthodox Church. In the West, Melania, daughter of a famous senatorial family of Rome, married a fellow aristocrat but made a pact with him to renounce their sexuality after their first two children died at birth. Although they were fabulously wealthy, Melania and her husband decided to liquidate their assets, free their slaves, and move to the Holy Land to live a life of asceticism. There she continued to exercise influence among aristocrats, even convincing the empress Aelia Eudocia to visit her in her retreat. Like Macrina and many other women, Melania was thus able to prove what her biographer Gerontius claimed, "that woman is not surpassed by man in anything that relates to virtue."

In late antiquity asceticism and piety had taken their place alongside martial valor and political achievement as a means to gain status and recognition.

Moreover, because asceticism was not a gendered cultural practice (at least, not to the degree that warfare and politics were), it was open to women as a way to win status. It was surely with this prospect at the back of her mind that the empress Pulcheria, older sister of the child emperor Theodosius II, committed herself to virginity as a young woman. This choice offered her an extraordinary claim to power during her brother's administration, not just because she avoided marriage entanglements that might have weakened her personal authority, but also because she exploited the commonly recognized value of asceticism in the period to gain the title Augusta and notable influence in the imperial court. Even after Theodosius II's death, Pulcheria continued to serve as the symbol of empire, so much so that her brother's successor Marcian legitimized his rule by marrying her. Indeed, the marriage itself demonstrated the power of her ascetic vows, for it was agreed to only on the condition that she would be allowed to remain a virgin. Pulcheria in many ways established a trend, not so much toward virginal empresses but rather toward powerful ones. Women played a greater role in the politics of the Byzantine court than they typically had in Rome.

THE "DECLINE AND FALL" OF THE ROMAN EMPIRE

Edward Gibbon, in his lengthy, celebrated study *The Decline and Fall of the Roman Empire*, argued that the empire fell prey to two forces: barbarism and Christianity. From the time of Augustus, he believed, emperors began using the military, and particularly their guard troops, to suppress the Roman people, and thus to supplant them as the functional citizen army that had once made Rome great. In his view, emperors increasingly turned to barbarians to man their forces, thus allowing external peoples to grow in strength even as Rome's citizens became effete and weak-willed. Meanwhile Christianity, Gibbon felt, encouraged the Roman people to place their trust in a transcendent otherworld, and thus to abandon their concern for the state. The church introduced an attachment to the irrational, and created a rival to the state's authority which undermined Rome's power and further weakened its empire in the face of the barbarian invasions.

From the moment of its publication (beginning in 1776), *The Decline and Fall* provoked strong reactions, positive and negative, and it continues to exercise tremendous influence on the popular imagination of the western world. Although scholars have since set aside many of Gibbon's arguments, his fundamental question still continues to confront those who study Rome's history: "Why did the Roman empire decline and fall?" Historians today are every bit as intent on answering that question as Gibbon was, and they have formulated a wealth of hypotheses, some related to Gibbon's, others not: Rome fell victim to a series of attacks initiated by the rise of Germanic peoples; it was overwhelmed by invasions set off by the arrival of the Huns in central Europe; it witnessed economic decline brought on by over-burdensome taxation or the rise of corruption; its economy collapsed as a result of labor shortages or restructuring; it suffered a dwindling of its elites, who were replaced by a military class that lost sight of the values that had made its culture great; it witnessed a decline at the local level as talent fled the cities for the growing imperial bureaucracy; it suffered a major population decline in the wake of a series of plagues; it succumbed to natural disasters caused by climate change, lead poisoning, or environmental destruction; it only truly collapsed with the Muslim conquests of the eighth century; it did not so much decline as transform itself into an ever-evolving cultural institution which survives even up to the present day.

None of these explanations has won anything like universal acceptance. Indeed, more recent studies have tended to marvel less at Rome's eventual decline and more at the very fact that its empire managed to survive as long as it did. Pondering Rome's decline and fall does in fact provoke some reflection about what it accomplished in assembling so large an empire—one larger than the greater Mediterranean region has witnessed ever since—and in holding it together for so long. This feat is especially surprising given the conclusions reached by recent studies about the nature of life around the Mediterranean. While it had long been argued that the Mediterranean provided a sort of common playing field with a uniform geography and climate for a relatively homogeneous set of cultures, recent work has drawn these assumptions into question. Rather, it points out, the micro-regional variations in geography, average rainfall, level of productivity, modes of subsistence, and linguistic and cultural expression across the Mediterranean basin are extraordinary and vast. Nor does the Mediterranean provide a particularly good platform for the control of the remarkably variable hinterlands to be found only a few days' journey from its shores.

It was an epic accomplishment, therefore, for Rome not only to have conquered the entire Mediterranean and much of its hinterland, but above all to have held this territory in a unified empire for 600 years. To do this, Rome needed to develop a powerful ideological framework supporting its claims to dominion, and to disseminate this outlook systematically to its various provinces. In other words, it needed to convince the many peoples living in its many regions that it was operating in their interests and, indeed, that Rome and Romanness were coterminous with their own self-identity. Egyptians and Britons, Africans and Greeks had to want to think of themselves as Romans for Rome's power to prevail. The spread and maintenance of this sense of common purpose were thus always a much greater accomplishment than Rome's physical expansion.

The decline of this sense of community and identity that set in during late antiquity was in many respects concomitant with the collapse of empire. This decline was in turn greatly accelerated by the barbarian invasions, which subverted Rome's overlordship of western Europe. The effects of the invasions as a catalyst for decline cannot be denied. An all-too-obvious vicious cycle developed as devastated provinces ceased paying taxes, imperial armies went unpaid, and Roman territory was left undefended in the face of further invasions. This process gained rapid momentum and led to the disappearance of the Roman state in the West within two generations.

Roman identity, however, did not vanish so rapidly. Newcomers were not especially averse to the adoption of Roman ways. The barbarian invaders were, for example, eager to link their power to the traditional state through the exchange of women in marriage. So, too, the barbarian taste for Roman military office confirms an acceptance of the ongoing importance of the Roman state as a source of authority and legitimacy. When the Visigothic king Alaric sought recognition as a Master of the Soldiers in 409, or Gundobad chose to carry the Roman title Patricius ("patrician") even after leaving Roman service to rule as king of the Burgundians in 474, both were aware that Roman titles and connections with the Roman state represented a source of power, even in their own cultures. In Italy, Spain, and Gaul barbarian leaders sought affirmation from local Roman aristocrats in the form of letters and panegyrics, and at various points fairly early in their histories the peoples here began using Latin for official documents and even for vernacular speech. They acted thus in no small measure because provincial Roman aristocrats were themselves integrated into the management of the new barbarian kingdoms. The Visigothic king Euric (466–484), for example, used the Gallo-Roman aristocrats Victorius as his Duke of Aquitania, Vincentius as his general in Spain and Italy, and Leo of Narbonne as advisor to his court in Tolosa (modern Toulouse).

As these cases suggest, however, Romans in turn were forced to adapt to new realities that required some degree of assimilation on their part to barbarian ways. Mundane changes in dress provide a telling example. Romans apparently took quite well to wearing barbarian clothes including furs and pants, so much so that emperors of the fourth century felt compelled to legislate against this practice. The assimilation of Roman to barbarian is also evidenced in instances of intermarriage (extending beyond the level of the nobility), as well as in the appointment of Romans to court offices, and even in the appointment of Romans to the office of emperor by barbarian leaders. We have seen that Alaric appointed Priscus Attalus emperor in 409. A further case occurred in 455 when the Gallo-Roman aristocrat Eparchius Avitus was named to the western throne by the Gothic court at Toulouse. Often the difference between barbarian and Roman was so subjective and blurred that it became virtually indistinct. The Bagaudae of northern Gaul, for example, were often classed as "barbarians" in spite of the fact that their uprising grew out of the local population.

As the Roman state contracted, the barbarian "successor kingdoms" stepped in to fill the void. Once these had introduced new governmental structures to settle disputes, apportion resources, bestow patronage, and provide for the common defense, it was only natural that the provincials looked to these new states for support, and gradually began to follow non-Roman social and political customs. While the upper echelons of Roman society without doubt hung on doggedly to at least some aspects of their culture, its language and literature in particular, they had little choice but to find strategies of accommodation to the situation in which they now found themselves. For the average peasant, life probably changed very little, or perhaps even improved, given the smaller demands placed on them by a much less exacting system of taxation.

Although 476 has been canonized as the year in which Rome fell, in most ways this was a non-event. In reality, Rome's fall from political supremacy in the West was a process that lasted over seventy years, so that this single occurrence represents only one step along a much longer path. It is even more important, however, to recognize that "Rome" continued to live on in the East long after 476. Indeed, this was in some sense the point of Odoacer's message to Constantinople after deposing Romulus Augustulus: "a single common emperor would be sufficient" for both East and West. Since at least 425 Constantinople had maintained effective primacy over the West, so it was logical for Odoacer to propose that the ruler in Constantinople sufficed for both halves of the empire. Constantine's new capital, self-consciously styled "the New Rome," had thus come to outshine its older forebear in power and prestige; by 476, it more clearly represented Rome than Rome itself. In some sense, loss of power to Constantinople is evidence that Rome had truly moved, as the title of this book suggests, from village to empire. By spreading its political, social, and cultural organization successfully to its provinces, Rome was able to take up residence elsewhere in the empire it had created, and thus to outlive itself. It was with complete sincerity and conviction that the Byzantines, who continued the tradition of Roman imperial succession down to 1453, referred to themselves as *Romaioi*. As far as they were concerned, they were the inheritors of the tradition of Romulus and Camillus, of Augustus and Constantine.

SUGGESTED READINGS

Brown, Peter R. L. 1988. *The Body and Society: Men, Women and Sexual Renunciation in Early Christianity*. New York: Columbia University Press.

Brown, Peter R. L. 2003 (ed. 2). *The Rise of Western Christendom: Triumph and Diversity, AD 200–1000*. Malden, MA, and Oxford: Blackwell.

Clark, Gillian. 1993. *Women in Late Antiquity: Pagan and Christian Lifestyles*. Oxford: Oxford University Press.

Gregory, Timothy E. 2005. *A History of Byzantium*. Malden, MA, and Oxford: Blackwell. Coverage spans late antiquity to the end of the Byzantine empire.

Halsall, Guy. 2007. *Barbarian Migrations and the Roman West, 376–568*. Cambridge: Cambridge University Press. Good summary of revisionist approaches to the barbarian migrations, emphasizing fluid identities and consensual, rather than confrontational, models for cultural change.

Harmless, William. 2004. *Desert Christians: An Introduction to the Literature of Early Monasticism*. Oxford: Oxford University Press.

Heather, Peter. 2006. *The Fall of the Roman Empire: A New History of Rome and the Barbarians*. Oxford: Oxford University Press. Nuanced restatement of the old orthodoxy that waves of barbarian invaders caused the Roman state to fall.

Horden, Peregrine, and Nicholas Purcell. 2000. *The Corrupting Sea: A Study of Mediterranean History*. Malden, MA, and Oxford: Blackwell. Comprehensive study of Mediterranean geography that emphasizes shifting patterns of connectivity across a varied landscape.

Hunt, E. David. 1982. *Holy Land Pilgrimage in the Later Roman Empire, AD 312–460*. Oxford: Oxford University Press.

Mathisen, Ralph W. 1993. *Roman Aristocrats in Barbarian Gaul: Strategies for Survival in an Age of Transition*. Austin, TX: University of Texas Press.

TIMELINE

4000 B.C. Emergence of agriculture

2000 Appearance of copper tools and ornaments

1800–1200 Bronze Age

1400–1100 Mycenaean contacts with Italy and Sicily

c. 1000 First undoubted traces of settlement at the site of Rome

900–700 Iron Age; Villanovan and Latial cultures

c. 800 Phoenicians found Carthage

c. 775 Greeks begin to settle in Italy and Sicily

c. 750 Formation of first city-states

700s Introduction of writing to Italy

c. 725–580 "Orientalizing" period in Italy

c. 700 Gradual adoption of hoplite warfare; cultivation of grape vines and olive trees spreads to central Italy

c. 700–500 "Princely" burials in northern and central Italy

700–400 Etruscan and Greek cities at their height in Italy (also Greek cities in Sicily)

753–510 Traditional dates for monarchy at Rome (seven kings in succession)

650–600 Construction of Forum Romanum and associated public buildings and spaces

c. 580–480 "Archaic" period in Italy

c. 500 Expulsion of Rome's last king, and establishment of the Republic; treaty between Carthage and Rome

c. 500–287 "Struggle of the Orders"

c. 450 Laws of the Twelve Tables are issued

c. 396 Romans take over Veii

c. 387 Warband of Gauls loots Rome

343–290 Samnite Wars: (343–341) First; (326–304) Second; (298–290) Third

341–338 Latin War

c. 280 Rome first issues its own coins

282–272 Rome at war with Tarentum and other communities in southern Italy; (280–275) King Pyrrhus of Epirus leads their forces

264–241 First Punic War, at the end of which Sicily becomes Rome's first "province"

237 Romans remove Carthaginians from Sardinia; (227) it becomes a province with Corsica

226 Carthaginians in Spain recognize the Ebro River as their limit

218–201 Second Punic War; Romans are defeated by Hannibal at (217) Lake Trasimene and (216) Cannae; (202) final defeat of Carthaginians at Zama

215–205 Rome's First Macedonian War

c. 211 Rome first mints silver *denarii*

204 Cult of *Magna Mater* is brought to Rome

198 Two Roman provinces are formed in Spain (Further, Nearer)

200–196 Second Macedonian War; (196) "Freedom" of the Greeks proclaimed

c. 200 Beginnings of historical writing at Rome; Roman elite engages with Greek literature, philosophy, rhetoric

c. 200–c. 170 Numerous colonies are established in both peninsular Italy and the Po Valley

195 Cato's consulship, and (to 194) command in Spain

192–189 Rome defeats Antiochus III in the Syrian War

186–183 Suppression of the cult of Bacchus in Italy

171–168 Third Macedonian War; end of its monarchy

168 Polybius comes to Rome as a hostage from Achaean League

mid-150s–130s Roman wars with Lusitanians and Celtiberians, ending (133) with capture of Numantia

149 "Extortion" court (*quaestio de repetundis*) is established

149–146 Third Punic War, ending with the destruction of Carthage; its territory becomes the province of Africa

149–148 After the suppression of Andriscus' rising, Macedon becomes a Roman province

146 Destruction of Corinth

130s Secret ballot is introduced in Roman assemblies

136–132 First Slave War in Sicily

133 Tribunate of Tiberius Gracchus

133 Kingdom of Pergamum is bequeathed to Rome and (129) becomes the province of Asia

123, 122 Tribunates of Gaius Gracchus, who (122) attempts to establish a colony (Junonia) on the site of Carthage

121 *Senatus Consultum Ultimum* authorizes elimination of Gaius Gracchus

121 Province of Transalpine Gaul is formed

113–101 Confrontation with Cimbri and Teutoni

112–105 War with Jugurtha in Numidia

c. 107–101 Major reform of the Roman army

107, 104, 103, 102, 101 Consulships of Marius

104–100 Second Slave War in Sicily

100 Tribunate of Saturninus and (sixth) consulship of Marius

91 Tribunate of Livius Drusus

91–87 Social (or Marsian) War; (90–89) extension of Roman citizenship throughout peninsular Italy; (88) tribunate of Sulpicius Rufus and Sulla's first march on Rome

90–85 War with Mithridates in Asia Minor and Greece; Sulla offers peace terms

87–84 After Marius and Cinna had both marched on Rome (87), Marius dies (86), Cinna works to restore stability, but is murdered (84)

86 Financial crisis: three quarters of all debts are cancelled

83–82 Sulla's second march on Rome; Pompey raises forces in support

82–81 Dictatorship of Sulla; proscriptions

80–73 Sertorius in Spain resists Sullan commanders (Pompey among them) until murdered

78–77 Despite marching on Rome, Lepidus fails to overturn key features of Sulla's program

75 Kingdom of Bithynia is bequeathed to Rome

74–63 Lucullus, then (from 66) Pompey, resume war against Mithridates

73–71 Slave revolt of Spartacus

70 Consulship of Crassus and Pompey; Cicero secures the condemnation of Verres for misgovernment in Sicily

c. 70 Earliest known construction of amphitheater in stone (at Pompeii)

67 Pompey suppresses piracy in the Mediterranean

65 Censorship of Crassus

64–63 Bithynia/Pontus, Cilicia, Syria are instituted or reshaped as provinces by Pompey (63); Mithridates dies

63 As consul, Cicero exposes Catiline's conspiracy; Julius Caesar is elected *pontifex maximus*

61–55 Pompey builds a theater complex in Campus Martius

60–59 Formation of "First Triumvirate" (Caesar, Crassus, Pompey)

59 Consulship of Julius Caesar

58 Tribunate of Clodius

58–57 Cato makes Cyprus a Roman province; Cicero in exile

58–51 Caesar campaigns in Gaul and (55–54) Britain; makes his accomplishments known through "commentaries"

56 "Triumvirs" meet at Luca to strengthen and extend their partnership

55 Consulship of Crassus and Pompey

54 Premature death of Julia

53 Crassus' army invades Parthia and is slaughtered at Carrhae

52 Death of Clodius; sole consulship of Pompey

51–50 Cicero governs Cilicia and Cyprus

50s or thereabouts Development of glass-blowing technology

49 (January) SCU is passed; Caesar crosses Rubicon River to invade Italy; (March) Pompey evacuates Italy; (March to fall) Caesar campaigns against Pompeians in Spain and besieges Massilia

48 Caesar holds (second) consulship, together with one-year dictatorship; debtors' rising in Italy is suppressed; (August) Pompey is defeated by Caesar at Pharsalus, and (September) killed on arrival in Egypt as fugitive

October 48–mid-47 Caesar in Alexandria establishes Cleopatra as ruler of Egypt, and fathers a son by her

47 (summer) Caesar defeats Pharnaces at Zela

Fall 47–mid-46 Campaign in Africa ends with Caesar's victory over Pompeians at Thapsus; Cato commits suicide

46 Caesar holds (third) consulship, and is appointed to ten-year dictatorship; new "Julian" calendar introduced; dedication of Forum Julium in Rome

Fall 46–mid-45 Second campaign in Spain ends with Caesar's victory over Pompeians at Munda

45 Caesar holds (fourth) consulship, and continues as dictator

44 Caesar holds (fifth) consulship, and (February) is made perpetual dictator; he becomes the first living Roman whose head appears on coins; his worship as a god is authorized; (March 15) he is assassinated

44 Lepidus becomes *pontifex maximus*; (May) Octavian arrives in Rome to claim his inheritance from Caesar

43 (April) Antony is repulsed from Mutina by both consuls, who lose their lives, and Octavian; (August) Octavian becomes consul; (November) formation of Second Triumvirate; Cicero is victim of ensuing proscriptions

42 (January) Deification of Julius Caesar; (fall) Antony and Octavian defeat Brutus and Cassius at Philippi

41 Perusine War; Antony meets Cleopatra, and fathers twins by her

40 Antony and Octavian redivide their control of the Roman world; Antony marries Octavia

39 Agreement is reached between Antony, Octavian, and Sextus Pompey

39–38 Parthian invasions of Syria and Asia Minor are repulsed

38 Octavian marries Livia

37 Second Triumvirate is renewed

36 Sextus Pompey is defeated by Octavian and Lepidus; Lepidus' attempt to eliminate Octavian results in his own exile; Antony's invasion of Parthia fails badly

35–34 Antony subdues Armenia; (34) "Donations of Alexandria"

32 Italy and West swear loyalty to Octavian; Antony divorces Octavia

31 (September) Octavian defeats Antony and Cleopatra at Actium

30 Octavian captures Alexandria; Antony and Cleopatra commit suicide; Egypt becomes a Roman province

29 Curia Julia is dedicated

27 "First Settlement"; Octavian is renamed Augustus

27–c. 1 B.C. Extension of Roman control in Spain, Alps, and central Europe to the Danube River; Raetia, Noricum, Dalmatia, Pannonia, Moesia are formed as provinces

25 Galatia becomes a Roman province

23 (July) "Second Settlement"; (fall) Marcellus dies

late 20s According to tradition, Vergil reads his *Aeneid* to Augustus

21 Marriage of Agrippa and Julia

20 Parthia returns legionary standards captured from Crassus and Antony

18–17 Augustus introduces legislation affecting marriage, childbearing, and adultery

17 Augustus adopts Gaius and Lucius; Secular Games

13 New conditions for army service are introduced

12 Agrippa dies; Augustus becomes *pontifex maximus* following the death of Lepidus

9 Drusus the Elder dies; endpoint of Livy's *History*; dedication of Ara Pacis

7 Monument at modern La Turbie commemorates Augustus' subjugation of "all the Alpine peoples"

6 B.C.–A.D. 2 Tiberius retires to Rhodes

2 B.C. Temple of Mars the Avenger is dedicated in Augustus' new Forum; title *Pater Patriae* is bestowed on him

A.D. 2 Lucius Caesar dies

4 Gaius Caesar dies; Augustus adopts Tiberius

6 Judaea becomes a Roman province

8 Augustus exiles Ovid to Tomis, where he remains until his death in 17

6–9 Rebellions in Germany, Dalmatia, Pannonia; (9) three Roman legions are massacred in Teutoburg Forest

14 Augustus dies, and is succeeded by Tiberius; promulgation of Augustus' *Res Gestae*; legions stationed in Germany and Pannonia mutiny

14–16/17 Germanicus campaigns in Germany

17 Cappadocia becomes a Roman province

17–19 Germanicus is dispatched to the East, and dies in Syria

20 Trial of Piso for the death of Germanicus

23 Drusus the Younger dies

23 Praetorian Guard is grouped together and based in Rome

26 Tiberius takes up residence on Capri

31 Sejanus (Praetorian Prefect since 14) is denounced and executed

33 Financial crisis, which Tiberius attempts to alleviate

37 Tiberius dies, and is succeeded by Gaius Caligula

38–40 Disturbances between Greeks and Jews in Alexandria

41 Assassination of Caligula, who is succeeded by Claudius

40s–50s Claudius constructs new harbor (Portus) north of Ostia

43 Britain and Mauretania become Roman provinces

46 Thrace becomes a Roman province

47–48 Claudius conducts a census

54 Claudius dies, and is succeeded by Nero

59 Nero orders the murder of his mother Agrippina

60 Boudica leads a rebellion in Britain

64 Great Fire of Rome; Christians are persecuted as scapegoats; extensive devastated area is appropriated by Nero for his Golden House

66 Nero crowns Tiridates King of Armenia in Rome

66 Nero visits Greece

66–73 First Jewish Revolt, culminating (70) in destruction of Temple in Jerusalem and (73) capture of Masada

67–68 Rising and defeat of Vindex in Gaul

68 (June) Nero commits suicide, and is succeeded by Galba

69 (early January) Legions in Germany support Vitellius for emperor; (mid-January) with Praetorians' support, Otho murders Galba and succeeds him; (April) defeated in battle at Bedriacum, Otho commits suicide, and is succeeded by Vitellius; (July) legions in the East and Pannonia support Vespasian for emperor; (October) Vitellius' army is defeated by Pannonian legions at Cremona; (December) Vitellius is killed, and is succeeded by Vespasian; temple of Jupiter Optimus Maximus on the Capitol is destroyed by fire

69–70 Germano-Gallic revolt

70 (October) Vespasian arrives in Rome as emperor

71 (June) Triumph of Vespasian and Titus to celebrate the fall of Jerusalem

73 Vespasian and Titus conduct a census

70s Vespasian builds the Temple of Peace in Rome, and begins the Colosseum; completion of Pliny the Elder's *Natural History*

70s–90s "Latin" status is awarded to Spanish communities

79 Vespasian dies, and is succeeded by Titus; eruption of Mt. Vesuvius

80 Fire devastates city of Rome

81 Titus dies, and is succeeded by Domitian

85–92 Domitian campaigns north of the Danube, especially against the Dacians

89 A rising by the commander in Upper Germany is suppressed

96 Domitian is assassinated and succeeded by Nerva

96–98 Nerva establishes *alimenta*

97 Nerva adopts Trajan

98 Nerva dies, and is succeeded by Trajan; completion of Tacitus, *Agricola*; and (c. 98) of Frontinus, *On the Aqueducts of Rome*

100 Trajan establishes colony at Thamugadi; (Sept.) Pliny the Younger delivers speech of thanks (*Panegyricus*) on becoming consul

101–102, 105–106 Dacian Wars; Dacia then becomes a Roman province

105–106 Arabia Petraea (Nabataea) becomes a Roman province

c. 111/112 Pliny the Younger's special governorship of Bithynia-Pontus

112–113 Forum of Trajan (112) and Column (113) are dedicated

113–117 Trajan campaigns to seize Armenia and Mesopotamia from Parthian control, and creates new provinces there

c. 115 Trajan adds an inner basin to Claudius' harbor at Portus

115–117 Second Jewish Revolt

117 Trajan dies, and is succeeded by Hadrian, who abandons territories seized from Parthia by Trajan

120s Hadrian builds "his" Wall across northern England, and defines the German–Raetian frontier by erecting wooden barrier

121–127, 128–131 Hadrian makes extended journeys empire-wide

130 Hadrian's favorite Antinous drowns in the Nile

131 Permanent Praetorian Edict ("Edictum Perpetuum") is instituted

132–135 Third Jewish Revolt (Bar Kokhba War)

138 Hadrian dies, and is succeeded by Antoninus Pius

139–142 Turf "Wall of Antoninus" is built across southern Scotland

c. 144 Aelius Aristides delivers his oration *To Rome*

150s Anti-Christian violence at Smyrna

161 Antoninus Pius dies, and is jointly succeeded by Marcus Aurelius and Lucius Verus

162–166 Lucius Verus campaigns against Parthia

mid 160s–190s In two main epidemics, plague sweeps through the empire

166–173, 176–180 First and Second Marcomannic Wars

169 Lucius Verus dies

175 Avidius Cassius proclaims himself emperor and briefly rules the East until assassinated

176 Marcus Aurelius makes his son Commodus co-emperor

177 Anti-Christian violence at Lugdunum

180 Marcus Aurelius dies, and is succeeded by Commodus, who abandons his father's attempts to secure territory north of the Danube

192 (Dec. 31) Commodus is assassinated

193 (Jan. 1) Pertinax becomes emperor, only to be killed in March; after an auction by the Praetorian Guard, Didius Julianus becomes emperor; only to be killed in June; Septimius Severus (supported by legions on Rhine and Danube) reaches Rome to replace him; Clodius Albinus (supported for emperor by legions in Britain) is appointed "Caesar" by Septimius Severus; legions in East support Pescennius Niger for emperor

193–194 Septimius Severus pursues and defeats Pescennius Niger

194–195, 197–199 Septimius Severus campaigns against Parthians

196–197 Septimius Severus defeats and kills Clodius Albinus at Lugdunum

190s Septimius Severus enlarges the forces in Rome, and stations others nearby; he lifts ban on marriage by soldiers

c. 200 Northern Mesopotamia and Osroene become Roman provinces

203 Arch of Septimius Severus and Septizodium are both dedicated at Rome; martyrdom of Perpetua at Carthage

208–211 Septimius Severus campaigns in northern Britain, where he dies, and is succeeded by his sons Caracalla and Geta

211 (December) Caracalla orders the murder of Geta

212 Caracalla extends Roman citizenship empire-wide (*Constitutio Antoniniana*)

213–214 Caracalla campaigns in Germany

216–217 Campaigns of Caracalla into Armenia and Parthia, during which he is assassinated

217 Macrinus (first *eques* to be emperor) replaces Caracalla

218 Macrinus is assassinated, and replaced by Elagabalus

222 Elagabalus is murdered, and succeeded by Severus Alexander

223 Praetorian Guard's murder of their Prefect Ulpian goes unpunished

224 Sasanian dynasty takes control of Parthia/Persia

229 Cassius Dio is consul with the emperor and ends his *Roman History* at this point

231–232 Severus Alexander regains Mesopotamia from Sasanian invaders

235 On campaign in Raetia, Severus Alexander and Julia Mamaea are assassinated by mutinous soldiers; their leader Maximinus replaces him

235–284 Age of Crisis

248 Celebration of Rome's thousandth anniversary

249–250 Decius initiates first empire-wide persecution of Christians

251 Decius killed in battle of Abrittus (Moesia) by Goths

257–259 Valerian's persecution of Christians

260 Sasanian King Shapur I captures Valerian

260–268 As sole emperor, Gallienus seeks to secure the core of the empire

260–274 "Gallic Empire" of Postumus exerts broad control over West

mid 260s–272 Odenaethus, and then his widow Zenobia, control East from Palmyra

270 Aurelian abandons province of Dacia

271 Aurelian fortifies Rome with encircling wall

272–273 Aurelian regains East from Zenobia

274 Aurelian regains all areas once controlled by Postumus

284 Diocletian becomes emperor

286 Maximian becomes co-emperor (Augustus) with Diocletian

287–293 Carausius rules Britain in defiance of Maximian

293 "Tetrarchy" formed: Galerius (under Diocletian) and Constantius (under Maximian) become Caesars

290s Provinces are redivided; civil and military positions are separated

296 Constantius regains Britain

297–298 Galerius defeats Sasanian forces and extends Roman territory in Mesopotamia

301–302 Coinage reform; Edict on Maximum Prices

303 "Great Persecution" of Christians (in West to 306, in East to 311)

305 Diocletian and Maximian abdicate; Constantius and Severus rule West, Galerius and Maximin Daia rule East

306 Constantius dies; Constantine is proclaimed Augustus in Britain; Maxentius is proclaimed Augustus in Rome

308 Conference at Carnuntum restores tetrarchy

311 Galerius issues "Edict of Toleration" permitting Christian worship

312 In a battle at the Milvian Bridge, Constantine defeats Maxentius and wins Rome; he disbands Praetorians and professes Christianity

313–324 Constantine rules West, Licinius the East; (313) together they issue "Edict of Milan," and unite to defeat Maximin Daia

313–314 Church councils at Rome (313) and Arles (314) adjudicate the Donatist controversy

315 Dedication of Rome's arch honoring Constantine; (c. 315) completion of Lactantius, *On the Deaths of the Persecutors*

324 Constantine defeats Licinius, becomes sole emperor, and initiates refoundation of Byzantium as his new capital of Constantinople; he promotes Christianity with growing confidence

325 First Ecumenical Council of Nicaea

c. 327 Construction of Church of the Holy Sepulcher in Jerusalem

330 Dedication of Constantinople

337 Constantine dies, and is succeeded by his sons: Constantine II in Gaul and Spain; Constans in Italy, Illyricum and Africa; Constantius II in East

340 Constantine II is killed in civil war

350 Constans is killed by Magnentius

353 Magnentius is defeated and killed by Constantius II

355 Julian is appointed Caesar in West

356 Death of Antony of Egypt; Athanasius composes *Life of Antony*

360 Julian is promoted to Augustus by his troops

361 Constantius II dies, and is succeeded by Julian

363 Julian is killed in battle with Persians; Jovian succeeds him, and surrenders northern Mesopotamia

364 Valentinian I and Valens become joint Augusti

375 Valentinian I dies, and is succeeded by sons Gratian and Valentinian II

378 Valens is killed by Goths at Battle of Adrianople, and is succeeded by Theodosius I in East; endpoint of Ammianus Marcellinus, *Histories*

381 Second Ecumenical Council of Constantinople

382 Theodosius I makes peace with Goths in Thrace

383–388 Magnus Maximus kills Gratian and rules in West until defeated by Theodosius I

390 Theodosius I does penance before Ambrose

392–394 Death of Valentinian II; Arbogast establishes Eugenius on throne

395 Theodosius I dies, and is succeeded by his sons: Honorius in West, Arcadius in East

399–400 Goths led by Gainas and Tribigild occupy Constantinople until expelled

402 Honorius transfers court from Milan to Ravenna, which becomes western capital

405–406 Ostrogoths invade Italy from Danube

406 Vandals, Alans, and Sueves invade Gaul and Spain from Rhine; Constantine "III" usurps power in Britain and Gaul

408 Arcadius dies, and is succeeded by Theodosius II; Stilicho is executed

410 Britain is abandoned by Roman army

410 (August) Visigoths under Alaric sack Rome

418 Settlement of Visigoths in Aquitania

423–425 Honorius dies, and is succeeded by Valentinian III

429–439 Vandals gain control of North Africa

431 Third Ecumenical Council of Ephesus

438 *Theodosian Code* is issued

450 Theodosius II dies, and is succeeded by Marcian

451 Aetius defeats Attila the Hun at Catalaunian Plains (Gaul); Fourth Ecumenical Council of Chalcedon

455 Valentinian III is assassinated; Gaiseric the Vandal sacks Rome

457 Marcian dies, and is succeeded by Leo I

467 Anthemius is imposed on Western throne; expedition against Vandals fails

474 Leo I dies, and is succeeded by his son-in-law Zeno

476 (September) Romulus Augustulus, last Western emperor, is deposed

489 Theodoric the Ostrogoth retakes Italy for the East and rules it as "King of the Romans"

527–565 Justinian rules Byzantine empire; he reconquers (533–534) Africa and (535–554) Italy

529–534 Justinian's *Corpus Iuris Civilis* is issued

GLOSSARY

[Most terms mentioned only once in the text are omitted here]

aedile—Four annual magistrates in the city of Rome, two of whom had to be plebeian. The office was originally a plebeian one, charged with oversight of the temple (*aedes*) established by the *plebs*. Later, duties came to include general oversight of trade, markets, weights and measures, public games (*ludi*), public grain supply, public buildings, and law and order in the city.

aerarium—Roman treasury and depository of state documents overseen by *quaestors*, situated in the Temple of Saturn in the Forum (*Forum Romanum*). In A.D. 6 Augustus established in addition the "military treasury" (*aerarium militare*) to pay the lump sums promised to legionaries on their discharge.

ager (*publicus, Gallicus,* etc.)—("land") *Ager publicus* ("public land") is property owned by the Roman state (as opposed to a private individual) that it could assign or lease (for rent), normally through the *censors*.

agger—("mound") A military rampart.

Agri Decumates—Territory that forms a re-entrant angle between the upper Rhine and Danube rivers.

Alexander the Great (356–323)—King of Macedon, whose astonishing conquest of the Persian Empire, and accompanying honors (worship among them), became the envy and inspiration of many Romans and others.

alimenta—Community-based child support schemes devised in the first century A.D. and funded both by emperors (especially Trajan in Italy) and by private benefactors.

ambitio, ambitus—("circuit" or "going round") The quest for public office by promising favors, paying voters, or giving them gifts. Unlike *ambitio* (legal canvassing), *ambitus* is illegal bribery of voters.

amicus, amicitia—("friend," "friendship") *Amicitia* signifies a cordial, cooperative relationship in Roman political and social life, although the relationship may only be short-term and the parties to it may not necessarily be on close personal terms otherwise. To be recognized as the *amicus* of a more powerful figure was an honor; by the same token, for the latter to withdraw his *amicitia* formally was a serious blow.

amphitheater—Oval-shaped structure (in wood, later stone) designed for gladiatorial and beast fights. The great one built by the Flavian emperors in Rome, and still partially standing today, came to be called the Colosseum in the Middle Ages, and others elsewhere are often referred to by that name.

amphora—Large, two-handled clay jar used to transport liquids such as wine, oil, and fish sauce in bulk.

annona—"Food supply," especially the supply of grain to the city of Rome (either free or at a regulated price).

Antonines—Line of emperors ruling from the accession of Antoninus Pius (138) through the death of Commodus (192). See Table 10.1.

antoninianus—Coin introduced by Caracalla in A.D. 215 as a double *denarius* (see below), although it weighed only as much as 1.5 *denarii*. In the mid-third century it became the standard Roman coin, and underwent successive weight reductions and debasements, bottoming out at 3 g and just under 2% silver by around 270.

ara—"Altar," erected in honor of one or more gods, where a sacrifice could be made.

Arians—Christians who accepted the theories of Arius that Christ was created after the beginning of the universe by God the Father and was inferior to him. Arianism was branded as heresy at the Council of Nicaea in 325; even so, aspects of Arian theology were adopted by various councils over the course of the fourth century, and retained in the theology of many Germanic Christian groups down to the sixth.

as (pl. *asses*)—Low-value Roman coin. See *denarius* below.

asceticism—(Greek *askesis*, "practice" or "training") Self-denial and mortification for the sake of spiritual improvement, practiced by some pagans and especially by Christians in late antiquity.

atrium (pl. *atria*)—Central reception room in a Roman house.

auctoritas—Unofficial influence exercised by, and prestige enjoyed by, those individuals or corporate bodies whose advice and recommendations gain special respect.

augur—See *auspicium*.

Augustales—Priests (usually freedmen) who took responsibility for the imperial cult in municipalities; often a group of six, hence the title *seviri* (or *sexviri*) *Augustales*.

Augustus—("revered") New *cognomen* taken by Octavian in 27 B.C., which later became a regular imperial title. Ancient writers connected it both to *auctoritas* and to augury (see *auspicium* below). In the third century, and particularly under the tetrarchy, *Augustus* came to distinguish senior rulers from their deputy counterparts, who were now termed *Caesares* (see below).

aureus (pl. *aurei*)—Gold coin valued at 25 *denarii* (see below).

auspicium—Divination, the search for and interpretation of signs in nature (good and bad) by *augurs*; the role of these priests was considered vital to the welfare of the Roman state.

auxilium—("aid") To give aid to fellow plebeians and their property was traditionally a key function for the tribunes (see below) to perform.

auxilia—Auxiliary troops (often cavalry or specialized fighters) who were to aid and relieve the legions (see below). Typically, these auxiliaries were noncitizens from the provinces.

beneficium (pl. *beneficia*)—("favor," "kindness") Special legal privilege or right granted to an individual or community. This noun is also used to describe political or military advancement.

Caesar—A *cognomen* (see below) which later became a regular imperial title. In the third century, and particularly from the time of the tetrarchs, it came to designate deputy emperors.

Campus Martius—("Field of Mars") Area at the Tiber River's "bend." During the Republic it lay beyond Rome's *pomerium*, and thus was used for meetings of the Centuriate assembly. Named after an early altar of Mars that was located here.

capitatio—See *iugatio*.

Capitolium (*Mons Capitolinus*)—("Capitoline Hill") Smallest of Rome's seven hills, located in the center of the city overlooking the *Forum Romanum*. On its height were the *arx* ("citadel") and the great temple of Jupiter Optimus Maximus ("Jupiter Best and Greatest").

censor—See *census*.

census—In the Republic, the official list of Roman citizens (only; *not* the entire population) used for voting, taxation, and recruitment of troops. The list was drawn up publicly by two *censors* every five years. Further duties of a political, financial, and social nature became attached to their office, which consequently became a very influential and prestigious one, even though its holders lacked *imperium*. From Augustus' time onwards, there were no more censors of the traditional type, and instead emperors periodically organized censuses which covered the entire empire and its population region by region.

centuria (pl. *centuriae*)—Voting units or "centuries" (193 total) into which the Roman citizen body was divided in the *comitia centuriata* ("Centuriate assembly"). Even though the literal meaning of *centuria* is a body of exactly one hundred men, in practice the centuries of the Centuriate assembly could vary greatly in size. However, the votes of each of them carried equal weight.

centurion—Title of the officers responsible for the day-to-day functioning of a Roman legion (see below).

Christianity—Religion inspired by Jesus Christ in the early first century A.D. It sprang from Judaism, but gradually separated from it in the course of developing a more distinct identity. However, like Judaism, it continued to require that its adherents be devoted exclusively to its one god.

circus (**Circus Maximus, Circus Flaminius**)—Long stadium rounded at one end, used mostly for chariot racing in public games (*ludi*) and religious festivals. Unlike the oval amphitheater, the circus was long and narrow with a racetrack running at the sides and a barrier or "spine" (*spina*) down the center. Spectators sat on benches at the curved end or along the sloped sides of the track. The Circus

Maximus ("Greatest Circus"), located between the Palatine and Aventine hills, was the oldest and largest circus in Rome, said to have been established under the kings in the sixth century. The Circus Flaminius, located in the Campus Martius, was built in 220 B.C.

clementia—"Clemency," willingness to pardon defeated enemies.

client (*cliens***, pl. ***clientes***)**—A free man who had ties (sometimes hereditary) to an individual of higher standing, termed his patron (*patronus*). Typically, clients received legal and political support, financial assistance, and even food from their patron; in return, they accompanied him when he appeared in public, as well as canvassing and voting for him when he ran for office.

client kingdom—A state usually on the fringes of Roman territory which remained independent, but whose ruler agreed to maintain and advance Roman interests; Rome offered protection in return. The choice of a new "client" or "friendly" king was normally subject to Roman approval.

cognomen **(pl. *cognomina*)**—Last component of the typical Roman *trinomina* ("three names"), representing the surname of a Roman family, e.g., Gaius Julius **Caesar**, who is of the Caesar family. A *cognomen* might also be acquired, and even become hereditary, through military distinction, e.g., Lucius Cornelius Scipio **Africanus**, following his victories in Africa. Some Roman families never had a *cognomen*; others had more than one. See also *praenomen, nomen.*

cohors—("cohort") Denotes a group of one kind or another, frequently a tactical unit within a legion, but also a governor's entourage, for example.

collegium—("group," "association") Denotes an organized group of many different kinds (religious, social, commercial, professional), including the groups (or "colleges") of priests such as augurs and pontiffs. In the tetrarchic period, the "association" of emperors.

colonia **(pl. *coloniae*)**—"Colony" or settlement (in Italy, or elsewhere in the Roman world) founded to settle discharged veterans or civilians eager to improve their prospects; each participant received a plot of land assigned by *triumviri coloniae deducendae*. After the early second century A.D., new foundations of this type were rare. However, the privileged civic status of *colonia* might still be awarded by an emperor to an existing community.

colonus **(pl. *coloni*)**—1) Farmer (especially a tenant) or country dweller; 2) inhabitant of a Roman *colonia*; 3) in the late empire, farmers bound to cultivate the parcels of land on which they and their ancestors were registered.

Colosseum—See amphitheater above.

comes **(pl. *comites*)**—"Companion," "adviser" (especially of the emperor), and (from the time of the tetrarchy) a high-ranking military commander or other official ("count").

comitatenses—("retinue troops") Soldiers in mobile units who accompanied the emperor or his generals in the large field armies characteristic of the later empire.

comitium **(pl. *comitia*)**—In all Roman communities, a designated place for citizens to meet when summoned by officials; at Rome, this was situated north of the Forum at the foot of the Capitoline hill. The plural *comitia* denotes such a citizen assembly itself.

commercium—1) "Business," "commerce"; also 2) the right of a Latin to own Roman land and to make a contract with a Roman that would be enforceable in a Roman lawcourt; the same right was sometimes granted to other non-Romans too.

concilium **(pl. *concilia*)**—"Assembly," especially that of Rome's plebeian citizens (*concilium plebis*). In addition, during the Principate, the term was used for the assemblies of delegates from cities within one or more provinces that met to discuss issues of common concern, and in particular to organize celebrations of the imperial cult. In Greek-speaking provinces the term used for such assemblies was the Greek *koinon* (pl. *koina*).

consilium—"Advice," and by extension the group that provided it, in particular to the emperor (hence *consilium principis*).

consistorium—("standing room council") The highest officers of state who formed the emperor's advisory council from Diocletian onwards.

constitutio Antoniniana—The legal enactment (*constitutio*) of A.D. 212 by which Caracalla (whose official name was Marcus Aurelius Antoninus) extended Roman citizenship to almost all the free inhabitants of the empire.

consul—Chief annual magistrate of the Roman Republic (always one of a pair).

contio **(pl. *contiones*)**—Public meeting convened by an officeholder to address a matter of current concern (legislative, judicial in particular). There could be discussion, but no binding vote of any kind.

conubium—Marriage, and the right to enter into a marriage recognized by Roman law. Both partners to such a marriage had to have either Roman citizenship or this right, which was given to Latins and sometimes to other non-Romans.

"crown tax"—Contributions that communities were required to send to the emperor on certain special occasions, especially his accession.

curator **(pl. *curatores*)**—General descriptive term for anyone who shoulders a special responsibility, above all in public life (thus to oversee food supply, or construction of an aqueduct, for example). Most notably, from the second century A.D., the term was used for high officials dispatched by emperors to intervene in the affairs of cities, or even a whole province, at a time of difficulty.

curia **(pl. *curiae*)**—1) The earliest group into which Roman citizens were divided; 2) the meeting place of a citizen unit or other group, in particular a senate or town council. The principal meeting place for Rome's own senate was the building called the Curia in the Forum.

curialis **(pl. *curiales*)**—See decurion.

cursus honorum—Literally "succession of offices," the prescribed series of magistracies which Roman senators sought to hold (subject to various regulations and restrictions) in order to become leading public figures.

Cynics—Philosophers who advocated living "according to nature," and hence were (in varying degrees) hostile to the established order, especially the Roman Principate.

damnatio memoriae—("damning of the memory") After the deaths of individuals declared by the senate to be enemies of the state (certain emperors especially), measures taken to blot out their memory; these could include destruction of images, erasure of names from public records, annulment of decisions.

dea, deus—Goddess, god.

decurion—City councilor, the equivalent at a local level to a senator at Rome. To serve thus, as at Rome, was a lifelong responsibility only open to wealthy, respectable citizens of the community. Decurions legislated on local regulations, oversaw public funds, offered benefactions (games, feasts, building projects, etc.), and aided in the collection of local and imperial taxes. During the late empire, decurions were termed *curiales*.

dediticii—Literally, individuals who have made a formal surrender (*deditio*) to Rome; in particular, from the second century A.D. onwards, the many peoples from outside the empire's borders who were admitted into it to settle. For whatever reason, Caracalla seems to have made a point of excluding *dediticii* from his grant of universal citizenship (*constitutio Antoniniana*).

demos—The citizen body of a community (Greek).

denarius (**pl.** *denarii*; **see also** *aureus, sestertius*)—Roman coin made of silver. Initially, during the Second Punic War (218–201), it weighed 4.5 g and was valued at 10 bronze *asses*. After this war, however, it was revalued at 16 bronze *asses* or 4 sesterces (4 *asses* = 1 *sestertius*). From the reign of Nero it weighed 3.4 g.

dictator—Magistrate appointed to take sole control of the state temporarily in order to overcome a crisis. He appointed a second-in-command (*magister equitum*) himself.

dignitas—"High rank," and hence the "esteem" due to the holder of it, a sense of respect about which ambitious Romans were prone to be very sensitive.

dilectus—Levy for choosing men to draft into the army.

diocese—A grouping of provinces controlled by a vicar (*vicarius*), who served as a deputy of the Praetorian Prefect (see below) and oversaw primarily fiscal concerns. Initially, Constantine and Licinius divided the empire into twelve dioceses early in the fourth century; later in the century, this division was modified to raise the number of dioceses to fourteen.

diploma (**pl.** *diplomata*)—Document comprising a pair of folded bronze tablets that certified the holder's privileges on discharge from military or naval service.

divus (**pl.** *divi*)—"Deified," used only of deceased humans who had been declared deified by the senate (thus members of the imperial family in particular).

Dominate (compare *dominus* **below)**—Period of more openly authoritarian rule instituted by Diocletian (284–305) after the Principate.

dominus—"Lord," "master."

Donatists—Group of North African Christians who argued that they had legitimate claim to church leadership because the recognized leaders were tainted with having "lapsed" during the Great Persecution (see below); the resulting schism lasted into the sixth century.

donative—Originally, money or loot distributed by a commander to his soldiers after a successful campaign. Later, a supplementary cash payment offered to soldiers to induce or cement their loyalty, especially by emperors on special occasions.

Druids—Priests (male and female) of the Celtic religion.

dux (**pl.** *duces*)—"General," "leader"; from the tetrarchic period onwards, an official title for generals with provincial or regional commands ("dukes").

ecclesiastical history—New form of historiography initiated by Eusebius of Caesarea in the early fourth century, focusing on the Christian church rather than the traditional topics of political and military affairs.

ecumenical council—"World council" of the church, at which major theological questions were decided. Held at Nicaea (325), Constantinople (381), Ephesus (431), and Chalcedon (451).

Edictum Perpetuum—("Perpetual Edict") Revised, permanent (from A.D. 129) version of the edicts issued by successive praetors.

eques (pl. *equites*)—("horseman," "knight"; also termed "equestrian") Member of the privileged group of Roman citizens who received the highest rating in a *census*; originally they served as cavalrymen in the army. From the 60s B.C. onwards, the group became a loose, self-selecting one: free birth, respectability, and wealth of at least 400,000 *sesterces* were essential qualifications. *Equites* ranked immediately below senators.

euergetism—("benefaction") The practice whereby wealthy leading citizens (decurions especially; see above) expended their personal resources to benefit communities at the local or regional level.

eunuchs—Castrated males, usually slaves or freedmen. Often employed as chamberlains of the emperor, some became important political figures in the late empire.

fasces—Bundle of rods surmounted by an axhead carried by official attendants (*lictores*) before a Roman magistrate as a symbol of his authority.

fasti—Calendar recording, say, recurrent events (e.g. religious festivals), or days on which different kinds of business could be conducted (e.g. meetings of citizen assemblies). Also chronological lists of past holders of an office (e.g. consulship, priesthood) or distinction (e.g. triumph).

feriae—A festival, or a day in the Roman calendar on which one could be held.

fides—"Good faith," the sense which Romans wished to convey to others that they were honorable and trustworthy. In law, fiduciary responsibility.

flamen, flaminica—"Priest," "priestess."

Flavians—Line of emperors begun by Titus Flavius Vespasianus that ruled from 69 to 96 (Vespasian and his two sons in succession, Titus and Domitian).

foederati—Independent foreign peoples bound by treaty (*foedus*) to serve alongside Roman armies, sometimes (especially during the late empire) in exchange for payment.

forum (pl. *fora*)—In all Roman communities, a designated area for conducting political, judicial, and commercial business, and hence usually a town's focal point. Rome itself, as well as other major cities, came to have more than one *forum*.

fossa—1) "Ditch;" 2) grave dug for an inhumation burial.

freedman—Freed (or "manumitted") slave. It was an exceptional feature of Roman law that almost all slaves freed by Roman owners automatically received not only freedom but also Roman citizenship. As citizens, needing a Roman name for the first time, freedmen customarily took the *nomen* of their former owner, who now became their *patronus*.

gens (pl. *gentes*)—Extended family or clan linked by a common ancestor.

gladiator—Participant in armed combat (of various types) staged for entertainment in an amphitheater (see above). Gladiators were often condemned criminals, slaves, or prisoners of war.

gloria—"Glory."

Great Persecution—The final and most extensive persecution against the Christians. Organized by the state, it was initiated on February 23, 303 and escalated through a series of four edicts, the last of which (in 304) required public sacrifice by all citizens. Throughout the East, the persecution was strictly enforced and continued until Galerius' Edict of Toleration in 311. In the West, it was fiercely enforced in North Africa and Italy down to 306, but only haltingly through the remaining provinces.

hagiography—Accounts of Christian saints. Such works include accounts of the trial and execution of martyrs (written from the second century A.D.), and biographies of other holy men and women (from the fourth century onwards).

Hellenistic—Adjective used to denote the period in the Greek world between Alexander the Great's time in the late fourth century B.C. and Octavian's final victory over Antony and Cleopatra in 31–30.

heresy—Religious dispute over issues of Christian doctrine, leading to the growth of rival factions in the church.

honestiores—("more honorable people") From the second century A.D. onwards, those considered by the authorities to merit greater respect, and (as defendants in court) more favorable consideration: in particular, senators, *equites*, town councilors, veterans, together with their families. The corresponding less privileged category was *humiliores* (see below).

hoplite—Greek armored infantryman who carried a heavy shield (*hoplon*) and fought in pitched battle as part of a massed formation (*phalanx*).

hostis—Any enemy of the Roman state, including a Roman citizen who takes up arms against it.

humiliores—("more lowly people") From the second century A.D., those considered by the authorities to merit only minimal respect. As defendants in court, they were likely to receive no more than summary justice, and, if convicted, harsh penalties, including corporal punishment. The corresponding more privileged category was *honestiores* (see above).

imago—Portrait (usually made of wax) of a distinguished ancestor; carried by descendants at family funerals and displayed in the *atrium* of the family home.

imperator—Originally, a title for a successful military commander. From Augustus' time it was used of the "emperor" (the English noun derives from the Latin), and from the Flavian period onwards *imperator* was a regular imperial title. At the same time, however, emperors might still take pride in the traditional acclamation that they received after a great victory during their rule; Claudius, for example, purposely boasted of a remarkable number of these "salutations" as *imperator*.

imperium—(from the verb *imperare*, "to command") Supreme authority in Rome's affairs vested in certain officeholders, who alone (among other prerogatives) could command troops and impose the death penalty. The *imperium* of emperors was specifically made *maius* ("greater") so that it outranked that of all other holders.

intercessio—A magistrate's right to halt or "veto" the activity of an equal or lower-ranking magistrate. Exceptionally, a tribune's power of *intercessio* extended to any magistrate and to the business of any session of the senate or an assembly.

interrex—A patrician who was chosen to conduct the election of new consuls when both died or left office without successors during the Republic.

Isis—Egyptian fertility goddess, the focus of a widespread cult.

iugatio vel capitatio—("acreage or head count") Taxation system initiated under Diocletian which calculated: 1) land tax based on the *iugum* ("yoke"), a standard unit assigned to lands proportional to their expected level of productivity; 2) head tax, based on the productive value of individuals measured by age, gender, and status.

iugerum (pl. *iugera*)—Unit of land measure. One *iugerum* = 0.25 hectare = 0.625 acre.

ius (pl. *iura*)—Legal right or privilege, legal status. Specifically, *ius Latii* denoted the various rights which any community or individual gained from Rome on being awarded "Latin status."

iustitium—Official temporary suspension of all public business at a time of crisis or mourning; sometimes imposed as a political device.

Judaism—Set of ancient Jewish religious and social practices—most notably, exclusive devotion to one god, male circumcision, observance of the Sabbath, and avoidance of nonkosher food.

Julio-Claudians—Line of emperors—descended from the Julian and Claudian families—ruling from Augustus in the 20s B.C. to Nero (died A.D. 68). See Table 8.1.

jurist—Expert interpreter of the law.

koinon—See *concilium*.

Lar (pl. *Lares*)—Household or family god, usually worshipped at domestic shrines. Certain *Lares* also protected the state and guarded travelers at crossroads.

Latin status (*ius Latii*)—See *ius* above.

laudatio—Public praise of an individual, especially in the form of a panegyric in prose or verse, or a eulogy at a funeral (*laudatio funebris*).

laus—"Praise."

legatus (pl. *legati*; **English "legate"**)—Commonly used term, which can denote in particular: 1) an envoy (dispatched by the senate, for example); 2) a senior military officer, often the commander of a legion; 3) a high-ranking assistant to a provincial governor; 4) from the time of Augustus, a provincial governor appointed directly by the emperor (as *his* "assistant," therefore).

legion—The standard large Roman military formation, comprising around 5,000 heavily armed infantry.

lex (pl. *leges*)—("law") Statute passed by a citizen assembly or issued by the emperor, and then generally known by the name(s) of its proposer(s): thus, for example, *lex Licinia-Sextia*.

lictor (pl. *lictores*)—Official attendant who escorted and assisted a Roman magistrate, in particular by carrying the *fasces* (see above) before him. The number of lictors to which magistrates were entitled varied according to their office.

limitanei—("border troops") In the late empire, soldiers stationed in permanent forts along the frontiers. To be distinguished from *comitatenses*.

lituus—Curved stick used by an *augur* (see *auspicium* above).

ludi—Public "games" such as beast hunts (*venationes*), gladiatorial shows, chariot races (*ludi circenses*), theatrical events (*ludi scaenici*), and mock naval battles. Such entertainments might be offered (usually free) by officials or private individuals, either on a regular basis (e.g. an annual religious festival) or as a special occasion (e.g. a funeral).

magister equitum—("master of cavalry") See *dictator*. In addition, as part of his military reforms, Constantine instituted a high-ranking commander of cavalry with this title (see *magister militum*).

magister militum—("master of soldiers") Highest-ranking general in the late empire, placed in command of *comitatenses* (see above). The titles of these generals (first appointed by Constantine) depended upon which particular force they led.

Magna Graecia—("Great Greece") Broad descriptive term for the whole region of southern Italy and Sicily colonized by Greeks from the eighth century B.C.

Magna Mater **("Great Mother," Cybele)**—Goddess whose cult was officially introduced to Rome from Asia Minor in 204 B.C.

maiestas—"Treason."

maius imperium—See *imperium* above.

Manichaeans—Religious group founded by Mani (c. 216–276), combining elements of Christianity, Judaism, and Zoroastrianism. Manichaeans propounded a dualist cosmology with light battling darkness, in which light could be freed through the ritual and ascetic practice of a religious elite, the "elect." They were persecuted from 302 (by Diocletian) until the end of the Roman empire.

manus **("hand") marriage**—An increasingly rare form of Roman marriage. It came to be regarded as unduly restrictive for the wife, because it placed both her person and property under her husband's absolute control.

monks—(Greek *monachoi*, "solitaries") Practitioners of Christian asceticism who believed in separating themselves from normal society and living lives of sexual and worldly renunciation, whether alone as hermits or in shared communities (monasteries).

Monophysites—Christians, mostly from Syria and Egypt, who refused to follow the findings of the Council of Chalcedon (451) that both human and divine aspects can be distinguished in Christ's nature. Instead, they formed their own group of believers in the "single nature" of Christ.

municipium **(pl. *municipia*)**—Descriptive term for the legal status of an autonomous city located in Roman territory, but governed by its own laws and city council, while obligated to assist Rome as an ally. Increasingly, these cities adopted institutions on the Roman model.

necropolis **(pl. *necropoleis*)**—(Greek "city of the dead") Area of a town where the dead were buried—traditionally outside the walls in order to protect the inhabitants from disease and the religious defilement of death.

negotiator **(pl. *negotiatores*)**—"Businessman."

Neoplatonism—Philosophy developed by Plotinus in the third century A.D., which endured until the sixth. It argued that the universe grew from a unified divine principle, "the One," and provided a monotheistic basis for pagan theology that aided in its reactions to Christianity.

new man—See *novus homo* below.

nobilis—(pl. *nobiles*) ("nobles") Rome's governing elite. More specifically, the members of those families with an ancestor who had attained the consulship.

nomen—(pl. *nomina*) ("name") Middle component of the typical Roman "three names," representing an individual's clan (*gens*); see also *cognomen* and *praenomen*.

novus homo—(pl. *novi homines*) ("new man") First member of a family to become a Roman senator. The higher he rose in the *cursus honorum*, the more remarkable his achievement was; for a *novus homo* to attain the consulship was especially difficult.

obelisk—(Greek *obeliskos*, "skewer") Tall and narrow monolithic columns, originally carved in Egypt, but regularly taken by Romans and dispersed in public architectural contexts, particularly on the *spina* of a *circus* (see above).

optimates, populares—Names used to describe the holders of contrasting political attitudes from the late second century B.C. *Optimates* ("the best people") continued to uphold traditional methods of competition among senators. *Populares* ("people's men"), on the other hand, sought wider popularity among the citizen body as a means of advancement.

origo—("origin") Line of descent, in particular a Roman citizen's community of origin, to which he owed political obligations (in addition to the ones he owed Rome); hence part of a citizen's political identity.

ovatio—Victory celebration in Rome awarded to a successful general, but on a distinctly lesser scale than a "triumph" (see below).

panegyric—See *laudatio* above.

papyrus—In Greek and Roman civilization, the equivalent of modern paper; sheets of it were made from strips of the pith of a plant which grew in the marshlands of Egypt's Nile delta.

pater patriae, also *parens patriae*—("father" or "parent of the fatherland") In origin, a special title awarded to an individual for extraordinary service to the state. It was bestowed on Augustus in 2 B.C., and almost all subsequent emperors took it, with the notable exception of Tiberius. It suggests the holder's role as *paterfamilias* ("father") of the state, and his *patria potestas* ("fatherly power") over Roman citizens.

paterfamilias—Male head of a family, usually a father or grandfather, if his marriage was valid in Roman law. In principle, he had complete legal authority (*patria potestas*) over the life, death, and freedom of his family.

patria potestas—("fatherly power") Legal authority of the male head of a family (*paterfamilias*) over his family and descendants, including other adult males, women, freedmen, slaves, and children. Terminated for children when a daughter was transferred to the power of her husband's family by marriage, or when a male descendant became independent (*sui iuris*) by legal procedure.

patrician—Member of the more privileged group of Roman citizens (in contrast to the *plebs*, or plebeian group, see below). Patrician status could only be gained by birth (at least, until emperors bestowed it).

patronus—("patron") See "client." Note that once a slave is freed by his owner, he becomes a freedman and the former owner becomes his patron.

pax Augusta—("Augustan peace") Descriptive term for the long period of relative peace and stability following Augustus' expansion and consolidation of the empire.

Penates—Roman spirits connected with the inner part of a private house.

peregrinus—("foreigner") Any free individual who is not a member of a Roman community.

"Perpetual Edict"—See Edictum Perpetuum.

plebs—Strictly speaking, the "plebeians," the less privileged group of Roman citizens (in contrast to patricians, see above). More generally, the term is also used of the common people anywhere, often dismissively.

podium—1) Supporting platform of a building or temple, from which public speeches were often delivered; 2) balcony of a theater or arena from which the emperor viewed the event; imperial dais.

polis (pl. *poleis*)—"City," "city state" (Greek).

pomerium—Sacred boundary of a city ritually marked by a priest. At Rome, a vital marker of the limit either side of which political and military authority could, or could not, be exercised.

pontifex (pl. *pontifices*)—("bridge builder," "pontiff") Member of one of the major groups or "colleges" of Roman priests, headed by the *pontifex maximus*; from the time of Augustus onwards, this headship was always taken by the emperor.

populares—See *optimates*.

populus (*Romanus*)—("people," "Roman people") Broad collective term for the citizen body of the Roman state, as in the standard formulation "Senate and People of Rome" (*Senatus Populusque Romanus*, SPQR).

porticus—1) Long (usually roofed) colonnade; 2) large, roofed market building with multiple rows of columns (such as the Porticus Aemilia in Rome's warehouse district); 3) courtyard enclosed on all four sides by rows of columns with colonnades (such as the Porticus of Octavia in the Campus Martius).

praenomen (pl. *praenomina*)—First component of the typical Roman "three names" (see also *nomen* and *cognomen*). The *praenomen* represents an individual's given or "first" name, and distinguishes members of the same family (e.g., **Marcus** Tullius Cicero, and his brother **Quintus** Tullius Cicero).

praetor—Annual magistracy with *imperium*, an important step in the *cursus honorum*. Its holders were placed in a variety of assignments, in particular to preside over lawcourts in Rome.

Praetorian Guard—Elite military force formed to serve as the emperor's bodyguard; it was instituted by Augustus, and disbanded by Constantine in 312.

Praetorian Prefect—Commander of the Praetorian Guard (see above), who exercised military and judicial authority second only to that of the emperor. Augustus maintained two Prefects simultaneously, but most emperors kept only one. From Constantine's reign onwards, Praetorian Prefects no longer had military authority, but they remained important judicial and administrative officials, numbering four or more at a time.

princeps (pl. *principes*)—("leading figure") During the Republic, an informal general term for those senators who carried the greatest weight in matters of state. *Princeps* therefore appealed to Augustus as the unassuming term that best fitted the position which he developed for himself. From this usage by Augustus stems "Principate," the descriptive term for the two and a half centuries during which the ideal of his nonauthoritarian style of rule was maintained (superseded by the "Dominate," see above).

princeps senatus—("leader of the senate") Informal title used for the senator whose name was placed first in the roll of senators when this was reviewed by the censors; to be distinguished from the broader usage of simply *princeps* (see above).

proconsul—Ex-consul who, at the end of his term in office, accepts an assignment (governorship of a province, for example) that continues, or "prorogues," his magistrate's authority for a set period.

procurator—("agent") In particular, an individual (often an *eques*) appointed by the emperor to manage property or to represent him in court.

proletarii—Roman citizens whose declaration of property at a census was too low to qualify them for military service; notionally, therefore, all they could contribute to the state was their children (*proles*).

propraetor—Ex-praetor who, at the end of his term in office, accepts an assignment (governorship of a province, for example) that continues, or "prorogues," his magistrate's authority for a set period.

proscription—Publication of a list of individuals who can be killed with impunity, and whose property is confiscated.

provincia—("province") The sphere of activity which a magistrate is assigned to exercise his authority; and hence, in particular, a foreign territory which he is required to oversee for Rome.

publicanus (pl. *publicani*)—Private individual who performs work for the Roman state under contract (construction, supply, tax collection, for example). The fulfilment of larger contracts might require a group of such individuals to work together as a "syndicate" (*societas*).

Punic—In Latin usage, Phoenician, hence Carthaginian.

quaestio (pl. *quaestiones*)—Tribunal or court for criminal matters, which could always be established as required in individual instances. In addition, between 149 and the late 80s B.C., a succession of permanent such courts (*quaestiones perpetuae*) with juries was established, each empowered to adjudicate a specific crime. The first was the *quaestio de repetundis* ("concerning items to be recovered"), which heard charges of extortion, embezzlement, and related crimes, brought against senators who had served in the provinces.

quaestor—Annual magistracy (without *imperium*), the first step in the *cursus honorum*. Holders could be placed in a variety of assignments in Rome or abroad, usually relating to the state's financial interests.

Regia—Sacred building in the Roman Forum between the Via Sacra and the Temple of Vesta, believed to have been built by king Numa. Residence of the king during the regal period, thereafter headquarters of the *pontifex maximus*.

relics—Objects (including body parts) associated with Christian martyrs or saints, preserved and venerated as religiously efficacious.

repetundae—See *quaestio* above.

rescript—An official response by the emperor to a legal question or petition. Even though rescripts usually addressed particular cases, they were still often held to have the force of general law.

rex—"King."

rostra—Raised platform in the Forum from which speeches were made; named after the prows (*rostra*) of captured enemy ships used for its decoration.

sacrosanctity—Attribute which made it a crime (subject to instant death) on the part of anyone who used violence towards its holder (a tribune of the *plebs*, for example).

Sasanians—Persian dynasty which seized power from the Parthians in A.D. 224. Reforms to taxation, law, and military organization allowed it to maintain very tight control of Mesopotamia and Iran. Its "King of Kings" Shapur I (240–272) invaded deep into Roman territory, and took many cities there, including Syrian Antioch; later, Shapur II (309-379) did likewise. In 260, Shapur I even captured the Roman emperor Valerian. United under a powerful religious ideology, Zoroastrianism (see below), the Sasanian empire reached its apex in the sixth century, but internal strife and attacks by the Byzantines weakened it, and it eventually fell to Arab Muslims by 651.

schism—Religious dispute over issues of leadership, leading to the growth of rival factions in the Christian church.

scholarii—("staff guards") Groups of imperial guardsmen newly formed under Constantine to replace the Praetorian Guard (see above).

Second Sophistic—Greek and Latin cultural and literary movement that spanned the mid-first to the third centuries A.D.; it drew its inspiration in particular from the teachers and researchers termed "sophists" in the Greek world of the fifth century B.C.

senatus—("senate") Advisory council first of Rome's kings, thereafter of the state's senior magistrates. Its role in affairs, and hence its *auctoritas*, came to be increasingly important, until it suffered challenges from powerful individuals during the last century of the Republic, and was eventually overshadowed by the emperors.

senatus consultum **(SC)**—"Resolution" or "decree of the senate."

sestertius **(English pl. "sesterces"; see also *denarius*)**—Roman coin originally of silver, but from Augustus' time minted in bronze. Often abbreviated "HS," because 1 *sestertius* was originally valued at 2.5 bronze *asses*; in Roman numerals, IIS or "HS" = 2.5.

Severans—Line of emperors ruling from the accession of Septimius Severus (193) through the death of Severus Alexander (235). See Table 11.1.

socius **(pl. *socii*)**—"Ally" (of the Roman state).

Sol Invictus—("Unconquered Sun") A deity worshipped from early in Roman history that became very popular in the third century A.D. This sun cult was promoted in particular by the emperors Elagabalus (his nickname derives from the Syrian name for the sun god), Aurelian, and Constantine.

solidus—Gold coin introduced by Constantine in 309 and weighing 4.5 g. It became the standard unit of taxation and account in the late empire.

Stoicism—Greek philosophical and ethical movement, some of whose adherents among Rome's upper classes objected to the autocratic style of certain emperors.

Struggle of the Orders—Prolonged struggle (early fifth to early third centuries B.C.) by Rome's plebeian citizens to overcome domination of the state's affairs by patricians.

suffect consul (or other officeholder)—Replacement elected to fill the remaining term of office when its original or "ordinary" holder died or resigned.

tabularium—("record-office") Rome's tabularium at the western end of the Forum was constructed in the early first century B.C.

Tetrarchy—("rule of four") Short-lived system of joint rule established by Diocletian (284–305), with an emperor (*Augustus*) in the West and another in the East, each with a deputy (*Caesar*).

toga—The undyed woolen robe that was the distinctive garment of adult Roman civilians; it could not be worn by non-Roman citizens. Holders of certain ranks and distinctions were entitled to wear togas that were decorated in various ways; consuls, for example, wore a *toga praetexta* that was bordered in purple.

tribune (*tribunus*, pl. *tribuni*)—From the early fifth century B.C., annually elected "tribunes of the plebs" (*tribuni plebis*) with their own authority (*tribunicia potestas*) were recognized as the leaders of the plebeian citizen body (*plebs*). In addition, and quite separately, "military tribunes" (*tribuni militum*) were army officers of sufficient importance for some of them even to be chosen as joint heads of state in certain years during the late fifth and early fourth centuries B.C. (*tribuni militum consulari potestate*). Thereafter, there continued to be army officerships with the title *tribunus militum*, but typically these were no longer of high rank.

tributum—A tax on property.

triumph—Voted by the senate to honor a general who had won an outstanding victory against a non-Roman enemy (no victory in a civil war could be recognized in this way); celebrated by a procession through Rome from the Campus Martius to the Capitoline hill. In these exceptional circumstances, the triumphant general (*triumphator*), dressed like the god Jupiter, rode in a chariot, and was permitted to march his army inside the *pomerium*.

triumvir **(pl. *triumviri*)**—Member of a group, or commission, of three men.

Twelve Tables—Rome's first set of written laws (around 450 B.C.).

Vestal virgins—Prestigious priestesses who performed the rites of Vesta (goddess of the hearth) from her shrine near the Regia in the Forum; maintenance of the sacred flame here was considered vital to Rome's survival.

via—Road.

vigiles **("watchmen")**—Paramilitary patrols of freedmen, instituted by Augustus to reduce the danger from outbreaks of fire in the city of Rome.

virtus—"Manly courage," more broadly "excellence" or "distinction" as demonstrated in service to the Roman state.

Zoroastrianism—Dualist religion of Persia, which held that the universe is a manifestation of the battle between the good god Ahura Mazda and his evil counterpart Angra Mainu. Elements of Zoroastrianism can be traced back to the fifth century B.C., but it gained particular importance as an imperial religion of the Sasanians (see above), who systematically established fire-temples in territories they controlled (fire was one of the seven sacred creations, capable of overcoming evil).

PRINCIPAL ANCIENT AUTHORS

This list aims to be no more than a concise identification of the principal authors mentioned in the book, together with a few anonymous writings (under their commonly used titles). The list omits nonhistorical authors whose writings are of lesser significance for modern readers new to Roman history, and historical authors whose work is entirely, or almost entirely, lost.

An English translation is cited only in those instances where none is readily available in any of the standard series, such as the Loeb Classical Library (Harvard University Press), Oxford World's Classics, Penguin Classics, Translated Texts for Historians (Liverpool University Press) or *The Early Church Fathers* website (http://www.ccel.org/fathers.html).

For further information in every case, consult, for example, the appropriate entry in *OCD* or *ODB*. A wide range of translated extracts from authors (including fragments), along with inscriptions, papyri, and coin legends, is assembled in sourcebooks such as Lewis, Naphtali, and Meyer Reinhold. 1990 (third edition). *Roman Civilization*, vol. 1 *The Republic and the Augustan Age*, vol. 2 *The Empire*. New York: Columbia University Press.

Acts of the Apostles: Fifth book of the New Testament, written by Luke, author of the third gospel, outlining the mission of the Church from Christ's ascension to Paul's visit to Rome around 62. This work—most likely to date to the 80s—was evidently not known to contemporary Roman authors.

*Publius **Aelius Aristides**: From the province of Asia, born in 118; became a leading practitioner of the Second Sophistic. His oration *To Rome*, praising Roman achievements and the benefits of Roman rule, dates to around 144. Translation: see citation in Source 11.1.

---

*Authors who write in Greek (rather than Latin) are asterisked.

Aurelius Ambrosius (**Ambrose**): born c. A.D. 339 in Trier, where his father served as Praetorian Prefect. Educated for a state career, he served as governor of Aemilia and Liguria before being chosen bishop of Milan in 374. He died in office in 397. His writings include theological and exegetical treatises as well as ninety-one letters, several to emperors and high officials.

Ammianus Marcellinus: Born c. A.D. 325, died c. 391. Probably from Syrian Antioch, he was a native Greek speaker who moved to Rome and published a history in Latin c. 390. It began with the reign of Trajan (thus continuing from Tacitus' *Histories*) and ended in 378. Only the last eighteen of its thirty-one books survive, covering the years 353–378. Ammianus was himself a soldier, and was thus able to write particularly vivid accounts of military affairs, some of which he witnessed personally.

*Appian: From Alexandria (Egypt), he rose high in the emperor's service and then (in the mid-second century A.D.) was able to devote himself to writing a Roman history, not all of which survives. His main focus is on the wars which Rome fought with the different peoples it conquered. His coverage of the Punic and Iberian wars is of special interest, likewise that of the civil wars between 133 and 35 B.C.

*Athanasius: Bishop of Alexandria from A.D. 328 until 373. He was a staunch defender of Nicene Orthodoxy who was exiled four times for confrontations with successive emperors over doctrine and church politics. He wrote a number of exegetical and theological treatises as well as several defenses against Arians. He is most famous for *The Life of Antony* (composed c. 356), a biography of this early ascetic leader, which offers the first true example of Christian "hagiography" (see Glossary); whether Athanasius in fact wrote this work, however, remains disputed.

Augustine: From Thagaste (Numidia), born A.D. 354 to a pagan father and Christian mother. Killed in 430 in the Vandal invasions of North Africa. He studied in Carthage and Italy, and experimented with Manichaeism and Neoplatonism (see Glossary) before converting firmly to Christianity in 387. Elected bishop of Hippo Regius in 395, he was to become the Latin writer whose works survive in greatest abundance from antiquity. They include letters, sermons, biblical exegesis, and his two masterworks: the *City of God* (twenty-two books, written after the sack of Rome in 410); and the narrative of his early personal life and conversion, the *Confessions*, written in 397.

Augustus, *Res Gestae*: see section in Chapter Eight.

Sextus **Aurelius Victor**: Late fourth-century compiler of brief outlines about each Roman emperor from Augustus to 360.

Book of Revelation: Last book of the New Testament, in all likelihood dating to the late first century A.D.; said to have been written by the Apostle John. In the tradition of apocalyptic, or "unveiling," literature which reveals the future, it offers a series of visions. Many of the images that these present may have some historical reference, but such meaning usually remains elusive. However, there is no mistaking the book's implacable hostility to Roman rule.

Gaius Julius **Caesar**: Caesar wrote (in the third person) an account or "commentary" about each of his first seven campaigning seasons in Gaul (58–52), and his subordinate officer Aulus Hirtius subsequently added an eighth account to cover the years 51–50. Together, they comprise the *Gallic War*. In similar vein, Caesar wrote an account, the *Civil War*, about his campaigns from January 49 to his arrival in Alexandria in October 48. Here he breaks off, but successive anonymous continuations—the "Alexandrian," "African," and "Spanish" wars—complete the narrative (to 45). Each of these three continuations seems to be by a different author; the "Alexandrian War" may be Hirtius' work.

*Cassius Dio: Second-generation senator from Bithynia, whose distinguished career culminated in his opening the year 229 as consul with the emperor Severus Alexander. Much of his immense *Roman History* from earliest times to that year is lost altogether, and much also survives only in abbreviated or excerpted form. However, we possess his coverage of 69 B.C. to A.D. 46 reasonably complete; within this span we gain our only year-by-year account of Augustus' career. The insights that Dio provides about his own times—from personal experience in the reign of Commodus onwards—are also valuable.

Marcus Tullius **Cicero**: Senator (*novus homo*) from Arpinum, born in 106 B.C., killed in the proscriptions of 43. He was an exceptionally active speaker and author. Quantities of his writings have survived, and furnish material of historical value—political and lawcourt speeches, works on rhetoric and philosophy, some poetry, and hundreds of letters, most of which are strictly private correspondence never intended for publication. "SB" signifies the recommended edition of the letters (with English translation) by David R. Shackleton Bailey.

Claudian: From Alexandria, he moved to Rome by A.D. 395 and established himself as a court poet to Arcadius and his general Stilicho. Composed a number of panegyrical and polemical poems in Latin which offer a somewhat distorted but colorful picture of political events down to 404.

*Dead Sea Scrolls: Texts that probably belonged to the library of a Jewish religious center at Qumran near the Dead Sea, and from 1947 onwards have been found in caves in the vicinity. A few of these texts are in Greek, but most are in Aramaic or Hebrew; they seem to have been written between the third century B.C. and the first century A.D.

Digest: A major part of the *Corpus Iuris Civilis*, the emperor Justinian's project (528–534) to restate Roman law in a more focused, consistent form. The bulk of the *Digest* comprises extracts from the writings of jurists active in the late second and early third centuries A.D. which are otherwise lost. Translation: Watson, Alan (ed.). 1987. *The Digest of Justinian*. Philadelphia: University of Pennsylvania Press.

*Diodorus Siculus: From Sicily, he lived in Rome from the 50s through the 20s B.C., but is not known to have been connected to prominent figures there. His lengthy *Universal History* spanned earliest times to 60 B.C., but only extracts of its coverage beyond 302 survive. Even so, some of these—on the slave revolts in Sicily, for example—are of exceptional importance.

*Dionysius of Halicarnassus: From Halicarnassus in Asia Minor, he migrated to Rome as a teacher of rhetoric around 30 B.C., but apparently never became a Roman citizen. Twenty years and more later, he issued his *Roman Antiquities*. Its coverage of Rome's history from earliest times to 441 survives complete, but we have only excerpts of the rest, which continued to the outbreak of the First Punic War in 264.

*Eunapius: Born c. A.D. 350 in Sardis. He wrote *Lives of the Sophists*, a collection of short biographies of late antique philosophers which survives, and a *History* covering the years 270 to 404; it contained praise of Julian and criticism of

Christian emperors, and survives only in fragments. Translation: Blockley, Roger C. 1983. *The Fragmentary Classicising Historians of the Later Roman Empire*. Liverpool: Francis Cairns.

*Eusebius: Born c. A.D. 263 and died c. 339 in Caesarea Maritima (Palestine), where he served as bishop from 313. Among his many surviving writings, the most useful are the first extant *Ecclesiastical History* (down to 324), the *Chronicle* (including a synchronic table of world history in columns down to 325), and the *Life of Constantine*.

Eutropius: Author of a rapid survey of Roman history issued in A.D. 369. This spans from Romulus to A.D. 364, and is most useful for its account of periods (such as the third century A.D.) otherwise thinly documented in the surviving record.

Sextus Pompeius **Festus**: Antiquarian of the late second century A.D., whose erudite scholarship sheds light on many archaic Roman practices. Much of his work is lost, however, and there is no English translation of what survives. "L" signifies the standard Latin text by Wallace M. Linsday.

Lucius Annaeus **Florus**: Mid-second century A.D. author of an outline of Roman history to the time of Augustus; this draws heavily on Livy's fuller record, and devotes particular attention to wars.

Sextus Julius **Frontinus**: Distinguished senator, whose career spanned the reigns of Nero to Trajan. Among other works, he wrote a handbook on the history, administration, and upkeep of the city of Rome's aqueducts after being appointed their superintendent by Nerva in 97.

Gaius: Teacher of law, whose introductory lectures delivered around A.D. 160 survive under the title *Institutes*. Translation: Gordon, William M. and Olive F. Robinson. 1988. *The Institutes of Gaius*. Ithaca, New York: Cornell University Press.

Aulus **Gellius**: Mid-second century A.D. intellectual, whose "miscellany book" entitled *Attic Nights* (after time spent in Attica, the territory of Athens) discusses a varied range of literary, historical, legal, and philosophical questions.

*Herodian: Author of uncertain origin and rank who wrote a Roman history in the mid-third century A.D. It covered the immediate past, from the death of Marcus Aurelius (180) to 238, the beginnings of the "Age of Crisis."

Historia Augusta: Lives of emperors from Hadrian through the mid-third century "Age of Crisis," loosely modeled after those of Suetonius (see Gaius Suetonius Tranquillus) and probably of late fourth century date. As they proceed, however, these Lives become increasingly unreliable and sensationalist. The work's own claim to be by six different writers is surely false, and no more than a reflection of the (single) author's teasing wit.

*John of Antioch: Sixth-century A.D. Greek author of a universal history. It sheds useful light on the fourth and fifth centuries, but survives only in two collections of fragments, the last of which relate to the reign of Anastasius (491–518).

*John Chrysostom: born c. A.D. 347 in Syrian Antioch; served as bishop of Constantinople from 398, but was exiled in 404 to Armenia, where he died in 407. His prolific writings include hundreds of sermons filled with incidental details on daily life.

*John Malalas: Sixth-century A.D. lawyer from Syrian Antioch. He wrote a *Chronicle* in plain style, covering world history to 563. It draws on earlier sources and preserves important information on Antioch, the Persian expedition of Julian, and particularly the reign of Justinian. Translation: Jeffreys, Elizabeth, Michael Jeffreys, and Roger Scott. 1986. *The Chronicle of John Malalas*. Melbourne: Australian Association for Byzantine Studies.

Jordanes: Sixth-century A.D. writer of barbarian background (Gothic or Alan, or both), who wrote a brief history of the Goths extending to the 550s. Translation: Mierow, Charles C. 1915. *The Gothic History of Jordanes*. Princeton: Princeton University Press.

*Flavius **Josephus**: Jewish aristocrat, priest, and leader in the First Jewish Revolt (66–73), until he defected to the Romans and was rewarded with citizenship by Vespasian (hence his Roman name Flavius). His extensive writings include a history of the revolt in which he took part (*Jewish War*), and a larger treatment of the Jews' entire history to that date (*Jewish Antiquities*).

*Julian: Born A.D. 331 in Constantinople, promoted to Caesar in 355, and Augustus in 360. Died on campaign in Persia in 363. His surviving writings include letters, speeches, philosophical treatises, poems, and satires like his *Beardhater* against the people of Syrian Antioch.

Justinianic Code: Part of Justinian's *Corpus Iuris Civilis* (see *Digest*). A collection of imperial laws issued in a first edition in 529 and a second in 534. These laws derive from emperors stretching from Hadrian to Justinian, and cover both private and imperial issues.

Decimus Junius **Juvenal**is: Early second century A.D. satirist of Roman society and its morals. His true identity is beyond recovery, and autobiographical statements that he makes should not be taken at face value.

Lactantius: Teacher of rhetoric at the imperial court, who (among other works) wrote *On the Deaths of the Persecutors* around 315. Its purpose—in a presentation that is far from objective—is to celebrate Christians' deliverance by Constantine, and to demonstrate that all the earlier emperors who persecuted them met a terrible fate. Translation: Creed, John L. 1984. *Lactantius, De Mortibus Persecutorum*. Oxford: Oxford University Press.

*Libanius: Born c. A.D. 314 in Syrian Antioch, where he died c. 394. An uncompromising pagan, he studied and taught rhetoric. Sixty-four orations by him survive, many addressed to emperors, or about them, especially his favorite Julian. In addition, over 1,500 of his letters survive.

Titus Livius (**Livy**): Native of Patavium in Cisalpine Gaul, probably born in 59 B.C. and died in A.D. 17, although it is possible that each of these dates should be five years earlier. Since he came to know both Augustus and Claudius personally, he must have spent time in Rome, but the circumstances are not recorded; there is no sign that he played a role in public life. His immense history, "Books from the Foundation of the City" (*Ab Urbe Condita Libri*), spanned Rome's origins to 9 B.C., but only two substantial portions of it survive—the opening books to 290, and coverage of the Second Punic War to the end of the Third Macedonian War (218–167).

*Olympiodorus: Born c. A.D. 380 in Egyptian Thebes, he traveled extensively before moving to Italy and joining the court of Honorius, who sent him on an embassy to the Huns (c. 412). His history covering Western affairs from 407 to 425 survives only in fragments. Translation: Blockley, Roger C. 1983. *The Fragmentary Classicising Historians of the Later Roman Empire*. Liverpool: Francis Cairns.

Orosius: Born c. A.D. 375 in Gallaecia (north-west Spain), he wrote a *History Against the Pagans* with the aim of refuting claims that in his day the Roman empire was suffering tragedies worse than it had in the past. The last of his seven books is useful for the history of the late fourth and early fifth centuries.

Panegyrics: An invaluable collection of twelve panegyric speeches (some anonymous) is a chance survival discovered in the fifteenth century. It preserves the speech of thanks that Pliny the Younger (see below) made on his entry to the consulship in A.D. 100. Otherwise, two of the speeches date to the late fourth century A.D., but the remaining nine all belong to the period of Diocletian and Constantine. Translation: Nixon, Charles E.V. and Barbara S. Rodgers. 1994. *In Praise of Later Roman Emperors: The* Panegyrici Latini. Berkeley, Los Angeles, London: University of California Press.

Aemilius **Papinian**us: Leading jurist of the early third century A.D. and close associate of the emperor Septimius Severus. Writings by him form a notable part of the *Digest* (see above).

Julius **Paul**us: Leading jurist of the early third century A.D., who worked closely with emperors from Septimius Severus to Severus Alexander. Writings by him form a notable part of the *Digest* (see above).

*Pausanias: From Asia Minor; his *Description of Greece*—of mid-second century A.D. date—offers an extensive treatment of many monuments and sanctuaries in the province of Achaia, together with their historical background. He had visited these sites personally, and proves to be an accurate observer.

Martyrdom of Perpetua: Anonymous account of the martyrdom—at Carthage in 203—of Perpetua, a Roman woman (young, respectable, married), and her female slave, Felicitas. The account incorporates impressions said to have been recorded by Perpetua herself. Translation: Ehrman, Bart D. (ed.). 1999. *After the New Testament: A Reader in Early Christianity*. Oxford: Oxford University Press, Chapter 3.8.

*Philo: A leader in the Jewish community at Alexandria (Egypt), and an expert philosopher in both the Jewish and Greek traditions. Among his voluminous surviving writings, two works—*Against Flaccus* [Prefect of Egypt, 32–38], and *Embassy to Gaius*—offer insight into the increasing ill-treatment of the Jewish community at Alexandria from the time of Augustus onwards. The latter work is Philo's vivid account of a Jewish embassy which he led to Gaius (Caligula) in Rome to plead with the emperor (in 39–40).

*Lucius Flavius **Philostratus**: Intellectual from the Aegean island of Lemnos, who studied at Athens and later lived in Rome, where he enjoyed the patronage of Julia Domna, wife of the emperor Septimius Severus. His admiring *Lives of the Sophists* illuminates the "Second Sophistic" movement.

Gaius Plinius Caecilius Secundus (**Pliny the Younger**): Senator (*novus homo*) from Comum (modern Como) in Cisalpine Gaul, born around 60, nephew of Pliny the Elder (see below), who raised him. He was promoted by Domitian, Nerva, and Trajan, and also had marked success as a trial advocate. A revised version of the traditional speech of thanks he made in the senate on taking up the consulship in September 100 survives (see under *Panegyrics* above). So do ten books of *Letters*. The last of these preserves official correspondence between Trajan and himself while serving in Bithynia-Pontus as a governor specially appointed by the emperor (around 111). The other nine books gather earlier private letters—rich, varied material, but all of it revised, if not composed, for publication.

Gaius Plinius Secundus (**Pliny the Elder**): *Eques*, uncle of Pliny the Younger (see above), who rose through the imperial service to become naval commander at Misenum on the Bay of Naples, and lost his life in 79 during a personal inspection of the eruption of Mt. Vesuvius. He was a polymath and an astonishingly productive author, but only his *Natural History* survives. An encyclopedia with even broader scope than its title might indicate, this work distils and preserves a staggering range of ancient learning.

*Plutarch: Born at Chaeronea in the province of Achaia, he chose to remain there as an active local figure, but also visited Rome and was well connected to leading Romans; his lifespan is at least A.D. 50–120. Many of his rhetorical and philosophical works survive, but for historians his *Lives* of outstanding statesmen and generals (written as pairs, a Greek figure matched and compared with a Roman) are of greater significance. There survive *Lives* of twenty-three such Romans—as far apart as Romulus and Antony—together with two (Otho, Vitellius) which are all that remain of an earlier set of imperial biographies.

*Polybius: Greek, born around 200, who as a young man took a leading role in the Achaean League, but after the Third Macedonian War (171–168) was deported to Rome as a hostage, where he forged close contacts with members of the elite; he supposedly lived to the age of eighty-two (around 118). The main purpose of Polybius' *History* is to explain what he views as Rome's meteoric rise to "world" dominion in the half-century between the onset of the Second Punic War (around 220) and the end of the Macedonian monarchy in 167. As background, however, he begins by treating the First Punic War, and continues to devote attention to events in Greece, Egypt, and elsewhere, that parallel developments in Italy. Eventually, too, he decided to extend his coverage to the destruction of Carthage and Corinth (146). Even so, only the first five of his final total of forty books survive complete, bringing the narrative down to 216, the year of Hannibal's victory at Cannae. Thereafter we possess no more than a varied accumulation of excerpts and abridgements.

*Priscus: Fifth-century A.D. historian from Panium in Thrace. He wrote a history of his own times that survives only in fragments, the most interesting of which describe his embassy from the court of Theodosius II to that of Attila the Hun in 448. Translation: Blockley, Roger C. 1983. *The Fragmentary Classicising Historians of the Later Roman Empire*. Liverpool: Francis Cairns.

Rufinus: Born c. A.D. 340 near Aquileia, traveled to Egypt and the Holy Land before returning to Italy. He translated many Greek Christian works into Latin, including Eusebius' *Ecclesiastical History*, which he then continued to 395 with two additional books. Translation: Amidon, Philip R. 1997. *The Church History of Rufinus of Aquileia, Books 10 and 11*. Oxford: Oxford University Press.

Gaius **Sallust**ius Crispus: Senator (*novus homo*) who served under Julius Caesar, but then turned to the writing of history until his death in the 30s B.C. Two short monographs survive, the *Jugurthine War* (112–105 B.C.) and the *Catilinarian War* (63–62 B.C.), both of them rhetorical and moralizing, but much admired in antiquity. Only some speeches and letters remain from a larger work, *Histories*, which began from the time of Sulla's death (78); where it ended, or was planned to end, is unknown.

*Socrates Scholasticus: Born c. A.D. 380 in Constantinople, he wrote an *Ecclesiastical History* covering the years 305–439; it offers much useful information on political, military, and foreign affairs.

*Sozomen: Born c. A.D. 400 in Bethelia near Gaza, and trained as a lawyer, he moved to Constantinople where he wrote an *Ecclesiastical History* covering the years 312–439. He relies on Socrates but adds plenty of material, especially on affairs in his native Palestine, on legal matters, and on pagan authors.

*Strabo: From Amaseia in Pontus, he made extensive travels, which included visits to Rome and Egypt. After writing history (now lost), he turned to composing a vast universal *Geography* during the time of Augustus and Tiberius, which survives. He intended it to be useful to the rulers of the Roman world in the changed conditions of the Principate.

Gaius **Suetonius** Tranquillus: *Eques*, probably from Africa, who worked closely with Trajan and Hadrian in high administrative positions, but was then dismissed by the latter emperor in the early 120s. He was also a prolific writer with antiquarian interests, whose engaging set of imperial biographies from Julius Caesar to Domitian survives. These *Lives* furnish important, often unconventional, testimony, especially in cases where little other material is available. It must be recognized, however, that Suetonius' interest in his own project seemingly cooled, because the *Lives* themselves become thinner as they advance.

Quintus Aurelius **Symmachus**: Born c. A.D. 340 and died 402 in Rome, one of the great statesmen and most prominent pagan leaders of the fourth century; proconsul of Africa in 373, consul in 391. He wrote a series of orations, including three imperial panegyrics, and numerous letters collected in ten books purposely organized to match those of Pliny the Younger (see above). Nine books contain personal correspondence, while the tenth offers forty-nine official reports (*relationes*) made to Valentinian II when Symmachus was Urban Prefect in Rome (384–385). Translation: Barrow, Reginald H. 1973. *Prefect and Emperor: The Relationes of Symmachus, A.D. 384*. Oxford: Oxford University Press.

*Synesius: born c. A.D. 370 in Cyrene, he served as bishop of Ptolemais in Libya from c. 410 until his death c. 414. He wrote a number of letters and poems, and a satirical speech *On Kingship* directed at the emperor Arcadius. Translation: Fitzgerald, Augustine. 1926. *The Letters of Synesius of Cyrene*. London: Oxford University Press.

Cornelius **Tacitus**: Senator (*novus homo*) from Cisalpine or Narbonese Gaul, born around 55 and active under the Flavian emperors, Nerva, and Trajan; consul in 97. His *Agricola*, a short commemorative biography of his father-in-law, dates to 98. He then wrote his *Histories*, which spans Vitellius' acclamation as emperor in January 69 to the assassination of Domitian in 96; only the extended narrative for 69 and part of 70 survives. His last work is the *Annals*, which was planned to span the accession of Tiberius in 14 to the death of Nero in 68. In the form we have the work, however, the end (from 66) is missing, along with the coverage of Caligula's entire rule and the first six years of that of Claudius (37–47).

Quintus Septimius Florens **Tertullian**us: African from Carthage, and prolific author, who during the late second and early third centuries used his outstanding literary abilities to explain and defend Christianity to educated Latin readers—as, for example, in his *On the Games* (*De Spectaculis*).

Theodosian Code: Compilation of imperial laws published in A.D. 438. As many as twenty-two scholars working in two teams took ten years to produce this work, which brings together more than 2,500 laws issued between 313 and 437. The Code represents the first attempt by the imperial government to publish its laws systematically. It serves as the basis for our knowledge of late Roman civil and administrative law, and as our main source of evidence for political careers in the fourth and fifth centuries. Translation: Pharr, Clyde. 1952. *The Theodosian Code and Novels*. Princeton: Princeton University Press.

Domitius **Ulpian**us: Leading jurist of the early third century A.D., who rose through the imperial service to become Praetorian Prefect in 223, but was soon murdered by the troops under his command. He was a prolific writer of books to expound Roman law, especially after the *Constitutio Antoniniana* of 212. Over two-fifths of Justinian's *Digest* (see above) comprises extracts from his work.

Valerius Maximus: Author of a substantial handbook of *Memorable Doings and Sayings*, dedicated to the emperor Tiberius, and perhaps issued during the 30s A.D.

Velleius Paterculus: Roman who first served in the army as an *eques*, and later served again as a senator, in both instances under Tiberius before he became emperor. In A.D. 30 he issued a summary history of Rome from earliest times to his own day in two books. The first of these—almost all lost—ended with the destruction of Carthage and Corinth (146).

*Zosimus: Imperial official, who around A.D. 500 issued a *New History* of the Roman Empire from the time of Augustus to the early fifth century. Remarkably for his time, his outlook is resolutely anti-Christian, and he therefore offers a rare window onto pagan perceptions of the religious changes of the late empire. Translation: Ridley, Ronald T. 1982. *Zosimus, New History*. Sydney: Australian Association for Byzantine Studies.

ART CREDITS

FIGURES

Fig 1.1: The Metropolitan Museum of Art/Art Resource, NY; Fig 1.2: after Small, Jocelyn P. 1971. "The banquet frieze from Poggio Civitate (Murlo)," *Studi Etruschi* 39, p. 28, fig. 1; Fig 1.3: after Nielsen, Erik and Kyle M. Phillips, Jr. 1976. "Poggio Civitate (Siena). Gli scavi del Bryn Mawr College dal 1966 al 1974," *Notizie degli Scavi di Antichità* 30, p. 115, fig. 1; Fig 1.4: Deutsches Archäologisches Institut, Rome; Fig 1.5: Ashmolean Museum, Oxford/ Bridgeman Art Library; Fig 1.6: after Östenberg, Carl E. 1975. *Case etrusche di Acquarossa.* Rome: Multigraphica Editrice, p. 182; Fig 1.7: Museo Archeologico di Villa Giulia, Rome, Italy/Bridgeman Art Gallery International; Fig 1.8: Fototeca Unione, American Academy in Rome; Fig 1.9: Scala/Art Resource, NY; Fig 2.1: Fototeca Unione, American Academy in Rome; Fig 2.2: Deutsches Archäologisches Institut, Rome; Fig 2.3: Soprintendenza Speciale per i Beni Archeologici; Fig 2.4: Alinari/Art Resource, NY; Fig 2.5: Scala/Ministero per i Beni e le Attività culturali/Art Resource, NY; Fig 3.1: (c) Araldo de Luca/CORBIS; Fig 3.2: (c) The Trustees of the British Museum; Fig 3.3: (c) The Trustees of the British Museum; Fig 3.4: after Keay, Simon J. 1988. *Roman Spain.* London: British Museum Publications, p. 41; Fig 4.1: Fototeca Unione, American Academy in Rome; Fig 4.2: after Zanker, Paul. 1998. *Pompeii: Public and Private Life.* Cambridge, MA: Harvard University Press, p. 36, fig. 5; Fig 4.3: Alinari/Art Resource, NY; Fig. 4.4 *Chiron* 12 (1982) Tafel 7 nos. 12 and 13; Fig 5.2: (c) The Trustees of the British Museum; Fig 5.3: after Coarelli, Filippo. 1987. *I Santuari del Lazio in Età Repubblicana.* Rome: La Nuova Italia Scientifica, p. 39, fig. 10; Fig 6.1a: Scala/Art Resource, NY; Fig 6.1b: Vanni/Art Resource, NY; Fig 6.2: Ny Carlsberg Glyptotek, Denmark; Fig 6.3: (c) The Trustees of the British Museum; Fig 6.4: Courtesy of Vladimir Kuznetsov; Fig 6.5: after Potter, Timothy W. 1987. *Roman Italy.* London: British Museum Publications, p. 105; Fig 6.6: Alinari/Art Resource, NY; Fig 7.1: Ancient Art and Architecture Collection Ltd; Fig 7.2a: after Higginbotham, James. 1997. *Piscinae: Artificial Fishponds in Roman Italy.* Chapel Hill: UNC Press, p. 153-154, Fig 62 & 63; Fig 7.2b: after Higginbotham, James. 1997. *Piscinae: Artificial Fishponds in*

Roman Italy. Chapel Hill: UNC Press, p. 153-154, Fig 62 & 63; Fig 7.2c: James Higginbotham; Fig 7.3: Getty Images; Fig 7.4: (c) The Trustees of the British Museum; Fig 7.5: Zandra Talbert; Fig 7.6: after Favro, Diane. 1996. *The Urban Image of Augustan Rome*. Cambridge: Cambridge University Press, p. 197, fig. 84; Fig 7.7a: Alinari/Art Resource, NY; Fig 7.7b: Deutsches Archäologisches Institut, Rome; Fig 7.7c: Fototeca Unione, American Academy in Rome; Fig 8.1: (c) The Trustees of the British Museum; Fig 8.2: The National Trust Photo Library; Fig 8.3a: ALEA (Archive of Late Egyptian Art-Robert Steven Bianchi); Fig 8.3b: Hunterian Museum at the University of Glasgow; Fig 8.3c: Vatican Museums 38511; Fig 8.4: (c) The Trustees of the British Museum; Fig 8.5a: after Murray, William M., and Photios M. Petsas. 1989. *Octavian's Campsite Memorial for the Actian War*. Philadelphia: American Philosophical Society, p. 89, fig. 55; Fig 8.5b: William M. Murray; Fig 8.5c: Istituto Centrale per il Catalogo e la Documentazione – MiBAC e British School at Rome; Fig 8.6: (c) The Trustees of the British Museum; Fig 8.7a: Ny Carlsberg Glyptotek, Denmark; Fig 8.7b: Alinari/Art Resource, NY; Fig 8.7c: Ancient Art and Architecture Collection Ltd; Fig 8.7d: Getty Images; Fig 8.7e: The National Trust Photo Library; Fig 8.7f: Walters Art Gallery; Fig 8.8: Walters Art Gallery; Fig 8.9a: (c) The Trustees of the British Museum; Fig 8.9b: (c) The Trustees of the British Museum; Fig 8.9c: (c) The Trustees of the British Museum; Fig 8.9d: Deutsches Archäologisches Institut, Rome; Fig 8.10: Foto Marburg/Art Resource, NY; Fig 8.11a-c: Christian Grovermann, Foto Stenger, GmbH Osnabrück, for Varusschlacht im Osnabrücker Land; Fig 8.12: Deutsches Archäologisches Institut, Rome; Fig 9.1: (c) The Trustees of the British Museum; Fig 9.2: Ali Dügenci/Aphrodisias Excavations, New York University; Fig 9.3: (c) The Trustees of the British Museum; Fig 9.4: Landesmuseum Mainz; Fig 9.5: Alinari/Art Resource; Fig 9.6: Museum of Serdica; Fig 9.7: Tomaž Lauko, Ptuj Municipal Museum (Slovenia); Fig 10.1: Scala/Art Resource, NY; Fig 10.2a: Alinari/Art Resource, NY; Fig 10.2b: Scala/Art Resource, NY; Fig 10.3: Roger Wood/Corbis; Fig 10.4: Scala/Art Resource, NY; Fig 10.5: Erich Lessing/Art Resource, NY; Fig 10.6: The Art Archive; Fig 10.7: Princeton University Art Museum; Fig 10.8a: Roger Wood/Corbis; Fig 10.8b: Pierre Belzeaux, Photo Researchers Inc.; Fig 10.9: Super Stock; Fig 11.1: (c) The Trustees of the British Museum; Fig 11.2: Alinari/Art Resource, NY; Fig 11.3: Deutsches Archäologisches Institut, Rome; Fig 11.4: Erich Lessing/Art Resource, NY; Fig 11.5: Staatliche Museen, Berlin/Bridgeman Art Library International; Fig 11.6: Gorsium Open-air Museum—Archaeological Garden. Hungarian National Museum/King St Stephen Museum of Székesfehérvár; Fig 11.7: Sandro Vanni/Corbis; Fig 12.1: Courtesy of the Oriental Institute of the University of Chicago; Fig 12.2: Vanni/Art Resource, NY; Fig 12.3: TongRo Image Stock/Alamy; Fig 12.4a: Photo by Branislav Strugar; Fig 12.5: Vanni/Art Resource, NY; Fig 13.1: Deutsches Archäologisches Institut, Rome; Fig 13.2: Vanni/Art Resource, NY; Fig 13.3a: (c) The Trustees of the British Museum; Fig 13.3b: American Numismatic Society; Fig 13.3c: Courtesy of Robert Bernobich; Fig 13.3d: American Numismatic Society; Fig 13.4: Vanni/Art Resource, NY; Fig 14.1: Alinari/Art Resource, NY; Fig 14.2: akg-images/Gerard Degeorge; Fig 14.3: Uppsala University Library; Fig 14.4a: Réunion des Musées Nationaux/Art Resource, NY; Fig 14.4b: akg-images/Bildarchiv Steffens.

PLATES

Plate 1a: Scala/Art Resource; Plate 1b: Vanni/Art Resource; Plate 3: Photo courtesy of Tom Bennett; Plate 4: Photo courtesy of Elizabeth Robinson; Plate 5a: Photo courtesy of RomanoImpero; Plate 5b: Photo courtesy of Cartomania; Plate 6: Photo courtesy of Richard Talbert; Plate 7: Werner Forman/Art Resource, NY; Plate 8a: Danita Delimont/Getty Images; Plate 8b: Digital Image (c) 2011 Museum Associates/

GAZETTEER

Ancient and modern names are not distinguished. Unless otherwise stated, numbers refer to pages. Where a feature, people or place is marked on several maps, not every instance may be listed; "etc" signifies such omissions. BP = Back endpaper map, FP = Front endpaper map.

557

INDEX

Most Roman males are listed by their nomen (middle of three names). Emperors and certain other well known figures are listed by the name normally used for them in English. A number in *italic* indicates a figure, a plate, a table, or its caption. The maps are indexed in the Gazetteer immediately above.

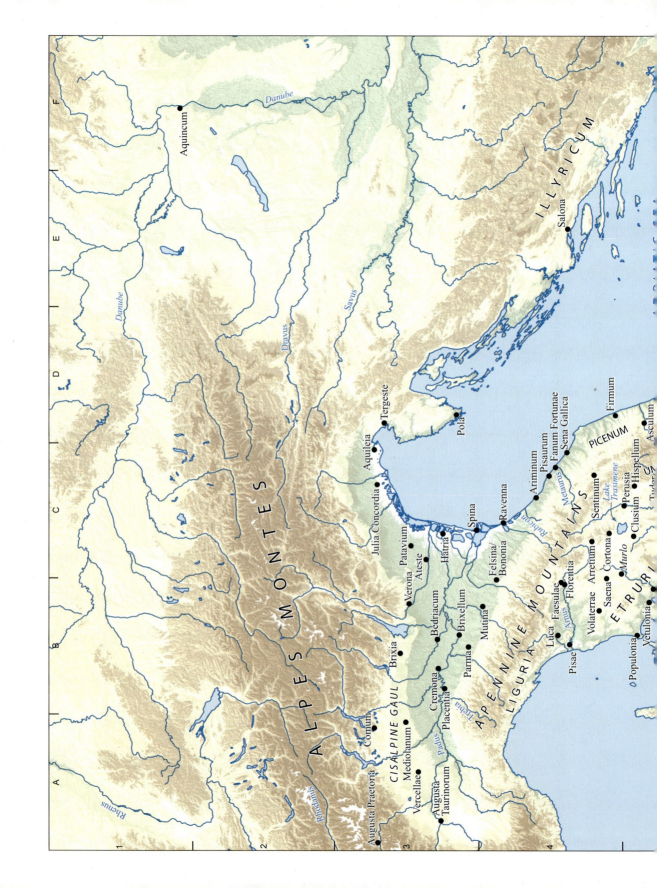